PENGUIN BOOKS

BENJAMIN FRANKLIN

Carl Van Doren, who was born in 1885 and died in 1950, was professor of English at Columbia University, literary editor of *The Nation*, and editor-in-chief of the Literary Guild, of which he was one of the founders. His other books include several volumes on American history, among them *The Great Rehearsal: The Story of the Making and Ratifying of the Constitution of the United States* (also available in a Compass edition); the autobiographical *An Illinois Boyhood*; and *Benjamin Franklin's Autobiographical Writings*, which Mr. Van Doren selected and edited.

Benjamin FRANKLIN

CARL VAN DOREN

PENGUIN BOOKS

PENGUIN BOOKS
Published by the Penguin Group
Penguin Books USA Inc.,
375 Hudson Street, New York, New York 10014, U.S.A.
Penguin Books Ltd, 27 Wrights Lane, London W8 5TZ, England
Penguin Books Australia Ltd, Ringwood, Victoria, Australia
Penguin Books Canada Ltd, 10 Alcorn Avenue,
Toronto, Ontario, Canada M4V 3B2
Penguin Books (N.Z.) Ltd, 182–190 Wairau Road,
Auckland 10, New Zealand

Penguin Books Ltd, Registered Offices:
Harmondsworth, Middlesex, England

First published in the United States of America
by The Viking Press, Inc., 1938
Compass Books Edition published 1964
Published in Penguin Books 1991

20 19 18 17 16 15 14 13

LIBRARY OF CONGRESS CATALOGING IN PUBLICATION DATA
Van Doren, Carl, 1885–1950.
Benjamin Franklin/Carl Van Doren.
p. cm.
Reprint. Originally published: New York: Viking Press, 1938.
Includes bibliographical references and index.
ISBN 0 14 01.5260 1
1. Franklin, Benjamin, 1706–1790.   2. Statesmen—United States—
Biography.   I. Title.
[E302.6.F8V36   1991]
973.3′092—dc20   90–27457

Printed in the United States of America

PREFACE

THIS is a long book. It could twice as easily have been three times as long. From Franklin's beginnings as a journalist at sixteen to his retirement from public affairs at eighty-two there was no break in his activity, and he was—and is—unsurpassed by any man in the range of his natural gifts and of the important uses he put them to. Many volumes have been written on many periods and phases of his career, and countless special studies. Yet not for three-quarters of a century has a biographer undertaken to bring the whole of Franklin's life, with all the precise details essential to it, into a single narrative large enough to do it justice. Thanks to later research it is now possible to correct and verify the earlier record at frequent points. But it is also difficult, with the new facts at hand, not to let it run beyond a readable length. This book, full as it is, is a biography cut with hard labour to the bone.

Franklin, the most widely read of autobiographers, is best known from his *Autobiography*, and therefore too little known. For in that masterpiece of memory and honesty he dealt with his years as a rising tradesman and did not reach his more memorable years as imperial prophet, revolutionary statesman, cosmopolitan diplomatist, scientist, wit, moralist, sage. He never found time to carry out the history of himself which he intended. But the materials which he would have used still exist, scattered in journals, letters, and miscellaneous writings through his manuscripts and his collected and uncollected works. Here at last they have been drawn together and arranged in something like the order he might have given them. Nor are they mere raw notes for a book. He seldom wrote a line without some characteristic touch of wit or grace. Most of these materials need no rewriting to make them match the unfinished story they continue. In effect, Franklin's autobiography is here completed on his own scale and in his own words.

The completed autobiography, with indispensable passages from the actual *Autobiography*, is what may be called the speaking voice in a new history of Franklin, seen not only as he saw himself but also as he may now be seen in the light of facts he did not tell or sometimes even know. Here first in any Franklin biography appear (in part) his *Elegy*, recently discovered and apparently his earliest writing that has survived; information about James Franklin's *New England Courant* based on the file kept, almost certainly, by Benjamin Franklin; an analysis of the hundreds of sayings of Poor Richard which Franklin left out of *The Way to Wealth*, thereby much narrowing his reputa-

tion as a maker and sharpener of adages; various details of his business, domestic life, and personal expenditures taken from manuscript
account books and advertisements in the *Pennsylvania Gazette*; a more
exact discussion than has hitherto been printed of his surreptitious
writings and of his *Reflections on Courtship and Marriage*; a critical
examination of the kite-flying episode; the narrative of Franklin's first
diplomatic mission, to the chiefs of the Ohio Indians at Carlisle; the
lifelong story of his affectionate friendship with Catherine Ray, with
unpublished letters from her; his campaign as a soldier, known in full
only to the readers of a single recent monograph; his record in Pennsylvania politics as shown in the executive and legislative journals of
the province; the insurance company's description of his house in
Philadelphia; an unpublished manuscript in which he outlined his
programme of opposition to the Stamp Act; a note on his meeting with
Baron Münchhausen and Raspe his chronicler; a circumstantial account of the Grand Ohio Company from which Franklin hoped to
make a fortune in land speculation; his acquaintance with James
Boswell; two fables by Franklin published in 1770 but lost sight of
till 1936; a comparison of the two versions of Wedderburn's attack on
Franklin, one as printed by the British government and one as remembered by Franklin's friends; the neglected record of his activities as
chairman of the Pennsylvania Committee of Safety; an unpublished
letter to General Schuyler written during the mission to Canada; an
accurate report of the conference with Lord Howe given directly from
the minutes; the amazing melodrama of the British spies who surrounded Franklin in Paris; new translations of three of his Passy
bagatelles, written by him, so far as is known, only in French; several
of the long-lost stories he was accustomed to tell his friends in France,
some of them later retold in his *Autobiography*; details of his administration as President of Pennsylvania; notes on his account with the
Bank of North America; proof that he could not have gone to Lancaster in June 1787; a minute record of his acts and opinions in the
Constitutional Convention; and accounts of the second century of his
famous bequests to Boston and Philadelphia.

Grateful acknowledgments are hereby made to the American Philosophical Society for permission to consult the Franklin Papers in the
Society's Library and to publish, for the first time, certain documents
and letters by and to Franklin; to the Historical Society of Pennsylvania for unfailing hospitality and assistance; to the Library of the
University of Pennsylvania for permission to study its Franklin Papers
and to reprint Franklin's *Elegy*; to the Philadelphia Contributionship
for information respecting Franklin and the founding of the company;
to the Pennsylvania Company (custodian of the records of the Bank
of North America) for transcripts from the Bank's ledgers; to the Free
Library of Philadelphia for an opportunity to examine books tempo-

rarily on exhibition there; to the National Archives at Washington for photographs of Franklin's signatures to the treaty of alliance with France and the treaty of peace with England; to the Cornell University Library for furnishing a photostatic copy of a manuscript of Franklin's last speech and permitting the use or reproduction of it; to the Yale University Library for special privileges with regard to the Mason-Franklin collection (now being catalogued and not generally accessible); to the John Carter Brown Library for permission to read the letters of Franklin to Catherine Ray; to the Frick Art Reference Library for assistance in the matter of Franklin portraits; to the Massachusetts Historical Society for courteous favours during a visit there; and to the Pennsylvania Academy of the Fine Arts, the Metropolitan Museum of Art, the New York Public Library, and the Fogg Art Museum of Harvard University for permission, elsewhere specifically acknowledged, to reproduce portraits of Franklin. Particular acknowledgments are due to Mrs. Charles Iselin for permission to examine and use the Passy-Chaillot correspondence between John Jay and his wife; to Dr. A. S. W. Rosenbach for permission to read Franklin's unpublished letters to Madame Brillon; and to Lt.-Colonel Ralph H. Isham for permission to quote from the *Private Papers of James Boswell*.

The final writing of the book called for almost daily use of the New York Public Library over a period of two years. It would be difficult to describe the expert interest and friendly patience of the members of the staff, no matter what burdens were laid upon them. It would be impossible to express in full the gratitude here imperfectly recorded.

The book could not have been written if, in the past twenty years or so, special students of Franklin had not continually added to what has become almost a Franklin science. Many of the facts now first brought into a narrative biography have already appeared in monographs and in articles in learned journals. Acknowledgments are made to all of these in the General Bibliography and Chapter References at the end of the volume. And at least the names must be gratefully given of at least a few of the friends, acquaintances, and strangers who have shared their knowledge or sources of knowledge with invariable generosity: Carl Becker, Julian P. Boyd, M. V. Brewington, Verner W. Crane, George Simpson Eddy, Andrew Keogh, Otto Kinkeldey, F. R. Kirkland, Bernhard Knollenberg, H. M. Lydenberg, Ethelwyn Manning, Dumas Malone, Frank Monaghan, S. E. Morison, J. Bennett Nolan, Morris Sadow, J. Somers Smith, Berthold A. Sorby, C. Seymour Thompson, Edith May Tilley, Lawrence C. Wroth.

This biography goes into detail because Franklin led a detailed life which in a general narrative loses colour and savour. But the chief aim of the book has been to restore to Franklin, so often remembered piecemeal in this or that of his diverse aspects, his magnificent central unity as a great and wise man moving through great and troubling events. No effort has been made to cut his nature to fit any simple scheme of what a good man ought to be. Here, as truly as it has been possible to find out, is what Franklin did, said, thought, and felt. Perhaps these things may help to rescue him from the dry, prim people who have claimed him as one of them. They praise his thrift. But he himself admitted that he could never learn frugality, and he practised it no longer than his poverty forced him to. They praise his prudence. But at seventy he became a leader of a revolution, and throughout his life he ran bold risks. They praise him for being a plain man. Hardly another man of affairs has ever been more devoted than Franklin to the pleasant graces. The dry, prim people seem to regard him as a treasure shut up in a savings bank to which they have the lawful key. I herewith give him back, in his grand dimensions, to his nation and the world.

CONTENTS

Penns. Franklin's illness. Presents for Philadelphia. Philosophic leisure. Cambridge. English Franklins. Tour in Scotland. Edinburgh scholars. Franklin made Dr. Franklin by the University of St. Andrews. Lord Kames. Propaganda against the proprietors. Temporary settlement with them. Canada and Franklin's Canada pamphlet. The Craven Street household. William Franklin's illegitimate son Temple. Visit to Holland and Belgium. Franklin's hoaxes. Varied philosophic interests. Scientific letters to Polly Stevenson. Franklin evolves the armonica. Oxford degrees to Franklin and his son. William Franklin made governor of New Jersey. Franklin returns to America.

Postal matters: Virginia to New Hampshire. Franklin and his daughter in New England. The Indian war called the conspiracy of Pontiac. Conflict between Philadelphia and the back counties. Massacre of the Conestoga Indians. Franklin's pamphlet. The frontier invades the capital. The governor takes refuge in Franklin's house, and Franklin quiets the rioters. Governor Penn hates Franklin more than ever. Franklin on the new colonial policy of the British government. Pennsylvania petitions the king to make it a royal province. Franklin drafts the petition, and signs it as Speaker of the Assembly. Franklin beaten in an uproarious election. Franklin builds a house. Again to England with the petition.

The petition submerged in the agitation over the Stamp Act. Opposition and passage. Further Franklin hoaxes. Franklin's original contribution to musical theory. Tumult over the Stamp Act in America. Franklin blamed. His wife and house threatened. Franklin chief spokesman for British-American propaganda in favor of repeal. Unprecedented debate in Parliament. Franklin before the House of Commons. Hero in his own historical comedy. The Stamp Act repealed. Franklin sees the repeal as patchwork legislation.

Franklin tells Joseph Priestley about the electrical kite. Franklin and John Pringle to Hanover. Baron Münchhausen. The Royal Society of Sciences at Göttingen. Franklin's English

son by Madame Caillot. Bagatelles for Madame Brillon. Madame Helvétius at Auteuil. Abigail Adams is shocked. Breakfast at Madame Helvétius's house. Stories Franklin told his French friends. Bagatelles for Madame Helvétius. Franklin proposes marriage to her. Franklin and women generally. Franklin and the great. Franklin and the Freemasons in France. Franklin and the constitutionalists. His little leisure for science. His works in German and Italian. Membership in learned societies. Franklin's private press at Passy. *Ça ira.*

Vergennes the impresario of the war. Conflict of interests between Spain and the United States. Imperial mediators. Shelburne opens with Franklin the first discussions of peace. Franklin's journal. Richard Oswald comes to Paris. Franklin suggests the cession of Canada. Franklin's fiction about British atrocities. Thomas Grenville comes to treat for England with France. Delays and confusion in the British ministry. John Jay arrives in Paris from Madrid. Franklin first outlines the American terms of peace. Jay's suspicions of Spain and France. Vergennes's position. Franklin's illness. Jay's terms. Adams arrives from Holland. The final negotiations without consultation with Vergennes. Franklin on fisheries and loyalists. The treaty signed in violation of instructions from Congress. Franklin informs Vergennes. Two masters cross swords. Franklin gets another loan from France. Independence from England, and from Europe.

Paris's first balloon ascension. Franklin sees the first ascent of human passengers. Franklin receives the first letter carried through the air. Franklin signs, with Sweden, the first treaty made by the United States after independence. Franklin's plan for transatlantic mail packets adopted by France and England. Post-war writings about America. The Society of the Cincinnati. Franklin and Mirabeau. Franklin on luxury, property, criminal law, war, and privateering. Treaty with Prussia. The royal commission for the investigation of mesmerism. Experiments at Passy. Further international honours. Franklin and his son. Franklin and Jefferson. Farewell to Passy. Visit to England, and farewell. Scientific writings on Franklin's last voyage to America.

THE UNITED STATES

Boston

Father and Son

FAMILIES break up when poor men emigrate. In January 1744 Josiah Franklin of Boston in New England wrote an inquiring letter across the Atlantic to a Captain Franklin in Oxfordshire. "By what intelligence I have received from my son at Philadelphia, and what intelligence I have had by a gentleman that comes pretty often to dinner here, I am pretty much inclined to believe that you are my brother's grandson that I lived with eleven years. I know of no advantage, neither do I propose any, to myself or you, by scraping acquaintance with you; but as father's children seemed to have more than common affection one for another, and I having the same affection as formerly, I shall rejoice to hear of the welfare of my brother's family, and I hope it will not be ungrateful to you, if we are related, to favour me with a few lines as opportunity presents.

"My brother John lived in Banbury, in Oxfordshire, and purchased a house by the mill," the letter went on. John Franklin had also inherited their father's freehold at Ecton in Northamptonshire, Josiah Franklin mistakenly thought. "Now I understand by the gentleman above mentioned that you sold land to the value of £500 sterling, which I suppose is about the value of what my father was possessed of. . . . I understand you also practise surveying, which my brother practised also, so that his instruments for art might fall to your portion also. Thus, sir, I have given you my conjecture, and if you'll send me an answer I shall count myself obliged to you."

"It's so long since I came away," the New England Franklin explained in a postscript, "that I have lost the knowledge of all our relations, having been in Boston sixty years last October. Whoever it be, I cannot expect to hold correspondence with you but a short time, being this New Year's day eighty-six years of age; but I have three sons which it's possible may be glad of the same friendship I may desire, and I believe would be glad if they can do you any service. They are John Franklin, tallow-chandler at Boston; Peet Franklin, at Newport, master of a vessel; and Benja. Franklin, at Philadelphia," where, as Captain Franklin knew, this son was postmaster.

Though Josiah Franklin might have the same affection as formerly, he had long outlived his brothers and was far removed from his English kin. For two centuries or more there had been Franklins at Ecton, where they had a farm of thirty acres and a forge, and where eldest son after eldest son had been a blacksmith. The next to the last of the line had had four sons: Thomas, John, Benjamin, and Josiah. Thomas was blacksmith and more: "a conveyancer, something of a lawyer, clerk of the county courts and clerk to the archdeacon in his visitations; a very leading man in all county affairs, and much employed in public business. He set on foot a subscription for erecting chimes in their steeple, and completed it. . . . He found out an easy method of saving their village meadows from being drowned. . . . His advice and counsel were sought for on all occasions, by all sorts of people."[1] The earliest Franklin to rise from village obscurity, more prosperous than any of their name had been before him, he seems a kind of first draft of the great Franklin. John Franklin, the second brother, left Ecton for Banbury, where he became a dyer, and where the brothers Benjamin and Josiah learned his trade. That "more than common affection" could not hold these Franklins together. The two elder adhered to the Church of England, the two younger turned to nonconformity. And now there was a New England which, especially to younger sons, held out better prospects than the Old. The Ecton clan dissolved when first Josiah and, much later, Benjamin crossed the Atlantic to Boston.

Benjamin Franklin knew the exact year neither of his father's birth nor of his arrival in America. Josiah Franklin's letter,[2] neglected by his son's biographers, fixes the first date at 1658 (January) and the second at 1683 (October). Married very young to an Anne whose surname is not known, Josiah was the father of a daughter when he was barely twenty, and had a son and another daughter when, not yet twenty-six, he put Ecton and Banbury behind him. Perfectly obscure in England, he would have been almost as obscure in New England if he had not had a famous son. Of all the records of his life that have come to light, the most numerous concern the births and baptisms of his children. After Elizabeth, Samuel, and Hannah, born in Banbury, came four more born in Boston: Josiah, Anne, Joseph, who lived five days in 1688, and another Joseph, born June 1689 and dead in fifteen days. Anne Franklin, three years older than her husband but still only thirty-four, died of her seventh child. The widower before the end of the year married Abiah Folger, twenty-two, daughter of Peter Folger of Nantucket. Josiah Franklin's American wife had ten children: John, Peter, Mary, James, Sarah, Ebenezer, Thomas, Benjamin, Lydia, and Jane. As Jane was a whole generation younger than Elizabeth, the first of these sons and daughters had grown up and gone away before the last were born, but Benjamin could remember thirteen sitting at his father's table at one time.

Although artisans and tradesmen left few records in that age, traces of Josiah Franklin appear in the documents of Boston. In 1685 he "owned the covenant"[3] at the Old South Church, which means that he had applied for membership. In 1691 he was occupying, as tenant, a small house in Milk Street directly opposite the church,[4] and in 1692 he was given permission to build what was possibly a shop, eight feet square, on the same lot.[5] In 1694 he was admitted to communion at the Old South, along with his wife Abiah. He had served the stern probation of nine years and was a church member, as not more than one man out of four or five in Boston then was. In February 1703, Samuel Sewall's diary notes, Ebenezer Franklin, sixteen months old, "was drowned in a tub of suds."[6] In September 1708 Sewall went to a Thursday evening prayer meeting at Josiah Franklin's house. " 'Tis the first time of meeting at his house since he joined."[7] In 1709 Josiah Franklin supplied the town of Boston with candles for the watch, enough to cost a pound.[8] In January 1712, the house in Milk Street having been sold, Josiah Franklin bought, for £320, a house at the corner of Union and Hanover Streets, where he lived the rest of his life, finally, it appears from his will, in two rooms.[9] In 1713 he was host to another prayer meeting, presumably in his new house.[10] In

February 1718 Samuel Sewall one Sunday "set York Tune" in church and the congregation "went out of it into St. David's." Sewall, who had been precentor at the Old South for twenty-four years, felt that he ought to give up his office to some more accurate singer. He told the minister that "Mr. White or Franklin might do it very well. The return of the gallery where Mr. Franklin sat was a place very convenient for it."[11] In April of that year, when two deacons were chosen, Josiah Franklin got ten votes, but two other men got more.[12]

Here are most of the known facts of Josiah Franklin's plain life. "He had an excellent constitution of body," his son wrote, "was of middle stature, but well set, and very strong; he was ingenious, could draw prettily, was skilled a little in music, and had a clear, pleasing voice, so that when he played psalm tunes on his violin and sung withal, as he sometimes did in an evening after the business of the day was over, it was extremely agreeable to hear. He had a mechanical genius too, and, on occasion, was very handy in the use of other tradesmen's tools; but his great excellence lay in a sound understanding and solid judgment in prudential matters, both in private and public affairs. In the latter, indeed, he was never employed, the numerous family he had to educate and the straitness of his circumstances keeping him close to his trade; but I remember well his being frequently visited by leading people, who consulted him for his opinion in affairs of the town or of the church he belonged to, and showed a good deal of respect for his judgment and advice; he was also much consulted by private persons about their affairs when any difficulty occurred, and frequently chosen an arbitrator between contending parties. At his table he liked to have, as often as he could, some sensible friend or neighbour to converse with, and always took care to start some ingenious or useful topic for discourse, which might tend to improve the minds of his children."[13] After his death his son told Peter Kalm of an experiment that Josiah Franklin had made. Living between two rivers, one with herring and one without, he caught spawn in one and carried it to the other. "It was hatched, and thereafter herring spawned there."[14]

Josiah Franklin was nearly fifty when his youngest son was born, and Benjamin, after he ran away from Boston to Philadelphia at seventeen, saw his father only three times. The father the son remembered was a busy maker and seller of soap and candles, seasoned and shrewd, orthodox but not too devout, cheerful among his houseful of children who with his trade and his church made up his existence. Most of the troubling events of his life were past. The wrench at leaving Ecton and Banbury, and the uncomfortable voyage. The anxiety at finding in Boston, with its five or six thousand people strictly ruled by ministers, magistrates, and merchants, that he could not make a living at his trade of dyer; and his decision to become a tallow-chandler. The deaths of two children and his wife within a year and a half. The discovery—by whom in that swarming house in Milk Street?—of the drowned child. His son Josiah's headstrong going off to sea and the long silence about him. Josiah was still at sea when his father bought the new house at Union and Hanover Streets and, moving his family there, took along with him the sign of the Blue Ball which had hung and now again hung before his door. But this was his own house, his last child was born soon after he bought it, and his son Benjamin was from the first the most promising of all his children.

II

Benjamin Franklin was born 6 January (17 January, New Style) 1706 in the house in Milk Street, and, born on Sunday, was carried that day across the winter street to be baptized in the Old South. He says, for a man so explicit and graphic about his later life, little about his first ten years. "My mother had likewise an excellent constitution; she suckled all her ten children."[15] Hardly another word about her, though he was always an affectionate son. She had been born in Nantucket, where her father was teacher, surveyor, weaver, miller, clerk of the town and court, and interpreter between whites and Indians. Her mother, Mary Morrils, had been an indentured servant whom Peter Folger had bought for twenty pounds and afterwards married. Abiah Franklin, married to a young widower with five small children, and with ten more of her own, was as much taken up as he with the cares of their family. "She was a discreet and virtuous woman," her son said on her tombstone. Her children and her epitaph and a few misspelled letters make up her recorded history.

Of his brothers and sisters in these early years Franklin says no more than appears in a single episode. "When I was a child of seven years old, my friends, on a holiday, filled my pockets with coppers. I went directly to a shop where they sold toys for children; and, being charmed with the sound of a whistle that I met by the way in the hands of another boy, I voluntarily offered and gave all my money for one. I then came home and went whistling all over the house, much pleased with my whistle, but disturbing all the family. My brothers and sisters and cousins, understanding the bargain I had made, told me I had given four times as much for it as it was worth; put me in mind what good things I might have bought with the rest of the money; and laughed at me so much for my folly that I cried with vexation; and the reflection gave me more chagrin than the whistle gave me pleasure."[16] If they teased him at other times as well, still he cherished no resentments or grievances. He was a genius in an ordinary family who was not bullied as an ugly duckling.

He was the special pet of his uncle Benjamin, who all the way from London sent his namesake didactic verses on the evils of war when the child was four years old and, the father had written to the uncle, was excited about soldiers. Benjamin, eight years older than his brother Josiah, had gone from Banbury to London and had not prospered. His wife had died and nine of his ten children, and his son Samuel had left him for New England. The lonely old man collected political pamphlets, listened to sermons and took them down in a shorthand he had invented, and poured himself out in tireless verse, always doggerel. When the nephew was nine the uncle came to Boston and lived for three or four years in Josiah Franklin's house. The promising boy was watched over by two old men.

The poetry of Benjamin took effect before the prose of Josiah. When the boy was seven he wrote some verses to go in a letter of his father's to London, and his uncle exulted, in answering verse, with hopeful praise. While the uncle was living at the Blue Ball the nephew began, in verse, his long life as a writer. He had already been apprenticed to his brother James the printer. "I now took a fancy to poetry, and made some little pieces; my brother, thinking it might turn to account, encouraged me and put me on composing occasional ballads. One was called *The Lighthouse Tragedy* and contained an account of the drowning of Captain Worthilake, with his two daughters; the other was a sailor's song, on the taking of Teach (or Blackbeard) the pirate. They were wretched stuff, in the Grub-Street-ballad style; and when they were printed he sent me about the town to sell them. The first sold wonderfully, the event being recent, having made a great noise."[17]

It was in November 1718. George Worthilake (or Worthylake), keeper of the first Boston light, was drowned with his wife and daughter (not his two daughters) on their way to town. They were "carried all together to the grave, with a very solemn funeral," and Cotton Mather preached. "I entertain the flock," he said of his sermon, "with as pungent and useful a discourse as I can."[18] Franklin, who often heard Cotton Mather, may have heard him on this day. That same month the pirate Blackbeard was killed off the coast of North Carolina, and within a few weeks the news had reached Boston, and Benjamin Franklin had run his ballad-making course.

The vogue of the ballads, now lost, "flattered my vanity; but my father discouraged me by ridiculing my performance, and telling me verse-makers were generally beggars. So I escaped being a poet, most probably a very bad one."[19] He escaped being a poet by never having been one, and he could take his father's advice because he was his father's son. Shakespeare and Milton and Dryden had not touched the Franklins. There was Peter Folger, who with "decent plainness and manly freedom" had written, "in the home-spun verse of that time and people,"[20] against intolerance and persecution. There was Uncle Benjamin, kind but a little fantastic, perpetually rhyming. There were the "foolish songs and ballads" which, Cotton Mather complained, "the hawkers and pedlars carry into all parts of the country." But in all this there was little to stir or fix the ambition of so reasonable a boy. Much as Josiah Franklin loved his brother Benjamin, he could not set much value on that Benjamin's verses. One poet in a family was enough. Ridiculing his son's ballads, the prudent tradesman was quietly opposing his brother's example. And in the conflict over the young

Benjamin, between the uncle and the father, the father in the end won with prose.

Such prudence as Josiah Franklin's was less prosaic than it may at first thought appear. It had tones of revolution in it. All those Franklins in Ecton, son after father, had gone on hammering at the same forge because they had little choice as to how they should live. Owning land, entering professions, holding office: these were for privileged men. Outside the circles of privilege in England life was hard. Unprivileged men made up the bulk of those who came to America, looking for security and freedom. In Boston Josiah Franklin found gentry and theocracy still in power, though the tight experiment was breaking up, becoming more flexible and more secular. He accepted his rank as a tradesman and lived in it with a firm self-respect. His trade was his security. He taught the trade to his sons John and Peter, and he grieved because his son Josiah disliked it and went to sea, where he was later lost. If a man prospered in a trade, their father thought, he could have a kind of freedom too. That is, he could save money, acquire property, and live as he liked. "Seest thou a man diligent in his calling, he shall stand before kings, he shall not stand before mean men." Even the privileged could not easily resist a man with money. If they did, he could disregard them. With what he had he could feel himself equal to them, and superior to those among them who shabbily held on to their rank when they had nothing else. The tide was rising against privilege, and Josiah Franklin, mild revolutionary, was rising with it. New England was kind to him. His eldest brother Thomas, back in Ecton, had had gentlemen and noblemen for patrons. Josiah Franklin in Boston, in spite of his huge family, with no help but from his trade, yet left a fortune a third as large as Thomas's. And as an old man, with leisure to write to remote Franklins to ask if they were related to him, he could with fatherly satisfaction speak of his substantial sons.

But this was when his youngest son was almost forty. Thirty years before Josiah Franklin had aimed at a profession for the boy. "I was put to the grammar school at eight years of age, my father intending to devote me, as the tithe of his sons, to the service of the Church. My early readiness in learning to read (which must have been very early, as I do not remember when I could not read), and the opinion of all his friends that I should certainly make a good scholar, encouraged him in this purpose of his. My uncle Benjamin, too, approved of it, and proposed to give me all his shorthand volumes of sermons, I suppose as a stock to set up with, if I would learn his character. I continued, however, at the grammar school not quite one year, though in that time I had risen gradually from the middle of the class of that year to be the head of it, in order to go with that into the third at the end of the year. But my father, in the meantime, from a view of the expense of a college education, which, having so large a family, he could not well afford, and the mean living many so educated were afterwards able to obtain—reasons that he gave to his friends in my hearing—altered his first intention, took me from the grammar school, and sent me to a school for writing and arithmetic kept by a then famous man, Mr. George Brownell. . . . I acquired fair writing pretty soon, but I failed in the arithmetic, and made no progress in it. At ten years old I was taken home to assist my father in his business."[21]

There are no records of Franklin's schooling except the few words he wrote about it. In his will he left a hundred pounds to the free schools of Boston, to which, he said, "I . . . owe my first instructions in literature," to provide annual silver medals for deserving pupils.[22] But he was almost as wholly self-taught as if he had never gone to school. Failing in arithmetic under a good teacher, he later took it up, during his studious apprenticeship, and mastered it. The little Latin he had got in one year at the grammar school (now the Boston Latin School) he neglected until, a printer in Philadelphia, he had learned to read French, Italian, and Spanish, and was surprised to find that they made Latin easy for him. He wondered if it was not the natural process. "If you can clamber and get to the top of a staircase without using the steps, you will more easily gain them in descending; but certainly, if you begin with the lowest you will with more ease ascend to the top."[23] All Franklin's education was a natural process. The most insatiable and acquisitive young mind in America was on the hunt for knowledge and would have found it in a desert.

Josiah Franklin was more important than schools in the education of his promising son. For a tradesman a trade was a school.

The father for two years was Benjamin's teacher, as he had been John's and Peter's, in the family trade. The boy was more restless than these brothers. He disliked tallow as much as his brother Josiah did, and like him wanted to go to sea: "living near the water, I was much in and about it, learnt early to swim well, and to manage boats; and when in a boat or canoe with other boys, I was commonly allowed to govern, especially in any case of difficulty."[24] Fearing the sea, the father, near sixty, looked about for a trade which would be more agreeable to the son. "He therefore sometimes took me to walk with him, and see joiners, bricklayers, braziers, etc., at their work, that he might observe my inclination, and endeavour to fix it on some trade or other on land. It has ever since been a pleasure to me to see good workmen handle their tools; and it has been useful to me, having learnt so much by it as to be able to do little jobs myself in my house when a workman could not readily be got, and to construct little machines for my experiments, while the intention of making the experiments was fresh and warm in my mind."[25] For a time the cutler's trade seemed best, and the boy was put in charge of his cousin Samuel, who had come from London and established himself in Boston. But Samuel, son of the uncle Benjamin, did not have his father's partiality and asked a fee which Josiah Franklin thought too high. He finally decided, because the boy was fond of books, to make him a printer and apprenticed him to his brother James, nine years older, who at twenty had learned printing in London and returned to Boston with types and press of his own. At last Benjamin Franklin had begun his real education.

In the five years more which the apprentice spent in Boston he still had the frequent counsel of his father, and not only as to industry, honesty, prudence. His father, discouraging his son from verse, gave him good and useful advice about his first prose. "I fell far short in elegance of expression, in method and in perspicuity, of which he convinced me by several instances. I saw the justice of his remarks, and thence grew more attentive to the manner in writing."[26] When the brothers quarrelled they consulted their father, who usually sided with Benjamin. But Benjamin was James's apprentice, and the father, for all his care, had yielded most of his authority to the elder brother.

Brother and Brother

I F THE terms of the apprenticeship were in the form then customary, they said that Benjamin Franklin, twelve years old in 1718, "with the consent of his parents, doth put himself apprentice to his brother," then twenty-one, "to learn his art, and with him, after the manner of an apprentice, to serve" until he should himself be twenty-one. "During which term the said apprentice his master faithfully shall or will serve, his secrets keep, his lawful commands everywhere gladly do. He shall do no damage to his said master nor see it to be done of others; but to his power shall let, or forthwith give notice to his said master of the same. The goods of his said master he shall not waste, nor the same without licence of him to any give or lend. Hurt to his said master he shall not do, cause, nor procure to be done. He shall neither buy nor sell without his master's licence. Taverns, inns, or alehouses he shall not haunt. At cards, dice, tables, or any other unlawful game he shall not play. Matrimony he shall not contract; nor from the service of his said master day nor night absent himself; but in all things as an honest and faithful apprentice shall and will demean and behave himself towards his said master and all his during the said term." James Franklin, acknowledging the receipt of ten pounds, agreed that he "the said apprentice in the art of a printer which he now useth, shall teach and instruct or cause to be taught and instructed the best way and manner that he can, finding and allowing unto the said apprentice meat, drink, washing, lodging, and all other necessaries during the said term." In the last year of this apprenticeship Benjamin was to have journeyman's wages.

Though his strongest hankering was for the sea, he preferred ink to tallow if he must stay on land, and he had the instinct to make the best of a bargain he could not avoid. With his quick

mind and accurate hands he was soon skilful at the trade in which
all his life he took a hearty pride. James Franklin's business got
only slowly under way. There were other printers in Boston, and
a provincial town, however bookish, of ten or twelve thousand
people did not have too much need of printing. The brothers did
odd jobs, printing a few pamphlets, the ballads which the younger
wrote, even linen, calico, or silk "in good figures, very lively and
durable colours, and without the offensive smell which commonly
attends the linens printed here." At the end of 1719 James Franklin
was engaged to print the *Boston Gazette* and printed forty numbers
of it. When it was taken away from him for another printer he
started a newspaper of his own, the *New England Courant*, in
August 1721.

Benjamin, then fifteen, was already well along in the course of
that self-education of which his *Autobiography* gives a classic and
incomparable account. "From a child I was fond of reading, and
all the little money that came into my hands was ever laid out in
books." Pleased with the *Pilgrim's Progress*, he bought the rest of
Bunyan "in separate little volumes," and sold them to buy forty
or fifty "chapmen's books," said to be by R. Burton—nobody
knows who the author actually was—and called *Historical Collections* though they were random miscellanies of history, travel,
fiction, science, biography, and wonders of all sorts. The omnivo-
rous boy read his father's books "of polemic divinity" and later
felt that his time had been wasted. He "read abundantly" in
Plutarch's *Lives*, and thought that time well spent. He read
Defoe's *Essay on Projects* and Cotton Mather's *Essays to Do Good*,
which both set him thinking.[1] Apprenticed to a printer, he had
access to more and better books. Booksellers' apprentices would
lend him their masters' books to read overnight. Matthew Adams,
a tradesman who came often to James Franklin's shop, took an
interest in Benjamin and gave him the run of a private library. He
studied arithmetic and navigation, grammar and logic, and read
Locke's *Essay Concerning Human Understanding* and Xenophon's
Memorabilia, along with such contemporary free-thinkers as
Shaftesbury and Collins.

He read not to pass the time but to get at what he needed, and while he was reading he was learning to write. "Prose writing has been of great use to me in the course of my life, and was a principal means of my advancement."[2] His writing grew out of his arguing with a friend, John Collins, who was more fluent than he and could seem to overcome without convincing him. Benjamin, after one of these debates, wrote down his arguments and sent them to his friend. Letters passed between them, and by chance fell into Josiah Franklin's critical hands. Benjamin "determined to endeavour at improvement."

"About this time I met with an odd volume of the *Spectator*. It was the third. I had never before seen any of them. I bought it, read it over and over, and was much delighted with it. I thought the writing excellent, and wished, if possible, to imitate it. With this view I took some of the papers, and, making short hints of the sentiment in each sentence, laid them by a few days, and then, without looking at the book, tried to complete the papers again, by expressing each hinted sentiment at length, and as fully as it had been expressed before, in any suitable words that should come to hand. Then I compared my *Spectator* with the original, discovered some of my faults, and corrected them. But I found I wanted a stock of words, or a readiness in recollecting and using them, which I thought I should have acquired if I had gone on making verses; since the continual occasion for words of the same import, but of different length, to suit the measure, or of different sound for the rhyme, would have laid me under a constant necessity of searching for variety, and also have tended to fix that variety in my mind, and make me master of it. Therefore I took some of the tales and turned them into verse; and, after a time, when I had pretty well forgotten the prose, turned them back again. I also sometimes jumbled my collection of hints into confusion, and after some weeks endeavoured to reduce them into the best order, before I began to form the full sentences and complete the paper. This was to teach me method in the arrangement of thoughts. By comparing my work afterwards with the original, I discovered many faults and amended them; but I sometimes had the pleasure of fancying that, in certain particulars of small import, I had been lucky enough to improve the method or the language, and this encouraged me to think I might possibly in time come to be a tolerable English writer, of which I was extremely ambitious."[3]

As he tried to improve the manner of his writing, so he tried to improve his manners. Out of admiration for Socrates he gave up the disputatious habits he had formed, "and put on the humble inquirer and doubter. And being then, from reading Shaftesbury and Collins, become a real doubter in many points of our religious doctrine, I found this method safest for myself and very embarrassing to those against whom I used it; therefore I took a delight in it, practised it continually, and grew very expert in drawing people, even of superior knowledge, into concessions the consequences of which they did not foresee; entangling them in difficulties out of which they could not extricate themselves, and so obtaining victories that neither myself nor my cause always deserved. I continued this method some few years, but gradually left it, retaining only the habit of expressing myself in terms of modest diffidence."[4]

For his studies Franklin needed both time and money. "My time for these exercises and for reading was at night, after work or before it began in the morning, or on Sundays, when I contrived to be in the printing-house alone, evading as much as I could the common attendance on public worship which my father used to exact of me when I was under his care, and which indeed I still thought a duty, though I could not, as it seemed to me, afford time to practise it." He saved money by becoming a vegetarian—after he had read Thomas Tryon's *The Way to Health*—and proposing to his brother "that if he would give me, weekly, half the money he paid for my board, I would board myself. He instantly agreed to it, and I presently found that I could save half what he paid me. This was an additional fund for buying books. But I had another advantage in it. My brother and the rest going from the printing-house to their meals, I remained there alone, and, dispatching presently my light repast, which was often no more than a biscuit or a slice of bread, a handful of raisins or a tart from the pastry-cook's, and a glass of water, had the rest of the time till their return for study, in which I made the greater progress, from that greater clearness of head and quicker apprehension which usually attend temperance in eating and drinking."[5]

Though Franklin, hungry for time in which to study, might stay away from church, he could not avoid the family prayers at home. Once, when the winter's provision of meat had been salted, he proposed that his father say grace over the whole cask once for all.[6] At morning and evening prayers the restless apprentice taught himself geography from the four large maps which hung on the walls of the solemn room.[7] So far as any record shows, his work and his studies were his whole life from twelve to sixteen. But it may have been during these years that he tried his earliest known experiments. "When I was a boy I made two oval palettes," he wrote long afterwards to Barbeu Dubourg, "each about ten inches long and six broad, with a hole for the thumb, in order to retain it fast in the palm of my hand. They much resembled a painter's palettes. In swimming I pushed the edges of these forward, and I struck the water with their flat surfaces as I drew them back. I remember I swam faster by means of these palettes, but they fatigued my wrists. I also fitted to the soles of my feet a kind of sandals; but I was not satisfied with them, because I observed that the stroke is partly given by the inside of the feet and the ankles, and not entirely with the soles of the feet. . . . When I was a boy, I amused myself one day with flying a paper kite; and, approaching the bank of a pond which was near a mile broad, I tied the string to a stake, and the kite ascended to a very considerable height above the pond, while I was swimming. In a little time, being desirous of amusing myself with my kite and enjoying at the same time the pleasure of swimming, I returned; and, loosing from the stake the string with the little stick which was fastened to it, went again into the water, where I found that, lying on my back and holding the stick in my hands, I was drawn along the surface of the water in a very agreeable manner. Having then engaged another boy to carry my clothes round the pond, to a place which I pointed out to him on the other side, I began to cross the pond with my kite, which carried me quite over without the least fatigue, and with the greatest pleasure imaginable. I was only obliged occasionally to halt a little in my course, and resist its progress, when it appeared that, by following too quick, I lowered the kite too much; by doing which I occasionally made it rise again. I have never since that time practised this singular mode of swimming."[8]

For either sports or experiments he was too ambitious to have much time, and his ambition seems to have kept him close to books. He barely mentions boys of his own age, only one by name, and no girl at all.

I I

The establishment of the *New England Courant* brought him, as apprentice to the printer, into his first touch with affairs. There were already two newspapers in Boston, the *Boston News Letter* and the *Boston Gazette*: semi-official, conservative, and dull. There were two because there had been a quarrel. The *News Letter* had been published by the postmaster, who could read the mail, learn the news, have it printed, and distribute his papers by his carriers. But when John Campbell lost his post in 1718, he refused to turn over the *News Letter* to his successor, William Brooker. Brooker, angry, started the *Gazette* and gave the printing of it to James Franklin. Within a year there was a third postmaster, Philip Musgrave, who took the printing away from Franklin. Franklin, now angry too, undertook a third newspaper. "I remember," his brother later wrote, "his being dissuaded by some of his friends from the undertaking, as being not likely to succeed. . . . He went on, however, with the undertaking, and after having worked in composing the types and printing off the sheets, I was employed to carry the papers through the streets to the customers."[9]

Not all James Franklin's friends dissuaded him. A new spirit was moving in Boston and there was a lively opposition which had hitherto had no voice. Episcopalians and deists alike resented the stubborn power of the Congregational churches. To men of easy temper the Puritanism of the Mathers and the magistrates seemed as old as Cromwell. John Checkley, bookseller and apothecary, had lived fifteen years in Europe, and in Boston had argued in favour of bishops and been harried and fined by the authorities. William Douglass, born in Scotland, had studied medicine at Edinburgh,

Leyden, and Paris, and had come to Boston with the only medical degree in America. These two more than any others encouraged James Franklin, who had learned his trade in the London of Addison and Steele, of popular freethinkers, of coffee houses and Grub Street. A bookselling apothecary (later a clergyman), a physician, and a printer put their heads together to give Boston a newspaper such as the town had never had before.

The first number appeared in the middle of a hot summer (7 August) when smallpox was epidemic, and the *Courant's* "chief design" was to "oppose the doubtful and dangerous practice"[10] of inoculation. Cotton Mather, who had heard from one of his slaves about inoculation in Africa and had read about inoculation in Constantinople, late in June suggested to Zabdiel Boylston that he try the experiment. Boylston inoculated two of his sons and two of his slaves, and went on to become the real hero of the plague and to leave the first masterly clinical report by an American physician. His venture caused uproar in Boston. The selectmen called him to account. Pamphlets and newspapers abused him. His life and Mather's were threatened. Mather, the apologist for the practice, got more blame than the practitioner.

Douglass, writing in the *Courant*[11] that inoculation had come from "the Greek old women," opposed it on medical grounds, like most of the Boston doctors. Knowing nothing of bacteriology, they saw only fantastic hocus-pocus in the new preventive. Let Cotton Mather go back to his witches. The Boston wits who quickly took to the new paper, and wrote for it, fell in with Douglass. They baited and twitted the Mathers. The Mathers answered back. A grandson of Increase Mather, Thomas Walter, once an intimate friend of Checkley but recently at odds with him, wrote a broadside answer (also printed by James Franklin) to the first number: *The Little-Compton Scourge; or, The Anti-Courant*. Walter, who must have had Checkley in mind, superciliously condemned the anonymous apothecary who talked of gentle readers but who could not hope to interest any but "men of passion and resentment." Checkley in the third *Courant* replied to this "obscene and fuddling Merry-Andrew" and accused him of drunkenness and debauchery. Although James Franklin promptly denied that any of his writers had ever meant to reflect on the clergy or the government,[12] and

Checkley wrote no more for the *Courant,* there could never be peace with the Mathers. Cotton Mather declared that "the practice of supporting and publishing every week a libel on purpose to lessen and blacken and burlesque the virtuous and principal ministers of religion in a country, and render the services of their ministry despicable, even detestable, to the people, is a wickedness that was never known before in any country, Christian, Turkish, or Pagan, on the face of the earth."[13] And he named the writers for the *Courant* the Hell-Fire Club.

The argument over inoculation ran as long as the epidemic lasted, but the *Courant* after a few numbers turned more and more to lighter themes. A Clan of Honest Wags wrote to the editor that they were tired of the paper's one subject and could do better themselves.[14] There was no such clan, as there was no actual Hell-Fire Club. There were an enterprising printer and two or three contributors at first, and soon others. This was enough to bring the *Spectator* to Boston and start a little war with dullness. "The publisher earnestly desires," the second *Courant* said, "his friends may favour him from time to time with some short pieces, serious, sarcastic, ludicrous, or otherwise amusing; or sometimes professedly dull (to accommodate some of his acquaintance) that this *Courant* may be of the more universal use." His friends did favour him. Every Monday the newspaper, usually a single sheet printed on both sides, listed the ships which had entered or left the port, and gave bits of news from other towns or colonies or from Europe. But the essence of the *Courant* was letters to the editor from Timothy Turnstone, Tom Penshallow, Tom Tram, Ichabod Henroost, Abigail Afterwit, Betty Frugal, Fanny Mournful, Homespun Jack, Tabitha Talkative, Dorothy Love, Philanthropus, Philomusus, Hypercarpus, Hypercriticus: all the Boston wits being as Addisonian as they could about Boston manners. Obliged to be careful about ministers and magistrates, they poked fun at rival editors and the postmaster. They hinted scandals. They ridiculed foppery, protested against extravagance, burlesqued pedantry, and talked again and again about the charms and follies of women.

The files of the *Courant* are dead now, except for rummaging antiquarians. But it is in the *Courant* for 2 April 1722 that Benjamin Franklin, sixteen, first speaks in prose known to be his. And he speaks, like the other contributors, under a disguise, calling himself Silence Dogood.

"Sir,

"It may not be improper in the first Place to inform your Readers, that I intend once a Fortnight to present them, by the Help of this Paper, with a short Epistle, which I presume will add somewhat to their Entertainment.

"And since it is observed, that the Generality of People, now a days, are unwilling either to commend or dispraise what they read, until they are in some measure informed who or what the Author of it is, whether he be *poor* or *rich*, *old* or *young*, a *Scollar* or a *Leather-Apron Man*, &c., and give their Opinion of the Performance, according to the Knowledge which they have of the Author's Circumstances, it may not be amiss to begin with a short Account of my past Life and present Condition, that the Reader may not be at a Loss to judge whether or no my Lucubrations are worth his reading."[15]

(Addison as Mr. Spectator had introduced himself: "I have observed that a reader seldom peruses a book with pleasure until he knows whether the writer of it be a black or a fair man, of a mild or choleric disposition, married or a bachelor, with other particulars of the like nature that conduce very much to the right understanding of an author." But Addison had not even thought of "poor or rich, old or young, a scholar or a leather-apron man.")

The whole character of Silence Dogood reveals, in stroke after stroke through three papers, the boy who imagined her. She had been born, she said, on shipboard on the way to New England, and her father had been lost on the voyage. Living in the country, not far from town, "I was bound out apprentice, that I might no longer be a charge to my indigent mother, who was put to hard shifts for a living." Her master was a minister who saw that she was taught needle-work, writing, and arithmetic, and, "observing that I took a more than ordinary delight in reading ingenious books, he gave me the free use of his library, which though it was but small yet it was well chose, to inform the understanding rightly and enable the mind to form great and noble ideas." In time the minister began to look for a wife and, after "several unsuccessful fruitless attempts on the more topping part of our sex," he chose his apprentice—as

Peter Folger had chosen his indentured servant, Benjamin's grand-mother. "As he had been a great benefactor (and in a manner a father to me), I could not well deny his request." Married, mother of three children, and widowed, Silence Dogood now lived quietly in the country. "I am an enemy to vice and a friend to virtue. I am of an extensive charity and a great forgiver of private injuries; a hearty lover of the clergy and all good men, and a mortal enemy to arbitrary government and unlimited power. . . . I have like-wise a natural inclination to observe and reprove the faults of others, at which I have an excellent faculty. . . . I now take up a resolution to do for the future all that lies in my way for the service of my countrymen."[16]

Franklin, "being still a boy, and suspecting that my brother would object to printing anything of mine in his paper if he knew it to be mine,"[17] had slipped his first letter from Silence Dogood under the door of the printing-house. And though what he had written pleased his brother and his friends, and Mrs. Dogood was welcomed, the apprentice kept his secret. Sometimes in his in-vented role, more often unconsciously as himself, he put his young thoughts into words.

Mrs. Dogood, having an allegorical dream about Harvard Col-lege, saw it with Franklin's eyes. Riches and Poverty kept the gate, and Poverty rejected those whom Riches did not recommend. Within the temple Learning sat on a high throne reached by diffi-cult steps. Most of the worshippers "contented themselves to sit at the foot with Madam Idleness and her maid Ignorance" until they had to ascend, when "they were fain to crave the assistance of those who had got up before them, and who, for the reward perhaps of a pint of milk or a piece of plum cake, lent the lubbers a helping hand and sat them, in the eyes of the world, upon a level with themselves. . . . Every beetle-skull seemed well satisfied with his own portion of learning, though perhaps he was e'en just as igno-rant as ever." Once out of the temple, "some I perceived took to merchandising, others to travelling, some to one thing, some to another, and some to nothing; and many of them from henceforth, for want of patrimony, lived as poor as church mice, being unable to dig and ashamed to beg, and to live by their wits it was impossible. . . . I reflected in my mind on the extreme folly of those parents who, blind to their children's dullness and insensible of the solidity of their skulls, because they think their purses can afford it will needs send them to the Temple of Learning, where, for want of a suitable genius, they learn little more than how to carry themselves handsomely and enter a room genteelly (which might as well be acquired at a dancing-school), and from whence they return, after abundance of trouble and charge, as great block-heads as ever, only more proud and self-conceited."[18]

The apprentice had once thought of Harvard and the ministry for himself, but now that he was a tradesman he smiled at them to prove how little he had missed and how sensibly he had preferred a better career. (He even knew enough Latin to furnish most of the Dogood papers with pertinent Latin mottoes.) And it was a re-formed poet, no Widow Dogood, who humorously took up the cause of New England poetry. Visitors to the country did not ex-pect good poetry there, but perhaps the reason was that it had so little native encouragement. Let it be encouraged by suitable encomiums.

"There has lately appeared among us a most excellent piece of poetry, entitled *An Elegy upon the Much Lamented Death of Mrs. Mehitabel Kitel, Wife of Mr. John Kitel of Salem, etc.* It may be justly said in its praise, without flattery to the author, that it is the most extraordinary piece that ever wrote in New England. The language is so soft and easy, the expression so moving and pathetic, but above all, the verse and numbers so charming and natural that it is almost beyond comparison. . . . And for the af-fecting part, I will leave your readers to judge if ever they read any lines that would sooner make them draw their breath and sigh, if not shed tears, than these following:

Come let us mourn, for we have lost a wife, a daughter, and a sister,
Who have lately taken flight, and greatly we have missed her.

"In another place:

Some little time before she yielded up her breath,
She said, I ne'er shall hear one sermon more on earth.
She kissed her husband some little time before she expired,
Then leaned her head the pillow on, just out of breath and tired.

"But the threefold appellation in the first line—

a wife, a daughter, and a sister—

must not pass unobserved. That line in the celebrated Watts—

Gunston the just, the generous, and the young—

is nothing comparable to it. The latter only mentions three quali-
fications of one person who was deceased, which could therefore
raise grief and compassion for but one. Whereas the former (our
most excellent poet) gives his reader a sort of an idea of the death
of three persons, viz.:

a wife, a daughter, and a sister,

which is three times as great a loss as the death of one and consequently must raise three times as much grief and compassion in
the reader.

"The author has (to his honor) invented a new species of poetry,
which wants a name and was never before known. . . . Now 'tis
pity that such an excellent piece should not be dignified with a
particular name; and seeing it cannot be called either Epic, Sap-
phic, Lyric, or Pindaric, nor any other name yet invented, I presume it may (in honor and remembrance of the dead) be called
the Kitelic."

For the benefit of New England poets who wrote nothing so
often as elegies, the critic offered *A Receipt to Make a New England Funeral Elegy.*

"*For the title of your elegy.* Of these you may have enough ready
made to your hands; but if you should choose to make it yourself,
you must be sure not to omit the words *ætatis suæ*, which will
beautify it exceedingly.

"*For the subject of your elegy.* Take one of your neighbours
who has lately departed this life; it is no great matter at what age
the party died, but it will be best if he went away suddenly, being
killed, drowned, or froze to death.

"Having chose the person, take all his virtues, excellencies,
etc., and if he have not enough, you may borrow some to make up
a sufficient quantity: to these add his last words, dying expressions,
etc., if they are to be had; mix all these together and be sure you

strain them well. Then season all with a handful or two of melancholy expressions, such as *dreadful, deadly, cruel cold death, unhappy fate, weeping eyes,* etc. Having mixed all these ingredients well, put them into the empty skull of some young Harvard (but in case you have ne'er a one at hand, you may use your own); there let them ferment for the space of a fortnight, and by that time they will be incorporated into a body, which take out; and having prepared a sufficient quantity of double rhymes, such as *power, flower; quiver, shiver; grieve us, leave us; tell you, excel you; expeditions, physicians; fatigue him, intrigue him,* etc., you must spread all upon paper, and if you can procure a scrap of Latin to put at the end, it will garnish it mightily; then having affixed your name at the bottom, with a *Mœstus composuit,* you will have an excellent elegy.

"*N. B.* This receipt will serve when a female is the subject of your elegy, provided you borrow a greater quantity of virtues, excellencies, etc."[19]

This was the most effective of all the Dogood papers. Other contributors caught at the name Kitelic and for months applied it again and again to bad native verse. Probably none of them knew that the parodist had himself written an elegy of the very kind he laughed at. Or so it seems from the manuscript *Elegy on My Sister Franklin,*[20] only recently discovered and now first mentioned in a Franklin biography. The precise date of the *Elegy* is still uncertain, and the name of the sister-in-law whose death called it forth. But the parody's ridicule of the Kitelic triple epithet "a wife, a daughter, and a sister" glanced at Franklin's own line:

> We've lost a Mother, Daughter, Sister kind;

and the general language of the *Elegy,* while less hackneyed than that of the parody, was high and turgid.

> Warm from my Breast surcharg'd with Grief & Woe
> These mellancholly Strains spontaneous flow
> Flow for a fav'rite Sister's sad Decease
> Flow for the worthiest of the female Race. . . .
> My dear my much-loved Sister!—O my Friend
> We in this World on nothing may depend:
> For soon as we esteem ourselves possest

Of every needful Thing to make us blest
Some Friend's Demise (like hers we now lament)
Casual Mischance, or tragical Event
Like an intrudent Guest will intervene
Frustrate our Hopes and mar our blissful Scene.
How weak! how vain! how void all mundane Joys
A Medley fraught with Nonsense, Shew and Noise
O what is Life which we so high esteem
A Bubble, Vapour, Shadow, fleeting Dream
From sordid Dust we sprang & surely must
Or soon or late return to native Dust
What mortal Man even in his best Estate
All Vanity, Pride, Folly and Deceit. . . .
Crowns have their Thorns and Opulence its **Bane**
And all our Pleasures their Alloy of Pain
All the Vicissitudes of Life declare
Uncertainty alone is certain here. . . .
No sublunary Blessings long endure
And from Death's Clutches nought can us ensure
Who o'er all Flesh maintains a sovereign Sway
And Millions fall his Victims every Day
Nor Worth, Wit, Beauty, Wealth or Power can free
From rigid Fate's immutable Decree. . . .
Else might this worthy Saint whose wayward Fate
We now deplore have claimed a longer Date
Of circling Years her Kin to serve and bless
Enjoy her Friends and Life's good Things possess. . . .
And tho I humbly trust our Friend deceas'd
Is wafted to the Saints eternal Rest
Yet her sad Exit maugre my Resolves
In Woe's profound Abyss my Soul involves
With Sighs & Groans my lab'ring Bosom swells
And down my cheeks Grief's mournful Stream impels
May Heaven forgive me if I ought offend
Whilst thus I mourn my dear departed Friend
Sure Heaven forbids not for our Friends to mourn
Nor to bedew with Tears their peaceful Urn.

These are perhaps the earliest surviving words of Franklin, written when he had not yet finally decided between poetry and prose. But by 25 June 1722, when he parodied such elegies as his, he had found an idiom fully natural to him and had things more urgent than Kitelic elegies to think about.

III

The anger of the Mathers had made the magistrates watchful. In the *Courant* for 11 June, James Franklin printed a fictitious letter from Newport which said that pirates had been seen off that coast. "We are advised from Boston that the government of the Massachusetts are fitting out a ship (the *Flying Horse*), to go after the pirates, to be commanded by Captain Peter Papillon, and 'tis thought he will sail some time this month, wind and weather permitting." The Council took this for contempt of the authorities, and James Franklin was arrested, examined, and committed to the stone jail in Boston: "I suppose," his brother explains, "because he would not discover his author. I too was taken up and examined before the Council; but, though I did not give them any satisfaction, they contented themselves with admonishing me, and dismissed me, considering me, perhaps, as an apprentice who was bound to keep his master's secrets."[21] After a week in prison James Franklin told the Council he was "truly sensible and heartily sorry," and after a month, when Dr. Boylston had certified that the offender's health had suffered from confinement, he was released. "It was no mitigation of my punishment," he wrote in a lively account of it in the *Courant*, "to think that better men than myself had been in prison before me. I know the late Governor Dudley was confined in the time of the Revolution; but I never could perceive that the gaol stank a whit the less for him."[22]

During the brother's absence Benjamin carried on the newspaper alone. In his eighth Dogood paper he spoke his mind in "an abstract from the *London Journal*": "Without freedom of thought there can be no such thing as wisdom; and no such thing as public liberty without freedom of speech; which is the right of every man as far as by it he does not hurt or control the right of another; and this is the only check it ought to suffer and the only bounds it ought to know. . . . Whoever would overthrow the liberty of a nation must begin by subduing the freeness of speech: a thing terrible to public traitors."[23] But the younger brother was shrewd as well as bold. Ever since the beginning of the *Courant* he had apparently kept a file of the paper, for himself or for the office, and had methodically entered in his own handwriting the names of the contributors. Either he had not entered the names for the offending issue and the one before it or he now destroyed them and substituted other copies. In any case, he gave up his careful habit, and after 28 May the file betrays no secrets.[24]

The six later Dogood papers had more and more of the apprentice in them. "It has been for some time a question with me whether a commonwealth suffers more by hypocritical pretenders to religion or by the openly profane. But some late thoughts of this nature have inclined me to think that the hypocrite is the more dangerous person of the two, especially if he sustains a post in the government. . . . A little religion, and a little honesty, goes a great way in courts. . . . If we have had, or are like to have, any instances of this nature in New England, we cannot better manifest our love to religion and the country than by setting the deceivers in a true light and undeceiving the deceived, however such discoveries may be represented by the ignorant or designing enemies of our peace and safety."[25] The apprentice put in the mouth of Mrs. Dogood an argument for insurance for widows, from Defoe, and another for old maids, but it must have been his observation not hers which lay back of his remarks on drinking.

" 'Tis true, drinking does not improve our faculties, but it enables us to use them; and therefore I conclude that much study and experience, and a little liquor, are of absolute necessity for some tempers, in order to make them accomplished orators. . . . The moderate use of liquor and a well-placed and well-regulated anger often produce this same effect; and some wits who cannot ordinarily talk but in broken sentences and false grammar do in the heat of passion express themselves with as much eloquence as warmth. . . . But after all it must be considered that no pleasure can give satisfaction or prove advantageous to a reasonable mind which is not attended with the restraints of reason. . . . 'Tis strange to see men of a regular conversation become rakish and profane when intoxicated with drink, and yet more surprising to observe that some who appear to be the most profligate wretches when sober become mighty religious in their cups, and will then, and at no other time, address their Maker but when they are destitute of reason and actually affronting Him. Some shrink in the wetting, and others swell to such an unusual bulk in their imaginations that they can in an instant understand all arts and sciences, by the liberal education of a little vivifying punch or a sufficient quantity of other exhilarating liquor. . . . It argues some shame in the drunkards themselves that they have invented numberless words and phrases to cover their folly, whose proper significations are harmless or have no signification at all. They are seldom known to be *drunk*, though they are very often *boozy, cogey, tipsy, foxed, merry, mellow, fuddled, groatable, confoundedly cut, see two moons*; are *among the Philistines, in a very good humor, see the sun*, or, *the sun has shone upon them;* they *clip the King's English*, are *almost froze, feverish, in their altitudes, pretty well entered*, etc. In short, every day produces some new word or phrase which might be added to the vocabulary of the tipplers. But I have chose to mention these few, because if at any time a man of sobriety and temperance happens to cut himself confoundedly, or is almost froze, or feverish, or accidentally sees the sun, etc., he may escape the imputation of being drunk, when his misfortune comes to be related."[26]

"In persons of a contemplative disposition," the apprentice wrote, "the most indifferent things provoke the exercise of the imagination; and the satisfactions which often arise to them thereby are a certain relief to the labor of the mind (when it has been intensely fixed on more substantial subjects) as well as to that of the body. In one of the late pleasant moonlight evenings"—this was in September—"I so far indulged in myself the humor of the town in walking abroad as to continue from my lodgings two or three hours later than usual. . . . I met a crowd of Tarpaulins and their doxies, linked to each other by the arms, who ran (by their own account) after the rate of *six knots an hour*, and bent their course toward the Common. Their eager and amorous emotions of body, occasioned by taking their mistresses *in tow*, they called *wild steerage;* and as a pair of them happened to trip and come to the ground, the company were called upon to *bring to*, for that Jack and Betty were *foundered*. But this fleet were not less comical than a company of females I soon after came up with, who, by throwing their heads to the right and left at everyone who passed by them, I concluded came out with no other design than to revive the spirit of love in disappointed bachelors, and expose themselves to sale to the first bidder. . . . As it grew later I observed that many pensive youths, with down looks and a slow pace, would be ever now and then crying out on the cruelty of their mistresses; others with a more rapid pace and cheerful air would be swinging their canes and clapping their cheeks, and whispering at certain intervals: 'I'm certain I shall have her! This is more than I expected! How charmingly she talks!' "[27]

The industrious apprentice had taken a few hours off from his work, his books, and his ambition, to look with sharp, humorous eyes at idlers. And, as if to prove that he was Benjamin Franklin, he added a little apologue on economy: "Upon the whole I conclude that our night-walkers are a set of people who contribute very much to the health and satisfaction of those who have been fatigued with business or study and occasionally observe their pretty gestures and impertinencies. But among men of business the shoemakers and other dealers in leather are doubly obliged to them, inasmuch as they exceedingly promote the consumption of their ware. And I have heard of a shoemaker who, upon being asked by a noted rambler whether he could tell how long her shoes would last, very prettily answered that he knew how many days she might wear them but not how many nights; because they were then put to a more violent and irregular service than when she employed herself in the common affairs of the house."

James Franklin had repented only enough to get out of prison, and the *Courant* kept up its opposition, now more to the magistrates than to the ministers. On 14 January 1723 a vigorous article resumed the theme of the Dogood paper which had argued that "hypocritical pretenders to religion" are worse for a commonwealth than the "openly profane." "There are many persons," this *Courant* said, "who seem to be more than ordinary religious, but yet are on several accounts worse, by far, than those who pretend to no religion at all." At once the Council struck again, and forbade James Franklin to print or publish his newspaper, "or any other pamphlet or paper of the like nature, except it first be supervised by the Secretary of this Province." The friends of the *Courant* met and, after weighing various stealthy schemes, decided that it should now be printed in the name of Benjamin Franklin. "To avoid the censure of the Assembly," the younger tells, "that might fall on him as still printing it by his apprentice, the contrivance was that my old indenture should be returned to me, with a full discharge on the back of it, to be shown on occasion; but to secure to him the benefit of my service, I was to sign new indentures for the remainder of the term, which were to be kept private. A very flimsy scheme it was; however, it was immediately executed."[28] The *Courant* for 11 February, as by the new publisher, announced a new policy. "The present undertaking . . . is designed purely for the diversion and merriment of the reader. Pieces of pleasancy and mirth have a secret charm in them to allay the heats and tumours of our spirits, and to make a man forget his restless resentments. They have a strange power to tune the harsh disorders of the soul, and to reduce us to a serene and placid state of mind. The main design of this weekly paper will be to entertain the town with the most comical and diverting incidents of humane life. . . . Nor shall we be wanting to fill up these papers with a grateful interspersion of more serious morals which may be drawn from the most ludicrous and odd parts of life."

This prospectus must have been by Benjamin Franklin, and so must have been an article, in the following number, on honours and titles of respect. It was a witty as well as mature apprentice who wrote: "In old time it was no disrespect for men and women to be called by their own names. Adam was never called Master Adam; we never read of Noah Esquire, Lot Knight and Baronet, nor the Right Honourable Abraham, Viscount Mesopotamia, Baron of Canaan. No, no, they were plain men, honest country graziers, that took care of their families and their flocks. Moses was a great prophet and Aaron a priest of the Lord; but we never read of the Reverend Moses nor the Right Reverend Father in God, Aaron, by Divine Providence Lord Archbishop of Israel. Thou never sawest Madam Rebecca in the Bible, my Lady Rachel; nor Mary, though a princess of the blood, after the death of Joseph called the Princess Dowager of Nazareth. No, plain Rebecca, Rachel, Mary,

or the Widow Mary, or the like. It was no incivility then to mention their naked names as they were expressed."

The *Courant* prospered under its discreeter policy, increased its
circulation, and raised its price. But it was not large enough to
have room in it for two Franklins. James, married to Ann Smith
in February, was a capable printer and journalist, but Benjamin at seventeen had the best mind in Boston and was the best
apprentice in the world. Though he could not know that, neither
could he help outgrowing his position and feeling uncomfortable
in it. James too was uncomfortable. The truth about the Dogood
papers had come out, the writer had been so much praised that his
master thought him vain, and now Benjamin, ostensibly the publisher and no longer an apprentice, had the advantage if he cared
to use it. He did. "I took upon me to assert my freedom," Benjamin admits, "presuming that he would not venture to produce
the new indentures. It was not fair in me to take this advantage,
and this I therefore reckon one of the first errata of my life; but
the unfairness of it weighed little with me when under the impressions of resentment for the blows his passion too often urged him
to bestow upon me, though he was otherwise not an ill-natured
man. Perhaps I was too saucy and provoking."[29]

An indenture of apprenticeship in 1723 was more than a simple
understanding. Master and apprentice were bound in what was
almost a trade sacrament, and Benjamin, leaving his master who
was also his brother, could not avoid a strong sense of guilt. But
neither could he any longer endure their incompatibility. Yet at
first he meant no more than to find journeyman work with one of
the other Boston printers. James stopped that by speaking first to
all of them. Masters must stand together even if brothers could
not. "I then thought of going to New York, as the nearest place
where there was a printer; and I was rather inclined to leave Boston
when I reflected that I had already made myself a little obnoxious
to the governing party, and . . . it was likely I might, if I stayed,
soon bring myself into scrapes; and farther, that my indiscreet
disputations about religion began to make me pointed at with
horror by good people as an infidel or atheist. I determined on the
point, but my father now siding with my brother, I was sensible
that, if I attempted to go openly, means would be used to prevent

me. My friend Collins, therefore, undertook to manage a little for me. He agreed with the captain of a New York sloop for my passage, under the notion of my being a young acquaintance of his that had got a naughty girl with child, whose friends would compel me to marry her, and therefore I could not appear or come away publicly. So I sold some of my books to raise a little money, was taken on board privately, and, as we had a fair wind, in three days I found myself in New York."[30]

That methodical file of the *Courant* which Benjamin Franklin had kept ends with the number for 16 September. Two weeks later a famous advertisement in the paper said: "James Franklin, printer in Queen's Street, wants a likely lad for an apprentice."

Philadelphia

Journeyman

MATHER BYLES, another Mather grandson who had written against the *Courant* and who was almost exactly Benjamin Franklin's age, was then at Harvard, and he stayed on in Boston to be its clerical wit and man of letters till the Revolution. Thomas Hutchinson, five years younger, that year entered Harvard, also to stay in Boston and in time become governor of Massachusetts. If either of these promising sons of the "governing party" had left Boston for New York or Philadelphia he would have carried letters of recommendation to ministers and officials anywhere he might go. The runaway apprentice, with no letters and little money, had all his fortunes in his fingers and his mind, but he was not too much worse off than the privileged boys would have been. As there was a kind of fraternity of the ruling caste from province to province, so was there a fraternity of tradesmen. Wherever Franklin could find a master printer he could be at home if there was work for him to do, and if there was work he could do it.

Furtive on his voyage to New York, he was still reasonable. Becalmed off Block Island, the sailors caught cod out of the sea and ate them. The vegetarian philosopher told himself that this was unprovoked murder, since none of the fish had injured any of the men. "But I had formerly been a great lover of fish, and, when this came hot out of the frying-pan, it smelt admirably well. I balanced some time between principle and inclination, till I recollected that, when the fish were opened, I saw smaller fish taken out of their stomachs; then thought I: 'If you eat one another, I don't see why we mayn't eat you.' So I dined upon cod very heartily, and continued to eat with other people, returning only now and then to a vegetable diet. So convenient a thing it is to be a reasonable creature, since it enables one to find or make a reason for everything one has a mind to do."[1]

New York, then still a smaller town than Boston, had no newspaper and only one printer, William Bradford, who had been the first printer in Philadelphia and, after trouble with the authorities there, government printer in New York for thirty years. Bradford could not use a new hand, but he said that his son Andrew Bradford in Philadelphia had just lost a journeyman by death and might need another. Franklin, leaving his chest to follow him, set out across the bay in a boat for Perth Amboy, to walk from there across New Jersey fifty miles to Burlington.

For this journey he is the sole historian.[2] "In crossing the bay we met with a squall that tore our rotten sails to pieces, prevented our getting into the Kill, and drove us upon Long Island. In our way, a drunken Dutchman, who was a passenger too, fell overboard; when he was sinking I reached through the water to his shock pate and drew him up so that we got him in again." The man had a Dutch (German?) *Pilgrim's Progress*, and Franklin, an expert even in a storm, thought it a better edition than he had ever seen in English. The surf made it impossible for the boat to land on Long Island, and they were obliged to lie at anchor overnight, all of them as wet as the Dutchman. "But, the wind abating the next day, we made a shift to reach Amboy before night, having been thirty hours on the water, without victuals or any drink but a bottle of filthy rum, and the water we sailed on being salt."

Feverish, he remembered something he had read, drank a great deal of cold water before he went to sleep, and woke up well the next morning. Having crossed the ferry at Perth Amboy, he walked till noon in the rain and then stopped for the rest of the day at a poor inn, "beginning now to wish that I had never left home." The second night he met an inn-keeper who "finding I had read a little, became very sociable and friendly." They talked about books and were friends thereafter as long as the inn-keeper lived. At Burlington on Franklin's third morning he found that the regular boat by which he meant to go down the Delaware to Philadelphia had left, and that there would be no other for three days. "An old woman in the town, of whom I had bought ginger-bread to eat on the water . . . invited me to lodge at her house. . . . She was very hospitable, gave me a dinner of ox-cheek with great good will, accepting only of a pot of ale in return." But, "walking in the evening by the side of the river," he saw another boat which, he learned, was on its way to Philadelphia "with several people in her." He joined them and they rowed downstream till midnight. Afraid they might pass the town in the dark, "we put toward the shore, got into a creek, landed near an old fence with the rails of which we made a fire, the night being cold, in October, and there we remained till daylight." At eight or nine o'clock on a Sunday morning they reached the Market Street wharf in Philadelphia.

"I was in my working dress, my best clothes being to come round by sea. I was dirty from my journey; my pockets were stuffed out with shirts and stockings; and I knew no soul nor where to look for lodging. I was fatigued with travelling, rowing, and want of rest; I was very hungry; and my whole stock of cash consisted of a Dutch dollar and about a shilling in copper. The latter I gave the people of the boat for my passage, who at first refused it, on account of my rowing; but I insisted on their taking it. A man being sometimes more generous when he has but a little money than when he has plenty, perhaps through fear of being thought to have but little.

"Then I walked up the street, gazing about till near the market house I met a boy with bread. I had made many a meal on bread, and, inquiring where he got it, I went immediately to the baker's he directed me to, in Second Street, and asked for biscuit, intending such as we had in Boston; but they, it seems, were not made in Philadelphia. Then I asked for a threepenny loaf, and was told they had none such. So, not considering or knowing the difference of money, and the greater cheapness nor the names of his bread, I bade him give me threepenny worth of any sort. He gave me, accordingly, three great puffy rolls. I was surprised at the quantity, but took it, and, having no room in my pockets, walked off with a roll under each arm, and eating the other. Thus I went up Market Street as far as Fourth Street, passing by the door of Mr. Read, my future wife's father; when she, standing at the door, saw me, and thought I made, as I certainly did, a most awkward, ridiculous appearance. Then I turned and went down Chestnut Street and part of Walnut Street, eating my roll all the way; and, coming round, found myself again at Market Street wharf, near the boat I came in, to which I went for a draught of the river water; and, being filled with one of my rolls, gave the other two to a woman and her child that came down the river in the boat with us, and were waiting to go farther."

He saw many "clean-dressed people" in the street all walking the same way and followed them to and into the Quaker meeting house near the market. In the Quaker silence he fell asleep till the meeting was over. "This was, therefore, the first house I was in, or slept in, in Philadelphia." Again in the street he met "a young Quaker man, whose countenance I liked," and asked him how to find lodgings. The young Quaker advised him against the Three Mariners, as not quite reputable, and took him to the Crooked Billet in Water Street. "Here I got a dinner; and, while I was eating it, several sly questions were asked me, as it seemed to be suspected from my youth and appearance that I might be some runaway." He slept all afternoon without undressing, had to be called to supper, went back to bed, and slept all night. Early the next day "I made myself as tidy as I could and went to Andrew Bradford the printer's."

Not only Andrew Bradford welcomed the boy but also Bradford's father, who had, it turned out, come from New York to Philadelphia on horseback. The three printers had breakfast together. Andrew Bradford had already hired a journeyman in place of the dead Aquila Rose, but he told Franklin there was another printer who had just opened a shop in town and might employ him. If not, he might lodge at Bradford's house and do odd jobs till something better came along. William Bradford went with Franklin to introduce him to the rival printer, Samuel Keimer. Keimer put a composing stick in Franklin's hand, watched him work a few minutes, and said that though he then had nothing for the boy to do, he would soon have. Not knowing who William Bradford was, Keimer boasted of his prospects, and the old man drew him out with artful questions. "I, who stood by and heard all, saw immediately that one of them was a crafty old sophister, and the other a mere novice."[3]

Franklin from the first had a poor opinion of both Andrew

Bradford, who seemed illiterate, and Keimer, who seemed eccentric and foolish. The young expert from Boston looked over Keimer's shop, the one "worn-out font of English," and the lame press which he had not yet used. Having done what could be done to put the press in order, and promising to come back later to help with the elegy on Aquila Rose which Keimer was composing direct from type, Franklin returned to Bradford's house for a few days and the work that Bradford could find for him. When Keimer had finished his elegy and had a pamphlet to reprint, he employed all Franklin's time. Not liking his journeyman to live in his rival's house, and having no furniture in his own, Keimer got lodgings for the future husband of Deborah Read in Deborah's father's house.

This first winter in Philadelphia Franklin enjoyed a freedom he had never felt before. Here he had no father to admonish and no brother to bully him. In Boston he had been an apprentice, a boy whom everybody knew and took for granted. In Philadelphia he was a skilled workman with his own money in his pocket. Being a stranger, he was something of a novelty. Coming from Boston, the largest city in the colonies, he was something of a notability among "the young people of the town, that were lovers of reading, with whom I spent my evenings very pleasantly."[4] There were sober Quakers in Philadelphia as there had been strict Puritans in Boston, but in both the young were still young. Philadelphia had not been founded by persecuting men and had no long tradition of theocracy. In the more tolerant town Franklin relaxed and expanded. If he read as hard as he had done for years, he does not say so. About Boston he speaks chiefly of his studies. About Philadelphia he speaks chiefly of his friends. And while he was charming them he was impressing them by his hard work and cool head.

He forgot Boston as much as he could and sent word of his whereabouts only to his friend Collins. But Franklin's brother-in-law Robert Holmes, master of a sloop that traded between Boston and Delaware, heard at New Castle that Benjamin was in Philadelphia and wrote to tell him how much his family and friends were concerned for him, and to urge him to go home again. Benjamin answered with a full account of his reasons for leaving Boston and for remaining where he was. It happened that Captain

Holmes, when the letter reached him, was in the company of the governor of Pennsylvania, Sir William Keith. The captain told the governor about the runaway and showed him the letter, which impressed him. He made large official promises to encourage and favour a young man who wrote so well. Let him set up a shop in Philadelphia and he could be printer to the government.

"This my brother-in-law afterwards told me in Boston, but I knew as yet nothing of it, when, one day, Keimer and I being at work together near the window, we saw the governor and another gentleman (which proved to be Colonel French, of New Castle), finely dressed, come directly across the street to our house, and heard them at the door. Keimer ran down immediately, thinking it a visit to him; but the governor inquired for me, came up, and with a condescension and politeness I had been quite unused to, made me many compliments, desired to be acquainted with me, blamed me kindly for not having made myself known to him when I first came to the place, and would have me away with him to the tavern, where he was going with Colonel French to taste, as he said, some excellent Madeira. I was not a little surprised, and Keimer stared like a pig poisoned."[5]

In the tavern the governor expounded his plans and offered to use his influence, as the colonel did too, to see that the proposed new shop should get the public printing for both Pennsylvania and Delaware. If Franklin had not enough capital to begin the business, as he had not, he might borrow it from his father. The governor would give him a letter which no doubt would persuade Josiah Franklin, and the son must leave for Boston by the next boat. In the meantime the matter must be kept a secret. So with a handsome air of patronage the placeman, who was on the whole a good governor, aristocratically, irresponsibly interfered with a life and started a genius on a new step of his career. The governor probably meant no harm. More likely he meant nothing much. He was a busybody in a provincial post and he had found a clever journeyman who was as good as a curiosity.

About the end of April 1724 Franklin sailed for Boston and arrived there, after "a blustering time at sea," an impenitent prodigal. The first surprise and welcome of the family over, he went to his brother's printing-house. "I was better dressed than ever while in his service, having a genteel new suit from head to foot, a watch, and my pockets lined with near five pounds sterling in silver. He received me not very frankly, looked me all over, and turned to his work again." Benjamin bragged to the journeymen about Philadelphia and his good luck. "One of them was asking what kind of money we had there, I produced a handful of silver and spread it before them, which was a kind of raree-show they had not been used to, paper being the money in Boston. Then I took an opportunity of letting them see my watch; and lastly (my brother still grum and silent), I gave them a piece of eight to drink, and took my leave." James Franklin told their mother that Benjamin "had insulted him in such a manner before his people that he could never forget or forgive it. In this, however, he was mistaken."[6]

Benjamin might ruffle his brother, but he could not persuade his father, who, when he had read the governor's sanguine words, thought him a man of little sense. Josiah Franklin wrote politely to Sir William, thanking him for his offer of patronage but saying he believed his son to be too young for so important and expensive a venture. The father still hoped that Benjamin might make peace with James. When he saw that this was hopeless for the present, he agreed to let the younger son go back to Philadelphia. Josiah Franklin, though he could not approve of Governor Keith's plans, was proud that his son had pleased a man of note in Pennsylvania, and "advised me to behave respectfully to the people there, endeavour to gain the general esteem, and avoid lampooning and libelling, to which he thought I had too much inclination; telling me that by steady industry and a prudent parsimony I might save enough by the time I was twenty-one to set me up; and that, if I came near the matter, he would help me out with the rest."[7]

Other men in Boston had advice to give, and Cotton Mather did not hold the *Courant* against the young man who called on him. "He received me in his library and, on my taking leave, showed me a shorter way out of the house through a narrow passage, which was crossed by a beam overhead. We were still talking as I withdrew, he accompanying me behind, when he said hastily: 'Stoop, stoop!' I did not understand him, till I felt my head hit against the beam. He was a man that never missed any occasion of giving instruction, and upon this he said to me: 'You are young, and have the world before you; stoop as you go through it, and you will miss many hard bumps.' "[8] Franklin was not too young to reflect on the dangers of carrying a head too high.

II

The second journey to Philadelphia was neither lonely nor stealthy. Collins, a clerk in the Boston post office, had decided to emigrate to the new country where his friend was prospering. He went ahead and was to join Franklin at New York. At Newport Benjamin stopped to visit his brother John, who "received me very affectionately, for he always loved me."[9] A friend of John Franklin, a man named Vernon, to whom somebody in Pennsylvania owed a debt of thirty-five pounds, asked the visitor to collect and keep it till he should be told how to remit it. Between Newport and New York Franklin flirted with two girls on board till a sensible Quaker matron warned him that they were bad. "When we arrived at New York they told me where they lived and invited me to come to see them; but I avoided it, and it was well I did; for the next day the captain missed a silver spoon and some other things that had been taken out of his cabin, and, knowing that these were a couple of strumpets, he got a warrant to search their lodgings, found the stolen goods, and had the thieves punished."[10]

Franklin had not, he says, guessed the character of the girls until the Quaker matron warned him, and then he did not at first think she could be right about them. He was at eighteen less read in women than in books. Books now brought him to the attention of another great man. William Burnet, governor of New York and New Jersey, son of Gilbert Burnet the historian and bishop, heard from the captain of the sloop that one of his passengers had many books with him—they were Franklin's and Collins's. Such luxuries were then so rare that a few would seem many to a ship captain and remarkable to a governor. Burnet sent for Franklin, showed him his own large library, and had a long talk with him about books and authors. "This was the second governor who had done me the honour to take notice of me; which, to a poor boy like me, was very pleasing."[11]

Collins, who had books too, could not go with Franklin to the governor's, because Collins was drunk, and had been every day since he got to New York. Not all young men have Franklin's head for freedom. The sober Franklin had to settle unpaid bills, for Collins had gambled and lost his savings, and had to meet the cost of getting both of them to Philadelphia. He could do this only by using some of Vernon's money which he collected on the way. Once they were in Philadelphia, Collins was still a burden. He went on "sotting with brandy," could not find work because of the reputation he soon got, lived at his friend's expense, and, knowing that Franklin had the Vernon money in charge, insisted on borrowing from it. Franklin, who felt that he had unsettled Collins's opinions and so was partly responsible for his bad habits, was as patient as he could be, but finally they quarrelled. The actual quarrel was one of those small affairs that are so unexpected and so violent when men have been too long at outs, whether they have yet admitted it or not. Franklin and his friend, with other companions, were in a boat on the Delaware, and Collins, drunk and fractious, refused to take his turn at the oars. Franklin said if Collins would not row the others, the others would not row him. "So he swore he would make me row, or throw me overboard; and coming along, stepping on the thwarts, toward me, when he came up and struck at me, I clapped my hand under his crutch and, rising, pitched him headforemost into the river. I knew he was a good swimmer, and so was under little concern for him; but before he could get round to lay hold on the boat, we had with a few strokes pulled her out of his reach; and ever when he drew near the boat, we asked if he would row, striking a few strokes to slide her away from him. He was ready to die for vexation, and obstinately would not promise to row. However, seeing him at last beginning to tire, we lifted him and brought him home dripping wet in the evening. We hardly exchanged a civil word afterwards."[12] Collins left for Barbados, promising to repay what he had borrowed, but Franklin never heard of him again.

This was the end of his first boyish friendship. He was changing from his single-minded Boston mode of life to one more daring and more confusing. Troubled by the knowledge that he had spent part of Vernon's money and might be called upon at any time to produce the whole of it, he was excited by the prospects that Governor Keith held out to him. If Josiah Franklin would not furnish the necessary capital, Sir William would do it himself. The printer had only to furnish an inventory of the stock that a good shop would require. Of course the thing must still be a secret between them. Franklin, without a confidant, had no chance to find out from others how liberal Keith could be with promises, and so trusted him completely. The stock would cost about a hundred pounds, the young man calculated. At once the governor had another plan. Let Franklin go to London to make his own selections and, perhaps, useful friendships among booksellers and stationers. No sooner thought about than decided upon. The governor told him to get ready to sail on the annual ship between Philadelphia and London which left that fall.

During the restless summer of 1724 Franklin "made some courtship" to Deborah Read. "I had a great respect and affection for her, and had some reason to believe she had the same for me";[13] so he remembered it when he was sixty-five. At eighteen, though his blood ran warmer, he seems to have raised no tumult over his love. That was for poets and men of leisure. For a tradesman marriage was a graver bargain. Deborah's mother—her father John Read died in September—thought the lovers too young to be married now, when Franklin was about to set out on a long voyage. If there was to be a marriage, it would be "more convenient" after he came back. The lovers consented, and may have been convinced.

Day after day in the shop Franklin amused himself by baiting Keimer, who in London had belonged to a noisy sect called the French Prophets and who was still full of old enthusiasms. He kept Saturday as the Sabbath and refused to trim his tremendous beard. Franklin played Socrates with him, and "trepanned him so often by questions apparently so distant from any point we had in hand, and yet by degrees led to the point and brought him into difficulties and contradictions, that at last he grew ridiculously cautious."[14] But he had to admire such skill in debate, and he proposed that they set up a new sect, he to preach the doctrines and Franklin to defend them against arguing opponents. The young unbeliever said he would accept Keimer's Saturdays and beards if Keimer, a glutton, would accept a vegetarian diet as a third tenet of their sect. "I promised myself some diversion in half starving him." For three months they tried the experiment together. Franklin, used to it and liking to save money, enjoyed his joke. "Keimer suffered grievously, tired of the project, longed for the flesh-pots of Egypt, and ordered a roast pig. He invited me and two women friends to dine with him; but, it being brought too soon upon table, he could not resist the temptation, and ate the whole before we came."[15]

Evening after evening the journeyman spent with his friends Charles Osborne, Joseph Watson, and James Ralph, who, like Keimer, are remembered chiefly or only because Franklin remembered them. All three of them were clerks. Watson was pious, the others more lax. Osborne was "sincere and affectionate to his friends, but, in literary matters, too fond of criticizing. Ralph was ingenious, genteel in his manners, and extremely eloquent; I think I never knew a prettier talker. Both of them"—Osborne and Ralph—"great admirers of poetry, and began to try their hands in little pieces. Many pleasant walks we four had together on Sundays into the woods, near Schuylkill, where we read to one another, and conferred on what we read."[16] Ralph was determined to go on being a poet and to make his fortune by it. Osborne assured him he had no genius and had better stick to business. "I approved the amusing one's self with poetry now and then, so far as to improve one's language, but no farther."[17]

Unable to agree in principle, they determined to test their actual gifts. All four at the next meeting would bring poems they had written, versions of the eighteenth Psalm, and compare them. Franklin was little interested and wrote nothing, but he read Ralph's version in advance and thought it had real merit. Ralph asked him to read it to the others as his own, because Osborne was not jealous of him and would be fairer to the poem if he did not think it Ralph's. "We met; Watson's performance was read; there were some beauties in it, but many defects. Osborne's was read; it was much better; Ralph did it justice; remarked some faults but applauded the beauties. He himself had nothing to produce. I was backward; seemed desirous of being excused; had not had sufficient time to correct, etc.; but no excuse could be admitted; produce I must. It was read and repeated; Watson and Osborne gave up the contest, and joined in applauding it. Ralph only made some criticisms and proposed some amendments, but I defended my text. Osborne was against Ralph, and told him he was no better a critic than poet, so he dropped the argument. As they two went home together, Osborne expressed himself still more strongly in favour of what he thought my production; having restrained himself before, as he said, lest I should think it flattery. 'But who would have imagined,' said he, 'that Franklin had been capable of such a performance; such painting, such force, such fire! In his common conversation he seems to have no choice of words; he hesitates and blunders; and yet, good God, how he writes!' When we next met, Ralph discovered the trick we had played him, and Osborne was a little laughed at."[18]

Ralph now finally resolved to be a poet. Franklin, who that summer was prudent about love, sly about laughter, and reasonable about poetry, put his passion into his ambition. He still had faith in the governor, who when in November the ship was ready to sail had not yet furnished him the letters of introduction and credit he had promised. Sir William, his secretary said, would be at New Castle before the ship and deliver the letters there. Franklin took leave of his friends and of Deborah, with whom he "interchanged some promises," and boarded the *London Hope* at Philadelphia. Ralph, who had left behind him a wife and a child a few months old, was with him. At New Castle there was a governor but no letters. Sir William, his secretary said, was busy, but the letters would be sent directly to the ship. Franklin was puzzled but still not suspicious. As if to reassure him, Colonel French came on board and paid the printer so much attention that he and Ralph, who had been assigned to the steerage as ordinary persons, were invited by the other gentlemen to come into the great cabin. Franklin supposed that Colonel French had brought the governor's letters. The captain of the ship said that all the mail was in the bag and was hard to get at but that any letters marked in Franklin's care would be given to him before they reached Eng-

land. Though they had bad weather, the young men got on pleasantly with the two iron-masters and the Quaker merchant in the
cabin. Thomas Denham the merchant took a special fancy to
Franklin. They reached London the day before Christmas.

There were no letters from the governor. Franklin, going to
Denham in his trouble, learned how undependable Keith was. "He
wished to please everybody; and, having little to give, he gave
expectations."[19] A victim of this gesturing habit, Franklin found
himself stranded in London, with no friends, and with only fifteen
pistoles (about twelve pounds) in money. But he had a trade and
he at once found work at Samuel Palmer's printing-house in
Bartholomew Close.

III

As he had had Collins from Boston on his hands in Philadelphia,
so now he had Ralph from Philadelphia on his hands in London.
Strong and stable young men often attract their looser friends, and
are attracted to them. While Franklin felt that he had unsettled
Ralph's opinions too, though Ralph was at least ten years older,
and had some responsibility for him, as for Collins, at the same
time the printer had a wayward strain in his constitution and more
than a little sympathy with the poet. "Ralph and I were insep-
arable companions. We took lodgings together in Little Britain at
three shillings and sixpence a week—as much as we could then
afford. . . . I was pretty diligent, but spent with Ralph a great
deal of my earnings in going to plays and other places of amusement."[20] Ralph had no money, and borrowed steadily from the
stock of pistoles till they were gone, and longer. He thought he
would be an actor, but was told he lacked talent. He wanted to
write a weekly paper like the *Spectator*, but could not find a publisher. He was willing to be a copyist for stationers and lawyers,
but there was no vacancy. His only success was with a milliner who
lived in the same house with the two friends. "She had been genteelly bred, was sensible and lively, and of most pleasing conversation. Ralph read plays to her in the evening, they grew intimate,
she took another lodging, and he followed her."[21] As she already

had a child and could not support the three of them, he went to Berkshire after a few months and became a schoolmaster. Since he thought this calling beneath him, and was afraid it might some day be remembered against him when he was famous, he used the obscure name of Franklin as a precautionary disguise.

Soon after they arrived in London, Ralph had said he did not intend to go back to his wife and child in Philadelphia, and Franklin, either in imitation or out of a similar urge to freedom, had written to Deborah Read—his one letter to her while he was abroad—that he was not likely to return soon. Up to this time there is no hint of any amatory ventures in his life, except for the two strumpets he flirted with on the sloop from Newport to New York and, possibly, the women with whom he and Keimer dined in Philadelphia. Now in London he grew bolder. Ralph's milliner, "having on his account lost her friends and business, was often in distresses, and used to send for me and borrow what I could spare to help her out of them. I grew fond of her company, and, being at that time under no religious restraint and presuming upon my importance to her, I attempted familiarities (another erratum) which she repulsed with a proper resentment, and acquainted him with my behaviour."[22] Ralph ceased to be a friend, and held that Franklin's conduct wiped out the debt, then twenty-seven pounds. Franklin, for all his economy, was generous. He had let Ralph have at least a third of his own year's income. But, with whatever sense of guilt, Franklin had the comfort of reflecting that Ralph had no money to pay and that the end of the friendship was the end of a burden. Their ways parted. Ralph wrote poems "till Pope cured him," as Franklin says, with a couplet in *The Dunciad*,[23] revised plays which had short runs, produced in his ballad-opera *The Fashionable Lady* (1730) the first play by an American to reach the London stage, was friend and assistant to Henry Fielding at the Little Theatre and in *The Champion*, and finally became an able political writer who helped Franklin, now forgiven, on one of his undertakings years later.

Franklin, accustomed only to small, provincial, transatlantic towns, lived for a year and a half in the capital of his world in one of its brilliant ages. At peace with France, England had grown rich and was growing richer. The Hanoverian succession was established, though the Old Pretender plotted futilely in Rome. Men of trade and money challenged the power of the landowning aristocracy. Walpole, canny and corrupt, held the reins of many offices. It was an age of luxury, fashion, and wit. The elegant Stanhope became Lord Chesterfield while Franklin was in London, and Voltaire took refuge there from his enemies in Paris. It was an age of intellect. Newton towered over British science. Bentley, England's greatest classical scholar, wrangled at Cambridge. Hogarth had set up on his own account and had published his first engraving. Fielding, fresh from Eton, was having his fling in London, where Samuel Richardson was a rising printer. Jonathan Wild was hanged in 1725, and Defoe, Grub Street's genius, wrote the rascal's life. Swift in 1726 came back for the first time from his Irish exile. He and Pope and Gay put their heads together in the war against dullness which they carried out in *Gulliver's Travels, The Dunciad,* and *Fables.*

It was a brilliant age—and Franklin was little closer to it at first hand than if he had been in Boston or Philadelphia. He read and heard of great men, barely saw or talked with them. But the unknown journeyman made friends any way he could. Setting type, at Palmer's, for William Wollaston's earnest treatise *The Religion of Nature Delineated*, the printer disagreed with the writer and composed *A Dissertation on Liberty and Necessity, Pleasure and Pain* which he printed himself in 1725, apparently during his first half-year in London. Wollaston, in answer to the deists, had attempted to prove with geometrical rigour that even if there had never been a divine revelation there would still be support and reason in nature itself for all the essential beliefs of orthodox religion. Some acts of men, he claimed to prove, are naturally good, some naturally bad, some naturally indifferent. Franklin, who at fifteen in Boston had been turned to a logical deism by reading the arguments against it, now was turned to an indulgent pantheism.

Since God was all-wise, all-good, all-powerful, and yet permitted the world to be what it was, therefore there could be no such things as natural virtues and vices. Men had no free-will, did what they must, and could not be blamed or praised for their behaviour. What moved them to action was the desire to avoid pain and experience pleasure. "I might here observe, how necessary a thing in the order and design of the universe this pain or uneasiness is, and how beautiful in its place! Let us but suppose it just now banished the world entirely, and consider the consequence of it: all the animal creation would immediately stand stock-still, exactly in the posture they were in the moment uneasiness departed: not a limb, not a finger would henceforth move; we should all be reduced to the condition of statues, dull and unactive; here I should continue to sit motionless with the pen in my hand thus—and neither leave my seat nor write one letter more." But pleasure and pain were exactly equal to one another. "The monarch is not more happy than the slave, nor the beggar more miserable than Crœsus. Suppose A, B, and C three distinct beings: A and B animate, capable of pleasure and pain, C an inanimate piece of matter, insensible of either. A receives ten degrees of pain, which are necessarily succeeded by ten degrees of pleasure; B receives fifteen of pain, and the consequent equal number of pleasure; C all the while lies unconcerned, and as he has not suffered the former, has no right to the latter. What can be more equal and more just than this?" Since there is no inequality of pain and pleasure in this life, there is no need to imagine another, better life to come. Even though the immaterial soul should somehow persist, it "must then necessarily cease to think or act, having nothing left to think or act upon. . . . And to cease to think is but little different from ceasing to be."[24]

"The order and course of things will not be affected by reasoning of this kind,"[25] Franklin broke off to say in the middle of his demonstration. He did not value metaphysics. He was a young Bostonian trying to find reasons for doing as he liked in London. If there were no such things as right and wrong, and no eternal rewards or punishments, what he might do would not matter. He could make himself as free as Ralph already was. The pamphlet was dedicated to Ralph. But the order and course of Franklin's own life cannot have been much affected. He worked hard for long hours every day. He read books from the bookseller's next door to the house in Little Britain. He was too temperate to drink, too economical to gamble. Since the more splendid vices were out of his reach, "foolish intrigues with low women"[26] must have been his only dissipations. And it is not certain, though it is likely, that they began in London.

His employer thought Franklin's principles abominable, but he could not help noticing a journeyman who could and would write a book. Franklin printed a hundred copies, gave a few of them to friends, and later burned the rest, "conceiving it might have an ill tendency."[27] One copy reached a surgeon named William Lyons, who often called on Franklin to talk with him, and who introduced him to men of similar opinions. At the Horns, an alehouse in Cheapside, he met Bernard Mandeville, author of *The Fable of the Bees*, "who had a club there, of which he was the soul, being a most facetious, entertaining companion. Lyons, too, introduced me to Dr. [Henry] Pemberton, at Batson's coffee house, who promised to give me an opportunity, some time or other, of seeing Sir Isaac Newton, of which I was extremely desirous; but this never happened."[28]

By his own initiative Franklin met Sir Hans Sloane, who had been secretary of the Royal Society and after Newton's death was to become president. To him Franklin wrote the earliest of his surviving letters, on 2 June 1725. "Sir: Having lately been in the no[r]thern parts of America, I have brought from thence a purse made of the stone asbestos, a piece of the stone, and a piece of wood, the pithy part of which is of the same nature, and called by the inhabitants salamander cotton. As you are noted to be a lover of curiosities, I have informed you of these; and if you have any inclination to purchase them, or see 'em, let me know your pleasure by a line directed for me at the Golden Fan in Little Britain, and I will wait upon you with them." He added what was perhaps a strategic postscript: "I expect to be out of town in two or three days, and therefore beg an immediate answer."[29] Sloane called on Franklin, invited him to Bloomsbury Square to see his treasures, and bought the North American curiosities.

Late in 1725 Franklin, now rid of Ralph, left Palmer's for James Watts's larger printing-house in Wild's Court near Lincoln's Inn Fields. Here, though there were nearly fifty printers, he was soon distinguished by his strength and speed. The others carried one large form of types up and down the stairs; he carried two.

"They wondered to see, from this and several instances, that the 'Water American' as they called me, was stronger than themselves, who drank strong beer. We had an alehouse boy who attended always in the house to supply the workmen. My companion at the press drank every day a pint before breakfast, a pint at breakfast with his bread and cheese, a pint between breakfast and dinner, a pint at dinner, a pint in the afternoon about six o'clock, and another when he had done his day's work. I thought it a detestable custom."[30] There was no more strength in a quart of beer, Franklin argued, than in a pennyworth of bread. Let his companion eat that and save his money.

The pressmen, among whom Franklin first worked at Watts's because he wanted exercise, kept on drinking, and he was transferred to the composing room. There the compositors demanded that he pay a kind of initiation fee of five shillings for liquor for all of them. He had already paid for his welcome by the pressmen, and refused to pay again. Though he held out two or three weeks, he suffered from so many "little pieces of private mischief" that he yielded, "convinced of the folly of being on ill terms with those one is to live with continually."[31] At once he became popular and influential. "From my example a great part of them left their muddling breakfast of beer and bread and cheese, finding they could with me be supplied from a neighbouring house with a large porringer of hot-water gruel, sprinkled with pepper, crumbed with bread, and a bit of butter in it, for the price of a pint of beer, viz., three halfpence. This was a more comfortable as well as cheaper breakfast, and kept their heads clearer."[32] Some of them continued to drink beer, exhausted their credit at the alehouse before the end of the week, and had to depend on Franklin. He claimed what was due him every Saturday night, sometimes as high as thirty shillings, his week's wages. This impressed them, and they enjoyed his satirical tongue. His master, because Franklin was always at work, never late on Monday, and very fast, gave him special jobs and often special pay.

He left his lodgings in Little Britain for a house in Duke Street. His landlady "was a widow, an elderly woman; had been bred a Protestant, being a clergyman's daughter, but was converted to the Catholic religion by her husband, whose memory she much revered; had lived much among people of distinction, and knew a thousand anecdotes of them as far back as the times of Charles the Second. She was lame in her knees with the gout, and therefore seldom stirred out of her room, so she sometimes wanted company; and she was so highly amusing that I was sure to spend an evening with her whenever she desired it. Our supper was only half an anchovy each, on a very little strip of bread and butter, and half a pint of ale between us; but the entertainment was in her conversation."[33] When he heard of lodgings nearer his work for two shillings a week, instead of the three and six he paid her, she let him stay for one and six, and he did not scruple to accept her offer. He was saving money to take him back to Philadelphia.

He made friends at the printing-house with a young man named Wygate, who was better educated than most printers. Franklin taught him and a friend of his to swim "at twice going into the river." They introduced him to some gentlemen from the country, and all of them went one day by water to Chelsea, in the late spring or early summer of 1726. "In our return, at the request of the company, whose curiosity Wygate had excited, I stripped and leaped into the river, and swam from near Chelsea to Blackfriars, performing on the way many feats of activity, both upon and under water, that surprised and pleased those to whom they were novelties. I had from a child been ever delighted with this exercise, had studied and practised all Thevenot's motions and positions, added some of my own, aiming at the graceful and easy as well as the useful. All these I took occasion of exhibiting to the company, and was much flattered by their admiration."[34] Sir William Wyndham, friend of Swift and Bolingbroke, heard of the feat, sent for Franklin, and asked him to teach Wyndham's two young sons to swim. Wygate, drawn to Franklin by his skill in the water as well as by his intellectual interests, proposed that they travel throughout Europe as journeymen printers. Both schemes tempted Franklin, but he had grown tired of London and remembered Pennsylvania. And now Denham, the merchant with whom he had crossed the Atlantic, suggested how he might return.

Denham, who had already made one fortune in America, intended to make another, by starting a store in Philadelphia. Franklin could be his clerk at fifty pounds a year, and, as soon as he learned the business, could go with a shipload of goods to the West Indies and earn handsome commissions. Though this meant that Franklin would have to give up, as he then thought, the trade in which he was expert, and to work at first for lower wages than a London compositor's, it also meant better prospects. He immediately agreed, and Denham advanced him ten pounds for his passage home. They sailed from Gravesend on the *Berkshire* 23 July 1726.

IV

(So far in this history, Franklin, speaking of himself in his own words, has almost always spoken in the words of the *Autobiography* which he wrote forty-five years after the departure from Gravesend, when he was sage and famous, and writing for his son, the governor of New Jersey. Perhaps then he tempered the account of his youth, saw his course as straighter than it was, left out or had forgotten his ranker appetites, remembered too clearly the mind and will which had outlasted the lost years. But now he speaks as he wrote at twenty in the journal he kept of his summer voyage.[35])

"*Friday, July 22, 1726.*—Yesterday in the afternoon we left London and came to anchor off Gravesend about eleven at night. I lay ashore all night, and this morning took a walk up to the Windmill Hill, from which I had an agreeable prospect of the country for above twenty miles round, and two or three reaches of the river, with ships and boats sailing both up and down, and Tilbury Fort on the other side, which commands the river and passage to London. This Gravesend is a cursed biting place; the chief dependence of the people being the advantage they make of imposing upon strangers. If you buy anything of them, and give half what they ask, you pay twice as much as the thing is worth. Thank God, we shall leave it tomorrow.

"*Saturday, July 23.*—This day we weighed anchor and fell down with the tide, there being little or no wind. In the afternoon we had a fresh gale that brought us down to Margate, where we shall lie at anchor this night. Most of the passengers are very sick. Saw several porpoises, etc.

"*Sunday, July 24.*—This morning we weighed anchor, and coming to the Downs, we set our pilot ashore at Deal, and passed through. And now, whilst I write this, sitting upon the quarter-deck, I have methinks one of the pleasantest scenes in the world before me. 'Tis a fine, clear day, and we are going away before the wind with an easy, pleasant gale. We have near fifteen sail of ships in sight, and I may say in company. On the left hand appears the coast of France at a distance, and on the right is the town and castle of Dover, with the green hills and chalky cliffs of England, to which we must now bid farewell. Albion, farewell!"

Fitful winds brought them on Wednesday to Spithead, where Denham and Franklin went ashore. Franklin, describing Portsmouth, commented on stories he had heard of a former lieutenant-governor. "It is a common maxim that without severe discipline 'tis impossible to govern the licentious rabble of soldiery. I own, indeed, that if a commander finds he has not those qualities in him that will make him beloved by his people, he ought by all means to make use of such methods as will make them fear him, since one or the other (or both) is absolutely necessary; but Alexander and Cæsar, those renowned generals, received more faithful service, and performed greater actions, by means of the love their soldiers bore them, than they could possibly have done if, instead of being beloved and respected, they had been hated and feared by those they commanded."

From Cowes the ship was to sail early Friday morning, but the wind was adverse, and Franklin with other restless or curious passengers went ashore to see Newport, the "metropolis" of the Isle of Wight, and Carisbrooke Castle, "which King Charles the First was confined in." About Charles and his fate Franklin said nothing. His eyes were for living sights. "I think Newport is chiefly remarkable for oysters, which they send to London and other places, where they are very much esteemed, being thought the best in England. The oyster merchants fetch them, as I am informed, from other places, and lay them upon certain beds in the river (the water of which is it seems excellently adapted for that purpose) a-fattening; and when they have lain a suitable time they are taken up again, and made fit for sale."

Franklin noticed that the monuments on the island were all cut from soft stone and that the inscriptions were none of them legible. At the castle: "The floors are several of them of plaster of Paris, the art of making which, the woman told us, was now lost. . . . There are several breaches in the ruinous walls, which are never repaired (I suppose they are purposely neglected). . . . There is a well in the middle of the Coop which they called the bottomless well, because of its great depth; but it is now half filled up with stones and rubbish, and is covered with two or three loose planks; yet a stone, as we tried, is near a quarter of a minute in falling before you hear it strike. But the well that supplies the inhabitants at present with water is in the lower castle, and is thirty fathoms deep. They draw their water with a great wheel, and with a bucket that holds near a barrel. It makes a great sound if you speak in it, and echoed the flute which we played over it very sweetly."

The young realist was a moralist. When he was told of a former governor of the island who had seemed a saint and yet turned out to be a villain: "What surprised me was that the silly old fellow, the keeper of the castle, who remembered him governor, should have so true a notion of his character as I perceived he had. In short, I believe it is impossible for a man, though he has all the cunning of a devil, to live and die a villain, and yet conceal it so well as to carry the name of an honest fellow to his grave with him, but some one, by some accident or other, shall discover him. Truth and sincerity have a certain distinguishing native lustre about them which cannot be perfectly counterfeited; they are like fire and flame, that cannot be painted."

The young moralist reflected about everything, even about the game of draughts (checkers) which he played all that Friday afternoon after they had come back to the ship. "It is a game I much delight in; but it requires a clear head, and undisturbed; and the persons playing, if they would play well, ought not much to regard the consequence of the game, for that diverts and withdraws the attention of the mind from the game itself, and makes the player liable to make many false moves; and I will venture to lay it down for an infallible rule, that if two persons equal in judgment play for a considerable sum, he that loves money most shall lose; his anxiety for the success of the game confounds him. Courage is almost as requisite for the good conduct of this game as in a real battle; for if the player imagines himself opposed by one that is much his superior in skill, his mind is so intent on the defensive part that an advantage passes unobserved."

Saturday the ship got as far as Yarmouth, still on the Isle of Wight, and several passengers went ashore to dine. All but three of them sat drinking after dinner. The three, including Franklin, went further inland, headed a creek and came down on the other side, and at dark found themselves cut off from Yarmouth by the stream. "We were told that it was our best way to go straight down to the mouth of the creek, and that there was a ferry boy that would carry us over to the town. But when we came to the house the lazy whelp was in bed and refused to rise and put us over; upon which we went down to the water-side, with a design to take his boat and go over by ourselves. We found it very difficult to get the boat, it being fastened to a stake, and the tide risen near fifty yards beyond it; I stripped all to my shirt to wade up to it; but missing the causeway, which was under water, I got up to my middle in mud. At last I came to the stake; but, to my great disappointment, found she was locked and chained. I endeavoured to draw the staple with one of the thole-pins, but in vain; I tried to pull up the stake, but to no purpose; so that, after an hour's fatigue and trouble in the wet and mud, I was forced to return without the boat.

"We had no money in our pockets, and therefore began to conclude to pass the night in some haystack, though the wind blew very cold and very hard. In the midst of these troubles one of us recollected that he had a horse-shoe in his pocket, which he found in his walk, and asked me if I could not wrench the staple out with that. I took it, went, tried, and succeeded, and brought the boat ashore to them. Now we rejoiced and all got in, and, when I had dressed myself, we put off. But the worst of our troubles was to come yet; for, it being high water and the tide over all the banks, though it was moonlight we could not discern the channel of the creek; but, rowing heedlessly straight forward, when we were got about half-way over, we found ourselves aground on a mud bank; and, striving to row her off by putting our oars in the mud, we broke one and there stuck fast, not having four inches of water. We were now in the utmost perplexity, not knowing what in the world to do; we could not tell whether the tide was rising or falling; but at length we plainly perceived it was ebb, and we could feel no deeper water within the reach of our oar.

"It was hard to lie in an open boat all night exposed to the wind and weather; but it was worse to think how foolish we should look in the morning, when the owner of the boat should catch us in that condition, where we must be exposed to the view of all the town. After we had strove and struggled for half an hour and more, we gave all over, and sat down with our hands before us, despairing to get off; for, if the tide had left us, we had been never the nearer; we must have sat in the boat, as the mud was too deep for us to walk ashore through it, being up to our necks. At last we bethought ourselves of some means of escaping, and two of us stripped and got out, and, thereby lightening the boat, we drew her upon our knees near fifty yards into deeper water; and then with much ado, having but one oar, we got safe ashore under the fort; and, having dressed ourselves and tied the man's boat, we went with great joy to the Queen's Head, where we left our companions, whom we found waiting for us, though it was very late. Our boat being gone on board, we were obliged to lie ashore all night; and thus ended our walk."

For six days the ship waited for favourable wind at Yarmouth or Cowes, and not until 5 August did they get away into the Channel. The next day: "In the afternoon I leaped overboard and swam round the ship to wash myself." On the 8th they saw the Lizard, and on the 9th took their leave of the land. Then for nine days there was nothing more remarkable than that "four dolphins followed the ship for some hours; we struck at them with the fizgig, but took none. . . .

"*Friday, August 19.*— . . . Yesterday, complaints being made that Mr. G——n, one of the passengers, had with a fraudulent design marked the cards, a court of justice was called immediately, and he was brought to his trial in form. A Dutchman, who could speak no English, deposed by his interpreter that, when our mess was on shore at Cowes, the prisoner at the bar marked all the court cards on the back with a pen.

"I have sometimes observed that we are apt to fancy the person that cannot speak intelligibly to us, proportionably stupid in understanding, and when we speak two or three words of English to a foreigner, it is louder than ordinary, as if we thought him deaf and that he had lost the use of his ears as well as his tongue. Something like this I imagine might be the case of Mr. G——n; he fancied the Dutchman could not see what he was about, because he could not understand English, and therefore boldly did it before his face.

"The evidence was plain and positive; the prisoner could not deny the fact, but replied in his defence that the cards he marked were not those we commonly played with, but an imperfect pack, which he afterwards gave to the cabin boy. The attorney-general observed to the court that it was not likely he should take pains to mark the cards without some ill design, or some further intention than just to give them to the boy when he had done, who understood nothing at all of cards. But another evidence, being called, deposed that he saw the prisoner in the main-top one day, when he thought himself unobserved, marking a pack of cards on the backs, some with the print of a dirty thumb, others with the top of his finger, etc. Now, there being but two packs on board, and the prisoner having just confessed the marking of one, the court perceived the case was plain. In fine the jury brought him in guilty, and he was condemned to be carried up to the round-top, and made fast there in view of the ship's company during the space of three hours, that being the place where the act was committed, and to pay a fine of two bottles of brandy. But the prisoner resisting authority and refusing to submit to punishment, one of the sailors stepped aloft and let down a rope to us, which we with much struggling made fast about his middle, and hoisted him up into the air, sprawling, by main force. We let him hang, cursing and swearing, for near a quarter of an hour; but at length, he crying out 'Murder!' and looking black in the face, the rope being overtort about his middle, we thought proper to let him down again; and our mess have excommunicated him till he pays his fine, refusing either to play, eat, drink, or converse with him. . . .

"*Thursday, August 25.*—Our excommunicated shipmate thinking proper to comply with the sentence the court passed upon him, and expressing himself willing to pay the fine, we have this morning received him into unity again. Man is a sociable being, and it

PLATO

is, for aught I know, one of the worst of punishments to be excluded from society. I have read abundance of fine things on the subject of solitude, and I know 'tis a common boast in the mouths of those that affect to be thought wise, that they are never less alone than when alone. I acknowledge solitude an agreeable refreshment to a busy mind; but were these thinking people obliged to be always alone, I am apt to think they would quickly find their very being insupportable to them. . . . One of the philosophers, I think it was Plato, used to say that he had rather be the veriest stupid block in nature than the possessor of all knowledge without some intelligent being to communicate it to.

"What I have said may in a measure account for some particulars in my present way of living here on board. Our company is in general very unsuitably mixed, to keep up the pleasure and spirit of conversation; and, if there are one or two pair of us that can sometimes entertain one another for half an hour agreeably, yet perhaps we are seldom in the humour for it together. I rise in the morning and read for an hour or two perhaps, and then reading grows tiresome. Want of exercise occasions want of appetite, so that eating and drinking afford but little pleasure. I tire myself with playing at draughts, then I go to cards; nay, there is no play so trifling or childish but we fly to it for entertainment. A contrary wind, I know not how, puts us all out of good humour; we grow sullen, silent, and reserved, and fret at each other upon every little occasion. 'Tis a common opinion among the ladies that if a man is ill-natured he infallibly discovers it when he is in liquor. But I, who have known many instances to the contrary, will teach them a more effectual method to discover the natural temper and disposition of their humble servants. Let the ladies make one long sea voyage with them, and if they have the least spark of ill-nature in them and conceal it to the end of the voyage, I will forfeit all my pretensions to their favour."

For the rest of the voyage, as if he had learned whatever there was to know about his human companions, Franklin gave more attention in his journal to nature than to man.

"*Tuesday, August 30.*—Contrary wind still. This evening, the moon being near full as she rose after eight o'clock, there appeared a rainbow in a western cloud, to windward of us. The first time I ever saw a rainbow in the night, caused by the moon. . . .

"*Friday, Sept*[*ember*] *2.*—This morning the wind changed; a little fair. We caught a couple of dolphins and fried them for dinner. They eat indifferent well. These fish make a glorious appearance in the water; their bodies are of a bright green, mixed with a silver colour, and their tails of a shining golden yellow; but all this vanishes presently after they are taken out of their element, and they change all over to a light grey. I observed that, cutting off pieces of a just-caught, living dolphin for baits, those pieces did not lose their lustre and fine colours when the dolphin died, but retained them perfectly. Everyone takes notice of that vulgar error of the painters, who always represent this fish monstrously crooked and deformed, when it is in reality as beautiful as any fish that swims. . . .

"*Wednesday, Sept*[*ember*] *14.*—This afternoon, about two o'clock, it being fair weather and almost calm, as we sat playing draughts upon deck we were surprised with a sudden and unusual darkness of the sun, which, as we could perceive, was only covered with a small, thin cloud; when that was passed by we discovered that that glorious luminary laboured under a very great eclipse. At least ten parts out of twelve of him were hid from our eyes, and we were apprehensive he would have been totally darkened. . . .

"*Wednesday, Sept*[*ember*] *21.*—This morning our steward was brought to the gears and whipped, for making an extravagant use of flour in the puddings, and for several other misdemeanours. It has been perfectly calm all this day, and very hot. I was determined to wash myself in the sea today, and should have done so had not the appearance of a shark, that mortal enemy to swimmers, deterred me; he seemed to be about five foot long, moves around the ship at some distance, in a slow, majestic manner, attended by near a dozen of those they call pilot fish, of different sizes; the largest of them is not so big as a small mackerel, and the smallest not bigger than my little finger. Two of these diminutive pilots keep just before his nose, and he seems to govern himself in his motions by their direction; while the rest surround him on every side indifferently. A shark is never seen without a retinue of these, who are his purveyors, discovering and distinguishing his prey for him; while he in turn gratefully protects them from the ravenous, hungry dolphin. . . .

"*Friday, September 23.*—This morning we spied a sail to wind-ward of us about two leagues· We showed our jack upon the ensign-staff and shortened sail for them till about noon, when she came up to us. She was a snow [brig] from Dublin, bound for New York, having upwards of fifty servants on board of both sexes; they all appeared upon deck, and seemed very much pleased at the sight of us. There is something strangely cheering to the spirits in the meeting of a ship at sea, containing a society of creatures of the same species and in the same circumstances with ourselves, after we had been long separated and excommunicated as it were from the rest of mankind. My heart fluttered in my breast with joy, when I saw so many human countenances, and I could scarce refrain from that kind of laughter which proceeds from some degree of inward pleasure. When we have been for a considerable time toss-ing on the vast waters, far from the sight of any land or ships, or any mortal creature but ourselves (except a few fish and sea birds), the whole world, for aught we know, may be under a second deluge, and we, like Noah and his company in the ark, the only surviving remnant of the human race. . . .

"I find our messmates in a better humour and more pleased with their present condition than they have been since they came out; which I take to proceed from the contemplation of the miserable circumstances of the passengers on board our neighbour, and mak-ing the comparison. We reckon ourselves in a kind of paradise, when we consider how they live, confined and stifled up with such a lousy, stinking rabble, in this hot sultry latitude."

The *Berkshire*, with only twenty-one on board, and the crowded snow "ran on very lovingly together" for a week, except when the wind separated them at night, and twice the snow's captain came on board the ship. On 25 September: "All our discourse now is of Philadelphia, and we begin to fancy ourselves ashore already." On the 27th: "I have laid a bowl of punch that we are in Phila-delphia next Saturday se'ennight; for we reckon ourselves not above one hundred and fifty leagues from land." (Franklin was too hopeful by three days.)

"*Wednesday, Sept[ember] 28.*—We had very variable winds and weather last night, accompanied with abundance of rain; and now the wind is come about westerly again, but we must bear it with patience. This afternoon we took up several branches of gulf-weed (with which the sea is spread all over, from the Western Isles to the coast of America); but one of these branches had something peculiar in it. In common with the rest, it had a leaf about three-quarters of an inch long, indented like a saw, and a small yellow berry, filled with nothing but wind; besides which it bore a fruit of the animal kind, very surprising to see. It was a small shell-fish like a heart, the stalk by which it proceeded from the branch being partly of a gristly kind. Upon this one branch of the weed there were near forty of these vegetable animals; the smallest of them, near the end, containing a substance somewhat like an oyster, but the larger were visibly animated, opening their shells every moment, and thrusting out a set of unformed claws, not unlike those of a crab; but the inner part was still a kind of soft jelly. Observing the weed more narrowly, I spied a very small crab crawling among it, about as big as the head of a ten-penny nail, and of a yellowish colour, like the weed itself. This gave me some reason to think that he was a native of the branch; that he had not long since been in the same condition with the rest of those little embryos that appeared in the shells, this being the method of their generation; and that, consequently, all the rest of this odd kind of fruit might be crabs in due time. To strengthen my conjecture I have resolved to keep the weed in salt water, renewing it every day till we come on shore, by this experiment to see whether any more crabs will be produced or not in this manner. . . . The various changes that silkworms, butterflies, and several other insects go through, make such alterations and metamorphoses not improbable.

"*Thursday, Sept[ember] 29.*—Upon shifting the water in which I had put the weed yesterday, I found another crab, much smaller than the former, who seemed to have newly left his habitation. But the weed begins to wither, and the rest of the embryos are dead. This new-comer fully convinces me that at least this sort of crabs are generated in this manner.

"*Friday, Sept[ember] 30.*—I sat up last night to observe an eclipse of the moon, which the calendar, calculated for London, informed us would happen at five o'clock in the morning. . . . It began with us about eleven last night, and continued till near two this morning, darkening her body about six digits, or one half; the middle of it being about half an hour after twelve, by which we may discover that we are in a meridian of about four hours and a half from London, or 67½ degrees of longitude, and consequently have not much above one hundred leagues to run. This is the second eclipse we have had within these fifteen days."

The bored shipmates had again something to talk about: their distance from Philadelphia. On 2 October: "I cannot help fancying the water is changed a little, as is usual when a ship comes within soundings, but 'tis probable I am mistaken; for there is but one besides myself of my opinion, and we are very apt to believe what we wish to be true." The next day: "The water is now very visibly changed to the eyes of all except the captain and mate, and they will by no means allow it; I suppose because they did not see it first. . . .

"*Tuesday, October 4.*—Last night we struck a dolphin, and this morning we found a flying-fish dead under the windlass. He is about the bigness of a small mackerel, a sharp head, a small mouth, and a tail forked somewhat like a dolphin, but the lowest branch much larger and longer than the other, and tinged with yellow. His back and sides of a darkish blue, his belly white, and his skin very thick. His wings are of a finny substance, about a span long, reaching when close to his body from an inch below his gills to an inch above his tail. When they fly it is straight forward (for they cannot readily turn) a yard or two above the water; and perhaps fifty yards is the furthest before they dip into the water again, for they cannot support themselves in the air any longer than while their wings continue wet. These flying-fish are the common prey of the dolphin, who is their mortal enemy. When he pursues them, they rise and fly; and he keeps close under them till they drop, and then snaps them up immediately. They generally fly in flocks, four or five, or perhaps a dozen together, and a dolphin is seldom caught without one or more in his belly."

Now Franklin's curiosity was all for signs that the ship was nearing home. On 4 October: "This afternoon we have seen abundance of grampuses, which are seldom far from land; but towards evening we had a more evident token, to wit, a little tired bird, something like a lark, came on board us, who certainly is an American, and 'tis likely was ashore this day." On 5 October: "This morning we saw a heron, who had lodged aboard last night. 'Tis a long-legged, long-necked bird, having, as they say, but one gut. They live upon fish, and will swallow a living eel thrice, sometimes, before it will remain in their body." On 7 October (gloomily): "For my part I know not what to think of it; we have run all this day at a great rate, and now night is come on we have no soundings. Sure the American continent is not all sunk under water since we left it." But on 9 October: "After dinner one of our mess went aloft to look out, and presently pronounced the long wished-for sound: LAND! LAND! In less than an hour we could descry it from the deck, appearing like tufts of trees. I could not discern it so soon as the rest; my eyes were dimmed with the suffusion of two small drops of joy.

"*Monday, October 10.*—This morning we stood in again for land; and we that had been here before all agreed that it was Cape Henlopen; about noon we were come very near, and to our great joy saw the pilot-boat come off to us, which was exceeding welcome. He brought on board about a peck of apples with him; they seemed the most delicious I ever tasted in my life; the salt provisions we had been used to gave them a relish. We had extraordinary fair wind all the afternoon, and ran above a hundred miles up the Delaware before ten at night. The country appears very pleasant to the eye, being covered with woods, except here and there a house and plantation. We cast anchor when the tide turned, about two miles below New Castle, and there lay till the morning tide.

"*Tuesday, October 11.*—This morning we weighed anchor with a gentle breeze and passed by New Castle, whence they hailed us and bade us welcome. It is extreme fine weather. The sun enlivens our stiff limbs with his glorious rays of warmth and brightness. The sky looks gay, with here and there a silver cloud. The fresh breezes from the woods refresh us; the immediate prospect of liberty, after so long and irksome confinement, ravishes us. In short, all things conspire to make this the most joyful day I ever knew. As we passed by Chester, some of the company went on shore,

impatient once more to tread on *terra firma*, and designing for
Philadelphia by land. Four of us remained on board, not caring
for the fatigue of travel when we knew the voyage had much
weakened us. About eight at night, the wind failing us, we cast
anchor at Redbank, six miles from Philadelphia, and thought we
must be obliged to lie on board that night; but, some young Philadelphians happening to be out upon their pleasure in a boat, they
came on board, and offered to take us up with them; we accepted
of their kind proposal, and about ten o'clock landed at Philadelphia, heartily congratulating each other upon our having happily
completed so tedious and dangerous a voyage. Thank God!"

4

~~~~~~

Master

DURING the voyage home Franklin drew up a plan by which he was to regulate his future conduct, and which he says he followed, on the whole, "quite through to old age." The original plan is missing from his journal. What resolutions he had made must now be guessed at, though they were possibly the ones printed long afterwards from a manuscript now apparently lost. "Those who write of the art of poetry teach us that if we would write what may be worth reading we ought always, before we begin, to form a regular plan and design of our piece; otherwise we shall be in danger of incongruity. I am apt to think it is the same as to life. I have never fixed a regular design as to life, by which means it has been a confused variety of different scenes. I am now entering upon a new one; let me therefore make some resolutions, and form some scheme of action, that henceforth I may live in all respects like a rational creature. 1. It is necessary for me to be extremely frugal for some time, till I have paid what I owe. 2. To endeavour to speak truth in every instance, to give nobody expectations that are not likely to be answered, but aim at sincerity in every word and action: the most amiable excellence in a rational being. 3. To apply myself industriously to whatever business I take in hand, and not divert my mind from my business by any foolish project of growing suddenly rich; for industry and patience are the surest means of plenty. 4. I resolve to speak ill of no man whatever, not even in a matter of truth; but rather by some means excuse the faults I hear charged upon others, and upon proper occasions speak all the good I know of everybody."[1]

Franklin's life for this first year in Philadelphia was not as he had planned. For four or five months he was busy in his new employment. Denham set up a general store in Water Street with the stock which he had brought from England, taught Franklin to keep accounts and to sell goods, and gave him affectionate counsel: They lived together like father and son. Franklin, who missed his own father, celebrated his twenty-first birthday by a high-sounding letter to his youngest and favourite sister Jane, then not yet fifteen but to be married the following July. He had heard, he said, that she had become a beauty and wanted to send her a present. "I had almost determined on a tea table; but when I considered that the character of a good housewife was far preferable to that of being only a pretty gentlewoman, I concluded to send you a spinning-wheel." He sent a moral reflection too. "Sister, farewell, and remember that modesty, as it makes the most homely virgin amiable and charming, so the want of it infallibly renders the most perfect beauty disagreeable and odious. But when that brightest of female virtues shines among other perfections of body and mind in the same person, it makes the woman more lovely than an angel. Excuse this freedom, and use the same with me."

Within a month after this letter both Denham and Franklin were taken seriously ill. "My distemper was a pleurisy, which very nearly carried me off. I suffered a great deal, gave up the point in my own mind, and was rather disappointed when I found myself recovering, regretting, in some degree, that I must now some time or other have all that disagreeable work to do over again."[2] Denham's ledger[3] shows that Franklin must have come home nearly penniless, for during his twenty weeks' work he had to be advanced cash and goods to the amount of three shillings and fivepence more than the six pounds which his wages came to. Denham, dying after a long sickness, forgave Franklin the unpaid balance and the ten pounds' passage money—or as Franklin says: "he left me a small legacy in a noncupative will." The journeyman who had left his trade went back to it.

Once more a printer, working for Keimer again, Franklin now lived only partly as he had before in Philadelphia. He had no secret patron. Keith had been removed from his post as governor and was shortly to leave the province. "I met him walking the streets as a common citizen. He seemed a little ashamed at seeing me, but passed without saying anything." Deborah Read, with her one letter from London, had lost hope of Franklin and had married a potter named Rogers, a good workman but a worthless man, with whom she had never been happy and from whom she was soon parted, after she heard he already had a wife. Franklin renewed his friendship with his former companions in poetry, but Watson died and Osborne went to the West Indies. At the printing-house Franklin was more than foreman. It did not take him long to understand that Keimer had hired him at high wages to be, in effect, teacher to the "raw, cheap hands" at work there, and to be dismissed when they had learned their trade. Franklin was as cheerful as he was skilful with his random crew. Three of them were young Pennsylvania farmers who had ambitiously come to Philadelphia: David Harry who later became Franklin's competitor, Hugh Meredith who became his partner, and Stephen Potts, his lifelong friend. Two of them were indentured servants: John, a wild Irishman who ran away, and George Webb, who had deserted Oxford after a year, gone to London to become an actor, spent all his money, and bound himself for his passage to be a servant in America, where Keimer had bought his time for four years from the captain of the ship. Franklin, besides instructing and disciplining them, took other responsibilities. "There was no letter-founder in America; I had seen types cast at James's in London, but without much attention to the manner; however, I now contrived a mould, made use of the letters we had as puncheons, struck the matrices in lead, and thus supplied in a pretty tolerable way all deficiencies. I also engraved several things on occasion; I made the ink; I was warehouseman, and everything."[4]

Serviceable as Franklin was, Keimer, short-tempered, short-sighted, after six months began looking for an excuse to let his foreman go, now that the shop had been put in order. "A trifle snapped our connexions; for, a great noise happening near the courthouse, I put my head out of the window to see what was the matter. Keimer, being in the street, looked up and saw me, called out to me in a loud voice and angry tone to mind my business, adding some reproachful words that nettled me the more for their publicity, all the neighbours who were looking out on the same occasion being witnesses how I was treated."[5] Keimer came indoors, the quarrel grew furious, and Franklin, waiving the quarter's notice that was due him, caught up his hat and left without the rest of his belongings.

Hugh Meredith brought them to Franklin that evening, and they talked over what was to be done. Franklin had begun to think of going back to Boston. Meredith, anxious not to lose so good and able a friend, urged him to stay in Philadelphia, wait for Keimer's certain failure, and succeed him. Though Franklin had no capital, Meredith's father had a high opinion of the young foreman, and might set the two up in business as equal partners, Franklin's skill counting for as much as Meredith's money. The father was just then in town and approved of the scheme, partly because his son had stopped drinking under his friend's influence. Franklin furnished the elder Meredith an inventory of what would be needed, and the order was sent off to London. It would of course be several months before the types and press could arrive. For a few days Franklin was idle. Then Keimer, "on a prospect of being employed to print some paper money in New Jersey, which would require cuts and various types that I only could supply, and apprehending Bradford might engage me and get the job from him,"[6] civilly, if interestedly, asked Franklin to forget the quarrel and return to work. Meredith strongly urged this, for his time with Keimer would not be up till the following spring, and he felt the need of more instruction. Franklin yielded in his friendly manner, which was both natural and astute. He contrived the first copperplate press in the country, and cut ornaments for the bills. With Keimer he went to Burlington, where he did the printing to the full satisfaction of the Assembly.

Keimer made money enough in Burlington to keep him going for a year or so more. Franklin made friends for a lifetime. The members of the committee who watched the printing to see that no unauthorized bills were struck off liked Franklin and felt his irresistible young charm. They asked him, not Keimer, to their houses and introduced him to others. At the end of three months he was on the best of terms with the secretary and the surveyor-general of the province and several members of the legislature. One shrewd old man, who knew nothing of Franklin's plans, prophesied that he would sooner or later take Keimer's business away from him and make a fortune. Not long after the printers were back in Philadelphia, early in 1728, the new equipment came. Meredith and Franklin, without telling Keimer they were to be his rivals, settled with him and left with his consent. They took a house in lower Market Street for twenty-four pounds a year, let a part of it to Thomas Godfrey, a mathematical glazier with whose family they were to board, and opened the new shop. Their first customer was a farmer who had been wandering through the streets looking for a printer and had been brought in by one of their friends. "This countryman's five shillings, being our first fruits, and coming so seasonably, gave me more pleasure than any crown I have since earned."[7]

II

No single thread of narrative can give a true account of Franklin's life during the years 1726–32, for he was leading three lives and—most of the time—something of a stealthy fourth, each distinct enough to call for a separate record and yet all of them closely involved in his total nature. There was his public life, beginning with his friendships in the club he organized in 1727, and continuing with larger and larger affairs as long as he lived. There was his inner life, which was at first much taken up with reflections on his own behaviour, and, after he had more or less settled that in his mind and habit, grew to an embracing curiosity about the whole moral and physical world. There was his life as workman—already told—and business man, which greatly occupied him and was to occupy him until, after twenty years in Philadelphia, he was able to retire from an activity he had never valued for itself. In time all three were to be fused in the spacious character of a sage in action, but in 1726–32 they were still distinct if not discrepant.

In business Franklin was extremely alert to the main chance, adaptable, resolute, crafty though not petty, and ruthless on occasion. But he had too ranging a mind to be taken up with his private concerns alone, and he genuinely desired the public welfare. Having neither wealth nor influence, he began where he could, using the tools he had. In the fall of 1727, about the time of his trouble with Keimer, he brought together the group called the Junto. Three besides Franklin—Hugh Meredith, Stephen Potts, and George Webb—were from Keimer's shop. Meredith was "a Welsh Pennsylvanian, thirty years of age, bred to country work; honest, sensible, had a great deal of solid observation, was something of a reader but given to drink. . . . Potts, a young countryman of full age, bred to the same, of uncommon natural parts, and great wit and humour, but a little idle. . . . Webb, an Oxford scholar . . . lively, witty, good-natured, and a pleasant companion, but idle, thoughtless, and imprudent to the last degree."[8]

With these were joined: "Joseph Breintnal, a copier of deeds for the scriveners, a good-natured, friendly, middle-aged man, a great lover of poetry, reading all he could meet with and writing some that was tolerable; very ingenious in many little knick-knackeries and of sensible conversation. Thomas Godfrey, a self-taught mathematician, great in his way, and afterward inventor of what is now called Hadley's quadrant. But he knew little out of his way, and was not a pleasing companion; as, like most great mathematicians I have met with, he expected universal precision in everything said, and was for ever denying or distinguishing upon trifles, to the disturbance of all conversation. He soon left us. Nicholas Scull, a surveyor, afterwards surveyor-general, who loved books and sometimes made a few verses. William Parsons, bred a shoemaker, but, loving reading, had acquired a considerable share of mathematics, which he first studied with a view to astrology, but he afterwards laughed at it. He also became a surveyor-general. William Maugridge, a joiner, a most exquisite mechanic, and a solid, sensible man. . . . Robert Grace, a young gentleman of some fortune, generous, lively, and witty; a lover of punning and of his friends. And William Coleman, then a merchant's clerk, about my age, who had the coolest, clearest head, the best heart, and the exactest morals of almost any man I ever met with. He became afterwards a merchant of great note, and one of our provincial judges."[9]

These solid, sensible, good-natured, ingenious—and inconspicuous—men were friends with whom Franklin already liked to talk, and it was a kind of economy to meet with them all at once at a tavern every Friday evening. There can be no doubt whose club it was. Franklin gave it form and direction. Many of the topics discussed were raised by him. The Junto was his benevolent lobby for the benefit of Philadelphia, and now and then for the advantage of Benjamin Franklin.

Somewhat unexpectedly, he seems to have borrowed the scheme of the Junto in part from Cotton Mather, who in Boston had originated neighbourhood benefit societies, one for every church, and had belonged to twenty of them. Mather had drawn up a set of ten questions to be read at each meeting, "with due pauses," as a guide to discussion.[10] Franklin, in his Rules for the Junto adopted in 1728, followed Mather. Some of the questions were much the same. Mather had asked: "Is there any matter to be humbly moved unto the legislative power, to be enacted into a law for public benefit?" Franklin asked: "Have you lately observed any defect in the laws of your country of which it would be proper to move the legislature for an amendment? Or do you know of any beneficial law that is wanting?" Mather: "Is there any particular person whose disorderly behaviour may be so scandalous and so notorious that we may do well to send unto the said person our charitable admonitions?" Franklin: "Do you know of a fellow-citizen who has lately done a worthy action, deserving praise or imitation; or who has lately committed an error proper for us to be warned against and avoid?" Mather: "Does there appear any instance of oppression or fraudulence in the dealings of any sort of people that may call for our essays to get it rectified?" Franklin: "Have you lately observed any encroachment on the just liberties of the people?" But Franklin has nothing like Mather's: "Can any further methods be devised that ignorance and wickedness may be chased from our people in general, and that household piety in particular may flourish among them?" And Mather has nothing like most of Franklin's twenty-four humane, secular, practical inquiries:

"1. Have you met with anything in the author you last read, remarkable or suitable to be communicated to the Junto, particularly in history, morality, poetry, physic, travels, mechanic arts, or other parts of knowledge? 2. What new story have you lately heard agreeable for telling in conversation? 3. Hath any citizen in your knowledge failed in his business lately, and what have you heard of the cause? 4. Have you lately heard of any citizen's thriving well, and by what means? . . . 7. What unhappy effects of intemperance have you lately observed or heard; of imprudence, of passion, or of any other vice or folly? 8. What happy effects of temperance, of prudence, of moderation, or of any other virtue? 9. Have you or any of your acquaintance been lately sick or wounded? If so, what remedies were used, and what were their effects? 10. Whom do you know that are shortly going voyages or journeys, if one should have occasion to send by them? . . . 12. Hath any deserving stranger arrived in town since last meeting that you have heard of? And what have you heard or observed of his character or merits? And whether, think you, it lies in the power of the Junto to oblige him, or encourage him as he deserves? 13. Do you know of any deserving young beginner lately set up, whom it lies in the power of the Junto any way to encourage? . . . 16. Hath anybody attacked your reputation lately? And what can the Junto do towards securing it? 17. Is there any man whose friendship you want, and which the Junto, or any of them, can procure for you? 18. Have you lately heard any member's character attacked, and how have you defended it? 19. Hath any man injured you, from whom it is in the power of the Junto to procure redress? 20. In what manner can the Junto, or any of them, assist you in any of your honourable designs? . . ."[11]

These questions were the Junto's weekly ritual. The members met first at a tavern, later in a room hired in a house belonging to Grace. Between questions there were, as in Boston, due pauses—in Philadelphia long enough to drink a glass of wine. The rules further required that "every member, in his turn, should produce one or more queries on any point of morals, politics, or natural philosophy, to be discussed by the company; and once in three months produce and read an essay of his own writing, on any subject he pleased. Our debates were to be under the direction of a president, and to be conducted in the sincere spirit of inquiry after truth, without fondness for dispute or desire of victory; and, to prevent warmth, all expressions of positiveness in opinions, or direct contradiction, were after some time made contraband, and prohibited under small pecuniary penalties."[12]

Franklin in his own queries asked the Junto things he was asking himself. "How shall we judge of the goodness of a writing? Or what qualities should a writing have to be good and perfect in its kind?" (He wrote out his own answer, and summed up: "It should be smooth, clear, and short.") "Can a man arrive at perfection in this life, as some believe; or is it impossible, as others believe?" "Wherein consists the happiness of a rational creature?" "What is wisdom?" ("The knowledge of what will be best for us on all occasions, and the best ways of attaining it.") "Is any man wise at all times and in all things?" ("No, but some are more frequently wise than others.") "Whether those meats and drinks are not the best that contain nothing in their natural taste, nor have anything added by art, so pleasing as to induce us to eat or drink when we are not thirsty or hungry, or after thirst and hunger are satisfied; water, for instance, for drink, and bread or the like for meat?" "Is there any difference between knowledge and prudence? If there is any, which of the two is most eligible?" "Is it justifiable to put private men to death, for the sake of public safety or tranquillity, who have committed no crime? As, in the case of the plague, to stop infection; or as in the case of the Welshmen here executed?" "If the sovereign power attempts to deprive a subject of his right (or, which is the same thing, of what he thinks his right), is it justifiable in him to resist, if he is able?" "Which is best: to make a friend of a wise and good man that is poor or of a rich man that is neither wise nor good?" "Does it not, in a general way, require great study and intense application for a poor man to become rich and powerful, if he would do it without the forfeiture of honesty?" "Does it not require as much pains, study, and application to become truly wise and strictly virtuous as to become rich?" "Whence comes the dew that stands on the outside of a tankard that has cold water in it in the summer time?"[13]

Many young men have organized clubs for talk and friendship, but only Franklin ever kept one alive for thirty years. He did not lose interest as most young men do, or tire of leadership. The Junto was his life enlarged and extended. It was convivial as well as philosophical. Once a month in the pleasant seasons the debaters met across the river for outdoor exercise. Once a year they had an anniversary dinner, with songs and healths. The Junto was practical as well as convivial. Perhaps, in the long run, the help the members gave each other had as much to do as anything with making it last. It was a secret brotherhood. New members had to stand up with their hands on their breasts and say they loved mankind in general and truth for truth's sake. But in the ritual questions many of the issues were more immediate. Strangers in Philadelphia were to be welcomed if they deserved it, young beginners in trade or business encouraged, reputations defended, friendships furthered, grievances redressed, useful information exchanged. Franklin himself was benefited. Breintnal brought the new printing-house its first large order. Grace and Coleman lent Franklin money to buy Meredith out. The Junto, commonly known at first as the Leather Apron, became the club of young, poor, enterprising men, as distinguished from the Merchants' Every Night, which was for the respectable and established, and the Bachelors, who were gay and suspected of being wicked. (Grace was a member of the Bachelors, and Webb, who wrote a poem called *Batchelors-Hall* which Franklin published.)

In time the Junto had so many applications for membership that it was at a loss to know how to limit itself to the twelve originally planned. Franklin, who preferred the convenient apostolic number, suggested that the Junto be kept as it was and that each member organize a subordinate club, "with the same rules respecting queries, etc., and without informing them of the connexion with the Junto. The advantages proposed were the improvement of so many more young citizens by the use of our institutions; our better acquaintance with the general sentiments of the inhabitants on any occasion, as the Junto member might propose what queries we should desire, and was to report to the Junto what passed in his separate club; the promotion of our particular interests in business by more extensive recommendation, and the increase of our influence in public affairs, and our power of doing good by spreading through the several clubs the sentiments of the Junto."[14] Only five or six of these subordinate clubs were founded.

The benevolent imperialism of the Junto did not go beyond these little clubs of artisans and tradesmen in Philadelphia, but Franklin for a few enthusiastic months had world-wide schemes. On 19 May 1731, about the time he became a Mason, he set down, in the library of the Junto which was also the room where the club held its meetings, his observations on his reading of history. The affairs of the world, he had observed, are carried on by parties. These parties act in their own interest or what they think their interest. Their different interests cause natural confusion. Within each party each man has his own private interest. As soon as a party has gained its general point, each man puts forth his special claim, and the party comes to confusion within itself. Few men act for the good of their country except when they can believe that their country's good is also theirs. Fewer men still act for the good of mankind. Consequently: "There seems to me at present to be great occasion for raising a United Party for Virtue, by forming the virtuous and good men of all nations into a regular body, to be governed by suitable good and wise rules, which good and wise men may probably be more unanimous in their obedience to, than common people are to common laws."[15]

The new sect was, much like the Junto, to be begun and spread by young single men joined in a secret society, each of whom should find other worthy members. "The members should engage to afford their advice, support, and assistance to each other in promoting one another's interests, business, and advancement in life. . . . For distinction, we should be called the Society of the Free and Easy: free, as being, by the general habit and practice of the virtues, free from the dominion of vice; and particularly, by the practice of industry and frugality, free from debt, which exposes a man to confinement and a species of slavery to his creditors."[16] Franklin was himself to write a kind of gospel for these free and easy saints, a book to be called *The Art of Virtue* which would not merely exhort to goodness but would show the precise means of achieving it. Almost thirty years later he was still hoping to write the book, which he told Lord Kames would be "adapted for universal use."[17] About his sect he did nothing but propose it to two young men who felt his enthusiasm. Then pressing matters intervened, and the Party for Virtue had to wait. Yet at eighty-two Franklin could say: "I am still of opinion that it was a practicable scheme, and might have been very useful, by forming a great number of good citizens; and I was not discouraged by the seeming magnitude of the undertaking, as I have always thought that one man of tolerable abilities may work great changes and accomplish great affairs among mankind, if he first forms a good plan and . . . makes the execution of that same plan his sole study and business."[18]

III

Remembering Franklin when he was old and canny, men forget that he was once young and passionate, romantic about the schemes which he realistically carried out, troubled by the conflict of many ideas in his fruitful mind, and ardently cherishing those he thought true and good. In London he had justified his looser impulses by arguing, against Wollaston, that men are machines driven by necessity and that there are no virtues and no vices in nature. But on his voyage home and during his first year or two in Philadelphia he decided that this argument was at fault. The freethinkers he had known best—Collins, Keith, Ralph—had all injured him, and he while a freethinker had behaved badly to his brother James, to Deborah Read, to Ralph's milliner, and to Vernon. There were in practice, perhaps in nature itself, such things as right and wrong. "Revelation had indeed no weight with me, as such; but I entertained an opinion that, though certain actions might not be bad because they were forbidden by it, or good because it commanded them, yet probably these actions might be forbidden because they were bad for us, or commanded because they were beneficial to us, in their own natures, all the circumstances of things considered."[19] His mind was too free to let him retreat to any contemporary sect, and he remained a deist. But neither was he able to be satisfied with a dry and niggling rationalism. Like Wollaston, he seems to have felt the need of some kind of ritual of worship. On 20 November 1728, the year Franklin formulated the Junto's rules, he settled upon his *Articles of Belief and Acts of Religion*[20] which served as his creed—though he later simplified that—and his private religious ceremony.

Believing that there is one Supreme Being, "Author and Father of the Gods themselves," he still held in 1728, again with Wollaston, that there are many lesser Gods, each in his system like a sun. To the God of his own system Franklin raised his "praise and adoration. . . . I conceive for many reasons that He is a good Being, and as I should be happy to have so wise, good, and powerful a Being my friend, let me consider in what manner I shall make myself most acceptable to Him. Next to the praise resulting from and due to His wisdom, I believe He is pleased and delights in the happiness of those He has created; and since without virtue man can have no happiness in this world, I firmly believe He delights to see me virtuous, because He is pleased when He sees me happy. And since He has created many things which seem purely designed for the delight of man, I believe He is not offended when He sees his children solace themselves in any manner of pleasant exercises and innocent delights; and I think no pleasure innocent that is to man hurtful. I love Him therefore for His Goodness, and I adore Him for His Wisdom."

After this statement of First Principles, the form of Adoration. "Being mindful that before I address the Deity my soul ought to be calm and serene, free from passion and perturbation, or otherwise elevated with rational joy and pleasure, I ought to use a countenance that expresses a filial respect, mixed with a kind of smiling that signifies inward joy and satisfaction and admiration. . . . O Creator, O Father! I believe that Thou art good and that Thou art pleased with the pleasure of Thy children.—Praised be Thy name for ever. By Thy power hast Thou made the glorious sun, with his attending worlds; from the energy of Thy mighty will they first received their prodigious motion, and by Thy wisdom hast Thou prescribed the wondrous laws by which they move.—Praised be Thy name for ever. . . . Thou abhorrest in Thy creatures treachery, deceit, malice, revenge, intemperance, and every other hurtful vice; but Thou art a lover of justice and sincerity, of friendship and benevolence, and every virtue. Thou art my friend, my father, and my benefactor.—Praised be Thy name, O God, for ever! Amen!" The Adoration concluded with "Milton's Hymn to the Creator" from *Paradise Lost*[21] and "the reading of some book, or part of a book, discoursing on and exciting to moral virtue."

Then the Petition and Thanks which completely reveal what the inner Franklin valued and desired.

"That I may be preserved from atheism and infidelity, impiety and profaneness, and in my addresses to Thee carefully avoid irreverence and ostentation, formality and odious hypocrisy,— Help me, O Father!

"That I may be loyal to my prince and faithful to my country, careful for its good, valiant in its defence, and obedient to its laws, abhorring treason as much as tyranny,—Help me, O Father!

"That I may to those above me be dutiful, humble, and submissive; avoiding pride, disrespect, and contumacy,—Help me, O Father!

"That I may to those below me be gracious, condescending, and forgiving, using clemency, protecting innocent distress, avoiding cruelty, harshness, and oppression, insolence, and unreasonable severity,—Help me, O Father!

"That I may refrain from censure, calumny, and detraction; that I may avoid and abhor deceit and envy, fraud, flattery, and hatred, malice, lying, and ingratitude,—Help me, O Father!

"That I may be sincere in friendship, faithful in trust, and impartial in judgment, watchful against pride and against anger (that momentary madness),—Help me, O Father!

"That I may be just in all my dealings, temperate in my pleasures, full of candour and ingenuity, humanity, and benevolence,— Help me, O Father!

"That I may be grateful to my benefactors, and generous to my friends, exercising charity and liberality to the poor and pity to the miserable,—Help me, O Father!

"That I may avoid avarice and ambition, jealousy and intemperance, falsehood, luxury, and lasciviousness,—Help me, O Father!

"That I may possess integrity and evenness of mind, resolution in difficulties, and fortitude under affliction; that I may be punctual in performing my promises, peaceable and prudent in my behaviour,—Help me, O Father!

"That I may have tenderness for the weak and reverent respect for the ancient; that I may be kind to my neighbours, goodnatured to my companions, and hospitable to strangers,—Help me, O Father!

"That I may be averse to talebearing, backbiting, detraction, slander and craft and overreaching, abhor extortion, perjury, and every kind of wickedness,—Help me, O Father!

"That I may be honest and open-hearted, gentle, merciful, and good, cheerful in spirit, rejoicing in the good of others,—Help me, O Father!

"That I may have a constant regard to honour and probity, that I may possess a perfect innocence and a good conscience, and at length become truly virtuous and magnanimous,—Help me, good God; help me, O Father!

"And forasmuch as ingratitude is one of the most odious of vices, let me be not unmindful gratefully to acknowledge the favours I receive from Heaven. . . .

"For peace and liberty, for food and raiment, for corn and wine and milk, and every kind of healthful nourishment,—Good God, I thank Thee!

"For the common benefits of air and light; for useful fire and delicious water,—Good God, I thank Thee!

"For knowledge and literature and every useful art, for my friends and their prosperity, and for the fewness of my enemies,—Good God, I thank Thee!

"For all Thy innumerable benefits; for life and reason and the use of speech; for health and joy and every pleasant hour,—My good God, I thank Thee!"

Though Franklin before he was twenty-three had so wide and serene a view of human behaviour, he had not yet resolved in himself the conflict between his instinct toward pleasure and his faith in reasonable virtue. He argued the matter out, some time in 1730, in two Socratic dialogues—suggested by *The Moralists* in Shaftesbury's *Characteristics*—which he read before the Junto and published in his newspaper.[22] The speakers were Philocles and Horatio, really two dramatic halves of Franklin.* Misfortune had sent Horatio, the man of pleasure, to philosophy for relief, and Philocles, the man of reason, told his friend that he had given more for pleasure than it was worth.

"*Hor[atio]*. That depends all upon opinion. Who shall judge what the pleasure is worth? Supposing a pleasing form of the fair kind strikes me so much that I can enjoy nothing without the

* See Notes, p. 808.

enjoyment of that one object. Or, that pleasure in general is so favourite a mistress that I will take her as men do their wives, for better or worse; mind no consequences, nor regarding what's to come. Why should I not do it?

"*Phil*[*ocles*]. Suppose, Horatio, that a friend of yours entered into the world about two-and-twenty, with a healthful vigorous body, and a fair plentiful estate of about five hundred pounds a year; and yet, before he had reached thirty, should, by following his pleasures and not, as you say, duly regarding consequences, have run out of his estate and disabled his body to that degree that he had neither the means nor capacity of enjoyment left, nor anything else to do but wisely shoot himself through the head to be at rest; what would you say to this unfortunate man's conduct? . . . Does that miserable son of pleasure appear as reasonable and lovely a being in your eyes as the man who, by prudently and rightly gratifying his natural passions, had preserved his body in full health, and his estate entire, and enjoyed both to a good old age, and then died with a thankful heart for the good things he had received . . . ? Say, Horatio, are these men equally wise and happy? And is everything to be measured by mere fancy and opinion, without considering whether that fancy or opinion be right?

"*Hor*. Hardly so neither, I think; yet sure the wise and good Author of Nature could never make us to plague us. He could never give us passions, on purpose to subdue and conquer 'em; nor produce this self of mine, or any other self, only that it may be denied; for that is denying the works of the great Creator Himself. Self-denial, then, which is what I suppose you mean by prudence, seems to me not only absurd but very dishonourable to that supreme Wisdom and Goodness. . . . Are we created sick, only to be commanded to be sound? Are we born under one law, our passions, and yet bound to another, that of reason? Answer me, Philocles, for I am warmly concerned for the honour of Nature, the mother of us all. . . .

"*Phil*. This, my dear Horatio, I have to say: that what you find fault with and clamour against, as the most terrible evil in the world, self-denial, is really the greatest good and the highest self-gratification. If, indeed, you use the word in the sense of some weak sour moralists, and much weaker divines, you'll have just reason to laugh at it. But if you take it as understood by philosophers and men of sense, you will presently see her charms, and fly to her embraces, notwithstanding her demure looks, as absolutely necessary to produce even your own darling sole good, pleasure; for self-denial is never a duty, or a reasonable action, but as 'tis a natural means of procuring more pleasure than you can taste without it. . . .

"*Hor.* . . . I'm impatient, and all on fire. Explain, therefore, in your beautiful, natural, easy way of reasoning, what I'm to understand by this grave lady of yours, with so forbidding, downcast looks, and yet so absolutely necessary to my pleasures. I stand ready to embrace her; for, you know, pleasure I court under all shapes and forms.

"*Phil.* . . . No created being can be all-wise, all-good, and all-powerful, because his powers and capacities are finite and limited; consequently, whatever is created must, in its own nature, be subject to error, irregularity, excess, and disorder. All intelligent, rational agents find in themselves a power of judging what kind of beings they are; what actions are proper to preserve 'em and what consequences will generally attend them, what pleasures they are formed for and to what degree their natures are capable of receiving them. All we have to do then, Horatio, is to consider, when we are surprised with a new object and passionately desire to enjoy it, whether the gratifying that passion be consistent with the gratifying other passions and appetites equal if not more necessary to us. And whether it consists with our happiness tomorrow, next week, or next year; for, as we all wish to live, we are obliged by reason to take as much care for our future as our present happiness and not build one upon the ruins of t'other. . . . So that this philosophical self-denial is only refusing to do an action which you strongly desire, because 'tis inconsistent with your health, fortunes, or circumstances in the world; or, in other words, because 'twould cost you more than 'twas worth. You would lose by it, as a man of pleasure."

So far in the first dialogue. In the second Philocles and Horatio had met again in the "delightful, awe-inspiring fields" after three or four months. Horatio, now convinced that self-denial is a pleasure, wanted further to be told what was the "constant, durable good" which he had heard Philocles speak of. "Pray explain what you mean; for I am not much used to this abstract way of reasoning." Philocles explained that the good of man is not natural and sensual, but rational and moral.

"*Phil.* Natural or sensual pleasure continues no longer than the action itself, but this divine or moral pleasure [doing good to others] continues when the action is over, and swells and grows upon your hand by reflection. The one is inconstant, unsatisfying, of short duration, and attended with numberless ills; the other is constant, yields full satisfactions, is durable, and no evils preceding, accompanying, or following it. But, if you inquire further into the cause of this difference, and would know why the moral pleasures are greater than the sensual; perhaps the reason is the same in all other creatures; that their happiness or chief good consists in acting up to their chief faculty, or that faculty which distinguishes them from all creatures of a different species. The chief faculty in a man is his reason, and consequently his chief good; or that which may be justly called his good consists not merely in action, but in reasonable action. By reasonable actions we understand those actions which are preservative of the human kind and naturally tend to produce real and unmixed happiness; and these actions, by way of distinction, we call actions morally good.

"*Hor.* . . . Pray tell me what is the real difference between natural good and ill, and moral good and ill. For I know several people who use the terms without ideas.

"*Phil.* That may be. The difference lies only in this: that natural good and ill is pleasure and pain; moral good and ill is pleasure or pain produced with intention and design; for 'tis the intention only that makes the agent morally good or bad.

"*Hor.* But may not a man, with a very good intention, do an ill action?

"*Phil.* Yes, but then he errs in his judgment, though his design be good. If his error is inevitable, or such as, all things considered, he could not help, he is inculpable; but if it arose through want of diligence in forming his judgment about the nature of human actions, he is immoral and culpable.

"*Hor.* I find, then, that in order to please ourselves rightly, or to do good to others morally, we should take great care of our opinions.

"*Phil.* Nothing concerns you more; for, as the happiness or real good of men consists in right action, and right action cannot be produced without right opinion, it behoves us, above all things in this world, to take care that our opinions of things be according to the nature of things. The foundation of all virtue and happiness is thinking rightly."

In this "beautiful, natural, easy way of reasoning" Franklin in Philadelphia answered his London arguments. There was more than reasoning in his dialogues; a zest for reason, a hunger for goodness, a passion for wisdom. "About this time [but perhaps a year or so later] I conceived the bold and arduous project of arriving at moral perfection. I wished to live without committing any fault at any time; I would conquer all that either natural inclination, custom, or company might lead me into. As I knew, or thought I knew, what was right and wrong, I did not see why I might not always do the one and avoid the other. But I soon found I had undertaken a task of more difficulty than I had imagined. While my care was employed in guarding against one fault, I was often surprised by another; habit took the advantage of inattention; inclination was sometimes too strong for reason. I concluded, at length, that the mere speculative conviction that it was our interest to be completely virtuous was not sufficient to prevent our slipping; and that the contrary habits must be broken, and good ones acquired and established, before we can have any dependence on a steady, uniform rectitude of conduct."[23]

(Franklin had told the Junto that he supposed "the perfection of anything to be only the greatest the nature of the thing is capable of. Different things have different degrees of perfection, and the same things at different times. Thus, a horse is more perfect than an oyster, yet the oyster may be a perfect oyster as well as the horse a perfect horse." People might properly insist that "a man in this life cannot be so perfect as an angel"; for "an angel, by being incorporeal, is allowed some perfections we are at present incapable of, and less liable to some imperfections than we are liable to. If they mean a man is not capable of being as perfect here as he is capable of being in heaven, that may be true likewise.

But that a man is not capable of being so perfect here as he is capable of being here is not sense."[24])

Like a scientist undertaking an experiment in a laboratory, Franklin worked out a scheme of desirable virtues and "annexed to each a short precept which fully expressed the extent I gave to its meaning.. . . . 1. *Temperance:* Eat not to dullness; drink not to elevation. 2. *Silence:* Speak not but what may benefit others or yourself; avoid trifling conversation. 3. *Order:* Let all your things have their places; let each part of your business have its time. 4. *Resolution:* Resolve to perform what you ought; perform without fail what you resolve. 5. *Frugality:* Make no expense but to do good to others or yourself; i.e., waste nothing. 6. *Industry:* Lose no time; be always employed in something useful; cut off all unnecessary actions. 7. *Sincerity:* Use no hurtful deceit; think innocently and justly, and, if you speak, speak accordingly. 8. *Justice:* Wrong none by doing injuries, or omitting the benefits that are your duty. 9. *Moderation:* Avoid extremes; forbear resenting injuries so much as you think they deserve. 10. *Cleanliness:* Tolerate no uncleanliness in body, clothes, or habitation. 11. *Tranquillity:* Be not disturbed at trifles, or at accidents common or unavoidable. 12. *Chastity:* Rarely use venery but for health or offspring, never to dullness, weakness, or the injury of your own or another's peace or reputation. 13. *Humility:* Imitate Jesus and Socrates."[25]

Franklin arranged his virtues in this order because he thought he would have to take them up one at a time and that success in one ought to help him with the next. "*Temperance* first, as it tends to procure that coolness and clearness of head which is so necessary where constant vigilance is to be kept up. . . . This being acquired and established, *Silence* would be more easy; and my desire being to gain knowledge at the same time that I improved in virtue, and considering that in conversation it was obtained rather by the use of the ears than of the tongue, and therefore wishing to break a habit I was getting into of prattling, punning, and joking, which only made me acceptable to trifling company, I gave *Silence* the second place. This and the next, *Order,* I expected would allow me more time for attending to my project and my studies. *Resolution,* once become habitual, would keep me firm in my endeavours to obtain all the subsequent virtues; *Frugality* and *Industry*, freeing me from my remaining debt and producing affluence and independence, would make more easy the practice of *Sincerity* and *Justice*, etc."[26] (What other moralist since the Greeks has ever so cheerfully taken it for granted that affluence might make it easier to practise sincerity, justice, moderation, cleanliness, tranquillity, chastity, and humility?)

Like a scientist in a laboratory, Franklin took careful notes of his experiment. "I made a little book, in which I allotted a page for each of the virtues. . . . I determined to give a week's strict attention to each of the virtues successively. Thus, in the first week, my great guard was to avoid every the least offence against *Temperance*, leaving the other virtues to their ordinary chance, only marking every evening the faults of the day. . . . Proceeding thus to the last, I could go through a course complete in thirteen weeks, and four courses in a year. And like him who, having a garden to weed, does not attempt to eradicate all the bad herbs at once, but works on one of the beds at a time, and, having accomplished the first, proceeds to a second, so I should have, I hoped, the encouraging pleasure of seeing on my pages the progress I made in virtue . . . till in the end, by a number of courses, I should be happy in viewing a clean book."[27]

He was surprised to find he had more faults than he had imagined, but pleased to see them diminish before he lost interest in his experiment in perfection and gradually gave it up. It was in respect to *Order* that he was most incorrigible. In business he had many interruptions, and with his "exceeding good memory" he found it easier to remember where things might be than to watch that they were kept where they belonged. But he did make a systematic programme for his usual day. He got up at five, washed, said his prayer to Powerful Goodness, planned the day's work, studied, and had breakfast till eight. From eight to twelve he worked at his business. From twelve to two he read, looked after his accounts, and dined. From two till six he worked again. From six to ten: "Put things in their place. Supper. Music or diversion, or conversation. Examination of the day."[28] Then he slept from ten to five again. He carried out this program as well as he could. Perhaps he was most successful with *Humility*. He had not included it on his list at first: "but a Quaker friend having kindly informed me that I was generally thought proud; that my pride showed itself frequently in conversation; that I was not content with being in the right when discussing any point but was over-bearing and rather insolent, of which he convinced me by mentioning several instances; I determined endeavouring to cure myself, if I could, of this vice or folly among the rest. . . . I cannot boast of much success in acquiring the reality of this virtue, but I had a good deal with regard to the appearance of it. I made it a rule to forbear all direct contradiction of the sentiments of others, and all positive assertion of my own. . . . I soon found the advantage of this change in my manner; the conversations I engaged in went on more pleasantly. The modest way in which I proposed my opinions procured them a readier reception and less contradiction; I had less mortification when I was found to be in the wrong; and I more easily prevailed with others to give up their mistakes and join with me when I happened to be in the right."[29]

Many of Franklin's friends might have wondered if they had known what were the virtues he so much desired. They would have supposed he already had enough temperance, order, resolution, frugality, industry, sincerity, justice, moderation, cleanliness, tranquillity for any man, and would not have supposed he set any such value as this on silence, chastity, humility. All of his friends in the Junto must have wondered when they heard that their amiable companion had even thought of reaching austere perfection. For, moving in the familiar, fallible world, he showed few signs of the inner life which ran incessantly through his studious days and nights, and from which his influence and charm rose to pour over Philadelphia.

I V

Franklin was not all mind and will. There was also his warm, indocile flesh. No certain early likeness of him survives, but what he outwardly was when he returned to Philadelphia may be imagined backwards from later portraits and various chance notes on his personal appearance. Strongly built, rounded like a swimmer or a wrestler, not angular like a runner, he was five feet nine or ten inches tall, with a large head and square, deft hands. His hair was blond or light brown, his eyes grey, full, and steady, his mouth wide and humorous with a pointed upper lip. His clothing was as clean as it was plain. Though he and others say he was hesitant in speech, he was prompt in action. On that bored voyage home he had been among those who tied the rope around the cheat and hoisted him up, and the one who by himself did the hard, wet work of commandeering the boat. Now back among old friends, and making new ones, he was restless with vitality.

Again as in London the chief impulse he could or did not regulate was sexual. He told his illegitimate son all that is known about whatever excesses there were "through this dangerous time of youth, and the hazardous situations I was sometimes in among strangers, remote from the eye and advice of my father. . . . That hard-to-be-governed passion of youth hurried me frequently into intrigues with low women that fell in my way, which were attended with some expense and great inconvenience, besides a continual risk to my health by a distemper which of all things I dreaded, though by great good luck I escaped it."[30] In his morning litany he could pray to be kept from lasciviousness, but when night came lust might come with it. Phrases of gallantry appear in his writings. Even Philocles speaks of even self-denial as a charming and desirable mistress. Franklin was then not a gallant and he seems not to have fallen in love. He went to women hungrily, secretly, and briefly.

But one of them bore him a son, in 1730 or early in 1731 (Franklin referred to him as nineteen in April 1750[31]). None of the scandal-hunters of that day could find out who the mother was, though an anonymous political enemy in 1764 alleged she was a maid named Barbara who had served in the Franklin household, for ten pounds a year, till her death "lately" and had been buried in an unmarked grave.[32] Subsequent antiquarians have not cleared up the mystery, which is still obscure when it is argued that the mother may have been Deborah Read, before or after she began to call herself Deborah Franklin.

Franklin had been gradually convinced that it was better to marry than to burn—or, as he later put it, that "a single man

resembles the odd half of a pair of scissors." In his search for a
wife he had begun near home, at first without intention. "I had
hitherto continued to board with Godfrey"—the disputative member of the Junto—"who lived in part of my house with his wife
and children, and had one side of the shop for his glazier's business,
though he worked little, being always absorbed in his mathematics.
Mrs. Godfrey projected a match for me with a relation's daughter,
took opportunities of bringing us often together, till a serious
courtship on my part ensued, the girl being in herself very deserving. The old folks encouraged me by continual invitations to
supper, and by leaving us together, till at length it was time to
explain. Mrs. Godfrey managed our little treaty. I let her know
that I expected as much money with their daughter as would pay
off my remaining debt for the printing-house, which I believe was
not then above a hundred pounds. She brought me word they had
no such sum to spare; I said they might mortgage their house in
the loan office. The answer to this, after some days, was that they
did not approve the match; that, on inquiry of Bradford, they had
been informed the business was not a profitable one . . . and,
therefore, I was forbidden the house and the daughter shut up."[33]

The business-like suitor did not feel sure that there had been a
change of sentiment in the business-like parents. Perhaps they
thought he could not do without the girl and might elope with her
and so forfeit any claim he had on them. He was not so far gone,
and he gave up his suit. "Mrs. Godfrey brought me afterwards
some more favourable account of their disposition, and would
have drawn me on again; but I declared absolutely my resolution
to have nothing more to do with that family. This was resented by
the Godfreys; we differed, and they removed, leaving me the whole
house, and I resolved to take no more inmates. . . .

"But this affair having turned my thoughts to marriage, I looked
round me and made overtures of acquaintance in other places; but
soon found that, the business of a printer being generally thought
a poor one, I was not to expect money with a wife, unless with
such a one as I should not otherwise think agreeable. . . . A
friendly correspondence as neighbours and old acquaintances had
continued between me and Mrs. Read's family, who all had a
regard for me from the time of my first lodging in their house. I

was often invited there and consulted in their affairs, wherein
I sometimes was of service. I pitied poor Miss Read's unfortunate
situation, who was generally dejected, seldom cheerful, and avoided
company. I considered my giddiness and inconstancy when in
London as in a great degree the cause of her unhappiness, though
the mother was good enough to think the fault more her own than
mine, as she had prevented our marrying before I went thither,
and persuaded the other match in my absence. Our mutual affection was revived, but there were now great objections to our union.
The match was indeed looked upon as invalid, a preceding wife
being said to be living in England; but this could not be easily
proved, because of the distance; and though there was a report of
his death"—Rogers had run away from his creditors to the West
Indies—"it was not certain. Then, though it should be true, he
had left many debts, which his successor might be called upon to
pay. We ventured, however, over all these difficulties, and I took
her to wife September 1st, 1730."[84]

This is the philosopher's bland version, written at the country
seat of the Bishop of St. Asaph's in 1771. In August 1730, just after
Franklin had published his dialogues concerning pleasure, he must
have been more troubled. By that time he could have known that
Barbara, or whoever it was, had had or was to have a child of his.
To scurry into marriage with Deborah was to risk her under-
standable anger when she should find out. Or if matters were otherwise, and it was she who was to have his child, the situation was
still troubling. Suppose Rogers were alive. For Deborah Rogers to
have a child by another man would be at least as bad as bigamy.
There was bound to be scandal. But of course it would be less if
the child appeared to be Franklin's and an unknown mother's. The
lusty philosopher could take all the blame. He did take it. The
child, born to whatever mother, lived in the new household as
William Franklin, supposed to be illegitimate but acknowledged
and cherished. Deborah may have had reason to be grateful, or she
may have been merely forgiving. It is now impossible to say which.
Because the couple could not be sure that Rogers was dead, they
were married at common law, without a ceremony or any record
at Christ Church, which she attended. The young widow, if she
was that, came to the house near the market as Franklin's wife, and

no more minded the irregularity than he did, or her mother who lived with them, or any of their friends. Deborah Franklin was a sturdy, handsome, high-coloured woman, untaught and sometimes turbulent, little interested in her husband's studies or speculations but devoted to him, economical and sensible. "She proved a good and faithful helpmate, assisted me much by attending the shop; we throve together, and have ever mutually endeavoured to make each other happy."[35]

The most unreasonable of Franklin's impulses had now been quieted by this most reasonable of marriages, and he was free to turn his whole mind and will to work.

V

Nothing in the history of Philadelphia gave Franklin a right to expect that the printer's trade would there be a way to wealth. Compared with Boston, the town was backward as to books. Few were sold, almost none printed except theological pamphlets and almanacs. Keimer, though Franklin ridiculed him, was enterprising. His folio history of the Quakers (1728), by William Sewel, was the most important book yet published in Pennsylvania, and his Epictetus (1729) the first translation of a classic writer published in America. He printed paper money in Burlington and he started a newspaper in Philadelphia. But when Franklin and Meredith left him in the spring of 1728, Keimer was shaky. He was not able to compete with Andrew Bradford, who as postmaster could use the carriers to distribute his newspaper, and who as printer for the government was given profitable work on the laws, minutes, proclamations, addresses, and ballots issued by authority. If there was little room in Philadelphia for a second printer, there must have seemed none for a third.

The third was Benjamin Franklin, who was more than a printer. He was the best writer in America. He had the Junto for sworn friends and backers. He was bringing to his first business a powerful and ambitious mind which had in it none of Keimer's eccentricity or Bradford's unadventurous security. From the outset Franklin aimed to pass, or to undo, his rivals.

For three years Keimer had been working on the Sewel, and the Quakers were impatient. Breintnal of the Junto, Franklin says, "procured us from the Quakers the printing forty sheets of their history, the rest being to be done by Keimer."[36] Breintnal may have thought of this himself, or he may have been acting on a hint from Franklin. The speed of the new printers was an argument against Keimer. "I composed . . . a sheet a day, and Meredith worked it off at press; it was often eleven at night, and sometimes later, before I finished my distribution for the next day's work, for the little jobs sent in by our other friends now and then put us back. But so determined I was to continue doing a sheet a day of the folio that one night when, having imposed my forms, I thought my day's work over, one of them by accident was broken and two pages reduced to pie, I immediately distributed it and composed it over again before I went to bed; and this industry, visible to our neighbours, began to give us character and credit."[37] The merchants at the Every Night Club talked about the promising young tradesmen.

Franklin, who had worked on the first lively newspaper in Boston, planned to begin one in Philadelphia, in competition with Bradford's *American Weekly Mercury*. In this scheme a member of the Junto did Franklin harm. Webb, "who had found a female friend that lent him wherewith to purchase his time of Keimer,"[38] came to Franklin and Meredith looking for employment as a journeyman. They could not then afford one, but Franklin thought they might later—and let out his secret. Webb took the secret to Keimer, who, to get ahead of Franklin, promptly announced a newspaper of his own, in October 1728, and in December published the first number of *The Universal Instructor in All Arts and Sciences: and Pennsylvania Gazette*. As Instructor he set out to reprint Chambers's *Cyclopædia*, fresh from London. As Gazette he had an address from the legislature of New Jersey to their governor and his reply, some news paragraphs, and one paid advertisement. He ran on for thirty-nine numbers, with his *Cyclopædia*, Defoe's *Religious Courtship*, news and advertisements, and various lighter matters, in prose and verse, which made his paper more interesting than Bradford's had been.

But not as interesting as the *Mercury* became in February, when

Franklin wrote every week as the Busy-Body, and twice more in March before he gave the series over to Breintnal. Franklin wrote to tease Keimer, who answered with sputtering abuse, and to keep readers away from him, even if they were "fixed on" the *Mercury*. The Busy-Body was easy and humorous, praising virtue and good temper. On 18 February he advised "Cretico, thou sour philosopher, thou cunning statesman," to "neglect those musty authors; let them be covered with dust and moulder on their proper shelves; and do thou apply thyself to a study much more profitable, the knowledge of mankind and of thyself." The Busy-Body approved Cato, "who appeared in the plainest country garb; his greatcoat was coarse and looked old and threadbare; his linen was homespun; his beard perhaps of seven days' growth; his shoes thick and heavy"—yet who was greeted with respect by every person in the room when recently he came to town, to a house where "were met men of the most note in this place. . . . A mixture of innocence and wisdom makes him ever seriously cheerful. His generous hospitality to strangers, according to his ability; his goodness, his charity, his courage in the cause of the oppressed, his fidelity in friendship, his humility, his honesty and sincerity, his moderation, and his loyalty to the government; his piety, his temperance, his love to mankind, his magnanimity, his public-spiritedness, and, in fine, his consummate virtue, make him justly deserve to be esteemed the glory of his country."[39]

The Busy-Body observed little incidents of the common life in Philadelphia which plenty of readers must have recognized though they were seeing them in print for the first time. There was the letter on 25 February from the imagined Patience, a single woman who kept a shop and was pestered by the visits of a friend who came too often and stayed too long. "She has two children that are just big enough to run about and do pretty mischief; these are continually along with Mamma, either in my room or shop, if I have ever so many customers or people with me about business. Sometimes they pull the books off my low shelves down to the ground, and perhaps where one of them has just been making water. My friend takes up the stuff and cries: 'Eh, thou little wicked mischievous rogue! But, however, it has done no great damage; 'tis only wet a little'; and so puts it up upon the shelf again. Sometimes they get to my cask of nails behind the counter and divert themselves, to my great vexation, with mixing my ten-penny and eight-penny and four-penny together. I endeavour to conceal my uneasiness as much as possible, and with a grave look go to sorting them out. She cries: 'Don't thee trouble thyself, neighbour; let them play a little; I'll put all to rights myself before I go.' But things are never so put to rights but that I find a great deal of work to do after they are gone. Thus, Sir, I have all the trouble and pesterment of children without the pleasure of—calling them my own."[40]

The Busy-Body on 27 March prudently ridiculed what seemed to the son of Josiah Franklin a grotesque folly: "There are among us great numbers of honest artificers and labouring people who, fed with a vain hope of growing suddenly rich, neglect their business, almost to the ruining of themselves and families, and voluntarily endure abundance of fatigue in a fruitless search after imaginary hidden treasure. They wander through the woods and bushes by day, to discover the marks and signs; at midnight they repair to the hopeful spot with spades and pickaxes; full of expectation, they labour violently, trembling at the same time in every joint through fear of certain malicious demons who are said to haunt and guard such places. At length a mighty hole is dug, and perhaps several cartloads of earth thrown out; but, alas, no cag or iron pot is found! No seaman's chest crammed with Spanish pistoles or weighty pieces of eight! Then they conclude that, through some mistake in the procedure, some rash word spoke, or some rule of art neglected, the guardian spirit had power to sink it deeper into the earth and convey it out of their reach. . . .

"This odd humour of digging for money, through a belief that much has been hid by pirates formerly frequenting the river, has for several years been mighty prevalent among us; insomuch that you can hardly walk half a mile out of town on any side without observing several pits dug with that design, and perhaps some lately opened. Men otherwise of very good sense have been drawn into this practice through an overweening desire of sudden wealth and an easy credulity of what they so earnestly wished might be true; while the rational and almost certain methods of acquiring riches by industry and frugality are neglected or forgotten. There seems to be some peculiar charm in the conceit of finding money; and if the sands of Schuylkill were so much mixed with small grains of gold that a man might in a day's time, with care and application, get together to the value of half a crown, I make no question but we should find several people employed there that can with ease earn five shillings a day at their proper trades. . . .

"Let honest Peter Buckram, who has long without success been a searcher after hidden money, reflect . . . and be reclaimed from this unaccountable folly. Let him consider that every stitch he takes, when he is on his shopboard, is picking up part of a grain of gold, that will in a few days' time amount to a pistole; and let Faber think the same of every nail he drives or every stroke with his plane. Such thoughts may make them industrious, and of consequence in time they may be wealthy. But how absurd it is to neglect a certain profit for such a ridiculous whimsy; to spend whole days at the George, in company with an idle pretender to astrology, contriving schemes to discover what was never hidden, and forget how carelessly business is managed at home in their absence; to leave their wives and a warm bed at midnight (no matter if it rain, hail, snow, or blow a hurricane, provided that be the critical hour), and fatigue themselves with the violent exercise of digging for what they shall never find, and perhaps getting a cold that may cost their lives, or at least disordering themselves so as to be fit for no business beside for some days after. Surely this is nothing less than the most egregious folly and madness.

"I shall conclude with the words of my discreet friend Agricola, of Chester County, when he gave his son a good plantation. 'My son,' says he, 'I give thee now a valuable parcel of land; I assure thee I have found a considerable quantity of gold by digging there; thee may'st do the same. But thee must carefully observe this: Never to dig more than plough-deep.' "[41]

Keimer could not write as well as Franklin, any more than any other American then could. But what drove Keimer out of Philadelphia was less his new rival than his own incompetence and bad management. He got deeper and deeper into debt. His creditors pressed him, and he loudly called it persecution. Epictetus could not save him. He was obliged to sell his newspaper to Franklin, and his printing-house to his former apprentice David Harry, whom Franklin had taught their trade. "I was at first apprehensive of a powerful rival in Harry, as his friends were very able and had a good deal of interest. I therefore proposed a partnership to him which he, fortunately for me, rejected with scorn. He was very proud, dressed like a gentleman, lived expensively, took much diversion and pleasure abroad, ran in debt, and neglected his business; upon which, all business left him, and, finding nothing to do, he followed Keimer to Barbados, taking the printing-house with him."[42]

On 2 October 1729 Franklin began to issue the newspaper with the simpler title *The Pennsylvania Gazette*. He dropped the encyclopædia and Defoe from its columns, limited it more strictly to the actual concerns of Pennsylvanians, wrote much for it himself, in time enormously increased the advertisements, and printed it with skill and some taste. "To publish a good newspaper," he said in his first preface, "is not so easy an undertaking as many people imagine it to be. The author of a gazette (in the opinion of the learned) ought to be qualified with an extensive acquaintance with languages, a great easiness and command of writing and relating things clearly and intelligibly, and in few words; he should be able to speak of war both by land and sea; be well acquainted with geography, with the history of the time, with the several interests of princes and states, the secrets of courts, and the manners and customs of all nations. Men thus accomplished are very rare in this remote part of the world."[43] Franklin hoped he might have all possible assistance from his friends.

But for many issues of the *Gazette* he was writer as well as printer. He wrote or rewrote the foreign and domestic news. He wrote letters to himself as editor and answered them. He wrote humorous squibs and advertisements. Both his former experience with the *New England Courant* and his maturing temper kept him discreet in what he said about the civil authorities. The clergy could not complain of *A Witch Trial at Mount Holly* in the *Gazette* for 22 October 1730.[44] Such actions were as ridiculous as this broad report of them. In matters of religion the *Gazette* was neither scoffing nor partisan. Yet Franklin was always insistent on the freedom of the press, and in *An Apology for Printers* on 10 June 1731[45] he made his position clear. Men have many opinions,

he said, and printers print them as a part of their business. They
are "educated in the belief that when men differ in opinion, both
sides ought equally to have the advantage of being heard by the
public; and that when truth and error have fair play, the former is
always an overmatch for the latter. Hence they cheerfully serve all
contending writers that pay them well, without regarding on
which side they are of the question in dispute. . . . If all printers
were determined not to print anything till they were sure it would
offend nobody, there would be very little printed." And there are
more bad and foolish things left unprinted than are ever printed.

With Keimer out of the way, Franklin had only Andrew Bradford for a rival. Bradford was postmaster and he ordered his
carriers not to take the *Gazette* to its subscribers. Franklin bribed
them to carry it secretly. Bradford did all the government printing
and made money by it. Franklin and Meredith in the first month
of the *Gazette* voluntarily printed an address from the Assembly to
the governor, which had been officially printed by Bradford, and
sent it to every member. Their work was so much better than
Bradford's that the members "were sensible of the difference; it
strengthened the hands of our friends in the House; and they
voted us their printer"[46] for 1730. From that time on Franklin
was the printer for Pennsylvania. This was less than two years after
Franklin and Meredith had set up their uncertain business.

Meredith had been little help. He was a poor workman and had
gone back to drinking. His father, who was to have advanced two
hundred pounds, had paid only half of it to the merchant who had
imported their equipment from London and who now brought
suit for the rest. In this trouble Franklin was heartened by his
Junto friends Grace and Coleman, who each separately came to
him and offered to let him have the money, but hoped he could
get rid of Hugh Meredith, "who, as they said, was often seen drunk
in the streets, and playing at low games in alehouses, much to our
discredit."[47] Franklin could hardly suggest this to Meredith. For
once Meredith helped. He said he could see he would never be a
printer, and he wanted to go back to farming. If Franklin would
repay the hundred pounds to the elder Meredith, assume the firm's
debts and settle Hugh Meredith's personal debts, and give him
thirty pounds and a new saddle on which to ride away to North

Carolina where land was cheap, he would turn over the whole business to his partner. Franklin borrowed half of what was needed, and had been offered, from Grace and half from Coleman, and the partnership was quietly dissolved 14 July 1730.

To the public eye of Philadelphia Franklin now became the complete tradesman. "In order to secure my credit and character . . . I took care not only to be in reality industrious and frugal but to avoid all appearances to the contrary. I dressed plainly; I was seen at no places of idle diversion. I never went out a-fishing or shooting; a book, indeed, sometimes debauched me from my work, but that was seldom, snug, and gave no scandal; and, to show that I was not above my business, I sometimes brought home the paper I purchased at the stores through the streets on a wheelbarrow."[48]

This is the first of the roles that Franklin strategically assumed, as he was to assume others later. For his character was never of one single piece, like, for example, Washington's. Franklin's was rich, flexible, dramatic. Personally ambitious, he was no less truly eager for the general good. Able to aim at moral perfection for himself, he was not in the least ascetic and he did not desire to isolate himself from the common life. He could be metaphysical when he cared to. In the very year he got rid of his partner Franklin wrote a speculative essay on prayer, though he did not print it. "The great uncertainty I found in metaphysical reasonings disgusted me, and I quitted that kind of reading and study for others more satisfactory."[49] But he remained a moralist, loving goodness and wisdom. He was not satisfied to think them out. He wanted to act and see them acted out. Desirable ends do not come of themselves. Men must conceive them, believe in them, further them, and execute them. Franklin was perfectly willing to bring touches of drama into his undertakings—even when, as at first, his end was only his reputation as a tradesman in a provincial town.

However wholly Franklin gave himself to his business he did not give up the Junto, which was his business too. During the winter of 1728–29 the members debated the question of paper money, which all the province was talking about. The balance of transatlantic trade was against Pennsylvania, and gold and silver were steadily drawn to England, leaving money scarce and prices

and interest high. Six years earlier the currency shortage had been
relieved by a small issue of paper money, which was now to be
called in. People who had money were opposed to the issue of
further paper, for fear of inflation, which had taken place in New
England and South Carolina. Debtors, traders, and workmen were
in favour of a still larger issue. Franklin—debtor, trader, and
workman—took his stand with them and broke off the Busy-Body
papers to write *A Modest Enquiry into the Nature and Necessity
of a Paper Currency*,[50] which, dated 3 April 1729, was probably the
first publication of the new firm. Unlike conservative economists,
he saw that gold and silver were in themselves commodities, bought
and sold like any other. "The riches of a country are to be valued
by the quantity of labour its inhabitants are able to purchase, and
not by the quantity of silver and gold they possess. . . . Trade in
general being nothing else but the exchange of labour for labour,
the value of things is . . . most justly measured by labour."
Pennsylvania had little gold and silver as security for paper, but it
had land. "As bills issued upon money security are money, so bills
issued upon land are, in effect, coined land." With this basic principle and this happy phrase—"coined land"—Franklin adroitly
argued for the need of a more plentiful medium of exchange, to
benefit land, labour, and trade. As he had read moralists and meta-
physicians, so had he, at twenty-three, read economists: particularly, it seems, Sir William Petty. But he had made his own observations and he wrote out of a local experience which his readers
understood. "It was well received by the common people in general; but the rich men disliked it, for it increased and strengthened
the clamour for more money, and they happening to have no
writers among them that were able to answer it, their opposition
slackened, and the point was carried by a majority in the House.
My friends there, who conceived I had been of some service,
thought fit to reward me by employing me in printing the money:
a very profitable job and a great help to me. This was another
advantage gained by my being able to write."[51] In the summer of
1731 he had planned to go to Boston, he told his sister, but "printing the paper money here has hindered me near two months."[52]

Franklin, with or without Meredith, was never an adventurous
publisher of books. In his first year he published Isaac Watts's

Psalms, which, he noted, did not sell as fast as Robin Hood's Songs by another printer. Franklin's German hymn book—the first printed in America—was aimed at the Germans in Pennsylvania, for whom in May 1732 he started the first German-American newspaper, the *Philadelphische Zeitung* edited by Louis Timothée, "language master," and short-lived. The *Batchelors-Hall* of George Webb in 1731 and the single-sheet *Almanacs* of Thomas Godfrey in 1729, 1730, 1731 (each for the following year) were by Junto members. On the whole Franklin published books chiefly for profit or for friendship, sometimes both at once. James Logan, the most eminent of the Quakers and the best scholar in Pennsylvania, had at first suspected the Junto and had written to Penn that the Leather Apron men were tools of Sir William Keith. Franklin soon made friends with Logan, and published his translations of *Cato's Moral Distichs* (1735) and of *Cato Major* (1744), which Franklin thought his masterpiece in the printer's art. *The Constitutions of the Free-Masons* (1734)—the first Masonic book printed in America—was for the members of the order, of which he became grand master in that same year. *Every Man His Own Doctor* (1734) and *The Gentleman's Farrier* (1735) were for profit and were profitable. Cadwallader Colden's *An Explication of the First Causes of Motion in Matter* (1745, with the actual imprint of Franklin's partner in New York) was partly for friendship, as was Aquila Rose's *Poems on Several Occasions* (1740), edited by Joseph Rose, who was Franklin's apprentice. Jonathan Edwards's *Distinguishing Marks of a Work of the Spirit of God* (1742), Increase Mather's *Soul-Saving Gospel Truths* (1743), and *The New England Psalter* (1744) were acts of piety for what Franklin called his native country. Defoe's *Family Instructor* (1740) and Richardson's *Pamela* (1744)—this the first novel published in America—were, though profitable too, tributes from Franklin to another projector and another printer. Nine-tenths of what Franklin printed, outside his official printing of legislative records, laws, treaties, his newspaper, and his almanacs, was theological and ephemeral. The most memorable books bearing his imprint (or Franklin and Hall's) now seem to be the folio Indian treaties, rich documents of a vanished age.

But he imported many books to sell in his shop. "If Mr. War-burton," Franklin wrote in 1744 to his friend William Strahan in London, "publishes a new edition of Pope, please to send it me as soon as it is out, 6 sets. That poet has many admirers here, and the reflection he somewhere casts on the plantations [colonies] as if they had a relish for such writers as Ward only, is injurious. Your authors know but little of the fame they have on this side of the ocean. We are a kind of posterity in respect to them. We read their works with perfect impartiality, being at too great a distance to be biased by the factions, parties, and prejudices that prevail among you. We know nothing of their personal failings; the blemishes in their character never reach us, and therefore the bright and amiable part strikes us with its full force. They have never offended us or any of our friends, and we have no competitions with them; therefore we praise and admire them without restraint. Whatever Thomson writes send me a dozen copies of. I had read no poetry for several years, and almost lost the relish of it, till I met with his *Seasons*. That charming poet has brought more tears of pleasure into my eyes than all I ever read before. I wish it were in my power to return him any part of the joy he has given me."[53] The same year Franklin issued a catalogue of "near 600 volumes" which he would sell "for ready money only" at the post office. They were books of divinity, history, law, mathematics, philosophy, physic, and poetry, in various languages, in folio, quarto, and octavo, and the titles represent the whole literature of the age.

Though Franklin in his earliest years as a tradesman might read in a way that was "snug, and gave no scandal," he was actually an avid, powerful reader of many books. There were always books in his inner life, books in his business, books in his friendships. At the Junto in 1730 he made a suggestion: "that, since our books were often referred to in our disquisitions upon the queries, it might be convenient to us to have them all together where we met, that upon occasion they might be consulted; and by thus clubbing our books to a common library, we should, while we liked to keep them together, have each of us the advantage of using the books of all the other members, which would be nearly as beneficial as if each owned the whole. It was liked and agreed to, and we filled one end of the room with such books as we could best spare. The number was not so great as we expected; and though they had been of great use, yet some inconveniences occurring for want of due care of them, the collection, after about a year, was separated and each took his books home again."⁵⁴

Franklin had a better plan. Why should the Junto not organize a subscription library for its own members and any other citizens of Philadelphia who might care to join with them? The Junto agreed. Franklin worked out the details of the scheme, Charles Brockden the scrivener put them in form, and the Instrument of Association was signed 1 July 1731. There were fifty subscribers who each paid in forty shillings and promised to pay ten shillings a year. Franklin's name stood first on the board of directors, who held their initial meeting at Nicholas Scull's house 8 November 1731. At the meeting of 29 March 1732 Thomas Godfrey reported that James Logan would be glad to give advice in the selection of their books. Two days later they had the list and forty-five pounds, which they sent off to Peter Collinson, a Quaker mercer in London who had friends in Philadelphia and was interested in American affairs.

The books came in October. On this or the second list were Pufendorf on jurisprudence, Hayes on fluxions, Keill on astronomy, Sidney on government, L'Hospital on conic sections, Gravesande on natural philosophy; Palladio, Evelyn, Addison, Xenophon's *Memorabilia*, Defoe's *Compleat English Tradesman*, *Gulliver's Travels*, the *Spectator, Tatler, Guardian*, Homer's *Iliad* and *Odyssey*, Dryden's *Virgil*, Bayle's *Critical Dictionary*; and Collinson's gifts: Newton's *Principia* and a dictionary of gardening. Franklin gave Montaigne's *Essays* and a black-letter reprint of the Magna Charta. They were installed in the Junto's quarters in Jones's Alley (or Pewter Platter Alley, now Church Street), where Louis Timothée was the Junto's fellow-tenant. He was chosen to be librarian, in attendance from two to three every Wednesday, and from ten to four on Saturdays. Any "civil gentlemen" might read the books, but only subscribers could take them out—and James Logan. Franklin on 11 December offered to print catalogues and present them to the members. The next year he was librarian for three months. The library had its headquarters at Grace's house, then William Parsons's, till April 1740 when it was moved to a room in the State House on a petition drawn up by Franklin, now clerk of the Assembly. He was its agent in London 1760–65. Absorbing the rival libraries in Philadelphia in 1769, the Library Company became a permanent memorial to the club of artisans and tradesmen who founded it, and to their leader who was not content to use and enjoy his books alone.

On 11 May 1732 the *Gazette* appeared for the first time as published by B. Franklin, not by Franklin and Meredith. The firm had so far not seemed secure enough to risk making it known that the venture was wholly in the hands of one young man without capital. Now the young man, now twenty-six, had paid or saw his way clear to paying all his debts: to Vernon (whose thirty-five pounds had haunted Franklin since 1724), to the elder Meredith, to Grace and Coleman. Throughout his life Franklin acutely dreaded debt, as a form of slavery. Yet he had had a shorter experience of it than most men. Only four years after he set up in business he was his own master.

VI

For Franklin 1732 was a busy and crucial year. His *Gazette* was profitable, and he had a hand in other *Gazettes* in South Carolina and Rhode Island. He was printer to Pennsylvania and printer on his own account. Besides the Junto there was the new library. Through the library and the Masons he was widening his acquaintance among Philadelphians more prominent than his Leather Apron friends. At home he had a shop in part of his house, where his wife helped him sell books and stationery and his mother-in-law sold the salves and ointments which she made. On 20 October his son Francis Folger was born. But all these were not enough, nor the letters which Franklin wrote for the *Gazette* that summer as from Anthony Afterwit, Celia Single, Alice Addertongue.[55] He wanted another outlet and another income, and, perhaps without realizing it, another character to play. He found them in the almanac which he published for the first time in December, in the character of Poor Richard.

Books might sell, almanacs were sure to. Many households in the colonies had no printed matter besides an almanac, but almost every one of them had that. An almanac had been the first thing printed in Pennsylvania, by William Bradford for Daniel Leeds. Almanacs, pocket-size and paper-bound, calculated the tides and the changes of the moon, and claimed to forecast the weather. Almanacs were calendars. They furnished astrology for those who believed in it. There were sometimes recipes in almanacs, and jokes and poems and maxims and odd facts of many sorts. The skimpy margins of the calendar pages were a diary. Children might learn to read from almanacs. The printer of a successful almanac could make money, and the compiler of it a reputation. Andrew Bradford had long issued the annual *American Almanac* of Titan Leeds. Another son of Daniel Leeds, Felix Leeds, was an almanac-maker too. Keimer had undertaken almanacs. And Franklin himself had published not only Thomas Godfrey's almanac for three years but also John Jerman's for 1731 and 1732.

Almanacs usually appeared in October or November for the following year. Franklin was late with his *Poor Richard, 1733.* The *Gazette* announced it as just published 19 December 1732 at five-pence a copy. Within three weeks there had had to be three impressions, and Richard Saunders quickly passed all his rival philomaths. The imaginary astrologer probably took his full name from an actual English Richard Saunders, compiler of the *Apollo Anglicanus*, though Denham's account book lists a Philadelphia Richard Saunders as one of the firm's customers. The suggestion of the more common name Poor Richard may have come from the *Poor Robin* almanac which James Franklin was issuing at Newport. The prophecy in the first *Poor Richard* that Titan Leeds would die 17 October 1733 is a deliberate echo of Swift's hoax on John Partridge twenty-five years before—Swift's hoax brought to Pennsylvania and persisted in by Franklin for years. But the essence of Poor Richard, his humorous, homely character, was Franklin's own creation. Here are Richard's opening words: "I might in this place attempt to gain thy favour by declaring that I write almanacs with no other view than that of the public good; but in that I should not be sincere, and men are now-a-days too wise to be deceived by pretences how specious soever. The plain truth of the matter is, I am excessive poor, and my wife, good woman, is, I tell her, excessive proud; she cannot bear, she says, to sit spinning in her shift of tow while I do nothing but gaze at the stars; and has threatened more than once to burn all my books and rattling-traps (as she calls my instruments) if I do not make some profitable use of them for the good of my family. The printer has offered me some considerable share of the profits, and I have thus begun to comply with my dame's desire."[56]

The next year Poor Richard was grateful for the profits he had made. "My wife has been enabled to get a pot of her own, and is no longer obliged to borrow one from a neighbour; nor have we ever since been without something of our own to put in it. She has also got a pair of shoes, two new shifts, and a new warm petticoat; and, for my part, I have bought a second-hand coat, so good that I am now not ashamed to go to town or be seen there. These things have rendered her temper so much more pacific than it used to be that I may say I have slept more, and more quietly, within this last year than in the three foregoing years put together."[57] His verses on feminine idleness in his almanac for 1733 were answered by her verses on masculine worthlessness in the almanac for 1734. The little tiff was kept up between them. In *Poor Richard* for 1738 the preface appeared as by Bridget Saunders, who had scratched out what Richard had written. "Cannot I have a little fault or two but all the country must see it in print?"[58] She had gone through the whole almanac in his absence and had put in better weather "for the goodwomen to dry their clothes in." Nor did she like some of his verses. He himself, he admitted in 1747, did not think too highly of them. "I know as well as thee that I am no poet born; and it is a trade I never learnt, nor indeed could learn."[59] He did not claim infallibility in his weather forecasts. "We modestly desire only the favourable allowance of a day or two before and a day or two after the precise day against which the weather is set."[60] Poor Richard was resentful toward people who said there was no such man as he. "This is not civil treatment, to endeavour to deprive me of my very being and reduce me to a nonentity in the opinion of the public. But so long as I know myself to walk about, eat, drink, and sleep, I am satisfied that there is really such a man as I am."[61] People who began to say, after half a dozen years, that he must have grown rich were equally wrong. His printer "runs away with the greatest part of the profit."[62] He suffered from the jealousy of rival philomaths, and was for ever pestered by persons who wanted private astrological advice from him. "The perpetual teasing of both neighbours and strangers to calculate nativities, give judgments on schemes, erect figures, discover thieves, detect horse-stealers, describe the route of runaways and strayed cattle; the crowd of visitors with a thousand trifling questions: Will my ship return safe? Will my mare win the race? Will her next colt be a pacer? When will my wife die? Who shall be my husband, and how long first? When is the best time to cut hair, trim cocks, or sow salad? These and the like impertinences I have now neither taste nor leisure for. I have had enough of 'em."[63] He preferred to live quietly in the country, telling no one where.

The almanac for 1748 and afterwards was called *Poor Richard Improved*, and was larger than before. It had become an institution. It sold ten thousand copies a year. Franklin in 1757, writing his preface for 1758, skimmed his almanacs for twenty-five years to make up a single harangue which Poor Richard said he had heard an old man deliver at an auction. This is *The Way to Wealth*, which stands with the *Autobiography* as the best and farthest known of all Franklin's writings, and which has been taken for the essence of his wisdom.

It is not that, and it gives only one aspect of the younger Franklin. Father Abraham at the auction is an old man talking about economy. He has chosen from Poor Richard the sayings which specially prove his point, and left out the rest. Having the last word, he has had almost the only word. *The Way to Wealth* has been endlessly reprinted, while the original almanacs were most of them worn out and thrown away, and the few that have survived are guarded like the bullion they are worth. Everybody knows the Poor Richard that has been saved in Father Abraham's speech. Nobody knows Poor Richard as he was in the racy years which made him known to his contemporaries. Franklin, remembering, said he had filled "all the little spaces" with "proverbial sentences, chiefly such as inculcated industry and frugality, as the means of procuring wealth and thereby securing virtue."[64] Poor Richard for 1739 had put the matter differently. "Be not thou disturbed, O grave and sober reader, if among the many serious sentences in my book thou findest me trifling now and then, and talking idly. In all the dishes I have hitherto cooked for thee, there is solid meat enough for thy money. There are scraps from the table of wisdom that will, if well digested, yield strong nourishment to thy mind. But squeamish stomachs cannot eat without pickles; which, 'tis true, are good for nothing else, but they provoke an appetite."[65]

The earlier Poor Richard was by no means always on the side of calculating prudence. "Never spare the parson's wine nor the baker's pudding" (1733). "Innocence is its own defence" (1733). "As charms are nonsense, nonsense is a charm" (1734). "What one relishes, nourishes" (1734). "He does not possess wealth; it possesses him" (1734). "Avarice and happiness never saw each other. How then should they become acquainted?" (1734). "Poverty wants some things, luxury many things, avarice all things" (1735). "There's more old drunkards than old doctors" (1736). "Wealth is not his that has it, but his that enjoys it" (1736). "He that can take rest is greater than he that can take cities" (1737). "Hast thou virtue? Acquire also the graces and beauties of virtue" (1738).

Poor Richard could say: "Nothing but money is sweeter than honey" (1735), but he spoke of many things besides. "Kings and bears often worry their keepers" (1733). "Hunger never saw bad bread" (1733). "Eat to live, and not live to eat" (1733). "Men and melons are hard to know" (1733). "There is no little enemy" (1733). "He's a fool that makes his doctor his heir" (1733). "The heart of the fool is in his mouth, but the mouth of the wise man is in his heart" (1733). "He that drinks fast pays slow" (1733). "Do good to thy friend to keep him, to thy enemy to gain him" (1734). "Where there's marriage without love there will be love without marriage" (1734). "He that is rich need not live sparingly, and he that can live sparingly need not be rich" (1734). "Approve not of him who commends all you say" (1735). "The family of fools is ancient" (1735). "Look before or you'll find yourself behind" (1735). "A lie stands on one leg, truth on two" (1735). "Sloth and silence are a fool's virtues" (1735). "Deny self for self's sake" (1735). "Opportunity is the great bawd" (1735). "An old young man will be a young old man" (1735). "He is no clown that drives the plough, but he that doth clownish things" (1736). "Now I have a sheep and a cow, everybody bids me good morrow" (1736). "The rotten apple spoils his companions" (1736). "Fish and visitors smell in three days" (1736). "He that has neither fools nor beggars among his kindred is the son of thunder-gust" (1736). "Admiration [wonder] is the daughter of ignorance" (1736). "Bargaining has neither friends nor relations" (1736). "He that can have patience can have what he will" (1736). "None preaches better than the ant, and she says nothing" (1736). "The absent are never without fault, nor the present without excuse" (1736). "Poverty, poetry, and new titles of honour make men ridiculous" (1736). "A countryman between two lawyers is like a fish between two cats" (1737). "Love and lordship hate companions" (1737). "There are no ugly loves nor handsome prisons" (1737). "The worst wheel of the cart makes the most noise" (1737). "Write with the learned, pronounce with the vulgar" (1738). "If you would not be forgotten as soon as you are dead and rotten, either write things worth reading or do things worth the writing" (1738). "Defer not thy well doing; be not like St. George, who is always a-horseback and never rides on" (1738). "As we must account for every idle word, so we must for every idle silence" (1738). "Fly pleasures and they'll follow you" (1738). "Time is an herb that cures all diseases" (1738). "He that would have a short Lent, let him borrow money to be repaid at Easter" (1738). "Eat to please thyself, but dress to please others" (1738). "The ancients tell us what is best; but we must learn from the moderns what is fittest" (1738).

Poor Richard in these gamy years spoke often of women, tenderly and cynically in turn. "A house without a woman and fire-light is like a body without soul or sprite" (1733).

> You cannot pluck roses without fear of thorns,
> Nor enjoy a fair wife without danger of horns (1734).

"Neither a fortress nor a m——d will hold out long after they begin to parley" (1734). "Marry your son when you will, but your daughter when you can" (1734). "A little house well filled, a little field well tilled, and a little wife well willed, are great riches" (1735).

> When ♂ [Mars] and ♀ [Venus] in conjunction lie,
> Then, maids, whate'er is asked of you deny (1735).

"A ship under sail and a big-bellied woman are the handsomest two things that can be seen common" (1735). "Let thy maidservant be faithful, strong, and homely" (1736). "He that takes a wife takes care" (1736). "Why does the blind man's wife paint herself?" (1736). "Keep your eyes wide open before marriage, half shut afterwards" (1738).

These varied sayings run through *Poor Richard* side by side with the stricter—and some of them later—maxims of prudence that Franklin put into Father Abraham's summary. (Those marked with a star are thought to be original with Franklin.[66]) "Fools make feasts, and wise men eat them" (1733). "Early to bed and early to rise makes a man healthy, wealthy, and wise" (1735). "Keep thy shop, and thy shop will keep thee" (1735). "God helps them that help themselves" (1736). "Creditors have better memories than debtors" (1736). *"An empty bag cannot stand upright" (1740). *"The sleeping fox catches no poultry. Up! Up!" (1743). *"If you'd have it done, go; if not, send" (1743). *"Experience keeps a dear school, yet fools will learn in no other" (1743). *"The used key is always bright" (1744). "When the well's dry, we know the worth of water" (1746). "For want of a nail the shoe is lost; for want of a shoe the horse is lost; for want of a horse the rider is lost" (1752). "In the affairs of this world, men are saved not by faith but by the want of it" (1754). *"Three removes is as bad as a fire" (1758).

Poor Richard took wisdom and wit where he could find them: from Dryden, Pope, Prior, Gay, Swift, Bacon, La Rochefoucauld, Rabelais, and many other known masters. There are sayings in Latin, Spanish, French, German, and Welsh. The rustic philosopher drew also on the stream of popular adages, whether already gathered into printed collections or still only current in ordinary speech. In this profusion and uncertainty of sources Poor Richard never hesitated to rework his texts to suit his purpose and his audience. Whatever passed through Franklin's mind brought away some of its qualities and its flavour. Writing, he thought, should be "smooth, clear, and short." The Scottish proverb: "Fat housekeepers make lean executors" he simplified to: "A fat kitchen, a lean will" (1733). Another proverb ran in its Scottish version: "A gloved cat was never a good hunter"; and in an English version: "A muffled cat is no good mouser." Franklin sharpened it: "The cat in gloves catches no mice" (1754). To what had been: "Many strokes fell great oaks" Franklin gave a more pointed antithesis: "Little strokes fell great oaks" (1751). "Three may keep counsel if two of them are away" became in his handling more cynical, and plainer, as: "Three may keep a secret if two of them are dead" (1735). There was a stock saying: "Good wits jump" which Swift put into the mouth of one of his foolish talkers in *Genteel and Ingenious Conversation*. Franklin laughingly dramatized it: "Great wits jump, says the poet, and hit his head against the post" (1735). "The king's cheese goes half away in parings" was an old fling at the wastefulness of courts. Franklin made another application: "The king's cheese is half wasted in parings; but no matter, 'tis made of the people's milk" (1735). And in one of his proverbs Franklin, proverbial for prudence, took the imprudent side. An Italian proverb had been translated into English as: "It is better to have an egg today than tomorrow a hen." Thomas Fuller in 1732 had firmly turned it to: "It is better to have a hen tomorrow than an egg today." Franklin turned it back to the spendthrift: "An egg today is better than a hen tomorrow" (1734).

There is one larger example of Franklin's method with his sources. In the almanac for 1739 he gave a *True Prognostication* which came direct from the *Pantagruelian Prognostication* at the end of the Urquhart-Motteux version of Rabelais. Of the eclipses of the year Pantagruel says in a rush of words: "Saturn will be retrograde, Venus direct, Mercury unfixed as quicksilver. . . . For this reason the crabs will go sidelong and the rope-makers backward . . . bacon will run away from pease in Lent; the belly will waddle before; the bum will sit down first; there will be not a bean left in a twelfth-cake, nor an ace in a flush; the dice will not run as you wish, though you cog them . . . brutes shall speak in several places; Shrovetide will have its day . . . such a hurly-burly was never seen since the devil was a little boy; and there will be above seven-and-twenty irregular verbs made this year, if Priscian do not hold them in. If God do not help us, we shall have our hands and hearts full." Poor Richard, writing for cramped pages, had to be brief. Writing for Pennsylvania, he left out the Catholic and medieval touches in Pantagruel, and put American notes in their place. "During the first visible eclipse," he wrote, "Saturn is retrograde; for which reason the crabs will go sidelong and the rope-makers backward. The belly will wag before, and the a—— shall sit down first. Mercury will have his share in these affairs, and so confound the speech of people that when a Pennsylvanian would say *panther* he shall say *painter*. When a New Yorker thinks to say *this* he shall say *diss*. And the people in New England and Cape May will not be able to say *cow* for their lives, but will be forced to say *keow* by a certain involuntary twist in the root of their tongues. No Connecticut man nor Marylander will be able to open his mouth this year but *Sir* shall be the first or the last syllable he pronounces, and sometimes both. Brutes shall speak in many places, and there will be above seven-and-twenty irregular verbs made this year, if grammar don't interpose.—Who can help these misfortunes!" And so on through the prognostication, fitting the original to fresh uses.

Franklin, creating the character of Poor Richard, also assumed it, as another role like that of the complete tradesman. The rising philosopher could not be for ever in his leather apron, behind his conscious wheelbarrow. He wanted to speak out. Young, he might not be listened to in his own person. As Poor Richard he had a dramatic licence to speak as he chose. He could pretend to be an astrologer and yet make fun of superstition. He could pretend to be old and wise, packing his almanac with wisdom in the verses and proverbs which were all he had space for. If he laid frequent stress on prudence, that was in part because the folk-wisdom on which he drew is largely prudence, which is the ordinary wisdom of ordinary men. At the same time, Franklin believed in prudence. He was not a mystic but a moralist, and the first law of his nature was order. Order in human life, he held, begins in the daily habits of men looking out for themselves. They must work to be happy, and save to be secure. There were plenty of mysteries about men, but industry and frugality were not mysterious. A man who practised them might go beyond them to more important things, as Franklin aimed to. Industry and frugality were the simple, natural road to freedom.

Franklin could see that the times called for Poor Richard's

counsel. Philadelphia had not yet become what he helped to make it. Besides the orderly Quakers and Germans there were many immigrants to that hopeful town who had been misfits in Europe and did not soon adjust themselves in America. They looked for the sudden riches they had been told about. They hunted for buried treasure. Disappointed, they drifted off to the back country or to the West Indies. Because some men profited by speculation, many men speculated, wasting time and money. In the shortage of skilled labour, so much work was badly done that the pride of craftsmanship was lost. People who had had no chance to save in England did not learn to save in Pennsylvania. They waited for miracles. Franklin, bred in settled Boston, felt that Philadelphia must be industrious and frugal before it could be anything else. This middle way was the way of the new world. Few men of privilege had come from Europe to America. They had not needed to emigrate. Few of the helpless European poor had come. They had not been able to. The colonists were "middling people" and they must work and save if they were to survive and prosper. Franklin as Poor Richard was merely insisting that the first thing to build in their house was the plain foundation. But with how much wit and charm he insisted!

VII

After 1732 the separate currents of Franklin's life drew gradually together in the single, broad stream which was his character moving through history. He had investigated his own mind till he knew it and was at home there. His physical existence was established in a comfortable marriage. Troubled by neither metaphysics nor lust, he turned from introspection to "more satisfactory studies." In 1733 he began to teach himself languages. He learned enough French, Italian, and Spanish to read what he wanted of them, and to make Latin easier. He learned to read German. Of these he could speak and write only French, inaccurately, but he commanded them all for his special object, which was to extend his knowledge in any humane direction. If the centre of his world was

Philadelphia, he would make it the centre of a large and liberal world.

How close together his business and his friendships ran appears from the accounts[68] he kept and from the minutes of the Library Company. A compositor whom Franklin had known in London, Thomas Whitemarsh, came to Philadelphia and took Meredith's place some time in 1730. The next year the Assembly of South Carolina voted a bounty of £1000 to encourage a printer to set up there. Franklin shipped Whitemarsh off to Charleston in September with "a printing-house and materials." The two were to be partners in the business and, presumably, in the bounty. The Assembly preferred another printer, the governor thought Whitemarsh the better workman. (Franklin even at a distance had a way with governors.) The bounty went to the rival, who had come from Boston, but he died in 1732 and left Whitemarsh sole printer to the government and editor of the *South Carolina Gazette*, started 8 January on the model of the *Gazette* in Philadelphia. Whitemarsh died of yellow fever in September 1733. South Carolina voted another bounty of £1000. Franklin sent Louis Timothée (who began to call himself Lewis Timothy) to Charleston.

Timothée was a French Protestant, married to a Dutch woman in Holland, who had come to Philadelphia in September 1731 and in October had advertised himself in Franklin's newspaper as ready to give lessons in French. He was one of the deserving newcomers whom the Junto encouraged. Being a printer, he seems to have succeeded Whitemarsh as Franklin's journeyman, and the following May had charge of the experimental, unsuccessful *Philadelphische Zeitung*. Living with his family in the house where the Junto met, he was chosen to be the Library Company's first librarian. When he went to South Carolina late in 1733, the terms of agreement were that Franklin should pay one-third of the expenses of the six-year partnership and take one-third of the profit. Timothy revived the *South Carolina Gazette*, became public printer, and published the laws of the province, with a few pamphlets and John Wesley's earliest *Collection of Psalms and Hymns* (1737). Franklin admired Timothy's learning but wished he were more systematic in his accounts. His widow, after Timothy died in 1738, ably carried on the partnership and bought the business for her son Peter. Franklin's influence did not end with his partnership. Peter Timothy helped found a library in Charleston in 1743, urged and defended the use of the lightning rod. He became provincial postmaster and clerk of the South Carolina Assembly, who corresponded with Franklin in London on public affairs and told him about his namesake Benjamin Franklin Timothy.[69]

A George Webb, perhaps the Junto's tricky Oxford scholar, applied for the first South Carolina bounty and got no part of it. Stephen Potts remained in Philadelphia as Franklin's bookbinder. Hugh Meredith came back from North Carolina by 1739 and for nine years had occasional small sums from Franklin, who finally engaged him to buy rags for paper. Meredith fell behind in his accounts and made off with some books Franklin had put in his hands to sell. When Franklin invented the stove that has since been named after him, he declined to patent it and turned the model over to Robert Grace to manufacture at his furnace in Chester County. To promote the sales Franklin wrote *An Account of the New-Invented Pennsylvanian Fire-Places* (1744)[70] and published it, but Grace paid for the printing. His stoves were on sale for at least a time at Franklin's post office. When Grace was in difficulties in 1749 Franklin helped him.[71]

Then there was Franklin's family. He sold in his shop the Crown soap that his brothers John and Peter made, and they sold books and paper for him in theirs. James Franklin had settled in 1727 in Newport, where he issued his almanac called *Poor Robin* and became printer for the colony. In September 1732 he undertook the *Rhode Island Gazette*, though it ran for only a year. Benjamin sent him three hundred almanacs the following August. (Now for a time there were *Gazettes* in Rhode Island, Pennsylvania, and South Carolina, all of them celebrating—advertising— Poor Richard.) During 1733 Franklin saw New England again. It was probably in the fall, for he gave his wife power of attorney on 30 August, as if he were to be away. "Having become easy in my circumstances, I made a journey thither to visit my relations, which I could not sooner well afford." For the first time he saw his sister Jane Mecom's children in Boston, one of whom was named Benjamin and was to become his uncle's apprentice and partner. "In returning, I called at Newport to see my brother, then settled there with his printing-house. Our former differences were forgotten, and our meeting was very cordial and affectionate. He was fast declining in his health, and requested of me that, in case of his death, which he apprehended not far distant [February 1735], I would take home his son, then but ten years of age, and bring him up to the printing business. This I accordingly performed, sending him a few years to school before I took him into the office. His mother carried on the business till he was grown up, when I assisted him with an assortment of new types, those of his father being in a manner worn out. Thus it was that I made my brother ample amends for the service I had deprived him of by leaving him so early."[72]

Ten years, and the runaway youngest son of the Franklins had become a second head of the family. Five years a tradesman, and Franklin was in easy circumstances though he had chosen one of the least promising trades in a provincial town. The industry and frugality about which he talked cannot account for his swift progress. That he talked about them so much makes it clear that they came less from his nature than from his discipline. Other men besides Franklin in Philadelphia were as industrious and as frugal as he. No other man had a mind so capacious and ingenious and incessant, so able at once to persuade and to charm. It was Franklin's luck that it was easier for him to be outstanding in Philadelphia than it would have been in London. But from the first he was outstanding, and he throve by the exercise of natural gifts of which Poor Richard could not tell the secrets.

Franklin's quick success did not slow down his business. By 1734 he was public printer for Delaware and New Jersey as he later was for Maryland also. His appointment to be clerk of the Pennsylvania Assembly in 1736—and until 1751—enabled him to make sure the government printing came to him. After he became postmaster at Philadelphia in 1737 he could use his own riders to distribute his own papers. The circulation of the *Gazette* increased, and the number of its advertisements. Franklin allowed Bradford to send his *Mercury* by the carriers until October 1739, when Alexander Spotswood, deputy postmaster-general, forbade it because Bradford had not yet turned in his accounts for the Philadelphia post office since 1734. Then there was a new clash between the rival printers.

The Gentleman's Magazine had been founded in London in 1731, and Franklin decided to follow its profitable lead in Philadelphia. For his editor he chose a lawyer named John Webbe who had contributed to the *Gazette* a series of *Essays on Government* long ascribed to Franklin. The two were to be partners in the venture, Franklin to pay all the expenses, Webbe to have 25 per cent of the profits on the sale of the first two thousand copies, 50 per cent on sales above that. Franklin, thinking of the magazine as a mere compilation which would call for only part of Webbe's time, thought these terms fair. Webbe hoped he could do better, and took the scheme to Bradford, as George Webb years before had taken the scheme for the *Gazette* to Keimer. Bradford on 6 November 1740 announced in the *Mercury* that he would begin to publish *The American Magazine* the following March. Franklin on 13 November announced in the *Gazette* that *The General Magazine and Historical Chronicle for All the British Plantations in America* would appear in January. "This magazine, in imitation of those in England, was long since projected; a correspondence is settled with intelligent men in most of the colonies. . . . It would not, indeed, have been published quite so soon, were it not that a person to whom the scheme was communicated in confidence has thought fit to advertise it in the last *Mercury*, without our participation; and probably with a view, by starting before us, to discourage us from prosecuting our first design and reap the advantage of it wholly to himself."[73] Webbe and Bradford, knowing Franklin's plans, had announced their magazine as cheaper than the one he had in mind. He now planned to sell his magazine not by the year's subscription but by the single copy, "sixpence sterling or ninepence Pennsylvania money."

Webbe angrily replied in three numbers of the *Mercury*. Franklin paid no attention until the third accused him of excluding Bradford's newspaper from the mails. Then the editor-postmaster published Spotswood's order, and pointed out that Webbe knew about it. Webbe retorted that Bradford, after being excluded, had bribed the riders to carry the *Mercury*, and that Franklin must have known about that. So, acrimoniously, the two printers raced to see who would be first with the first magazine in America. The *American Magazine* seems to have been three days ahead of the *General Magazine*, of which the first issue seems to have come out 16 February 1741, dated January. Bradford's ran for three monthly issues, Franklin's for six. Both were unsuccessful; Franklin did not mention his magazine in his *Autobiography*, and most of his biographers have done no more than mention it.

In part this is because Franklin wrote little himself for what was a repository of matters from many sources. As in the *Gazette*, he did not so much take sides as let both sides have their say. The three chief topics dealt with were the war which had broken out between England and Spain, the problem of paper currency, and the Great Awakening as recently proclaimed by George Whitefield. Along with state papers Franklin reprinted news, miscellaneous extracts from books and pamphlets, essays, dialogues, characters, poems. The *General Magazine* is a curious anthology of American literary primitives for 1741. And the department called *Historical Chronicle* is still a useful survey of events month by month for half a year.

Franklin, unsuccessful for once at home, turned to New York. One of his printers was James Parker, a former apprentice to William Bradford, who in 1733 had run away to Philadelphia. On 20 February 1742 Franklin and Parker formed a silent partnership. Franklin was to equip his former journeyman with a press and types, transport them to New York, pay a third of the expenses of the business there, and receive a third of the profits. William Bradford retired. Parker (and the silent Franklin) took over the *New York Gazette* and in 1743 became public printer for that province. In 1746 Parker was made librarian of the Corporation of the City of New York. A better printer than Franklin, he had a career something like his master's and partner's: printer, librarian, postmaster, captain of a troop of horse, lay reader, controller of the North American post office, and eventually judge. Printer for New York and New Jersey, he was also printer for Yale College, and at his shop (and Franklin's) in New Haven he established the *Connecticut Gazette* 12 April 1755. By that time Franklin had retired from active business, but his capital still had partners.

Two of them were his nephews. James Franklin's son James after his father's death had come to Philadelphia, gone to school, and been apprenticed to his uncle 5 November 1740. He was to serve for seven years for "sufficient meat, drink, clothes, lodging, and washing fitting for an apprentice," and at the end of his term was to have "one good new suit of clothes, besides his common apparel."[74] When that time came he went back to Newport, with his new types, to the business which his mother with his uncle's help had kept going since his father died. Benjamin Mecom, Jane Franklin's son, born 1732, went to serve his apprenticeship with Parker in New York. In 1748 Franklin sent Thomas Smith, a journeyman who had worked for him both in New York and Philadelphia, to St. John in Antigua, to open its first printing-house and to start the *Antigua Gazette* about September of that year. But Smith died in the summer of 1752, and Franklin in August sent Benjamin Mecom to take his place. "That island," Franklin wrote reassuringly on 14 September to his sister and her husband in Boston, "is reckoned one of the healthiest in the West Indies. My late partner there enjoyed perfect health for four years, till he grew careless and got to sitting up late in taverns, which I have cautioned Benny to avoid. . . . He has the place on the same terms with his predecessor, who, I understand, cleared from five to six hundred pistoles during the four years he lived there. I have recommended him to some gentlemen of note for their patronage and advice."[75]

Benjamin Mecom, not yet twenty when he went to be almost his own master in Antigua, was too much a Franklin not to be restless. As printer he had the Leeward Islands to himself. He revived the *Antigua Gazette*, and published it till June 1756. But he disliked the long leash on which he felt he ran. Franklin explained in a patient letter to his sister on 28 June 1756. He had sent Benny, he said, as his partner, for one-third of the profits. "After this, finding him diligent and careful, for his encouragement I relinquished that agreement and let him know that, as you were removed into a dearer house, if he paid you yearly a certain sum, I forget what it was, towards discharging your rent, and another small sum to me, in sugar and rum for my family use, he need keep no farther accounts of the profits but should enjoy all the rest himself." The total was not above twenty pounds a year, and Franklin intended to give Benjamin the printing-house as soon as he should prove that he was stable.

"This proposal of paying you and me a certain annual sum did not please him; and he wrote to desire I would explicitly tell him how long that annual payment was to continue . . . and finally insisted that I would name a certain sum that I would take for the printing-house, and allow him to pay it off in parts as he could, and then the yearly payments to cease; for, though he had a high esteem for me, yet he loved freedom, and his spirit would not bear dependence on any man, though he were the best man living."[76] This letter came to Philadelphia when Franklin was away, and could not be answered promptly. Benjamin Mecom resolved to leave Antigua. Buying the press outright, he moved it early in 1757 to Boston, where he was something of a beau among the printers, with ruffles, wig, and gloves. In March 1758 he issued the first separate edition of *Father Abraham's Speech* from *Poor Richard Improved*. But he did not prosper. He removed his press to New York in 1763, with no better fortune. Leaving his own press in storage, he rented Parker's (really Franklin's) in New Haven, where he was also Parker's deputy in the post office. But there, and later in Philadelphia and in Burlington, Mecom was too little a Franklin to make his way, and finally went mad about 1776.

At one time or another Franklin had partnerships with William Smith in Dominica (where he founded the *Freeport Gazette*), with a printer named Daniel in Kingston, Jamaica, and perhaps with other printers in North Carolina and Georgia. Nearer home he had for partners his wife's relative William Dunlap, Samuel Holland, and John Henry Miller at Lancaster, and in Philadelphia Gotthard Armbruester (1747–50), Johannes Boehm (1749–51), and Anthony Armbruester (1754–58) for his German publications. One of these was the brief *Hoch Teutsche und Englische Zeitung* which in 1752 gave its readers news from the *Pennsylvania Gazette* in two languages. But most of his partnerships after 1748, however numerous, were slight affairs, almost as much to encourage printing and printers as to bring a return on his money.

His principal partners were James Parker in New York (and New Jersey and Connecticut) and David Hall in Philadelphia. Hall had learned his trade in Edinburgh and then had gone to Watts's in London, where he met William Strahan, later Franklin's correspondent. Strahan recommended Hall to Franklin, and Franklin invited him to come to America in 1743, agreeing either to make him partner or to employ him for a year and pay his passage back to England if he wanted to go. Hall came, and Franklin at once found him "obliging, discreet, industrious, and honest." Perhaps he had something to do with making Logan's *Cato Major* the next year Franklin's masterpiece in the printer's art. They shipped five hundred copies of the book to Strahan in London. (Strahan turned them over to a bookseller who as late as 1781 had never accounted for them.) Hall became foreman, and *Poor Richard* for 1748 became *Poor Richard Improved*. On 29 January 1748 Franklin wrote to Cadwallader Colden that he had a partner, and on 29 September: "I too am taking the proper measures for obtaining leisure to enjoy life and my friends, more than heretofore, having put my printing-house under the care of my partner, David Hall, absolutely left off bookselling, and removed to a more quiet part of town."[77] For eighteen years the partnership paid Franklin an average of £467 a year, and the firm was known as Franklin and Hall till 1766.[78]

So long as he lived by printing Franklin was satisfied to have his work neat and readable, and barely went beyond this. During his later years in England and France he became interested in fine printing and had some of the best European printers among his friends. Printing was his trade. He had chosen it as a boy under the eye of his father, who thought a man's trade should be his pride. It was that for the son, who began his will: "I, Benjamin Franklin, Printer, late Minister Plenipotentiary from the United States of America to the Court of France, now President of Pennsylvania. . . ."[79] Printer first, then ambassador. And at the other end of his career, in 1728 when he set up in business, he had written for himself the most famous of American epitaphs,[80] humorously in the language of his trade:

The Body of
B Franklin Printer,
(Like the Cover of an old Book
Its Contents torn out
And stript of its Lettering & Gilding)
Lies here, Food for Worms.
But the Work shall not be lost;
For it will, (as he believ'd) appear once more,
In a new and more elegant Edition
Revised and corrected,
By the Author.

Philadelphian

FOR the twenty years 1728–48 Franklin, like any tradesman of his time, worked and lived in the same house, near the busy courthouse and the noisy market. While the Godfreys were still his tenants, Franklin with Meredith shared their living quarters above the shop, which Godfrey shared as glazier. After the Godfreys and Meredith had left and Franklin had married, the new household and the growing business filled the premises. There were the young couple and Deborah's mother, with her salves and ointments, and soon the mysterious son William. The apprentice Joseph Rose must have lived with them, and probably for a time the journeyman Thomas Whitemarsh. Two years after the marriage Francis Folger was born, and before or after his death four years later, Franklin's nephew James came from Newport, first to be sent to school with William and then to succeed young Rose as apprentice. A brother and a sister of Deborah seem also to have lived with the Franklins for uncertain periods. Their daughter Sarah was born 31 August (11 September, New Style) 1743 and baptized at Christ Church 5 October. It is likely that various journeymen lodged and boarded in the house.

Though the household was mixed it was compact. Franklin at first seldom entertained his friends at home, but saw them at taverns or, chiefly, at the meetings of the Junto. He and his wife had little to do with other tradesmen, except on business. The more formal gentry of Philadelphia long looked, condescendingly if approvingly, on Franklin as a tradesman, and never accepted his wife or included her in invitations to their houses. Her life was her husband, her children, and her house and shop. Nor was Franklin during these years away from home as much as may be thought. He had no daily journeys to and from his work. He simply got up and came downstairs, to his press, his shop, his accounts, and, after 1737, his post office. His house was his plain castle, his study, his laboratory, and a place to stand while he moved his world.

Paragraphs and advertisements in the *Gazette* tell much of what is known about his private life. In December 1734, when his sons were four and two years old, he advertised for "a servant . . . that is a scholar and can teach children reading, writing, and arithmetic." When William was twelve he (that is, his father for him) advertised on 17 June 1742: "Strayed, about two months ago, from the Northern Liberties of this city, a small bay mare branded IW on the near shoulder and buttock. She, being but little and barefooted, cannot be supposed to have gone far; therefore if any of the town boys find her and bring her to the subscriber, they shall, for their trouble, have the liberty to ride her when they please." Not many young tradesmen's sons in Philadelphia had ponies to ride or, like Francis, their portraits painted in early childhood. Francis died of smallpox on 21 November 1736. Franklin, a humorous and indulgent father but a conscientious citizen, in the *Gazette* for 6–13 December corrected the false report that the child had died from being inoculated: "inasmuch as some people are by that report (joined with others of the like kind, and perhaps equally groundless) deterred from having that operation performed on their children. I do hereby sincerely declare that he was not inoculated but received the distemper in the common way of infection; and I suppose the report could only arise from its being my known opinion that inoculation was a safe and beneficial practice; and from my having said among my acquaintance that I intended to have the child inoculated as soon as he should have recovered sufficient strength from a flux with which he had been long afflicted." In *Poor Richard* for the next year Franklin among the adages and jokes put his saddest verses:

> The Thracian infant, entering into life,
> Both parents mourn for, both receive with grief;
> The Thracian infant snatched by Death away,
> Both parents to the grave with joy convey.
>
> This, Greece and Rome, you with derision view,
> This is mere Thracian ignorance to you;

But if you weigh the custom you despise,
This Thracian ignorance may teach the wise.

(Long afterwards Franklin wrote to his sister Jane that his grandson "brings often afresh to my mind the idea of my son Franky, though now dead thirty-six years, whom I have seldom since seen equalled in everything, and whom to this day I cannot think of without a sigh."[1])

In the *Gazette* Franklin regularly and amusingly reminded his subscribers that the paper ought to be paid for. When he had lent books and they had not been returned, he advertised them as missing, perhaps only pretending that he had forgotten who had them. Deborah Franklin's prayer book was taken out of her pew in Christ Church, and the newspaper for 23–30 June 1737 said: "The person who took it is desired to open it and read the Eighth Commandment, and afterwards return it into the same pew again; upon which no further notice will be taken." In February 1739, according to an announcement on the 22d, William Lloyd, who had been a schoolmaster and claimed to know Latin and Greek, stole a half-worn sagathy [silk and wool or silk and cotton] coat from Franklin's house, "four fine homespun shirts, a fine Holland shirt ruffled at the hands and bosom, a pair of black broadcloth breeches, new seated and lined with leather; two pair of good worsted stockings, one of a dark colour and the other a lightish blue, a coarse cambric handkerchief marked with an F in red silk, a new pair of calfskin shoes." Franklin had already begun to be, as the French police noted years later, particular about his linen, but his sagathy coat was not as new as the frugal new seat and leather lining of his broadcloth breeches. His wife's clothes, stolen in 1750, were gayer: "a woman's long scarlet coat, with double cape; a woman's gown of printed cotton, of the sort called brocade, very remarkable, the ground dark with large red roses and other large red and yellow flowers and smaller blue and white flowers, with many green leaves," according to the *Gazette* for 1 November.

Traces of Franklin as printer and scientist now and then appeared in his advertisements. In November 1738 "a small manuscript treatise upon the dry gripes" had been dropped somewhere in the streets, and the owner asked that it be brought, if found, to the printer for a handsome reward. This was presumably Thomas

Cadwalader's *An Essay on the West-India Dry Gripes* which Franklin published in 1745, and which may have led to his own important observations on lead poisoning—caused in this case by the
lead pipes through which Jamaica rum was distilled. The following
June Franklin's apprentice Joseph Rose announced that, "with
the leave of my master," he had undertaken to collect and print
his father's poems, and in return for each manuscript sent him he
would give a printed book when the work was finished. In August
somebody, probably Franklin, had lost "a magnifying glass set in a
cup of wood about the bigness of a tailor's thimble." And in the
first issue for that year the public was informed: "Benjamin Franklin, printer, is removed from the house he lately dwelt in, four
doors nearer the river, on the same side of the street."[2] The *Gazette*
had made the official announcement, on 27 October 1737 that "the
post office of Philadelphia is now kept at B. Franklin's, in Market
Street."

The *Gazette* gives a running account of what Franklin had to
sell in the shop which he opened about the time of his marriage.
Though his stock was never perhaps as large in a single week as
may appear, he sold as time went on many things besides stationery
and books in a lively confusion of sights and smells, indoors and
out: soap, ballads, slates and pencils, ink and ink powders, pounce
and pounce boxes, sealing wax, wafers, lead pencils, fountain pens
(what they then were is not known), quills for pens, ink horns,
sand glasses, mezzotints, maps, sack (Spanish wine), lampblack,
chocolate, linseed oil, coffee, powdered mustard, compasses and
scales, patent medicines, dividers and protractors, a second-hand
chaise, another with four wheels, Rhode Island cheese and cod fish,
quadrants, fore-staffs, nocturnals, mariners' compasses, lumber,
edgings, scarlet cloth, black broadcloth, white stockings, duck, iron
stoves, a horse for riding or driving, tea, saffron, lottery tickets,
mackerel by the barrel, a copper still, spermaceti, palm oil, spectacles, a fishing net. Franklin also bought linen rags to send to
paper-mills: 55,476 pounds between 1735 and 1741.[3]

At his shop he was a kind of general trader, offering for sale the
unexpired time of indentured servants. "A servant man's time for
near three years, to be disposed of. He is a joiner by trade and a
very good workman." "A likely servant maid's time for four years

to be disposed of. She works well with her needle." "A very good tailor, having one year and ten months to run; fit for either town or country business. And a servant lad for six years, fit for country business." "To be sold for her passage. A likely young woman, well clothed, can sew and do household work. Term of time as you can agree with her. N. B. Her passage is £8. Also a breeding Negro woman about twenty years of age. Can do any household work."[4] For Franklin dealt in slaves too, sold for other owners or bought by him as an investment. The servants in his household were usually white, though Deborah in her old age had a little slave boy to whom she was much attached. "A likely Negro wench about fifteen years old, has had the smallpox, been in the country above a year and talks English. Inquire of the printer hereof." "A likely young Negro fellow about nineteen or twenty years of age, to be disposed of. He is very fit for labour, being used to plantation work, and has had the smallpox." "Two likely young Negroes, one a lad about nineteen, the other a girl of fifteen."[5]

His shop was as full of goods as his head was of ideas. Here was a philosopher who could not really be interrupted. Interruptions came, and he dealt with them one by one, punctually and effortlessly, and then went back to the real business of his mind: moral reflections, foreign languages, varied sciences, the comfort and safety of Philadelphia and of mankind in general. His mind was a federation of purposes, working harmoniously together. Other philosophers might be dark and profound, but Franklin moved serenely through the visible world, trying to understand it all. Other men of action might lay single plans and endlessly persist in them, but Franklin met occasions as they rose and acted on them with a far-sighted opportunism. His mind grew as his world grew.

II

Franklin's projects for the good of the public came naturally out of his own experience and character. Wanting more books than he had or could afford, he planned and furthered a library which would supply books for him and everybody. Disliking all waste that might be avoided, he next set about a scheme for the control of fire, the fiercest enemy of property. Boston managed its fires better than Philadelphia. Franklin, back from his visit to his native town, talked with the members of the Junto. When they agreed with him that something should be done, he wrote a letter to himself and published it 4 February 1735 in the *Gazette*, as from an old citizen, on *Protection of Towns from Fire*.[6] People should be careful, the old citizen said, about carrying coals from room to room or up and downstairs, "unless in a warming-pan shut," and about narrow hearths and wooden mouldings on the sides of fire-places. Chimney sweeps should be licensed by the mayor, and responsible for their work. So much for prevention. As to putting fires out, let them consider "the example of a city in a neighbour-ing province. There is, as I am well informed, a club or society of active men belonging to each fire engine, whose business is to attend all fires with it whenever they happen." Such men became skilled from practice. They had quarterly meetings at which they talked over what they had learned. "Since the establishment of this regulation it seems there has been no extraordinary fire in that place; and I wish there never may be any here." The old citizen hoped that Philadelphia would remember that "an ounce of pre-vention is worth a pound of cure."

The town read, and agreed with the Junto and Franklin. A volunteer company of thirty men was formed. They equipped themselves with "leather buckets, with strong bags and baskets (for packing and transporting of goods), which were to be brought to every fire" They met once a month and spent "a social evening together, in discoursing and communicating such ideas as occurred to us upon the subject of fires. . . . Many more desiring to be admitted than we thought convenient for one company, they were advised to form another, which was accordingly done; and this went on, one new company being formed after another, till they became so numerous as to include most of the inhabitants who were men of property."[7] The Union Fire Company, formed by Franklin 7 December 1736, was the first of the companies which made Philadelphia, so far as fires were concerned, one of the safest cities in the world.

After firemen, policemen. "The city watch was one of the first things that I conceived to want regulation. It was managed by the constables of the respective wards in turn; the constable warned a number of housekeepers [householders] to attend him for the night. Those who chose never to attend paid him six shillings a year to be excused, which was supposed to be for hiring substitutes, but was in reality much more than was necessary for that purpose, and made the constableship a place of profit; and the constable, for a little drink, often got such ragamuffins about him as a watch that respectable housekeepers did not choose to mix with. Walking the rounds, too, was often neglected and most of the nights spent in tippling. I thereupon wrote a paper to be read in Junto, representing these irregularities, but insisting more particularly on the inequality of the six-shilling tax of the constables, respecting the circumstances of those who paid it, since a poor widow housekeeper, all whose property to be guarded by the watch did not perhaps exceed the value of fifty pounds, paid as much as the wealthiest merchant, who had thousands of pounds' worth in his stores."[8] Proposing that the tax be equitable, Franklin urged also that the city choose proper watchmen and pay them for regular services. His programme, approved by the central Junto, was taken to the lesser clubs—the Vine, the Union, the Band—and made to seem to have originated there. These plans were carried out less promptly than those for fire companies, and dragged on for years. Franklin had here not only to bring in something new but also to get rid of something already in existence.

Thoroughly secular, though no longer anti-clerical, Franklin worked little through the churches. Their traditions made them too rigid, and their sects too discordant, for his purposes. He seldom went to church, because Sunday was still his day for study. But he had been brought up a Presbyterian, and he was once persuaded by the minister of that denomination to attend its services for five Sundays. Franklin found the sermons "very dry, uninteresting, and unedifying, since not a single moral principle was inculcated or enforced, their aim seeming to be rather to make us Presbyterians than good citizens."[9] They were, he thought, not worth the reading they cost him. A livelier preacher, named Hemphill, came to Philadelphia from Ireland and preached sermons which Franklin liked for their emphasis on good works. The orthodox Presbyterians disapproved. "I became his zealous partisan, and contributed all

I could to raise a party in his favour. . . . There was much scribbling pro and con upon the occasion; and, finding that though an elegant preacher he was but a poor writer, I lent him my pen and wrote for him two or three pamphlets."[10] The orthodox party triumphed when it was learned that Hemphill had purloined his sermons from English books, though Franklin thought good sermons preferable to bad, no matter who had written them. Hemphill "left us in search elsewhere of better fortune, and I quitted the congregation, never joining it after, though I continued many years my subscription for the support of its ministers."[11] The Franklin family had a pew in the Episcopalian Christ Church, where the two younger children were baptized and they and both their parents were buried. Franklin gave help in the church's business affairs, subscribed to the building fund, and served (1752–53) as one of the managers of a lottery to raise money for a steeple and a chime of bells.

Freemasonry, secret, sociable, and unified, was more congenial than churches to Franklin. The earliest known lodge in America was St. John's in Philadelphia, and its earliest records are dated 1730. Franklin seems not to have been among the first members, but the *Gazette* was alert. On 8 December of that year it had an article pretending to reveal the Masonic mysteries. Franklin became a Mason in February. On 13 May he admitted that he had been in error in December. In June 1732 he drafted the lodge's by-laws. On the 24th of that month he became warden, and two years later on the same day (St. John the Baptist's day) grand master of St. John's lodge, a month after he had printed the *Constitutions*, the first Masonic book in America. From 1735 to 1738 he was the lodge's secretary. On 10 June 1749 he was elected grand master of the province, and the next year, yielding that post to William Allen the chief justice, became deputy grand master. He seems to have been always active in Masonic affairs, met with the lodge in Boston when he was there, and had a notable part in the building of the first Masonic temple in America, dedicated on 24 June 1755 while Braddock was on his way to his defeat.[12]

In the *Gazette* is Franklin's story of an outrageous episode which, though only a burlesque of the Masonic ritual and utterly disavowed by St. John's lodge, was blamed on the Masons, Franklin among them. Evan Jones, a chemist, had a gullible apprentice, Daniel Rees, who wanted to be a Mason. Jones and some of his friends in June 1737 pretended to initiate the boy. In the ceremony a bowl of burning rum was thrown at him and he was fatally burned. Jones was tried for murder and acquitted; for manslaughter and found guilty, and sentenced to be burned in the hand. Bradford in the *Mercury* charged Franklin with having been present and having relished the tragic buffoonery, including the blasphemous oath the boy had sworn.[13] Franklin answered the charges in his newspaper for 7–15 February 1738:

"Some time in June last Mr. Danby, Mr. Alrihs, and myself were appointed by the Court of Common Pleas as auditors to settle an affair between Dr. Jones and Armstrong Smith, then depending in said Court. We met accordingly at a tavern in Market Street on the Saturday morning before the tragedy was acted in the doctor's cellar. Dr. Jones appeared, and R——n[14] as his attorney, but Smith could not readily be found. While we waited for Smith in order to hear both parties together, the doctor and R——n began to entertain us with an account of some diversion they had lately had with the doctor's apprentice, who being desirous of being made a Freemason, they had persuaded him they could make him one, and accordingly had taught him several ridiculous signs, words, and ceremonies, of which he was very fond. 'Tis true I laughed (and perhaps heartily, as my manner is) at the beginning of their relation; but when they came to those circumstances of their giving him a violent purge, leading him to kiss J.'s posteriors, and administering to him the diabolical oath which R——n read to us, I grew indeed serious, as I suppose the most merry man (not inclined to mischief) would on such an occasion. Nor did any one of the company except the doctor and R——n themselves seem in the least pleased with the affair, but the contrary. Mr. Danby in particular said that if they had done such things in England they would be prosecuted. Mr. Alrihs, that he did not believe they could stand by it. And myself, that when the young man came to know how he had been imposed on, he would never forgive them.

"But the doctor and R——n went on to tell us that they designed to have yet some further diversion, on pretence of raising him to a higher degree in Masonry. R——n said it was intended to introduce him blindfolded and stripped into a room where the company, being each provided with a rod or switch, should chastise him smartly; which the doctor opposed, and said he had a better invention. They would have a game of snapdragon in a dark cellar, where some figures should be dressed up, that by the pale light of burning brandy would appear horrible and frighten him d——bly. Soon after the discourse, the young man himself coming in to speak with his master, the doctor pointed at me, and said to him: 'Daniel, that gentleman is a Freemason. Make a sign to him.' Which whether he did or not, I cannot tell; for I was so far from encouraging him in the delusion, or taking him by the hand, or calling him brother and welcoming him into the fraternity, as is said, that I turned my head to avoid seeing him make his pretended sign, and looked out of the window into the garden.

"And all those circumstances, with that of my desiring to have notice that I might be present at the snapdragon, are absolutely false and groundless. I was acquainted with him, and had a respect for the young lad's father, and thought it a pity his son should be so imposed upon; and therefore followed the lad downstairs to the door when he went out, with a design to call him back and give a hint of the imposition; but he was gone out of sight and I never saw him afterwards; for the Monday night following, the affair in the cellar was transacted which proved his death. As to the paper or oath, I did desire R——n when he had read it to let me see it; and, finding it a piece of a very extraordinary nature, I told him I was desirous to show it to some of my acquaintance, and so put it in my pocket. I communicated it to one who mentioned it to others, and so many people flocked to my house for a sight of it that it grew troublesome; and therefore when the mayor sent for it, I was glad of the opportunity to be discharged from it. Nor do I yet conceive that it was my duty to conceal or destroy it. And being subpœnaed on the trial as a witness for the king, I appeared and gave my evidence fully, freely, and impartially, as I think it becomes an honest man to do."[15] To the truth of this statement of the case John Danby and Harmanus Alrihs made affidavit.

In Boston, where there was now a lodge of Masons, the *News Letter* published Bradford's account of the scandalous accident, and Franklin's parents were troubled. They wrote to ask not only about Freemasonry but about his religious opinions. Franklin on 13 April answered both of them in a letter to his father, "When the natural weakness and imperfection of human understanding is considered, the unavoidable influence of education, custom, books, and company upon our ways of thinking, I imagine a man must have a good deal of vanity who believes, and a good deal of boldness who affirms, that all the doctrines he holds are true, and all he rejects are false. And perhaps the same may be justly said of every sect, church, and society of men, when they assume to themselves that infallibility which they deny to the Pope and councils. I think opinions should be judged of by their influences and effects; and, if a man holds none that tend to make him less virtuous or more vicious, it may be concluded he holds none that are dangerous; which I hope is the case with me.

"I am sorry you should have any uneasiness on my account; and if it were a thing possible for one to alter his opinions in order to please another, I know none whom I ought more willingly to oblige in that respect than yourselves. But, since it is no more in a man's power to think than to look like another, methinks all that should be expected from me is to keep my mind open to conviction, to hear patiently and examine attentively, whatever is offered me for that end; and, if after all I continue in the same errors, I believe your usual charity will induce you to rather pity and excuse than blame me. In the meantime your care and concern for me is what I am very thankful for.

"My mother grieves that one of her sons is an Arian, another an Arminian. What an Arminian or an Arian is, I cannot say that I very well know. The truth is, I make such distinctions very little my study. I think vital religion has always suffered when orthodoxy is more regarded than virtue; and the Scriptures assure me that at the last day we shall not be examined what we thought but what we did; and our recommendation will not be that we said 'Lord! Lord!' but that we did good to our fellow-creatures. See Matt. xxv.

"As to the Freemasons, I know no way of giving my mother a better account of them than she seems to have at present, since it is not allowed that women should be admitted into that secret society. She has, I must confess, on that account some reason to be displeased with it; but for anything else, I must entreat her to suspend her judgment till she is better informed, unless she will believe me when I assure her that they are in general a very harmless sort of people, and have no principles or practices that are inconsistent with religion and good manners."[16]

While Franklin was writing these tactful, affectionate words, which comforted his father and mother, George Whitefield was on his way from England to Georgia. The Great Awakening had begun with Jonathan Edwards at Northampton, Massachusetts, four years before, and John Wesley in Georgia had planted the first American seeds of Methodism. (Timothy—Franklin's partner in Charleston—published Wesley's first hymns.) But Edwards stayed in Massachusetts, and Wesley went back to England. The chief preacher of the Awakening was Whitefield, who from Georgia to Massachusetts called upon sinners to repent and upon drowsy Christians to rise and glow. When he came to Philadelphia late in 1739, Franklin took a philosopher's and a philanthropist's interest in him. "The multitudes of all sects and denominations that attended his sermons were enormous, and it was matter of speculation to me, who was one of the number, to observe the extraordinary influence of his oratory on his hearers, and how much they admired and respected him notwithstanding his common abuse of them by assuring them that they were naturally half beasts and half devils. It was wonderful to see the change soon made in the manners of our inhabitants. From being thoughtless or indifferent about religion, it seemed as if all the world were growing religious, so that one could not walk through the town in an evening without hearing psalms sung in different families of every street."[17]

Franklin, himself no public speaker, carefully noted Whitefield's oratory. "He had a loud and clear voice, and articulated his words and sentences so perfectly that he might be heard and understood at a great distance, especially as his auditories, however numerous, observed the most exact silence. He preached one evening from the top of the courthouse steps, which are in the middle of Market Street and on the west side of Second Street, which crosses it at right angles. Being among the hindmost in Market Street, I had the curiosity to learn how far he could be heard, by retiring backwards down the street towards the river;

and I found his voice distinct till I came near Front Street, when some noise in that street obscured it. Imagining then a semicircle, of which my distance should be the radius, and that it were filled with auditors to each of whom I allowed two square feet, I computed that he might be heard by more than thirty thousand. This reconciled me to the newspaper accounts of his having preached to twenty-five thousand people in the fields, and to the ancient stories of generals haranguing whole armies, of which I had sometimes doubted."[18]

It was an advantage to Whitefield, Franklin realized, that as an itinerant he could preach old sermons to new audiences. "His delivery . . . was so improved by frequent repetitions that every accent, every emphasis, every modulation of voice was so perfectly well turned and well placed that, without being interested in the subject, one could not help being pleased with the discourse; a pleasure of much the same kind with that received from an excellent piece of music."[19] Yet Franklin could be moved in spite of his cool reason. Talking to Whitefield, he had refused to contribute to the scheme for building an orphanage in Georgia out of money raised in Philadelphia. Georgia lacked materials and workmen, and it would be more expensive to send them there than to build the orphanage in Philadelphia and bring the children to it. "I happened soon after to attend one of his sermons, in the course of which I perceived he intended to finish with a collection, and I silently resolved he should get nothing from me. I had in my pocket a handful of copper money, three or four silver dollars, and five pistoles in gold. As he proceeded I began to soften, and concluded to give the coppers. Another stroke of his oratory made me ashamed of that, and determined me to give the silver. And he finished so admirably that I emptied my pocket wholly into the collector's dish, gold and all."[20]

The preacher and the philosopher were on the friendliest terms. Franklin printed Whitefield's sermons, gave him worldly counsel, and invited him to lodge in the crowded quarters above the press and shop in Market Street. When the regular clergy refused their pulpits to the evangelist, Franklin had a hand in buying ground and building a house "expressly for the use of any preacher of any religious persuasion who might desire to say something to the people at Philadelphia; the design in building not being to accommodate any particular sect, but the inhabitants in general; so that even if the Mufti of Constantinople were to send a missionary to preach Mohammedanism to us, he would find a pulpit at his service."[21] Perhaps not many Philadelphians had so large a conception of the building's possible use. Its original trustees came one from each sect, though after the Moravian had died, the others chose Franklin as "merely an honest man and of no sect at all."[22] Whitefield prayed for Franklin's conversion, "but never had the satisfaction of believing that his prayers were heard."[23]

Yet Whitefield, stirring the colonies and making them aware of one another as they heard about his long, tumultuous progress through town after town, sharpened in Franklin his interest in "all the British plantations in America" for which he planned the *General Magazine* announced the month Whitefield left Philadelphia for Georgia again. Franklin was becoming intercolonial. As clerk of the Assembly since 1736 he had been kept attentive to Pennsylvania affairs. As postmaster since 1737 he had been made to think often of more than Pennsylvania. The mails were still irregular, but the line stretched now from Boston to Charleston and passed both ways through Philadelphia. Ships from Europe, from the West Indies, and from other continental ports brought bags of mail to his post office, which was a corner of his shop. On the day each week when the mail left, north and south, he might have to give his whole time to it. Franklin had a chance to read other newspapers besides his own. In particular he watched to see what men of learning there were in America and what they did. He had an impulse to bring them somehow together as he had brought the members of the Junto when he was a journeyman. He printed a circular letter dated 14 May 1743 and sent it to various correspondents, proposing that they unite to form the American Philosophical Society.[24]

What he had in mind was unmistakably an intercolonial Junto. Philadelphia was to be the centre of the society, and there were always to be at Philadelphia seven members—a physician, a botanist, a mathematician, a chemist, a mechanician, a geographer, and a general natural philosopher—besides the president, treasurer, and secretary. (Of the first ten members in Philadelphia, five are known to have belonged to the Junto.) The Philadelphia members were to meet once a month, or oftener, transact their philosophical business, consider such reports or queries as might have been sent in by correspondents, and arrange to keep all the members informed of what all of them were doing. Quarterly abstracts of valuable communications were to be sent, postage-free, to each member, who was to pay an annual piece of eight (worth about one dollar).

"The first drudgery of settling new colonies," Franklin said, "which confines the attention of people to mere necessaries, is now pretty well over; and there are many in every province in circumstances that set them at ease and afford leisure to cultivate the finer arts and improve the common stock of knowledge." The extent of the country kept them apart and ignorant of each other's speculations. What was needed was systematic correspondence among them, through the society, on such subjects as these: "all new-discovered plants, herbs, trees, roots, their virtues, uses, etc.; methods of propagating them, and making such as are useful, but particular to some plantations, more general; improvements of vegetable juices, as ciders, wines, etc.; new methods of curing or preventing diseases; all new-discovered fossils in different countries, as mines, minerals, and quarries; new and useful improvements in any branch of mathematics; new discoveries in chemistry, such as improvements in distillation, brewing, and assaying of ores; new mechanical inventions for saving labour, as mills and carriages, and for raising and conveying of water, draining of meadows, etc.; all new arts, trades, and manufactures that may be proposed or thought of; surveys, maps, and charts of particular parts of the sea coasts or inland countries; course and junctions of rivers and great roads, situation of lakes and mountains, nature of the soil and productions; new methods of improving the breed of useful animals; introducing other sorts from foreign countries; new improvements in planting, gardening, and clearing land; and all philosophical experiments that let light into the nature of things, tend to increase the power of man over matter, and multiply the conveniences or pleasures of life. . . .

"Benjamin Franklin, the writer of this Proposal, offers himself to serve the Society as their secretary, till they shall be provided with one more capable."

Franklin could offer to act as secretary, which he knew would be the Society's most laborious and responsible post, because he himself, like the colonies, now saw the end of the "first drudgery" of his business. Most men as prosperous as he would have lost interest in philosophy. He was more interested than ever. Most philosophers with as many irons in the fire as he still had would have thought themselves distracted. Franklin was specialized to versatility. His inquiring temper did not call for isolation. It was important that new things should be known, not that he himself should find them out. He was philanthropist and publicist as well as scientist. Let as many men as possible pool their knowledge for the good of all men, and he would serve them in any way that might be needed.

That summer he visited New England again, and could do little about his proposal till November. Then he went seriously to work, and by April 1744 the Society was organized in Philadelphia and had had several meetings. Of his Junto friends, Thomas Godfrey was the Society's mathematician, Samuel Rhoads its mechanician, William Parsons its geographer, and William Coleman its treasurer—and Franklin its secretary. Besides these, there were Thomas Hopkinson as president, Thomas Bond as physician, John Bartram as botanist, and Phineas Bond as general natural philosopher. Among them were able men. Godfrey had already invented his quadrant and had been recognized by the Royal Society. John Bartram was well under way in his career as, Linnæus said, the greatest "natural botanist" in the contemporary world. Thomas Bond, an excellent physician, was soon to plan and, with Franklin's help, establish the Pennsylvania Hospital. As corresponding members the Society had Robert Hunter Morris, chief justice of New Jersey, and Archibald Home, its secretary, and John Coxe and Hugh Martyn of Trenton. In New York the first member was James Alexander, lawyer and member of the Council, who had defended Peter Zenger in his famous trial. "And there are a number of others," Franklin wrote on 5 April 1744 to Cadwallader

Colden,[25] "in Virginia, Maryland, Carolina, and the New England colonies, who we expect to join us as soon as they are acquainted that the Society has begun to form itself."

The Society was less active for years than Franklin had hoped it would be. "The members . . . here are very idle gentlemen," he wrote to Colden after a year and a half. "They will take no pains."[26] Their meetings were perhaps irregular, minutes were not always kept, and no proceedings or abstracts were published. Franklin's satisfaction in his scheme came chiefly from the correspondence between him and Colden, begun after the two had met accidentally on the road during the summer of 1743. Colden, official and scholar in New York, had written his important *History of the Five Indian Nations* (1727), had classified the plants on and around his Orange County manor according to the Linnæan system, and was almost equally at home in mathematics, medicine, physics, and mental and moral philosophy. He invented—independently if not first—the process now called stereotyping, and asked Franklin for his opinion of it. He wrote about the pores of the skin, and Franklin not only answered in detail but worked out mechanical experiments to prove his point. Franklin asked Colden if the diurnal motion of the earth might not cause ships sailing across the Atlantic to be slower on the westward than on the eastward voyage.[27] Colden thought not. Franklin was unpretending. "I ought to study the sciences I dabble in before I presume to set pen to paper."[28] He was "very willing and ready" to print Colden's *Explication of the First Causes of Motion in Matter, and of the Cause of Gravitation* (1745) "at my own expense and risk. If I can be the means of communicating anything valuable to the world, I do not always think of gaining, or even of saving, by my business." At the end of 1745 he had resolved to publish an *American Philosophical Miscellany*, monthly or quarterly, himself to do all the work and take all the responsibility. Colden had proposed the miscellany, Franklin was to carry it out.[29] It went no further than proposal and resolution.

Writing his account of the Pennsylvanian fireplace (Franklin stove), the inventor remembered that he was a member of the American Philosophical Society which he was then organizing.

Though this was a pamphlet to help Robert Grace sell the stoves he manufactured on Franklin's model, and Grace paid the printer's bill, Franklin fortified his treatise with learned notes, one of them in Latin. He began with a scientific explanation of how heated air rises and cold air comes in to take its place. He described the various heating arrangements then in use, especially the "improved" fireplaces with small openings which caused such draughts of cold air: "it rushes in at every crevice so strongly as to make a continual whistling or howling; and 'tis very uncomfortable as well as dangerous to sit against any such crevice. . . . Women, particularly, from this cause (as they sit much in the house) get colds in the head, rheums, and defluxions, which fall into their jaws and gums, and have destroyed early many a fine set of teeth in these northern colonies. Great and bright fires do also very much contribute to damage the eyes, dry and shrivel the skin, and bring on early the appearances of old age."[30] Having artfully appealed to women, Franklin went on to explain as if to mechanics, with the help of the drawings by Lewis Evans, precisely how the Pennsylvanian fireplace was constructed. Then one by one he gave fourteen advantages, and answered the objections that had been raised. After this, as if his argument were complete and unanswerable, he directed workmen how to install the new stoves. And of course there was the saving in fuel. "My common room, I know, is made twice as warm as it used to be, with a quarter of the wood I formerly consumed there."[31] This was in November 1744. Franklin and his family and friends had "used warm rooms for these four winters past."[32] He must have invented his stove in 1740—not, as is commonly said, in 1742. But he did not publish his account of it till there was a Philosophical Society in Philadelphia.

He seems to have left no record but a circumstantial legend of how he introduced the yellow willow (*Salix vitellina*) to America. The legend says that he found an imported, discarded osier basket sprouting in Dock creek and planted some of the shoots in Isaac (or Charles) Norris's garden, where they grew and made the tree generally known.[33]

III

Before there was a Philosophical Society Franklin's own scientific interests, like those of the colonies, had been dispersed and casual. His mind, growing tired of business and relieved by the coming of David Hall to be his foreman, swung in inquisitive directions. Though it was patient, it seems never to have known fatigue or languor. Forced to sit idle, as he sometimes was in dragging sessions of the Assembly, he would work out mathematical puzzles. "Being one day in the country at the house of our common friend, the late learned Mr. Logan," Franklin told Peter Collinson some time after Logan's death in 1751, "he showed me a folio French book filled with magic squares, wrote, if I forget not, by one M. Frénicle [Bernard Frénicle de Bessy], in which, he said, the author had discovered great ingenuity and dexterity in the management of numbers; and, though several other foreigners had distinguished themselves in the same way, he did not recollect that any one Englishman had done anything of the kind remarkable. I said it was perhaps a mark of the good sense of our English mathematicians that they would not spend their time in things that were merely *difficiles nugæ*, incapable of any useful application. He answered that many of the arithmetical or mathematical questions publicly proposed and answered in England were equally trifling and useless. 'Perhaps the considering and answering such questions,' I replied, 'may not be altogether useless, if it produces by practice an habitual readiness and exactness in mathematical disquisitions, which readiness may on many occasions be of real use.' 'In the same way,' says he, 'may the making of these squares be of use.' I then confessed to him that in my younger days, having once some leisure which I still think I might have employed more usefully, I had amused myself in making these kind of magic squares, and at length had acquired such a knack at it that I could fill the cells of any magic square, of reasonable size, with a series of numbers as fast as I could write them, disposed in such a manner as that the sums of every row, horizontal, perpendicular, or diagonal, should be equal; but not being satisfied with these, which I looked on as common and easy things, I had imposed on myself more difficult tasks, and succeeded in making other magic squares with a variety of properties, and much more curious. He then showed me several in the same book, of an uncommon and more curious kind; but, as I thought none of them equal to some I remembered to have made, he desired me to let him see them; and, accordingly, the next time I visited him, I carried him a square of 8 which I found among my old papers, and which I will now give you, with an account of its properties. . . .

52	61	4	13	20	29	36	45
14	3	62	51	46	35	30	19
53	60	5	12	21	28	37	44
11	6	59	54	43	38	27	22
55	58	7	10	23	26	39	42
9	8	57	56	41	40	25	24
50	63	2	15	18	31	34	47
16	1	64	49	48	33	32	17

"The properties are: (1) That every straight row, horizontal or vertical, of 8 numbers added together makes 260, and half each row half 260. (2) That the bent row of 8 numbers, ascending and descending diagonally, viz., from 16 ascending to 10, and from 23 descending to 17, and every one of its parallel bent rows of 8 numbers, make 260. Also the bent row from 52, descending to 54, and from 43 ascending to 45, and every one of its parallel bent rows of 8 numbers, make 260. Also the bent row from 45 to 43 descending to the left, and from 23 to 17 descending to the right, and every one of its parallel bent rows of 8 numbers, make 260. Also the bent row from 52 to 54 descending to the right, and from 10 to 16 descending to the left, and every one of its parallel bent rows of

8 numbers, make 260. Also the parallel bent rows next to the above-mentioned, which are shortened to 3 numbers ascending and 3 descending, etc., as from 53 to 4 ascending, and from 29 to 44 descending, make, with the 2 corner numbers, 260. Also the 2 numbers, 14, 61 ascending, and 36, 19 descending, with the lower 4 numbers situated like them, viz., 50, 1 descending and 32, 47 ascending, make 260. And, lastly, the 4 corner numbers, with the 4 middle numbers, make 260. . . .

"Mr. Logan then showed me an old arithmetical book in quarto, wrote, I think, by one [Michel] Stifelius, which contained a square of 16 that he said he should imagine must have been a work of great labour; but if I forget not, it had only the common properties of making the same sum, viz., 2056, in every row, horizontal, vertical, and diagonal. Not willing to be outdone by Mr. Stifelius, even in the size of my square, I went home and made that evening the following magical square of 16, which, besides having all the properties of the foregoing square of 8, i.e., it would make the 2056 in all the same rows and diagonals, had this added: that a four-square hole being cut in a piece of paper of such a size as to take in and show through it just 16 of the little squares, when laid on the greater square, the sum of the 16 numbers so appearing through the hole, wherever it was placed on the greater square, should likewise make 2056. This I sent to our friend the next morning, who, after some days, sent it back in a letter with these words: 'I return to thee thy astonishing or most stupendous piece of the magical square, in which'—but the compliment is too extravagant, and therefore, for his sake as well as my own, I ought not to repeat it. Nor is it necessary; for I make no question but you will readily allow this square of 16 to be the most magically magical of any magic square ever made by any magician."[34] (But Barbeu Dubourg, when he was translating Franklin's works twenty years later, found two mistakes in the square.[35])

Just when Franklin made his early magic square of 8 or his later of 16 is not certain, but neither can have been far from the years when he was turning from business to science without having yet found a subject which compelled him. In the transition he became something of a man of pleasure in sober Philadelphia. Comfortable

200	217	232	249	8	25	40	57	72	89	104	121	136	153	168	181
58	39	26	7	250	231	218	199	186	167	154	135	122	103	90	71
198	219	230	251	6	27	38	59	70	91	102	123	134	155	166	187
60	37	28	5	252	229	220	197	188	165	156	133	124	101	92	69
201	216	233	248	9	24	41	56	73	88	105	120	137	152	169	184
55	42	23	10	247	234	215	202	183	170	151	138	119	106	87	74
203	214	235	246	11	22	43	54	75	86	107	118	139	150	171	182
53	44	21	12	245	236	213	204	181	172	149	140	117	108	85	76
205	212	237	244	13	20	45	52	77	84	109	116	141	148	173	180
51	46	19	14	243	238	241	206	179	174	147	142	115	110	83	78
207	210	239	242	15	18	47	50	79	82	111	114	143	146	175	178
49	48	17	16	241	240	209	208	177	176	145	144	113	112	81	80
196	221	228	253	4	29	36	61	68	93	100	125	132	157	164	189
62	35	30	3	254	227	222	195	190	163	158	131	126	99	94	67
194	223	226	255	2	31	34	63	66	95	98	127	130	159	162	191
64	33	32	1	256	225	224	193	192	161	160	129	128	97	96	65

at home, he was convivial in taverns, where he drank rum and
Madeira, sang songs, and wrote some.

> The antediluvians were all very sober,
> For they had no wine and they brewed no October;
> All wicked, bad livers, on mischief still thinking,
> For there can't be good living where there is not good drinking.
>> Derry-down.

> 'Twas honest old Noah first planted the vine,
> And mended his morals by drinking its wine;
> And thenceforth justly the drinking of water decried;
> For he knew that all mankind by drinking it died.
>> Derry-down.[36]

Wine and friendship were better than love.

> Fair Venus calls; her voice obey;
> In beauty's arms spend night and day.
> The joys of love all joys excel,
> And loving's certainly doing well.

>> *Chorus*

>> Oh! no!
>> Not so!
>> For honest souls know
>> Friends and a bottle still bear the bell.

> Then let us get money, like bees lay up honey;
> We'll build us new hives and store each cell.
> The sight of our treasure shall yield us great pleasure;
> We'll count it and chink it and jingle it well.

>> *Chorus*. Oh! no! etc.

> If this does not fit ye, let's govern the city;
> In power is pleasure no tongue can tell.
> By crowds though you're teased, your pride shall be pleased,
> And this can make Lucifer happy in hell.

>> *Chorus*. Oh! no! etc.

> Then toss off your glasses and scorn the dull asses
> Who, missing the kernel, still gnaw the shell;
> What's love, rule, or riches? Wise Solomon teaches
> They're vanity, vanity, vanity still.

Chorus

That's true!
He knew!
He'd tried them all through;
Friends and a bottle still bore the bell.[87]

Another song domestically celebrated a love nearer home than Venus. At a supper of the Junto or of some other convivial club it was laughingly pointed out that they were all married men and yet were singing the praise of poets' mistresses. The next morning at breakfast John Bard—who left Philadelphia for New York in 1746—received a new and proper song from Franklin, who asked him to be ready to sing it at the next meeting.

Of their Chloes and Phyllises poets may prate,
  I sing my plain country Joan,
These twelve years my wife, still the joy of my life;
  Blest day that I made her my own.
        My dear friends, etc.

Not a word of her face, of her shape, of her air,
  Or of flames or of darts you shall hear;
I beauty admire but virtue I prize,
  That fades not in seventy years.

Am I loaded with care, she takes off a large share,
  That the burden ne'er makes me to reel;
Does good fortune arrive, the joy of my wife
  Quite doubles the pleasure I feel. . . .

Some faults have we all, and so has my Joan,
  But then they're exceedingly small;
And now I'm grown used to them, so like my own,
  I scarcely can see them at all. . . .[38]

And in a fourth, which was not by Franklin, he took a special, philosophical delight of which in old age he told a friend. "I like . . . the concluding sentiment in the old song called *The Old Man's Wish*, wherein, after wishing for a warm house in a country town, an easy horse, some good authors, ingenious and cheerful companions, a pudding on Sundays, with stout ale and a bottle of Burgundy, etc., etc., in separate stanzas, each ending with this burden:

> May I govern my passions with absolute sway,
> Grow wiser and better as my strength wears away,
> Without gout or stone, by a gentle decay,

he adds:

> With courage undaunted may I face my last day,
> And when I am gone may the better sort say:
> In the morning when sober, in the evening when mellow,
> He's gone and has left not behind him his fellow.
>   For he governed his passions, etc. . . .

I have sung that wishing song a thousand times when I was young."[39]

Every year in *Poor Richard* Franklin put into print for his town or country readers the notes he had made on human life, from observation or reading. His song in praise of fellowship had a prose version: "Great beauty, great strength, and great riches are really and truly of no great use; a right heart exceeds all" (1739). In his almanac he first announced his reasonable view of the nature of sin: "Sin is not hurtful because it is forbidden, but it is forbidden because it is hurtful" (1739). "He that falls in love with himself will have no rivals" (1739). "Proclaim not all thou knowest, all thou owest, all thou hast, nor all thou canst" (1739). "Thou hadst better eat salt with the philosophers of Greece than sugar with the courtiers of Italy" (1740). "Some are justly laughed at for keeping their money foolishly, others for spending it idly; he is the greatest fool that lays it out in a purchase of repentance" (1740). "Learn of the skilful; he that teaches himself hath a fool for a master" (1741). "Lying rides upon debt's back" (1741). "Up, sluggard, and waste not life; in the grave will be sleeping enough" (1741). Once he referred by name to himself:

> Ben beats his pate and fancies wit will come;
> But he may knock, there's nobody at home (1742).

(Poor Richard was smiling at his creator.) "He that riseth late must trot all day, and shall scarce overtake his business at night" (1742).

"Sloth (like rust) consumes faster than labour wears" (1744). "The eye of a master will do more work than his hand" (1744). "Help, hands; for I have no lands" (1745). "Light-heeled mothers make leaden-heeled daughters" (1745). "What's proper is becoming: See the blacksmith with his white silk apron" (1746). "The most exquisite folly is made of wisdom spun too fine" (1746). "A life of leisure and a life of laziness are two things" (1746).

This last note for the almanac of 1746 Franklin made in 1745. His father died that year, and the son wrote two of the jocular pieces which, though not in his collected works, have surreptitiously been kept alive in manuscript copies and—lately—private and less private printings.

Writing on 17 August to the lawyer James Read, Franklin took a scholar's liberties in a learned language. "I have been reading your letter over again, and, since you desire an answer, I sit me down to write you; yet as I write in the market, [it] will I believe be but a short one, though I may be long about it. . . . Your copy of Kempis must be a corrupt one if it has that passage as you quote it: *in omnibus requiem quæsivi, sed non inveni, nisi in angulo cum libello.* The good father understood *requiem* (pleasure) better, and wrote *in angulo cum puella.* Correct it thus without hesitation. I know there is another reading, *in angulo puellæ*; but this reject, though more to the point, as an expression too indelicate."[40] There were too many interruptions in the market, and Franklin had to be brief, in English.

The best known of his surreptitious writings, *Advice to a Young Man on the Choice of a Mistress,* is in the form of a letter to a friend dated 25 June. "I know of no medicine fit to diminish," he began, "the violent natural inclinations you mention; and if I did, I think I should not communicate it to you. Marriage is the proper remedy. It is the most natural state of man, and therefore the state in which you are most likely to find solid happiness. . . . It is the man and woman united that make the complete human being. Separate, she wants his force of body and strength of reason; he, her softness, sensibility, and acute discernment. Together they are more likely to succeed in the world. A single man has not nearly the value he would have in a state of union. He is an incomplete animal. He resembles the odd half of a pair of scissors. . . .

But if you will not take this counsel, and persist in thinking a commerce with the sex inevitable, then I repeat my former advice, that in all your amours you should prefer old women to young ones." One by one Franklin gave his sensible reasons, which were much like Lord Chesterfield's, though homelier.

"Because they have more knowledge of the world, and their minds are better stored with observations, their conversation is more improving and more lastingly agreeable. . . . Because there is no hazard of children. . . . Because through more experience they are more prudent and discreet in conducting an intrigue. . . . Because in every animal that walks upright, the deficiency of the fluids that fill the muscles appears first in the highest part. The face first grows lank and wrinkled; then the neck; then the breast and arms; the lower parts continuing to the last as plump as ever: so that covering all above with a basket, and regarding only what is below the girdle, it is impossible of two women to know an old one from a young one. . . . Because the sin is less. The debauching a virgin may be her ruin and make her for life unhappy. . . . Because the compunction is less. The having made a young girl miserable may give you frequent bitter reflection; none of which can attend the making an old woman happy. . . . And lastly, they are so grateful! Thus much for my paradox. But still I advise you to marry directly."[41]

(To this same year has wrongly been ascribed the broadest of Franklin's surreptitious pieces, *A Letter to the Royal Academy at Brussels,* which was written in France after that academy was founded in 1772. On 23 January 1782, writing to William Carmichael from Passy, Franklin gave permission to print any of his "little scribblings" except this one; "which, having several English puns in it, cannot be translated, and besides has too much *grossièreté* to be borne by the polite readers of this nation."[42] On 16 September 1783 Franklin sent a copy of the letter to Richard Price in London, as "a little jocular paper I wrote some years since in ridicule of a prize question given out by a certain academy on this side the water." Price showed it to Priestley, and the two clergymen were "entertained with the pleasantry of it."[43] It was a burlesque of such preposterous scientific schemes as Rabelais and Swift had ridiculed. "Let it be considered of how small importance

to mankind, or to how small part of mankind have been useful,
those discoveries in science that have heretofore made philosophers
famous. Are there twenty men in Europe this day the happier, or
even the easier, for any knowledge they have picked out of
Aristotle? What comfort can the vortices of Descartes give to a man
who has whirlwinds in his bowels? The knowledge of Newton's
mutual attraction of the particles of matter, can it afford ease to
him who is racked by their mutual repulsion and the cruel disten-
sions of occasion?" Broadly but gravely, Franklin proposed re-
searches which might make crepitation less distressing to individuals, more agreeable to society. "The generous soul who now
endeavours to find out whether the friends he entertains like best
claret or Burgundy, champagne or Madeira, would then inquire
also whether they chose [the perfume of] musk or lily, rose or
bergamot, and provide accordingly."44)

In 1746 Franklin wrote the *Reflections on Courtship and Marriage* which, though the first of his books to be published in Europe
(Edinburgh, 1750), has been steadily neglected by his editors and
biographers. The printer, who was Franklin, pretended not to
know who the author was: the manuscript had come secretly to the
press and may not have been meant for publication. It was in the
form of two letters to a friend, carrying on one side of an argument
started "the other day" among a group of bachelors, most of whom
had thought women ignorant and vain, a peril and a nuisance to
men. The anonymous writer, also Franklin, defended women.
Given the same education as men, he thought, they would be as
reasonable and sensible. But usually they were untaught, and they
were courted with flattery and nonsense. Look at courtship. Too
often it was undertaken for mercenary reasons or in headstrong
desire. Franklin thought that interest was a more common motive
than passion. Interested suitors did not tell the truth about themselves, and so made later disappointments likely. Passionate suitors
were in such haste that there was no chance for friendship to
develop. But friendship was the only sound basis for marriage—
reasonable friendship. "Marriage, or an union of the sexes, though
it be in itself one of the smallest societies, is the original fountain
from whence the greatest and most extensive governments have
derived their beings. 'Tis a monarchical one, having reason for its

legislator and prince: an authority more noble and sublime than any other state can boast of."[45] Neither reason nor nature prescribed who should rule in marriage, and men had the right only if they were more reasonable than women. Marriage was a voluntary contract, binding on both parties to it, for the sake of their common welfare and pleasure.

Franklin was specific. Married persons should avoid petty quarrelling. "What fermentations and heats often arise from breaking of china, disordering a room, dinner not being ready at a precise hour, and a thousand other such impertinent bagatelles. . . . These sort of matrimonial squabbles put one in mind of a little venomous insect they have in the West Indies, like a gnat, who when they bite create a great itching which, if much scratched, raises an inflammation so malignant that a leg has been lost by it, and sometimes mortifications ensue that have been attended with death."[46] Husband and wife, punctilious in their manners, must also be scrupulous about their persons. Here, suddenly, Franklin sounds a little like Swift, with his modern nerves: "Let us survey the morning dress of some women. Downstairs they come, pulling up their ungartered, dirty stockings; slipshod, with naked heels peeping out; no stays or other decent conveniency, but all flip-flop; a sort of a clout thrown about the neck, without form or decency; a tumbled, discoloured mob or nightcap, half on and half off, with the frowzy hair hanging in sweaty ringlets, staring like Medusa with her serpents; shrugging up her petticoats, that are sweeping the ground and scarce tied on; hands unwashed, teeth furred, and eyes crusted—but I beg your pardon, I'll go no farther with this sluttish picture, which I am afraid has already turned your stomach."[47] Swift, fastidious to the point of sickness, had just died or was dying when Franklin wrote. Franklin was stronger, and his disgust lasted only for a paragraph, but at the end of his *Reflections* he printed Swift's *Letter to a Very Young Lady on Her Marriage* with its grim advice.

More like Franklin was *The Speech of Polly Baker*,[48] which, written in Philadelphia, somehow got to England and was printed in the *Gentleman's Magazine* for April 1747. Being prosecuted the fifth time "at Connecticut near Boston in New England" for having a bastard child, the heroine robustly defended herself for following the laws of her nature if not of the province. "Abstracted from the law, I cannot conceive (may it please your honours) what the nature of my offence is. I have brought five fine children into the world, at the risk of my life; I have maintained them well by my own industry, without burdening the township, and would have done it better if it had not been for the heavy charges and fines I have paid. Can it be a crime (in the nature of things, I mean) to add to the king's subjects, in a new country that really wants people? . . . How can it be believed that heaven is angry at my having children, when to the little done by me towards it, God has been pleased to add His divine skill and admirable workmanship in the formation of their bodies and crowned the whole by furnishing them with rational and immortal souls? . . . If you, gentlemen, must be making laws, do not turn natural and useful actions into crimes by your prohibitions." Let them think of her first seducer, who was now a magistrate. Let them think of "the great and growing number of bachelors" who "by their manner of living leave unproduced (which is little better than murder) hundreds of their posterity to the thousandth generation. Is not this a greater offence against the public good than mine? Compel them, then, by law, either to marriage or to pay double the fine of fornication every year. What must poor young women do, whom customs and nature forbid to solicit the men, and who cannot force themselves upon husbands, when the laws take no care to provide them any and yet severely punish them if they do their duty without them? The duty of the first and great command of nature and nature's God, increase and multiply; a duty from the steady performance of which nothing has been able to deter me, but for its sake I have hazarded the loss of the public esteem and have frequently endured public disgrace and punishment; and therefore ought, in my humble opinion, instead of a whipping to have a statue erected to my memory." The court was so much impressed by her argument that the next day she was married to one of the judges—by whom she had fifteen children.

It is hardly accident that Franklin's salty year came when, just before and after forty, he had at last a clear sense of the leisure toward which he had long been working. It is no wonder that his spirits rose or that in cheerful moments he amused himself and his friends with philosophical ribaldries. A philosopher who had arrived at freedom might take his ease in the lively world. But Franklin had no impulse to be merely a provincial wit and man of pleasure, and soon he had an important ruling passion. "In 1746, being at Boston, I met there with a Dr. Spence, who was lately arrived from Scotland and showed me some electric experiments. They were imperfectly performed, as he was not very expert; but, being on a subject quite new to me, they equally surprised and pleased me."[49] At home again, Franklin himself began to experiment. Spence came to Philadelphia, and Franklin bought his apparatus. Collinson sent more to the Library Company. Franklin gave up the winter to electricity. "I never was before engaged in any study that so totally engrossed my attention and my time as this has lately done," he wrote to Collinson 28 March 1747; "for, what with making experiments when I can be alone, and repeating them to my friends and acquaintance who, from the novelty of the thing, come continually in crowds to see them, I have during some months past had little leisure for anything else."[50]

6

∞∞

Electrician

NOW that electricity has become a daily commonplace it is hard to realize what fresh, strange news it was when Franklin first thought—perhaps first heard—of it in Boston in the summer of 1746. Before that year he might have known that various bodies may be electrified by rubbing, so that they will attract lighter objects, and that the attracting force may be transferred to other bodies. He might have read of frictional machines, mounted rotating spheres of sulphur or glass, which could be used to charge insulated conductors with what was called the electric fluid. European scientists already distinguished two kinds of electricity: vitreous, produced on glass rubbed with silk, and resinous, produced on resin rubbed with wool or fur. But not until January 1746 had Pieter van Musschenbroek at Leyden discovered the electric bottle later known as the Leyden jar, the simplest and for years the only known condenser, which was the basis of early electrical research. William Watson in London quickly followed Musschenbroek in his experiments and concluded that all bodies contained electricity: uncharged bodies the normal or equilibrium amount, charged bodies more or less than that as they contained vitreous or resinous electricity, or vice versa. Franklin in the fall or winter of the year went forward from the year's chief discovery in science.

"My house," he says, "was continually full, for some time, with people who came to see these new wonders. To divide a little this encumbrance among my friends, I caused a number of similar tubes"—similar to the one Collinson had sent the Library Company—"to be blown at our glass-house, with which they furnished themselves, so that we had at length several performers."[1] Philip Syng, a member of the Junto and a skilled silversmith, contrived a machine to save them labour. "The European papers on electricity," Franklin wrote in the earliest of the reports which he regularly made to Collinson, "frequently speak of rubbing the tube as a fatiguing exercise. Our spheres are fixed on iron axes which pass through them. At one end of the axis there is a small handle with which you turn the sphere like a common grindstone."[2] Thomas Hopkinson, president of the American Philosophical Society, first noticed that points "throw off the electrical fire." Ebenezer Kinnersley, a Baptist minister with no pastorate, discovered that the Leyden jar could be electrified as strongly through the tinfoil coating as through the wire leading into it, and independently rediscovered the "contrary electricities" of glass and sulphur. His lectures—planned and encouraged by Franklin—in Philadelphia, Boston, Newport, and New York during 1751–52 made Kinnersley's experiments nearly as famous in America as Franklin's.

But Franklin, carefully crediting his friends with whatever they found out, was the real master of the new knowledge. In his busy house in Market Street, working with such pieces of apparatus as a saltcellar, a vinegar cruet, a pump handle, or the gold on the binding of a book, and "little machines I had roughly made for myself,"[3] he had the most spacious views and the most painstaking methods. Within a few months he could write to Collinson, on 28 March 1747, that "we have observed some particular phenomena that we look upon to be new."[4] By 11 July, when he wrote at length, he had already hit upon two of his fundamental contributions: his conception of electricity as a single fluid, and his substitution of the terms positive and negative, or plus and minus, for vitreous and resinous electricity; and he was full of "the wonderful effect of pointed bodies, both in drawing off and throwing off the electrical fire,"[5] which was to suggest the lightning rod.

Within another month he had written Collinson two more long letters, and then on 14 August sent a hurried note after them. "On some further experiments since, I have observed a phenomenon or two that I cannot at present account for on the principle laid down in those letters, and am therefore become a little diffident of my hypothesis and ashamed that I expressed myself in so positive a manner. In going on with these experiments how many pretty systems do we build which we soon find ourselves obliged to destroy! If there is no other use discovered of electricity, this however is something considerable, that it may help to make a vain man humble. I must now request that you would not expose those letters; or if you communicate them to any friends you would at least conceal my name."[6] In a letter dated 1 September, he began: "The necessary trouble of copying long letters which perhaps, when they come to your hands, may contain nothing new or worth your reading (so quick is the progress made with you in electricity) half discourages me from writing any more on that subject."[7] Yet again he wrote at some length, this time brilliant observations on the Leyden jar, which was still mysterious. Then public affairs, particularly the defence of the province against the French, claimed him, and for a year he had little time for science. But on 29 September 1748 he had retired from his printing business and moved to his new house at the corner of Race and Second Streets, and could write to Cadwallader Colden: "I am in a fair way of having no other tasks than such as I shall like to give myself and of enjoying what I look upon as a great happiness: leisure to read, study, make experiments, and converse at large with such ingenious and worthy men as are pleased to honour me with their friendship or acquaintance."[8] The winter of 1748–49 was as fruitful as that of 1746–47.

In the report to Collinson of 29 April 1749 Franklin, continuing his observation on the Leyden jar, first pointed out the great part played by the dielectric—the glass—and told of making, for the first time in history, "what we called an electrical battery, consisting of eleven panes of large sash-glass, armed with thin leaden plates pasted on each side, placed vertically and supported at two inches' distance on silk cords, with thick hooks of leaden wire, one from each side, standing upright, distant from each other, and convenient communications of wire and chain from the giving side of one pane to the receiving side of the other; that so the whole might be charged together and with the same labour as one single pane."[9] How important these matters were he could not know. He gave nearly as much space to telling of devices he and his friends had worked out to astound the curious. "Chagrined a little that we have been hitherto able to produce nothing in this way of use to mankind, and the hot weather coming on when electrical experiments are not so agreeable, it is proposed to put an end to them for this season, somewhat humorously, in a party of pleasure on the banks of Schuylkill. Spirits, at the same time, are to be fired by a spark sent from side to side through the river, without any other conductor than the water: an experiment which we some time since performed, to the amazement of many. A turkey is to be killed for our dinner by the electrical shock, and roasted by the electrical jack, before a fire kindled by the electrified bottle; when the healths of all the famous electricians in England, Holland, France, and Germany are to be drank in electrified bumpers, under the discharge of guns from the electrical battery."[10]

Later that year Franklin made an entry in "the minutes I used to keep of the experiments I made, with memorandums of such as I purposed to make. . . . *November 7, 1749.* Electrical fluid agrees with lightning in these particulars. 1. Giving light. 2. Colour of the light. 3. Crooked direction. 4. Swift motion. 5. Being conducted by metals. 6. Crack or noise in exploding. 7. Subsisting in water or ice. 8. Rending bodies it passes through. 9. Destroying animals. 10. Melting metals. 11. Firing inflammable substances. 12. Sulphureous smell. The electric fluid is attracted by points. We do not know whether this property is in lightning. But since they agree in all particulars wherein we can already compare them, is it not probable they agree likewise in this? Let the experiment be made."[11] Other scientists before Franklin had suspected that lightning was electricity. He set out to find a method of proving it.

A use for the discovery was promptly in his mind. It cannot have been more than a few weeks before he wrote a letter which Collinson sent to the *Gentleman's Magazine* for May 1750, where it has eluded Franklin's editors. "There is something, however, in the experiments of points, sending off or drawing on the electrical fire, which has not been fully explained, and which I intend to supply in my next. For the doctrine of points is very curious, and the effects of them truly wonderful; and, from what I have observed on experiments, I am of opinion that houses, ships, and even towers and churches may be effectually secured from the strokes of lightning by their means; for if, instead of the round balls of wood or metal which are commonly placed on the tops of weathercocks, vanes, or spindles of churches, spires, or masts, there should be a

rod of iron eight or ten feet in length, sharpened gradually to a
point like a needle, and gilt to prevent rusting, or divided into a
number of points, which would be better, the electrical fire would,
I think, be drawn out of a cloud silently, before it could come near
enough to strike; and a light would be seen at the point, like the
sailors' corpuzante [corposant: St. Elmo's fire]. This may seem
whimsical, but let it pass for the present until I send the experiments at large." Here is Franklin's earliest suggestion of the lightning rod, made when he seems not yet to have thought of the need
of a ground wire.

Now he turned his attention to thunder-storms—which he
called thunder-gusts—and wrote out a new hypothesis for Collinson which, though undated, must belong to the first half of 1750.
Franklin then supposed that clouds formed over the ocean had
more electricity in them than clouds formed over the land, and
that when they came close enough together their different charges
were equalized by the passage of lightning between them. "If two
gun barrels electrified will strike at two inches' distance, and make
a loud snap, to what a great distance may 10,000 acres of electrified
cloud strike and give its fire, and how loud must be that crack?"[12]
When clouds came close to the earth their electricity was discharged through "high hills and high trees, lofty towers, spires,
masts of ships, chimneys, etc., as so many prominencies and
points."[13]

By 29 July 1750 Franklin was ready to draw up for Collinson,
who had sent the first electrical tube, and Thomas Penn, who had
sent the Library Company "a complete electrical apparatus," a
summary of the *Opinions and Conjectures, concerning the Properties and Effects of the Electrical Matter, Arising from Experiments and Observations, Made at Philadelphia, 1749.* Now, nine
months after he had privately determined to make his great experiment, he publicly proposed it, through Collinson to the Royal
Society. Let the experiment be made. Make the truth useful to
mankind. "Nor is it of much importance to us to know the manner
in which nature executes her laws: 'tis enough if we know the laws
themselves. 'Tis of real use to know that china left in the air unsupported will fall and break; but how it comes to fall, and why it

breaks, are matters of speculation. 'Tis a pleasure indeed to know them, but we can preserve our china without it."

Now repeating his suggestion of lightning rods, Franklin provided also for "a wire down the outside of the building into the ground, or down round one of the shrouds of a ship and down her side till it reaches the water. . . . To determine the question whether the clouds that contain lightning are electrified or not, I would propose an experiment to be tried where it may be done conveniently. On the top of some high tower or steeple place a kind of sentry box . . . big enough to contain a man and an electrical stand [an insulator]. From the middle of the stand let an iron rod rise and pass bending out of the door, and then upright twenty or thirty feet, pointed very sharp at the end. If the electrical stand be kept clean and dry, a man standing on it when such clouds are passing low might be electrified and afford sparks, the rod drawing fire to him from a cloud. If any danger to the man should be apprehended (though I think there would be none), let him stand on the floor of his box and now and then bring near to the rod the loop of a wire that has one end fastened to the leads, he holding it by a wax handle; so the sparks, if the rod is electrified, will strike from the rod to the wire and not affect him."[14]

Franklin did not know enough about lightning to know how dangerous such an experiment might be, and the experience he had two days before Christmas the same year did not disturb his plans. "Being about to kill a turkey by the shock from two large glass jars, containing as much electrical fire as forty common phials, I inadvertently took the whole through my own arms and body, by receiving the fire from the united top wires with one hand while the other held a chain connected with the outsides of both jars. The company present (whose talking to me, and to one another, I suppose occasioned my inattention to what I was about) say that the flash was very great and the crack as loud as a pistol; yet, my senses being instantly gone, I neither saw the one nor heard the other; nor did I feel the stroke on my hand. . . . I then felt what I know not well how to describe: a universal blow throughout my whole body from head to foot, which seemed within as well as without; after which the first thing I took notice of was a violent quick shaking of my body, which gradually remitting, my sense as gradually returned. . . . That part of my hand and fingers which held the chain was left white, as though the blood had been driven out, and remained so eight or ten minutes after, feeling like dead flesh; and I had a numbness in my arms and the back of my neck which continued till the next morning but wore off. . . . I am ashamed to have been guilty of so notorious a blunder; a match for that of the Irishman . . . who, being about to steal powder, made a hole in the cask with a hot iron." "The greatest known effects of common lightning," Franklin thought the next year, might be exceeded by linking up enough electric bottles, "which a few years since could not have been believed and even now may seem to many a little extravagant to suppose. So we are got beyond the skill of Rabelais's devils of two years old, who, he humorously says, had only learnt to thunder and lighten a little round the head of a cabbage."[15]

Again Franklin, soon to be a member of the Assembly and active in the founding of a new college and a new hospital, was drawn away from philosophic leisure. The Royal Society listened to his papers, offered to it by Collinson, but did not value them enough to publish them in full. "One paper, which I wrote for Mr. Kinnersley, on the sameness of lightning with electricity, I sent to Dr. Mitchel [John Mitchell, who had been Franklin's correspondent while living in Virginia], an acquaintance of mine and one of the members also of that society, who wrote me word that it had been read, but was laughed at by the connoisseurs."[16] John Fothergill, a London physician who was later to be one of Franklin's best friends in England, urged that the electrical letters be printed. Collinson turned them over to Edward Cave for his *Gentleman's Magazine*, but he issued them in a separate pamphlet as *Experiments and Observations on Electricity, Made at Philadelphia in America* (1751), with a preface by Fothergill. Watson, Franklin's English rival in electrical research, read an abstract of the pamphlet to the Royal Society on 6 June of that year, in which he asked the members to notice how much Franklin's observations "coincide with and support those which I some time since communicated to the Society," but said not a word about the experiment to find out if lightning was electricity and could be prevented by iron rods from doing mischief. (Franklin in his own copy of the pamphlet carefully credited Hopkinson, Kinnersley, and Syng with the discoveries they had made.[17])

France was more hospitable to the new idea. A bad translation of Franklin's book came into the hands of Buffon, then keeper of the Jardin du Roi, who advised Thomas-François D'Alibard to make a better version, published in Paris early in 1752. Scientists and public were at once excited. The king himself saw the "Philadelphian experiments" performed by "M. de Lor, master of experimental philosophy." Buffon, D'Alibard, and de Lor determined to carry out the greater experiment which Franklin had proposed. D'Alibard, first to be successful, did nothing that might not have been done in Philadelphia. In a garden at Marly, six leagues from Paris, he set up an iron rod, an inch through and forty feet long, pointed with brass. Having no cake of resin with which to insulate it from the ground, he used a stool which was merely a squared plank with three wine bottles for legs. At twenty minutes past two on the afternoon of 10 May 1752, there was a single clap of thunder followed by hail. D'Alibard was just then absent. A former dragoon named Coiffier, left to watch the experiment, heard the thunder and hurried to the rod with an electric phial. Sparks came from the iron with a crackling sound. Coiffier sent a child for the prior of Marly, who had heard the thunder and was already on his way. Meeting the child in the road, he began to run. The villagers, believing that Coiffier had been killed, ran after the prior through the beating hail. Terrified, they stood back ten or a dozen paces from the rod, but in broad daylight they could see the sparks and hear the crackling while Raulet the prior drew off all the electric fire. He sat down and wrote a letter which Coiffier took to D'Alibard, who three days later made his report to the Académie Royale des Sciences. Following the course which Franklin had outlined, he said, he had arrived at incontestable proof. Franklin's idea was no longer a conjecture.[18]

On 18 May the experiment was repeated by de Lor in Paris. The Abbé Mazéas was commanded by the king to send word to the Royal Society in London that he greatly applauded Franklin and Collinson. John Canton made a successful experiment in London 20 July. In England as well as France, and in Belgium, Franklin's theory was proved again and again during the summer of 1752. He was famous in Europe before he knew it in America.

II

Before that he had thought of another way of proving his theory, and with the help of his electrical kite had drawn lightning from a cloud. The episode of the kite, so firm and fixed in legend, turns out to be dim and mystifying in fact. Franklin himself never wrote the story of the most dramatic of his experiments. All that is known about what he did on that famous day, of no known date, comes from Joseph Priestley's account, published fifteen years afterwards but read in manuscript by Franklin, who must have given Priestley the precise, familiar details.

"As every circumstance relating to so capital a discovery (the greatest, perhaps, since the time of Sir Isaac Newton) cannot but give pleasure to all my readers, I shall endeavour to gratify them with the communication of a few particulars which I have from the best authority.

"The Doctor, having published his method of verifying his hypothesis concerning the sameness of electricity with the matter of lightning, was waiting for the erection of a spire [on Christ Church] in Philadelphia to carry his views into execution; not imagining that a pointed rod of a moderate height could answer the purpose; when it occurred to him that by means of a common kite he could have better access to the regions of thunder than by any spire whatever. Preparing, therefore, a large silk handkerchief and two cross-sticks of a proper length on which to extend it, he took the opportunity of the first approaching thunder-storm to take a walk in the fields, in which there was a shed convenient for his purpose. But, dreading the ridicule which too commonly attends unsuccessful attempts in science, he communicated his intended experiment to nobody but his son"—then twenty-one, not a child as in the traditional illustrations of the scene—"who assisted him in raising the kite.

"The kite being raised, a considerable time elapsed before there was any appearance of its being electrified. One very promising cloud had passed over it without any effect; when, at length, just as he was beginning to despair of his contrivance, he observed some loose threads of the hempen string to stand erect, and to avoid one another, just as if they had been suspended on a common conductor. Struck with this promising appearance, he immediately presented his knuckle to the key, and (let the reader judge of the exquisite pleasure he must have felt at that moment) the discovery was complete. He perceived a very evident electric spark. Others succeeded, even before the string was wet, so as to put the matter past all dispute, and when the rain had wet the string he collected electric fire very copiously. This happened in June 1752, a month after the electricians in France had verified the same theory, but before he heard of anything they had done."[19]

Priestley, writing what he could have learned only from Franklin, and writing under Franklin's eye, could hardly have invented these minute circumstances. Nor is Franklin, with his powerful and exact memory, likely to have been wrong. If he had wanted— what was quite out of character for him—to claim more credit for originality than he deserved, he might as well have said he flew the kite before his theory had been verified in France. Instead, he allowed the French a month's priority. Yet there is this mystery about the matter: Franklin, who knew how startling the discovery was, and who had a genius for promptly making drama out of news, kept the electrical kite a secret till October. He mentioned it to none of his correspondents. He wrote nothing about it in the *Gazette*, and apparently did not tell Kinnersley, who lectured on electricity in Philadelphia during September without reference to this latest triumph.

Can Franklin deliberately have kept his secret till October so that he might publish at the same time, or almost the same time, in his newspaper and in his almanac the two most important pieces of his year's news? That is what he did. On 19 October his first account of the *Electrical Kite* appeared in the *Gazette*. The same issue advertised as in the press the new *Poor Richard* for 1753, which contained Franklin's first positive statement of *How to Secure Houses, etc., from Lightning*.

"As frequent mention," he wrote in the *Gazette*, "is made in public papers from Europe of the success of the Philadelphia experiment for drawing the electric fire from clouds by means of pointed rods of iron erected on high buildings, etc., it may be agreeable to the curious to be informed that the same experiment has succeeded in Philadelphia, though made in a different and more easy manner, which is as follows:

"Make a small cross of two light strips of cedar, the arms so long as to reach to the four corners of a large thin silk handkerchief when extended; tie the corners of the handkerchief to the extremities of the cross, so you have the body of a kite; which, being properly accommodated with a tail, loop, and string, will rise in the air, like those made of paper; but this, being of silk, is fitter to bear the wet and wind of a thunder-gust without tearing. To the top of the upright stick of the cross is to be fixed a very sharp-pointed wire, rising a foot or more above the wood. To the end of the twine, next the hand, is to be tied a silk ribbon, and where the silk and twine join, a key may be fastened. This kite is to be raised when a thunder-gust appears to be coming on, and the person who holds the string must stand within a door or window, or under some cover, so that the silk ribbon may not be wet; and care must be taken that the twine does not touch the frame of the door or window. As soon as any of the thunder-clouds come over the kite, the pointed wire will draw the electric fire from them, and the kite, with all the twine, will be electrified, and the loose filaments of the twine will stand out every way and be attracted by an approaching finger. And when the rain has wet the kite and twine, so that it can conduct the electric fire freely, you will find it stream out plentifully from the key on the approach of your knuckle. At this key the phial may be charged; and from electric fire thus obtained, spirits may be kindled, and all the other electric experiments may be performed which are usually done by the help of a rubbed glass globe or tube, and thereby the sameness of the electric matter with that of lightning completely demonstrated."[20]

"It has pleased God in His goodness to mankind," Franklin said in *Poor Richard*, "at length to discover to them the means of securing their habitations and other buildings from mischief by thunder and lightning. The method is this: Provide a small iron rod (it may be made of the rod-iron used by the nailers) but of such a length that, one end being three or four feet in the moist ground, the other may be six or eight feet above the highest part of the building. To the upper end of the rod fasten about a foot of brass wire the size of a common knitting-needle, sharpened to a fine point; the rod may be secured to the house by a few small staples. If the house or barn be long, there may be a rod and point at each end, and a middling wire along the ridge from one to the other. A house thus furnished will not be damaged by lightning, it being attracted by the points and passing through the metal into the ground without hurting anything. Vessels, also, having a sharp-pointed rod fixed on the top of their masts, with a wire from the foot of the rod reaching down, round one of the shrouds, to the water, will not be hurt by lightning."

Again a question: Why were these two epoch-making announcements so circumspectly worded? Franklin described the kite experiment, but said only that it had succeeded in Philadelphia, not that he himself had performed it. (In all his later writings he mentions it but once, in that section of the *Autobiography*, written in 1788, which refers to D'Alibard and de Lor: "I will not swell this narrative with an account of that capital experiment, nor of the infinite pleasure I received in the success of a similar one I made soon after at Philadelphia, as both are to be found in the histories of electricity."[21]) Speaking of lightning rods, Franklin said that a method of securing houses had been discovered, not that it had been put into practice by him, or in America. So far as his words in *Poor Richard* go, he might have been depending on the report from France that the experiments of the best naturalists there confirmed his theory of points as "a preservative against thunder." This he could have read in the *Gentleman's Magazine* for May, which he had seen by 14 September[22] and possibly earlier.

Every simple explanation of the kite mystery leaves it still confused. Franklin, it has been guessed by cynics, invented the whole story. This is quite out of keeping with his record in science, in which he elsewhere appears always truthful and unpretending. It has been guessed by kinder sceptics that Franklin, talking with Priestley after fifteen years, mistook the month in which he had made his discovery: that he made it as he said, but in September. The important thing about his recollection is not that he flew the kite in June but that he flew it before he knew of the experiments in France. After that there was no need for Franklin to verify an experiment which had been satisfactorily verified, and it would not have been like him to do it. The chances that he did not do it at all are nearly as good as that he did it when proof was no longer called for. By 14 September he certainly knew about the French experiments, and had probably flown his kite. Yet he did not make the kite public in the *Gazette* till *Poor Richard* was ready with its news of lightning rods. A man who could keep such a secret for five weeks could as easily have kept it for four months.

Whether Franklin is supposed to have flown the most famous of all kites in June, or later, or never, little is known about him through this mysterious time. "We have had excessive hot weather now near two weeks," he wrote to Susanna Wright on 11 July. "This town is a mere oven. . . . I languish for the country, for air and shade and leisure and converse, but fate has doomed me to be stifled and roasted and teased to death in a city."[23] "Business sometimes obliges one to postpone philosophical amusements," he wrote to John Perkins on 13 August. "Whatever I have wrote of that kind are really, as they are entitled, but conjectures and suppositions; which ought always to give place when careful observation militates against them. I own I have too strong a penchant to the building of hypotheses; they indulge my natural indolence. I wish I had more of your patience and accuracy in making observations, on which alone true philosophy can be founded."[24] Writing to Cadwallader Colden on 14 September, Franklin, in answer to a letter written in May, apologized for his neglect of their correspondence, but said nothing about the kite, and left Colden to hear about it from the newspapers. That same month Franklin "erected an iron rod to draw the lightning down into my house, in order to make some experiments on it, with two bells to give notice when the rod should be electrified."[25]

His rod was "fixed to the top of my chimney and extending about nine feet above it. From the foot of this rod a wire (the thickness of a goose-quill) came through a covered glass tube in the roof and down through the well of the staircase; the lower end connected with the iron spear of a pump. On the staircase opposite to my chamber door the wire was divided; the ends separated about six inches, a little bell on each end; and between the bells a little brass ball, suspended by a silk thread, to play between and strike the bells when clouds passed with electricity in them. After having frequently drawn sparks and charged bottles from the bell of the upper wise, I was one night awaked by loud cracks on the staircase. Starting up and opening the door, I perceived that the brass ball, instead of vibrating as usual between the bells, was repelled and kept at a distance from both; while the fire passed, sometimes in very large, quick cracks from bell to bell, and sometimes in a continued, dense, white stream, seemingly as large as my finger, whereby the whole staircase was inlightened as with sunshine, so that one might see to pick up a pin."[26] Those bells rang in his house for years.

Though he had, it seems, put up his rod chiefly to get electricity for experiments without the work of making it by laborious friction, he also thought it protected his house, as other rods protected other houses in Philadelphia that year.[27] When on 1 October he wrote to Collinson about the kite he added a postscript about lightning rods. "I was pleased to hear of the success of my experiments in France, and that they begin to use points upon their buildings. We had before that placed them upon our academy and state house spires."[28] This is the earliest American reference to lightning rods in actual use. Printing a copy of this letter in the *Gazette* for the 19th (of course long before the original reached Collinson and the Royal Society), Franklin left off the postscript. The rods on the academy and state house were already known to Philadelphia. When they were put up is not clear from Franklin's "before that" in the postscript to Collinson. Did he mean before the French began to "erect points upon their buildings" in May or before he heard about it in September or earlier? If it was before May, why did he wait till September to install the rod on his house? The whole chronology of the episode is guesswork. But it may with some reason be guessed: (1) that Franklin, having proposed the experiment which D'Alibard verified in May, was waiting for the high Christ Church spire which he thought he needed; (2) that in June he thought of another method of proving his theory and flew his kite; (3) that he then, without giving away his kite secret, suggested the rods on the lower spires, as much to obtain electricity as to safeguard the buildings; (4) and that he came to the idea of a rod on his house only after he had learned from the French that no greater height was needed. He felt certain enough of the value of such rods to recommend them confidently in *Poor Richard* the next month. But not till eight years later did Kinnersley report to Franklin, then in London, that a house in Philadelphia had unmistakably been struck by lightning and saved by his invention.[29]

Franklin suggested if he did not erect the first lightning rod, and he probably flew the first electrical kite, but there are little mysteries about both his proof of his great conjecture and his application of it.

III

In 1752–53 these were not mysteries but wonders. A man in Philadelphia in America, bred a tradesman, remote from the learned world, had hit upon a secret which enabled him, and other men, to catch and tame the lightning, so dread that it was still mythological. To the public, as it gradually heard about him, he seemed a magician. To scientists, from the first, he seemed a master. He had resounding praise from France, even the applause of the king. When Franklin learned of this he felt, he told Jared Eliot on 12 April 1753, like the girl in the *Tatler* "who was observed to grow suddenly proud, and none could guess the reason, till it came to be known that she had got on a new pair of garters."[30] His account of the electrical kite was read at the Royal Society 21 December, almost as soon as it could get to London, and was published in the *Transactions* for that year. Harvard gave him the honorary degree of Master of Arts in July 1753. Yale followed with the same degree in September, and William and Mary in April 1756. The Royal Society on 30 November 1753 awarded him the Sir Godfrey Copley gold medal "on account of his curious experiments and observations on electricity," and on 29 May 1756 elected him a member of the Society. "I had not the least expectation," he told Collinson, "of ever arriving at that honour."[31] Giovanni Battista Beccaria made Franklin quickly known and accepted in the schools of Italy. His electrical writings were translated not only into French but also into German (1758) and Italian (1774). Throughout Europe he stood first among electricians, as electricity, for an excited time, stood first among scientific marvels. The Swedish physicist G. W. Richmann in St. Petersburg put up an experimental rod in July 1753 and was killed—as Franklin might have been if his kite or his rod had happened to draw a heavy bolt of lightning. Kinnersley in Philadelphia in 1754 took the trouble to explain in his lectures that lightning rods were not presumptuous or irreligious. On this point there were controversies.

Wonders could not run through the world then as they can now, thanks to electricity, but Franklin's fame reached far beyond those who did or could read his books, understand his ingenious experiments, and enjoy his easy, natural expositions. He had made one of the most dramatic guesses in the history of science, and he had verified his guess with a boy's plaything. He had applied his knowledge to making men's houses, barns, ships safe from an incalculable danger. With what seemed the simplest key he had unlocked one of the darkest and most terrifying doors in the unknown universe. Here was another hero of the human race, even as against the terrifying gods. Franklin, Kant said, was a new Prometheus who had stolen fire from heaven.

In the six years between the summer of 1746, when Franklin first saw electrical experiments in Boston, and the summer of 1752, when he flew the electrical kite in Philadelphia, he made all his fundamental contributions to electricity. He made them because he had a fundamental mind, which almost at once mastered the general problem as it then existed and went deeper into it than any observer had yet gone. He found electricity a curiosity and left it a science. Indolence, he thought, disposed him too much to the building of hypotheses, and he claimed only to have been lucky in his guesses. His procedure came from the nature and method of his mind. But there was more in his science than a few bold conjectures. He steadily insisted on the need of painstaking experiments, scrupulous accuracy, and a stubborn refusal to surmise what the tested facts did not warrant. He regretted his weakness in mathematics and the frequent interruptions which broke off the chain of thought which he believed should be continuous in a scientist. Nobody ever gave more grateful attention than Franklin to experiments which contradicted this or that theory of his, or more readily accepted them if he was convinced that he had been in error. His hypotheses grew as his facts accumulated. It did not matter to him who got the credit. "These thoughts, my dear friend," he wrote to Collinson at the end of his letter about lightning rods, "are many of them crude and hasty; and if I were merely ambitious of acquiring some reputation in philosophy I ought to keep them by me till corrected and improved by time and farther experience. But since even short hints and imperfect experiments in any new branch of science, being communicated, have oftentimes a good effect, in exciting the attention of the ingenious to the subject, and so become the occasion of more exact disquisition and more complete discoveries; you are at liberty to communicate this paper to whom you please; it being of more importance that knowledge should increase than that your friend should be thought an accurate philosopher."[32]

As Franklin was not ambitious, neither did he expect too much from the world, which he knew as few scientists have known it. "There are everywhere a number of people who, being totally destitute of any inventive faculty themselves, do not readily conceive that others may possess it," he wrote to John Lining on 18 March 1755. "They think of inventions as miracles: there might be such formerly, but they are ceased. With these, everyone who offers a new invention is deemed a pretender: he had it from some other country or from some book. A man of their own acquaintance, one who has no more sense than themselves, could not possibly, in their opinion, have been the inventor of anything. They are confirmed, too, in these sentiments by frequent instances of pretensions to invention which vanity is daily producing. That vanity too, though an incitement to invention, is at the same time the pest of inventors. Jealousy and envy deny the merit or the novelty of your invention; but vanity, when the novelty and merit are established, claims it for its own. . . . Thus through envy, jealousy, and the vanity of competitors for fame, the origin of many of the most extraordinary inventions, though produced within but a few centuries past, is involved in doubt and uncertainty. We scarce know to whom we are indebted for the compass and for spectacles; nor have even paper and printing, that record everything else, been able to preserve with certainty the name and reputation of their inventors. One would not, therefore, of all faculties or qualities of the mind, wish for a friend or a child that he should have that of invention. For his attempts to benefit mankind in that way, however well imagined, if they do not succeed, expose him, though very unjustly, to general ridicule and contempt; and if they do succeed, to envy, robbery, and abuse."[33]

It may have been knowledge of the world as much as modesty that kept Franklin from being too explicit or emphatic about his own inventions. Having no envy, jealousy, or vanity in himself, he would not run the risk of needlessly rousing them in others. When the Abbé Nollet, preceptor to the royal family in France, attacked the theories from America, Franklin did not, after a little reflection, bother to answer him. "I concluded to let my papers shift for themselves, believing it was better to spend what time I could spare from public business in making new experiments than in disputing about those already made."[34] He refused to patent the lightning rod, often called the Franklin rod, or to profit by it. Though he never lost sight of what was being done in electricity during his whole lifetime, he was perfectly willing to have his contributions to it absorbed in the enlarging science. They were absorbed, and it is now difficult to trace the details of his influence. His Principia made only a beginning.

But in one discoverable respect he still survives wherever electricity is spoken of. Franklin appears to have been the first to use, at least in print in English, these electrical terms: armature, battery, brush, charged, charging, condense, conductor, discharge, electrical fire, electrical shock, electrician, electrified, electrify, electrized, Leyden bottle, minus (negative or negatively), negatively, non-conducting, non-conductor, non-electric, plus (positive or positively), stroke (electric shock), uncharged.[35] The Philadelphia Prometheus with his kite was also an American Adam in his electrical garden.

I V

Franklin was more conspicuous, and more methodical, in electricity than in any other branch of science, but his scientific curiosity swung freely in all directions. At twenty, on his voyage from London to Philadelphia, he was already a scientist, acute in observing and precise in reporting what he saw. During his heavy years of business as a printer he had little time for scientific studies, though even then he thought often about "natural philosophy," and made friends with such experts as he had a chance to meet— particularly the men who became the first members of the American Philosophical Society. Franklin, offering himself as secretary, did not pretend to be an expert himself. Yet in the year he proposed the Society, 1743, he made an observation which ranks him with the first and best meteorologists. He had not as Poor Richard forecast the weather annually since 1732 for nothing.

"We were to have an eclipse of the moon at Philadelphia, on a Friday evening [21 October] about nine o'clock. I intended to observe it, but was prevented by a north-east storm which came on about seven with thick clouds, as usual, that quite obscured the whole hemisphere. Yet when the post brought us the Boston newspaper, giving an account of the effects of the same storm in those parts, I found the beginning of the eclipse had been well observed there, though Boston lies north-east of Philadelphia about four hundred miles. This puzzled me, because the storm began with us so soon as to prevent any observation; and being a north-east storm, I imagined it must have begun rather sooner in places farther to the north-eastward than it did at Philadelphia. I therefore mentioned it in a letter to my brother who lived at Boston; and he informed me that the storm did not begin with them till near eleven o'clock, so that they had a good observation of the eclipse. And upon comparing all the other accounts I received from the several colonies, of the time of beginning of the same storm . . . I found the beginning to be always later the farther north-eastward. . . .

"From thence I formed an idea of the cause of these storms,

which I would explain by a familiar instance or two. Suppose a
long canal of water stopped at the end by a gate. The water is quite
at rest till the gate is open, then it begins to move out through the
gate; the water next the gate is first in motion, and moves towards
the gate; the water next to the first water moves next, and so on successively till the water at the head of the canal is in motion, which
is last of all. In this case all the water moves indeed towards the
gate, but the successive times of beginning motion are the contrary
way, viz., from the gate backwards to the head of the canal. Again,
suppose the air in a chamber at rest, no current through the room
till you make a fire in the chimney. Immediately the air in the
chimney, being rarefied by the fire, rises; the air next the chimney
flows in to supply its place, moving towards the chimney; and in
consequence the rest of the air successively, quite back to the door.
Thus to produce our north-east storms I suppose some great heat
and rarefaction of the air in or about the Gulf of Mexico; the air
thence rising has its place supplied by the next more northern,
cooler, and therefore denser and heavier air; that, being in motion,
is followed by the next more northern air, etc., etc., in a successive
current, to which current our coast and inland ridge of mountains
give the direction of north-east, as they lie north-east and south-
west."[36]

Franklin's alert, conjecturing mind here shows itself working in
its most characteristic ways. Concerned with an eclipse, he noticed
a storm. He read about it in the newspapers and wrote a letter
to his brother asking for more information. Other accounts came
from other colonies. He compared them all, reflected upon them,
and worked out his hypothesis. It was continental in scope, but
he reduced it to the simple image of water in a canal or air in
a room. Submitting his explanation to John Perkins, Franklin
said: "If my hypothesis is not the truth, it is at least as naked. For
I have not with some of our learned moderns disguised my nonsense in Greek, clothed it in algebra, or adorned it with fluxions.
You have it *in puris naturalibus*."[37] He threw off his powerful idea
and left other men to realize that he had taken a first step toward
a knowledge of the great whirling wind systems now known as
cyclones and anticyclones.

In 1744 Franklin, who had begun his correspondence with Cadwallader Colden on the subject of stereotyping, expounded the philosophy as well as the construction of the Pennsylvanian fire-places, and in a letter to his father and mother answered their questions about various remedies for sickness. During 1745 he discussed with Colden the pores of the skin and the circulation of the blood. Electricity absorbed him in 1746–47, but five days after his first important letter to Collinson, Franklin wrote with more than usual variety to Jared Eliot, clergyman and physician and farmer in Connecticut, soon to become the most widely read colonial writer on agriculture. Franklin told him about oil mills in Pennsylvania, the price of linseed oil, the kind of land used for hemp, and the weather for that summer and the two past; and offered his new opinion about north-east storms. He agreed with Eliot as to the source of most springs, but had another theory concerning springs on the sides of mountains. "Now I mention mountains, it occurs [to me] to tell you that the great Appalachian Mountains, which run from York River, back of these colonies, to the Bay of Mexico, show in many places, near the highest parts of them, strata of sea-shells; in some places the marks of them are in the solid rock. It is certainly the wreck of a world we live on! We have specimens of these sea-shell rocks, broken off near the tops of these mountains, brought and deposited in our Library as curiosities. If you have not seen the like, I'll send you a piece. Farther about mountains (for ideas will string themselves like ropes of onions); when I was once riding in your country, Mr. Walker showed me at a distance the bluff side or end of a mountain which appeared striped from top to bottom, and told me the stone or rock of that mountain was divided by nature into pillars; of this I should be glad to have a particular account from you. I think I was somewhere near New Haven when I saw it."[38] Then Franklin shifted to what seemed to him the bad economics of a law Connecticut had just passed to lay a tax on goods imported from neighbouring colonies.

For a year he was taken up with public affairs, but in 1748 he told the Swedish botanist Peter Kalm, sent by Linnæus to America, about the ways of ants which Franklin had observed. Believing that they had something like speech, he had tried an experiment. Ants had got into a little earthen pot of molasses in a closet. He shook out all but one of them and hung the pot by a string from a nail in the ceiling. When the ant had eaten enough, it managed to find its way up the string to the ceiling and down the wall to the floor. Within half an hour a swarm of ants arrived, as if they had been told the news, followed the course the pioneer ant had taken, ate till they finished the molasses, and then left by string and ceiling.[39] Franklin observed the pigeons in the box, big enough for six pair, nailed against the wall of his house. "Though they bred as fast as my neighbours' pigeons," he wrote to Samuel Johnson on 23 August 1750, "I never had more than six pair, the old and strong driving out the young and weak, and obliging them to seek new habitations. At length I put up an additional box with compartments for entertaining twelve pair more; and it was soon filled with inhabitants, by the overflowing of my first box and of others in the neighbourhood."[40]

About the time he retired from business Franklin bought a farm of three hundred acres near Burlington, New Jersey, and planned to "indulge myself," he wrote to Jared Eliot,* "in that kind of life which was most agreeable. My fortune (thank God) is such that I can enjoy all the necessaries and many of the indulgencies of life; but I think that in duty to my children I ought so to manage that the profits of my farm may balance the loss my income will suffer by my retreat into it." He began at once to develop and enrich his land, particularly "a meadow on which there had never been much timber, but it was always overflowed. The soil of it is very fine, and black about three foot; then it comes to a fat bluish clay; of this meadow I have about eighty acres, forty of which had been ditched and mowed. . . . This meadow had been ditched and planted with Indian corn, of which it produced about sixty bushels per acre. I first scoured up my ditches and drains, and took off all the weeds; then I ploughed it and sowed it with oats in the last of May [apparently 1748]. In July I mowed them down, together with the weeds which grew plentifully among them, and they made good fodder. I immediately ploughed it again and kept harrowing till there was an appearance of rain; and, on the 23d of August, I sowed near thirty acres with red clover and herd-grass, allowing six quarts of herd-grass and four pounds of red clover to an acre in most parts of it; in other parts, four quarts herd-grass and three

* See Notes, p. 808.

pounds red clover. The red clover came up in four days and the herd-grass in six days; and I now find that where I allowed the most seed it protects itself the better against the frost." He was surprised that "the herd-grass, whose roots are small and spread near the surface, should be less affected by the frost than the red clover, whose roots I measured in the last of October, and found that many of their taproots penetrated five inches, and from its sides threw out near thirty horizontal roots, some of which were six inches long, and branched."[41] In other letters to Jared Eliot, Franklin asked many acute questions about farming. "Since for want of skill in agriculture I cannot converse with you pertinently on that valuable subject,"[42] Franklin explained, he took pains to introduce Eliot to Collinson and John Bartram, who were experts.

Franklin was one of the earliest Americans to perceive that the agricultural resources of the country should not be wasted, and that farming must be something of a business and a science as well as a way of life. His arguments and his example seemed to him to have had little effect. "If the farmers in your neighbourhood," he wrote to Eliot, "are as unwilling to leave the beaten road of their ancestors as they are near me, it will be difficult to persuade them to attempt any improvement."[43] Farmers were not as flexible as traders or as open-minded as philosophers. Franklin was both by nature and experience a city man, and not suited to the rural tempo. Public affairs drew him back to Philadelphia. But though he soon gave up the hope of living on his farm (the exact whereabouts of which is now not known), he urged that farming and gardening be taught in the new academy which he was founding while he farmed, and he remained all his life a realistic friend of agriculture.

From 1748 to 1752 Franklin's varied experiments in electricity, his farm, his official duties, and the academy and hospital took almost all his time and filled almost all his letters, though here and there his general curiosity showed itself fresh and persistent. Then on 23 April 1752 he wrote about air and light to Cadwallader Colden. "I must own I am much in the dark about light. I am not satisfied with the doctrine that supposes particles of matter called light, continually driven off from the sun's surface with a swiftness so prodigious. Must not the smallest particle conceivable have, with such a motion, a force exceeding that of a 24-pounder discharged from a cannon? . . . May not all the phenomena of light be more conveniently solved by supposing universal space filled with a subtle elastic fluid which, when at rest, is not visible, but whose vibrations affect that fine sense the eye as those of air do the grosser organs of the ear? We do not, in the case of sound, imagine that any sonorous particles are thrown off from a bell, for instance, and fly in straight lines to the ear; why must we imagine that luminous particles leave the sun and proceed to the eye? . . . It is well we are not, as poor Galileo was, subject to the Inquisition for philosophical heresy. My whispers against the orthodox doctrine, in private letters, would be dangerous."[44] Whether he knew that Huygens had already propounded the wave theory of light is not clear, but Franklin did know that the corpuscular theory, with its flying particles, was orthodox. Heretically he embraced the theory of the future. He was on ground more native to him—that is, humane or practical, not metaphysical—when in December of that year he devised for the use of his brother John in Boston the first flexible catheter known to American—though not to European—medical history.[45] "I went immediately to the silversmith's and gave directions for making one (sitting by till it was finished) that it might be ready for this post."[46]

After 1753, when Franklin became Postmaster-General, he had less leisure for science than ever, though he kept up his electrical correspondence with Collinson. Somewhat as if he were taking leave of a happy chapter of his life, he made up, in November of that year, "a small philosophical packet" of letters which, recently but at unknown times, he had written to various philosophical friends in America. His observations, suppositions, and conjectures were most of them in physics and meteorology, simple in language and close to daily experience. "My desk and its lock are, I suppose, of the same temperament [temperature] when they have long been exposed to the same air; but now, if I lay my hand on the wood, it does not seem so cold to me as the lock; because (as I imagine) wood is not so good a conductor, to receive and convey away the heat from my skin and the adjacent flesh, as metal is. Take a piece of wood of the size and shape of a dollar between the thumb and fingers of one hand, and a dollar in like manner with the other hand; place the edges of both, at the same time, in the flame of a candle; and though the edge of the wooden piece takes flame and the metal piece does not, yet you will be obliged to drop the latter before the former, it conducting the heat more suddenly to your fingers. Thus we can without pain handle glass and china cups filled with hot liquors, as tea, etc., but not silver ones. A silver teapot must have a wooden handle. Perhaps it is for the same reason that woollen garments keep the body warmer than linen ones equally thick; woollen keeping the natural heat in, or, in other words, not conducting it out to the air."[47]

Nowhere throughout this first scientific period of his does Franklin appear so nearly full length and to the life as in his accounts of a whirlwind which he observed in 1755. "Being in Maryland, riding with Colonel Tasker and some other gentleman to his country seat where I and my son were entertained by that amiable and worthy man with great hospitality and kindness, we saw, in the vale below us, a small whirlwind beginning in the road and showing itself by the dust it raised and contained. It appeared in the form of a sugar loaf, spinning on its point, moving up the hill towards us, and enlarging as it came forward. When it passed by us, its smaller part near the ground appeared no bigger than a common barrel, but, widening upwards, it seemed at forty or fifty feet high to be twenty or thirty feet in diameter. The rest of the company stood looking after it, but, my curiosity being stronger, I followed it, riding close by its side, and observed its licking up in its progress all the dust that was under its smaller part. As it is a common opinion that a shot fired through a water-spout will break it, I tried to break this little whirlwind by striking my whip frequently through it, but without any effect. Soon after, it quitted the road and took into the woods, growing every moment larger and stronger, raising instead of dust the old dry leaves with which the ground was thick covered, and making a great noise with them and the branches of the trees, bending some tall trees round in a circle swiftly and very surprisingly, though the progressive motion of the whirl was not so swift but that a man on foot might have kept pace with it; but the circular motion was amazingly rapid. By the leaves it was now filled with I could plainly perceive that the current of air they were driven by moved upwards in a spiral line;

and when I saw the trunks and bodies of large trees enveloped in the passing whirl, which continued entire after it had left them, I no longer wondered that my whip had no effect on it in its smaller state. I accompanied it about three-quarters of a mile, till some limbs of dead trees, broken off by the whirl, flying about and falling near me, made me more apprehensive of danger; and then I stopped, looking at the top of it as it went on, which was visible by means of the leaves contained in it for a very great height above the trees. Many of the leaves, as they got loose from the upper and widest part, were scattered in the wind; but so great was their height in the air that they appeared no bigger than flies.

"My son, who was by this time come up with me, followed the whirlwind till it left the woods and crossed an old tobacco field, where, finding neither dust nor leaves to take up, it gradually became invisible below as it went away over that field. The course of the general wind then blowing was along with us as we travelled, and the progressive motion of the whirlwind was in a direction nearly opposite, though it did not keep a straight line nor was its progressive motion uniform, it making little sallies on either hand as it went, proceeding sometimes faster and sometimes slower, and seeming sometimes for a few seconds almost stationary, then starting forward pretty fast again. When we rejoined the company, they were admiring the vast height of the leaves now brought by the common wind over our heads. These leaves accompanied us as we travelled, some falling now and then about us, and some not reaching the ground till we had gone near three miles from the place where we first saw the whirlwind begin.

"Upon my asking Colonel Tasker if such whirlwinds were common in Maryland, he answered pleasantly: 'No, not at all common; but we got this on purpose to treat Mr. Franklin.' "[48]

"The rest of the company stood looking after it, but, my curiosity being stronger, I followed it, riding close by its side." This is a little symbolical history of Franklin as scientist. Going about his ordinary affairs, he was more curious than ordinary men and followed up what they only looked at. The ants he observed were in his closet, the pigeons in a box on the wall of his house. To warm his house, he devised a new kind of stove. To protect his house, he thought of the lightning rod. Watching the weather, he followed in his mind the course of a north-east storm for a thousand miles. Out of sympathy for his ailing brother he fashioned his catheter. Science came so naturally to him that he blamed himself for not being more patient and systematic. Actually he was, during his first electrical years, as patient and systematic in his studies of electricity as any of the scholars he surpassed. He surpassed them by the speed and reach of the hypotheses of which he spoke slightingly. Franklin, for all his home-made machines to experiment with and his homely inventions and his eagerness to make scientific knowledge immediately useful to mankind, was magnificent in outlook. He saw sea-shells from the top of a mountain, and saw time stretch out behind him in the great age of the earth. He guessed that light could not come from the sun in particles but on waves in the ether. On the hypothesis that lightning was electricity he built the bolder one that it could be proved. In the one metaphysical sentence in his writings on electricity he referred to "adoring that wisdom which had made all things by weight and measure."[49] Secular as he was, he had often a vision, not unlike religion's, of an enormous universe of order and law which sometime might be understood. Immortal secrets for mortal men. In the meantime, he could be delighted, reasonable, and humorous about the mysteries.

Pennsylvanian

SINCE 1739 England had been at war with Spain over British smuggling in Spanish America, and since 1744 with France over the Austrian succession. Neither war, before 1747, had come close to Pennsylvania. The northern colonies protected it from the French in Canada, the southern colonies from the Spanish in Florida and the Caribbean. Enemy ships cruised off the coast, but none of them had found its long and difficult way up the Delaware to Philadelphia. Then in July 1747 French and Spanish privateers appeared in the bay, plundered two plantations only a little below New Castle, captured a ship coming in from Antigua, and murdered its captain. Franklin, in the midst of his electrical experiments, was concerned for the safety of the thriving city and the rich province. War was a hazard like fire or lightning, and like them to be guarded against. Philadelphia had no fort, no artillery, no militia. The Quakers, who dominated the Assembly, would not vote money to make war. They had no quarrel with Spain or France, and they had always been at peace with the Indians. Let men who started wars finish them. The richer merchants in Philadelphia refused to give money to protect Quaker property along with their own. The Germans on their quiet farms usually sided with the Quakers. The Scotch-Irish, still further in the interior, did not feel that the danger to the seaboard capital particularly threatened them. The men who called for defensive action were not a party, and they had as many plans as minds. Franklin left his philosophical inquiries for a political problem.

"I determined to try what might be done by a voluntary association of the people. To promote this I first wrote and published a pamphlet entitled *Plain Truth*, in which I stated our defenceless situation in strong lights, with the necessity of union and discipline for our defence, and promised to propose in a few days an association to be generally signed for that purpose. The pamphlet had a sudden and surprising effect. I was called upon for the instrument of association, and, having settled the draft of it with a few friends, I appointed a meeting of the citizens in the large building [built for Whitefield]. . . . The house was pretty full; I had prepared a number of printed copies, and provided pens and ink dispersed all over the room. I harangued them a little on the subject, read the paper and explained it, and then distributed the copies, which were eagerly signed, not the least objection being made. When the company separated and the papers were collected, we found above twelve hundred hands."[1]

So Franklin tersely told the story in 1788. In earlier detail it is more interesting and more revealing. Rumours from the West Indies said in the fall of 1747 that six French privateers, and perhaps others, had made a plot to come together the next year and sack Philadelphia. The Quakers were not unanimous in their stand against any war whatever. Some of them, including James Logan, thought defensive war was justified. They had helped fit out a privateer to drive away the raiders the past summer, and now faced being excommunicated if they would not recant. Liberal Quakers were disaffected, and the other sects disgusted. Franklin saw the situation as an opportunity. He talked with William Coleman of the Junto, Thomas Hopkinson of the American Philosophical Society, and Tench Francis, attorney-general. Together they agreed that Franklin should, as an anonymous tradesman, write against Quakers and merchants both, and so, it was hoped, bring the general run of people into unity in their own defence. He would print all sides of the controversy in the *Gazette*, at his own expense, and if his newspaper would not hold what was written, he would issue pamphlets and send them to his subscribers. First he printed, in the *Gazette*, verses in praise of Robert Barclay, and next a passage from Barclay's *Apology* on self-defence. Then came Franklin's own pamphlet: *Plain Truth; or, Serious Considerations on the Present State of the City of Philadelphia and Province of Pennsylvania. By a Tradesman of Philadelphia.*[2] It was published on Wednesday, 17 November.

Again Franklin assumed a dramatic role. He could be, in his

argument, as homely as Poor Richard or he could quote Scripture. Though a Philadelphian, his tradesman was also very much a Pennsylvanian. The danger was not entirely from the sea. Suppose the French should arouse the Indians against the back country. "Perhaps some in the city, towns, and plantations near the river may say to themselves: 'An Indian war on the frontiers will not affect us; the enemy will never come near our habitations; let those concerned take care of themselves.' And others who live in the country, when they are told of the danger the city is in from attempts by sea, may say: 'What is that to us? The enemy will be satisfied with the plunder of the town, and never think it worth his while to visit our plantations; let the town take care of itself.' These are not mere suppositions, for I have heard some talk in this strange manner. But are these the sentiments of true Pennsylvanians, of fellow-countrymen, or even of men that have common sense or goodness? Is not the whole province one body?" It was to the interest of all the people that trade should go on by sea and life and property be secure on land. No help would come from the Quakers with their religious principles—"may they long enjoy them," the tradesman said. Nor from the merchants, obstinately unwilling to raise money if the Quakers would not. "Till of late I could scarce believe the story of him who refused to pump in a sinking ship because one on board whom he hated would be saved by it as well as himself." No, the "middling people, the farmers, shopkeepers, and tradesmen of this city and country" must do whatever was to be done. The tradesman had faith in them. " 'Tis computed that we have at least (exclusive of the Quakers) 60,000 fighting men, acquainted with firearms, many of them hunters and marksmen, hardy and bold." English, Scotch-Irish, German—they were all descended from races famous in war. If their leaders would not act, they themselves could and would. The tradesman had a project which in a few days he would lay before them if they cared to hear it.

The response was so quick and favourable that Franklin called a meeting, but it was not the large public affair which he speaks of in the *Autobiography*. First a caucus. On Saturday about a hundred men, mostly tradesmen, gathered in Chancellor's sail-loft, according to Richard Peters.[3] Franklin, after telling them they had taken the lead in every useful undertaking for the good of the city, such as the Library and the fire companies, pulled the draft of the proposed Association out of his pocket and read it to them. They were ready to sign at once. Franklin thought it wiser to "offer it, at least, to the gentlemen, and, if they come into it, well and good." On Monday, according to the *Gazette*, the plan was laid "before a great meeting of the principal gentlemen, merchants, and others at Roberts's Coffee House." The gentlemen were as ready as the tradesmen. On their motion the Association—that is, the document to be signed by the volunteers—was printed for use at the large building the next night. As Franklin in his *Autobiography* remembered it, there were twelve hundred signers. But a few days after the meeting he told Peters the number would soon be a thousand, as the *Gazette* had already promised. Peters, provincial secretary, at once wrote the whole story to John and Richard Penn. Franklin had kept him informed through William Allen, soon to be chief justice. The founders of the new Association thought it was no trespass on the rights of the proprietors, and hoped they would send cannon for the fort.

The Association spread through the province till there were more than ten thousand members of the volunteer militia. They furnished themselves with arms, formed companies and regiments, chose their own officers, and met every week for drill. "The women, by subscriptions among themselves, provided silk colours which they presented to the companies, painted with different devices and mottoes which I supplied."[4] The Philadelphia companies, through their officers, chose Franklin for colonel, but he thought himself unfit and recommended another man, who was elected. Franklin's son William, now sixteen, had tried to ship on a privateer, and, balked in this, had been allowed in June 1746 to join—as ensign—one of the four companies raised in Pennsylvania for a campaign against Canada. They had spent the winter of 1746–47 at Albany. Franklin on 28 November 1747 ordered from Strahan "Folard's Polybius in French; it is in six volumes quarto and costs about three guineas"[5]—as a kind of textbook for his soldier son. The father helped organize a lottery to build a fort below the city and furnish it with cannon. Having no heavy guns, they bought thirty-nine from Boston, and ordered more from London in addition to whatever the proprietors might or might not send as a gift. The London guns would be till summer in coming. Franklin wrote at once to Colden to find out whether New York would lend guns for the spring, when more privateers might be expected. Four commissioners, including Franklin, went to New York to make their request to the governor, George Clinton. "He at first refused us peremptorily; but at dinner with his council, where there was great drinking of Madeira wine as the custom of that place then was, he softened by degrees, and said he would lend us six. After a few more bumpers he advanced to ten; and at length he very good-naturedly conceded eighteen. They were fine cannon, 18-pounders, with their carriages, which we soon [April 1748] transported and mounted on our battery, where the Associators kept a nightly guard while the war lasted, and among the rest I regularly took my turn of duty there as a common soldier."[6]

The peace that year gave Franklin a prospect of leisure again. He wrote to Strahan 19 October not to send the Polybius, since his son had given up military life. He himself refused to be named in 1748 for the Assembly. But his skill and zeal in recent affairs had made him too well known to be long an undisturbed philosopher. Heretofore Franklin had worked quietly, through the Junto, the Library Company, the fire companies, the Masonic lodge, the American Philosophical Society, and his post as clerk of the Assembly—which was only a minor office. Now he was, though not an official, a public man. He had enlarged his scope, not changed his methods. Feeling the general apprehension, he had moved to precipitate and focus it in a policy of defence. He had talked it over with his friends. He had widened it through his own class, the tradesmen, and carried it to the gentlemen and merchants, and on to the entire province. First to suggest the scheme, he was first among those who put it into execution. It was probably he who thought of buying guns from Boston, and certainly he who bought from his brother John, in June, "drums and sundry warlike implements." It was the philosophical Franklin who proposed Pennsylvania's first fast day, Thursday, 7 January 1748, and drew up the proclamation in a language partly borrowed from theological New England: "Forasmuch as it is the duty of mankind on all suitable occasions to acknowledge their dependence on the Divine Being, to give thanks for the mercies received, and no less to deprecate His Judgments and humbly pray for His protection . . . That Almighty God would mercifully interpose and still the rage of war among the nations and put a stop to the effusion of Christian blood . . . That He would bless, prosper, and preserve all the British colonies, and particularly that He would take this province under His protection, confound the designs and defeat the attempts of its enemies, and unite our hearts and strengthen our hands in every undertaking that may be for the public good, and for our defence and security in this time of danger; That He would graciously please to bless the succeeding year with health, peace, and plenty, and enable us to make a right use of His late afflicting hand in a sincere and thorough reformation of our lives and manners."[7]

In all this Franklin seems to have made the fewest enemies. The liberal Quakers were his friends, and the merchants gladly joined his Association. The governor and his council took Franklin into their confidence as they had never taken a tradesman before. However much he might want to be a philosopher, he had become too much a public man to be left out of office. "The governor put me into the commission of the peace [1749, 1752]; the corporation of the city chose me of the common council [4 October 1748] and soon after an alderman [1 October 1751]; and the citizens at large chose me a burgess to represent them in Assembly [1751]."[8] The Freemasons in 1749 elected him Grand Master of Pennsylvania.

Franklin's retirement from business increased the demands made on him by the public. Philosophy was not a career in Pennsylvania. If a man was rich and free he should be useful. By provincial standards Franklin was rich. A housemaid got ten pounds a year, a clerk twenty-five, a tutor in the academy sixty or seventy. The salary offered Samuel Johnson to be head of the English school was one hundred pounds sterling, and the chief justice received two hundred. The governor, the great man of the province, was paid a thousand pounds. Franklin had five hundred from David Hall, and possibly as much again from his partnerships elsewhere, his post office, his farm, his city real estate, and his money at interest. He had wanted wealth only that he might be free, and to be free only that he might be useful. There was in him no more of the solitary scholar than of the brooding mystic. He was a man of action, whether in science or morals or politics. He disliked waste and disorder. Pennsylvania, with its mixture of races and its rapid growth and its irregular development, seemed to him disorderly. In that confusion he thought in forms—in forms which life might take. Greatly as he loved and valued science, he could not resist the claims of society. The choice was so close in his mind that he felt he was compelled by outward pressure. It was the pressure of his own instinct. As a public man he could also play a part. And Franklin in public life was as naturally actor as writer.

Pennsylvania, he thought, should have a college. Massachusetts had Harvard, Connecticut had Yale, Virginia had William and Mary, and the College of New Jersey (later Princeton) had just been founded. As early as 1743 Franklin had drawn up a proposal for an academy, but had been busy and not too sure of himself, and had laid his project temporarily aside. "Peace being concluded, and the Association business therefore at an end, I turned my thoughts again to the affair of establishing an academy. The first step I took was to associate in the design a number of active friends, of whom the Junto furnished a good part; the next was to write and publish a pamphlet, entitled *Proposals Relating to the Education of Youth in Pennsylvania*."[9]

Plain Truth had been dramatic and artful. The *Proposals* was straightforward and serious. The first settlers, Franklin said, had been many of them well educated in Europe, but education in the colony had been neglected. It was time to remedy the neglect. He proposed that "some persons of leisure and public spirit" be incorporated to found and conduct an academy. "That the members of the corporation make it their pleasure, and in some degree their business, to visit the academy often, encourage and countenance the youth, countenance and assist the masters, and by all means in their power advance the usefulness and reputation of the design; that they look on the students as in some sort their children, treat them with familiarity and affection, and, when they have behaved well and gone through their studies and are to enter the world, zealously unite and make all the interest that can be made to establish them whether in business, offices, marriages, or any other thing for their advantage, preferably to all other persons whatsoever, even of equal merit." This was the old method of the Junto applied to a new enterprise. The academy should be properly housed—"if it may be, not far from a river, having a garden, orchard, meadow, and a field or two"—and should have a library "with maps of all countries, globes, some mathematical instruments, an apparatus for experiments in natural philosophy and for mechanics; prints of all kinds, prospects, buildings, machines, etc." The students should "diet together plainly, temperately, and frugally," and "be frequently exercised in running, leaping, wrestling, and swimming." A long footnote cited Milton, Locke, and others on the benefits of exercise. On swimming Franklin was in part his own authority: " 'Tis supposed that every parent would be glad to have their children skilled in swimming, if it might be learnt in a place chosen for its safety and under the eye of a careful person. . . . 'Tis some advantage besides, to be free from the slavish terrors many of those feel who cannot swim, when they are obliged to be on the water even in crossing a ferry."

"As to their studies, it would be well if they could be taught everything that is useful and everything that is ornamental. But art is long and their time is short. It is therefore proposed that they learn those things that are likely to be most useful and most ornamental, regard being had to the several professions for which they are intended." Franklin was explicit. "All should be taught to write a fair hand, and swift, as that is useful to all." He stressed the need of drawing, both in text and footnote. "Drawing is a kind of universal language, understood by all nations. A man may often express his ideas, even to his own countrymen, more clearly with a lead pencil or bit of chalk than with his tongue. And many can understand a figure that do not comprehend a description in words, though ever so properly chosen. . . . Drawing is no less useful to a mechanic than to a gentleman. . . . By a little skill of this kind the workman may perfect his own idea of the thing to be done before he begins to work; and show a draft for the encouragement and satisfaction of his employer." The academy should teach "arithmetic, accounts, and some of the first principles of geometry and astronomy. . . . Not only the skill but the habit of keeping accounts should be acquired by all as being necessary to all. . . . The English language might be taught by grammar; in which some of our best writers, as Tillotson, Addison, Pope, Algernon Sidney, *Cato's Letters,* etc., should be classics. The styles principally to be cultivated being the clear and the concise. Reading should also be taught, and pronouncing, properly, distinctly, emphatically; not with an even tone, which underdoes, nor a theatrical, which overdoes nature." Much attention should be paid to writing and public speaking. "Almost all kinds of useful knowledge," Franklin thought, could be learned through the reading of history: geography, chronology, ancient customs, morality. "Indeed, the general natural tendency of reading good history must be to fix in the minds of youth deep impressions of the beauty and usefulness of virtue of all kinds, public spirit, fortitude, etc." Reading history might make students eager to learn Greek and Latin, or French, German, and Spanish. "And though all should not be compelled to learn Latin, Greek, or the modern foreign languages, yet none that have an ardent desire to learn them should be refused; their English, arithmetic, and other studies absolutely necessary being at the same time not neglected."

Franklin urged that the students read histories of nature and of commerce, "of the invention of arts, rise of manufactures, progress of trade, change of its seats, with the reasons, causes, etc." This would lead to a curiosity about mechanics, "that art by which weak men perform such wonders, labour is saved, manufactures expedited, etc." "While they are reading natural history, might not a little gardening, planting, grafting, inoculating, etc., be taught and practised; and every now and then excursions made to the neighbouring plantations of the best farmers, their methods observed and reasoned upon for the information of youth? The improvement of agriculture being useful to all, and skill in it no disparagement to any."

And finally: "With the whole should be constantly inculcated and cultivated that benignity of mind which shows itself in searching for and seizing every opportunity to serve and oblige, and is the foundation of what is called good breeding."[10]

This was an exuberant programme for boys from eight to sixteen. In a day of rigid classical schools, Franklin took his stand with reformers like Milton and Locke and the most advanced contemporary Americans. His programme, if carried out, would have made all the students young philosophers. Every theorist designs his model school somewhat in his own image. But Franklin's aim was rather to give Philadelphia an academy than to settle in advance what should be taught there. He distributed his pamphlet "among the principal inhabitants gratis; and as soon as I could suppose their minds a little prepared by the perusal of it, I set on foot a subscription for opening and supporting an academy; it was to be paid in quotas yearly for five years; by so dividing it, I judged the subscription might be larger; and I believe it was so, amounting to no less, if I remember right, than five thousand pounds."[11] A board of twenty-four trustees was formed and on 13 November 1749 elected Franklin president, a position he held till 1756. They promptly hired a house, engaged masters, and opened the Academy.

"The scholars increasing fast, the house was soon found too small, and we were looking out for a piece of ground, properly situated, with intention to build, when Providence threw into our way a large house, already built, which with a few alterations might well serve our purpose. This was the building . . . erected by the hearers of Mr. Whitefield. . . . The enthusiasm which existed when the house was built had long since abated, and its trustees had not been able to procure fresh contributions for paying the ground-rent and discharging some other debts the building had occasioned, which embarrassed them greatly. Being now a member of both sets of trustees, that for the building and that for the Academy, I had a good opportunity of negotiating with both, and brought them finally to an agreement by which the trustees for the building were to cede it to those of the Academy, the latter undertaking to discharge the debt, to keep for ever open in the building a large hall for occasional preachers, according to the original intention, and maintain a free school for the instruction of poor children. . . . By dividing the great and lofty hall into stories, and different rooms above and below for the several schools, and purchasing some additional ground, the whole was soon made fit for our purpose and the scholars removed into the building. The care and trouble of agreeing with the workmen, purchasing materials, and superintending the work, fell upon me."[12]

Upon him, too, fell the work of developing the English school and of finding a director for it. His ideas at first went "no farther than to procure the means of a good English education . . . and I had good reason to know that this was a prevailing part of the motives for subscribing with most of the original benefactors."[13] But the richest and most learned among the subscribers insisted on a Latin school and assigned to the head of it the title of Rector of the Academy, with a salary of two hundred pounds as against one hundred for the English master. Franklin wrote out his detailed *Idea of the English School*,[14] in which he remembered how he had learned to write in Boston: "They may now, besides continuing to write letters, begin to write little essays in prose, and sometimes in verse, not to make them poets, but for this reason, that nothing acquaints a lad so speedily with variety of expression as the necessity of finding such words and phrases as will suit with the measure, sound, and rhyme of verse, and at the same time well express the sentiment. . . . Where the judgment is not ripe enough for forming new essays, let the sentiments of a *Spectator* be given, and required to be clothed in a scholar's own words."

During the summer of 1750 Franklin visited Samuel Johnson, then minister of the Episcopal church at Stratford, Connecticut, later first president of King's College (now Columbia). By letters after his return Franklin tried to persuade Johnson to undertake the English school, without success. The partisans of the English school had to see it neglected in spite of all Franklin and they could do. The Academy was opened 7 January 1751, and the charity school 16 September. In 1753 the Trustees of the Academy and Charitable School in the Province of Pennsylvania were incorporated by the proprietors, and two years later the corporate name became the Trustees of the College, Academy, and Charitable School. Franklin, as president till 1756, had a hand in all its affairs. But after William Smith became first Provost, in 1756, of the College, Academy, and Charitable School, Franklin, though he was a trustee for the rest of his life, had less influence, and between him and Smith, on political grounds, there came to be intense enmity.

The Pennsylvania Hospital was proposed not by Franklin but by Thomas Bond, the physician among the first ten members of the American Philosophical Society. Bond, born in Maryland, had come back from his studies in Paris to practise in the rising town of Philadelphia, and by 1750 had decided that the province should have a hospital for the sick and insane. "He was zealous and active in endeavouring to procure subscriptions for it, but, the proposal being a novelty in America and at first not well understood, he met with but small success. At length he came to me with the compliment that he found there was no such thing as carrying a public-spirited project through without my being concerned in it. 'For,' says he, 'I am often asked by those to whom I propose subscribing: Have you consulted Franklin about this business? And what does he think of it? And when I tell them that I have not (supposing it rather out of your line), they do not subscribe, but say they will consider of it.' I inquired into the nature and probable utility of his scheme, and, receiving from him a very satisfactory explanation, I not only subscribed to it myself but engaged heartily in the design of procuring subscriptions from others."[15]

Though Franklin as printer had already published medical books, and as general philosopher had discussed medical matters with various correspondents from Boston to Charleston, he was not an expert in medicine. But he was an expert in promotion. He got together a meeting of citizens to consider Bond's scheme. It had to be explained to a community which had never seen any medical care outside of private houses except in prisons or almshouses. Franklin wrote about the hospital in the *Gazette* for 8 and 15 August 1751. "The subscriptions afterwards were more free and generous; but, beginning to flag, I saw they would be insufficient without some assistance from the Assembly, and therefore proposed to petition for it, which was done." Franklin—who gave £25—had actually already drawn up the petition 23 January 1751 and seen it presented to the Assembly, of which he was clerk. "The country members did not at first relish the project; they objected that it could only be serviceable to the city, and therefore the citizens alone should be at the expense of it; and they doubted whether the citizens themselves generally approved of it." Franklin, clerk and lobbyist, persuaded the country members to vote £2000 to the hospital, on condition the subscribers raised an equal amount—which the legislators thought unlikely. Franklin drafted the conditional bill. "The members who had opposed the grant, and now conceived they might have the credit of being charitable without the expense, agreed to its passage; and then, in soliciting subscriptions among the people, we urged the conditional promise of the law as an additional motive to give, since every man's donation would be doubled; thus the clause worked both ways. The subscriptions accordingly soon exceeded the requisite sum, and we claimed and received the public gift, which enabled us to carry the design into execution. . . . I do not remember any of my political manœuvres the success of which gave me at the time more pleasure, or wherein, after thinking of it, I more easily excused myself for having made some use of cunning."[16]

Member from the first of the board of managers, Franklin on 28 May 1754 furnished them with the manuscript of *Some Account of the Pennsylvania Hospital* which he had written at their request, and which by their order was at once printed by Franklin and Hall. Its opening sentence was a whole history of their beginnings: "About the end of the year 1750 some persons who had frequent opportunities of observing the distress of such distempered poor as from time to time came to Philadelphia for the advice and assistance of the physicians and surgeons of that city; how difficult it was for them to procure suitable lodgings and other conveniences proper for their respective cases and how expensive the providing good and careful nurses and other attendants for want whereof many must suffer greatly, and some probably perish, that might otherwise have been restored to health and comfort and become useful to themselves, their families, and the public for many years after; and considering moreover that even the poor inhabitants of this city though they had homes were therein but badly accommodated in sickness and could not be so well and so easily taken care of in their separate habitations as they might be in one convenient house, under one inspection and in the hands of skilful practitioners; and several of the inhabitants of the prov-

ince who unhappily became disordered in their senses wandered
about to the terror of their neighbours, there being no place
(except the house of correction) in which they might be confined
and subjected to proper management for their recovery, and that
house was by no means fitted for such purposes; did charitably
consult together and confer with their friends and acquaintances
on the best means of relieving the distressed under those circumstances."

On 28 May 1755, when the corner stone of the "convenient and
handsome" new hospital building was laid in Eighth Street, between Spruce and Pine, it had an inscription written by Franklin
in the language of a philanthropic deism.

In the year of CHRIST

MDCCLV

GEORGE the second happily reigning
(For he sought the happiness of his people)

PHILADELPHIA flourishing

(For its inhabitants were publick spirited)
This Building,
By the bounty of the Government,
And of many private persons,
Was piously founded
For the relief of the sick and miserable;
May the God of Mercies
Bless the Undertaking.

On 30 June of that year he was elected president of the board, and
he presided at the first meeting held in the new building. (During
the next year he was absent eleven times from the managers' meetings, and twice late.) And when, as agent for Pennsylvania, he left
for England in 1757, he was requested by the trustees to use his
interest there to solicit donations whenever he had a chance.

It was a matter of course that when a group of Philadelphia
business men met 13 April 1752 to organize the first American fire
insurance company Franklin was one of the twelve directors
chosen, and that his name stood at the head of the list next to that
of Governor Hamilton. The *Gazette* published notices for the

Insurance Office, and Franklin and Hall printed the policies. Franklin insured two houses by policies 19 and 20 in the company, which is still in existence as the Philadelphia Contributionship for the Insurance of Houses from Loss by Fire. It was no less a matter of course that he had a principal share in sending the *Argo*, Captain Charles Swaine, from Philadelphia in 1753 on the first American voyage of Arctic exploration. Franklin had become interested in the Hudson Bay region from reading the controversial writings of Arthur Dobbs and Christopher Middleton in 1744, and had in his preface to *Poor Richard* for 1748 given some account of northern winters. "And now, my tender reader, thou that shudderest when the wind blows a little at N-West, and criest: ''Tis extrrrrrreme cohohold! 'Tis terrrrrrible cohold!' what dost thou think of removing to that delightful country? Or dost thou not rather choose to stay in Pennsylvania, thanking God that He has caused thy lines to fall in pleasant places?" But after the British expedition of 1746–47 Franklin took the lead in organizing another in Philadelphia, to find if possible the Northwest passage—and to win the reward of £20,000 which Parliament had offered for proof that such a passage existed. Neither Swaine's first voyage, March–November 1753, nor his second the next year met with success. But here were the beginnings of a long chapter in the history of American adventure.[17]

II

On 12 April 1750 Franklin wrote in more than usual detail to his mother, then eighty-three and within two years of her death. "We read your writing very easily," he assured her. "I never met with a word in your letters but what I could readily understand; for, though the hand is not always the best"—she had apologized for it—"the sense makes everything plain. My leg which you inquire after is now quite well. I shall keep those servants [slaves]; but the man not in my own house. I have hired him out to the man that takes care of my Dutch printing office, who agrees to keep him in victuals and clothes and pay me a dollar a week for his work. His wife, since that affair, behaves exceeding well; but we conclude to sell them both the first good opportunity, for we do not like Negro servants. . . .

"As to your grandchildren, Will is now nineteen years of age, a tall proper youth, and much of a beau. He acquired a habit of idleness on the expedition, but begins of late to apply himself to business, and I hope will become an industrious man. He imagined his father had got enough for him, but I have assured him that I intend to spend what little I have myself, if it please God that I live long enough; and, as he by no means wants sense, he can see by my going on that I am like to be as good as my word. Sally grows a fine girl, and is extremely industrious with her needle and delights in her book." Sarah Franklin was not yet seven. "She is of a most affectionate temper and perfectly dutiful and obliging to her parents, and to all. Perhaps I flatter myself too much, but I have hopes that she will prove an ingenious, sensible, notable, and worthy woman, like her Aunt Jenny. She goes now to the dancing school.

"For my own part, at present I pass my time agreeably enough. I enjoy, through mercy, a tolerable share of health. I read a great deal, ride a little, do a little business for myself, more for others, retire when I can, and go into company when I please; so the years roll round, and the last will come, when I would rather have it said 'He lived usefully' than 'He died rich.' "

Philosophers writing to their mothers, like other men, tell what they think their mothers would most like to hear, and Franklin told rather about his household than about the lightning rod he had just proposed or the academy he was helping to found or the public demands on his jealous time. There was an air of leisure about his letter, for he was then freer than he had recently been or was soon to be again. Retired from business, he had not yet seriously entered politics. That came with his election to the Assembly the year following.

His clerkship had been a long apprenticeship, since 15 October 1736. On that day, the day after the Assembly convened for its annual session, the members voted not to reappoint Joseph Growdon, their former clerk. Then, the record says: "A petition from Benjamin Franklin was presented to the House, and read, setting forth that he hath been informed this House have a disposition to change their clerk, and if so, he humbly offers his service to them in that station. Resolved, that Benjamin Franklin be appointed clerk to the House of Representatives for the current year. And he was called in and qualified accordingly."[18] The record hints what it does not say. Printer to the province, publisher of a newspaper, active in the affairs of the Library Company and the fire companies, Franklin had won the favour of men in the Assembly who had, before the session, already decided on his appointment. His petition was a form, and he was probably waiting outside the door of the legislative chamber. Perhaps Stephen Potts was with him, his friend of the Junto and his bookbinder, that day appointed door-keeper of the Assembly. Franklin at once began his duties, and for fifteen years wrote the record of provincial legislation in his strong, smooth prose.

The Assembly met annually in October and sat, as a rule, for irregular periods during October, January, May, and August, though special sessions might be called for special business. Franklin was only an observer, necessarily a close one. "Besides the pay for the immediate service as clerk, the place gave me a better opportunity of keeping up an interest among the members, which secured me the business of printing the votes, laws, paper money, and other occasional jobs for the public that, on the whole, were very profitable."[19] When a new member the next year brought forward another candidate for clerk, and spoke against Franklin, the printer dealt philosophically with the opposition. Having heard that the member "had in his library a certain very scarce and curious book, I wrote a note to him, expressing my desire of perusing that book, and requesting that he would do me the favour of lending it to me for a few days. He sent it immediately, and I returned it in about a week with another note, expressing strongly my sense of the favour. When we next met in the House, he spoke to me (which he had never done before), and with great civility; and he ever after manifested a readiness to serve me on all occasions, so that we became great friends and our friendship continued to his death. This is another instance of the truth of an old maxim I had learned, which says: 'He that has once done you a kindness will be more ready to do you another than he whom you yourself have obliged.' "[20]

Franklin wanted to keep his post because he got money by it, but he seems for ten years to have taken no traceable interest in the legislation he recorded. When debate was long and tiresome, he made magic squares to pass the time. On 4 July 1744 he wrote to Strahan: "We have seldom any news on our side of the globe that can be interesting to you or yours. All our affairs are *petit*. They have a miniature resemblance only, of the grand things of Europe. Our governments, parliaments, wars, treaties, expeditions, fashions, etc., though matters of great and serious consequence to us, can seem but trifles to you. Four days since, our naval force received a terrible blow. Fifty sail of the line destroyed would scarce be a greater loss to Britain than that to us—and yet 'twas only a 20-gun ship sunk, and about one hundred men drowned, just as she was going out to sea on a privateering voyage. . . . A treaty is now holding at Newtown, in Lancaster County, a place sixty miles west of this city, between the governments of Virginia, Maryland, and Pennsylvania on one side, and the united Five Nations of Indians on the other. I will send you an account of it when printed, as the method of doing business with those barbarians may perhaps afford you some amusement."[21]

Writing to his brother John in Boston in March 1745, Franklin was humorous about the New England expedition against the fortress of Louisbourg in Cape Breton. "Fortified towns are hard nuts to crack; and your teeth have not been accustomed to it. . . . But some seem to think forts are as easy taken as snuff. . . . You have a fast and prayer day for that purpose; in which I compute five hundred thousand petitions were offered up to the same effect in New England, which, added to the petitions of every family morning and evening, multiplied by the number of days since January 25th, make forty-five millions of prayers; which, set against the prayers of a few priests in the garrison, to the Virgin Mary, give a vast balance in your favour. If you do not succeed, I fear I shall have but an indifferent opinion of Presbyterian prayers, in such cases, as long as I live. Indeed, in attacking strong towns I should have more dependence on works than on faith."[22]

A year later and Franklin was grave about the war. There were enemy privateers too near for humour. William Franklin, whom his affectionate and indulgent father was bringing up as a gentleman, was a boyish ensign in another expedition against Canada. Franklin sided strongly with the governor in his policy of defence. Another year, and Franklin, despairing of legislation, had set about organizing the volunteer militia.

In the swift accumulation of offices which followed his first success, his duties as common councilman and alderman of Philadelphia made slight demands on him. "The office of justice of the peace I tried a little, by attending a few courts and sitting on the bench to hear causes, but, finding that more knowledge of the common law than I possessed was necessary to act in the situation with credit, I gradually withdrew from it, excusing myself by my being obliged to attend the higher duties of a legislator in the Assembly."[23] As clerk on 13 August 1751, Franklin himself may have entered in the minutes: "Benjamin Franklin being returned a representative to serve in Assembly for the city of Philadelphia, he was qualified and took his seat accordingly."[24] The next entry was the petition of William Franklin, then twenty, to be appointed to the vacant clerkship, to which he was promptly chosen and qualified. At once the elder Franklin was as much involved in Assembly business as if he had been member, not merely clerk, for the past fifteen years.

That same day he was put on a committee to draft a bill dealing with the exclusion of criminals from the province. It was a matter on which he had already written in the *Gazette* for 9 May.[25] As Americanus, he aimed a bitter arrow at the British government, which insisted on exporting felons to the colonies, no matter how the colonies protested. It was, the mother country said, for the "improvement and well peopling" of America. Such parental concern, Americanus thought, called for some kind of filial acknowledgment, and at least the offer of repayment. Americanus had a plan. "In some of the uninhabited parts of these provinces there are numbers of the venomous reptiles we call rattle-snakes: felons-convict from the beginning of the world. These, whenever we meet with them, we put to death, by virtue of an old law: Thou shalt bruise his head. But as this is a sanguinary law, and may seem too cruel; and as, however mischievous those creatures are with us, they may possibly change their natures if they were to change the climate; I would humbly propose that this general sentence of death be changed for transportation. In the spring of the year, when they first creep out of their holes, they are feeble, heavy, slow, and easily taken; and if a small bounty were allowed per head, some thousands might be collected annually and transported to Britain. There I would propose to have them carefully distributed in St. James's Park, in the Spring Gardens and other places of pleasure about London; in the gardens of all the nobility and gentry throughout the nation; but particularly in the gardens of the prime ministers, the lords of trade, and members of Parliament, for to them we are most particularly obliged."

There might be some difficulties in the scheme, but no worse than went with the transporting of felons to America. "Let not private interests obstruct public utility. Our mother knows what is best for us. What is a little housebreaking, shoplifting, or highway robbing; what is a son now and then corrupted and hanged, a daughter debauched and poxed, a wife stabbed or a husband's throat cut, or a child's brains beat out with an axe, compared with this improvement and well peopling of the colonies?" Whatever damage the rattle-snakes might do might be offset by their good example. "May not the honest, rough British gentry, by a familiarity with these reptiles, learn to creep and to insinuate and to slaver and to wriggle into place (and perhaps to poison such as stand in their way): qualities of no small advantage to courtiers?" This would be a just trade as well as gratitude for a favour. "Rattlesnakes seem the most suitable returns for the human serpents sent to us by our mother country. In this, however, as in every other branch of trade, she will have the advantage of us. She will reap equal benefits without equal risk of the inconveniences and dangers. For the rattle-snake gives warning before he attempts his mischief; which the convict does not." (With this ominous image, Franklin sounded his own earliest warning to the British government of the colonies.)

Now as a member of the Assembly he helped draft the bill repealing provincial legislation which had imposed a duty upon felons sent to Pennsylvania. His first session dealt with other matters which had concerned him as a private citizen. The Speaker reported that the subscriptions to the hospital had reached £2000, and that he had signed an order for a like amount due from the

Assembly. The bill to regulate the city watch, proposed by Franklin, came before the House. On his second day as member, he was sent, with the influential Quaker merchant Israel Pemberton, to carry a message to the governor, and two days later Franklin was assigned to the committee to frame an answer to the governor's message. Within a year he served on both the most honourable and the most laborious committees: to wait upon the governor and to see that the Great Seal was affixed to the laws; to revise the minutes before they were printed, to review the whole history and present need of paper money, and to search the records of the Assembly to find out what share of the Indian expenses had been borne by the province and what by the proprietors. Franklin was on the Committee of Aggrievances and the Committee of Correspondence; on committees to study official fees, to consider the petition of the bakers as to the price of bread, to regulate the number of dogs in the city, and to recommend where it would be best to undertake the first bridge across the Schuylkill.

Many and minute as Franklin's legislative interests were during this and the next five years, there were only three general issues: the Indians, paper currency, and the taxation of the proprietary lands. On the first of these issues the Assembly and the governor, representing the proprietors, were already at deadlock. It was the current phase of an old conflict. Pennsylvania had the most famous of all the colonial constitutions, and on the whole the best. William Penn and the original settlers had thought of the colony as a "holy experiment," an asylum for Quakers and other persecuted men. The heirs of Penn, no longer Quakers, thought of their province as a source of revenue. Belated feudal lords of the domain, they received large sums from leases and quit-rents, and on their unsold land had the benefit of steadily rising prices. The Pennsylvanians had not the temper of feudal vassals. Realizing—to put the matter in its simplest terms—that they by their risks and labours were making the proprietors rich and richer, they asked the proprietors to contribute to the cost of the provincial government, particularly in its dealings with the Indians. The proprietors took the position that they were no more obliged to help meet the public charges than any royal governor of any other colony would be. The Pennsylvanians held that the Penns were not like royal governors, but were owners and therefore beneficiaries of the province. The Penns believed that they were legally in the right. The Pennsylvanians were sure that they had reason and justice in their favour.

What made the conflict sharp and tense in 1751, the year Franklin became a member of the Assembly, was the new restlessness of the Indians beyond the Alleghenies, in the region which is now western Pennsylvania and eastern Ohio. Because the claims of Pennsylvania and Virginia to this territory had not yet been adjusted, few settlers had moved into it, but traders were active there, and the Indians were troubled. They knew they were no longer dealing with men like William Penn, scrupulous and generous. The friendly Six Nations (to the earlier Five the Tuscarora had been added), who were a kind of buffer confederacy between the English and the French, felt themselves invaded from both sides. The English were crossing the mountains. The French were laying claim to the Ohio valley and planning, or soon to plan, a line of forts from Niagara to the junction of the Allegheny and the Monongahela. Since the French and English were temporarily at peace, neither did more than try to win the Indians by presents, which were degenerating into bribes. Almost the whole of Pennsylvania's Indian expenses went to the cost of these gifts and the accompanying ceremonies. It was this which the Assembly had in mind when, ten days after Franklin took his seat, his committee wrote to the proprietors, over the head of the governor, asking them to accept as rightly theirs a stated share, year by year, of the Indian expenses. The proprietors refused, after delaying their answer till the early part of 1753.

In October 1751 Franklin's committee brought in, and the Assembly passed, a bill for the issue of £40,000 of paper money, reduced to £20,000 when the governor returned it without his assent. The smaller amount was no more satisfactory to him than the larger. Parliament, he pointed out, was opposed to the increase of paper currency in the northern colonies, though no binding act had been passed. For two years messages went back and forth between Assembly and governor, without result. Franklin was in prophetic opposition to both proprietors and Parliament.

As quickly as he had become first among electricians, Franklin became first among Pennsylvania politicians. He appears to have spoken seldom, for he thought he spoke badly. He worked, rather, behind the scenes, shaping opinions, harmonizing differences, and at last summing up in incomparable and irresistible statements. By the end of 1753 he was far on his way to being head of the Assembly, sourly regarded by the Penns as a tribune of the people. His recognition abroad, that year, helped his prestige at home. The Royal Society's medal, the honorary degrees from Harvard and Yale, and his appointment as Deputy Postmaster-General for all the colonies could not be overlooked. And he had helped negotiate his first treaty.

III

"The year following [1752]," he inaccurately says in his *Autobiography*, "a treaty being to be held with the Indians at Carlisle, the governor sent a message to the House, proposing that they should nominate some of their members, to be joined with some members of council, as commissioners for that purpose. The House named the Speaker (Mr. Norris) and myself; and, being commissioned, we went to Carlisle and met the Indians accordingly."[26] Again Franklin had forgotten details, including the date, and his biographers, without curiosity as to the original records, have neglected one of the most graphic episodes of his Philadelphia years.

On 20 September 1753 Governor Hamilton of Pennsylvania received a letter from William Fairfax of Virginia, written at Winchester. He had been in conference, he said, with certain chiefs of the Six Nations and their allies, who were returning to their troubled country and would be glad, on their journey, to meet the governor at Carlisle on or before the 22nd. As the Assembly was not then in session, Hamilton called together the members who were in town. There were six of them, including the Speaker and Franklin. Since Governor Dinwiddie of Virginia had not met the Indians at Winchester, Hamilton chose not to go in person but to send commissioners instead. He chose Richard Peters, secretary of the Council, and Isaac Norris and Benjamin Franklin from the

Assembly. Governor, councillors, and assemblymen, meeting on the 21st, decided that the commissioners must take presents with them, to be bought out of a fund of £800 already voted by the Assembly and now at the disposal of the governor. Commissioned the next day, the three left on horseback, followed by wagons loaded with goods for the Indians. (The list of goods is not given, but they probably included, as at other times, blankets, coats, shoes, ruffled shirts, bolts of coloured cloth, guns, powder, lead, flints, knives—and rum.) Riding hard, the commissioners followed the Lancaster turnpike, crossed the Susquehanna either at Harris's Ferry, now Harrisburg, or at Wright's Ferry, now Columbia, and took the rough trail to Carlisle, settled two years before. They arrived the 26th. The Indians, later than they had expected to be, came the same day. Nearly a hundred of them, men, women, and children, were lodged in temporary cabins built outside the town.

The commissioners, who did not officially know what the Indians had come for, had been instructed only to renew, ratify, and confirm the league of amity already existing. But George Croghan of Carlisle, the principal Indian trader of Pennsylvania, and Andrew Montour, part Huron, part Seneca, and assistant interpreter for the province, had been at Winchester, and they assured the commissioners that the party from the Ohio country included "some of the most considerable persons" of the Six Nations, Delawares, Shawnee, Miami (then usually called Twightwees), and Wyandots. The commissioners met the Indians in a kind of preliminary council and bade them welcome through Montour and Conrad Weiser, Pennsylvania's chief interpreter. Business had to wait upon ceremony. The Delawares and the Miami had lost several warriors killed by the French and their Indians, and all the chiefs of the Wyandots had lately died. "It became necessary to condole their loss, and no business could be begun, agreeable to the Indian customs, till the condolences were passed; and as these could not be made with the usual ceremonies for want of the goods, which were not arrived, and it was uncertain when they would," the commissioners asked Scarouady, an Oneida chief who was spokesman for the Six Nations, whether the Indians would accept ceremonial belts and strings and "lists of the particular goods intended to be given, with assurances of their delivery as soon as they should come." The cautious Scarouady "frankly declared that the Indians could not proceed to business while the blood remained on their garments, and that the condolences could not be accepted unless the goods intended to cover the graves were actually spread on the ground before them."[27]

Messengers were sent out to hurry up the wagons, and the commissioners talked informally with Scarouady and the chiefs of the Delawares and the Shawnee. They learned that the Indians, alarmed by the advance of the French to the Ohio, had twice warned them not to come further. Then, after a council fire at Logstown (near Pittsburgh), the chief men of the tribes had divided into two parties, one to confer with Virginia and Pennsylvania, the other to carry to the French the third and final warning. If the party led by the Senecan Half King (Scruniyatha) were rebuffed, the Indians friendly to the English must make war on the French. The commissioners understood the savage diplomats. They wanted presents to keep them friendly. Croghan told the commissioners what Virginia had given. The Pennsylvanians decided the goods in the wagons were not enough, and bought more in Carlisle "at the Philadelphia price." On 1 October word came that the Half King's warning had had no effect, and the wagons arrived before daylight. The ceremony of condolences was set for eleven o'clock.

(Not Fenimore Cooper tells the story, but the Pennsylvania commissioners,[28] one of them Benjamin Franklin, who that same year printed, in one of Franklin and Hall's monumental folios, *A Treaty Held with the Ohio Indians at Carlisle in October, 1753.*)

Present at the ceremony were the three commissioners, twelve deputies from the Six Nations, three from the Delawares, fifteen from the Shawnee, three from the Miami, and the interpreters Weiser and Montour; also the members of the Assembly from Cumberland County, and magistrates, gentlemen, and freeholders of that frontier. The goods for the day's presents were already laid out on the ground. The commissioners produced their commission as evidence of their authority to treat. They announced that the Six Nations would join with them in the condolences, and that Scarouady would speak for all of them. "Here the commissioners gave a string of wampum." Scarouady spoke to the Miami and

Shawnee. "I and my brother Onas [William Penn, or after him any governor of Pennsylvania] join together to speak to you, as we know that your seats at home are bloody. We wipe away the blood and set your seats in order at your council fire, that you may sit and consult again in peace and comfort as formerly, that you may hold the ancient union and strengthen it, and continue your old friendly correspondence." Here a string was given. Again Scarouady: "Brethren Twightwees and Shawonese: We suppose that the blood is now washed off. We jointly with our brother Onas dig a grave for your warriors killed in your country, and we bury their bones decently, wrapping them up in these blankets, and with these we cover their graves." Here goods were given. "Brethren Twightwees and Shawonese: I and my brother Onas jointly condole with the chiefs of your towns, your women, and children, for the loss you have sustained. We wipe your tears from your eyes that you may see the sun, and that everything may become pleasant and clear to your sight, and we desire you would mourn no more." Here a belt was given. Then the whole ceremony was repeated, spoken now to the Delawares and Wyandots.

The council of the second day was again ceremonial. The commissioners gave the Indians a belt of wampum on which were six figures representing the Six Nations, the Delawares, the Shawnee, the Wyandots, the Miami, and Pennsylvania, in token of the absolute unity which they agreed to keep for ever. The Philadelphians tactfully urged dispatch. The Indians took their time. On the third day Scarouady said what the Indians really meant. Let the English remain on their own side of the mountains. Croghan would represent the Indians, and the Pennsylvanians through their own agent could deal with him. If the French were troubled by the number of Pennsylvania traders in the neutral territory, so were the Indians. They wanted only three trading posts, as had been agreed. The goods the English sold were too dear. Honest and sober traders might be able to sell their goods cheaper, and might bring valuable goods like powder and lead, not flour and rum. Scarouady spoke strongly against the sale of rum, which ruined the Indians. On the fourth and last day the commissioners agreed in principle to the three trading posts, but said they must consult their government. For the sake of the Indians, the goods would not all be delivered now, but·put in charge of Croghan till it was sure they were safe. That evening the Indians, given the rum they had been refused while the treaty was going on, all got drunk.

Neither an anthropologist nor a romancer, Franklin looked upon the Indians always with the humane curiosity and natural respect which he felt for any people whose way of life was different from his own. He admired the Iroquois confederation, and plainly had it in mind in his earliest discussion of the need of union among the colonies. "It would be a strange thing if Six Nations of ignorant savages should be capable of forming a scheme for such an union, and be able to execute it in such a manner as that it has subsisted ages and appears indissoluble; and yet that a like union should be impracticable for ten or a dozen English colonies, to whom it is more necessary and must be more advantageous, and who cannot be supposed to want an equal understanding of their interests."[29] Franklin seems not to have expected that the Indians would become civilized. He took a philosophical pleasure in their preference for the savage state. Nor did he foresee the conflict of cultures which would at last destroy even the powerful Six Nations. Always, so far as his imagination saw, there would be a frontier, with a forest for forest men. The Indians' worst enemy was alcohol, which in excess Franklin thought an enemy to anybody. As between the Indians and the white settlers, he sympathized with the Indians. It was not they who broke treaties or drove greedy bargains or presumed on superior strength. He believed with William Penn that civilized justice and savage justice were much the same and could live side by side in peace. What was needed was equitable agreements between the two races, and honest trading.

This backwoods mission of 1753 was the beginning of Franklin's career in diplomacy.

Intercolonial

FRANKLIN said in his *Autobiography* that his rule as to public office was "never ask, never refuse, nor ever resign."[1] But he had petitioned, at least in form, for his clerkship in the Assembly, and he unquestionably asked for the office of Deputy Postmaster-General. On 21 May 1751, the month he proposed trading American rattle-snakes for British convicts, he wrote to Peter Collinson in London, who might have influence with the postal authorities.[2] Elliot Benger of Virginia, then in charge of the colonial post office, was thought to be near death (he died that same year), and William Allen, chief justice of Pennsylvania, was recommending Franklin as his successor. "I am quite a stranger," Franklin said, "to the manner of managing these applications." He left it in the hands of Collinson and Allen's London correspondent, who was authorized to spend as much as £300 for any needed perquisites, fees, and charges. "However, the less it costs the better, as 'tis for life only, which is a very uncertain tenure." "The place has been commonly reputed worth about £150 a year, but would otherwise be very suitable to me, particularly as it would enable me to execute a scheme long since formed . . . which I hope would soon produce something agreeable to you and all lovers of useful knowledge, for I have now a large acquaintance among ingenious men in America. I need not tell you that Philadelphia, being the centre of the continent colonies and having constant communication with the West India islands, is by much a fitter place for the situation of a general post office than Virginia, and that it would be some reputation to our province to have it established here. I would only add that, as I have a respect for Mr. Benger, I should be glad the application were so managed as not to give him any offence if he should recover."

The scheme long since formed was the American Philosophical Society which Franklin had proposed ten years before. Although it had not been as active as he wished, and his electrical and political interests had somewhat diverted him from general philosophy, he had always cherished the idea of the Society, his larger Junto. He wanted to bring and keep more and more ingenious men in touch with one another, not only in Philadelphia but throughout the colonies. One of the difficulties was the slow, expensive, and undependable postal system. That would have to be developed, and the secretary of the Society thought he could do it. As Philadelphia was the focus of the Society, so might it be of the post office in America. Franklin was a citizen of Philadelphia and desired to make the city important in every way possible. As to himself, he could not expect much profit, and for four years he did hard work without it. But there was genuine prestige in being an officer of the Crown, and this post would give him a better opportunity than any other to extend his acquaintance with the whole American world.

In the month of his letter to Collinson, Franklin bought a house from the Read family in Market Street, "a little above the prison," and the following January he moved his post office to it from the printing-house of Franklin and Hall.³ At the Philadelphia office he had the help of his wife and later a clerk. He himself was, under Benger, controller of the colonial posts, auditing the accounts of the local postmasters and carrying out intercolonial plans. Benger died, and Franklin, as controller, in the summer of 1753 spent ten weeks in New England chiefly on postal affairs. Then on 10 August the heads of the British post office appointed Franklin and William Hunter, postmaster of Williamsburg and publisher of the *Virginia Gazette*, to be joint "Deputy Postmaster and Manager of all His Majesty's Provinces and Dominions on the Continent of North America," at a salary of £600 a year between them, "to be paid out of the money arising from the postage of letters"— that is, if there should be any money left above expenses. The general post office had been in Virginia since 1730. Williamsburg for the southern colonies and Philadelphia for the northern divided the postal system between them. The two men worked in harmony, and Franklin thought Hunter an able man. But Hunter was handicapped by ill health, and the principal responsibility fell on Franklin.

The news of Franklin's appointment can hardly have reached him before his return from Carlisle. He promptly made his son postmaster of Philadelphia, and the next year promoted him to be controller. William Franklin gave up the postmastership to Joseph Read, Deborah Franklin's relative, who later yielded it to Peter Franklin, brought from Boston. John Franklin remained in Boston, postmaster there from 1754, and after his death in January 1756 was succeeded by his widow, so far as is known the first woman to hold a public office in America. For several months after October 1753 Benjamin Franklin was much occupied with the Pennsylvania Assembly and the Albany Congress and could take only the first steps in postal matters. But he found time to work out, apparently at once, a full, explicit, and yet simple system of accounting, had forms and instructions printed, and sent them to all the local postmasters. He had, as controller, lately improved the service in Philadelphia. Within a year he had improved it between Philadelphia and the towns to the north. Philadelphia and New York were to have, from March to October, three mails a week each way instead of one, and two in any but the worst weather. A letter could go to Boston and bring an answer to Philadelphia in three weeks. During 1754 Franklin visited all the post offices in the northern colonies, and during 1755–56 those in Maryland and Virginia, becoming acquainted with the postmasters, systematizing their accounts, studying their special difficulties, surveying and selecting roads, fords, ferries. By the time he sailed for England with his son in 1757, still holding his Crown office but leaving his partner James Parker in New York as controller, Franklin had completely reorganized the colonial post office. The receipts for the fourth year were greater than for the first three put together. After four years more, with Parker still controller, Franklin and Hunter in 1761 could pay back to themselves what they had advanced, and could remit to the post office in London the first money that the American department had ever earned.

Most of the changes which Franklin introduced were founded on his own experience in Philadelphia. He had been given Bradford's place because Bradford was irregular in his accounts. Franklin, careful about accounting, required that all the postmasters be careful too, and furnished them with a uniform system. He had long printed in the *Gazette* the names of persons who had letters waiting for them, and he now introduced this practice in other towns which had newspapers. In Philadelphia he established, in 1753, what was called the penny post. Letters which were not called for on the day the post arrived were sent the next day by the penny postman—there was only one—for an extra fee. Franklin encouraged the same local delivery in other large towns. Letters advertised in newspapers and not claimed were after three months forwarded to the central office in Philadelphia. This was the beginning of the Dead Letter Office in America. Though Franklin as postmaster at Philadelphia had used his riders to distribute his newspaper free, he thought the arrangement monopolistic, and abolished it. All newspapers might be sent by mail, and all of them must pay postage. What was most valuable among his reforms, he made the postmasters and riders from Maine to South Carolina aware of the unity and vitality of the postal service, and by his improvements in the speed and safety of the mails led them to be increasingly used. No one man before him had ever done so much to draw the scattered colonies together.

I I

Franklin's workman-like improvements of the post office were characteristic outward acts of his powerful imagination. To realize how much the colonies, remote and self-centred, had in common, he had to be a philosopher, imaginatively conceiving the large design into which the raw facts fitted. To plan to unite them, with all their provincial separatisms, into a common enterprise, he had to be a statesman. But in being philosopher and statesman he did not cease to be Franklin, instinctively working with familiar tools. In Europe the social contract might be a more or less metaphysical theory. In America it, or something like it, was ordinary practice. Associations of men everywhere, from the first settlement, had regularly come together to do what was beyond the strength or capacity of individuals. Mutual help was taken for granted. The members of the Junto were young tradesmen in a town, but in forming their club they were not essentially different from pioneers building a stockade for their general defence, or farmers assembling to raise the frame of a house for one of them. Nor was the American Philosophical Society different, except that its scale was more than local. It was a club of like-minded men working together for mutual help and public benefit. But Franklin's views had grown steadily larger during the fifteen years between the Junto and the Society, and when, in 1751, he looked toward the office of Deputy Postmaster-General, they were larger still. A month before he wrote to Collinson he had already outlined his first tentative plan for a union of the colonies.

It was a specific plan for defence against the Indians, whose latest threat was not to any single colony but to all the English alike. The matter came up in the way of business. Archibald Kennedy, a member of the governor's council in New York, had written a pamphlet, *The Importance of Gaining and Preserving the Friendship of the Indians to the British Interest Considered,* and had given it to James Parker to be printed. Parker sent the manuscript to his Philadelphia partner for an opinion. Franklin, replying on 20 March 1751 and heartily approving, offered further suggestions. "The union of the colonies, however necessary, I apprehend is not to be brought about by the means that have hitherto been used for that purpose. A governor of one colony, who happens from some circumstance in his own government to see the necessity of such an union, writes his sentiments of the matter to the other governors, and desires them to recommend it to their respective assemblies. They accordingly lay the letters before those assemblies and perhaps recommend the proposal in general words. But governors are often on ill terms with their assemblies, and seldom are the men that have the most influence among them. And perhaps some governors, though they openly recommend the scheme, may privately throw cold water on it, as thinking additional public charges will make their people less able or less willing to give to them. Or perhaps they do not clearly see the necessity of it, and therefore do not very earnestly press the consideration of it; and no one being present that has the affair at heart, to back it, to answer and remove objections, etc., 'tis easily dropped, and nothing is done. . . .

"Now if you were to pick out half a dozen men of good understanding and address, and furnish them with a reasonable scheme and proper instructions, and send them in the nature of ambassadors to the other colonies, where they might apply particularly to all the leading men and by proper management get them to engage in promoting the scheme; where, by being present, they would have the opportunity of pressing the affair both in public and private, obviating difficulties as they arise, answering objections as soon as they are made, before they spread and gather strength in the minds of the people, etc., etc.; I imagine such an union might thereby be made and established. For reasonable, sensible men can always make a reasonable scheme appear such to other reasonable men, if they take pains and have time and opportunity for it; unless from some circumstances their honesty and good intentions are suspected. A voluntary union entered into by the colonies themselves, I think, would be preferable to one imposed by Parliament; for it would be perhaps not much more difficult to procure, and more easy to alter and improve as circumstances should require and experience direct."[4]

As to the details of his scheme, Franklin proposed an intercolonial council of Indian affairs and defence, made up of representatives from all the colonies, with a governor appointed by the Crown. The money needed might best be raised, he thought, by an excise on strong liquors, and the amount paid by each colony might determine the number of its representatives. The council would decide what was to be done, and their governor, acting for the Crown, would put it into execution. To avoid jealousy among the colonies, the council might meet in turn in the various capitals. This would also serve to make the members familiar with other colonies besides their own. The details are less important than Franklin's central idea that the union should originate with the colonies themselves and should carry out their plans with their money, after they had reasonably agreed.

There was more than political shrewdness in his idea. Back of it lay a large, new conception of the whole of American life. That same year, in his *Observations concerning the Increase of Mankind, Peopling of Countries, etc.,*[5] Franklin laid down first principles which were to colour much of his later social thought and action. Though he did not publish it till 1755, he sent it to other members of the American Philosophical Society, at least Bartram and Colden, for their opinions. He had, being Franklin, an immediate occasion: the Parliamentary act of 1750 restricting, on the complaint of British iron-masters, the manufacture of iron in Pennsylvania. But he wrote like a philosopher, looking behind politics to find something fundamental in the national behaviour. He studied it in the people themselves, in the basic matter of the increase of population.

America was no more like Europe in this respect, he said, than the country was like cities. Europe, like cities, was crowded with men who because of the difficulty of making a living might put off marriage or not marry at all, and so kept the population down. In America there was room. "So vast is the territory . . . that it will require many ages to settle it fully. . . . No man continues long a labourer for others, but gets a plantation of his own. No man continues long a journeyman to a trade, but goes among these new settlers and sets up for himself." Marriages were more common in America, and earlier, than in Europe, and the population doubled, he thought, and would go on doubling every twenty years. Labour could not, in the circumstances, become cheap, and England need not fear the competition of her colonies in "trades that depend on labour, manufactures, etc." Whatever the British might think, slave labour was expensive: "reckon . . . the interest on the first purchase of a slave, the insurance or risk on his life, his clothing and diet, expenses in his sickness and loss of time, loss by his neglect of business (neglect is natural to the man who is not to be benefited by his own care or diligence), expense of a driver to keep him at work, and his pilfering from time to time (almost every slave being by nature a thief)." Americans bought slaves only because they might be owned and used "as long as a man pleases, or has occasion for their labour; while hired men are continually leaving their masters." But America with its growing population was a growing market for manufactures, whether British or American. "Therefore Britain should not too much restrain manufactures in her colonies. A wise and good mother will not do it. To distress is to weaken, and weakening the children weakens the whole family."

Almost half a century before Malthus, Franklin saw that the means of subsistence determined the increase of population, through its effect on the ease or difficulty of marriage. "There is, in short, no bound to the prolific nature of plants or animals but what is made by their crowding and interfering with each other's means of subsistence. Was the face of the earth vacant of other plants, it might be gradually sowed and overspread with one kind only; as, for instance, with fennel. And were it empty of other inhabitants, it might in a few ages be replenished from one nation only; as, for instance, with Englishmen. Thus there are supposed to be now upwards of one million English souls in North America (though 'tis thought scarce 80,000 have been brought over sea), and yet perhaps there is not one fewer in Britain, but rather many more, on account of the employment the colonies afford to manufacturers at home. This million, doubling suppose but once in twenty-five years, will in another century be more than the people of England, and the greatest number of Englishmen will be on this side the water. What an accession of power to the British Empire by sea as well as land! What increase of trade and navigation! What numbers of ships and seamen! . . . How important an affair then to Britain is the present treaty for settling the bounds between her colonies and the French, and how careful should she be to secure room enough, since on the room depends so much the increase of her people."

Here is the earliest clear statement of the function of the American frontier. By giving room enough, Franklin thought, it would furnish opportunity for many ages of unchecked human increase and prosperity. Thanks to it, life in America had an enormous future—the life of the whole country, not merely of this or that colony. It could not be regulated from London, because static England would not understand dynamic America. Americans who knew their own natures must make their own rules. But Franklin had still no notion of American independence except for local rights and responsibilities within the frame of empire. The American frontier was the British frontier, and rising America a part of widening Britain.

In the midst of his imaginative imperialism he had a touch of Anglo-Saxon insularity, and in the first edition of his *Increase of Mankind*—though not the later ones—he questioned the admission of any but Englishmen to the colonies. "Why should the Palatine boors be suffered to swarm into our settlements and, by herding together, establish their language and manners to the exclusion of ours? Why should Pennsylvania, founded by the English, become a colony of aliens, who will shortly be so numerous as to Germanize us, instead of our Anglifying them?" Franklin was at the time resentful of the Pennsylvania Germans, who were politically backward and intractable, economically below English standards. But he ended his remarks, though with bad ethnology, yet with better temper. "The number of purely white people in the world is proportionably very small. All Africa is black or tawny; Asia chiefly tawny; America (exclusive of the newcomers) wholly so. And in Europe the Spaniards, Italians, French, Russians, and Swedes are generally of what we call a swarthy complexion; as are the Germans also, the Saxons only excepted, who with the English make the principal body of white people on the face of the earth. I could wish their numbers were increased. And while we are, as I may call it, scouring our planet by clearing America of woods and so making this side of our globe reflect a brighter light to the eyes of inhabitants in Mars or Venus, why should we in the sight of superior beings darken its people? Why increase the sons of Africa by planting them in America, where we have so fair an opportunity, by excluding all blacks and tawnys, of increasing the lovely red and white? But perhaps I am partial to the complexion of my country, for such kind of partiality is natural to mankind."[6] (It should be noted that Franklin in 1755 was a trustee, with some of the most eminent citizens of Pennsylvania, of a charitable scheme to provide relief and instruction for poor German settlers.)

In any case, the English colonies must know where the boundary lay between them and the French. Both nations assumed that the English had a right to the Atlantic seaboard east of the Alleghenies, and the French to Canada and Louisiana. But the domain of the

Six Nations, reaching vaguely from the mountains to the Mississippi, had no boundaries, and upon it French and English alike
steadily encroached, trading with the Indians for furs. The English, perhaps more numerous, went as individuals, little controlled
by their governments. The French, with their official expedition to
the Ohio to build forts in 1753, seemed to challenge the English
as well as the Six Nations. Virginia was first to act on the appeal the
Indian chiefs brought to Winchester. Governor Dinwiddie sent
George Washington, then twenty-one, with an ultimatum to the
French commandant in November, the month after Franklin met
the Indians at Carlisle. Washington was no more successful with
the French than the Half King had been, and the Indians at the
council fire at Logstown, seeing that the French in the Ohio region
were stronger than the English, were wary about pledges to their
old allies. Dinwiddie dispatched a few men to build an English
fort at the forks of the Ohio, and commissioned Washington to go
with reinforcements as soon as the Virginia militia could be ready.
Word was sent to Governor Hamilton that the Pennsylvania forces
might join the Virginians on the Potomac early in March 1754.

The Pennsylvania Assembly, meeting in February 1754, would
not be hurried. As they understood the letter of instruction to the
governor which had come from the British secretary of state, they
were asked to defend the colony from invasion by the subjects of
any foreign power, but were to make use of armed force only
within English territory. They thought it important to find out
whether the French forts were within it. For the present, the
Assembly chose not to join too quickly with Virginia in what
might turn out to be aggressive action. They believed that Pennsylvania must take some blame for its conduct in the Indian trade,
"carried on (some few excepted) by the vilest of our own inhabitants and convicts imported by Great Britain and Ireland."[7] As
matters stood, the Assembly refused to vote money "for the king's
use"—as the Quakers put it—till after word had come in May that
the Virginia fort was in the hands of the French. Then, though
£10,000 was voted, there was a conflict between the Assembly and
the governor as to the terms on which it was to be raised. The
governor said he was bound by the will of Parliament; the Assembly believed he was bound by the supposed interest of the pro-

prietors. Claiming the sole right to decide on the amounts and terms of money bills, the Assembly adjourned without action. But they agreed with the governor that commissioners should be sent to Albany to join with commissioners from other colonies in a new treaty with the Six Nations. John Penn, a grandson of William Penn, and Richard Peters were chosen from the council, Isaac Norris and Franklin from the Assembly. Their commissions were dated 30 May, and on 17 June they arrived in Albany, where they lodged in the house of James Stevenson.

The conference had been called by the Board of Trade. Presents were to be given to the Six Nations from the king, and Governor De Lancey of New York was to be in charge of the ceremony of "burying the hatchet and renewing the covenant chain." Since other colonies were concerned, New Hampshire, Massachusetts, New Jersey, Pennsylvania, Maryland, and Virginia had been asked to take part in the treaty. Virginia was too much occupied, and New Jersey neglected the invitation. Rhode Island and Connecticut had chosen commissioners without being invited. In the six months since the summons had been received in America, there had been time to think of the possibility of a union of the colonies for security and defence. Nobody had thought more about it than Benjamin Franklin. In his *Gazette* of 9 May he published—and had probably drawn—what appears to be the first American cartoon. It was a rough picture of a joint snake in eight pieces, marked with the initials of New England, New York, New Jersey, Pennsylvania, Maryland, Virginia, North Carolina, South Carolina, and with the caption: "Join or Die."

In New York on the way to Albany Franklin talked with Kennedy and with James Alexander, member of the New York Council and of the American Philosophical Society, and wrote out for him and for Cadwallader Colden, to whom Alexander was to send it, the *Short Hints towards a Scheme for Uniting the Northern Colonies.*[8] Since 1751 Franklin had made few changes in his first scheme. The union was to be planned by the commissioners at Albany as representatives of their various assemblies, and established, not imposed, by act of Parliament. The governor-general was to be a military man and have his salary as well as his appointment from the Crown. Besides Indian affairs, Franklin now thought, the making and supporting of new settlements and the equipping of vessels to protect the coast might be in the hands of the union. But he seems not to have gone into minute detail, and he went to Albany with only the large outlines of his scheme in mind.

The conference was to have begun on 14 June. Some of the delegates were unavoidably late, and the Mohawks led by Hendrick (Tiyanoga) were deliberately so. On the 19th the commissioners met at the state house: five from New York including the governor, five from Massachusetts, four from New Hampshire, three from Connecticut, two from Rhode Island, two from Maryland, and the four from Pennsylvania. The members of the New York council met with them. The first day a committee was chosen to draft the speech which the governor was to make to the Indians. It was not finally agreed upon till the 27th, and not delivered till two days later. In the meantime the commissioners had other business. On the third day of the session they had a dispute over precedence among them, and decided that in their transactions the colonies should be named in their geographical order from north to south. On the 24th, while the governor was considering the speech that had been drawn up for him, the commissioners resolved that some kind of colonial union was necessary, and assigned a committee: Theodore Atkinson from New Hampshire, Thomas Hutchinson from Massachusetts, Stephen Hopkins from Rhode Island, William Pitkin from Connecticut, William Smith from New York, Benjamin Franklin from Pennsylvania, and Benjamin Tasker from Maryland. On the 28th the committee brought in what it called "short hints" for a plan, and copies were made by other commissioners. The next day the whole Congress adjourned to hear the governor's speech.

He offered the familiar condolences and ceremonial wampum, and particularly urged the Six Nations not to let themselves be dispersed and weakened but to "collect yourselves together and dwell in your national castles." The honours of the occasion went to the Mohawk sachem Hendrick, answering with bitter candour. "You have asked us the reason of our living in this dispersed manner. The reason is your neglecting us for these three years past." Here he took a stick and threw it over his head. "You have thus thrown us behind your backs and disregarded us; whereas the French are a subtile and vigilant people, ever using their utmost endeavours to seduce and bring our people over to them." The Six Nations, he said, had not sold their land to the French or given them leave to invade it. "The governor of Virginia and the governor of Canada are both quarrelling about lands they think belong to us; and such a quarrel as this may end in our destruction. They fight who shall have the land." Virginia and Pennsylvania also had invaded the territory of the Six Nations. Yet toward the French the English were slack and craven. "Look about your country and see. You have no fortifications about you. . . . 'Tis but a step from Canada hither, and the French may easily come and turn you out of doors. Brethren, you desired us to speak from the bottom of our hearts, and we shall do it. . . . Look at the French; they are men; they are fortifying everywhere. But, we are ashamed to say it, you are all like women, bare and open, without any fortifications."[9]

There were other speeches back and forth between the governor and the assembled Indians. John Penn for the Pennsylvania proprietors and Richard Peters for the council made a separate treaty, at their own lodgings, with the Six Nations. For a thousand pieces of eight paid down, and the promise of another thousand when the land should be settled, they bought a great tract west of the mountains which, not too accurately described, was meant to extend Pennsylvania to Lake Erie and the Ohio. The commissioners at large were displeased with the entertainment which the Pennsylvanians gave the Indians at the state house.[10] The general treaty was much the same as all the treaties before it. Though the Six Nations renewed their covenant with the English, nothing was decided between the colonists and the doomed aborigines, who were merely given presents to keep them peaceful in the face of extinction. While speeches were being made at Albany, Washington surrendered to the French at Fort Necessity, and the struggle of the English with the French for North America began.

Side by side with the treaty went on daily debates about the scheme of union. Such plans had been thought of before this, and Franklin was not the only commissioner who had brought one with him. But his was preferred, with some changes which he accepted, against his judgment, in order to carry his main point. On 9 July he was asked to prepare a draft of the Plan "as now concluded upon." That afternoon he was absent from the Congress, writing, but the next day his draft was read, adopted, and ordered transmitted to the assemblies, not only of the colonies represented by commissioners but also of New Jersey, Virginia, and the Carolinas.

Not one of them approved, because none of them, in the current state of colonial jealousy and separatism, was willing to yield so much power to a general council. Even the Pennsylvania Assembly, which managed to take it up when Franklin was not present, paid no attention to the Plan.[11] Without the agreement of the colonies, the matter never came before the royal government, which probably would not have approved it either. "The assemblies," Franklin wrote long afterward with some dramatic exaggeration, "did not adopt it, as they all thought there was too much prerogative in it; and in England it was judged to have too much of the democratic. . . . The different and contrary reasons of dislike to my plan makes me suspect that it was really the true medium; and I am still of opinion that it would have been happy for both sides of the water if it had been adopted. The colonies, so united, would have been sufficiently strong to have defended themselves; there would have been no need of troops from England; of course, the subsequent pretence for taxing America and the bloody contest it occasioned would have been avoided. But such mistakes are not new; history is full of the errors of states and princes. . . . Those who govern, having much business on their hands, do not generally like to take the trouble of considering and carrying into execution new projects. The best public measures are therefore seldom adopted from previous wisdom, but are forced by the occasion."[12]

Whatever Franklin's disappointment, he had made valuable friendships with influential men from other colonies, and had been first among them in a statesman-like design. Talking with them, thinking always of the colonies as a whole, he formed during 1754 his mature conception of the British Empire and its American colonies. They were to be one country with nothing but an ocean between them. The colonial territory, he thought, should be enlarged and consolidated. Soon after the Albany Congress he drew up a *Plan for Settling Two Western Colonies in North America*.[13] If the English were to increase, they must have room and subsistence, which were both to be found beyond the mountains. Let the French establish themselves there, and they would be a perpetual danger: "set the Indians on to harass our frontiers, kill and scalp our people, and drive in the advanced settlers"; and so, by cutting down subsistence for the English, "discourage our marriages and keep our people from increasing; thus (if the expression may be allowed) killing thousands of our children before they are born." The English must move into the disputed territory to protect what they already had. "A single old colony does not seem strong enough to extend itself otherwise than inch by inch." The two barrier colonies that Franklin planned would have to be settled by the older colonies acting in concert, as under the Albany scheme, or else by charter from England. One of them would have a port on Lake Erie, the other would lie along the lower Scioto: "there being for forty miles on each side of it, and quite up to its heads, a body of all rich land; the finest spot of its bigness in all North America, and has the particular advantage of sea coal in plenty (even above ground in two places) for fuel, when the woods are gone." There would be trade with the Indians, whose land would be bought from them, and shipping on the lakes, and peace and population and prosperity—all still within the British Empire.

But Americans must have a principal hand in governing themselves. Franklin, in New York and New England from September to the following January, talked at Boston during December with William Shirley, governor of Massachusetts, who had his own plan of union. Under it the colonial assemblies would have little power, and the money for defence would come from taxes laid on the colonies by Parliament. The objections which Franklin raised he wrote out in three letters to the governor[14] which, twenty years before the Revolution, had in them the essence of the whole Revolutionary argument.

"Excluding the people of the colonies from all share in the choice of the grand council would probably give extreme dissatisfaction, as well as taxing them by act of Parliament, where they have no representative. In matters of general concern to the people, and especially where burdens are to be laid upon them, it is of use to consider what they will be apt to think and say as well as what they ought to think." The colonists were loyal subjects of the king, Franklin believed, and willing to vote money for defence, but they thought they were better judges of how much they needed and could afford than "the Parliament of England at so great a distance." Parliament might be misinformed by the colonial governors and their councils, whom the colonists by no means always trusted. As to taxes, "it is supposed an undoubted right of Englishmen not to be taxed but by their own consent given through their representatives." So long as the colonies were not represented in Parliament, compelling them to pay money without their consent "would be rather like raising contributions in an enemy's country than taxing of Englishmen for their own public benefit." But Americans were not foreigners. "The British colonies bordering on the French are properly frontiers of the British Empire; and the frontiers of an empire are properly defended at the joint expense of the body of the people." Americans already paid many and heavy indirect taxes to Britain. The British acts restraining American trade with other countries and forbidding colonial manufactures kept prices high, for the benefit of British merchants, manufacturers, and people, who thus in effect paid their own taxes out of American pockets. "These kind of secondary taxes, however, we do not complain of, though we have no share in the laying or disposing of them; but to pay immediate heavy taxes, in the laying, appropriation, and disposition of which we have no part, and which perhaps we may know to be as unnecessary as grievous, must seem hard measure to Englishmen who cannot conceive that, by hazarding their lives and fortunes in subduing and settling new countries, extending the dominion and increasing the commerce of the mother nation, they have forfeited the native rights of Britons."

Even if the colonies were not allowed many representatives in Parliament, Franklin hoped there would be enough of them "to occasion those laws to be better and more impartially considered, and perhaps to overcome the interests of a petty corporation or of any particular set of artificers or traders in England"—like the iron-masters—"who heretofore seem, in some instances, to have been more regarded than all the colonies. . . . I should hope, too, that by such a union the people of Great Britain and the people of the colonies would learn to consider themselves as not belonging to a different community with different interests, but to one community with one interest; which I imagine would contribute to strengthen the whole and greatly lessen the danger of future separations."

With one of his simple, powerful illustrations Franklin summed up his argument for the unity of the Empire and the natural rights of the Americans. "Could the Goodwin Sands be laid dry by banks, and land equal to a large country thereby gained to England and presently filled with English inhabitants, would it be right to deprive such inhabitants of the common privileges enjoyed by other Englishmen: the right of vending their produce in the same ports, or of making their own shoes, because a merchant or shoemaker living on the old land might fancy it more to his advantage to trade or make shoes for them? Would this be right, even if the land were gained at the expense of the state? And would it not seem less right, if the charge and labour of gaining the additional territory to Britain had been borne by the settlers themselves? And would not the hardship appear yet greater if the people of the new country should be allowed no representatives in the Parliament enacting such impositions?

"Now I look on the colonies as so many counties gained to Great Britain, and more advantageous to it than if they had been gained out of the seas around its coasts and joined to its land. For, being in different climates, they afford greater variety of produce; and, being separated by the ocean, they increase much more its shipping and seamen. And since they are all included in the British Empire, which has only extended itself by their means; and the strength and wealth of the parts are the strength and wealth of the whole; what imports it to the general state whether a merchant, a smith, or a hatter grow rich in Old or New England? And if, through increase of people, two smiths are wanted for one employed before, why may not the new smith be allowed to live and thrive in the new country as well as the old one in the old? In fine, why should the countenance of a state be partially afforded to its people, unless it be most in favour of those who have most merit?

And if there be any difference, those who have most contributed to enlarge Britain's empire and commerce, increase her strength, her wealth, and the numbers of her people, at the risk of their own lives and private fortunes in new and strange countries, methinks ought rather to expect some preference."

III

From these large, clear speculations in Boston Franklin returned in January or early February 1755 to the angry politics of Philadelphia. Hamilton had been succeeded by Robert Hunter Morris, but the conflict between governor and Assembly remained the same. Morris, like Hamilton, was under bond to veto any legislation that might threaten the interests of the proprietors. When the Assembly voted £20,000 for the king's use in the war with the French and Indians, to be raised by striking paper money redeemable in ten years out of the excise, the governor amended the period to five years, in deference to a Parliamentary act which applied to New England but not to Pennsylvania. The proprietors thought it to their interest, the Assembly supposed, to stand well with the royal government from which they held their grant of the province, and to maintain the province's credit. But the Assembly saw nothing illegal in their money bill, and they believed they were better judges of their credit than the governor was. They alone, under their constitution, had the authority to say what money should be voted for public use. The governor, trying to amend the bill, was encroaching upon one of their most cherished rights. No matter what the emergency, they refused to surrender to him. Their constitution was not less important to them than their soil. If they were to protect the province they must keep it worth protecting. It was as much their duty to defend their liberties as to resist the French. Stubborn messages went back and forth, those from the Assembly written by Franklin.

Meanwhile the war got under way, after the British and French had each decided that the other had begun it. The British planned expeditions from New York and New England against Niagara, Crown Point, and Acadia, and in December 1754 shipped two regiments of British regulars to Virginia, to march beyond the mountains and recapture the stronghold at the forks of the Ohio which the French now called Fort Duquesne. The regulars landed in February at Hampton. The general in command, Edward Braddock of the Coldstream Guards, conferred at Alexandria in April with the governors of Massachusetts, New York, Pennsylvania, Maryland, and Virginia. This was as near to union as the colonies ever came before the Revolution, though the conference had little in common with the Albany Plan. The burden of supplying and transporting Braddock's army fell particularly on Virginia, Maryland, and Pennsylvania. The pacifist Quakers voted—or allowed to be voted—as much money for the king's use as the warlike Virginians. Since Governor Morris still objected to the Assembly's terms, they borrowed not only £5000 for Braddock but also £10,000 for the northern expeditions. (Josiah Quincy came from Boston to arrange for the money to be used in the north, and he owed his success, he thought, to Franklin, once a Bostonian.) And while Virginia furnished Braddock the most promising young soldier in America, Pennsylvania furnished America's most farsighted statesman, most eminent scientist, most gifted writer—to find wagons for the march.

Ostensibly Franklin went as Postmaster-General, to arrange with Braddock the best method of communicating with the governors with whom he would constantly have to deal. This special postal service was to be paid for by the Pennsylvania Assembly, which had heard that Braddock had a violent prejudice against Quakers on account of their principles; it turned out that he was sure the Pennsylvanians were selling provisions to the French. Since Braddock was commander-in-chief of all the forces raised or to be raised in America, Pennsylvania could not prudently risk his disfavour.

"My son accompanied me on this journey. We found the general at Frederictown [Frederick, Maryland], waiting impatiently for the return of those he had sent through the back parts of Maryland and Virginia to collect wagons. I stayed with him several days, dined with him daily, and had full opportunity of removing all his prejudices, by the information of what the Assembly had before his arrival actually done, and were still willing to do, to facilitate his operations." But Franklin, though he might remove Braddock's prejudices against Pennsylvania, could not touch his deeper bias as a professional British soldier of a rigid school. "In conversation with him one day, he was giving me some account of his intended progress. 'After taking Fort Duquesne,' says he, 'I am to proceed to Niagara; and, having taken that, to Frontenac, if the season will allow time; and I suppose it will, for Duquesne can hardly detain me above three or four days; and then I see nothing that can obstruct my march to Niagara.' Having before revolved in my mind the long line his army must make in their march by a very narrow road, to be cut for them through the woods and bushes, and also what I had read of a former defeat of fifteen hundred French who invaded the Iroquois country, I had conceived some doubts and some fears for the event of the campaign. But I ventured only to say: 'To be sure, sir, if you arrive well before Duquesne, with these fine troops, so well provided with artillery, that place, not yet completely fortified and as we hear with no very strong garrison, can probably make but a short resistance. The only danger I apprehend of obstruction to your march is from ambuscades of Indians, who, by constant practice, are dexterous in laying and executing them; and the slender line, near four miles long, which your army must make, may expose it to be attacked by surprise in its flanks, and to be cut like a thread into several pieces, which, from their distance, cannot come up in time to support each other.' He smiled at my ignorance and replied: 'These savages may, indeed, be a formidable enemy to your raw American militia, but upon the king's regular and disciplined troops, sir, it is impossible they should make any impression.' I was conscious of an impropriety in my disputing with a military man in matters of his profession, and said no more."[15]

In civil matters Franklin was at home. When Braddock could get together only 25 transport wagons in Maryland, Franklin thought he might do better in Pennsylvania. With instructions and money he went to Lancaster, and he and his son within two weeks had assembled, in Lancaster, York, and Cumberland Counties, 150 wagons with four horses each and 259 pack horses, and had sent them off to the rendezvous at Will's Creek. In addition to the eight hundred pounds Franklin had been furnished with, he advanced two hundred more. "The advertisement promised payment according to the valuation, in case any wagon or horse should be lost. The owners, however, alleging they did not know General Braddock or what dependence might be had on his promise, insisted on my bond for the performance, which I accordingly gave them."[16] The commander-in-chief of all the British forces in America had less credit with the colonists than their own postmaster. Franklin took up also the case of the subalterns, who "were generally not in affluence, and could ill afford, in this dear country, to lay in the stores that might be necessary in so long a march, through a wilderness, where nothing was to be purchased."[17] William Franklin, who had been a subaltern himself, made a list of "necessaries and refreshments," and his father sent it off to a committee of the Assembly that had some money on hand. The committee made a present to every officer, with a horse to carry it, of a parcel containing six pounds each of rice, raisins, chocolate, coffee, loaf sugar, and "good Muscovada" sugar; one pound each of green and bohea tea; a half-pound of pepper, a half-dozen dried tongues, and a half-hundredweight of the best white biscuit; one Gloucester cheese; two well-cured hams; twenty pounds of good butter; one bottle of flour of mustard and one quart of white wine vinegar; two gallons of Jamaica spirits; and two dozen of old Madeira wine. Braddock was so much pleased by Franklin's activities that he engaged his further services in sending supplies after the army on its march. Franklin advanced more than a thousand pounds of his own money.

Braddock marched away into the fateful forest, cutting what was later to be famous as the National Road. Franklin in Philadelphia had during June a few days of leisure. He sent off to Collinson the "philosophical packet" which he had made up in November 1753 but had been too busy to send before this. John Bartram had brought Franklin a box which was to go to Collinson, and Franklin would fill the "little vacancy" in it: a few sheets of asbestos paper, some candles which "give a whiter flame than that of any other kind of candle," "a few cakes of American soap made of myrtle wax, said to be the best soap in the world for shaving or washing fine linens"; the notes he had made last winter describing a woodchuck, when "one of them was killed in the garden of an old inn I put up at" in New England. No countryman, he had not known what it was, but Bartram recognized it from the description as a ground hog. Franklin had broken his thermometer and had invented a way to mend it, not very successfully. Here were ten copies of the pamphlet on the Pennsylvanian fireplaces. Some day he would muster up a full account of the Philadelphia voyages in search of the Northwest Passage. He included a letter for D'Alibard, in Paris, on electrical matters, reporting at length the effects of a stroke of lightning on a church at Newbury in New England. He ran through all the questions that Collinson had written him in letters so far unanswered, and he requested that Collinson "would send my wife satin sufficient for a gown, somewhat darker than the enclosed pattern."[18]

That June Franklin had a new clerk whose diary throws a little light on the private life of the Franklins. Daniel Fisher, a needy Englishman, had come from Williamsburg in May looking for work. Unable to find any, he wrote a note to Franklin on 4 June and promptly got an answer asking him to tea the same day. Franklin engaged him and sent him to lodge in the house of a neighbour. The next afternoon Fisher, coming down from his room, found Deborah Franklin sitting at the foot of the neighbour's stairway, loudly complaining that "all the world claimed a privilege of troubling her Pappy (so she usually calls Mr. Franklin) with their calamities and distresses." Afterwards, when Fisher knew her better, he discovered that she was jealous of William, whom she thought his father preferred to her and Sally, though Fisher could see no signs of this. "I have often," Fisher noted, "seen [William] pass to and from his father's apartment upon business (for he does not eat, drink, or sleep in the house) without the least compliment between Mrs. Franklin and him or any sort of notice taken of each other, till one day, as I was sitting with her in the passage when the young gentleman came by, she exclaimed to me (he not hearing): 'Mr. Fisher, there goes the greatest villain upon earth!' This greatly confounded and perplexed me, but did not hinder her from pursuing her invectives in the foulest terms I ever heard from a gentlewoman."[19] (Here is evidence which more than any other makes it hard to believe that William was secretly Deborah's own son.) Fisher while he was Franklin's clerk made copies of the *Observations concerning the Increase of Mankind*, first published that year in Boston, and of a long and grateful letter from Braddock to Franklin. On 24 June the Freemasons, who had hitherto met in taverns, dedicated their own building with high ceremony. At the banquet the toast to the success of Braddock was the thirteenth.

In the letter to Collinson of 26 June Franklin wrote that he was sick of politics. "I like neither the governor's conduct nor the Assembly's; and, having some share in the confidence of both, I have endeavoured to reconcile 'em, but in vain; and between 'em they make me very uneasy. . . . If my being able now and then to influence a good measure did not keep up my spirits, I should be ready to swear never to serve again as assemblyman, since both sides expect more from me than they ought, and blame me sometimes for not doing what I am not able to do, as well as for not preventing what was not in my power to prevent."[20] Indeed, he wrote on 27 August: "I abhor these altercations, and if I did not love the country and the people would remove immediately into a more quiet government, Connecticut, where I am also happy enough to have many friends."[21]

The consequences of Braddock's defeat on 9 July, with the slaughter of over two-thirds of his officers and over half of his men, kept Franklin in Pennsylvania. At once he was more involved in politics than ever. The Assembly, voting £50,000 for defence, proposed to tax proprietors as well as people, and the conflict raised new angers. Franklin faced ruin till October, when Governor Shirley, who had succeeded Braddock as commander-in-chief, ordered payment for the horses and wagons for which Franklin was surety, in the amount of nearly £20,000. There was general terror in the province. The French, with no British to withstand them, might attack in force. The Indians, encouraged by the French victory, turned against the frontier English. Though the Six Nations officially kept faith, some of their warriors joined the French. The Delawares had been implacable ever since 1737, when Thomas Penn cheated them in the Walking Purchase. Now they took revenge. The western Indians resented the separate treaty made with the Pennsylvanians at Albany. They were as hostile as the Delawares. With no British army to defend it, Pennsylvania must have militia. Those citizens who demanded vigorous action abused the peaceful Quakers.

Franklin could have seen in the tumult few evidences of the imperial unity he had imagined. For lack of a common plan among the colonies, the British government had sent an army that had proved worse than useless. Braddock had fought clansmen in the Highlands, but knew and would learn nothing about fighting Indians, and he offended the friendly Indians who joined him as scouts. Years of service in the Coldstream Guards had not taught Braddock how to deal with colonials. He too plainly showed them how much he despised what he thought their inefficiency and selfishness. Franklin's help, he wrote to the secretary of state, was "almost the only instance of address and fidelity which I have seen in all these provinces." And possibly Franklin's help had been a handicap. Washington, Braddock's aide, would not have burdened the march with so many wagons or so many horses carrying "necessaries and refreshments" for the subalterns. If Braddock had taken colonial advice, he need not have been surprised and defeated. But no Briton liked to take colonial advice in American affairs. Braddock was hardly more to blame than the government which had sent him on a campaign so badly planned at home. Nor had the colonies been willing, after Albany, to sink their special interests in the general interest. If Britain did not understand her colonies, neither did they understand each other. The Empire was far from being one country yet.

Interlude

THE crowded, troubled year 1755 saw the beginning of Franklin's affectionate friendship with Catherine Ray, the first of the younger women who from his fiftieth year to the end of his life delighted in his ageless charm and adored him. Since his marriage in 1730 Franklin had had, so far as is known, no close friendships among women. All his surviving letters written before 1755 were to men except those to his mother and his sister Jane, and two to Susanna Wright, sister of John and James Wright, whom Franklin had visited at their house called Hempfield near Wright's Ferry on the Susquehanna. Business, study, science, public welfare, politics, and masculine friendships had apparently absorbed him. But in Rhode Island in January 1755, on his way back from Boston, he met Catherine Ray.

The letters between them, the only records of their friendship, do not make clear the circumstances of their meeting. She was then twenty-three, daughter of Simon Ray of Block Island, and through her mother, Deborah Greene, related to the Greenes of Warwick, one of the most notable families in the province. Her sister Judith was married to Thomas Hubbard of Boston, where Franklin must have known her. Another sister, Anne, was married to Samuel Ward of Westerly, on the Pawcatuck River between Rhode Island and Connecticut. Franklin, taking his time to visit as he went, may have met Catherine Ray in Newport, among the many Wards who lived there, or in Westerly at Anne Ward's. Somewhere he took a longish journey with Catherine; somewhere he watched her making sugar plums and said her hands were sweet; somewhere he talked to her of favours which she refused him, though she was rather pleased than vexed by his boldness. They parted on the shore of Block Island sound, she to cross the water to her home, he to return to Westerly. He was a conjurer, she said. He left her under a spell, and he was hardly gone when she wrote after him, on 20 January.

This letter, and the three that followed it, are all missing from Franklin's careful files. She later thought them indiscreet, and he may have thought so too. When, on 4 March, he first wrote to her, he put a prudent if tender distance between them. "It gives me great pleasure," he said, "to hear that you got home safe and well that day. I thought too much was hazarded, when I saw you put off to sea in that very little skiff, tossed by every wave. But the call was strong and just, a sick parent. I stood on the shore and looked after you till I could no longer distinguish you, even with my glass; then returned to your sister's, praying for your safe passage. Towards evening all agreed that you must certainly be arrived before that time, the weather having been so favourable; which made me more easy and cheerful, for I had been truly concerned for you.

"I left New England slowly, and with great reluctance. Short day's journeys and loitering visits on the road, for three or four weeks, manifested my unwillingness to quit a country in which I drew my first breath, spent my earliest and most pleasant days, and had now received so many fresh marks of the people's goodness and benevolence, in the kind and affectionate treatment I had everywhere met with. I almost forgot I had a home, till I was more than half-way towards it; till I had, one by one, parted with all my New England friends and was got into the western borders of Connecticut, among mere strangers. Then, like an old man who, having buried all he loved in this world, begins to think of heaven, I began to think of and wish for home; and, as I drew nearer, I found the attraction stronger and stronger. My diligence and speed increased with my impatience. I drove on violently and made such long stretches that a very few days brought me to my own house and to the arms of my good old wife and children, where I remain, thanks to God, at present well and happy.

"Persons subject to the *hyp* complain of the north-east wind as increasing their malady. But since you promised to send me kisses in that wind, and I find you"—in her first letter?—"as good as your word, it is to me the gayest wind that blows and gives me the best spirits. I write this during a north-east storm of snow, the greatest we have had this winter. Your favours come mixed with the snowy fleeces, which are as pure as your virgin innocence, white as your lovely bosom—and as cold. But let it warm towards some worthy young man, and may heaven bless you both with every kind of happiness.

"I desired Miss Anna Ward to send you over a little book I left with her, for your amusement in that lonely island. My respects to your good father and mother and sister. Let me hear often of your welfare, since it is not likely I shall ever again have the pleasure of seeing you. Accept mine and my wife's sincere thanks for the many civilities I receive from you and your relations; and do me the justice to believe me, dear girl, your affectionate, faithful friend and humble servant."[1]

The day before he wrote, Catherine had written a second letter. It and the two after it, at four-week intervals, reached him when he was deep in the Braddock business, and he did not answer. On 28 June she wrote, in distress and anxiety, her fifth letter, which is the earliest that survives from her and has hitherto not been published: "Dear, dear Sir: Excuse my writing when I tell you it is the great regard I have for you will not let me be silent, for absence rather increases than lessens my affection. Then, my not receiving one line from you in answer to three of my last letters—March the 3d and 31st and April the 28th—gives me a vast deal of uneasiness and occasioned many tears, for surely I have wrote too much and you are affronted with me, or have not received my letters, in which I have said a thousand things that nothing should have tempted me to [have] said to anybody else, for I knew they would be safe with you. I'll only beg the favour of one line [*illegible*] what is become of my letters. Tell me you are well and forgive and love me one-thousandth part so well as I do you, and then I will be contented and promise an amendment. It is with the greatest reluctance I shall finish my letter without telling you of some great alterations since my last. But you have my promise, so I will pray God to bless you with the best of blessings, and subscribe myself, dear sir, your most sincere, affectionate, and obliged friend." Then she added: "My proper respects to Mrs. Franklin and daughter." And again she added, in the margin: "Pray take care of your health and accept the sugar plums. They are every one sweetened as you used to like."[2]

Her uneasy question did not reach Franklin for three months, and he let the whole summer pass, what with Braddock's defeat and the uproar in Pennsylvania, before he answered the three letters in which she was afraid she had said too much. Then on 11 September, while the Assembly was adjourned, he began his second and longest letter to her: "Begone, business, for an hour, and let me chat a little with my Katy." He explained that her first letter had reached him just before he set out on a long journey, and the others while he was away, and that since then a "perpetual hurry of public affairs" had forced him to neglect his "private correspondences, even those that afforded me the greatest pleasure." If he had thought her letters indiscreet, he showed no signs of it, only teasing her about her confidences, which he seemed to take for granted.

"You ask in your last, how I do and what I am doing, and whether everybody loves me yet and why I make them do so.

"In regard to the first, I can say, thanks to God, that I do not remember I was ever better. I still relish all the pleasures of life that a temperate man can in reason desire, and through favour I have them all in my power. . . . As to the second question, I must confess (but don't you be jealous) that many more people love me now than ever did before; for since I saw you I have been enabled to do some general services to the country and to the army for which both have thanked and praised me, and say they love me. They say so as you used to do; and if I were to ask any favours of them, they would perhaps as readily refuse me; so that I find little real advantage in being beloved, but it pleases my humour.

"Now it is four months since I have been favoured with a single line from you; but I will not be angry with you, because it is my fault. I ran in debt to you three or four letters; and as I did not pay, you would not trust me any more, and you had some reason. But believe me I am honest; and though I should never make equal returns, you shall see I will keep fair accounts. Equal returns I can never make, though I should write to you by every post; for the pleasure I receive from one of yours is more than you can have from two of mine. The small news, the domestic occurrences among our friends, the natural pictures you draw of persons, the sensible observations and reflections you make, and the easy chatty manner in which you express everything, all contribute to heighten the pleasure; and the more as they remind me of those hours and miles that we talked away so agreeably, even in a winter journey, a wrong road, and a soaking shower.

"I long to hear whether you have continued ever since in that monastery [Block Island] or have broke into the world again, doing pretty mischief; how the lady Wards do, and how many of them are married, or about it; what is become of Mr. B—— and Mr. L——, and what the state of your heart is at this instant. But that, perhaps, I ought not to know; and therefore I will not conjure, as you sometimes say I do. If I could conjure, it should be to know what was that oddest question about me that ever was thought of, which you tell me a lady had just sent to ask you.

"I commend your prudent resolutions in the article of granting favours to lovers. But if I were courting you I could not hardly approve such conduct. I should even be malicious enough to say you were too knowing, and tell you the old story of the Girl and the Miller. I enclose you the songs you write for, and with them your Spanish letter with a translation. I honour that honest Spaniard for loving you. It showed the goodness of his taste and judgment. But you must forget him, and bless some worthy young Englishman.

"You have spun a long thread, five thousand and twenty-two yards. It will reach almost from Rhode Island hither. I wish I had hold of one end of it, to pull you to me. But you would break it rather than come. The cords of love and friendship are longer and stronger, and in times past have drawn me farther; even back from England to Philadelphia. I guess that some of the same kind will one day draw you out of that island.

"I was extremely pleased with the turf you sent me. The Irish people who have seen it say it is the right sort; but I cannot learn that we have anything like it here. The cheeses, particularly one of them, were excellent. All our friends have tasted it, and all agree that it exceeds any English cheese they ever tasted. Mrs. Franklin was very proud that a young lady should have so much regard for her old husband as to send him such a present. We talk of you every time it comes to table. She is sure you are a sensible girl, and a notable housewife, and talks of bequeathing me to you as a legacy; but I ought to wish you a better, and hope she will live these hundred years; for we are grown old together, and if she has any faults I am so used to 'em that I don't perceive 'em. . . . Indeed, I begin to think she has none, as I think of you. And since she is willing I should love you as much as you are willing to be loved by me, let us join in wishing the old lady a long life and a happy."

He sent her his wife's compliments, and his own to her parents, whom he did not know. And he too added a postscript: "Sally says: 'Papa, my love to Miss Katy.' If it was not quite unreasonable, I should desire you to write to me every post, whether you hear from me or not. As to your spelling, don't let those laughing girls put you out of conceit with it. It is the best in the world, for every letter of it stands for something."[3]

(That same day Franklin wrote to Thomas Hancock in Boston, proposing an annual subscription to buy books for the Harvard library. Franklin sent an order on his brother John for four pistoles for the fund. " 'Tis but a trifle compared with my hearty good will and respect to the college; but a small seed properly sown sometimes produces a large and fruitful tree."[4] The subscription was never started, and Franklin's order, never cashed, is still in the Harvard College archives.)

To Catherine Ray's worried letter, when it finally got to Philadelphia, Franklin sent a lively answer on 16 October, as if to reassure her. "Your favour of the 28th of June came to hand but the 28th of September, just three months after it was written. I had, two weeks before, wrote you a long chat and sent it to the care of your brother Ward. I hear you are now in Boston, gay and lovely as usual. Let me give you some fatherly advice. Kill no more pigeons than you can eat. Be a good girl and don't forget your catechism. Go constantly to meeting—or church—till you get a good husband; then stay at home, and nurse the children, and live like a Christian. Spend your spare hours in sober whisk [whist], prayers, or learning to cipher. You must practise *addition* to your husband's estate, by industry and frugality; *subtraction* of all unnecessary expenses; *multiplication* (I would gladly have taught you that myself, but you thought it was time enough, and wouldn't learn), he will soon make you a mistress of it. As to *division,* I say with Brother Paul, 'Let there be no division among ye.' But as your good sister Hubbard (my love to her) is well acquainted with the rule of two, I hope you will become an expert in the rule of three; that when I have again the pleasure of seeing you, I may find you like my grapevine, surrounded with clusters, plump, juicy, blushing, pretty little rogues, like their mamma. Adieu. The bell rings [the Assembly was then in session], and I must go among the grave ones and talk politics. . . . P.S. The plums came safe, and were so sweet from the cause you mentioned that I could scarce taste the sugar."[5]

Franklin's side of the early friendship between him and Catherine Ray is clearer than hers, but hers is not too hard to guess at. Her sister Judith had been married at nineteen, her sister Anne at seventeen, her younger sister Phebe at twenty-one or sooner. Catherine at twenty-four (July 1755) was still at home on the lonely island. Franklin was the most interesting man she had ever met: the most interesting because the most interested. A famous scientist, an officer of the Crown, he gave her the same close attention and imaginative understanding that he gave to electricity or business or politics. His frank attraction to her person went with an exciting admiration for her mind. Finding herself important in his experienced, humorous eyes, she felt important in her own, and naturally told him her small secrets, which he did not seem to think were small. Given more opportunity, she might easily have become a Vanessa to his Swift. But this was New England, this was Franklin. In answer to her impetuous letters he wrote blandly from Philadelphia about his wife and daughter, doubted that he would ever see his charming friend again, and urged her to marry some suitable young man.

The following summer she sent a short note to say that she expected to see Franklin soon in Boston and so would not write a long letter. "I know not when I shall enjoy that pleasure," he said on 26 August about a Boston meeting, "being more involved in public affairs than ever; so that I cannot be so long out of the province as such a journey requires; therefore, dear girl, write me all your little news, for it is extremely entertaining to me." He would not let it appear that he thought her in Boston on account of him. "Your apology for being in Boston, that you must visit that sister once a year, makes me suspect you are [t]here for some other reason [some other man], for why should you think your being there would need an excuse to me, when you know that I know how dearly you loved that sister? Don't offer to hide your heart from me. You know I can conjure. Give my best respects to your sister, and tell her and all your other sisters and brothers that they must behave very kindly to you and love you dearly, or else I'll send a young gentleman to steal and run away with you, who shall bring you to a country from whence they shall never hear a word from you, without paying postage."[6]

They did not meet again till July 1763, when she had been married since 1758 to William Greene and had borne two of her six children. Franklin, who had been in England for five of the intervening years, visited her and her husband at their farm in Warwick on the way to Boston. Sally Franklin was with her father, and would have liked to stay a week. After that the friends saw each other no more than twice, once in 1775 when Franklin went to Cambridge to confer with Washington, and again in 1776 when Catherine Greene visited Franklin in Philadelphia with her husband. Catherine's affection embraced Franklin's sister Jane, who when Boston was besieged by the British took refuge with the Greenes in Warwick. (Jane's granddaughter married a brother of General Nathanael Greene, who was Catherine's nephew.) Franklin's affection embraced Catherine's eldest son Ray Greene, who was sent in 1775 with Franklin from Warwick to Philadelphia to enter the Academy, where in the overwhelming year 1776 his mother's friend looked after him as if he were a grandson. Though Franklin and Catherine Greene met so seldom, their devoted friendship never grew less, and they exchanged, from time to time for more than thirty years, letters which are as delightful as any in the language. Long lapses made no difference to them, nor the long distances between them. Her sister's husband Samuel Ward was three times governor of the province, and after independence her own husband was for eight years governor of the state. But she seldom mentioned public affairs, any more than Franklin did.

They wrote about their families and casually about themselves—the two selves that had met and loved each other and needed nothing else to keep their affection perfectly alive. One of his letters, she said, "gave me great pleasure, as it gave me fresh proof of your own dear self." She called him, in that formal age, "my dearly beloved friend," sent him "as much love as you wish," and signed herself "your friend that loves you dearly." After many years she told him: "I impute great part of the happiness of my life to the pleasing lessons you gave me in that journey."[7] Franklin at eighty-three wrote her: "Among the felicities of my life I reckon your friendship, which I shall remember with pleasure as long as that life lasts."[8]

Soldier

THE frontier was close to Philadelphia in 1755, and seemed to come ominously closer. Raiding Indians from the Ohio slipped through the forests of the back counties less than a hundred miles away. The frontier towns were little molested, for the Indians did not come in force. But during the years of peace many settlers, particularly German and Scotch-Irish, had taken up isolated farms. Whole families were killed and scalped, with no one to defend them or even to spread the news. Till the end of summer the raiders were cautious, not sure what plans the colony was making for defence. By fall they had become so bold and struck so often that the whole frontier was in a panic. Crowding in the towns, the refugees called for protection by the government. There was confusion in Philadelphia. The Quakers who dominated the Assembly were a minority of the whole people, and a growing majority angrily demanded that the matter of defence be taken out of the hands of pacifists. Others in the majority saw in the legislative deadlock only a tedious wrangling over negligible points of law. The Indians had crossed the mountains. Let the needed money be voted now and the principle agreed on later. The Assembly was blamed almost as much as the governor. If this was no time to delay, neither was it a time to keep up an obstinate animosity to the proprietors. They too had partisans in Philadelphia. A good many conservatives stood with the proprietary government because it was the government, and established, and British. Others were under obligation to the proprietors, or looked for favours from them. William Smith, provost of the Academy, who hoped that the colonies might have a bishop and he a bishopric, attacked the Quakers—and incidentally Franklin, who liked the Quakers and respected their scruples without sharing them. Smith and the governor and Richard Peters all wrote to Thomas Penn about the misdeeds of Franklin, that crafty leader of the presumptuous Assembly.

It is not entirely clear how far Franklin went with the Assembly in its stern principles. He seems to have tried to bring them and the governor to terms. Drafting the Assembly's messages, he had to present the Assembly's opinion, whether he had directed it or not. Leader or merely spokesman, he could not move much faster than the majority. But it was he who worked out the schemes which temporarily reconciled the antagonists in November. He drew up a militia bill which the Quakers would pass and the governor would sign. As to taxing the proprietary lands, he held as strongly as anybody that the proprietors should pay their share, since their property was being defended along with the rest. But when the proprietors offered to contribute £5000, as a gift not as a tax, he persuaded the Assembly to accept it as offered, only stipulating that they alone had the right to grant supplies to the Crown and to limit such grants "as to the matter, manner, measure, and time." The Assembly voted £60,000 and the governor assented.

On 25 November the Assembly passed the militia act[1] and ordered the money bill. The act, unmistakably in the language of Franklin, said that the people called Quakers, while they would not bear arms themselves nor compel others to do it, yet would not compel men of other principles not to bear arms. Therefore the Assembly made it lawful for the freemen of the province to form themselves into companies and elect their officers, subject to the approval of the governor or commander-in-chief; and for the officers of the companies to elect the officers of the regiments to which the companies should be assigned; and for the whole body of officers to establish articles of war and courts-martial which, when the enlisted men had voluntarily signed them, should be binding. Unlike the Association which Franklin had organized in 1747, this militia had a legal status, but it was still democratic. No matter what military men might think in general, Franklin was sure that colonial soldiers would serve best under officers they themselves had chosen.

A committee of seven was appointed by the Assembly to manage the funds raised for defence. With Franklin as its head, the committee sat every day of the week. There was immediate need of action. News came that the night before the militia act was passed and the defence money voted, a war party of Shawnee had attacked the Moravian mission village of Gnadenhuetten, seventy-five miles north-west of Philadelphia, had killed all the people who could not escape into the forest, and had burned the buildings. Hundreds of German farmers and their families from Northampton and Berks Counties had already streamed into Philadelphia, to say they would no longer be a buffer to the English settled nearer the city. If the frontier were not protected, the Germans would leave it and quarter themselves on the inhabitants of a safer neighbour-hood. Governor Morris received two of the Germans and told them that the proprietors had given £5000 for defence. The whole dele-gation then marched to the Assembly, where Franklin spoke to them so reassuringly that they returned to their villages and farms.

Whatever might be expected of Franklin's militia, which the military men thought absurd, there was bound to be delay in organizing the democratic companies. Soldiers were needed at once, and the committee ordered that three hundred men be enlisted in the provincial forces, to serve with pay as rangers on the frontier or in the blockhouses which were to be built. Frank-lin wrote for the *Gazette* his skilful explanation of the militia scheme in the form of *A Dialogue between X, Y, and Z concerning the Present State of Affairs in Pennsylvania.*[2] This appeared 18 December. The same day he set out with fifty provincial cavalry-men and three Conestoga wagons for Bethlehem, the chief town of the Moravians. With him were James Hamilton, formerly gov-ernor and still a member of the Council, and Joseph Fox, the Quaker chairman of the Assembly's committee of accounts. By rank Hamilton was leader of the expedition, and he went partly to keep an eye on Franklin and report to the governor. But after a week or so of deference to the man of rank, the man of genius was in charge, with his son as his aide. More or less sedentary by habit, fifty, and fat, Franklin seems to have taken as naturally to this rough campaigning as to prose or business or science or poli-tics. Though he had no military title, the Moravians called him General Franklin.

The line of defence ran from Easton on the Delaware south-west through Bethlehem on the Lehigh to Reading on the Schuylkill. Behind them lay the protecting range of the Blue mountains, cut between the Schuylkill and the Delaware only at the gap through which the Lehigh entered. Bethlehem was inside the Lehigh gap, but its mission at Gnadenhuetten had been just outside it, a natural point of attack by raiders from beyond the mountains. It was also a natural stronghold. If the French were allowed to build a fort there, they could harry the whole province and withstand an army many times their number advancing through the narrow defile from Northampton County. There must be a garrison to hold the site of the ruined village. But raiding Indians were sure to creep through the passes and fall upon pioneer families or weak settlements. The committee undertook to raise and station companies of provincial soldiers at intervals all the way from Easton to Reading, on the line of defence inside the mountains.

Two days of hard riding over a bad road brought the commissioners with their cavalry to Bethlehem, the little commune of Moravian quietists settled there since 1741, now under the headship of Augustus Gottlieb Spangenberg. "I was surprised," Franklin later remembered, "to find it in so good a posture of defence; the destruction of Gnadenhut had made them apprehend danger. The principal buildings were defended by a stockade; they had purchased a quantity of arms and ammunition from New York, and had even placed quantities of small paving stones between the windows of their high stone houses, for their women to throw down upon the heads of any Indians that should attempt to force into them."[3] The normal population of five hundred had been increased to three times as many by refugees from Moravian farms and missions, all of them frightened by a rumour that the town was to be attacked by an army of Indians on Christmas Day. But the commissioners, finding Bethlehem partly prepared, spent only a single night there, at the Crown Inn on the south side of the Lehigh, and the next morning crossed the river and went on to Easton. There William Parsons, one of the earliest members of the Junto and lately surveyor-general of the province, was laying out the town which had just been founded by the Penns at the forks of the Lehigh and the Delaware.

Without the Moravian discipline of Bethlehem, Easton was in

terrified disorder. Refugees filled all the houses. The stores of food were nearly gone, and the people, thinking themselves abandoned by the government, were ready to give up the town and look for safety in Philadelphia. There was much drinking and quarrelling. Franklin promptly organized a guard, with Parsons commissioned as major, put sentries at the ends of the principal streets, set up a patrol around the town to watch for signs of Indians, cleared away the bushes as far as a musket would carry from the outlying houses, and arranged for runners to be sent regularly to distant farms. At the same time he and the commissioners enlisted about two hundred men in the provincial forces. Enlistment was slow, and the governor's friends were pleased to see that the people did not rush to arms as Franklin had said they would under his militia act. The governor's friends might have laughed loudly among themselves if they had seen a letter which Franklin wrote at Easton to his friend Conrad Weiser at Reading, suggesting that dogs be used against the Indians. "They should be large, strong, and fierce; and every dog led in a slip string, to prevent their tiring themselves by running out and in, and discovering the party by barking at squirrels, etc. Only when the party come near thick woods and suspicious places, they should turn out a dog or two to search them. In case of meeting a party of the enemy, the dogs are all then to be turned loose and set on. They will be fresher and finer for having been previously confined, and will confound the enemy a good deal, and be very serviceable. This was the Spanish method of guarding their marches."[4]

After ten days at Easton the commissioners set out for Reading by way of Bethlehem, escorted by their cavalrymen. Reinforcements from other counties had joined them while they were in Northampton and they had been able not only to leave a guard there but also to send two companies across the mountains. On the afternoon of 30 December the party arrived in Bethlehem, where Franklin for the first time met Bishop Spangenberg, who became his friend. The next day they rode on by the King's Highway towards Reading, which they reached early New Year's afternoon. They had come to confer with Governor Morris, who was later to meet certain friendly Indian chiefs at Harris's Ferry. The governor had been in New York consulting with the governors of Massachusetts and New Jersey, although his Assembly had thought he was needed in his own province. It had not been pleasant for the governor, returning to Philadelphia, to find that the militia companies there had chosen Franklin for their colonel, or that, while the Council hesitated to approve this dubious choice, the militia made such a demonstration before the governor's house that he felt forced to promise he would confirm it.

The conference at Reading, then a hundred log houses jumbled around a large, muddy central square, took up the treaty with the friendly Indians, various measures of local defence, and the problem of the Germans, who the English thought, quite without reason, were making terms with the French. Franklin had intended to go from Reading back to Philadelphia, but on 3 January a runner came from Bethlehem with word that the soldiers recently sent to Gnadenhuetten had been surprised by Indians on New Year's Day and driven, those who were alive, through the Lehigh gap. The frontier was again exposed at its most vulnerable point. The first act of the conference was to offer a bounty of forty pieces of eight for the scalp of any Indian enemy killed in battle. The next was to decide that one of the commissioners must hurry to Bethlehem and then to Gnadenhuetten to rebuild the fort. The choice fell upon Franklin. While Hamilton and Fox accompanied the governor to make their peaceful treaty, Franklin on 6 January turned back on a harder and more dangerous errand. By the governor's commission, issued the day before, Franklin was given—though no military rank—dictatorial powers in Northampton County, to organize and rule it, distribute munitions, and appoint or dismiss officers of the forces. Half the cavalry escorted the governor's party, and half Franklin, who still had his son as his aide.

On the second day of his journey to Bethlehem he stopped at the encampment of the soldiers who had got away from Gnadenhuetten, and talked with their captain. Then to Bethlehem that afternoon, by a road crowded with the wagons of refugees. Bishop Spangenberg waited on the new commander-in-chief in the name of the congregation. Lodged at the house of Timothy Horsfield, an Englishman who was assistant to Spangenberg, Franklin spent a week in Bethlehem, directing civilian relief, assembling men to march to Gnadenhuetten, and disposing troops to guard the townships inside the mountains. For Captain Vanetta (John Van Etten) Franklin wrote out detailed and typical instructions on 12 January. "You are to proceed immediately to raise a company of foot, consisting of thirty able men including two sergeants, with which you are to protect the inhabitants of Upper Smithfield, assisting them while they thresh out and secure their corn, and scouting from time to time as you judge necessary on the outside of the settlements, with such of the inhabitants as may join you, to discover the enemy's approaches and repel their attacks. . . . You are to keep a diary or journal of every day's transactions, and an exact account of the time when each man enters himself with you; and if any man desert or die, you are to note the time in your journal, and the time of engaging a new man in his place, and submit your journal to the inspection of the governor when required. . . . You are to acquaint the men that if in their ranging they meet with or are at any time attacked by the enemy, and kill any of them, forty dollars will be allowed and paid by the government for each scalp of an Indian enemy so killed, the same being produced with proper attestations. . . . You are to take care that your stores and provisions are not wasted. . . . You are to keep good order among your men, and prevent drunkenness and other immoralities, as much as may be, and not suffer them to do any injury to the inhabitants whom they come to protect. . . . You are to take good care that the men keep their arms clean and in good order, and that their powder be always kept dry and fit for use."[5]

During this driven week in Bethlehem the commissioner was enough of a philosopher to inquire a little into the customs of the Moravians. "I found they worked for a common stock, eat at common tables, and slept in common dormitories, great numbers together. In the dormitories I observed loopholes, at certain distances all along just under the ceiling, which I thought judiciously placed for change of air. I was at their church, where I was entertained with good music, the organ being accompanied with violins, hautboys, clarinets, etc." This was on the evening of Saturday, 10 January. On Sunday Franklin had the seat of honour below the choir loft, and, according to a Moravian diarist, was very attentive to the service. Bethlehem had the first municipal waterworks

in America, which must have interested Franklin, and a co-
operative store. But what he remembered best for his *Autobiography* was the fact that the Moravian marriages were sometimes,
though not often, decided by lot. "I objected, if the matches were
not made by the mutual choice of the parties, some of them may
chance to be very unhappy. 'And so they may,' answered my in-
former, 'if you let the parties choose for themselves': which, indeed, I could not deny."[6]

But the real business of the expedition was the fort at Gnadenhuetten, twenty miles from Bethlehem. On the morning of 15
January Franklin wrote to his wife that they would move that day.
"We shall have with us about one hundred and thirty men, and
shall endeavour to act cautiously, so as to give the enemy no advantage through our negligence. Make yourselves therefore easy.
Give my hearty love to all friends."[7] Besides his soldiers Franklin
had a company of skilled axemen, frontier farmers, to cut down
trees for the stockade, seven wagons with six horses each, a doctor,
and a chaplain. The line of march followed the Lehigh. William
Franklin led the advance through the pass. After him came the
cavalry escort from Philadelphia, the survivors of Gnadenhuetten
now returning to their post, then Franklin, the chaplain, and the
wagons and baggage, and finally a rearguard of two companies.
Scouts ranged the hills on either side. On the second night from
Bethlehem they had good quarters at the tavern of Nicholas Up-
linger. The next day was Franklin's fiftieth birthday. "We began
to march towards Gnadenhuetten and proceeded near two miles;
but it seeming to set in for a rainy day, the men unprovided with
greatcoats, and many unable to secure effectually their arms from
the wet, we thought it most advisable to face about and return to
our former quarters, where the men might dry themselves and be
warm; whereas had they proceeded they would have come in wet
to Gnadenhuetten, where shelter and opportunity of drying themselves that night was uncertain. In fact, it rained all day, and we
were all pleased that we had not proceeded.

"The next day, being Sunday, we marched hither [to Gnaden-
huetten], where we arrived about two in the afternoon, and before
five had enclosed our camp with a strong breastwork, musket-
proof, and with the boards brought here before by my order from

Drucker's mill, got ourselves under some shelter from the weather."
That evening they buried the dead who still lay exposed among
the ruins of the mission. "Monday was so dark with a thick fog
all day that we could neither look out for a place to build nor see
where materials were to be had. Tuesday morning we looked
around us, pitched on a place, marked out our fort on the ground,
and by ten o'clock began to cut timber for stockades and to dig
the ground. By three in the afternoon the logs were all cut and
many of them hauled to the spot, the ditch dug to set them in
three feet deep, and that evening many were pointed and set up.
The next day we were hindered by rain most of the day. Thursday
we resumed our work, and before night were pretty well enclosed,
and on Friday morning the stockado was finished and part of the
platform within erected, which was completed the next morning."[8]

The fort, the simple stockade of the American frontier, was one
hundred and twenty-five feet long by fifty wide. It took seventy
axes five hours to cut down the trees they needed. "Seeing the trees
fall so fast, I had the curiosity to look at my watch when two men
began to cut at a pine; in six minutes they had it upon the
ground, and I found it of fourteen inches diameter. Each pine
made three palisades of eighteen feet long, pointed at one end."[9]
While axes chopped, spades dug the ditch which marked the walls
of the fort. Though it was cold and wet, the ground could hardly
have been frozen, for the ditch was ready as soon as the trees. The
wagons, with the bodies taken off, brought up the palisades, which
averaged a foot thick. Set firmly in the ground, side by side, they
made a wall twelve feet high which was strong enough to keep
out Indians who had no cannon. Inside the wall a platform six
feet from the ground ran the whole length, for the defenders to
stand on in case of an attack. There was a well in the enclosure,
and mounted at two corners were swivel guns. It was hardy work.
This was January in the mountains, and the men had no overcoats
or tents. They lived in the roughest huts till they could build
barracks within the fort. But Franklin noted that they were ill-
humoured only on the days when the rain kept them idle.

On the second Sunday they hoisted a flag, fired off all their
muskets and the two swivels, and named the place Fort Allen
after the chief justice. (It stood in what is now a park in Weiss-

port.) That day Franklin wrote to his wife that the fort was defensible and "we have every day more convenient living." Food had arrived from Philadelphia. "We have enjoyed your roast beef, and this day began on the roast veal. All agree that they are the best that ever were of the kind. Your citizens, that have their dinners hot and hot, know nothing of good eating. We find it in much greater perfection when the kitchen is four score miles from the dining room. The apples are extremely welcome, and do bravely eat after our salt pork; the minced pies are not yet come to hand, but I suppose we shall find them among the things expected up from Bethlehem on Tuesday; the capillaire [a medicinal cordial] is excellent, but, none of us having taken cold as yet, we have only tasted it. As for our lodging, it is on deal featherbeds, in warm blankets."[10] If Franklin, used to his comfortable house, felt the hardships of the frontier he barely mentioned them, and always humorously.

"We had for our chaplain," he later remembered, "a zealous Presbyterian minister, Mr. Beatty, who complained to me that the men did not generally attend his prayers and exhortations. When they enlisted they were promised, besides pay and provisions, a gill of rum a day, which was punctually served out to them, half in the morning and half in the evening; and I observed they were as punctual in attending to receive it; upon which I said to Mr. Beatty: 'It is perhaps below the dignity of your profession to act as steward of the rum; but if you were to deal it out, and only just after prayers, you would have them all about you.' He liked the thought, undertook the office, and, with the help of a few hands to measure out the liquor, executed it to satisfaction; and never were prayers more generally and more punctually attended."[11]

During the second week the expedition built two other stockades, Fort Norris fifteen miles to the east of Fort Allen, Fort Franklin the same distance to the west. Besides the forts, Franklin had various military problems on his hands. There were now thirteen companies in the Northampton forces, about five hundred men, scattered from Gnadenhuetten to Easton. He was responsible for seeing that they were armed, provisioned, and kept in touch with one another. Stealthy raids went on while he was at Gnadenhuetten, and survivors and refugees had to be cared for.

The hut in which he slept at night on the pine floor along with his fellow-officers was crowded all day with business. "I thought to have wrote you a long letter," he told his wife 30 January, "but here comes in a number of people, from different parts, that have business with me and interrupt me; we have but one room, and that quite public."[12] He went with scouting parties in search of Indians in the woods. They found none, but they came upon cold campfires, holes dug in the ground for charcoal cut off burnt logs. The Indians had watched the white men building their fort, but thought them too strong to attack.

Politics called Franklin back to Philadelphia sooner than he had expected. Though the Assembly was adjourned to 3 March, the governor suddenly convened it for 3 February. Franklin at Fort Allen had only two days' notice. "I resolved to return; the more willingly, as a New England officer, Colonel Clapham, experienced in Indian warfare, being on a visit to our establishment, consented to accept the command. I gave him a commission and, parading the garrison, had it read before them; and introduced him to them as an officer who from his skill in military affairs was much more fit to command them than myself; and, giving them a little exhortation, took my leave. I was escorted as far as Bethlehem, where I rested a few days to recover from the fatigue I had undergone. The first night, being in a good bed, I could hardly sleep, it was so different from my hard lodging on the floor of our hunt at Gnadenhut wrapt only in a blanket or two."[13]

So Franklin remembered. Actually, Colonel Clapham had come to Fort Allen in the deliberate hope of succeeding Franklin. And the Moravian records show that Franklin arrived in Bethlehem on the afternoon of 4 February, had his horse shod and his bridle mended, and went on the next morning. He and his son, in spite of the bad roads, were in Philadelphia that night.

Though the little campaign had ended, and Franklin turned at once to the affairs of the Assembly, he was still the choice of the Philadelphia militia for their colonel. Within two weeks he was formally elected, and confirmed in his post by the reluctant governor on 24 February. The governor could not help himself in view of Franklin's services and popularity, but there was lively opposition in the Council and among the governor's friends. In

England Thomas Penn, increasingly suspicious of Franklin, had taken steps which he hoped would lead to Franklin's dismissal from the post office unless he changed his attitude toward the governor—that is, the proprietors. Franklin accepted his election and believed in the militia. "The first time I reviewed my regiment they accompanied me to my house, and would salute me with some rounds fired before my door, which shook down and broke several glasses of my electrical apparatus."[14] On 16 March the regiment was paraded for the governor to review on Society Hill, and the *Gazette* said that "so grand an appearance was never seen in Pennsylvania." The next day Franklin left for Virginia to confer with Hunter. "Twenty officers of my regiment, with about thirty grenadiers, presented themselves on horseback at my door just as I was going to mount, to accompany me to the ferry about three miles from town. Till we got to the end of the street, which is about two hundred yards, the grenadiers took it in their heads to ride with their swords drawn, but then they put them up peaceably into their scabbards, without hurting or even terrifying man, woman, or child; and from the ferry where we took leave and parted they all returned as quietly to their homes. This was the only instance of the kind; for though a greater number met me at my return, they did not ride with drawn swords, having been told that ceremony was improper, unless to compliment some person of great distinction. I who am totally ignorant of military ceremonies, and above all things averse to making show and parade or doing any useless thing that can serve only to excite envy or provoke malice, suffered at the time much more pain than I enjoyed pleasure and have never since given an opportunity for anything of the sort."[15]

Thomas Penn was pettishly incensed by these honours to Franklin, whom from England Penn saw as an upstart with an army of his own in Pennsylvania. While the news was being written to Penn, Franklin was in Williamsburg, "as gay as a bird," he told his wife on 30 March, "not beginning yet to long for home, the worry of perpetual business being yet fresh in my memory. . . . Virginia is a pleasant country, now in full spring; the people extremely obliging and polite."[16] On 2 April he was given his honorary degree from William and Mary, and on the 10th made a burgess and freeman of the borough of Norfolk. Back to the May sitting of the Assembly, he went in June to New York with an address to Governor Shirley, who was returning to England, to be succeeded as commander-in-chief of the British forces by Lord Loudoun, who arrived in July. Though Franklin had several interviews with Lord Loudoun, he was not wholly taken up with military affairs. He amused himself with the idea that he and George Whitefield, who had written that he would like to be a chaplain in the American army, might be employed by the Crown to settle a colony on the Ohio. "Life, like a dramatic piece, should not only be conducted with regularity but methinks it should finish handsomely. Being now in the last act, I begin to cast about for something fit to end with. Or if mine be more properly compared to an epigram, as some of its few lines are barely tolerable, I am very desirous of concluding with a bright point."[17] But when Franklin returned to Philadelphia he returned to the dragging conflict between governor and Assembly, and soon heard that he was in worse favour than ever with the proprietors. "I am not much concerned by that," he wrote cheerfully to Collinson on 5 November, "because if I have offended them by acting right, I can, whenever I please, reverse their displeasure by acting wrong."[18]

The governor and the proprietors tried by various arts to win Franklin over. Morris, who objected to Franklin as colonel, proposed after his expedition to the frontier that he lead an army to capture Fort Duquesne, with the rank of general. Franklin knew the governor wanted only to enlist him and his influence on the government side: "probably he might think that my popularity would facilitate the raising of the men, and my influence in Assembly the grant of money to pay them, and that, perhaps, without taxing the proprietary estate."[19] There is reason to guess that the proprietors had some influence with the Royal Society, which now elected Franklin to membership. There was no better reason for this than there had been for more than two years past, except that by 29 May several letters had come to London about his stubbornness and his militia. Certainly when Morris was superseded by William Denny in August, the new governor brought with him the Society's gold medal which had been awarded to Franklin in November 1753, but never sent to him. This Denny "presented to me at an entertainment given him by the city. He accompanied it with very polite expressions of his esteem for me, having, as he said, been long acquainted with my character. After dinner, when the company as was customary at that time were engaged in drinking, he took me aside into another room, and acquainted me that he had been advised by his friends in England to cultivate a friendship with me as one who was capable of giving him the best advice and of contributing most effectually to the making his administration easy; that he therefore desired of all things to have a good understanding with me, and he begged me to be assured of his readiness on all occasions to render me every service that might be in his power. He said much to me, also, of the proprietor's good disposition towards the province, and of the advantage it might be to us all, and to me in particular, if the opposition that had been so long continued to his measures was dropped, and harmony restored between him and the people; in effecting which it was thought no one could be more serviceable than myself; and I might depend on adequate acknowledgments and recompenses, etc., etc. The drinkers, finding we did not return immediately to the table, sent us a decanter of Madeira which the governor made liberal use of, and in proportion became more profuse of his solicitations and promises."[20]

The philosopher was not beguiled by the politician. He was a better politician himself. Franklin had not raised the militia or gone to the frontier because he was ambitious in the way the proprietors thought. Northampton County had been invaded by savages and must be defended. Franklin could never see chaos without thinking of order. The role of soldier was new to him, and he took a dramatic pleasure in it. But organizing his thirteen companies was hardly different from organizing the post office. He had not really ceased to be a civilian, and he felt the least chagrin when the militia act was repealed in England and all the commissions died with it. It was like the proprietors, he may have thought, to make an issue of so small a matter as his military episode. What interested him was the right of the whole province to have some say in governing itself without what he thought the selfish interference of distant, unimaginative landlords. He did not yet see how much revolution was implicit in the Assembly's stand against the proprietors and their antiquated tenure.

II

The war went on between the Assembly and the governor. The Assembly had voted money for defence. The governor wanted to take offensive steps. Against the will of the Quakers in the Assembly he declared war on the Delawares on 14 April, with the abominable provision to which the commissioners for the defence fund agreed: "I do hereby declare and promise that there shall be paid out of the said sixty thousand pounds to all and every person and persons, as well Indians as Christians, not in the pay of the province, the several and respective premiums and bounties following, that is to say: For every male Indian enemy above twelve years old who shall be taken prisoner and delivered at any fort garrisoned by the troops in the pay of this province or at any of the county towns to the keepers of the common jails there, the sum of one hundred and fifty Spanish dollars or pieces of eight; For the scalp of every male Indian enemy above the age of twelve years, produced as evidence of their being killed, the sum of one hundred and thirty pieces of eight; For every female Indian taken prisoner and brought in as aforesaid, and for every male Indian prisoner under the age of twelve years taken and brought in as aforesaid, one hundred and thirty pieces of eight; For the scalp of every Indian woman produced as evidence of their being killed, the sum of fifty pieces of eight; And for every English subject that has been taken and carried from this province into captivity, that shall be recovered and brought in and delivered at the city of Philadelphia, the sum of one hundred and fifty pieces, but nothing for their scalps."[21] Officers and soldiers in the pay of the province were to have only half the amounts.

In a situation so desperate that it seemed to call for these pitiless measures the Quakers in the Assembly began to leave it rather than take part. Six of them resigned that year, and enough later to give non-Quakers the majority. When it came to voting money again, the governor still would not assent to any taxing of the proprietary estates. The £5000 which the proprietors had offered, it now appeared, was to be collected in Pennsylvania out of unpaid money due them as quit-rents, about which the proprietors had had a great deal of trouble with their careless, unwilling tenants. The Assembly could act as collectors, and could advance whatever sums were slow in coming in. The Assembly insisted on their rights, the governor resisted under his instructions. Morris was succeeded in August by Denny, who turned out to be equally bound by the proprietors. In September the Assembly voted £30,000 on the governor's terms, yielding their rights only for this emergency, and resolving that it was necessary to send a remonstrance to England.

By the end of 1756 the province was in more danger than ever. The French still held Duquesne, and in August had taken the British fort at Oswego. In November a party of Indians had surprised Fort Allen, killed, captured, or driven away the garrison, and burned the village as well as Franklin's stockade—at a time when Franklin was with Denny at Easton making a treaty with the friendly Tedyuskung, who called himself king of the Delawares.[22] The Lehigh gap lay open to the French. The governor in December asked £125,000 for the coming year. The Assembly voted £100,000 on terms which they thought liberal though just. The governor in January vetoed the bill, and said that he would transmit a copy of it to the king. The Assembly resolved on 28 January to send commissioners to England to present their cause, and the next day named the Speaker and Franklin. Isaac Norris on 3 February pleaded his age and ill-health. Franklin said he was willing to go as soon as the Assembly required. They excused Norris for the present and resolved that Franklin "do first go over." The Assembly prepared another bill. The governor held out. Lord Loudoun came to Philadelphia in March and conferred with Franklin and the governor. Franklin offered the Assembly's arguments, the governor the proprietors' instructions. Loudoun "finally . . . rather chose to urge the compliance of the Assembly; and he entreated me to use my endeavours with them for that purpose, declaring that he would spare none of the king's troops for the defence of our frontiers, and that if we did not continue to provide for that defence ourselves they must remain exposed to the enemy."[23] Franklin persuaded the Assembly, conceding the occasion but not the principle, to make the bill conform, and the governor assented. On 4 April Franklin left for the packet at New York, with his son, who had resigned from his clerkship, and a dozen friends, who rode with them as far as Trenton.

Summary of an American

SOMEBODY who may have been Robert Feke of Newport or John Greenwood of Boston had painted the earliest known portrait of Franklin about the time he retired from business. Not long before leaving for England he is said to have sat for another portrait said to be by Matthew Pratt, whose father was a tradesman and a member of the Library Company. Franklin had not yet, both portraits show, grown to that look of benevolence, sometimes shy and always sage, which is familiar from his later likenesses. He was not in appearance unmistakably a philosopher. His eyes were open, full, and bold, the line of his mouth straight and even a little hard. His heavy chin was stubborn if not assertive. He still had the marks of the self-made man which he was, not yet refined to the ripe native genius which Europe took him for. He looked successful rather than superior.

In various respects he was the quintessence of provincial America. Born of the "middling people," he had emerged from his class without deserting it, and he never pretended or wanted to belong to the aristocracy. He had prospered along with many other men in Pennsylvania and in the other colonies. Though he talked about frugal living and was indifferent to hardships on his travels, he lived comfortably at home, liked rum punch and Madeira, and was on his way to gout. In his impulse toward intellectual pursuits he was not too much ahead of his society. There had been a dozen ambitious young tradesmen in his Junto, and enough men of learning in America to make up, however slowly, the American Philosophical Society. A large part of his leisure had always been devoted to the concerns of the common life: warming houses with his stove, protecting them against fire with his volunteer firemen and his lightning rod; persuading Philadelphia to pave its streets and to light and guard them at night (the bill for the lights and the watch was before the Assembly when Franklin went to England); founding a library and an academy and a hospital and a fire insurance company; urging the homely virtues through the maxims of Poor Richard; defending the frontiers against the Indians; and in the Assembly powerfully upholding the rights of the whole people as against the special interests of the proprietors and their friends.

In himself Franklin summed up the growing tendency toward intercolonial understanding. He had been born in New England, and he remembered it in Pennsylvania. His brother's widow was postmaster in Boston, and his brother in Philadelphia. One of his partners was postmaster in New Haven, and the son of another in Charleston. Franklin's partner in New York was controller of the colonial post office. Through William Hunter, joint Deputy Postmaster-General, Franklin was in touch with Virginia. He had planned with Washington in 1756 to persuade the two colonies to unite in building the road between Philadelphia and Winchester. No other man in America had seen so much of it as Franklin at first hand or had so wide an acquaintance among its influential men. His beginnings in intercolonial affairs had been made with his newspaper, his almanac, his partnerships, his magazine, none of which was so important as his philosophical correspondence and widening reputation. By 1757 he had long made peace with Harvard and was friendly with its president and professors, and he was on the best of terms with Yale. He had received honorary degrees from the three chief colleges in America, and had himself been largely responsible for the college in Pennsylvania. As philosopher and scientist he was friend or correspondent of most of the best scholars in America, except Jonathan Edwards, who died the next year.

The world of learning in America was more open to talent than the world of government. Offices were likely to go by birth, favor, or influence. Franklin owed his place in the post office in part to the recommendation of Chief Justice Allen, who now bitterly disapproved of Franklin's opposition to the proprietors. Other men who had encouraged the young tradesman must have regretted it as they saw him rise to a power they could not have foreseen. Most of them had been born or educated in Great Britain. Franklin belonged to a generation bred in America, aware of its changing circumstances, and slowly coming to feel that it must have a new status in the Empire. He had so strong a popular support in Pennsylvania that the conservative party could not keep him out of the government, or dispense with his special services when he was in it. At Albany he had been the only tradesman on the committee to draw up the Plan of Union, but his plan had been chosen over that of any of the others, even of Thomas Hutchinson. Though governors might not take Franklin's advice, they had to listen to him. If they had only known, they were listening to ideas which were to become a continental groundswell of opinion. But Franklin was still early with his ideas about labour, land, population, the frontier, colonial union, and self-government. Now fifty-one, he was to be seventy when he signed the Declaration of Independence, eighty-one when he signed the Constitution. Of his great associates in the founding of the Republic, Washington in 1757 was twenty-five, John Adams twenty-two, Jefferson fourteen, Madison six years, and Hamilton six months old.

II

Franklin did not have to go far from Philadelphia to run again into the British confusion which was the cause of much colonial discontent. Lord Loudoun, who was assembling a fleet in New York to lead against Louisbourg, controlled the packets for England. Franklin had already missed one, carrying his sea stores, while he conferred with Loudoun and Morris in Philadelphia. In New York Loudoun, genuinely overwhelmed with the details of the undertaking, said day after day that the London packet would sail at once. Two packets were waiting when Franklin arrived, and a third came in while he waited. "Passengers were engaged in all, and some extremely impatient to be gone, and the merchants uneasy about their letters and the orders they had given for insurance (it being wartime) for fall goods; but their anxiety availed nothing; his lordship's letters were not ready; and yet whoever waited on him found him always at his desk, pen in hand, and concluded he must write abundantly. . . . This daily expectation of sailing, and all the three packets going down to Sandy Hook to join the fleet there, the passengers thought it best to be on board, lest by a sudden order the ship should sail and they be left behind. There, if I remember right, we were about six weeks consuming our sea stores and obliged to procure more."[1]

Senseless delay was hard on Franklin. "I have been very low-spirited all day," he wrote to his wife after seven weeks. "This tedious state of uncertainty has almost worn out my patience. Except the two or three weeks at Woodbridge, I know not when I have spent time so uselessly."[2] The weeks at Woodbridge, New Jersey, he had spent at the house of his New York partner, James Parker, where Deborah and Sally Franklin joined him. With them and his son, and some unnamed "gentlemen and ladies" from New York, Franklin early in May led "a little excursion in the Jerseys," to Newark, Passaic Falls, and the Schuyler copper mines. William had not had "the least idea that views so agreeably enchanting were to be met with in America."[3] Perhaps the amusements of New York, with John Temple and James Abercrombie (son of the British general) and a gentleman from Rhode Island and an Irish beau from Philadelphia (where William had not met him), all of whom were waiting for the packet,[4] were consolation enough for Franklin's son, who wrote gallant letters to Elizabeth Graeme, whom in fact he was deserting.

Franklin had several conferences with Loudoun about the indentured servants in Pennsylvania who had been enlisted in the army with no compensation to their masters. Loudoun had countless reasons for leaving the matter unsettled. Franklin applied for the balance still due him for the provisions furnished Braddock, particularly since the delay in New York was being expensive. Loudoun promised to give an order on the paymaster, then repeatedly put off doing it. When Franklin protested, Loudoun made it clear that he was sure Franklin must already have made money out of the job and should not complain about a little delay. "I assured him that was not my case, and that I had not pocketed a farthing; but he appeared clearly not to believe me; and, indeed, I have since learnt that immense fortunes are often made in such employments."[5] Franklin reflected that Braddock and Loudoun were hardly better than Morris and Denny. If Britain could or would not spare more competent men to administer the colonies, the colonists must do more of it themselves.

From 4 April when Franklin left Philadelphia to 26 July when he reached London was the longest period of idleness he had known since he was first apprenticed to his brother. In New York, never knowing when the ship might sail, he could undertake little more than letters, and he wrote more letters than he is known ever to have written before in that length of time. He wrote to his wife on 27 May asking her to send him his best spectacles which he had forgotten, and to deliver to Parker two books which Franklin carefully directed her to. "In my room on the folio shelf between the clock and our bedchamber and not far from the clock, stands a folio called the *Gardener's Dictionary* by P. Miller. And on the same side of the room, on the lowest shelf or lowest but one, near the middle and by the side of a little partition, you will find standing, or rather lying on its fore edge, a quarto pamphlet covered with blue paper, called a *Treatise of Cider-Making*."[6] He wrote to her about various matters of business, and sent her and Sally the most affectionate messages. He wrote three times to his sister Jane in Boston, discussing the future of his nephews, and gently agreeing that Elizabeth Dowse, the eldest of all the Franklin brothers and sisters and then eighty, must be allowed to go on living in her own house. "As having their own way is one of the greatest comforts of life to old people, I think their friends should endeavour to accommodate them in that as well as in anything else. When they have lived long in a house it becomes natural to them; they are almost as closely connected with it as a tortoise with its shell; old folks and old trees, if you remove them, it is ten to one that you kill them."[7] He wrote in detail to Isaac Norris about Loudoun and the case of the indentured servants.

Colonel Henry Bouquet, whom Franklin had met in Philadelphia, was going to South Carolina. He had given Franklin letters of introduction to men in London, and Franklin gave him letters to his friends Alexander Garden and John Lining, both physicians, in Charleston. "I regret much," Franklin wrote to Bouquet, "that through your business and mine I could enjoy so little of your conversation in Philadelphia. How happy are the folks in heaven, who, 'tis said, having nothing to do but to talk with one another, except now and then a little singing and drinking of *aqua vitæ*."[8] To Garden, after whom Linnæus named the gardenia, Franklin wrote that he hoped to return from England by way of Charleston, to see his friends there. To Lining, Franklin wrote at length about certain phenomena of heat and cold, particularly the effects of evaporation which a correspondent in Glasgow had reported to him. "I have not had leisure to repeat and examine more than the first and easiest of them, viz., Wet the ball of a thermometer by a feather dipped in spirit of wine which has been kept in the same room and has, of course, the same degree of heat or cold. The mercury sinks presently three or four degrees, and the quicker if during the evaporation you blow on the ball with a bellows; a second wetting and blowing, when the mercury is down, carries it yet lower. I think I did not get it lower than five or six degrees from where it naturally stood, which was at that time sixty."[9] From there Franklin went on to observations of his own on the different conductivity of different substances.

At last about the middle of June the fleet and convoy sailed from New York. The packets for five days attended Loudoun's flagship, to take on his dispatches when his interminable writing should be done. Then, though two of the packets were kept with the fleet as far as Halifax, Franklin's was released and steered for England. "Our captain of the packet had boasted much, before we sailed, of the swiftness of his ship; unfortunately, when we came to sea, she proved the dullest of ninety six sail, to his no small mortification. After many conjectures respecting the cause, when we were near another ship almost as dull as ours, which, however, gained upon us, the captain ordered all hands to come aft and stand as near the ensign-staff as possible. We were, passengers included, about forty persons. While we stood there, the ship mended her pace and soon left her neighbour far behind, which proved clearly what our captain suspected: that she was loaded too much by the head. The casks of water, it seems, had been all placed forward; these he therefore ordered to be moved further aft, on which the ship recovered her character and proved the best sailer in the fleet."[10] Franklin speculated on the nautical assumption, at the time, that it could never be known how a ship would sail till she was built and could be tested. The trouble was, the philosopher decided, that "one man builds the hull, another rigs her, a third lades her and sails her. No one of these has the advantage of knowing all the ideas and experience of the others, and therefore cannot draw just conclusions from a combination of the whole."[11] What was called for was a set of accurate experiments on all such matters, jointly undertaken and carried out to a common end. Nothing was alien to this philosopher, whose countrymen were soon to develop faster ships than had ever sailed before.

During the voyage Franklin, with more time than usual on his hands, wrote more than a usual preface for his next year's almanac. It was to be a summary of Poor Richard's counsels on economy. Poor Richard, he told his readers in the new preface dated 7 July, had seldom had the pleasure of being quoted by other learned authors, though in conversation he had sometimes quoted himself. But at an auction he had recently heard an old man, called Father Abraham, make a speech drawn almost altogether from Poor Richard. This preface was that speech. Here were the best economical maxims from the almanacs of twenty-five years. Either because Franklin had no file with him and was quoting from memory, or more likely because he wanted to give a sharper point to the adages, he several times revised his text. In 1740 he had written: "An empty bag cannot stand upright." In 1750 he had elaborated it: " 'Tis hard (but glorious) to be poor and honest. An empty sack can hardly stand upright; but if it does, 'tis a stout one." Now he gave the proverb its final form: " 'Tis hard for an empty bag to stand upright." In 1743 he had written: "If you'd have it done, go; if not, send." Now he tried to make this clearer, and made it weaker: "If you would have your business done, go; if not, send." He changed the person of pronouns, the tenses of verbs; he put in a few proverbs that had not appeared before: among them the famous: "Three removes is as good as a fire"; and the homely: "Always taking out of the meal-tub and never putting in soon comes to the bottom." And all of them were dramatically fitted to the character of Father Abraham.

If he had a file of *Poor Richard* with him, Franklin, turning through it, might have noticed that he had touched many topics in the past ten years of his public life. *"What maintains one vice would bring up two children" (1747). "Lost time is never found again" (1748). "The muses love the morning" (1748). "He is not well bred that cannot bear ill-breeding in others" (1748). "The end of passion is the beginning of repentance" (1749). "Many foxes grow grey, but few grow good" (1749). "Having been poor is no shame, but being ashamed of it is" (1749). "Doing an injury puts you below your enemy; revenging one makes you but even with him; forgiving it sets you above him" (1749). "Discontented minds and fevers of the body are not to be cured by changing beds or businesses" (1750). "Men would live by their wits, but break for want of stock" (1750). *"We may give advice, but we cannot give conduct" (1750). "Cunning proceeds from want of capacity" (1750). "Old boys have their playthings as well as young ones; the difference is only in the price" (1752). "The brave and the wise can both pity and excuse when cowards and fools show no mercy" (1752). " 'Tis against some men's principle to pay interest, and seems against others' interest to pay principal" (1753). "He that best understands the world least likes it" (1753). "Anger is never without a reason, but seldom with a good one" (1753). "The bell calls others to church, but itself never minds the sermon" (1754). "Cut the wings of your hopes and hens, lest they lead you a weary dance after them" (1754). "Love your neighbour, yet don't pull down your hedge" (1754). "When prosperity was well mounted, she let go the bridle, and soon came tumbling out of the saddle" (1754). "An hundred thieves cannot strip one naked man, especially if his skin's off" (1755). "It is ill manners to silence a fool, and cruelty to let him go on" (1757). "Retirement does not always secure virtue. Lot was upright in the city, wicked in the mountains" (1757). When Franklin had finished his preface he added a variety of maxims for the body of the almanac for 1758. *"Half a truth is often a great lie." "The first mistake in public business is the going into it." "In a corrupt age the putting the world in order would breed confusion; then e'en mind your own business."

But for the summary preface Franklin chose only the maxims of worldly prudence suitable to the occasion. Such a preface could not be left to wear out in an old almanac, along with the earlier issues of *Poor Richard*. Benjamin Mecom, Franklin's nephew in Boston, published it separately as *Father Abraham's Speech* the

following March. Under that and its later title *The Way to Wealth*
it spread throughout the colonies and followed Franklin to Europe.
Translated into many languages, it long ago passed from literature
into the general human speech.

Later in July the packet was several times chased by French
privateers. Near Falmouth the captain determined to run the last
night to avoid the enemy, "who often cruised near the entrance of
the channel. Accordingly all the sail was set that we could possibly
make, and, the wind being very fresh and fair, we went right before
it and made great way. . . . We had a watchman placed in the
bow, to whom they often called: 'Look well out before there,' and
he as often answered: 'Aye, aye'; but perhaps had his eyes shut and
was half asleep at the time, they sometimes answering, as is said,
mechanically; for he did not see a light just before us which had
been hid by the studding-sails from the man at the helm and from
the rest of the watch, but by an accidental yaw of the ship was
discovered and occasioned a great alarm, we being very near it,
the light appearing to me as big as a cart wheel. It was midnight,
and our captain fast asleep; but Captain Kennedy, jumping up on
deck and seeing the danger, ordered the ship to wear around, all
sails standing; an operation dangerous to the masts, but it carried
us clear and we escaped shipwreck, for we were running right upon
the rocks upon which the lighthouse was erected. This deliverance
impressed me strongly with the utility of lighthouses, and made me
resolve to encourage the building more of them in America if I
should live to return there.

"In the morning it was found by the soundings, etc., that we
were near our port, but a thick fog hid the land from our sight.
About nine o'clock the fog began to rise and seemed to be lifted
up from the water like the curtain at a playhouse, discovering
underneath the town of Falmouth, the vessels in its harbour, and
the fields that surrounded it. . . . I set out immediately with my
son for London, and we only stopped a little by the way to view
Stonehenge on Salisbury Plain and Lord Pembroke's house and
gardens, with his very curious antiquities at Wilton. We arrived
in London the 27th [26th] of July 1757."[12]

London

Agent

FRANKLIN'S reputation as a scientist had gone ahead of him to London. A member since April 1756 of the Royal Society, he had been member also since September of the Premium Society, for the encouragement of arts, manufactures, and commerce, now known as the Society of Arts. On 27 November of that year he had written that he was sending twenty guineas "to be applied in premiums for some improvement in Britain, as a grateful though small return for your most kind and generous intentions of encouraging improvements in America. I flatter myself, from that part of your plan, that those jealousies of her colonies which were formerly entertained by the mother country begin to subside. . . . Never be discouraged by any apprehension that arts are come to such perfection in England as to be incapable of farther improvement. As yet, the quantity of human knowledge bears no proportion to the quantity of human ignorance."[1] Both his societies were prepared to welcome him, as were scientists on the Continent. Beccaria from Turin saluted Franklin as "vir præclarissime" in a Latin letter of welcome dated 24 December 1757.[2]

But Franklin, that man of friendships, had few personal friends in London, and those mostly by correspondence. He had reported to Peter Collinson, Quaker, merchant, and member of the Royal Society, all his observations on electricity. He had for fourteen years exchanged letters with William Strahan, printer already of Johnson's dictionary and the first volumes of Hume's history and later of Adam Smith, Gibbon, Robertson, and Blackstone. The two printers had more than trade and business in common. They sent each other news about their families, and ever since Sally Franklin was six or seven had humorously planned a marriage between her and Strahan's son William, who was three years older.

Even before Franklin told the Assembly he would go to London as
their agent, he hurried letters off to Collinson and Strahan. "Our
Assembly," he told Strahan, "talk of sending me to England
speedily. Then look out sharp, and if a fat old fellow should come
to your printing house and request a little smouting [job work],
depend upon it 'tis your affectionate friend and humble servant."[3]

When Franklin and his son reached London late on 26 July
they spent the first night at Collinson's house at Mill Hill. Strahan
called on them the next day. Both Collinson and Strahan were
instantly captivated by the philosopher. "For my own part,"
Strahan wrote to Deborah Franklin, "I never saw a man who was,
in every respect, so perfectly agreeable to me. Some are amiable
in one view, some in another, he in all. . . . Your son I really
think one of the prettiest young gentlemen I ever knew from
America."[4] After a few days at the Bear Inn the father and son
found lodgings with Margaret Stevenson, a widow living with her
daughter Mary at 7 (later 36) Craven Street, Strand, where Franklin stayed as long as he was in London. He had four rooms, and
lived handsomely, with two servants he had brought from Philadelphia. Nor did the philosopher disregard the London fashions.
His account books show that the earliest expenses of the new
household were for stationery, shoes, and wigs, linen to be made up
into shirts, and cambric for William's handkerchiefs. There were
a sword and sword blade to be mended, and such varied purchases
as spectacles and a glass, a watch at auction, mourning swords, a
sword knot, two pairs of silver shoe and knee buckles, two razors
and a case, and copies of the *Gentleman's Magazine*. William,
whose wants were greater than his father's, was entered in the
Middle Temple to study for the bar.

Franklin promptly took up the mission on which he had come
to London. First he consulted John Fothergill, the Scottish doctor
who had urged that the Philadelphia letters on electricity be
printed. Fothergill thought Franklin should not complain immediately to the government but should first apply to the proprietors.
While Fothergill was arranging a meeting with them, Collinson
arranged that Franklin should go with John Hanbury, "the great
Virginia merchant," to call on Lord Granville, president of the
Privy Council. Granville was disturbing to the agent who had

come to plead the cause of the Assembly. "The Council," Granville said, and Franklin reported to Isaac Norris, "is over all the colonies; your last resort is to the Council to decide your differences, and you must be sensible it is for your good, for otherwise you often would not obtain justice. The king in council is legislator of the colonies; and when His Majesty's instructions come there, they are the law of the land . . . and as such ought to be obeyed."[5] "I told his lordship this was new doctrine to me. I had always understood from our charters that our laws were to be made by our assemblies, to be presented indeed to the king for his royal assent, but that being once given the king could not repeal or alter them. And as the assemblies could not make permanent laws without his assent, so neither could he make a law for them without theirs. He assured me I was totally mistaken."[6] Franklin, come to appeal from the proprietors to the king, found that one of the king's ministers thought very much like a proprietor.

The meeting at Thomas Penn's house in Spring Garden about the middle of August was polite but hostile. Franklin presented the Heads of Complaint that he had brought, and was told to reduce them to writing. When he did this on 20 August, the paper was turned over to Ferdinand John Paris, "a proud, angry man," who had drafted many of the proprietarial messages to the Assembly and bitterly resented Franklin's stinging answers. The Penns asked the agent to deal with their lawyer. Franklin refused to treat with anybody but them. They claimed they could not find out from the complaint what the Assembly meant and wanted. Would Franklin draw up a supply bill such as the Assembly would approve? He said he had no authority to do that, and declined to. They then, on Paris's suggestion, referred the document to the attorney-general and the solicitor-general for an opinion. As this was August and the royal lawyers were out of town, nothing could be done at once. Not until November 1758 did the proprietors have an answer ready, and then they sent it to the Assembly, snubbing Franklin, who they said had handled the affair without due formality or candour. Franklin could think of no informality on his part except that he had not, in his paper, addressed them as True and Absolute Proprietaries of the Province of Pennsylvania. He had been only setting down for their convenience what he had already said in conversation. Whatever excuses they gave, the truth is that they heartily disliked him for his past record and his present firmness. After all, he was dangerous, as spokesman of the Assembly, to their pockets, their prerogative, and their peace of mind.

Franklin was not behind them in dislike. He said to Thomas Penn that the original charter of the province gave the Assembly "all the powers and privileges of an assembly according to the rights of free-born subjects of England, and as is usual in any of the British plantations in America. 'Yes,' says he, 'but if my father granted privileges he was not by the royal charter empowered to grant, nothing can be claimed by such grant.' I said: 'Then if your father had no right to grant the privileges he pretended to grant, and published all over Europe as granted, those who came to settle in the province on the faith of that grant, and in expectation of enjoying the privileges contained in it, were deceived, cheated, and betrayed.' He answered that they should have themselves looked to that; that the royal charter was no secret; they who came into the province on his father's offer of privileges, if they were deceived, it was their own fault. And that he said with a kind of triumphing, laughing insolence, such as a low jockey might do when a purchaser complained that he had cheated him on a horse. I was astonished to see him thus meanly give up his father's character, and conceived at that moment a more cordial and thorough contempt for him than I ever felt for any man living, a contempt that I cannot express in words, but I believe my countenance expressed it strongly, and that his brother, who was looking at me, must have observed it. However, finding myself grow warm, I made no other answer to this than that the poor people were no lawyers themselves and, confiding in his father, did not think it necessary to consult any."[7]

Impatiently waiting, Franklin had a serious illness that lasted eight weeks. About the first of September, he told his wife, he had "a violent cold and something of a fever" for a day or two, and then thought he had recovered. "However, it was not long before I had another severe cold which continued longer than the first, attended by great pain in my head, the top of which was very hot and, when the pain went off, very sore and tender. These fits of pain continued sometimes longer than at others; seldom less than twelve hours, and once thirty-six hours. I was now and then a little delirious; they cupped me on the back of the head, which seemed to ease me for the present; I took a great deal of bark [cinchona] both in substance and infusion; and, too soon thinking myself well, I ventured out twice to do a little business and forward the service I am engaged in, and both times got fresh cold and fell down again. My good doctor [Fothergill] grew very angry with me, for acting contrary to his cautions and directions, and obliged me to promise more observance for the future. He attended me very carefully and affectionately; and the good lady of the house nursed me kindly. Billy was also of great service to me, in going from place to place where I could not go myself, and Peter was very diligent and attentive. I took so much bark in various ways that I began to abhor it; I durst not take a vomit for fear of my head; but at last I was seized one morning with a vomiting and purging, the latter of which continued the greater part of the day, and I believe was a kind of crisis to the distemper, carrying it clear off; for ever since I feel quite lightsome, and am every day gathering strength; so I hope my seasoning is over and that I shall enjoy better health during the rest of my stay in England."

This was written on 22 November, when Fothergill had allowed Franklin to think of letters again. He ran on cheerfully at length, replying to all he had heard from his wife and sending her bits of gossip. He had been visiting with Shirley, the former governor of Massachusetts. William Hunter, Franklin's associate in the colonial post office, was in England, and he and his sister wanted to be remembered to Mrs. Franklin. James Ralph, after all these years, was friendly and obliging. Though he was glad to hear about his daughter and grandchildren in America, he did not want his present wife to know that he had them. On 3 December Franklin added a long postscript. "It is now twelve days since I began to write this letter, and I still continue well, but have not yet quite recovered my strength, flesh, or spirits. I every day drink a glass of infusion of bark in wine, by way of prevention, and hope my fever will no more return; on fair days, which are but few, I venture out about noon. The agreeable conversation I meet with among men of learning, and the notice taken of me by persons of distinction, are the principal things that soothe me for the present, under this painful absence from my family and friends."[8]

He had intended if he had been well, he said in the same post-script, to go round among the shops for "some pretty things for you and my dear good Sally (whose little hands you say eased your headache) to send by this ship, but I must now defer it to the next, having only got a crimson satin cloak for you, the newest fashion, and the black silk for Sally; but Billy sends her a scarlet feather, muff, and tippet, and a box of fashionable linen for her dress." By February Franklin, with the help of his landlady, had got together and shipped two cases of presents, which he described in affec-tionate, perhaps homesick detail.[9] He sent some English china: "melons and leaves for a dessert of fruit and cream, or the like; a bowl remarkable for the neatness of the figures, made at Bow near this city; some coffee cups of the same; a Worcester bowl, ordinary. To show the difference of workmanship, there is something from all the china works in England; and one old true china basin mended, of an odd colour. The same box contains four silver salt ladles, newest but ugliest fashion; a little instrument to core apples; another to make little turnips out of great ones; six coarse diaper breakfast cloths: they are to spread on the tea table, for nobody here breakfasts on the naked table, but on the cloth set a large tea board with the cups. There is also a little basket, a present from Mrs. Stevenson to Sally, and a pair of garters for you, which were knit by the young lady, her daughter, who favoured me with a pair of the same kind, the only ones I have been able to wear; as they need not be bound tight, the ridges in them preventing their slip-ping. We send them therefore as a curiosity, for the form more than for the value. Goody Smith may, if she pleases, make such for me hereafter, and they will suit her own fat knees. My love to her."

He sent, further, carpet "for a best room floor" which he had thought of himself, and bedticks, blankets, tablecloths, napkins, and sheeting which Deborah had ordered. "There is also fifty-six yards of cotton printed curiously from copperplates, a new inven-tion, to make bed and window curtains; and seven yards chair bottoms, printed in the same way, very neat. These were my fancy; but Mrs. Stevenson tells me I did wrong not to buy both of the same colour. Also seven yards of printed cotton, blue ground, to make you a gown. I bought it by candle-light, and liked it then, but not so well afterwards. If you do not fancy it, send it as a present from me to sister Jenny. There is a better gown for you, of flowered tissue, sixteen yards, of Mrs. Stevenson's fancy, cost nine guineas; and I think it a great beauty."

Then there were steel snuffers, snuff-stand, and extinguishers, music William had bought for his sister, and two sets of books her father sent her: the *World* and the *Connoisseur*. The silk blankets were "of a new kind, were just taken in a French prize, and such were never seen in England before; they are called blankets, but I think will be very neat to cover a summer bed, instead of a quilt or counterpane. I had no choice, so you will excuse the soil on some of the folds; your neighbour Forster can get it off. I also forgot, among the china, to mention a large fine jug for beer, to stand in the cooler. I fell in love with it at first sight; for I thought it looked like a fat jolly dame, clean and tidy, with a neat blue and white calico gown on, good-natured and lovely, and put me in mind of—somebody." And there was a whole box of table glass of various sorts. He was buying a set of china, silver-handled knives and forks, and silver candle-sticks; "but these I shall keep here to use till my return, as I am obliged sometimes to entertain polite company." The harpsichord he had planned to buy for Sally, for forty guineas, he had given up on the advice of a musical friend, who told him a new one could never be depended on, "though made by the best hands." It was not the cost that mattered to the indulgent father. He paid forty-two guineas for the harpsichord he bought in June.

On 30 November he was well enough to go to the Royal Society's feast, and then frequently by coach to the White Lion, to Montague House where the British Museum had recently been installed, and to the houses of his friends. Before Christmas he had hired a coach of his own for twelve guineas a month. "I found that every time I walked out I got fresh cold; and the hackney coaches at this end of the town, where most people keep their own, are the worst in the whole city, miserable, dirty, broken, shabby things, unfit to go into when dressed clean, and such as one would be ashamed to get out of at any gentleman's door."[10] In his comfortable lodgings with the friendly Mrs. Stevenson and her daughter, with his promising, dashing son, with his servant Peter who soon learned the town well enough to go on errands anywhere, with the slave King who waited incompetently on William and ran away after a year, Franklin settled down in a household not too much unlike that in Philadelphia. Strahan wrote to Deborah Franklin urging her to come over. Her husband was sure she would never in any circumstances cross the ocean. Nor did he insist. First he expected to return to America the following spring. Then he thought his work would take a summer, then a year. It was five years before he set out for home. After a few months he was as much at home in London as anywhere.

Now, while the Penns and the lawyers procrastinated, Franklin had a year or so of something like philosophic leisure. He had brought with him, or devised in London, the most powerful electric machine ever seen there. Lord Charles Cavendish and others judged that the spark it threw was nine inches long. A copy was owned by Lord Morton.[11] Franklin on 21 December 1757 wrote out for John Pringle, who had already produced his classic treatise on military medicine and sanitation and was to be president of the Royal Society, an account of the effects of electricity on paralytics in Pennsylvania. "I never knew any advantage from electricity in palsies that was permanent. And how far the apparent temporary advantage might arise from the exercise in the patients' journey, and coming daily to my house, or from the spirits given by the hope of success, enabling them to exert more strength in moving their limbs, I will not pretend to say."[12] Franklin invented a curious clock, economical but not quite practical, which a new friend, James Ferguson, improved in 1758 to Franklin's generous satisfaction.[13] He was on the friendliest terms with John Canton, who first in England had got lightning from the sky. Franklin bought electrical equipment for Harvard, and himself took pains to prepare it and to furnish careful instructions.[14]

In May 1758 he went to Cambridge with his son, and there performed experiments in evaporation with John Hadley, professor of chemistry. Using ether instead of spirits on the ball of Hadley's thermometer, they got the temperature down to twenty-five degrees below freezing. "From this experiment," Franklin wrote to John

Lining in Charleston on 17 June, "one may see the possibility of freezing a man to death on a warm summer's day, if he were to stand in a passage through which the wind blew briskly, and to be wet frequently with ether." Franklin's mind ranged over the subject. In India, he had heard, they kept water cool by evaporation. "Even our common sailors seem to have had some notion of this property; for I remember that, being at sea when I was a youth, I observed one of the sailors, during a calm in the night, often wetting his finger in his mouth and then holding it up in the air, to discover, as he said, if the air had any motion and from which side it came; and this he expected to do by finding one side of his finger grow suddenly cold, and from that side he should look for the next wind; which I then laughed at as a fancy."

Franklin remembered the hot Sunday at Philadelphia in July 1750. "When the thermometer was up at 100 in the shade, I sat in my chamber without exercise, only reading or writing, with no other clothes on than a shirt and a pair of long linen drawers, the windows all open, and a brisk wind blowing through the house; the sweat ran off the backs of my hands, and my shirt was so often wet as to induce me to call for dry ones to put on. . . . But . . . my body never grew so hot as the air that surrounded it or the inanimate objects immersed in the same air. . . . May not this be a reason why our reapers in Pennsylvania, working in the open field in the clear hot sunshine common in our harvest time, find themselves well able to go through that labour without being much incommoded by the heat while they continue to sweat, and while they supply matter for keeping up that sweat by drinking frequently of a thin evaporable liquor, water mixed with rum; but if the sweat stops, they drop, and sometimes die suddenly if a sweating is not again brought on by drinking that liquor, or, as some rather choose in that case, a kind of hot punch made of water mixed with honey and a considerable proportion of vinegar?" Perhaps Negroes sweat more than white men and so could bear the sun's heat better; "if that is a fact, as it is said to be." Might not even the earth itself, under the summer sun, be cooled by evaporation? "To these queries of imagination, I will only add one practical observation: that wherever it is thought proper to give ease in cases of painful inflammation in the flesh (as from burnings or the like) by cooling the part, linen cloths wet with spirit and applied to the part inflamed will produce the coolness required better than if wet with water and will continue it longer."[15]

Franklin enjoyed his visit to Cambridge so much that, "as all the great folks were out of town and public business at a stand," he went back for commencement early in July. He and his son "were present at all the ceremonies, dined every day in their halls, and my vanity was not a little gratified by the particular regard showed me by the chancellor and vice-chancellor of the University and the heads of colleges." From Cambridge, after commencement, the Franklins set out for Northampton, to visit, like so many later Americans, the homes of their forefathers. At Wellingborough they found Mary Fisher, a daughter of Thomas Franklin, who remembered when Josiah Franklin and his family left for New England. The American Franklins went to Ecton, where the English Franklins had lived so long on their small freehold. "The land is now added to another farm, and a school kept in the house. It is a decayed old stone building, but still known by the name of Franklin House." The rector of the parish showed them the parish register, "in which were the births, marriages, and burials of our ancestors for two hundred years, as early as his book began." The rector's wife showed them the Franklin gravestones in the church-yard, "which were so covered with moss that we could not read the letters till she ordered a hard brush and basin of water with which Peter scoured them clean, and then Billy copied them." Then the father and son went to Birmingham and looked up Deborah's relations, who were in even a smaller way than the Franklins.[16] John Baskerville, the fine printer in Birmingham, interested the plain printer from Philadelphia. Franklin, who the year before had sent the Baskerville Virgil as a gift to Harvard, now put the name of Isaac Norris in the list of subscribers to the Baskerville Milton.

In London again in September he heard that two of his old Junto friends had died: Stephen Potts, who had remained a book-binder, and William Parsons, who had become surveyor-general. "Odd characters, both of them," Franklin wrote to Hugh Roberts, who had sent the news. "Parsons a wise man that often acted fool-ishly; Potts a wit that seldom acted wisely. If *enough* were the means to make a man happy, one had always the means of happiness without ever enjoying the thing; the other had always the thing without ever possessing the means. Parsons even in his prosperity always fretting; Potts in the midst of his poverty always laughing. It seems, then, that happiness in this life rather depends on internals than externals; and that, besides the natural effects of wisdom and virtue, vice and folly, there is such a thing as a happy or an unhappy constitution."[17] In December Franklin, who had as happy a constitution as any in the world, was busy with the art and science of chimneys. He had reduced the opening of his fireplace in Craven Street to three feet by two and had invented an iron frame with a sliding plate which acted as a draught, with the result that he got more heat from less fuel. "Several of my acquaintance, having seen this simple machine in my room, have imitated it in their own houses, and it seems likely to become pretty common." The effect of chimneys upon ventilation, he thought, had been too little studied.[18]

In January 1758 the odd rumour got back to Boston that Franklin had been made a baronet and governor of Pennsylvania. A more appropriate honour came on 12 February 1759 when the University of St. Andrews conferred on him the degree of doctor of laws, and gave him the only title he ever had. Three of his best friends in London—Strahan, Fothergill, and Pringle—were Scots, and later in that year he made a long and happy tour in Scotland. Most of his letters for 1759 have been lost, and the scant records tell little but that he was made burgess and guildbrother of Edinburgh on 5 September and one day the same month had supper at the house of William Robertson with Adam Smith, William Cullen, Alexander Carlyle, and other men of learning unnamed. By Edinburgh standards Franklin seemed reserved that evening,[19] less sociable than his son, who was with them. But Franklin knew that this was a notable year in Scotland. David Hume, the acutest thinker in Great Britain, keeper of the Advocates' Library in Edinburgh, in 1759 published the third and fourth volumes of his history of England; Robertson, soon to become principal of the University, his history of Scotland; Adam Smith, still professor at Glasgow, his *Theory of the Moral Sentiments*. Franklin was a moralist and thought history the most useful of moral studies. And there were scientists in Edinburgh. Cullen, professor of chemistry, had made important experiments on the production of cold by evaporation. Franklin and his son visited Sir Alexander Dick, president of the College of Physicians, at Prestonfield. John Anderson, professor of natural philosophy at Glasgow, accompanied the travellers through Perth to St. Andrews where Dr. Franklin received his diploma. At St. Andrews one of the students, Lord Cardross, was sick with a fever. His doctor prescribed that he be blistered. Franklin, asked for an opinion, advised against it. Cardross, later the earl of Buchan, always insisted that Franklin had probably saved his life.[20]

The closest friendship which Franklin brought away from his journey to Scotland was with Lord Kames, judge of session in Edinburgh, the man whose life Boswell—with his genius for recognizing character—wanted most to write after Johnson's. In Berwick on their way to London the Franklins stopped at Kames for several days, and their host and hostess went with them part of their way to York. Franklin, back in London at the end of the year after some weeks in Yorkshire and Lincolnshire, still regretted that he had not urged Lord and Lady Kames to come further. "Our conversation," he wrote for himself and his son, "till we came to York was chiefly a recollection of that we had seen and heard, the pleasure we had enjoyed, and the kindnesses we had received in Scotland, and how far that country had exceeded our expectations. On the whole, I must say I think the time we spent there was six weeks of the *densest* happiness I have met with in any part of my life; and the agreeable and instructive society we found there in such plenty has left so pleasing an impression on my memory that, did not strong connexions draw me elsewhere, I believe Scotland would be the country I should choose to spend the remainder of my days in."

And to Kames, in the same letter, Franklin turned aside from friendly compliments to speak for a moment of his imperial vision. "I have long been of opinion that the foundations of the future grandeur and stability of the British Empire lie in America; and though, like other foundations, they are low and little seen, they are nevertheless broad and strong enough to support the greatest political structure human wisdom ever yet erected."[21]

II

Only William Pitt among the men in power in England had this imperial vision, and Pitt was carrying on an enormous war in India and Europe as well as in America. "I made several attempts," Franklin later wrote, "to be introduced to Lord Chatham (at that time first minister) on account of my Pennsylvania business, but without success. He was then too great a man, or too much occupied in affairs of greater moment."[22] To Pitt, Franklin was merely the agent of a remote colony squabbling with its proprietors. Arthur Onslow, Speaker of the House of Commons, saw that the liberties of Englishmen were possibly at stake, but Charles Yorke, the solicitor-general, stood for the prerogative of the proprietors as well as of the Crown. "You may conjecture," Franklin wrote to Isaac Norris on 19 March 1759, "what reception a petition concerning privileges from the colonies may meet with from those who think that even the people of England have too many."[23] Charles Pratt, the attorney-general, was friendly though discreet, but he saw trouble ahead. Some day, he told Franklin during 1758, the Americans for all they said of their loyalty and affection would set up for independence. Franklin insisted that "no such idea was ever entertained by the Americans, nor will any such ever enter their heads, unless you grossly abuse them." That, Pratt said, might well happen and bring the outcome he foresaw.[24]

While waiting for an answer from the proprietors, Franklin did more than wait. Besides talking with everybody he saw who might have influence, he turned to the press, about which he knew so much, to get at public opinion, with which he was so expert. He aimed, he wrote to the Assembly on 10 June 1758, at "removing the prejudices that art and accident have spread among the people of this country against us, and obtaining for us the good opinion of the bulk of mankind without doors."[25] In the first days of his illness in September 1757 he had William write a letter to the *Citizen* in refutation of the anonymous abuses of Pennsylvania which had appeared, and which Franklin believed came from the proprietors. He paid a pound to have the letter printed. As soon as he was well he planned a book which should cover the whole ground of the quarrel: *An Historical Review of the Constitution and Government of Pennsylvania.* William "furnished most of the materials," James Ralph had a hand in preparing it for the press, and Strahan printed it, at Franklin's expense. Franklin "looked over the manuscript, but was not permitted to alter everything I did not wholly approve." "It was wrote," he told Norris on 9 June 1759, "by a gentleman said to be one of the best pens in England, and who interests himself in the concerns of America, but will not be known."[26] The man was Richard Jackson, an English lawyer who wrote secretly because he was hoping to become a member of Parliament through the favour of the ministry and did not want to run the risk of alienating them. The book was nearly ready by June 1758, but was held up for about a year.

In the meantime there were other colonial incidents. William Moore, who had a brother in the House of Commons and had been appointed by the proprietors to be justice of the peace in Chester County, was arrested in January 1758 by the sergeant-at-arms of the Pennsylvania Assembly on the charge that he had libelled them, and William Smith, provost of the Academy, at the same time for aiding Moore. They spent three months in jail, where Smith taught his classes. After their release by order of the supreme court, Smith carried their case to London, where he arrived in January 1759. He argued that the Quakers had prosecuted him and Moore, both good Churchmen, because they had urged the need of defence in Pennsylvania, and that the Assembly did not have the constitutional right to punish libel. While he waited for his hearing before the attorney-general and the solicitor-general, Smith talked everywhere bitterly against the Quakers. They were, he said, persecuting Churchmen to avenge themselves on Thomas Penn, who had ceased to be a Quaker. Fellow-Churchmen quickly took Smith's side, and skirmished to get him the degree of doctor of divinity from Oxford on the recommendation of the Archbishop of Canterbury and five other bishops. This he was given in March, six weeks after Franklin, a dissenter, had received his Scottish degree. Smith was as bitter against Franklin as against the Quakers. He did not deserve, Smith said, even his reputation as a scientist, but had stolen his ideas about electricity from Ebenezer Kinnersley in Philadelphia. Though Franklin was angry and fought back, he had the better temper and had a philosophical last word when, four years later, he wrote: "I made that man my enemy by doing him too much kindness. 'Tis the honestest way of acquiring an enemy. And, since 'tis convenient to have at least one enemy, who by his readiness to revile one on all occasions may make one careful of one's conduct, I shall keep him an enemy for that purpose."[27] But in June 1759 the Privy Council ruled that the Assembly, in punishing the libels, had unwarrantably assumed powers which did not belong to them.

The proprietors came off less well in the matter of the Delawares. With the help of certain Quakers, and under the leadership of Tedyuskung, the Delawares, now officially at peace with Pennsylvania, had settled on the Susquehanna in the Wyoming district. The Penns claimed the land. Tedyuskung asked to see their title deeds. At the council held at Easton in July–August 1757 Tedyuskung had had a clerk, Charles Thomson, and his minutes did not read the same as the proprietors'. The Assembly sent Thomson's record to Franklin, asking him to consult the ministry. Thomas Penn saw Granville and Halifax, also a member of the Privy Council, and misrepresented the facts to them. Franklin changed their opinions. At the hearing before the Board of Trade on 15 May 1759 Franklin asked the proprietors to show their deeds to the Board. They protested, thinking he did not know the contents, and saying he wanted them only to pick holes. He surprised Penn, and Paris, by producing copies of the deeds and freely turning them over to Halifax. The Board took the case out of the hands of the proprietors and referred it to Sir William Johnson of New York, superintendent of the Six Nations under the Crown, who allowed the Delawares to stay at Wyoming.

Steadily, adroitly, Franklin harried the proprietors. Before the hearing on the Delawares he had published Thomson's *Enquiry into the Causes of the Alienation of the Delaware and Shawonese Indians from the British Interest*, and before the hearing on Smith and Moore, the *Historical Review*. Penn was furious. "When I meet him anywhere," Franklin told Isaac Norris on 9 June, "there appears in his wretched countenance a strange mixture of hatred, anger, fear, and vexation."[28] The *Historical Review* contained a passage which must have cut the Penns like poisoned knives. "And who or what are these proprietaries? In the province, unsizable subjects and unsufficient lords. At home, gentlemen it is true, but gentlemen so very private that in the herd of gentry they are hardly to be found; not in court, not in office, not in Parliament."[29] Though Jackson had written this, the Penns supposed the insult came from Franklin, as well as the whole treatise which, polemically but powerfully, condemned their government of Pennsylvania. They were rather ordinary men, fairly conscientious, who had had a great deal of trouble with their province and derived by no means so much income from it as was commonly thought. With the prejudices of their class, they thought of themselves as owning Pennsylvania, with no more responsibility toward it than they might be pleased to feel. And here they were being bullied in the name of liberty, as it seemed to them, not only by the contumacious Assembly but also by the crafty, incessant man of genius who had come to London to turn public opinion against them and take away their prerogative.

The Assembly did not bother to discuss the answer which the Penns made them, through the governor not Franklin, in February 1759. Denny assented in April to a money bill for £100,000 which at last levied taxes on the lands of the proprietors. He was not sued on his bond, as he and governors before him had been afraid to be, but he left his office and entered the British army. The bill was sent to England for the royal assent, and the Penns opposed it. The Privy Council's Committee for Plantation Affairs in June 1760 reported against it as "manifestly offensive to natural justice, to the laws of England, and to the royal prerogative." Franklin, intending soon to leave for Ireland and then Scotland again, was kept in England all summer. Though he had never met Pitt, and knew of Pitt's imperious temper, Franklin boldly wrote to him, adding an audacious postscript as from one man to another. "Between you and I, it is said that we may look upon them all to be a pack of d——d r——ls, and that unless we bribe them all higher than our adversaries can do, and condescend to every piece of dirty work they require, we shall never be able to attain common justice at their hands."[30] He ran his pen through the postscript, but left it legible.

The proprietors contended that if they were put at the mercy of the province's assessors they would be ruined. Franklin and his lawyers pointed out that the £100,000 had been issued as paper money which was now in general circulation, and that to repeal the bill and make the paper worthless would ruin the province. Finally Lord Mansfield, chief justice and member of the Privy Council, at one of the hearings "rose and, beckoning me, took me into the clerk's chamber while the lawyers were pleading, and asked me if I was really of opinion that no injury would be done to the proprietary estate in the execution of the act. I said certainly. 'Then,' says he, 'you can have little objection to enter into an engagement to assure that point.' I answered: 'None at all.' He then called in Paris, and after some discourse his lordship's proposition was accepted on both sides."[31] On 28 August the Committee for Plantation Affairs reported in favour of the act, if it should be amended as Franklin engaged, for the Assembly, it would be. The essential provisions of the compromise were that the unsurveyed lands of the proprietors should not be taxed and their surveyed lands be taxed at no higher rate than other lands of the same kind. The act went before the king in council on 2 September and was allowed. On the whole the proprietors thought compromise better than repeal. To the Assembly Franklin's compromise seemed their triumph. What the Penns had to pay the first year was only about one-fiftieth of the total sum raised by taxation. The money was less than the principle. The Assembly had won, what they had long claimed, the right to tax all the property in the province, with no feudal exemption for the True and Absolute Proprietaries. The king himself paid taxes in England.

Franklin and his son left London about the middle of September, for Coventry, where they were on the 27th, then planning to go to Cheshire, Wales, Bristol, and fashionable Bath. Little further is known about their tour except that Franklin says they visited Liverpool and Glasgow and in Birmingham he made some electrical experiments with Matthew Boulton.[32] In London by the middle of November, Franklin made no move to return to Philadelphia. On the death in March 1759 of Richard Partridge, one of Franklin's associates in the agency, Franklin had asked that Richard Jackson, soon to be elected to Parliament for the con-

joint borough of Weymouth and Melcombe Regis, be appointed
chief agent. There would be both advantage and prestige for the
province in having a member of the House to represent them.
Jackson was willing, but not the Assembly. Franklin remained in
London, official agent for Pennsylvania and more and more the
unofficial voice of America.

III

Brilliantly directed by Pitt, the war in America had changed the
face of colonial affairs. Duquesne and Louisbourg were taken from
the French in 1758, and in September 1759 Wolfe captured Quebec. The whole of Canada submitted in 1760. Franklin set himself
at once to work to convince both authorities and public in Britain
that Canada must be permanently English. Already there had
been pamphlets in London on whether Canada should be kept or
Guadeloupe, which also had been taken from the French. Canada
seemed to many Englishmen no better than a hopeless wilderness.
Guadeloupe was a sugar island in the comparatively rich and populous West Indies. Franklin entered the argument with another
pamphlet, *The Interest of Great Britain Considered with Regard
to her Colonies and the Acquisitions of Canada and Guadeloupe,*[33]
written with possibly some help from Richard Jackson and published in London by May or June 1760. To it was added Franklin's
earlier *Observations concerning the Increase of Mankind.* Whatever Jackson contributed, the imperial vision was Franklin's.
Canada must be English so that the English colonies could be
secure. But this was not solely a colonial problem. The colonies
were the western frontier of the British Empire. To secure them
was to secure the Empire, to the benefit of all its people.

Now on a larger stage Franklin said very much what he had
written in Philadelphia in 1751 and published in Boston in 1755.
Given territory enough, the English in America would multiply
till they would soon be more numerous than those in Europe. Such
an increase to the nation could not be neglected. It meant riches,
power, and splendour. There was no danger, as some men in England thought, that the colonies would drain off the population of

the mother country. The seed of the English was already planted in America and would grow of itself, without further emigration. Nor was there a danger that the colonies would become, as some men in England feared, rivals to the English in manufactures. Where land was free and easy to get, the people would remain agricultural, even though the Americans in some centuries might number a hundred million. This would be an immense outlet for British industry, and British ships would carry British goods. Canada, as a part of the continental system, had a future which Guadeloupe could not have. As to the chance that the colonies might some day revolt and become enemies of England, that was a prospect too remote and unlikely to be thought of. "If they could not agree to unite for their defence against the French and Indians, who were perpetually harassing their settlements, burning their buildings, and murdering their people; can it reasonably be supposed there is any danger of their uniting against their own nation, which protects and encourages them, with which they have so many connexions and ties of blood, interest, and affection, and which 'tis well known they all love much more than they love one another? . . . I will venture to say an union amongst them for such a purpose is not merely improbable, it is impossible; and if the union of the whole is impossible, the attempt of a part must be madness; as those colonies that did not join the rebellion would join the mother country in suppressing it.

"When I say such an union is impossible, I mean without the most grievous tyranny and oppression. People who have property in a country which they may lose, and privileges which they may endanger, are generally disposed to be quiet, and even to bear much rather than hazard all. While the government is mild and just, while important civil and religious rights are secure, such subjects will be dutiful and obedient. The waves do not rise but when the winds blow."[34]

If there was in this a note of warning, Franklin did not intend it, for he had still no thought of the British government as "tyranny and oppression." He believed that England misunderstood America and the true relations between them, but he believed that all the misunderstandings could be cleared up by the reasonable arguments which he had to offer. His pamphlet was published the same year in Dublin, Boston (by his nephew Benjamin Mecom), and Philadelphia, and had second editions the year following in Boston and London. It is supposed to have had some influence, and at least the treaty of Paris did return Guadeloupe to France and keep Canada for the English. But the influence of an unofficial philosopher is always hard to trace. In Craven Street and at the Pennsylvania Coffee House, at many other houses and other clubs, Franklin talked steadily, quietly, persuasively, and charmingly about America: the need of winning it entirely from the French, of allowing it to flourish without British interference with its trade, of thinking of it as part of the Empire not as detached and dependent colonies, of extending to it the ancient rights of Englishmen. He was himself his own best argument. "America," Hume wrote to Franklin, "has sent us many good things, gold, silver, sugar, tobacco, indigo, etc.; but you are the first philosopher, and indeed the first great man of letters, for whom we are beholden to her."[35] No British contempt or indifference could easily hold out against an American who in any company had to be taken as an equal for knowledge, wit, and charm.

Though his friends knew that he was Deputy Postmaster-General for the colonies, they seldom thought about it. He was merely another of the many men who, in the comfortable manner of the age, held American offices but lived in England. When Hunter died in 1761 Franklin was continued in office with John Foxcroft of Virginia as his colleague. The two were jointly appointed in October. Nor did Franklin's philosophical friends know much about his domestic life in Craven Street. Always a man who moved in various circles of acquaintance, he was likely to keep them reticently separate. Mrs. Stevenson's house became Franklin's little court, where he amiably made the laws but was himself pliable to the women: Margaret Stevenson almost his sister, Mary almost his daughter. He encouraged a match between Mary Stevenson and William, but it came to nothing. The "hard-to-be-governed passion of youth" which had driven Franklin to obscure intrigues in Philadelphia drove William to the same courses in London, and early in 1760 some unknown woman bore him an illegitimate son who was called William Temple. Whatever the philosopher's disappointment, he serenely accepted his grandson and in time took him into his own household.

From November 1760 to August 1762 Franklin seems to have kept close to London, except during August–September 1761 when he went with William on a short visit to Belgium and Holland. They marvelled at the churches in Ghent and Bruges, and the cosmopolitan born in Boston reflected that religion could be more agreeable than he had been brought up to realize. "When I travelled in Flanders," he afterwards wrote to Jared Ingersoll in Connecticut, "I thought of your excessively strict observation of Sunday; and that a man could hardly travel on that day among you upon his lawful occasions without hazard of punishment; while, where I was, every one travelled, if he pleased, or diverted himself in any other way; and in the afternoon both high and low went to the play or the opera, where there was plenty of singing, fiddling, and dancing. I looked round for God's judgments, but saw no signs of them. The cities were well built and full of inhabitants, the markets filled with plenty, the people well favoured and well clothed, the fields well tilled, the cattle fat and strong, the fences, houses, and windows all in repair, and no Old Tenor anywhere in the country; which would almost make one suspect that the Deity is not so angry at that offence as a New England justice."[36]

In Brussels the scientist was welcomed by the Prince of Lorraine and shown his physics laboratory. In Leyden Franklin visited with Musschenbroek, whose electric bottle the American had understood better than its discoverer. (Musschenbroek the year before had drawn up a list of all the important European writings on electricity and sent it to Franklin in London.) At The Hague the Franklins dined with the British ambassador, who was Joseph Yorke, brother of the solicitor-general already known to the agent from Pennsylvania. And in Amsterdam Franklin, as he wrote his wife from Utrecht on 14 September, "met with Mr. Crellius and his daughter that was formerly Mrs. Neigh; her husband, Dr. Neigh, died in Carolina, and she is married again and lives very well in that city. They treated us with great civility and kindness."[37] The travellers were back in London in time for the coronation of George III, whom Franklin saw as a virtuous, generous young king.

Now, if Franklin had really desired it and had been a more systematic moralist, he might have written his *Art of Virtue*, planned as early as 1732 in the days when he was aiming at perfection. "The materials have been growing ever since," he wrote to Lord Kames in November 1761. "The form only is now to be given; in which I purpose employing my first leisure, after my return to my other country."[38] But he found it more pleasant to be a philosopher than to write philosophy, and he put off finishing, or even beginning, his little treatise. He amused himself with grave hoaxes. Somewhere he came upon a story about tolerance which has been traced back to the Persian of Sadi's *Bustan*, and which apparently entered English in Jeremy Taylor's *Liberty of Prophesying*. Franklin turned the story into Biblical language as *A Parable against Persecution*,[39] and, having memorized it, used to pretend to read it from the fifty-first chapter of Genesis. He had it printed and bound up in his own Bible to prove that it was genuine. Only his close friends were in the secret. To the *Chronicle* some time in 1760 Franklin sent what he said was an extract from a book written in 1629 by a Spanish Jesuit.[40] In a chapter *Of the Means of Disposing the Enemie to Peace* the imaginary author advised the king of Spain to spread propaganda in England by hiring Englishmen to speak and write against the further continuance of the war which Spain was waging. This, Franklin implied, was what the king of France was possibly now doing. In an enlightened age, Franklin said he was sure, the British would not be tricked but would go on to a safe, advantageous, and honourable peace—that is, though he did not say it, till America could be rid of the French.

In these two years of relative leisure Franklin's mind ranged widely if casually through the fields of speculation. With the poets, dramatists, novelists, and general men of letters he was little acquainted. The age of Pope and Swift had passed. Fielding had died in 1754, Richardson died in 1761. The age of Johnson, Boswell, Goldsmith, Sterne, Burke, Gibbon had not yet taken form. Edinburgh was on the whole as eminent in literature as London. To

Hume in Edinburgh Franklin wrote a letter on literary matters. He had sent Hume the pamphlet on Canada and Guadeloupe, and Hume, answering that he had now changed his mind about America, admonished the American on points of usage. Franklin on 27 September 1760 thanked him for the serviceable admonition. "The 'pejorate' and the 'colonize,' since they are not in common use here, I give up as bad; for certainly in writings intended for persuasion and for general information one cannot be too clear; and every expression in the least obscure is a fault. The 'unshakable' too, though clear, I give up as rather low. The introducing new words, where we are already possessed of old ones sufficiently expressive, I confess must be generally wrong, as it tends to change the language; yet at the same time I cannot but wish the usage of our tongue permitted making new words, when we want them, by composition of old ones whose meanings are already well understood. The German allows of it, and it is a common practice with their writers. Many of our present English words were originally so made; and many of the Latin words. In point of clearness such compound words would have the advantage of any we can borrow from the ancient or from foreign languages. For instance, the word 'inaccessible,' though long in use among us, is not yet, I dare say, so universally understood by our people as the word 'uncomeatable' would immediately be, which we are not allowed to write. But I hope, with you, that we shall always in America make the best English of this island our standard, and I believe it will be so. I assure you it often gives me pleasure to reflect how greatly the audience (if I may so term it) of a good English writer will, in another century or two, be increased by the increase of English people in our colonies."[41]

Of the three words Franklin promised to give up, two—"colonize" and "unshakable"—have lived down all conservative objections. He was surer in his practice than in his doctrine. Hume, questioning Franklin's vocabulary, accepted his prophecy, and seven years later urged Gibbon to write in English not in French. "Our solid and increasing establishments in America, where we needlessly dread the inundation of barbarians, promise a superior stability and duration to the English language." Gibbon answered that he did not aim "to instruct or amuse our posterity on the other side of the Atlantic ocean," but he wrote his great history in English.[42]

Franklin wrote to Hume in detail about the "shortest and simplest method of securing buildings, etc., from the mischiefs of lightning."[43] Hume turned the letter over to the Philosophical Society in Edinburgh, and it was read before them and published among their transactions. To Sir Alexander Dick and to Lord Kames, Franklin wrote about the improvement of fireplaces and the cure of smoky chimneys. He explained to Alexander Small his theory of the origin of north-east storms, discussed legible typography with John Baskerville, reported to Ebenezer Kinnersley on recent developments in electricity, made notes on his own experiment in melting powdered amber, and commented on the nature of fire and the source of the rock salt found in mines. His most engaging scientific observations were in the letters he wrote to Mary Stevenson.

Whether or not Franklin's match-making and William's son had anything to do with it, the girl had left Craven Street by May 1759 to live with an aunt at Wanstead in Essex. At her own suggestion, Franklin agreed on 1 May 1760 to make natural philosophy the regular subject of their correspondence. "But why will you," he asked her, "by the cultivation of your mind make yourself still more amiable and a more desirable companion for a man of understanding when you are determined, as I hear, to live single? If we enter, as you propose, into moral as well as natural philosophy, I fancy when I have fully established my authority as a tutor I shall take upon me to lecture you a little on that chapter of duty." In the meantime, he advised her to read the books he should recommend to her and write him her observations or questions.[44]

Her first question was about the working of the barometer, and her first observation on the usefulness of insects. Franklin, replying on 11 June, put in a sly sentence which it probably amused him to think she would not catch, but he was otherwise sober enough. "Superficial minds are apt to despise those who make that part of the creation [insects] their study, as mere triflers; but certainly the world has been much obliged to them. Under the care and management of man, the labours of the little silkworm afford employ-

ment and subsistence to thousands of families and become an
immense article of commerce. The bee, too, yields us its delicious
honey, and its wax useful to a multitude of purposes. Another
insect, it is said, produces the cochineal from whence we have our
rich scarlet dye. The usefulness of the cantharides, or Spanish flies,
in medicine is known to all, and thousands owe their lives to that
knowledge. By human industry and observation other properties
of other insects may possibly be hereafter discovered, and of equal
utility. A thorough acquaintance with the nature of these little
creatures may also enable mankind to prevent the increase of such
as are noxious, or secure us against the mischiefs they occasion."
He went on to tell her what he had heard from "a Swedish gentleman of good credit" about how Linnæus had safeguarded timber
against ship-worms. But once more Franklin warned her not to let
her scientific curiosity make her forget her common duties. "Nicholas Gimcrack . . . who neglected his family to pursue butterflies,
was a just object of ridicule, and we must give him up as fair game
to the satirist."[45]

During the summer Polly—as she was usually called—wrote to
Franklin from Bristol to ask him why the water at that place,
though cold at the spring, became warm by pumping. "It will be
most prudent in me to forbear attempting to answer," he said on
13 September, "till by a more circumstantial account you assure
me of the fact. I own I should expect that operation to warm, not
so much the water pumped, as the person pumping." But he did
not want to seem to snub or tease her, and he said that he had
learned from a woman, in one of Selden's books, not "to give
reasons before one is sure of facts." The letter which followed was
the longest and the most technical of the series, on tides in rivers.
Franklin realized that he had perhaps lost sight of his reader in his
own interest in the theme, and he ended with an exquisite apology.
"After writing six folio pages of philosophy to a young girl, is it
necessary to finish such a letter with a compliment? Is not such a
letter of itself a compliment?"[46]

Of all the matters he discussed with her, the most original was
his experiment to test the effect of the sun's heat on clothing. "Since
I cannot find the notes of my experiment to send you I must give it
as well as I can from memory. . . . I took a number of little

square pieces of broadcloth from a tailor's pattern card, of various colours. There were black, deep blue, lighter blue, green, purple, red, yellow, white, and other colours or shades of colours. I laid them all out upon the snow in a bright sunshiny morning. In a few hours (I cannot now be exact as to the time) the black, being warmed most by the sun, was sunk so low as to be below the stroke of the sun's rays; the dark blue almost as low, the lighter blue not quite so much as the dark, the other colours less as they were lighter; and the quite white remained on the surface of the snow, not having entered it at all.

"What signifies philosophy that does not apply to some use? May we not learn from hence that black clothes are not so fit to wear in a hot sunny climate or season as white ones? . . . That soldiers and seamen, who must march and labour in the sun, should in the East or West Indies have an uniform of white? That summer hats, for men or women, should be white, as repelling that heat which gives headaches to many and to some the fatal stroke that the French call the *coup de soleil*?"[47] Here, a century before Europeans learned generally to wear light-coloured clothing in the tropics, Franklin pointed out the manifest advantage of it, with the simplest kind of experiment to prove his point.

If it was like Franklin to put some of his acutest observations into affectionate letters to a girl of twenty-one, so was it like him to take the hand he took in a pamphlet, now exceedingly rare, on smallpox by William Heberden. Heberden, the first to describe *angina pectoris*, was a distinguished doctor in London whom Franklin met soon after he arrived. Talking together about smallpox, Franklin told Heberden of inoculation as practised in Boston and Philadelphia. Then Franklin persuaded Heberden to write, in the midst of many interruptions, *Some Account of the Success of Inoculation for the Small-Pox in England and America Together with Plain Instructions, by Which Any Person May Be Enabled to Perform the Operation and Conduct the Patient through the Distemper* (1759). Heberden had it printed at his own expense—Strahan was the printer—and to the eight pages of the pamphlet Franklin added four more as a preface.[48] He sent 1500 copies to David Hall in Philadelphia to be given away. There was no longer any doubt, he said in his preface, as to the value of inoculation. But "scruples of conscience weigh with many concerning the lawfulness of the practice; and if one parent or near relation is against it, the other does not choose to inoculate a child without free consent of all parties, lest in case of a disastrous event perpetual blame should follow. These scruples a sensible clergy may in time remove. The expense of having the operation performed by a surgeon weighs with others, for that has been pretty high in some parts of America; and when a common tradesman or artificer has a number in his family to have the distemper, it amounts to more money than he can well spare." This pamphlet, Franklin thought, might teach poor parents how to inoculate their own children. Heberden, desiring no personal credit, had not signed his name. Franklin, afraid a nameless physician might be disregarded, divulged it in the preface.

On 13 July 1762 Franklin, about to leave Europe, wrote a farewell letter to Beccaria in Turin, thanking him for his support of Franklin's electrical opinions. "I wish I could in return entertain you with anything new of mine on that subject; but I have not lately pursued it. Nor do I know of anyone here that is at present much engaged in it. Perhaps, however, it may be agreeable to you, as you live in a musical country, to have an account of the new instrument lately added here to the great number that charming science was before possessed of. As it is an instrument that seems peculiarly adapted to Italian music, especially that of the soft and plaintive kind, I will endeavour to give you such a description of it, and of the manner of constructing it, that you or any of your friends may be enabled to imitate it, if you incline to do so, without being at the expense and trouble of the many experiments I have made in endeavouring to bring it to its present perfection." The new instrument was based upon the musical glasses invented by Richard Puckeridge [Pockrich] in 1743. "He collected a number of glasses of different sizes, fixed them near each other on a table, and tuned them by putting into them water, more or less as each note required. The tones were brought out by passing his fingers round their brims. He was unfortunately burnt here, with his instrument, in a fire which consumed the house he lived in

[1759]. Mr. E. [Edmund Hussey] Delaval, a most ingenious member of our Royal Society, made one in imitation of it, with a better choice and form of glasses, which was the first I saw or heard."

Franklin may or may not have known that the musical glasses (*Glasspiel*) were already much used in Germany, and that Gluck himself had played a concerto of his own on them, with full orchestral accompaniment, in London as early as 1746. The instrument came to Franklin's knowledge through the Royal Society, and Franklin was a scientist as well as a lover of music. "Being charmed by the sweetness of its tones and the music he produced from it, I wished only to see the glasses disposed in a more convenient form, and brought together in a narrower compass, so as to admit of a greater number of tunes and all within reach of hand to a person sitting before the instrument." Instead of using beer glasses set on a table, Franklin had special glasses blown in the shape of hemispheres, with a hole in the middle, the largest glass nine inches in diameter and the smallest three. From them he chose thirty-seven, "which are sufficient for three octaves with all the semitones," and tuned them by grinding as it was needed, "often trying the glass by a well-tuned harpsichord." Then he mounted them on an iron spindle running through the holes in their centres, the largest glass at one end of the spindle and each next smaller one partly within the larger but not touching it. This spindle was laid horizontal in a long case on four legs, something like a harpsichord. The player, sitting before the instrument, revolved the spindle with a treadle like that on a spinning-wheel, and touched the edges of the moving glasses with his fingers. "The advantages of this instrument are that its tones are incomparably sweet beyond those of any other; that they may be swelled and softened at pleasure by stronger or weaker pressures of the finger, and continued at any length; and that the instrument, being once well tuned, never again wants tuning. In honour of your musical language," Franklin concluded his letter to Beccaria, "I have borrowed from it the name of this instrument, calling it the armonica."[49]

The harmonica—as it came generally to be spelled—had a sudden vogue that lasted for years. Copies of the instrument were made in London, on Franklin's specifications, and sold for forty guineas. Marianne Davies gave public performances on the har-

monica in England early in 1762, travelled with it to Italy, and
introduced it to the imperial court at Vienna, where Gluck was
now chapel-master, and Marie Antoinette became one of her
pupils. Metastasio composed an ode which was sung by Cecilia
Davies at a royal wedding, while Marianne played on the "nuovo
istrumento di musica . . . inventata dal celebre Dottore Franklin."⁵⁰ By December 1764 the harmonica had got to Philadelphia,
and was for the first time heard in public at the Assembly Room in
Lodge Alley. More was made of the instrument in Germany and
Austria than elsewhere. Franklin was long as famous among German musicians for his harmonica as among German electricians for
his lightning rod. There were virtuosos celebrated for their skill
on the harmonica, and various mechanical improvements, adap-
tations, and imitations. Mozart and Beethoven, not to mention
lesser men, composed music for it. Then the vogue as suddenly
ceased, about 1800, with no reason given except that the vibration
of the glasses harrowed the nerves of the performers.⁵¹

Because the harmonica has become obsolete Franklin is seldom
thought of in connexion with music, but he both delighted in it
and thought clearly and critically about it. At the Junto he had
taken his turn in singing, and had written words for familiar airs.
Somehow or other, sooner or later, he found time to learn to play
the harp, the guitar, and the violin, as well as the harmonica, with
which he pleased his friends in London and Paris. One of his
earliest acquaintances in London on this visit was John Stanley,
organist to the Society of the Inner Temple. Now, after so many
years of business and science and politics and war, in the midst of
diplomacy, the philosopher was free to choose his satisfactions.
Music was high among them. Nothing he wrote between 1757 and
1762, no experiment he undertook and carried out, absorbed him
more happily than his musical invention.

By January 1762 Franklin had determined to return to Philadelphia the coming summer, though, since England was still at
war with France, he would have to wait for a safe convoy. He had
stayed longer than his errand needed, and he could not help being
restless in even the most entertaining leisure. He had of course not
yet become the public figure he was to be on his second mission to
England. His postmastership and his agency were little posts in

the great world, and his reputation as philosopher and person had not spread far beyond the circle of his friends. But, while he waited for a convoy, Oxford on 22 February voted that Franklin should be given the degree of doctor of civil laws *honoris causa* whenever he should be pleased to visit the university. He came the end of April and at a convocation on the 30th the illustrious Benjamin Franklin, Esquire, Agent of the Province of Pennsylvania at the Court of His Most Serene Majesty, Postmaster-General of North America, and Fellow of the Royal Society (*Ornatissimus Vir Benjaminus Franklin Armiger, Provinciæ Pensylvaniæ Deputatus, ad Curiam Serenissimi Regis Legatus, Tabellariorum per Americam Septentrionalem Præfectus Generalis, necnon Regiæ Societatis Socius*) was admitted to the degree, and William Franklin at the same time to the degree of master of arts. William Smith, doctor of divinity for three years and recently arrived from Philadelphia, that month wrote an angry letter to the president of St. John's College. The letter reached Franklin, and he and Smith met at Strahan's house, where Smith agreed that he had been misinformed and rancorous and promised to write another letter withdrawing his charges. He did not write it, but spread the news in London and Oxford that Franklin had lost many of his friends in Philadelphia.[52]

Franklin's friends in England could hardly let him go. Strahan two years before had formally proposed a marriage between his son and Franklin's daughter, and Franklin had sent the proposal to his wife. She refused to cross the ocean or to part with Sally. That plan of Strahan's to hold Franklin fell through. Now Strahan used every further plan and argument he could think of. But, Franklin wrote him on 20 July, "I feel here like a thing out of its place, and useless because it is out of its place. How then can I any longer be happy in England? You have great power of persuasion, and might easily prevail on me to do anything; but not any longer to do nothing. I must go home."[53] Yet still Franklin wavered. In that same letter he said he was leaving London for ever. Three days later he admitted that Strahan's "almost irresistible eloquence" was "secretly supported and backed by my own treacherous inclinations."[54] On 23 August, writing from Portsmouth where he had gone to take his ship, he yielded still more. "The attraction of reason is at present for the other side of the water, but that of inclination will be for this side. You know which usually prevails. I shall probably make but this one vibration and settle here for ever. Nothing will prevent it if I can, as I hope, prevail with Mrs. F. to accompany me, especially if we have a peace."⁵⁵ But his ship sailed almost at once. "I am going," he wrote to Lord Kames, "from the old world to the new; and I fancy I feel like those who are leaving this world for the next: grief at the parting; fear of the passage; hope of the future. These different passions all affect their minds at once; and these have *tendered* me down exceedingly."⁵⁶

"We had a long passage near ten weeks from Portsmouth to this place," he reported to Strahan from Philadelphia, "but it was a pleasant one; for we had ten sail in company and a man-of-war to protect us; we had pleasant weather and fair winds, and frequently visited and dined from ship to ship; we called too at the delightful island of Madeira, by way of half-way house, where we replenished our stores and took in many refreshments. It was the time of their vintage, and we hung the ceiling of the cabin with bunches of fine grapes which served as a dessert for dinner for some weeks afterwards. The reason of our being so long at sea was that, sailing with a convoy, we could none of us go faster than the slowest, being obliged every day to shorten sail or lay by till they came up. This was the only inconvenience of our having company, which was abundantly made up to us by the sense of greater safety, the mutual good offices daily exchanged, and the other pleasures of society."⁵⁷

And also to Strahan: "I got home well the first of November, and had the happiness to find my little family perfectly well, and that Dr. Smith's reports of the diminution of my friends were all false. My house has been full of a succession of them from morning to night ever since my arrival, congratulating me on my return with the utmost cordiality and affection. My fellow-citizens, while I was on the sea, had at the annual election chosen me unanimously, as they had done every year while I was in England, to be their representative in Assembly, and would, they say, if I had not disappointed them by coming privately to town, have met me with five hundred horse."⁵⁸

William Franklin had not come with his father. Before the convoy sailed the son had been appointed governor of New Jersey, by Lord Halifax, president of the Board of Trade, at the request of Lord Bute, secretary of state and favorite minister of George III. The new governor was married in September to Elizabeth Downes, born in the West Indies. There is no good reason to doubt that the ministry had in mind that if Franklin's son were a governor, Franklin might be more tractable to the governor, and the proprietors, of Pennsylvania. Thomas Penn believed he would.

Speaker

HAPPY as he was to be at home again, Franklin could not help missing England, which had more learning, wit, and elegance than Pennsylvania, and had known how to pay more pleasing honours to the philosopher than his own province did. "Of all the enviable things England has," Franklin wrote to Mary Stevenson on 25 March 1763, "I envy it most its people. Why should that petty island, which compared to America is but like a stepping-stone in a brook, scarce enough of it above water to keep one's shoes dry; why, I say, should that little island enjoy in almost every neighbourhood more sensible, virtuous, and elegant minds than we can collect in ranging a hundred leagues of our vast forests? But 'tis said the arts delight to travel westward. You have effectually defended us in this glorious war, and in time you will improve us. After the first cares for the necessaries of life are over"—Franklin had used almost the same words in his proposal for the American Philosophical Society twenty years before—"we shall come to think of the embellishments. Already some of our young geniuses begin to lisp attempts at painting, poetry, and music."[1] He sent her, and other English friends, various specimens of American verse which he hoped might find favour in England. He thought he would himself soon follow them. "In two years at farthest," he wrote to Strahan on 7 December 1762, "I hope to settle all my affairs in such a manner as that I *may* then conveniently remove to England—provided we can persuade the good woman to cross the seas."[2]

The conflict with the proprietors had made Franklin fresh enemies in Philadelphia, who spread the news that he had lived extravagantly in England and wasted public money. But in February, rendering his account to the Assembly, Franklin charged

them with only £714 10s. 7d. of the £1500 that had been voted
for his use. They allowed him the sum charged for expenses, let
him keep the £1500 voted, and added as much more; that is,
£3000 for his five years. His enemies could not call this extravagance. His friends in the Assembly realized how much he had done
in England, and on 19 February they resolved that the Speaker,
from the chair, should thank their agent "as well for the faithful
discharge of his duty to this province in particular as for the many
and important services done to America in general." His personal
friends continued to welcome him. Catherine Ray, now Catherine
Greene, wrote eagerly from Rhode Island, inviting him to visit
her. They seem not to have kept up their correspondence while
he was in England, though she had written occasional letters to
Deborah Franklin. In January Franklin promised Catherine that
if he went to New England the next summer, as he planned, he
would not fail to stop at Warwick on his way.

William Franklin came back to America in February and took
up his office as governor of New Jersey. In spite of some resentment, he made friends with almost his father's ease. He was
escorted to Perth Amboy, alternately with Burlington the capital,
by many of the gentry in sleighs and by the Middlesex troop of
horse, and was greeted with congratulatory addresses by the cor-
porations of towns, the college (Princeton), and the clergy. Franklin looked on with lively satisfaction. "I am just returned," he
wrote to Strahan on 28 March, "from a journey I made through
his government, and had the pleasure of seeing him received
everywhere with the utmost respect and even affection of all ranks
of people."[3] The governor fixed his residence at Burlington, where
his father, a runaway apprentice, forty years before had caught a
chance boat for the last stage of his journey to Philadelphia.

Much of Franklin's first year in America was given up to the
affairs of the post office. Now that Canada was English, some sort
of postal communication between New York and Montreal and
Quebec had to be arranged, and a better schedule of packets to
carry the mails between England and the colonies. The mails, for
the first time in America, were made to travel night and day from
Philadelphia to New York and back, and later the same service

was extended to Boston. Franklin inspected post offices from southern Virginia to eastern New England. In April and May 1763 he spent three or four weeks in Virginia, where he met his new colleague John Foxcroft. In June Franklin was in New York. On the way from Philadelphia he had attended a public dinner given for his son and his wife in Elizabethtown (Elizabeth). In New York Franklin's time was taken up with Cadwallader Colden, now governor, Lord Stirling (William Alexander), and Jeffery Amherst, commander-in-chief of the British forces in America and sinecure governor of Virginia. They talked, presumably, of the new outbreak among the western Indians, whom Amherst wanted to exterminate.

Sally Franklin, almost twenty, joined her father in New York, and the two went to New England together. Before they got to Warwick, or while they were there, Franklin had a fall from his horse, and Catherine Greene tenderly nursed him. Sally would have liked to stay longer, but her father's plans would not allow it. When they left for Providence, and Boston, the Greenes accompanied them part of the way, as Lord and Lady Kames had accompanied Franklin and William on the road toward York. Catherine urged her guests to stop again on their return. But Franklin, on a trip to Portsmouth or back, early in September had another fall and dislocated his shoulder. "I am not yet able to travel rough roads," he wrote to Catherine on the 5th, "and must lie by awhile, as I can neither hold reins nor whip with my right hand till it grows stronger."[4] Three weeks later he was still in Boston, his arm still painful. About the first of November he was in Philadelphia, resting from sixteen hundred miles of travel. The daughter of Sir Alexander Dick in Edinburgh had sent Sally some Scottish songs, and Franklin and his daughter delighted in them. "She sings the songs to her harpsichord, and I play some of the softest tunes on my armonica, with which entertainment our people here are quite charmed, and conceive the Scottish tunes to be the finest in the world."[5]

II

The treaty of Paris in February 1763 made peace between England and France but not between the colonists and the Indians. If anything, the Indians were worse off than before. While the war lasted they had been courted and bribed by both French and English, and furnished with guns, goods, and rum. Now, though the territory from the Alleghenies to the Mississippi was reserved to them, their supplies were suddenly cut off. Even the Six Nations were restless, and among the tribes that had been favourable to the French the summer of 1763 saw the general uprising which is classically, if not quite accurately, called the conspiracy of Pontiac, who was chief of the Ottawa. French traders told the Indians that the English occupation was only temporary, and encouraged them to keep up their raids. The Indians could see for themselves that the frontier forts were gruffly held by the English, and rightly guessed that more and more settlers would follow the soldiers, take up the land, and drive the hunters off. Whether organized by Pontiac or acting independently, the western Indians attacked the English on the long front from Detroit to Fort Pitt. These two posts held out, but during May and June every other garrison west of Niagara was surprised and massacred. The Indians were desperate in the face of extinction, and went to all lengths in the savage cruelty which was their rule of warfare. Nor were the English much behind them. General Amherst, who had cut off the Indian supplies, suggested, perhaps before the uprising, that blankets inoculated with smallpox might be sent among the Indians "to extirpate this execrable race," and he thought well of the scheme to hunt them down with dogs.

If the British commander-in-chief could entertain these ruthless plans, it is no wonder that the actual frontiersmen made war as furiously as the Indians. With the forts on the Ohio taken, war parties again, as after Braddock's defeat, ravaged the whole of Pennsylvania as far east as the Conococheague valley and the Blue mountains. Carlisle and Shippensburg were filled with refugees. James Smith, who had been captured by the Indians while working on Braddock's road and had lived among them for four years, formed a company of volunteer defenders who called themselves the Black Boys and, naked and painted, ranged the Conococheague district in Cumberland County. In Lancaster County certain Scotch-Irish settlers of Paxton and Donegal townships, Presbyterian fanatics who called themselves the Paxton Boys, turned their fury against the friendly Indians living at peace within the province. The Indians under the protection of the Moravians near Bethlehem were safely moved to Philadelphia. But in December fifty or more of the Paxton Boys fell upon the quiet village of the Conestoga Indians near Lancaster and murdered the six they found at home. The remaining fourteen, who had been away selling their baskets, brooms, and bowls among the neighbouring whites, were collected by the sheriff and lodged in the workhouse at Lancaster. The rioters two days after Christmas broke open the workhouse and put old and young to the hatchet; "then," according to Franklin, "mounted their horses, huzza'd in triumph as if they had gained a victory, and rode off—unmolested."

John Penn, governor since November, issued two proclamations ordering the arrest of the criminals and offering a reward. Nothing came of it. The people of Lancaster who were not terrorized approved or excused the murders. The bloody mob grew into an army of several hundred men that moved on Philadelphia, citing Scripture to justify their furious purpose to wipe out the Moravian Indians. The frontier counties cherished old and bitter grievances. The capital, they thought, coldly and selfishly neglected them. Three companies of regular troops, the Royal Americans, had been called from Cumberland to Philadelphia to guard the Indian refugees, at a time when other Indians were murdering whole families in Cumberland. Indians were Indians, the rioters said, with vendetta logic. "Who ever proclaimed war," two of their spokesmen asked, "with part of a nation, and not with the whole?" The Moravian Indians had plotted with the enemy and were as guilty as any. Yet the government was doing more for them than for its own people on the border. The expedition under Colonel Bouquet, then being planned, was not against the enemy on the nearer frontier, but against the Indians at the forks of the Muskingum in Ohio. (The rioters could not see that it was the best

strategy to strike at the distant towns which were the source of all
the raiding parties.) The Scotch-Irish blamed the Quakers for their
long weakness—kindness—toward the Indians, and accused them
even now of profitably trading with the savages. The five back
counties had only ten members in the Assembly as against twenty-
six from the three home counties and Philadelphia. Helpless in
the legislature, the frontier had taken to arms, the rebels said. And
they demanded a bounty for scalps. The lack of that encouragement had "damped the spirits of many brave men" who would
otherwise have invaded the enemy country.

There was enough raw reason in their claims to divide public
opinion. The eastern Presbyterians were inclined to side with
them, some of the more righteous Churchmen, the Indian-hating
rabble, and, it was suspected, Penn and his Council, out of proprietarial animosity toward the Quakers. Franklin, more open to
true reason than any other man in Pennsylvania, saw that, whatever else the rising was, it was first of all riot and murder. In
January he wrote his warm and moving *Narrative of the Late
Massacres in Lancaster County*.[6]

He began with the most intimate simplicity, as if he were taking
up a topic already on everybody's tongue—as it was. "These Indians were the remains of a tribe of the Six Nations settled at
Conestoga and thence called Conestoga Indians. On the first
arrival of the English in Pennsylvania, messengers from this tribe
came to welcome them, with presents of venison, corn, and skins;
and the whole tribe entered into a treaty of friendship with the
first proprietor, William Penn, which was to last 'as long as the
sun should shine or the waters run in the rivers.'" Most of the
surviving members of the tribe had English names, and Franklin
gave the names and characters of half of them. He told the story
of the two massacres in plain, unsparing words. "There are some
(I am ashamed to hear it)," he went on, "who would extenuate
the enormous wickedness of these actions by saying: 'The inhabitants of the frontiers are exasperated with the murder of their
relations by the enemy Indians in the present war.' It is possible.
But though this might justify their going out into the woods, to
seek for those enemies and avenge upon them those murders, it
can never justify their turning into the heart of the country to

murder their friends. If an Indian injures me, does it follow that I may revenge that injury on all Indians? It is well known that Indians are of different tribes, nations, and languages, as well as the white people. In Europe, if the French, who are white people, should injure the Dutch, are they to revenge it on the English, because they too are white people? The only crime of these poor wretches seems to have been that they had a reddish-brown skin and black hair; and some people of that sort, it seems, had murdered some of our relations. If it be right to kill men for such a reason, then, should any man with a freckled face and red hair kill a wife or child of mine, it would be right for me to revenge it by killing all the freckled red-haired men, women, and children I could afterwards anywhere meet with."

Here in terms of everyday experience he answered the arguments of the Paxton Boys. He went through history to find examples of hospitality and mercy, among Greeks, Turks, Arabs, Moors, Spaniards, Negroes, and Indians themselves. "I beg that I may not be understood as framing apologies for all Indians. I am far from desiring to lessen the laudable spirit of resentment in my countrymen against those now at war with us, so far as is justified by their perfidy and inhumanity. I would only observe that the Six Nations, as a body, have kept faith with the English ever since we knew them, now near an hundred years; and that the governing part of those people have had notions of honour, whatever may be the case with the rum-debauched, trader-corrupted vagabonds and thieves on the Susquehanna and Ohio, at present in arms against us." The Conestoga Indians who had been murdered, and the Moravian Indians who were threatened, had been charged with numberless crimes: "all which stories are well known, by those who know the Indians best, to be pure inventions, contrived by bad people either to excite each other to join in the murder or, since it was committed, to justify it; and believed only by the weak and credulous." What had old Shehaes, so old he had been present at Penn's treaty in 1701, done that he should have been cut to pieces in his bed? "What could he or the other poor old men and women do? What had little boys and girls done? What could children of a year old, babes at the breast, what could they do that they too must be shot and hatcheted? And in their parents' arms! This is done by no civilized nation in Europe. Do we come to America to learn and practise the manners of barbarians? But this, barbarians as they are, they practise against their enemies only, not against their friends. . . .

"Unhappy people, to have lived in such times and by such neighbours!" They would have been safe among the ancient heathen, the Turks, the Saracens, the Moors, the Spanish, the Negroes. "In short, it appears they would have been safe in any part of the known world except in the neighbourhood of the Christian white savages of Peckstang and Donegal!"

The pamphlet made Franklin more enemies than friends, but it helped discredit the rioters in Philadelphia, where many citizens besides the Quakers resolved that the Moravian Indians should not be murdered or the city invaded. In the panic that filled the people as the rioters approached, Franklin kept his head. Another governor had to turn to the philosopher—also one of the commissioners for defence—to ask his aid in defending the city. Franklin organized another Association, "signed . . . first myself, and was followed by several hundreds who took arms accordingly. The governor offered me the command of them, but I chose to carry a musket and strengthen his authority by setting an example of obedience to his order." Besides the three companies of regular soldiers, there were eight of the Associators and a battery of artillery. The governor asked the Assembly for a riot act, and it was drawn, voted, and made a law the same day: 3 February. On the 6th and 7th there was no quorum in the Assembly. On the 8th the Speaker and fifteen members met and at once adjourned, "the city being suddenly alarmed by a report that a number of rioters were approaching in a hostile manner." The governor, much as he hated Franklin, "did me the honour, in an alarm, to run to my house at midnight, with his councillors at his heels, for advice, and made it his headquarters."[7] The rioters, finding the ford over the Schuylkill guarded, turned north, crossed the river at another ford, and came boisterously to Germantown, eight or ten miles from Philadelphia. There they halted, and Franklin, at the request of the governor, went out with three other men to meet them. "The fighting face we put on and the reasonings we used with the insurgents . . . turned them back and restored quiet to the city."[8] By the 11th they had been dispersed. "And within four-and-twenty hours," Franklin wrote to Fothergill in London on 14 March, "your old friend was a common soldier, a councillor, a kind of dictator, an ambassador to a country mob, and, on his returning home, nobody again."[9] The grandson of William Penn proclaimed a bounty for Indian scalps, male or female.

The whole episode made the antagonism between Franklin and John Penn complete. Franklin told Fothergill that Penn's conduct—"his dropping all inquiries after the murderers and his answering the disputes of the rioters privately," and his insults to the Assembly—had brought "him and his government into sudden contempt. All regard for him in the Assembly is lost. All hopes of happiness under a proprietary government are at an end." And Penn on 5 May wrote to his uncle Thomas: "There will never be any prospect of ease and happiness while that villain [Franklin] has the liberty of spreading about the poison of that inveterate malice and ill nature which is deeply implanted in his own black heart."[10]

III

Absorbed in war and politics in Pennsylvania, Franklin for a year had little time to give to what was happening in London. No man is always a prophet, and Franklin at the end of 1763 still had romantic notions about George III. "You now fear for our virtuous young king," said a letter to Strahan on 19 December, "that the faction forming will overpower him and render his reign uncomfortable. On the contrary, I am of opinion that his virtue and the consciousness of his sincere intentions to make his people happy will give him firmness and steadiness in his measures and in the support of the honest friends he has chosen to serve him; and when that firmness is fully perceived, faction will dissolve and be dissipated like a morning fog before the rising sun, leaving the rest of the day clear with a sky serene and cloudless."[11]

But when the firm king's honest friend George Grenville in the following March had announced the new programme for taxing the colonies and regulating their trade, including the Stamp Act as then proposed, Franklin saw injustice and danger at once. "Our opinions or inclinations," he wrote to Collinson on 30 April, "if they had been known, would perhaps have weighed but little among you. We are in your hands as clay in the hands of the potter: and so in one more particular than is generally considered; for as the potter cannot waste or spoil his clay without injuring himself, so I think there is scarce anything you can do that may be hurtful to us but what will be as much or more so to you. This must be our chief security; for interest with you we have but little. The West Indians vastly outweigh us of the northern colonies. What we get above a subsistence we lay out with you for your manufactures. Therefore what you get from us in taxes you must lose in trade. The cat can yield but her skin. And as you must have the whole hide, if you first cut thongs out of it 'tis at your own expense. . . .

"Let me tell you a piece of news that, though it might displease a very respectable body among you, the button-makers, will be agreeable to yourself as a virtuoso. It is, that we have discovered a beach in a bay several miles round, the pebbles of which are all in the form of buttons, whence it is called Button Mould Bay. . . . But I think I must not mention this place, lest some Englishman get a patent for this button mine, as one did for the coal mine at Louisbourg, and, by neither suffering others to work it nor working it himself, deprive us of the advantage God and nature seem to have intended us. As we have now got buttons, 'tis something towards our clothing; and who knows but in time we may find out where to get cloth?—for as to our being always supplied by you, 'tis folly to expect it. Only consider the rate of our increase, and tell me if you can increase your wool in that proportion, and where, in your little island, you can feed the sheep. Nature has put bounds to your abilities, though none to your desires. Britain would, if she could, manufacture and trade for all the world; England for all Britain; London for all England; and every Londoner for all London. So selfish is the human mind. But 'tis well there is One above that rules these matters with a more equal hand. He that is pleased to feed the ravens will undoubtedly take care to prevent a monopoly of the carrion."[12]

Sharply as Franklin here spoke of the colonial policy of the new ministers, he had nevertheless made up his mind that Pennsylvania would be better off in their hands than in the hands of the proprietors. The conflict between the Assembly and the governor had come at last to a breaking-point. After the riot the Assembly promptly passed a militia bill and a money bill, and the governor as promptly vetoed them. He insisted on appointing the militia officers himself, without allowing the men the share in choosing them which the bill provided. The money bill, he insisted, must contain the exact words of the provision of the Privy Council "that the located uncultivated lands belonging to the proprietaries shall not be assessed higher than the lowest rate at which any located uncultivated lands belonging to the inhabitants shall be assessed." The Assembly objected to this strict construction, preferred to frame their bill in their language, and, whatever the Privy Council might have ruled, resented the claims of the proprietors to be taxed at lower rates than other landowners. The bill went back and forth for a month without agreement. On 24 March the Assembly sent it to Governor Penn with a message, probably written by Franklin, in strong, insulting terms. If any ill consequences came from the delay at this crucial time, the message said, "they will undoubtedly add to that load of obloquy and guilt the proprietary family is already burdened with, and bring their government (a government which is always meanly making use of public distress to extort something from the people for its own private advantage) into (if possible) still greater contempt." That same day the Assembly passed twenty-six resolutions, of which the last said that the Assembly would adjourn and consult their constituents as to "whether an humble address should be drawn up and transmitted to his Majesty, praying that he would be graciously pleased to take the people of this province under his immediate protection and government."[13]

During the recess Franklin wrote his pamphlet *Cool Thoughts on the Present Situation of Our Public Affairs*, which on the night of 12 April was distributed by hand throughout the town. "Considering all circumstances," he said, "I am at length inclined to think that the cause of these miserable contentions is not to be sought for merely in the depravity and selfishness of human minds. For though it is not unlikely that in these, as well as in other disputes, there are faults on both sides, every glowing coal being apt to inflame its opposite; yet I see no reason to suppose that all proprietary rulers are worse men than other rulers, nor that all people in proprietary governments are worse people than those in other governments. I suspect, therefore, that the cause is radical, interwoven in the constitution and so become of the very nature of proprietary governments; and will therefore produce its effects as long as such governments continue. And, as some physicians say every animal body brings into the world among its original stamina the seeds of that disease that shall finally produce its dissolution, so the political body of a proprietary government contains those convulsive principles that will at length destroy it."[14]

There were not many cool thoughts in Pennsylvania. The proposed change had a revolutionary look to it, and feeling was violent on both sides. The friends of the governor, the men who were officials under the proprietors or hoped to be, and the comfortable aristocracy of Philadelphia wanted the government to remain as it was. So did the Presbyterians, afraid a royal government might bring an established church, a bishop, and tithes. The Churchmen and the Germans were divided. The Quakers and the Moravians favoured the change. The leader of the opposition was John Dickinson, a young lawyer who admitted the evils of the proprietary rule but held there was no good reason to think—as there was not—that the ministry would send better governors than the proprietors had sent. Just now, Dickinson argued, when a new imperial policy threatened the colonies, Pennsylvania could not afford to give up the constitution which had long protected it. Franklin, urging the change, had for his lieutenant another young lawyer, Joseph Galloway, who had more or less taken Franklin's place in the Assembly during his absence in England. Galloway seems to have believed with Franklin that George III, "who has no views but for the good of his people, will thenceforth appoint the governor, who, unshackled by proprietary instructions, will be at liberty to join with the Assembly in enacting wholesome laws."[15]

When the Assembly met again in May the governor was as obdurate as ever, and the money bill for £55,000 had finally to be passed on his terms. The real business of the session was the petition to the king to assume the government of the province. When the debate was at its angry height, Isaac Norris, whose daughter had married John Dickinson, resigned the office of Speaker which he had honourably held for fourteen years. Franklin was immediately and unanimously elected to succeed him, on 26 May, and it was Franklin who as Speaker signed the petition, which he had drafted.[16]

Franklin, for years the spokesman for the Assembly, presided as Speaker for only the few days left in May and again during the short session in September. The members went to the constituents, and the campaign before the election of 1 October was noisy and venomous. Dickinson published his speech in the May debate as a pamphlet, with a preface by William Smith. Galloway published his, with a long preface by Franklin[17] which was a powerful defence of the Assembly full of abrasive sarcasm aimed at its enemies. Smith had composed an elaborate epitaph, in the manner of the time, for William Penn, all of its complimentary phrases drawn, he said, from the minutes of the Assembly. Franklin composed another on the sons, "in the lapidary style" and not complimentary, drawn mostly from the same minutes. He was answered in the anonymous pamphlet—one long epitaph—*What Is Sauce for a Goose Is Also Sauce for a Gander*, which, not content to accuse him of every public villainy, raked up the private scandal of his son's birth. The Germans were not allowed to forget that he had called them "Palatine boors," nor the Scotch-Irish of Paxton and Donegal townships that he had called them "Christian white savages." He was the target of cartoons, squibs in the newspapers, malicious tongues, none of which he then troubled himself to answer—though another anonymous pamphlet *The Scribler* praised him in the highest terms and savagely abused his enemies. (But Franklin found time to write a preface for *Poor Richard Improved* for 1765, in which he pointed out that if the British government laid new duties on American trade, Americans could go without British manufactures and supply themselves.[18])

Franklin and Galloway, both candidates for seats from the city of Philadelphia, managed the campaign for their party, which was called the Old Ticket. On election day the polls were opened at nine in the morning, and the slow stream of voters crowded the high steps of the state house till nearly midnight. About three the next morning the managers of the New Ticket moved to close, but the Old Ticket would not agree. They still had a reserve of aged and crippled voters who could not come in a crowd but who now, between three and six, were brought in chairs and litters. The New Ticket men sent out for laggard citizens, as far away as Germantown, and got more than the Old. The polls were closed at three in the afternoon, and when the votes were counted it was found that Franklin and Galloway had been beaten, by twenty-five votes among nearly four thousand. Charles Pettit, a spirited observer, wrote to Joseph Reed in London: "Mr. Franklin died like a philosopher. But Mr. Galloway agonized in death, like a mortal deist who has no hopes of a future existence."[19]

Though the Old party lost Philadelphia, they had a majority in the Assembly, and in the next session they not only resolved, against vehement opposition, to present the petition to the king but also chose Franklin, on 26 October, to go as agent to manage the difficult affair with Richard Jackson, who had been agent for the province since Franklin's return from England. The opposition brought in a remonstrance against the choice, and Franklin answered them, on 5 November, in his *Remarks on a Late Protest*. He ended with a philosopher's gesture, which he so well knew how to make disarming—and infuriating. "I am now to take leave (perhaps a last leave) of the country I love and in which I have spent the greatest part of my life. *Esto perpetua.* I wish every kind of prosperity to my friends; and I forgive my enemies."[20]

There was no money in the provincial treasury. The Assembly authorized a loan, and £1100 was raised by subscription within a few hours. Franklin would take only £500. As he had not hesitated to accept the appointment, neither did he delay his going. Deborah still refused to cross the ocean, and would not consent to sending Sally with him, which he would have liked. He left behind him the new house being built for them on the south side of Market Street, between Third and Fourth. (It was thirty-four feet square, the insurance survey noted, built of brick, three stories high, with three rooms to a floor and the kitchen in the cellar, had two "large painhouses with trusses at each end," and was insured in 1766 for £500.[21]) Whatever he had said in his *Remarks*, he expected to be gone no more than a few months, not ten years. On 7 November he set out for his ship at Chester, sixteen miles away, with three hundred friends on horseback. Galloway and two others stayed on board with him as far as New Castle. "Tell our friends that dined with us on the turtle," he wrote to Deborah from the Isle of Wight on 9 December, "that the kind prayer they then put up for thirty days' fair wind for me was favourably heard and answered, we being just thirty days from land to land."[22] He went at once to London and Craven Street, where he found only a maid at home and surprised Margaret Stevenson when she came in. Back in Philadelphia the proprietary party kept up its abuse of him. When his friends heard that he had got safely to England, bells rang till midnight, healths were drunk, and Hugh Roberts of the Junto sat up late telling anecdotes of the forty years he had known Franklin.

Authority on America

AGAIN as in 1757 Franklin caught cold soon after he arrived in London, and had a troubling cough that lasted into January. But before Parliament met on the 10th as well as afterwards he was busy with his mission. It called for all the arts of strategy. The Penns had influence, and many politicians instinctively sided with the English proprietors as against the insubordinate Pennsylvanians. Richard Jackson, Franklin's colleague, thought the Assembly's move unwise. As a member of Parliament he knew its temper, and he was very close to Grenville, then head of the ministry. Jackson believed that the Penns in any case would not long be allowed to own and rule the province but would be required to sell it to the Crown, to be administered like the other colonies. It would be wiser to wait and let the change come of itself than to force the issue and so perhaps stir up a stubborn resentment. Jackson and Franklin had been instructed by the Assembly to be sure that the change, if granted, did not cost the people any of the liberties guaranteed them by their constitution

Franklin walked everywhere on eggshells. He had to lobby for the change without making concessions and yet without irritating the ministers. It was essential that he stand well with them. He wanted to keep his place in the post office, and he knew that the Penns were doing their best to get him dismissed. He had at the same time to further the petition and to resist the passage of the Stamp Act. If he pressed either point too hard he might have to yield on the other. Most of all, he was faithful to his imperial vision and his old desire to bring the separated parts of the Empire together in a friendly understanding. That at best would take time and have to be done, he thought, through the quiet courses of reason.

The Pennsylvania matter was lost in the larger issue. Though Franklin in February supposed he would be home by the end of summer, he found the Privy Council steadily indifferent or averse even to hearing the petition, which was not laid before them till November. Then they said the king had no power to interfere between proprietors and people. If this was partly a legal answer, it was also partly political. The outcry against the Stamp Act was at its height, and the ministry in no mood to let Americans say how they should be governed. The decision was postponed and the affair dragged on, intermittently, until after the Revolution, when Pennsylvania voted the Penns £130,000 and the British government settled on the head of the family an annual pension of £4000. During these ten years the Assembly's petition was among Franklin's lesser troubles.

The opposition to the Stamp Act absorbed him early and, again, late in 1765. News of the proposal of March 1764 had reached Philadelphia while Franklin was still a member of the Assembly, and he knew the colonists felt that this was the wrong method for raising money in America. If British taxes were heavy on account of the recent war, so were American taxes. The Americans were willing to pay for their defence, but they wanted to be consulted and to vote the needed money in their assemblies as they had always done. Otherwise the Stamp Act would be a tax imposed upon them by a legislature in which they were not represented, in plain violation of their ancient rights. In London Franklin found no understanding of the American attitude. The Parliamentary majority had thought less of upholding American rights than of reducing British taxes. Country squires, appalled by the national debt, had heard that the colonies were now rich, had come to hold that the colonies owed more than gratitude to the mother country for protecting them from the French, and had easily agreed that the colonies should be taxed without too much concern for their metaphysical objections. Grenville, brother-in-law to Pitt, took his budget seriously and had set himself to correct the laxity of colonial administration, especially in the customs. From London the American assemblies did not look so important as the Americans seemed to think them. After all there was only one Parliament, and while it might be policy to pay some attention to the notions of the little parliaments overseas, in the end the responsibility must be taken by the ministry in London. And back of these was George III, obstinately bound to be king of all his people, for what he considered their own good, and to draw even the remote Americans into the great circle of royal sway and order.

Before bringing in the Stamp Act in February 1765 Grenville on the 2nd heard the protests of the colonial agents. He told them he had the task of managing the national revenue and he saw no better way of assigning Americans their rightful share than the present tax. Could the agents suggest one? Franklin thought the "usual constitutional way" would be better; that is, through requisitions from the king and responsive votes from the assemblies. Grenville asked whether the various assemblies would agree on the sum each colony should raise of the total. The agents could not promise that they would. Grenville said he believed that the Stamp Act would be a fair and equal tax. When the agents insisted that if Parliament taxed the colonies their assemblies might lose their importance and be neglected. Grenville answered that nothing of the sort was intended by the act. He must proceed with it, and he hoped the Americans would be moderate. They could not hope to gain anything from England by agitation.

The Stamp Act was brought before the House of Commons and hardly debated. Jackson, agent for Pennsylvania, and Irish, doubted the expediency of the measure. Isaac Barré, also Irish, who had fought with Wolfe at Quebec, on 6 February burst out with a fiery defence of the colonists. "They planted by your care!" Jared Ingersoll reported that Barré said in answer to Charles Townshend: "No; your oppression planted them in America. They fled from your tyranny to a then uncultivated, inhospitable country. . . . They nourished by your indulgence! They grew by your neglect of them. . . . They protected by your arms! They have nobly taken up arms in your defence; have exerted their valour amidst their constant and laborious industry for the defence of a country whose frontier was drenched in blood while its interior parts yielded all its little savings to your emolument." He called them "sons of liberty." The English majority was not affected by his Irish eloquence. On the 13th the Stamp bill was read for the first time without discussion. Franklin the next day wrote to John Ross in Philadelphia: "The Stamp Act, notwithstanding all the opposition we have been able to give it, will pass. Every step in the law, every newspaper, advertisement, and almanac is severely taxed. If this should, as I imagine it will, occasion less law and less printing, it will fall particularly hard on us lawyers and printers."[1] Believing that nothing else could be done to stop the act, Franklin had already accepted it and was quietly urging other measures which he thought might offset it: among them, a repeal of the act which had prohibited the issue of paper money in the colonies, and the establishment of an American currency.

As he said it would, the Stamp Act passed the House, was approved by the Lords, and on 22 March received the king's assent by commission, the king having had his first attack of insanity. The act was to go into effect 1 November. It required that stamps, of specified costs, be put on almost every legal paper, from one shilling on any document concerned with proceedings in ecclesiastical courts to six pounds on any grant or privilege from a governor. The stamp for a college degree was to cost two pounds. For a bill of lading, fourpence. For an appointment to an office worth twenty pounds a year, ten shillings; more than twenty pounds a year, four pounds. For a liquor licence, four pounds. For a pack of cards, one shilling. For a pair of dice, ten shillings. For a newspaper on a half-sheet of paper, one halfpenny; on a whole sheet, one penny. For a pamphlet, one shilling. For an advertisement, two shillings. For an almanac, twopence. And so on through fifty-five articles.

Franklin, on the day he wrote to Ross that the bill would pass, wrote also to say that he had ordered for David Hall a hundred reams of large half-sheets for use in printing the *Pennsylvania Gazette* at the lower rate. "Some days after the Stamp Act was passed, to which I had given all the opposition I could, with Mr. Grenville, I received a note from Mr. Whately, his secretary, desiring to see me the next morning. I waited upon him accordingly, and found with him several other colony agents. He acquainted us that Mr. Grenville was desirous to make the execution of the act as little inconvenient and disagreeable to the Americans as possible; and therefore did not think of sending stamp officers from hence, but wished to have discreet and reputable persons appointed in each province from among the inhabitants, such as would be acceptable to them; for, as they were to pay the tax, he thought strangers should not have the emoluments. Mr. Whately therefore wished us to name for our respective colonies, informing us that Mr. Grenville would be obliged to us for pointing out to him honest and responsible men, and would pay great regard to our nominations."[2] Though this was obviously a politic and ingratiating move of Grenville's, Franklin saw no harm in it. Since the act was to be a law in America, it might best be administered by Americans. He nominated his friend John Hughes for Pennsylvania, and advised Jared Ingersoll, then agent for Connecticut, to accept the post of stamp officer in that province.

Franklin misjudged his countrymen. He did not expect them to resist the Stamp Act so violently as they did, and their violence surprised as well as disturbed him, when news of it began to reach England. These were not the quiet courses of reason. Disagreeable as the Stamp Act was, he thought it better to submit to it while working for its repeal. For him, it was only a single setback in a general campaign for imperial unity. The mistake had been made in London. American resistance meant British resentment, and was certain to delay the mutual understanding which he had at heart. Let Americans be as philosophical as they could. "Depend upon it, my good neighbour," he wrote to Charles Thomson on 11 July, "I took every step in my power to prevent the passing of the Stamp Act. Nobody could be more concerned in interest than myself to oppose it sincerely and heartily. But the tide was too strong against us. The nation was provoked by American claims of independence, and all parties joined in resolving by this act to settle the point. We might as well have hindered the sun's setting. That we could not do. But since 'tis down, my friend, and it may be long before it rises again, let us make as good a night of it as we can. We may still light candles. Frugality and industry will go a great way toward indemnifying us. Idleness and pride tax with a heavier hand than kings and parliaments; if we can get rid of the former, we may easily bear the latter."[3]

II

Between the passage of the act and the arrival in London of the angry news from America Franklin had a touch of gout that kept him in Craven Street for nearly two weeks in late spring and gave him time for other things besides his daily politics. Humour was fundamental in him. Calling himself "A Traveller," on 20 May he sent to a newspaper his grave defence of newswriters, who might not tell the truth but who made talk.

"Englishmen, Sir, are too apt to be silent when they have nothing to say; too apt to be sullen when they are silent; and when they are sullen, to hang themselves." And some of the things the newswriters told, "I can assure you, on the faith of a traveller, are serious truths." For instance, the stories from America of the manufactures which were being established there to take trade away from England. "The very tails of the American sheep are so laden with wool that each has a little car or wagon on four little wheels, to support and keep it from trailing on the ground. Would they caulk their ships, would they fill their beds, would they even litter their horses with wool if it were not both plenty and cheap? . . . Their engaging three hundred silk throwsters here in one week, for New York, was treated as a fable because, forsooth, they have 'no silk there to throw.' Those who made this objection perhaps did not know that at the same time the agents from the king of Spain were at Quebec to contract for a thousand pieces of cannon to be made there for the fortification of Mexico and at New York engaging the annual supply of woven floor carpets for their West India houses, other agents from the emperor of China were at Boston treating about an exchange of raw silk for wool, to be carried in Chinese junks through the Straits of Magellan.

"And yet all this is as certainly true as the account, said to be from Quebec, in all the papers of last week, that the inhabitants of Canada are making preparations for a cod and whale fishery this 'summer in the upper lakes.' Ignorant people may object that the upper lakes are fresh and that cod and whale are salt-water fish.

But let them know, Sir, that cod, like other fish when attacked by their enemies, fly into any water where they can be safest; that whales, when they have a mind to eat cod, pursue them wherever they fly; and that the grand leap of a whale in that chase up the fall of Niagara is esteemed, by all who have seen it, as one of the finest spectacles in nature. Really, Sir, the world is grown too incredulous. It is like the pendulum, ever swinging from one extreme to another. Formerly everything printed was believed, because it was in print. Now things seem to be disbelieved for just the very same reason. Wise men wonder at the present growth of infidelity. They should have considered, when they taught people to doubt the authority of newspapers and the truth of predictions in almanacs, that the next step might be a disbelief in the well-vouched accounts of ghosts, witches, and doubts even of the truths of the Creed."[4]

Franklin reworked the magic circle which he had made years ago and sent it to his electrical friend John Canton, carefully using inks of different colours. He wrote to Sir Alexander Dick recommending to him young Samuel Bard of New York, then studying in Edinburgh. (Bard, afterwards president of the College of Physicians and Surgeons in New York, was the son of John Bard for whom Franklin in Philadelphia had written his best known drinking song. Samuel Bard on his way to England in 1761 had been captured by the French and held till he could send word to Franklin, who helped to bring about his release.[5]) To Lord Kames, at his request, Franklin on 2 June wrote "my history from the time I set sail for America" in 1762, a compact masterpiece of autobiography. "Here I have been ever since," he went on, "engaged in . . . public affairs relating to America, which are like to continue some time longer upon my hands; but I promise you that, when I am quit of these, I will engage in no other; and that, as soon as I have recovered the ease and leisure I hope for, the task you require of me, of finishing my *Art of Virtue*, shall be performed. In the meantime, I must request you would excuse me on this consideration, that the powers of the mind are possessed by different men in different degrees, and that everyone cannot, like Lord Kames, intermix literary pursuits and important business without prejudice to either."

Franklin, who had been reading Lord Kames's *Elements of Criticism*, wished his friend had "examined more fully the subject of music." Franklin's own taste ran to simple airs, but he had reasons for his preference. His comments on melody were fresh and original ideas about it which psychologists were not to develop for a hundred years. "The reason why Scotch tunes have lived so long and will probably live for ever (if they escape being stifled in modern affected ornament) is merely this, that they are really compositions of melody and harmony united, or rather that their melody is harmony. I mean the simple tunes sung by a single voice. As this will appear paradoxical I must explain my meaning. In common acceptation, indeed, only an agreeable succession of sounds is called melody, and only the coexistence of agreeing sounds, harmony. But, since the memory is capable of retaining for some moments a perfect idea of the pitch of a past sound, so as to compare with it the pitch of a succeeding sound and judge truly of their agreement or disagreement, there may and does arise from thence a sense of harmony between the present and the past sounds, equally pleasing with that between two present sounds. . . .

"That we have a most perfect idea of a sound just past I might appeal to all acquainted with music, who know how easy it is to repeat a sound in the same pitch with one just heard. In tuning an instrument, a good ear can as easily determine that two strings are in unison by sounding them separately as by sounding them together; their disagreement is also as easily, I believe I may say more easily and better, distinguished when sounded separately; for when sounded together, though you know by the beating that one is higher than the other, you cannot tell which it is. I have ascribed to memory the ability of comparing the pitch of a present tone with that of one past. But if there should be, as possibly there may be, something in the ear similar to what we find in the eye, that ability would not be entirely owing to memory. Possibly the vibrations given to the auditory nerves by a particular sound may actually continue some time after the cause of those vibrations is past, and the agreement or disagreement of a subsequent sound become by comparison with them more discernible. For the impression made on the visual nerves by a luminous object will continue for twenty or thirty seconds. Sitting in a room, look earnestly at the middle of a window a little while when the day is bright, and then shut your eyes; the figure of the window will still remain in the eye, and so distinct that you may count the panes. . . .

"Farther, when we consider by whom these ancient tunes were composed and how they were first performed, we shall see that each harmonical succession of sounds was natural and even necessary in their construction. They were composed by the minstrels of those days to be played on the harp accompanied by the voice. The harp was strung with wire, which gives a sound of long continuance, and had no contrivance, like that in the modern harpsichord, by which the sound of the preceding could be stopped the moment a succeeding note began. To avoid actual discord it was therefore necessary that the succeeding emphatic note should be a chord with the preceding, as their sounds must exist at the same time. Hence arose the beauty in those tunes that has so long pleased and will please for ever, though men scarce know why. . . . Most tunes of late composition, not having this natural harmony united with their melody, have recourse to the artificial harmony of a bass and other accompanying parts. This support, in my opinion, the old tunes do not need, and are rather confused than aided by it."[6]

Two days later Franklin was writing domestically to his wife about the new house into which, after many delays on the part of the builder, she had moved, though she was still unsettled. "I could have wished to have been present at the finishing of the kitchen, as it is a mere machine and, being new to you, I think you will scarce know how to work it; the several contrivances to carry off steam and smell and smoke not being fully explained to you. The oven I suppose was put up by the written directions in my former letter. You mention nothing of the furnace. If that iron one is not set, let it alone till my return, when I shall bring a more convenient copper one. . . . I cannot but complain in my mind of Mr. Smith that the house is so long unfit for you to get into, the fences not put up, nor the other necessary articles got ready. The well I expected would have been dug in the winter, but I hear nothing of it. You should have gardened long before the date of your last, but it seems the rubbish was not removed. I am much obliged to my good old friends that did me the honour to remember me in the unfinished kitchen. I hope soon to drink with them in the parlour."[7]

III

When Grenville was succeeded by the milder Rockingham as first minister in July Franklin thought more about the prospects for a change from proprietary government than about the possibility of getting the Stamp Act repealed. And on 9 August he could still write to John Hughes of the need of reason and even of submission. "The rashness of the Assembly in Virginia is amazing. I hope, however, that ours will keep within the bounds of prudence and moderation; for that is the only way to lighten or get clear of our burdens. As to the Stamp Act, though we purpose doing our endeavour to get it repealed, yet the success is uncertain. . . . A firm loyalty to the Crown and faithful adherence to the government of this nation, which it is the safety as well as honour of the colonies to be connected with, will always be the wisest course for you and I to take, whatever may be the madness of the populace or their blind leaders, who can only bring themselves and country into trouble and draw on greater burthens by acts of rebellious tendency."[8]

By an irony of which Franklin was then possibly unaware, and which none of his biographers has noted, he had remotely had a hand in the American uproar. The defiant resolutions which Patrick Henry moved in the Virginia House of Burgesses on 29 May seemed too treasonable to be printed in Williamsburg, Philadelphia, or New York, but first appeared in the *Newport Mercury* for 24 June. And the *Mercury* had been founded by the younger James Franklin, now dead, who had learned his trade as apprentice to his uncle Benjamin.

Whoever first printed the Virginia Resolves, they were bound to reach the public. Reprinted the next week in Boston, still in a version more inflammatory than the one which had been voted in Virginia, they became, as the governor of Massachusetts said, "an alarum bell to the disaffected" from Halifax to St. Augustine. The assemblies might be generally temperate in their protests, but the people were outspoken. While the General Court of Massachusetts was calling an intercolonial congress to meet in New York in October, groups of unofficial men in various colonies were being organized as Sons of Liberty. Colonel Barré had called Americans that in Parliament, and they enthusiastically welcomed the name.

It was a large name, for the colonists did not think the Stamp Act a small issue. They had long been used to having their trade regulated by the British government, on the old assumption that colonies existed, economically, to furnish raw materials to the mother country and a market for manufactured goods. Franklin in his letters to Governor Shirley in 1754 had studied the system with penetrating eyes, and had pointed out that it was not only selfish on the part of Britain but actually short-sighted. To regulate the colonial trade too strictly was to reduce the volume of it, at the cost of American prosperity and British profits. But the acts of 1764 were stricter than any before them. Besides new duties on non-British goods imported to the colonies, there were new collectors, who made it difficult to get round the unpleasant law by smuggling. The Sugar Act undertook to limit the West Indian trade to the British islands, which did not produce as much molasses as the northern colonies required. Rum distilled from molasses was a universal beverage in America, and it was the currency used in trading with the Indians for furs and in Africa for slaves. With these trades hampered by the lack of rum, and with non-British markets cut off in the West Indies, the northern colonies could not make the money which they paid for British manufactures. Their whole economic life was upset. And they knew it was purely for the benefit of the British sugar planters, whose influence with Parliament had shaped the act.

While this was a grievance, the Stamp Act was an outrage, the Americans thought and said over and over during 1765 while they waited for it to go into effect in November, more and more firmly bent on resisting it. That the revenue produced was to be spent in America for the support of soldiers to defend the frontier did not matter. However it might be explained, it was a direct tax, and it had not been laid upon them by their assemblies. They alone had the right to vote public money, and they had maintained the right in many conflicts with their governors. Parliament, laying a tax upon the colonies without consulting them, was no better than a governor. Even Parliament could not tax Americans, who had no representative in Parliament. Their right not to be taxed without being represented was constitutional, fundamental, and sacred. Much of their reasoning was inexact, but their feelings were clear and sharp. The French and Indian war, which had made the British government think of the colonies as important enough to be taxed, had made the Americans think of themselves as important enough to say how they should be taxed. Though they had still a traditional affection for the homeland and the king, this did not in the same degree extend to Parliament, which the Americans knew, as honest men in England knew, was a corrupt and arrogant oligarchy. The Stamp Act was not merely disputed legislation. It was an encroachment of prerogative. The Americans at large looked upon Parliament somewhat as the Pennsylvanians looked upon the proprietors.

The news which reached England during the latter part of 1765 was diversified but mostly of one meaning. The nine colonies that sent delegates to the Stamp Act Congress of October had come nearer to intercolonial accord than so many colonies had ever come before. Mild as their resolutions were, they seemed to the Lords of Trade to set a dangerous precedent. The Congress, not prompted by royal officials like that at Albany eleven years before, was extralegal, a kind of dignified mutiny. Riots had broken out, from New Hampshire to South Carolina, after the names of the stamp distributors were published in America in August. The rioters were worst in Boston, but Franklin's friends Ingersoll in Connecticut and Hughes in Pennsylvania were both threatened by mobs and both forced to resign. Before the act went into effect there were no officers left to carry it out. When the stamps arrived, very few were used. Business went on without them or did not go on at all. As a protest against the revenue acts there had been widespread agreements to boycott British goods, and threats to begin manufacturing in America. Merchants stopped importing, and could not always pay for what they had ordered. Debtors were in distress, men out of work, restive and turbulent. The effects were felt in Britain, where the American trade was said to have been cut in half. British manufacturers, merchants, shippers, and tradesmen began to join with Americans in opposition to the acts.

For Franklin the Stamp Act was nearly a catastrophe. His enemies in Philadelphia caught at the occasion. They said, at that long, slow distance, that he had framed the act himself, encouraged its passage, and profited by it. He had, they said, got money for recommending stamp officers, and he had been promised a high post under the Crown. This was the agent who had gone to London for the redress of Pennsylvania's grievances. And this was a worse grievance than the Penns had ever thought of. Some of the anger which the Philadelphia rioters showed John Hughes was aimed at Franklin. There was talk of setting fire to his new house. William Franklin hurried from Burlington and urged his mother and sister to take refuge with him in New Jersey. Deborah Franklin let Sally go, but she herself would not move. One of her brothers came to stay with her, and one of her husband's nephews. She had them bring guns, and, she wrote to London, "we turned one room into a magazine. I ordered some sort of defence upstairs, such as I could manage myself." She knew she had offended nobody and she was sure her husband had not. And she believed that if there were any trouble she would have more friends than enemies.

Franklin on 8 July wrote to a friend that the malice of his adversaries was harmless: "all their arrows . . . have been like those that Rabelais speaks of, which were headed with butter hardened in the sun."[9] But as matters became worse he could not help being seriously concerned. Trying to draw two parts of the Empire together, he found himself suspected by each of being a partisan of the other. He had to choose between antagonists. As to his choice he was never in the least doubt. Though he made no excuses for the American rioters, he was on the side of the Americans. His change was in tactics, not in principles. What America was saying now he had said years ago in his letters to Shirley. But he seems to have believed that a just and stable imperial unity might be brought about by intelligent reasoning in London and through the voluntary decision of the British government to be unselfish and far-sighted about America. He had foreseen the time when America would be more populous than Britain and the balance of empire lie west of the Atlantic. That time, he knew, had not come, and yet the precocious Americans were already demanding their rights and ready to resist what seemed a violation of them. Quickly shifting his ground, he cited the American demands as proof of his argument that unity in the Empire depended upon local government in America and representation in Parliament.

The violence reported from the colonies made his work difficult. Their outcries sounded above his quiet voice, urging reason and wisdom. Parliament, which had expected nothing of the kind, was startled into resentment and persistence. The Grenville ministry had fallen for causes unconnected with the Stamp Act, and the new and weak ministry of Rockingham had not at first taken a stand on it. In the confusion of current politics there was no person or party to whom Franklin could go, to enlighten and persuade. This was not science or philosophy. This was a political situation, and he was faced with a whole patchwork of passions and interests. Grenville and his adherents in the opposition were unwilling to admit that they had blundered. The king saw in the American protests a threat to his plans for personal rule, and grew more stubborn than ever. The king's friends would vote with the king. The lawyers insisted on the strict legality of the act. The landowners held out for the simple reason that the act promised to reduce their taxes by making the colonies support the British forces in America. And London swarmed with placemen who realized that the more the British took a hand in colonial control the more places there would be for them.

Against none of these could Franklin hope to make much headway in arguing for the repeal of the Stamp Act. He had to try to win a majority without them. Pitt was supposed to be in favour of repeal, but he had refused to join the Rockingham ministry. The ministry was eager to discredit Grenville's policy, and it had liberal Whig opinions, but it was divided and its hold was insecure. Franklin, who had been close to Grenville through Richard Jackson, was close to Rockingham through his private secretary Edmund Burke, who was Irish, philosophical, friendly to Americans and Quakers, and was just entering Parliament as member for Wendover. There were of course not enough liberals and philosophers in power to repeal the unwise act. Franklin had to appeal to ordinary politicians by talking of their interests or the interests of their constituents. "I was extremely busy," he told Lord Kames, "attending members of both Houses, informing, explaining, consulting, disputing, in a continual hurry from morning to night."[10] His prestige as a philosopher, his enormous knowledge of American affairs, his skill in persuasive argument, his wide acquaintance, and his knack at getting along with all sorts of people made him first among all those who were working for repeal. But his principal strength came from his association with the British manufacturers, merchants, shippers, and tradesmen who were suffering from the consequences of the act. They too were victims of the landowning oligarchy who legislated for their own advantage and despised the commercial class. This was Franklin's class. He understood such men, and they him. Though they were still little represented in Parliament, they were rising men and they had an increasing influence on public opinion. The problem was to organize and present that opinion with such force that the landowners would not dare to overlook it. Franklin was the American spokesman for an American-British propaganda.

From August 1765 to the following January there are only scant and broken records of what Franklin was doing, thinking, saying. As if he had somehow gone underground, he worked cautiously and anonymously, calling the least attention to himself. No need to remind Americans that the propagandist was a Crown officer or the British that he was agent for Pennsylvania. But he gave his whole time and strength to the undertaking. He dined with Rockingham, he conferred with Lord Dartmouth. In a manuscript now first published,[11] apparently written during this busy hiatus, he set down the outline of his argument, probably as he had to repeat it many times. "We do not dispute your power," he said as if he were addressing the House of Commons. "We know we cannot in any form support a contest with you. Not only in arms, etc., our superiors infinitely; but in abilities of mind, knowledge, cultivated reason, etc. We cannot subsist without your friendship and protection, etc. But the greater you are, and the more we are in your power, the more careful you should be to do nothing but what is right.

"Internal tax. Freemen to be taxed by their representatives.

People of America fond of liberty. Suppose themselves to enjoy much of it. Will think all lost. They fear the example. 'Tis raising contributions on them (they will say) as in a conquered country. Right they should contribute, but they will do as much as they can afford voluntarily if properly called on. At present they love Britain [he had first written "England" and then wrote "Britain" above it], are fond of British people, British customs, modes, books, manufactures. A disgust of all these will ensue. Trade will suffer more than the tax profits. They will grow obstinately frugal.

"Post office rates no tax. Service done at a much cheaper rate. It is only a *quantum meruit*. Equity and justice wins hearts and secures dominions. The disgust occasioned by this tax will sow the seeds and lay the foundation of future disunion, misery, etc. False ideas given of their wealth by officers entertained at their houses. All their profits [?] centre in Britain. It is depriving subjects of the only means in their power to show their loyalty to their sovereign. Would the Commons like to have the Lords lay all the taxes on them, though they were to lay them ever so justly and equitably? People will make less conscience of smuggling.

"It is not wise to do it. Everything one has a right to do is not best to be done. More money will be got by voluntary grant. People will give from affection rather more than they can spare.

"Three ways of avoiding these inconveniences:

"1. By allowing each colony to send members to Parliament. The reasons. It will prevent their clamour. They are as numerous as North Britons, and will in a little time be as wealthy. Therefore deserve to be represented. Representation useful two ways. It brings information and knowledge to the great council. It conveys back to the remote parts of the empire the reasons of public conduct; thus prevents discontents and insurrection arising from want of or misinformation. The more extended an empire this becomes the more necessary. 'Tis cheaper than armies and garrisons to keep such countries in quiet; and the people themselves are at the expense. It will draw the most wealthy people to live in London, and their wealth with them, for such only can afford to be P[arliament] m[emb]ers or create patronage. It will for ever preserve the union which otherwise may be various ways broken, as by division in the royal family, etc. If members are allowed to each colony, perhaps at present all may not like to send them; some from the expense, etc. Yet these will then have little right to complain. Their omission is a tacit empowering the rest to proceed without them.

"2. By empowering them to send delegate from each assembly to a common council, of which council the sums to be asked. This practicable. Albany Plan.

"3. By the paper money scheme."

In these notes Franklin did not mention the Stamp Act by name. It was merely one of the internal taxes which Parliament had no right to lay on the colonies, so long as they were unrepresented. Representation meant more to him than repeal. The act might be temporary, the repeal temporary. What was needed was a lasting principle of agreement and a consolidating union. But by the end of the year he seems to have given up hope that any fundamental measures would be taken. The other colonial agents insisted on repeal as soon as possible. Franklin's British allies wanted a general trade reform, but they agreed to concentrate on the Stamp Act, which Franklin came to call "the mother of mischief." On 4 December many of the merchants trading to North America met at the King's Arms tavern and chose a committee, with Barlow Trecothick—who had lived in Boston—as chairman, to bring their cause before Parliament. They drummed up petitions for repeal from trading towns throughout the kingdom: Bristol, Liverpool, Halifax, Leeds, Lancaster, Leicester, Bradford, Frome, Birmingham, Coventry, Macclesfield, Wolverhampton, Stourbridge, Dudley, Minehead, Taunton, Witney, Newcastle, Glasgow, Chippenham, Nottingham. They arranged for the House of Commons to give a hearing to witnesses who could testify to the bad effects of the act.

Parliament met briefly on 17 December and again on 14 January, to plunge into long and fierce debate. Grenville and the opposition strenuously resisted any change in the colonial policy which they had begun. Parliament was sovereign, and the right of taxation was an essential part of its power. The Americans talked of liberty, but what they wanted was stingily to pay as little as possible. Their high talk was only a pretence to justify their illegal and riotous misbehaviour. If Parliament yielded now, there was no telling how far the Americans would go. Repeal would be humiliation to Parliament, treachery to Britain. On the side of the ministry and their friends Burke made his first speech, in favour of the colonists, and Pitt showed his mighty hand. Franklin, who seems to have been present on 14 January, reported Pitt's speech to Strahan. "Mr. Pitt spoke some time before one could divine on which side of the question relating to America he would be; but, beginning first to mention the Stamp Act by the soft term of that 'unhappy act,' he went on, and every time he had occasion to mention it, it was by a term still stronger, as 'unconstitutional,' 'unjust,' 'oppressive,' etc., till he finally declared in express terms that the British Parliament had in his opinion no right to raise internal taxes in America, though it had to regulate their commerce and even restrain their manufactures."[12] These were Franklin's opinions, almost in Franklin's words. But Franklin knew that Burke had only his eloquence with which to move Parliament, and that Pitt, out of the ministry, had less power with the members than with the public, who would not vote. The king and the king's friends were unalterably set against repeal, some of the ministers, and as many of the landowners as could not be reached by the pressure of the commercial groups. And there were any number who held what Franklin on 6 January called the "mistaken opinion that the honour and dignity of government is better supported by persisting in a wrong measure once entered into than by rectifying an error as soon as it is discovered."[13]

"I am excessively hurried," Franklin wrote to his wife on 22 February, "being, every hour that I am awake, either abroad to speak with members of Parliament or taken up with people coming to me at home concerning our American affairs."[14] Throughout the debate he never rested. He carried it from Parliament to the public and wrote anonymous letters to the newspapers, shrewd and biting. He now for the first time published, in Strahan's *London Chronicle* for 6–8 February, his letters to Shirley, the most thoroughgoing statement of the American position that London had ever read. He encouraged others to write on American affairs. With a stage manager's foresight he laid plans for the time when he should be allowed to speak out in his own person. On 3 February he was ordered to attend the House of Commons, which was sitting as a committee of the whole to hear the crowd of witnesses whom the merchants had produced. On the 13th he was excused from further attendance. On that day, and it may be also on the day before, the most renowned American had come to the bar and answered the House's questions about America.[15]

I V

Franklin was known by sight or reputation to the members, or most of them, but the Speaker asked him, for the record: "What is your name and place of abode?" And he answered: "Franklin, of Philadelphia." Then promptly his friends, the friends of repeal, took up the exposition of their cause. Grave as the issue was, the examination was in form almost a historical comedy, with the philosopher who had helped direct it now playing the chief part. He knew what questions his friends would ask, and had his answers ready. As to his adversaries' questions, he would have to improvise. No point was likely to come up that he had not thought how to meet.

James Hewitt led off. Member for Coventry, he was the son of a mercer and draper of that town, which manufactured ribbons and worsteds and had protested against the Stamp Act which made Americans resolve to do without them.

"*Q*. Do the Americans pay any considerable taxes among themselves?

"*A*. Certainly many, and very heavy taxes."

Hewitt asked what the taxes were in Pennsylvania, for what purposes they were laid, and how long they were to continue. Franklin answered with quiet precision, stressing the debt contracted in the recent war.

"*Q*. Was it not expected that the debt would have been sooner discharged?

"*A*. It was, when the peace was made with France and Spain. But, a fresh war breaking out with the Indians, a fresh load of debt was incurred; and the taxes, of course, continued longer by a new law.

"*Q*. Are not all the people very able to pay those taxes?

"*A*. No. The frontier counties, all along the continent, having been frequently ravaged by the enemy and greatly impoverished, are able to pay very little tax. And therefore, in consideration of their distresses, our late tax laws do expressly favour those counties,. excusing the sufferers; and I suppose the same is done in other governments."

Hewitt, who had given Franklin a chance to say that the Americans were already paying heavily for the imperial war, and also for a war of their own, was followed by John Huske, member for Maldon. Huske had been born in New Hampshire, the son of Ellis Huske who for twenty years was postmaster of Boston.

"*Q*. Are you not concerned in the management of the post office in America?

"*A*. Yes. I am Deputy Postmaster-General of North America.

"*Q*. Don't you think the distribution of stamps by post to all the inhabitants very practicable, if there was no opposition?

"*A*. The posts only go along the sea coasts; they do not, except in a few instances, go back into the country; and if they did, sending for stamps by post would occasion an expense of postage amounting, in many cases, to much more than that of the stamps themselves. . . .

"*Q*. From the thinness of the back settlements, would not the Stamp Act be extremely inconvenient to the inhabitants, if executed?

"*A*. To be sure it would; as many of the inhabitants could not get stamps when they had occasion for them without taking long journeys and spending perhaps three or four pounds that the Crown might get sixpence."

Here "one of the late administration, an adversary," who must have seen how Huske was playing into Franklin's hands, interrupted the artful dialogue.

"*Q*. Are not the colonies, from their circumstances, very able to pay the stamp duty?

"*A*. In my opinion there is not gold and silver enough in the colonies to pay the stamp duty for one year.

"*Q*. Don't you know that the money arising from the stamps was all to be laid out in America?

"*A*. I know it is appropriated by the act to the American service;

but it will be spent in the conquered colonies [Canada and Florida], where the soldiers are, not in the colonies that pay it.

"*Q*. Is there not a balance of trade due from the colonies where the troops are posted that will bring back the money to the old colonies?

"*A*. I think not. I believe very little will come back. I know of no trade likely to bring it back. I think it would come from the colonies where it was spent directly to England."

Huske resumed his questioning, about the dissatisfaction of the Pennsylvania Germans with the act and the number of white men in America. This was to make American resistance seem formidable. In answer to another question Franklin explained how Pennsylvania, which exported little to the British Isles, paid for its imports. "The balance is paid by our produce carried to the West Indies and sold in our own islands or to the French, Spaniards, Dutch, and Danes; by the same carried to other colonies in North America, as to New England, Nova Scotia, Newfoundland, Carolina, and Georgia; by the same carried to different parts of Europe, as Spain, Portugal, and Italy. In all which places we receive either money, bills of exchange, or commodities that suit for remittance to Britain; which, together with all the profits on the industry of our merchants and mariners, arising in these circuitous voyages, and the freights made by their ships, centre finally in Britain to discharge the balance and pay for British manufactures continually used in the province or sold to foreigners by our traders."

At this point Huske asked a question which was omitted from the record. "There had been," Franklin later remembered,[16] "a considerable party in the House for saving the honour and right of Parliament by retaining the act and yet making it tolerable to America, by reducing it to a stamp on commissions for profitable offices and on cards and dice. I had, in conversation with many of them, objected to this, as it would require an establishment for the distributors which would be a great expense, as the stamps would not be sufficient to pay them, and so the odium and contention would be kept up for nothing. The notion of amending, however, still continued, and one of the most active of the members for promoting it told me he was sure I could, if I would, assist them to amend the act in such a manner that America should have little

or no objection to it. 'I must confess,' says I, 'I have thought of one
amendment; if you will make it the act may remain and yet the
Americans will be quieted. It is a very small amendment, too; it is
only the change of a single word.' 'Aye,' says he, 'what is that?' 'It
is in that clause where it is said that from and after the first day of
November one thousand seven hundred and sixty-five, there shall
be paid, etc. The amendment I would propose is, for *one* read
two, and then all the rest of the act may stand as it does. I believe
it will give nobody in America any uneasiness.' Mr. Huske had
heard of this, and, desiring to bring out the same answer in the
House, asked me whether I could not propose a small amendment
that would make the act palatable. But, as I thought the answer he
wanted too light and ludicrous for the House, I evaded the
question."

Grenville, Franklin afterwards thought it had been, brought the
discussion sharply back from trade to justice.

"*Q.* Do you think it right that America should be protected by
this country and pay no part of the expense?

"*A.* That is not the case. The colonies raised, clothed, and paid,
during the last war, near 25,000 men and spent many millions.

"*Q.* Were you not reimbursed by Parliament?

"*A.* We were only reimbursed what, in your opinion, we had
advanced beyond our proportion, or beyond what might be reasonably expected from us; and it was a very small part of what we
spent. Pennsylvania, in particular, disbursed about £500,000, and
the reimbursements in the whole did not exceed £60,000."

The examination swung to the amount of taxes in Pennsylvania
and the rate of exchange. Then somebody, who may have been
either friend or adversary: "Do you not think the people of
America would submit to pay the stamp duty if it was moderated?"
And Franklin said: "No, never, unless compelled by force of arms."

Robert Nugent, ambitious poet, assiduous politician, rich from
marrying three rich widows, member for Bristol, and that year to
become Viscount Clare and president of the Board of Trade, fluttered into the argument. ("His drift," Franklin said, "was to establish a notion he had entertained, that the people in America had
a crafty mode of discouraging the English trade by heavy taxes on
merchants."[17])

"*Q*. Do not they, as much as possible, shift the tax off from land, to ease that, and lay the burden heavier on trade?

"*A*. I have never understood it so. I never heard such a thing suggested. And indeed an attempt of that kind could answer no purpose. The merchant or trader is always skilled in figures, and ready with his pen and ink. If unequal burdens are laid on his trade, he puts an additional price on his goods; and the consumers, who are chiefly landholders, finally pay the greatest part, if not the whole."

The answer made the questioner look silly. Grey Cooper, lawyer, pamphleteer, supporter of Rockingham, and a secretary of the treasury, went on with questions for which Franklin had some of his neatest answers.

"*Q*. What was the temper of America towards Great Britain before the year 1763?

"*A*. The best in the world. They submitted willingly to the government of the Crown, and paid, in all their courts, obedience to acts of Parliament. Numerous as the people are in the several provinces, they cost you nothing in forts, citadels, garrisons, or armies to keep them in subjection. They were governed by this country at the expense only of a little pen, ink, and paper. They were led by a thread. They had not only a respect but an affection for Great Britain; for its laws, its customs and manners, and even a fondness for its fashions, that greatly increased the commerce. Natives of Britain were always treated with particular regard; to be an Old England man was, of itself, a character of some respect and gave a kind of rank among them.

"*Q*. And what is their temper now?

"*A*. Oh, very much altered. . . .

"*Q*. In what light did the people of America use to consider the Parliament of Great Britain?

"*A*. They considered the Parliament as the great bulwark and security of their liberties and privileges, and always spoke of it with the utmost respect and veneration. Arbitrary ministers, they thought, might possibly at times attempt to oppress them; but they relied on it that Parliament on application would always give redress. . . .

"*Q*. And have they not still the same respect for Parliament?

"*A*. No, it is greatly lessened.

"*Q*. To what causes is that owing?

"*A*. To a concurrence of causes: the restraints lately laid on their trade by which the bringing of foreign gold and silver into the colonies was prevented; the prohibition of making paper money among themselves, and then demanding a new and heavy tax by stamps; taking away, at the same time, trials by juries and refusing to receive and hear their humble petitions."

Cooper or other friends gave Franklin a chance to say, what he had written long ago, that the population of America doubled every twenty-five years, but their demand for manufactures increased at a much more rapid rate. Nugent asked about the increase of population, and Franklin accounted for it by the early marriages in America. Then, Nugent asked, were not "the lower ranks of people more at their ease in America than in England"—implying, more able to pay taxes? Franklin told him merely: "They may be so, if they are sober and diligent, as they are better paid for their labour."

Friends and adversaries asked whether a modified Stamp Act or a future tax laid on the same principle would be more acceptable to Americans, and Franklin said no. They would never submit, never pay.

"*Q*. Have you not heard of the resolutions of this House, and of the House of Lords, asserting the right of Parliament relating to America, including a power to tax the people there?

"*A*. Yes, I have heard of such resolutions.

"*Q*. What will be the opinion of the Americans on those resolutions?

"*A*. They will think them unconstitutional and unjust.

"*Q*. Was it an opinion in America before 1763 that the Parliament had no right to lay taxes and duties there?

"*A*. I never heard any objection to the right of laying duties to regulate commerce; but a right to lay internal taxes was never supposed to be in Parliament, as we are not represented there.

"*Q*. On what do you found your opinion that the people in America made any such distinction?

"*A*. I know that whenever the subject has occurred in conversation where I have been present, it has appeared to be the opinion of everyone that we could not be taxed by a Parliament where we were not represented. But the payment of duties laid by an act of Parliament, as regulations of commerce, was never disputed."

Someone brought up the point that the colonial governors and assemblies had often been at odds over voting public money.

"*Q*. . . . In case a governor, acting by instruction, should call on an assembly to raise the necessary supplies, and the assembly should refuse to do it, do you not think it would then be for the good of the people, as well as necessary to the government, that the Parliament should tax them?

"*A*. I do not think it would be necessary. If an assembly could possibly be so absurd as to refuse raising the supplies necessary for the maintenance of government among them, they could not long remain in such a situation; the disorders and confusion occasioned by it must soon bring them to reason.

"*Q*. If it should not, ought not the right to be in Great Britain of applying the remedy?

"*A*. A right, only to be used in such a case, I should have no objection to; supposing it to be used merely for the good of the people of the colony.

"*Q*. But who is to judge of that: Britain or the colony?

"*A*. Those that feel can judge best."

Now the opposition for some time led the questioning. In particular they challenged Franklin's delicate—and dangerous—distinction between internal and external taxes. If the colonists were allowed to decide upon their internal taxes, they might later make the same claim for such external taxes as duties regulating their commerce.

"*Q*. You say the colonies have always submitted to external taxes and object to the right of Parliament only in laying internal taxes. Now can you show that there is any kind of difference between the two taxes to the colony on which they may be laid?

"*A*. I think the difference is very great. An external tax is a duty laid on commodities imported; that duty is added to the first cost and other charges on the commodity and, when it is offered for sale, makes a part of the price. If the people do not like it at that price, they refuse it; they are not obliged to pay it. But an internal tax is forced from the people without their consent, if not laid by their own representatives. The Stamp Act says we shall have no commerce, make no exchange of property with each other, neither purchase nor grant nor recover debts; we shall neither marry nor make our wills; unless we pay such and such sums; and thus it is intended to extort our money from us or ruin us by the consequences of refusing to pay it.

"*Q.* But supposing the external tax or duty to be laid on the necessaries of life imported into your colony, will not that be the same thing in its effects as an internal tax?

"*A.* I do not know a single article imported into the northern colonies but what they can either do without or make themselves."

This was true, Franklin explained, even of cloth. (He knew that the British wool-growers and cloth-makers had suffered greatly from the American boycott.) The Americans had given up eating lamb to increase the amount of wool in the country. "The people will all spin and work for themselves in their own houses." The southern colonists did not need much wool. "Their winters are short and not very severe; and they can very well clothe themselves with linen and cotton for the rest of the year."

The questioning turned sharply back to the matter of repeal and Parliament's claim of a right to tax the Americans.

"*Q.* Considering the resolutions of Parliament as to the right, do you think, if the Stamp Act is repealed, that the North Americans will be satisfied? . . .

"*A.* I think the resolutions of right will give them very little concern if they are never attempted to be carried into practice. The colonies will probably consider themselves in the same situation, in that respect, with Ireland; they know you claim the same right with Ireland, but you never exercise it. And they may believe you never will exercise it in the colonies unless on some very extraordinary occasion.

"*Q.* But who are to be the judges of that extraordinary occasion? Is not the Parliament?

"*A.* Though the Parliament may judge of the occasion, the people will think it can never exercise such right till representatives from the colonies are admitted into Parliament; and that, whenever the occasion arises, representatives will be ordered."

More questions on certain details of American legislation, and then the friends of repeal again, on more dramatic aspects of the issue.

"*Q.* Can anything less than a military force carry the Stamp Act into execution?

"*A.* I do not see how a military force can be applied to that purpose.

"*Q.* Why may it not?

"*A.* Suppose a military force sent into America, they will find nobody in arms; what then are they to do? They cannot force a man to take stamps who chooses to do without them. They will not find a rebellion; they may indeed make one.

"*Q.* If the act is not repealed, what do you think will be the consequences?

"*A.* The total loss of the respect and affection the people of America bear to this country, and of all the commerce that depends on that respect and affection."

With a run of questions the opposition asked Franklin how the Americans would get along without British imports, if internal taxes were laid.

"*Q.* Then no regulation with a tax would be submitted to?

"*A.* Their opinion is that when aids to the Crown are wanted they are to be asked of the several assemblies, according to the old established usage; who will, as they always have done, grant them freely. And that their money ought not to be given away, without their consent, by persons at a distance, unacquainted with their circumstances and abilities. The granting aids to the Crown is the only means they have of recommending themselves to their sovereign; and they think it extremely hard and unjust that a body of men in which they have no representatives should make a merit to itself of giving and granting what is not its own but theirs; and deprive them of a right they esteem of the utmost value and importance, as it is the security of all their other rights."

Grenville asked: "But is not the post office, which they have long received, a tax as well as a regulation?"

"*A.* No. The money paid for the postage of a letter is not of the nature of a tax; it is merely a *quantum meruit* for a service done; no person is compellable to pay the money if he does not choose to receive the service. A man may still, as before the act, send his letter by a servant, a special messenger, or a friend if he thinks it cheaper or safer.

"*Q.* But do they not consider the regulations of the post office, by the act of last year, as a tax?

"*A.* By the regulations of last year the rate of postage was generally abated near thirty per cent through all America; they certainly cannot consider such abatement as a tax."

Grenville retreated before a self-evident fact. The opposition asked if the Americans would distinguish between an excise on goods consumed and a duty on goods imported. Franklin said they would. "An excise is unconnected with any service done, and is merely an aid, which they think ought to be asked of them, and granted by them, if they are to pay it; and can be granted for them by no other persons whatsoever whom they have not empowered for that purpose."

"*Q.* You say they do not object to the right of Parliament in laying duties on goods to be paid on their importation. Now is there any kind of difference between a duty on the importation of goods and an excise on their consumption?

"*A.* Yes, a very material one. An excise, for the reasons I have just mentioned, they think you can have no right to lay within their country. But the sea is yours; you maintain by your fleets the safety of navigation on it and keep it clear of pirates; you may have therefore a natural and equitable right to some toll or duty on merchandise carried through that part of your dominions, towards defraying the expense you are at in ships to maintain the safety of that carriage. . . .

"*Q.* Supposing the Stamp Act continued, and enforced, do you imagine that ill-humour will induce the Americans to give as much for worse manufactures of their own, and use them, preferably to better of ours?

"*A.* Yes, I think so. People will pay as freely to gratify one passion as another, their resentment as their pride."

Franklin thought the act could not be enforced because the stamps could not be distributed. "The principal distributors, who were to have had a considerable profit on the whole, have not thought it worth while to continue in the office; and I think it impossible to find sub-distributors, fit to be trusted, who for the trifling profit that must come to their share would incur the odium and run the hazard that would attend it; and if they could be found I think it impracticable to protect the stamps in so many distant and remote places.

"*Q*. But in places where they could be protected, would not the people use them rather than remain in such a situation, unable to obtain any right or recover by law any debt?

"*A*. It is hard to say what they would do. I can only judge what other people will think and how they will act by what I feel within myself. I have a great many debts due to me in America, and I had rather they should remain unrecoverable by any law than submit to the Stamp Act. They will be debts of honour. In my opinion the people will either continue in that situation or find some way to extricate themselves; perhaps by generally agreeing to proceed in the courts without stamps."

Once more friends intervened and pressed a point which most members did not want to face.

"*Q*. What do you think a sufficient military force to protect the distribution of stamps in every part of America?

"*A*. A very great force; I can't say what, if the disposition of America is for a general resistance.

"*Q*. What is the number of men in America able to bear arms, or of disciplined militia?

"*A*. There are, I suppose, at least ——"

The question was instantly objected to, and Franklin withdrew. When he came back the friends of repeal asked him miscellaneous questions about American manufactures until the opposition again took up their persistent theme.

"*Q*. If the Stamp Act should be repealed would not the Americans think they could oblige the Parliament to repeal every external tax law now in force?

"*A*. It is hard to answer questions of what people at such a distance will think.

"*Q*. But what do you imagine they will think were the motives of repealing the act?

"*A*. I suppose they will think that it was repealed from a conviction of its inexpediency; and they will rely upon it that while the same inexpediency subsists you will never attempt to make such another."

An adversary asked a muddled question and Franklin gave him a dry, sly answer that must have made the House laugh.

"*Q.* If the act should be repealed, and the legislature should show its resentment to the opposers of the Stamp Act, would the colonies acquiesce in the authority of the legislature? What is your opinion they would do?

"*A.* I don't doubt at all that if the legislature repeal the act the colonies will acquiesce in the authority."

Then a friend, with a question to which Franklin's answer was as near a speech as he ever made.

"*Q.* But if the legislature should think fit to ascertain its right to lay taxes, by an act laying a small tax contrary to their opinion, would they submit to pay the tax?

"*A.* The proceedings of the people in America have been considered too much together. The proceedings of the assemblies have been very different from those of the mobs, and should be distinguished, as having no connexion with each other. The assemblies have only peaceably resolved what they take to be their rights; they have taken no measures for opposition by force; they have not built a fort, raised a man, or provided a grain of ammunition, in order to such opposition. The ringleaders of riots they think ought to be punished; they would punish them themselves if they could. . . . But as to an internal tax, how small soever, laid by the legislature here on the people there, while they have no representatives in this legislature, I think it will never be submitted to. They will oppose it to the last. They do not consider it at all necessary for you to raise money on them by your taxes; because they are, and always have been, ready to raise money by taxes among themselves and to grant large sums, equal to their abilities, upon requisition from the Crown. . . . America has been greatly misrepresented and abused here, in papers and pamphlets and speeches, as ungrateful and unreasonable and unjust; in having put this nation to immense expense for their defence and refusing to bear any part of that expense. The colonies raised, paid, and clothed near 25,000 men during the last war; a number equal to those sent from Britain, and far beyond their proportion; they went deeply into debt in doing this, and all their taxes and estates are mortgaged for many years to come for discharging that debt. Government here was at that time very sensible of this. The colonies were recommended to Parliament. Every year the king sent down to this House a written message to this purpose: that His Majesty, being highly sensible of the zeal and vigour with which his faithful subjects in North America had exerted themselves in defence of His Majesty's just rights and possessions, recommended it to this House to take the same into consideration and enable him to give them a proper compensation. You will find those messages on your own journals every year of the war to the very last; and you did accordingly give £200,000 annually to the Crown, to be distributed in such compensation to the colonies.

"This is the strongest of all proofs that the colonies, far from being unwilling to bear a share in the burden, did exceed their proportion; for if they had done less, or had only equalled their proportion, there would have been no room or reason for compensation. Indeed, the sums reimbursed them were by no means adequate to the expense they incurred beyond their proportion; but they never murmured at that; they esteemed their sovereign's approbation of their zeal and fidelity, and the approbation of this House, far beyond any other kind of compensation."

Charles Townshend, paymaster of the forces in the Rockingham ministry, asked a question.

"*Q.* But suppose Great Britain should be engaged in a war in Europe, would North America contribute to the support of it?

"*A.* I do think they would as far as their circumstances would permit. They consider themselves as a part of the British Empire, and as having one common interest with it; they may be looked on here as foreigners, but they do not consider themselves as such. They are zealous for the honour and prosperity of this nation; and, while they are well used, will always be ready to support it, as far as their little power goes. . . . They make no distinction of wars, as to their duty of assisting them. I know the last war is commonly spoke of here as entered into for the defence, or for the sake, of the people in America. I think it is quite misunderstood. It began about the limits between Canada and Nova Scotia; about territories to which the Crown indeed laid claim but which were not claimed by any British colony; none of the lands had been granted to any colonist; we had therefore no particular concern or interest in that dispute. As to the Ohio, the contest there began about your right of trading in the Indian country, a right you had by the treaty of Utrecht, which the French infringed; they seized the traders and their goods, which were your manufactures; they took a fort which a company of your merchants and their factors and correspondents had erected there to secure that trade. Braddock was sent there with an army to retake that fort, which was looked on here as another encroachment on the king's territory, and to protect your trade. It was not till after his defeat that the colonies were attacked. They were before in perfect peace with both French and Indians; the troops were not, therefore, sent for their defence.

"The trade with the Indians, though carried on in America, is not an American interest. The people of America are chiefly farmers and planters; scarce anything that they raise or produce is an article of commerce with the Indians. The Indian trade is a British interest; it is carried on with British manufactures, for the profit of British merchants and manufacturers; therefore the war, as it commenced for the defence of territories of the Crown the property of no American, and for the defence of a trade purely British, was really a British war; and yet the people of America made no scruple of contributing their utmost towards carrying it on and bringing it to a happy conclusion."

Nugent was shocked at hearing Franklin boldly turn the tables and call the recent war a British war, in which the British had rather been dutifully helped than magnanimously helping. "You will not deny," Nugent asked, "that the preceding war, the war with Spain, was entered into for the sake of America; was it not occasioned by captures made in the American seas?" "Yes," Franklin told him; "captures of ships carrying on the British trade there with British manufactures." (Again Nugent had been made to look silly. He "made a violent speech next day upon this examination, in which he said: 'We have often experienced Austrian ingratitude, and yet we assisted Portugal; we experienced Portuguese ingratitude, and yet we assisted America. But what is Austrian ingratitude, what is the ingratitude of Portugal, compared to this of America?

We have fought, bled, and ruined ourselves, to conquer for them; and now they come and tell us to our noses, even at the bar of this House, that they were not obliged to us, etc.' But his clamour was very little minded,"[18] Franklin remembered. Nor did Nugent hold a grudge. "He took me home from court," Franklin wrote to his son two years later, "that I might dine with him, as he said, alone and talk over American affairs. . . . He gave me a great deal of flummery; saying that, though at my examination I answered some of his questions a little pertly, yet he liked me, from that day, for the spirit I showed in defence of my country; and at parting, after we had drank a bottle and a half of claret each, he hugged and kissed me, protesting he never in his life met with a man he was so much in love with."[19])

Grenville insisted that the war with the Indians since the treaty with France had been a war for America only. Franklin firmly replied that it "was rather a consequence or remains of the former war, the Indians not having been thoroughly pacified." It had been fought and ended chiefly with American men and money. And Americans did not need British help against the Indians. "They defended themselves when they were but a handful and the Indians much more numerous. . . . They are very able to defend themselves."

Welbore Ellis, member for Aylesbury, vice-treasurer of Ireland, asked constitutional questions and got constitutional answers.

"*Q.* Do you think the assemblies have a right to levy money on the subject there, to grant to the Crown?

"*A.* I certainly think so; they have always done so.

"*Q.* Are they acquainted with the declaration of rights? And do they know that, by that statute, money is not to be raised on the subject but by consent of Parliament?

"*A.* They are very well acquainted with it.

"*Q.* How then can they think they have a right to levy money for the Crown, or for any other than local purposes?

"*A.* They understand that clause to relate to subjects only within the realm; that no money can be levied on them for the Crown but by consent of Parliament. The colonies are not supposed to be within the realm; they have assemblies of their own, which are their parliaments, and they are, in that respect, in the same situation with Ireland. When money is to be raised for the Crown upon the subject in Ireland or in the colonies, the consent is given in the Parliament in Ireland or in the assemblies in the colonies. They think the Parliament of Great Britain cannot properly give that consent till it has representatives from America; for the petition of right expressly says it is to be by common consent in Parliament; and the people of America have no representatives in Parliament to make a part of that common consent."

Legally Franklin was here on ticklish ground, finding justification for the American stand less in the written law than in a doctrine of natural rights. A little later, speaking of the Pennsylvanians under their charter but referring to Americans in general, he said that they were entitled "to all the privileges and liberties of Englishmen": among them, not to be taxed except by their own consent. An adversary pushed him to what now seems a prophetic warning.

"*Q.* Are there any words in that charter that justify that construction?

"*A.* 'The common rights of Englishmen,' as declared by Magna Charta and the petition of right, all justify it.

"*Q.* Does the distinction between internal and external taxes exist in the words of the charter?

"*A.* No, I believe not.

"*Q.* Then may they not, by the same interpretation, object to the Parliament's right of external taxation?

"*A.* They never have hitherto. Many arguments have been lately used here to show them that there is no difference, and that, if you have no right to tax them internally, you have none to tax them externally, or make any other law to bind them. At present they do not reason so; but in time they may possibly be convinced by these arguments."

Here was the dramatic last word of the examination, though friends and adversaries, adherents of both Grenville and Rockingham, asked a few more scattering questions, mostly going over ground already covered. "I have answered that," Franklin quietly said to one of them. And at the very end came two questions and their answers which must have been rehearsed as if for the descending curtain in a theatre.

"*Q*. What used to be the pride of the Americans?

"*A*. To indulge in the fashions and manufactures of Great Britain.

"*Q*. What is now their pride?

"*A*. To wear their old clothes over again till they can make new ones."

V

This was on 13 February. On the 21st the repealing bill was moved. It passed the House, was carried through the Lords, and received the royal assent on 8 March. The repeal was so popular that in the happy tumult most people in both England and America paid little attention to the accompanying act which declared that Parliament had the right to enact laws binding the British colonies "in all cases whatsoever"—even taxes. The Rockingham ministry had made this compromise with their opponents. The king gave only a sullen assent to what he thought humiliating. Most of the Scotch, most of the bishops, most of the Tories voted against repeal. To get a majority the ministry had had to offer repeal as an expedient for an extraordinary occasion, yielded by Parliament without any surrender of its supreme authority. Parliament, many members thought, must stand by its rights as the Americans by theirs. And, on another level of opinion, Parliament must save its face.

"There are claimers enough," Franklin told Charles Thomson on 27 September, "of merits in obtaining the repeal. But, if I live to see you, I will let you know what an escape we had in the beginning of the affair, and how much we were obliged to what the profane would call luck and the pious, Providence."[20] If he ever told the story, with all its personal and political ins and outs, at least he never told it for the public. The chief credit belongs to the merchants trading to America. It was not wisdom that brought about the repeal, but interest. The petitions from America did less than the boycott there, with its effect on the sensitive nerves of British trade. Franklin's wisdom included prudence. Talking about the rights of Americans, genuinely and profoundly as he believed in them, he never forgot to tell the British that if they alienated the colonies they would lose more in trade than they would gain in taxes. This, backed by the petitions of the merchants and the trading towns, was the convincing argument of his examination.

But no other man alive could have delivered the argument as Franklin did. The most backward squire from the remotest county, the most obliging placeman chosen for a pocket borough, would have heard of Franklin the philosopher. Now here he was at the bar of the House, a philosopher who had the affairs of a continent—from statistics to sentiments—at the end of his tongue. Nobody else had ever known or thought so much about America. The members could not surprise Franklin with any question for which he had not a reasoned and pointed answer. If they pressed him hard he was firm. If they tried to catch him he turned the answer deftly on the questioner. No matter how the discourse wandered, he brought it always back to simple fundamental points. When he was subtle he seemed only to be making those points scrupulously clear. He did not hurry or overwhelm his hearers with eloquence. Reasoning was his persuasion. Even though they disagreed with him, they admired his knowledge, assurance, spirit, and temper. And some of them must have valued the art of the scene which had been staged for them.

Franklin, whose arts were silent ones, had never before spoken so long before so large an audience, and he never did again. His answers were hardly oratory, but they brought him an orator's triumph. The Rockingham ministry was grateful. Taken down as spoken, the *Examination* was published in London, the same year in Boston, New London, New York, Philadelphia (in German as well as English), and Williamsburg, and the next year in French at Strasbourg. In the jubilations over repeal in America Franklin was its hero. He had upheld the cause of America before Parliament and won a great victory for his countrymen. In Pennsylvania even the proprietary party had to admit some good in him. In Philadelphia the coffee houses gave presents to every man on the ship that brought the news. Punch and beer were free to anybody who would drink the health of the king. Three hundred gentlemen in the State House, guests of the governor and the mayor, toasted

Franklin and resolved that on the king's birthday in June they would all wear suits of British manufacture and give their home-spun to the poor. On the birthday the salutes were fired from a barge named the *Franklin*.

"As the Stamp Act is at length repealed," Franklin wrote to his wife on 6 April, "I am willing you should have a new gown, which you may suppose I did not send sooner as I knew you would not like to be finer than your neighbours unless in a gown of your own spinning. Had the trade between the two countries totally ceased, it was a comfort to me to recollect that I had once been clothed from head to foot in woollen and linen of my wife's manufacture, that I never was prouder of any dress in my life, and that she and her daughter might do it again if it was necessary. I told the Parliament that it was my opinion, before the old clothes of the Americans were worn out they might have new ones of their own making. And indeed if they had all as many clothes as your old man has, that would not be very unlikely, for I think you and George reckoned when I was last at home at least twenty pair of old breeches. Joking apart, I have sent you a fine piece of Pompadour satin, fourteen yards, cost eleven shillings a yard; a silk negligee and petticoat of brocaded lutestring for my dear Sally, with two dozen gloves, four bottles of lavender water." Mrs. Stevenson had again helped him to buy presents for his wife and daughter: lace, three ells of cambric, three damask tablecloths, crimson mohair for curtains, "a large true Turkey carpet cost ten guineas for the dining parlour," some oiled silk, and "a gimcrack corkscrew which you must get some brother gimcrack to show you the use of. . . . I send you also a box with three fine cheeses. Perhaps a bit of them may be left when I come home."[21]

The repeal quieted America, and most Americans seemed to be satisfied. Franklin was still uneasy. Repeal was patchwork legislation. Nothing had been done to establish the imperial union which he saw as the basis of imperial harmony. In January, and perhaps before, he had come to doubt that there would ever be any such union. And on 9 May he wrote to Cadwallader Evans that it was now probably too late to hope for it. "The Parliament here do at present think too highly of themselves to admit representatives from us, if we should ask it; and, when they will be desirous of granting it, we shall think too highly of ourselves to accept of it. It would certainly contribute to the strength of the whole if Ireland and all the dominions were united and consolidated under one common council for general purposes, each retaining its own particular council or parliament for its domestic concerns. But this should have been more early provided for. In the infancy of our foreign establishments it was neglected, or not thought of. And now the affair is nearly in the situation of Friar Bacon's project of making a brazen wall round England for its eternal security. His servant, Friar Bungay, slept while the brazen head, which was to dictate how it might be done, said 'Time is' and 'Time was.' He only waked to hear it say 'Time is past.' An explosion followed that tumbled their house about the conjurer's ears."[22]

❦❦

Agent-General

DURING the winter of repeal Joseph Priestley came to
London from Warrington, where he was classical tutor in
a dissenting academy and had already begun his studies in electricity and chemistry. Franklin, never too busy to help a young
man of promise, undertook to furnish the books which Priestley
needed for his history of electricity, and told him details of the kite
experiment which had not been communicated to the Royal
Academy: how Franklin had been waiting for a taller spire than
Philadelphia had; how he had walked with his son to a field where
there was a convenient shed; how he had seen one cloud pass over
without effect and had begun to despair; and how he had felt an
exquisite pleasure when his knuckle drew a spark from the key.
Franklin read the manuscript of Priestley's book as it was written,
and had a hand in Priestley's election to the Royal Academy.
Priestley became one of the warmest friends of America. Franklin,
after the repeal, had a little leisure for science. Beccaria had sent
the Royal Society his account of new electrical experiments,
through Franklin, and the Society asked him to return Beccaria its
thanks. "I am pleased to hear," Franklin said, "that you read
English although you do not write it. That is my case with the
Italian. We can therefore correspond with greater facility, if it
pleases you, each of us writing in his own language."[1]

John Pringle, now Sir John and physician to the queen, went in
June to Pyrmont in Hanover to drink the waters, famous for their
iron, and Franklin with him. "I hope more from the air and exercise," he wrote to his wife on 13 June, "having been used, as you
know, to have a journey once a year, the want of which last year
has I believe hurt me, so that though I was not quite to say sick
I was often ailing last winter and through the spring. . . . I pur-

pose to leave him at Pyrmont and visit some of the principal cities nearest to it, and call for him again when the time for our return draws nigh"—which must be within eight weeks because the queen was soon to be confined. They left London the next day. If the travellers separated, it was not for long. At Pyrmont, or somewhere in Hanover, they met the prodigious Freiherr von Münchhausen, who had already retired from the wars to his estate at Bodenwerder and begun to amuse his friends with his stories; and they met also Rudolf Erich Raspe, who was later to make the stories famous in English as Baron Munchausen's.[2] The baron gave Pringle and Franklin letters to various learned men at the University of Göttingen, which George II had founded.

The Royal Society of Sciences elected Franklin and Pringle to membership, and they attended a meeting at Göttingen on 19 July. Hanover, like the colonies, had the same king as England, and the Hanoverians were full of questions. Franklin told Johann David Michaelis that the population of America doubled every twenty-five years. Michaelis thought, in spite of what Franklin said, that the colonies would sooner or later become independent. Interest would prove stronger than affection. They talked of the giant Patagonians about whom Franklin and Pringle had heard in London from John Byron, the poet's grandfather, just back from a voyage around the world. The prince of Schwarzburg-Rudolstadt sent a messenger to carry his salutations to Franklin at Göttingen, but Franklin had gone. In Hanover the travellers visited Johann Friedrich Hartmann, head of the royal hospital, who showed them his powerful electrical apparatus. Franklin was interested in a contrivance called a pulse-glass, and took one back to London, where he arrived by the middle of August. Though he had been warmly received and had enjoyed his holiday, he seems to have got no notable new ideas and made no special friends. His chief souvenir of the journey, besides his membership in the Hanoverian Royal Society, was his pulse-glass, copied and improved in London: a sealed glass tube, half filled with water, in which the bubbles behaved in a way to astonish visiting philosophers and the water would boil from the heat of a hand holding one of the hollow glass balls at either end of the tube.

Before going to Hanover Franklin had asked the Pennsylvania

Assembly to let him return to America. They appointed him agent for another year, and he stayed on in Craven Street. His household was now larger by a child, another Sally Franklin. She and her father Thomas Franklin, a dyer in Leicestershire, were the only Franklins in England descended from the brothers who had not crossed the Atlantic. Her father "brought her to town to see me in the spring, and Mrs. Stevenson persuaded him to leave the child under her care for a little schooling and improvement while I went abroad. When I returned I found her indeed much improved and grown a fine girl. She is sensible and of a sweet, obliging temper."[3] Then thirteen, she lived most of the time in Craven Street, a second daughter to Franklin, till she was married seven years later to James Pearce, a young farmer who lived in Surrey, twelve miles from London. When not at school William Franklin's illegitimate son Temple also was often with his hospitable grandfather. In July 1766 Franklin's last brother, Peter, died in Philadelphia, and Franklin gave careful attention to the widow's affairs. There had been a strain of poetry in Peter, as in other members of the family. In his old age he composed a ballad and sent it to his famous brother in London, asking him to have it set to music. Franklin thought that "if you had given it to some country girl in the heart of the Massachusetts, who has never heard any other than psalm tunes or *Chevy Chace*, the *Children in the Woods*, the *Spanish Lady*, and such old simple ditties, but has naturally a good ear, she might more probably have made a pleasing popular tune for you than any of our masters here and more proper for your purpose."[4]

For years Franklin had been open-handed to his brothers and sisters, his cousins, nephews, and nieces, but now at sixty he himself was worried about money. The partnership with David Hall ended in 1766, and with it an annual five hundred pounds or so. "A great source of our income is cut off," Franklin wrote to his wife on 22 June 1767; "and if I should lose the post office, which among the many changes here is far from being unlikely, we should be reduced to our rents and interests of money for a subsistence, which will by no means afford the chargeable housekeeping and entertainments we have been used to. For my own part I live here as frugally as possible not to be destitute of the comforts of life, making no dinners for anybody and contenting myself with a single dish when I dine at home; and yet such is the dearness of living here in every article that my expenses amaze me. I see too by the sums you have received in my absence that yours are very great, and I am very sensible that your situation naturally brings you a great many visitors, which occasion an expense not easily to be avoided, especially when one has been long in the practice and habit of it. But when people's incomes are lessened, if they cannot proportionably lessen their outgoings they must come to poverty. If we were young enough to begin business again it might be another matter; but I doubt we are past it; and business not well managed ruins one faster than no business."

In the circumstances they could not, Franklin thought, do more than fit their daughter "handsomely out in clothes and furniture, not exceeding in the whole five hundred pounds of value," on her marriage with Richard Bache. Bache, born in Yorkshire, was a merchant thirty years old who had come to Philadelphia from New York. William thought him a fortune-hunter, and so wrote to London. But Bache won Sally's heart and her mother's consent, which Franklin, who did not know him, ratified. "I can only say that if he proves a good husband to her, and a good son to me, he shall find me as good a father as I can be. . . . For the rest, they must depend as you and I did, on their own industry and care."[5] If Bache's business did not justify an early marriage, Sally might come to London and return with her father, Franklin suggested on 5 August. But Sally, twenty-four, handsome, robust (when she ordered gloves from London she asked for the largest size), blond like her father and high-coloured like her mother, remained in Philadelphia and was married in October. The ships in the harbour ran up their flags to celebrate the wedding.

Franklin's anxieties did not last too long. He kept his place in the post office and his agency for Pennsylvania, and was successively chosen agent also for Georgia in 1768, for New Jersey in 1769, and for Massachusetts in 1770. The total salaries, sometimes paid months or even years late, amounted to £1500, which more than made up for the Hall partnership, though Franklin freely spent his own money in the service of his missions. If the Revolution had been longer delayed, or had not come, he would probably have been agent-general for the colonies. In effect he was that. He was an ambassador from America before America had the right to send one.

II

Nothing should be clearer about the Revolution than that the English colonists had ceased to be British before they realized it. Their whole history had bred in them a sense of differentiation and self-sufficiency which guided their instincts even against their wills. Their wills drove them to protest their loyalty, which indeed was supported by many pleasant sentiments. But they had left the old country out of one discontent or another, and neither success nor failure in the new entirely reconciled them to what they had left behind. In America they had all been shaped by other ways of life to other habits, and some of them to other conscious precepts. No prince of the blood, hardly a lord temporal or spiritual, had accompanied the migration. The feudal impulses withered away in America. The British government looked upon the colonies almost purely as an asset, until 1760 not a very valuable one, and ran them, badly, like a business. They had ill luck with too many of the soldiers they first sent out—the bungling Braddock and the dilatory Loudoun—and the colonial governors were likely to be inferior in everything but rank to the Americans opposed to them. As late as 1768, when the imperial government needed prestige in America as never before, they sent Lord Botetourt, amiable but showy, fraudulent, and dishonoured, to hold Virginia against Washington, Jefferson, and George Mason. There were of course better soldiers and governors from Britain than these. But no number of able military or political administrators could have corrected the grievance which the Americans came increasingly to feel they had in the British commercial policy.

To use a later term, they felt increasingly after 1763 that they were exploited through the regulation of their trade and the restraint of their manufactures. Because exploitation had long been the rule of the colonial system and had only begun to be scrutinized, the colonists had at the outset no full and logical array of reasons to bring against it. Economics had not yet evolved a language which was authoritative and widely understood. The Americans in their dissatisfaction had to fall back—at least did fall back—upon the language of politics, and talked about constitutions, the privileges of subjects, the rights of man. Such matters seemed to them, whether they reflected or not, more dignified than the matter which lay at the back of their minds: that Americans were forced to work for British profits. Feeling partly on one plane, and almost always talking on another, they were sometimes contradictory. Their rich and lofty political eloquence clouded their economic realism. The British could answer this American eloquence as much as they liked, but the Americans were still vigilant and unyielding to encroachment upon their liberty and to trespass upon their property. To touch their ways of making a living was to touch their ways of life.

Parliament too was stubborn. Nothing could shake the conviction of the majority that the colonies were selfishly refusing to pay their share of the imperial expenses, which they could well afford and ought to pay. The landowners who had conceded the repeal of the Stamp Act, under pressure from the British manufacturers and merchants, knew that though trade might be better because of repeal the land taxes would be higher. They felt a double resentment toward the colonies, with their petitions and riots. The feeling grew that it was time to take the colonies in hand, tax them as they deserved, and keep them in order. The Rockingham ministry went out in July 1766, while Franklin was in Hanover. The king and Pitt, now Lord Chatham, agreed upon a coalition cabinet which, in spite of Pitt, had as little character as any in English history. To make the trouble worse, Chatham was overwhelmed by his old malady the gout. "It is said that his constitution is totally destroyed and gone," Franklin wrote to Cadwallader Evans on 5 May 1767, "partly through the violence of the disease and partly through his own quacking with it."[6] During his illness the leadership of the government was deftly seized by the adroit Charles Townshend, chancellor of the exchequer, who had voted both for the Stamp Act and for its repeal, and who in January 1767 light-heartedly promised the House of Commons that he would find revenue in America for its own military establishment, for the benefit of the land tax at home. His colleagues in the ministry, who had made no such plans, were too much surprised to check him. One of the most irresponsible politicians in England almost single-handed set going a fantastic series of political blunders.

What made it possible was not only that Chatham had lost the reins but also that there was exasperating news from America. New York had refused to provide for the British soldiers sent there by the Quartering Act which had been a part of Grenville's policy. Headquarters for the American forces, the province had been asked to support several regiments, much more than its share, not because they were needed for its defence but because it was convenient to keep them at a strategic point, for use in Canada, the frontier, or the West Indies. The New York Assembly would not vote the money asked for. Parliament was at once in a mood to back Townshend. In May he brought in his dangerous measures. The New York Assembly was to be suspended; that is, the governor was forbidden to give his assent to any legislation till the soldiers were provided for. Commissioners for the customs were to be sent from England to America, to be sure the duties were collected. New duties were to be laid on glass, painters' colours, paper, and tea. The annual revenue, estimated at less than £40,000, was to go to the Crown for a civil list to pay governors and judges. This would make administration easier, and would make places for the placemen.

Franklin saw every sign of danger ahead. The import duties, though laid as external taxes, were plainly for revenue. Money taken from the Americans, without their consent, would pay British officials to govern the colonies without dependence on their legislatures. This was not the road to imperial unity. The two countries were slipping farther and farther apart. "It becomes a matter of great importance," Franklin wrote to Lord Kames on 11 April, "that clear ideas should be formed on solid principles, both in Britain and America, of the true political relation between them and the mutual duties belonging to that relation. . . . I am fully persuaded, with you, that a consolidating union, by a fair and equal representation of all the parts of this empire in Parliament, is the only firm basis on which its political grandeur and prosperity can be founded. Ireland once wished it, but now rejects it. The time has been when the colonies might have been pleased with it; they are now indifferent about it; and if it is much longer delayed they too will refuse it. But the pride of this people cannot bear the thought of it, and therefore it will be delayed. Every man in England seems to consider himself as a piece of a sovereign over America; seems to jostle himself into the throne with the king, and talks of 'our subjects in the colonies.' The Parliament cannot well and wisely make laws suited to the colonies without being properly and truly informed of their circumstances, abilities, temper, etc. This it cannot be without representatives from thence; and yet it is fond of this power and averse to the only means of acquiring the necessary knowledge for exercising it; which is desiring to be omnipotent without being omniscient. . . .

"I have lived so great a part of my life in Britain, and formed so many friendships in it, that I love it and sincerely wish it prosperity; and therefore wish to see that union, on which alone I think it can be secured and established. As to America, the advantages of such a union to her are not so apparent. She may suffer at present under the arbitrary power of this country; she may suffer awhile in a separation from it; but these are temporary evils that she will outgrow. Scotland and Ireland are differently circumstanced. Confined by the sea, they can scarcely increase in numbers, wealth, and strength so as to overbalance England. But America, an immense territory, favoured by nature with all advantages of climate, soil, great navigable rivers, and lakes, etc., must become a great country, populous and mighty; and will, in a less time than is generally conceived, be able to shake off shackles that may be imposed on her and perhaps place them on the imposers. In the meantime, every act of oppression will sour their tempers, lessen greatly—if not annihilate—the profits of your commerce with them, and hasten their final revolt; for the seeds of liberty are universally found there, and nothing can eradicate them. And yet there remains among that people so much respect, veneration, and affection for Britain that, if cultivated prudently, with kind usage and tenderness for their privileges, they might be easily governed still for ages, without force or any considerable expense. But I do not see here a sufficient quantity of the wisdom that is necessary to produce such a conduct, and I lament the want of it."[7]

(The letter did not reach Lord Kames. It had possibly been intercepted by the authorities, who had begun to think it prudent to keep an eye on Franklin.)

It was hard for him to admit that there was not enough wisdom for his imperial design, or perhaps that wisdom was not enough. He still did not lose hope. But there were immediate concerns to occupy him from day to day. Even before the Stamp Act had been passed, early in 1765, he seems to have proposed to Grenville the issue of an American paper currency, to bear interest which would help the British to meet their American expenses. "This I then thought would be a lighter and more bearable tax than the stamps, because those that pay it have an equivalent in the use of the money; and that it would at the same time furnish us with a currency which we much wanted."[8] The plan would not have been more acceptable to the Americans than the Stamp Act itself, for it was essentially another internal tax. It is fortunate that Franklin kept the matter of his proposal a secret except from Joseph Galloway, who told it only to William Franklin. Franklin's enemies in Pennsylvania would have found it another proof that he had capitulated to the ministry. He gave up the idea that the American currency might bear interest, and by June 1767 had assured the Chatham-Townshend ministry that "no colony would make money on those terms, and that the benefits arising to the commerce of this country [England] in America from a plentiful currency would therefore be lost." But he worked for the repeal of the act which restrained paper money in America, and which was not repealed.

Franklin was closer to the Earl of Shelburne, secretary of state for the colonies, than he had ever been to any British minister. Shelburne was young and generous, a friend to America, and an admirer of the philosopher who was twice his age. The minister, who had a spacious programme for new colonies in the western territory, some time in 1767 showed Franklin a plan for dealing with the Indians who would be affected; and the philosopher commented on it. America was larger, he quietly suggested, than the British realized. "The Indians under the care of the northern superintendent border on the colonies of Nova Scotia, Quebec, New Hampshire, Massachusetts, Connecticut, New York, New

Jersey, Pennsylvania, Maryland, Virginia; the superintendent's residence, remote from several of these, may occasion great inconvenience if his consent is always to be necessary." As to the scheme for having a chief from each tribe living constantly at the commissary: "Provision must then be made for his maintenance, as particular Indians have no estates, but live by hunting, and their public has no funds. Being used to rambling, it would perhaps not be easy to find one who would be obliged to this constant residence."

Nor would it be easy to fix prices. "There may be differences of fineness, goodness, and value in the goods of different traders, and the like in the peltry of different Indians, that cannot be properly allowed for by general tariffs. It seems contrary to the nature of commerce for government to interfere in the prices of commodities. Trade is a voluntary thing between buyer and seller, in every article of which each exercises his own judgment and is to please himself. Suppose either trader or Indian is dissatisfied with the tariff and refuses barter on those terms; are the refusers to be compelled?" Debts, Franklin thought, could hardly be collected in the forest as in England. "The Indian trade, so far as credit is concerned, has hitherto been carried on wholly upon honour. They have among themselves no such thing as prisons or confinement for debt. . . . Our legal method of compulsion is by imprisonment. The Indians cannot and will not imprison one another; and if we attempt to imprison them I apprehend it would be generally disliked by the nations, and occasion breaches. They have such high ideas of personal liberty, and such slight ones of the value of personal property, that they would think the disproportion monstrous between the liberty of a man and a debt of a few shillings; and that it would be excessively inequitable and unjust to take away the one for a default in payment of the other. . . . Debts of honour are generally paid as well as any other debts. Where no compulsion can be used, it is more disgraceful to be dishonest."[9]

Franklin had something besides a philosopher's interest in these matters. White settlers were pressing over the mountains into the lands assigned to the Indians by the British government in 1763. George Croghan, the Indian trader, had in 1765 proposed to Sir William Johnson, the Indian superintendent, that a company be formed to buy land of the French settlers still in Illinois. Thomas Gage, commander-in-chief in America, liked the project but thought he must not be a partner. In 1766 the members of the Philadelphia firm of Baynton, Wharton & Morgan, merchants trading to the Indian country, met with Joseph Galloway, William Franklin, John Hughes, and Croghan to organize the venture. William Franklin, who was a politician, suggested that instead of buying land from the French they petition the British Crown for it. They then or later decided to ask for a tract of 1,200,000 acres within the territory bounded by the Ohio, Mississippi, Wisconsin, and Wabash rivers and agree to settle one white Protestant person there for every hundred acres. They invited Johnson, a Crown officer, to join them, and Franklin in London, who was to find English investors and present the scheme to the ministry. Here was something like Franklin's old plan for barrier colonies in the form of a speculation.

Shelburne thought with Franklin about the need and importance of extending the Empire westward. The boundary between the Indians and the whites would be fixed—without too much attention to the wishes of the Indians—and colonies established. In August 1767 Franklin dined with Shelburne and one other guest, General Henry Seymour Conway, who had moved the repeal of the Stamp Act and was now a secretary of state. The two friendly ministers told Franklin that they thought of taking the management of Indian affairs out of the hands of the Crown and returning it to the separate colonies. "I took the opportunity," Franklin wrote to his son on the 24th, "of urging it as one means of saving expense in supporting the outposts, that a settlement should be made in the Illinois country; expatiated on the various advantages, viz., furnishing provisions cheaper to the garrisons, securing the country, retaining the trade, raising a strength there which, on occasion of a future war, might easily be poured down the Mississippi upon the lower country and into the Bay of Mexico, to be used against Cuba or Mexico itself. I mentioned your plan, its being approved by Sir William Johnson, the readiness and ability of the gentlemen concerned to carry the settlement into execution, with very little expense to the Crown, etc. The secretaries appeared finally to be fully convinced, and there remained no obstacle but the Board of Trade, which was to be brought over privately before the matter should be referred to them officially."[10]

III

A week later the lobbyist left England to be a philosopher in France. He travelled again with his "steady, good friend" Pringle, and took with him many letters of introduction from Durand of the French legation in London. Durand was "extremely curious to inform himself in the affairs of America," Franklin wrote the day he set out from London; "pretends to have a great esteem for me, on account of the abilities shown in my examination; has desired to have all my political writings, invited me to dine with him, was very inquisitive, treated me with great civility, makes me visits, etc. I fancy that intriguing nation would like very well to meddle on occasion, and blow up the coals between Britain and her colonies; but I hope we shall give them no opportunity."[11]

As Franklin had written for Polly Stevenson some of his best scientific observations, so now on 14 September he wrote her the best account of his journey. "All the way to Dover we were furnished with post chaises, hung so as to lean forward, the top coming down over one's eyes like a hood as if to prevent one's seeing the country; which being one of my great pleasures, I was engaged in perpetual disputes with the inn-keepers, hostlers, and postilions, about getting the straps taken up a hole or so before and let down as much behind, they insisting that the chaise leaning forward was an ease to the horses and that the contrary would kill them. I suppose the chaise leaning forward looks to them like a willingness to go forward, and that its hanging back shows a reluctance. They added other reasons that were no reasons at all, and made me, as upon a hundred other occasions, almost wish that mankind had never been endowed with a reasoning faculty, since they know so little how to make use of it and so often mislead themselves by it; and that they had been furnished with a good sensible instinct instead of it."

From Dover they crossed to Calais. "Various impositions we suffered from boatmen, porters, etc., on both sides the water. I know not which are most rapacious, the English or the French, but the latter have, with their knavery, the most politeness. The roads we found equally good with ours in England, in some places paved with smooth stone, like our new streets, for many miles together, and rows of trees on each side, yet there are no turnpikes. But then the poor peasants complained to us grievously that they were obliged to work upon the roads full two months in the year, without being paid for their labour. Whether this is truth, or whether like Englishmen they grumble cause or no cause, I have not yet been fully able to inform myself."

He noticed that most of the women were dark, though in Paris some of them were fair, "who I think are not whitened by art." Polly would be interested in the Paris fashions, and Franklin was interested in everything. "As to rouge, they don't pretend to imitate nature in laying it on. There is no gradual diminution of the colour, from the full bloom in the middle of the cheek to the faint tint near the sides, nor does it show differently in different faces. I have not had the honour of being at any lady's toilet to see how it is laid on, but I fancy I can tell you how it is or may be done. Cut a hole of three inches diameter in a piece of paper; place it on the side of your face in such a manner as that the top of the hole may be just under your eye; then with a brush dipped in the colour paint face and paper together; so when the paper is taken off there will remain a round patch of red exactly the form of the hole. This is the mode, from the actresses on the stage upwards through all ranks of ladies to the princesses of the blood; but it stops there, the queen not using it, having in the serenity, complacence, and benignity that shine so eminently in—or rather through—her countenance, sufficient beauty, though now an old woman, to do extremely well without it.

"You see I speak of the queen as if I had seen her, and so I have; for you must know I have been at court. We went to Versailles last Sunday and had the honour of being presented to the king; he spoke to both of us very graciously and cheerfully, is a handsome man, has a very lively look, and appears younger than he is. In the evening we were at the *grand couvert*, where the family sup in public. . . . The table was . . . half a hollow square, the service gold. . . . Their distance from each other was such as that other chairs might have been placed between any two of them [the king and queen and four daughters]. An officer of the court brought us up through the crowd of spectators, and placed Sir John so as to stand between the king and Madame Adelaide and me between the queen and Madame Victoire. The king talked a good deal to Sir John, asking many questions about our royal family; and did me too the honour of taking some notice of me. That's saying enough, for I would not have you think me so much pleased with this king and queen as to have a whit less regard than I used to have for ours. No Frenchman shall go beyond me in thinking my own king and queen the very best in the world, and the most amiable."

Franklin thought Versailles splendid but ill-kept. "The water-works are out of repair, and so is great part of the front next the town, looking, with its shabby half-brick walls and broken windows, not much better than the houses in Durham Yard. There is, in short, both at Versailles and Paris a prodigious mixture of magnificence and negligence, with every kind of elegance except that of cleanliness and what we call tidiness. Though I must do Paris the justice to say that in two points of cleanliness they exceed us. The water they drink, though from the river, they render as pure as that of the best spring by filtering it through cisterns filled with sand; and the streets by constant sweeping are fit to walk in, though there is no paved footpath." More people walked in Paris than in London, he noticed, and the streets were not crowded with coaches and chairs. Umbrellas were carried by both men and women. The stones of the pavements, "being generally cubes, when worn on one side may be turned and become new."

Paris might look untidy to Franklin, used to Philadelphia and Boston, but he thought French manners better than English. "It seems to be a point settled here universally that strangers are to be treated with respect; and one has just the same deference shown here by being a stranger as in England by being a lady. The custom house officers at Porte St. Denis, as we entered Paris, were about to seize two dozen of excellent Bordeaux wine given us at Boulogne and which we had brought with us; but, as soon as they found we were strangers, it was immediately remitted on that account. At the church of Notre Dame, where we went to see a magnificent illumination, with figures, etc., for the deceased Dauphiness, we found an immense crowd who were kept out by guards; but, the officer being told that we were strangers from England, he immediately admitted us, accompanied us, and showed us everything. Why don't we practise this urbanity to Frenchmen? Why should they be allowed to outdo us in anything?"

He had seen an exhibition of pictures, but did not feel "connoisseur enough to judge which has most merit." He had been to theatres to hear plays and operas. "Though the weather has been hot, and the houses full, one is not incommoded by the heat so much as with us in winter. They must have some way of changing the air that we are not acquainted with. I shall inquire into it." Quadrille was out of fashion, "and English whisk all the mode at Paris and the court."

"Travelling," he reflected, "is one way of lengthening life, at least in appearance. It is but about a fortnight since we left London, but the variety of scenes we have gone through makes it seem equal to six months living in one place. Perhaps I have suffered a greater change, too, in my own person than I could have done in six years at home. I had not been here six days before my tailor and perruquier had transformed me into a Frenchman. Only think what a figure I make in a little bag-wig and naked ears! They told me I was become twenty years younger, and looked very *galante*. So, being in Paris, where the mode is to be sacredly followed, I was once very near making love to my friend's wife."[12]

It may be guessed that Durand of the legation in London had a good deal to do with the courtesy which Franklin was shown by the French officials. But as scientist he needed no official recommendations. "The time I spent in Paris and in the improving conversation and agreeable society of so many learned and ingenious men" afterwards seemed to him "like a pleasing dream from which I was sorry to be awaked by finding myself again at London."[13] D'Alibard, who had first carried out Franklin's suggestion and had got lightning from a cloud, and his wife delighted Franklin with many hospitalities. There were French scientists who were proud to be known as *franklinistes*, and Joseph-Étienne Berthier declared that France was as much Franklin's country as England: a father was in his own country when his children lived there. (Franklin the next year furthered Berthier's election to the Royal Society.) At the house of the Marquis de Courtanvaux, soldier and member of the French Academy of Sciences, Franklin met the Abbé Chappe d'Auteroche, astronomer and traveller, and told him of the elephant [mastodon] tusks and teeth which George Croghan had shipped to London from the Ohio country. (After Franklin's return he sent one of the teeth to the abbé, and asked if any like it had been found in Siberia.)

At the request of his friends in Paris Franklin wrote a paper on lightning and the way Americans secured their houses from it.[14] He began with the clearest statement of the general principles involved and ended with the homeliest advice. "A person apprehensive of danger from lightning, happening during the time of thunder to be in a house not so secured, will do well to avoid sitting near the chimney, near a looking-glass, or any gilt picture or wainscot; the safest place is in the middle of the room (so it be not under a metal lustre suspended by a chain), sitting in one chair and laying the feet up in another. It is still safer to bring two or three mattresses or beds [then usually feathers] into the middle of the room and, folding them double, place the chair upon them; for, they not being so good conductors as the walls, the lightning will not choose an interrupted course through the air of the room and bedding when it can go through a continued better conductor the wall. But where it can be had, a hammock or swinging bed suspended by silk cords equally distant from the walls on every side and from the ceiling and floor above and below affords the safest situation a person can have in any room whatever; and what indeed may be deemed quite free from danger of any stroke by lightning."

To Franklin the most important friends he made in Paris were not electricians but economists. During the first week in October, just before he left for London, he met François Quesnay, physician to the king, and leader of the school which the next year began to be called the physiocrats. Franklin missed seeing Pierre-Samuel du Pont de Nemours, the member of the group who gave it its name, but he enjoyed the "civilities" of the Marquis de Mirabeau (father of the revolutionary orator). Franklin had hitherto, it seems, heard little about the physiocrats, or they about him.

Economics, as a science, stood almost where electricity had stood twenty years before. But the French economists admired Franklin as a philosopher, and they had read the report of his examination before the House of Commons. They greeted him as a kind of living document from America. He found that they had reduced to something like a system the world of economic phenomena in which he had made random independent observations. Opinions which had hitherto moved separately through his mind were precipitated into order.

Within a few months he could write in a letter to Philadelphia, as his own opinion, what was essentially an epitome of the physiocratic doctrine. "After all, this country [England] is fond of manufactures beyond their real value, for the true source of riches is husbandry. Agriculture is truly productive of new wealth; manufacturers only change forms and, whatever value they give to the materials they work upon, they in the meantime consume an equal value in provisions, etc. So that riches are not increased by manufacturing; the only advantage is that provisions in the shape of manufactures are more easily carried for sale to foreign markets."[15] And a year later he drew his new conclusions to the sharpest point. "There seem to be but three ways for a nation to acquire wealth. The first is by war, as the Romans did, in plundering their conquered neighbours. This is robbery. The second by commerce, which is generally cheating. The third by agriculture, the only honest way, wherein man receives a real increase of the seed thrown into the ground, in a kind of continual miracle."[16]

Here was more than doctrine for Franklin. As he lost hope in the imperial union on which he had set his heart, he came to be dramatically aware of differences between Britain and America. The trouble was not only that they were far apart in miles, but also that they were forced by nature to be unlike. The boundless continent could live by agriculture, the true source of prosperity, while the narrow islands must confine themselves largely to manufactures and trading. It would be increasingly hard, Franklin thought, to reconcile the two interests. And his thinking as well as his feeling inclined him more and more to the side of the Americans. French economics had done as much to win him away from England as French politeness.

IV

On his way to London he was delayed for a week at Calais, by bad weather in the Channel, and wished he had spent the week in Paris. He found in London that there had been changes in the ministry. Townshend had died in September, to be succeeded by Lord North, who was in effect the king's agent in the House of Commons. George III had got the government firmly in his own hands, and by the aid of patronage and bribes could command a Parliamentary majority. Conway, always friendly to America, left office, and Shelburne, Franklin's young friend, gave up the management of American affairs to Lord Hillsborough, who had less interest in western colonies. The new commissioners of customs under the Townshend acts had sailed for Boston, instructed to put an end to smuggling and collect the duties which were to furnish a revenue from the stubborn colonies.

Franklin resumed his quiet, ceaseless efforts in behalf of America which led Josiah Tucker, dean of Gloucester, to declare that "Dr. Franklin wanted to remove the seat of government to America; that, says he, is his constant plan."[17] On 24 November Franklin published a paper *On Smuggling*[18] which, while he called it stealing, he said was hardly confined to America. The English never hesitated to avoid payment of duties when they could, even though they had made their own laws, as the Americans had not. "When I hear them exclaiming against the Americans, and, for every little infringement on the acts of trade or obstruction given by a petty mob to an officer of our customs in that country, calling for vengeance against the whole people as rebels and traitors, I cannot help thinking that there are still those in the world who can see a mote in their brother's eye while they do not discern a beam in their own." Toward the end of the year Franklin was once somewhere "in a large company in which were some members of Parliament." There he gave "satisfaction to all by what I alleged in explanation of the conduct of the Americans, and, to show that they were not quite so unreasonable as they appeared to be, I was advised by several present to make my sentiments public, not only for the sake of America but as it would be some ease to our friends here."[19] On 7 January he contributed to Strahan's *London Chronicle* his famous *Causes of the American Discontents before 1768.*[20]

Griffith Jones, the editor of the *Chronicle*, was cautious. "He has drawn the teeth and pared the nails of my paper," Franklin wrote his son two days later, "so that it can neither scratch nor bite. It seems only to paw and mumble."[21] Where Franklin had said that the Stamp Act "odiously militated" against American sentiments he was made to say merely "militated." His expression "an officious governor," referring to Bernard of Massachusetts, became "a G——r." His "force money from you" was changed to "raise money on you." Governors, he had written, were "frequently" men of vicious characters; his adverb was printed as "sometimes." In place of "new duties, professedly for such disagreeable, and to them appearing dangerous purposes," the *Chronicle* had only "new duties professedly for such disagreeable purposes." "The late Chancellor of the Exchequer, desirous of ingratiating himself with the opposition, or driven to it by their clamours," appeared as "a person lately in high office," since Grenville was still alive. The "frivolous complaint" of the Virginia merchants was modified to the "slight complaint." The editor struck out entirely Franklin's comment on the sending of convicts to the plantations: "an insult aggravated by that barbarous, ill-placed sarcasm in a report of the Board of Trade, when one of the provinces complained of the act. 'It is necessary that it should be continued for the better peopling of Your Majesty's colonies.' " (Or so the original is thought to have read, on the evidence of the fuller version published in America in 1774 as *The Causes of the Present Distractions in America Explained: in Two Letters to a Merchant in London. By F—— B——.*)

Even in that fuller version (here exactly followed instead of the *Chronicle's*, which all Franklin's editors have reprinted) the *Causes* meant to be conciliatory. It had in the *Chronicle* no signature but the F+S which Franklin sometimes used in his propaganda, nor was it clearly offered as the work of an American. But it took for its motto a sentence (slightly misquoted and called a proverb) from Franklin's Canada pamphlet of eight years before: "The waves never rise but when the winds blow." And it kept close to the position he had held before the Commons. He went over the familiar arguments discreetly, not so much asserting them as explaining to the English what the Americans thought and why they thought so. "I do not undertake here to support these opinions of the Americans; they have been refuted by a late act of Parliament, declaring its own power; which very Parliament, however, showed wisely so much tender regard to those inveterate prejudices as to repeal a tax that had odiously militated against them. And those prejudices are still so fixed and rooted in the Americans that, it is supposed, not a single man among them has been convinced of his error, by that act of Parliament."

He explained that the Americans, though willing to vote taxes in their assemblies upon proper requisition from the Crown, incurably believed that their right to grant their own money was "essential to English liberty." They had been pleased by the repeal of the Stamp Act into adapting themselves to the Quartering Act, which they looked upon as a temporary measure. But the Townshend acts, expressly intended to raise money for the support of the Crown officials in America and so make them independent of the assemblies, appeared to the Americans not only to tax them without their consent but also to put them under arbitrary rule from England, and renewed the "grievances, which from their respect and love for this country, they had long borne, and seemed almost willing to forget. They reflected how lightly the interest of all America had been esteemed here, when the interests of a few inhabitants of Great Britain happened to have the smallest competition with it." Americans could not import wine, oil, and fruit direct from Portugal, but must ship it by way of England in order that a few British merchants trading with Portugal might have their commissions. On the complaint of a few British merchants trading with Virginia nine colonies had been restrained from issuing paper money. A few British manufacturers of hats, nails, and steel had been able to prevent the manufacture of those articles in America. "Reflecting on these things, the Americans said to one another (their newspapers are full of discourses) these people are not content with making a monopoly of us . . . but now they have as good as declared they have a right to tax us, *ad libitum*, internally and externally; and that our constitutions and liberties shall all be taken away if we do not submit to that claim." "It is time then," Franklin said the Americans were saying, "to take care of ourselves, by the best means in our power. Let us unite in solemn resolutions and engagements with and to each other, that we will give these new officers as little trouble as possible by not consuming the British manufactures, on which they are to levy the duties. Let us agree to consume no more of their expensive gew-gaws; let us live frugally; and let us industriously manufacture what we can for ourselves."

The Americans were loyal, Franklin insisted. "Scotland has had its rebellions, and England its plots, against the present royal family; but America is untainted with those crimes; there is in it scarce a man, there is not a single native of our country who is not firmly attached to his King by principle and by affection. But a new kind of loyalty seems to be required of us, a loyalty to Parliament; a loyalty that is to extend, it seems, to a surrender of all our properties, whenever a House of Commons, in which there is not a single member of our choosing, shall think fit to grant them away without our consent, and to a patient suffering the loss of our privileges as Englishmen, if we cannot submit to make such surrender. We were separated too far from Britain by the ocean, but we were united strongly to it by respect and love, so that we could at any time freely have spent our lives and little fortunes in its cause. But this unhappy new system of politics tends to dissolve those bands of union and to sever us for ever. Woe to the man that first adopted it! Both countries will long have cause to execrate his memory." (The editor of the *Chronicle* omitted these last two sentences.)[22]

The *Causes*, even as edited by the *Chronicle* and widely reprinted, satisfied neither the Americans, who thought it pro-British, nor the British, who thought it pro-American. Franklin had written partly as an unofficial ambassador bent on reconciling the two countries, and partly as a philosopher who trusted reason. In his own mind he was more radical. The trouble over the Stamp Act had forced him to examine his opinions as to the relation between Britain and America. He had concluded that, by established custom and natural right if not by written law, the authority over the colonies was vested in the Crown, not in Parliament. The people of America and Britain were equally subjects of the king, but the Americans were not subject to the British. "Great Britain is not a sovereign," he wrote in the margin of a pamphlet he was studying. "The Parliament has power only within the realm."[23] Again: "The sovereignty of the Crown I understand. The sovereignty of the British legislature out of Britain I do not understand."[24] And again: "The British state is only the island of Great Britain. The British legislature are undoubtedly the only proper judges of what concerns the welfare of that state; but the Irish legislature are the proper judges of what concerns the Irish state, and the American legislatures of what concerns the American states respectively."[25] Look at history: "While an Englishman resides in England he is undoubtedly subject to its laws. If he goes into a foreign country he is subject to the laws and government he finds there. If he finds no government or laws there, he is subject there to none till he and his companions, if he has any, make laws for themselves. And this was the case of the first settlers in America. Otherwise and if they carried the English laws and power of Parliament with them, what advantages could the Puritans propose to themselves by going, since they would have been as subject to bishops, spiritual courts, tithes, and statutes relating to the church in America as in England? Can the dean [of Gloucester] or his principles tell how it happens that those laws, the game acts, the statutes for labourers, and an infinity of others made before and since the emigration, are not in force in America nor ever were?"[26] The Americans had the same right to their assemblies as the British to their Parliament, and the assemblies were not inferior to the Parliament but equal to it. Parliament had no more right to lay American taxes than the assemblies would have to lay British taxes.

Holding these opinions, Franklin could not long persist in his distinction between taxes as external and internal. In April 1767, before the Townshend acts were brought in, he had written to Lord Kames that "it seems necessary for the common good of the Empire that a power be lodged somewhere to regulate its general commerce; this can be placed nowhere so properly as in the Parliament of Great Britain."[27] But the Townshend acts, pretending to regulate commerce, had been as plainly designed to raise revenue as the Stamp Act had. By 13 March 1768 Franklin had privately gone further than the Americans—particularly John Dickinson and Samuel Adams—who were still admitting the right of Parliament to lay external taxes but protesting against specific measures. "The more I have thought and read on the subject," he wrote to his son that day, "the more I find myself confirmed in opinion that no middle doctrine can be well maintained; I mean, not clearly with intelligible arguments. Something might be made of either of the extremes: that Parliament has the right to make all laws for us, or that it has the power to make no laws for us; and I think the arguments for the latter more numerous and weighty than those for the former. Supposing that doctrine established, the colonies would then be so many separate states, only subject to the same king, as England and Scotland were before the union. And then the question would be, whether a union like that with Scotland would or would not be advantageous to the whole." Franklin had no doubt it would be, but he thoroughly doubted that it would ever be brought about. "As to my own sentiments, I am weary of suggesting them to so many different inattentive heads, though I must continue to do it while I stay among them."[28]

Again he wanted to go home, but again he stayed on about his various businesses. The divided ministry did not quite know what to do with him: whether to dismiss him from the American post office, and so get rid of him; or to promote him to some British post and so make use of him or, possibly, bridle his arguments. The ministry moved softly in the spring of 1768, after Shelburne had been succeeded by Hillsborough. Franklin's friend Grey Cooper, a secretary of the treasury, sent word that the Duke of Grafton, first minister, had heard from the Earl of Sandwich, postmaster-general, that Franklin's office suffered from his absence in England, and that, it seemed to Sandwich, Franklin ought either to return to America or else resign. Grafton "wished him (Mr. Cooper) to mention this to me, and to say to me at the same time that though my going to my post might remove the objection, yet if I choose rather to remain in England my merit was such, in his opinion, as to entitle me to something better here, and it should not be his fault if I was not well provided for." Franklin knew well enough that Sandwich's objection was less to the deputy's

absence from America than to his devotion to it. But Franklin
was a schooled office-holder, and he duly left his card on the duke,
as Cooper asked him to. "When I went next to the treasury, his
Grace not being there, Mr. Cooper carried me to Lord North,
chancellor of the exchequer, who said very obligingly, after talking
of some American affairs: 'I am told by Mr. Cooper that you are
not unwilling to stay with us. I hope we shall find some way of
making it worth your while.' I thanked his lordship and said I
should stay with pleasure if I could any ways be useful to government. He made me a compliment and I took my leave, Mr. Cooper
carrying me away with him to his country house at Richmond to
dine and stay all night."

The following Thursday Franklin dined at the King's Arms
with "the gentlemen of the post office," and talked with Anthony
Todd, the secretary. Todd told him that Sandwich had asked why
there should be two deputies for America. But when Franklin
said that he was going home, "which I still say to everybody, not
knowing but that what is intimated above may fail of taking
effect, he looked blank and seemed disconcerted a little, which
makes me think some friend of his was to have been vested in the
office; but this is surmise only." Franklin was not likely to have
been wrong in his guess as to the meaning of Todd's look. The
postal authorities probably expected that Franklin would resign
in the prospect of a better office, and had already thought of his
successor.

Nothing came of the better office. Though Grafton, pleased by
Franklin's paper on smuggling, might have wanted to see Franklin
an under-secretary for American affairs, continuing Shelburne's
plans, Franklin had too many enemies and his promotion was put
off and gradually dropped. "That day I received another letter
from Mr. Cooper, directing me to be at the Duke of Grafton's
next morning, whose porter had orders to let me in. I went accordingly, and was immediately admitted. But his Grace, being then
engaged in some unexpected business, with much condescension
and politeness made that apology for his not discoursing with me
then, but wished me to be at the treasury at twelve the next Tuesday. I went accordingly, when Mr. Cooper told me something had
called the duke into the country." If the negotiations dragged out

further, nothing definite is known of them. Franklin, writing to his son on 2 July, when the matter had not ended, was half indifferent. "Though I did not think fit to decline any favour so great a man expressed an inclination to do me, because at court if one shows an unwillingness to be obliged it is often construed as a mark of mental hostility and one makes an enemy; yet so great is my inclination to be at home, and at rest, that I shall not be sorry if this business falls through and I am suffered to retire to my old post; nor indeed very sorry if they take that from me too on account of my zeal for America, in which some of my friends have hinted that I have been too open. . . . If Mr. Grenville comes into power again, in any department respecting America, I must refuse to accept of anything that may seem to put me in his power, because I apprehend a breach between the two countries. . . . I am now myself grown so old as to feel much less than formerly the spur of ambition, and if it were not for the flattering expectation that by being fixed here I might more effectually serve my country, I should certainly determine for retirement, without a moment's hesitation."[29]

V

For four eventful years Franklin uneventfully if incessantly served his country in England as agent and peacemaker. His conception of America did not change. It was by right an independent state—or set of states—which was entitled to make its own laws and to choose how far it should belong to the union of the British Empire under the sovereignty of the Crown. He knew he was almost alone in this conception, and he could not hope that it would soon, or ever, be generally accepted in Great Britain. But he could keep his eyes on the course of Parliament and use all the influence he could bring upon the ministers to prevent legislation which, by depriving the Americans of their rights or outraging their sentiments, would widen and hasten the breach which he feared.

He came to be less troubled by the American excesses than he had been during the Stamp Act agitation. News reached London that the people in Boston were lawlessly resisting the customs officials there, and that troops had been called for. But London was rioting too, over John Wilkes whom the king was determined to keep out of Parliament. "Even this capital," Franklin wrote to John Ross on 14 May 1768, "the residence of the king, is now a daily scene of lawless riot and confusion. Mobs patrolling the streets at noonday, some knocking all down that will not roar for Wilkes and liberty; courts of justice afraid to give judgment against him; coal-heavers and porters pulling down the houses of coal merchants that refuse to give them more wages; sawyers destroying sawmills; sailors unrigging all the outward-bound ships and suffering none to sail till merchants agree to raise their pay; watermen destroying private boats and threatening bridges; soldiers firing among the mobs and killing men, women, and children; which seems only to have produced a universal sullenness that looks like a great black cloud coming on, ready to burst in a general tempest. What the event will be God only knows. But some punishment seems preparing for a people who are ungratefully abusing the best constitution and the best king any nation was ever blessed with, intent on nothing but luxury, licentiousness, power, places, pensions, and plunder."[30]

Franklin still cherished his idea that the king was just and magnanimous, and he knew that most enlightened Englishmen thought about the Americans much as Franklin did. But the enlightened Englishmen were not in power. After Chatham resigned from his nominal office in 1768 the ministry became more and more conservative. Hillsborough, charged with American affairs, was as bungling as Braddock and as hard for Franklin to work with. In February 1768 the Massachusetts Assembly sent a circular letter to the other American assemblies suggesting concerted opposition to the Townshend acts in the form of petitions to the British government. Hillsborough demanded that the Massachusetts Assembly rescind its action or be dissolved, and he directed the governors of the other colonies to dissolve their assemblies if they responded favourably to the Massachusetts appeal. The Massachusetts Assembly refused. Other assemblies sided with them. Parliament in the winter of 1768–69 went to such angry lengths as to propose— merely—that the Americans most active in resistance be brought to England and tried for treason under a disused statute of Henry

VIII. This brought outbursts of something very near rebellion throughout America, and the spread of non-importation agreements like those which had caused the repeal of the Stamp Act. Virginia took its place beside Massachusetts. Washington, almost new to politics, introduced into the House of Burgesses the Virginia Resolves of 1769, drawn up by George Mason and signed not only by Washington but also by Thomas Jefferson, now twenty-six, who had just taken his seat in the legislature.

Perhaps some large, liberal wisdom might still have restored unity and peace, but nothing of the kind appeared to dominate the bitter controversy. More than ever the king was determined to be the king, the ministry to persist in a policy supported by the Declaratory Act, Parliament to uphold its claim to be the supreme legislative authority of the Empire, whatever the colonial assemblies might pretend. The manufacturers who had protested against the Stamp Act had been alienated by the threat of American manufactures, and the merchants by the desire of the Americans to take over a part of the American trade. The British public, once for all convinced that the Americans were only trying to get out of paying their share of governmental expenses, were irritated by American talk about liberty and infuriated by American abuse of Britain. In America there was another complex of interests and animosities. The colonies were far from being united in a compact opposition. The majority of Americans still thought of themselves as loyal to the Crown and were unable to imagine themselves as outside the Empire. By no means all of them felt certain that their own officials, who also could be incompetent and corrupt, would govern better than the British. The regulation of their trade had been so long practised that it was more or less accepted, and this did not seem necessarily the time for demanding that it end. As to economic exploitation, the Americans were not so much objecting to it on principle as wanting to have their commercial system centred more profitably in America, where if exploiting was to be done it could be done by Americans. And between the countries there was perpetual, lagging misinformation across the ocean over which nothing travelled more rapidly and steadily than mutual abuse.

The ministers who in October 1768 had sent eight ships of war and two battalions (later reinforced) to quiet Boston and compel it to pay its customs duties were not altogether unreasonable. When they saw that the extraordinary military expenses of the first year were at least five thousand times the amount which the Townshend acts produced in revenue from the whole of America, they perceived that the acts were not worth the trouble they had caused. Hillsborough in 1769 informed the colonial governors that no further taxes would be laid for revenue, and the unpopular governor of Massachusetts, Francis Bernard, was recalled—with a baronetcy. On the question of repeal the ministry was still divided. North, who wanted to repeal all the duties, cast the deciding vote to retain the duty on tea, out of deference to the relentless wishes of the king. The right to tax must be kept up. When North brought the bill before Parliament on 5 March 1770, even Grenville was opposed to the pinchbeck compromise, and only the king's friends, bribed and true, made the passage of it possible. That very day in Boston a squad of British soldiers, hectored by a crowd, fired into it and killed four men. The Boston Massacre, as the episode was called in America, raised a colonial tumult. But the event of the day was the act passed in London. The conflict between Britain and America had been narrowed to a single point, trifling in itself but showing how ominous the conflict was if this pedantry of legislation could put and hold the countries so far apart.

Franklin, watching Parliament, thought it "was bad policy when they attempted to heal our differences by repealing part of the duties only; as it is bad surgery to leave splinters in a wound which must prevent its healing or in time occasion it to open afresh."[31] In December he heard that he had been appointed agent for the Assembly of Massachusetts. On 17 January he presented himself in his new capacity to Hillsborough, whose character, in Franklin's opinion, was made of "conceit, wrong-headedness, obstinacy, and passion," and who "perplexed and embarrassed" American affairs by his "perverse and senseless management." Franklin's journal gives a more lifelike account than any other of what the philosopher must have had to endure day after day from lords in office.

"I went this morning to wait on Lord Hillsborough. The porter at first denied his lordship, on which I left my name and drove off.

But before the coach got out of the square the coachman heard a call, turned, and went back to the door, when the porter came and said: 'His lordship will see you, sir.' I was shown into the levee room, where I found Governor Bernard [recalled from Massachusetts], who, I understand, attends there constantly. Several other gentlemen were there attending, with whom I sat down a few minutes, when Secretary Pownall [John Pownall of the Board of Trade] came out to us and said his lordship desired I would come in.

"I was pleased with this ready admission and preference, having sometimes waited three or four hours for my turn; and, being pleased, I could more easily put on the open, cheerful countenance that my friends advised me to wear. His lordship came towards me and said: 'I was dressing in order to go to court; but, hearing that you were at the door, who are a man of business, I determined to see you immediately.' I thanked his lordship and said that at present my business was not much; it was only to pay my respects to his lordship and to acquaint him with my appointment by the House of Representatives of Massachusetts Bay to be their agent here, in which station if I could be of any service—I was going on to say, to the public, I should be very happy; but this lordship, whose countenance changed at my naming that province, cut me short by saying, with something between a smile and a sneer:

"*L. H.* I must set you right there, Mr. Franklin. You are not agent.

"*B. F.* Why, my lord?

"*L. H.* You are not appointed.

"*B. F.* I do not understand your lordship. I have the appointment in my pocket.

"*L. H.* You are mistaken; I have later and better advices. I have a letter from Governor Hutchinson; he would not give his assent to the bill.

"*B. F.* There was no bill, my lord; it was a vote of the House.

"*L. H.* There was a bill presented to the governor for the purpose of appointing you and another, one Dr. Lee [Arthur Lee], I think he is called, to which the governor refused his assent.

"*B. F.* I cannot understand this, my lord; I think there must be some mistake in it. Is your lordship quite sure that you have such a letter?

"*L. H.* I will convince you of it directly. (*Rings the bell.*) Mr. Pownall will come in and satisfy you.

"*B. F.* It is not necessary that I should now detain your lordship from dressing. You are going to court. I will wait on your lordship another time.

"*L. H.* No, stay; he will come immediately. (*To the servant.*) Tell Mr. Pownall I want him. (*Mr. Pownall comes in.*) Have you not at hand Governor Hutchinson's letter, mentioning his refusing his assent to the bill for appointing Dr. Franklin agent?

"*Sec. P.* My lord?

"*L. H.* Is there not such a letter?

"*Sec. P.* No, my lord. There is a letter relating to some bill for the payment of a salary to Mr. De Berdt [the former agent], and I think to some other agent, to which the governor had refused his assent.

"*L. H.* And there is nothing in the letter to the purpose I mention?

"*Sec. P.* No, my lord.

"*B. F.* I thought it could not well be, my lord; as my letters are by the last ships, and they mention no such thing. Here is the authentic copy of the vote of the House appointing me, in which there is no mention of any act intended. Will your lordship please to look at it? (*With seeming unwillingness he takes it, but does not look into it.*)

"*L. H.* An information of this kind is not properly brought to me as secretary of state. The Board of Trade is the proper place.

"*B. F.* I will leave the paper then with Mr. Pownall to be ——

"*L. H.* (*Hastily*) To what end would you leave it with him?

"*B. F.* To be entered on the minutes of that board, as usual.

"*L. H.* (*Angrily*) It shall not be entered there. No such paper shall be entered there while I have anything to do with the business of that board. The House of Representatives has no right to appoint an agent. We shall take no notice of any agents but such as are appointed by acts of Assembly to which the governor gives his assent. We have had confusion enough already. Here is one agent appointed by the Council, another by the House of Representatives. Which of these is agent for the province? Who are we to hear in provincial affairs? An agent appointed by act of Assembly we can understand. No other will be attended to for the future, I can assure you.

"*B. F.* I cannot conceive, my lord, why the consent of the governor should be thought necessary to the appointment of an agent for the people. It seems to me that ——

"*L. H.* (*With a mixed look of anger and contempt*) I shall not enter into a dispute with *you*, sir, upon this subject.

"*B. F.* I beg your lordship's pardon; I do not presume to dispute with your lordship; I would only say that it seems to me that every body of men who cannot appear in person where business relating to them may be transacted should have a right to appear by an agent. The concurrence of the governor does not seem to me necessary. It is the business of the people that is to be done; he is not one of them; he is himself an agent.

"*L. H.* (*Hastily*) Whose agent is he?

"*B. F.* The king's, my lord.

"*L. H.* No such matter. He is one of the corporation by the province charter. No agent can be appointed but by an act, nor any act pass without his assent. Besides, this proceeding is directly contrary to express instructions.

"*B. F.* I did not know there had been such instructions. I am not concerned in any offence against them, and ——

"*L. H.* Yes, your offering such a paper to be entered is an offence against them. (*Folding it up again without having read a word of it.*) No such appointment shall be entered. When I came into the administration of American affairs I found them in great disorder. By my firmness they are now something mended; and while I have the honour to hold the seals I shall continue the same conduct, the same firmness. I think my duty to the master I serve, and to the government of this nation, requires it of me. If that conduct is not approved, they may take my office from me when they please. I shall make them a bow and thank them; I shall resign with pleasure. That gentleman knows it (*pointing to Mr. Pownall*), but while I continue in it I shall resolutely persevere in the same firmness. (*Spoken with great warmth, and turning pale in his discourse, as if he was angry at something or somebody besides the agent, and of more consequence to himself.)*

"B. F. (*Reaching out his hand for the paper, which his lordship returned to him*) I beg your lordship's pardon for taking up so much of your time. It is, I believe, of no great importance whether the appointment is acknowledged or not, for I have not the least conception that an agent can *at present* be of any use to any of the colonies. I shall therefore give your lordship no further trouble. (*Withdrew.*)"

Angry as he was, Hillsborough had ears. "I have since heard," Franklin wrote to Samuel Cooper on 5 February, "that his lordship took great offence at some of my last words, which he calls extremely rude and abusive. He assured a friend of mine that they were equivalent to telling him to his face that the colonies could expect neither favour nor justice during his administration. I find he did not mistake me."[32]

As agent for Massachusetts Franklin was strongly on the American side in that colony. In Pennsylvania, even when he was leading the Assembly, he had now and then intervened between legislature and governor; but his chief correspondents in Boston, Thomas Cushing and the Rev. Samuel Cooper, were always anti-British, and Franklin with them. In a letter to the Committee of Correspondence (Cushing, James Otis, and Samuel Adams) written 15 May 1771 Franklin forecast the steps of oppression and revolution which he thought could hardly be avoided.

"I think one may clearly see, in the system of customs to be exacted in America by act of Parliament, the seeds sown of a total disunion of the two countries, though as yet that event may be at a considerable distance. The course and natural progress seems to be, first, the appointment of needy men as officers, for others do not care to leave England; then, their necessities make them rapacious, their office makes them proud and insolent, their insolence and rapacity make them odious, and, being conscious that they are hated, they become malicious; their malice urges them to a continual abuse of the inhabitants in their letters to administration, representing them as disaffected and rebellious, and (to encourage the use of severity) as weak, divided, timid, and cowardly. Government believes all; thinks it necessary to support and countenance its officers; their quarrelling with the people is deemed a mark and consequence of their fidelity; they are therefore more highly rewarded, and this makes their conduct still more insolent and provoking.

"The resentment of the people will, at times and on particular incidents, burst into outrages and violence upon such officers, and this naturally draws down severity and acts of further oppression from hence. The more the people are dissatisfied the more rigour will be thought necessary; severe punishments will be inflicted to terrify; rights and privileges will be abolished; greater force will then be required to secure execution and submission; the expense will become enormous; it will then be thought proper, by fresh exactions, to make the people defray it; thence the British nation and government will become odious, and subjection to it will be deemed no longer tolerable; war ensues, and the bloody struggle will end in absolute slavery to America or ruin to Britain by the loss of her colonies: the latter most probable, from America's growing strength and magnitude. . . .

"I do not pretend to the gift of prophecy. History shows that by these steps great empires have crumbled heretofore; and the late transactions we have so much cause to complain of show that we are in the same train, and that without a greater share of prudence and wisdom than we have seen both sides to be possessed of we shall probably come to the same conclusion."[33]

The disruption of the Empire still seemed to Franklin a catastrophe, to be postponed as long as possible. Patience and discretion might find some wise settlement of the conflict. Suppose Britain should give up all but the fewest duties, as "a regulation of trade for the general advantage," and America should enforce and collect them by laws of their own and their own officers. Britain would keep its right to lay duties and America its right to make its own laws. "This would alone destroy those seeds of disunion, and both countries might thence continue much longer to grow great together, more secure by their united strength and more formidable to their common enemies." But Franklin thought the scheme would break down before the fondness of the British government for appointing "friends and dependants to profitable offices." This was the form which exploitation took among politicians. What else was Hillsborough's demand that the colonial agents be approved by the colonial governors—that is, be creatures of the administration?

The antagonism between Franklin and Hillsborough continued. About the middle of October, nine months after their sharp interview, Franklin was in Ireland, where he had gone with Richard Jackson. Hillsborough, whose title was in the Irish peerage, was then at Dublin. The two met at dinner at the lord lieutenant's. "He was extremely civil," Franklin wrote to his son on 30 January 1772, "wonderfully so to me whom he had not long before abused to Mr. Strahan as a factious, turbulent fellow, always in mischief, a republican, enemy to the king's service, and what not."[34] Nothing would do but Franklin must call at Hillsborough's house on his journey northward to Belfast. Franklin was unwilling to go, but he was also unwilling to seem as rude as he would have to if he did not stop, since his road led past Hillsborough's door. He did stop, and was "detained by a thousand civilities from Tuesday to Sunday." Hillsborough was "attentive in everything that might make my stay in his house agreeable, and put his eldest son Lord Kilwarling into his phaeton with me, to drive me a round of forty miles that I might see the country, the seats, manufactures, etc., covering me with his own greatcoat lest I should take cold."[35]

Hillsborough, talking to Franklin, blamed England for its policy of restraining manufactures in Ireland. When Franklin pointed out that this was England's policy towards America, Hillsborough insisted that he thought it ought not to be. He was the friend of American manufactures, he said, and had done nothing to remind Parliament of their growth. He hoped to see wine and silk produced in America. He asked for advice in forming a government for Newfoundland. Franklin was not impressed by what he believed was Hillsborough's effort to recommend himself through Franklin to the colonies. "All which I could not but wonder at," the agent reported to Thomas Cushing on 13 January 1772, "knowing that he likes neither them nor me; and I thought it inexplicable but on the supposition that he apprehended an approaching storm and was desirous of lessening beforehand the number of enemies he had so imprudently created. But if he takes no steps towards withdrawing the troops, repealing the duties, restoring the castle [in Boston harbour], or recalling the offensive instructions, I shall think all the plausible behaviour I have described is meant only, by patting and stroking the horse, to make him more patient while the reins are drawn tighter and the spurs set deeper into his sides."[36]

"As Lord Hillsborough in fact got nothing out of me," Franklin wrote to his son on 19 August, "I should rather suppose he threw me away as an orange that would yield no juice and therefore not worth more squeezing. When I had been a little while returned to London I waited on him to thank him for his civilities in Ireland, and to discourse with him on a Georgia affair. The porter told me he was not at home. I left my card, went another time, and received the same answer, though I knew he was at home, a friend of mine being with him. After intermissions of a week each, I made two more visits and received the same answer. The last time was on a levee day, when a number of carriages were at his door. My coachman, driving up, alighted and was opening the coach door when the porter, seeing me, came out and surlily chid the coachman for opening the door before he had inquired whether my lord was at home; and then, turning to me, said: 'My lord is not at home.' I have never since been nigh him, and we have only abused one another at a distance."[37]

Franklin's journey in the latter part of 1771 was the longest he ever made in the British Isles, and the most important. Though he went chiefly for his health, he was not allowed to forget that he was a public figure. In Dublin he attended two sessions of the Irish Parliament. Jackson, a member of the Parliament in England, was admitted by courtesy to the floor, and Franklin expected to go to the gallery. But "the Speaker stood up and acquainted the House that he understood there was in town an American gentleman of (as he was pleased to say) distinguished character and merit, a member or delegate of some of the Parliaments of that country, who was desirous of being present at the debates of this House; that there was a rule of the House for admitting members of English Parliaments and that he did suppose the House would consider the American assemblies as English Parliaments; but, as this was the first instance, he had chosen not to give any order in it without first receiving their directions. On the question the whole

House gave a loud unanimous aye; when two members came to me without the bar, where I was standing, led me in, and placed me very honourably."[38] Franklin hoped that the American assemblies would be as courteous to any visiting member of the Irish Parliament. He could not help feeling the difference between the Irish and the English in this respect.

Though Franklin talked with members of both parties in Ireland, the courtiers and the patriots, his sympathies were with the patriots, who were all friends of America. He said everything he could to confirm them in this friendship, for the Americans looked to Ireland for support in their conflict with the English Parliament. The Irish were watching America. They too had long endured the repressive regulation of their trade by England. They too claimed the right to make their own laws and lay their own taxes. If the Americans held out, Ireland would be encouraged and benefited. If the Americans lost, Ireland would lose with them. For Franklin the poverty and misery of the Irish people were an example of what might come to America if the old colonial system of exploitation were kept up. America must defend itself from such a future. America and Ireland had a common cause against England. Franklin later suggested to American correspondents that the colonies should not refuse trade with Ireland, as with England, but should import Irish linen as before and furnish Ireland with flaxseed.

He stayed a longer time in Ireland than he had meant his whole journey to last, when he left London after the middle of August. It was two months before he got to Edinburgh. "Through storms and floods I arrived here on Saturday night, late, and was lodged miserably in an inn," he wrote to Strahan on 27 October. "But that excellent Christian David Hume, agreeable to the precepts of the Gospel, has received the stranger, and I now live with him at his house in the new town most happily."[39] He thought he would be there no more than two weeks, but again he prolonged his stay, among the congenial Scots. "In Scotland I spent five days with Lord Kames at his seat . . . two or three days at Glasgow, two days at Carron Iron Works, and the rest of the month in and about Edinburgh, lodging at David Hume's, who entertained me with the greatest kindness and hospitality, as did Lord Kames and his

lady."[40] On 25 November he was at Preston in Lancashire, visiting
the mother and sister of Richard Bache. Franklin's son-in-law had
come to England, and the two men, who first met at Preston,
travelled together to London, which they reached about the end
of the month.

Bache had thought that Franklin might help him to a political
post, and had brought a thousand pounds in case he should have
to pay for an appointment, in the manner of the time. Franklin
advised him to put his money into goods and open a store in
Philadelphia, in the north room of the Franklin house where the
Baches lived. "I am of opinion," Franklin wrote to his daughter
on 29 January, "that almost any profession a man has been educated in is preferable to an office held at pleasure, as rendering
him more independent, more a freeman, and less subject to the
caprices of superiors. And I think that in keeping a store, if it be
where you dwell, you can be serviceable to him as your mother
was to me; for you are not deficient in capacity, and I hope are
not too proud. . . . For your encouragement I can assure you
that there is scarce a merchant of opulence in your town whom I
do not remember a young beginner with as little to go on and no
better prospects than Mr. Bache. That his voyage hither might not
be quite fruitless I have given him £200 sterling, with which I
wish you good luck."[41]

The journey had been pleasant and had greatly improved Franklin's health and spirits. But its chief effect upon him had been to
strengthen his belief that the Americans had a better way of life
than the British and must insist on maintaining it. "I have lately
made a tour through Ireland and Scotland," he wrote to Joshua
Babcock in Rhode Island on 13 January. "In those countries a
small part of society are landlords, great noblemen, and gentlemen,
extremely opulent, living in the highest affluence and magnificence; the bulk of the people tenants, living in the most sordid
wretchedness in dirty hovels of mud and straw and clothed only
in rags.

"I thought often of the happiness of New England, where every
man is a freeholder, has a vote in public affairs, lives in a tidy,
warm house, has plenty of good food and fuel, with whole clothes
from head to foot, the manufacture perhaps of his own family.

Long may they continue in this situation! But if they should ever envy the trade of these countries I can put them in a way to obtain a share of it. Let them with three-fourths of the people of Ireland live the year round on potatoes and buttermilk, without shirts; then may their merchants export beef, butter, and linen. Let them, with the generality of the common people of Scotland, go barefoot; then they may make large exports in shoes and stockings. And if they will be content to wear rags, like the spinners and weavers of England, they may make cloths and stuffs for all parts of the world.

"Farther, if my countrymen should ever wish for the honour of having among them a gentry enormously wealthy, let them sell their farms and pay racked rents; the scale of the landlords will rise as that of the tenants is depressed, who will soon become poor, tattered, dirty, and abject in spirit. Had I never been in the American colonies, but was to form my judgment of civil society by what I have lately seen, I should never advise a nation of savages to admit of civilization; for I assure you that in the possession and enjoyment of the various comforts of life, compared to these people every Indian is a gentleman; and the effect of this kind of civil society seems only to be the depressing multitudes below the savage state that a few may be raised above it."[42]

(Franklin knew that Americans, talking about liberty and wellbeing, left their slaves out of account, and that the slaves furnished the English an effective counter-charge. In *A Conversation between an Englishman, a Scotchman, and an American, on the Subject of Slavery,* published in January 1770 but only recently identified as his,[43] he had said what he could say about the evil. "In truth there is not, take North America through, perhaps one family in a hundred that has a slave in it. Many thousands abhor the slave trade . . . conscientiously avoid being concerned with it, and do everything in their power to abolish it." British traders "bring the slaves to us and tempt us to purchase them. I do not justify our falling into temptation." The receiver of stolen goods was as bad as the thief. But should not the forgotten reverse of the maxim be remembered: that the thief was as bad as the receiver? With further casuistry Franklin argued that the Scottish colliers, and even British soldiers and sailors, were not much better off than

American slaves. Slavery itself he did not defend. All slavery was bad. No country which had any kind of slavery in it had a right to accuse any other country of having any other kind of slavery.)

VI

When Franklin set out on his long tour through Ireland and Scotland he had reason to expect that the matter of the western colony would soon be favourably settled. The scheme had changed and grown since 1767, and in 1771 intricately involved British policy and British officials. In November 1768 the Crown, represented by Sir William Johnson, made a treaty with the Six Nations at Fort Stanwix, to fix the boundary between the English and the Indians. Through the engineering, apparently, of the Philadelphia members of the Illinois company, the Indians were persuaded to cede land in what is now West Virginia to compensate various Indian traders, including Baynton, Wharton & Morgan, for damage done to them by the Delawares and Shawnee in the Pontiac uprising. Samuel Wharton went to London early in the next year to urge the company's project. He was "exceedingly active and industrious in soliciting it," Franklin wrote to John Foxcroft on 4 February 1772, "and in drawing up memorials and papers to support the application, remove objections, etc. But though I have not been equally active (it not being thought proper that I should appear much in the solicitation since I became a little obnoxious to the ministry on account of my letters to America), yet I suppose my advice may have been thought of some use, since it has been asked on every step; and I believe that, being longer and better known here than Mr. Wharton, I may have lent some weight to his negotiations by joining in the affair, from the greater confidence men are apt to place in one they know than in a stranger."[44]

Wharton's advantage as lobbyist was simply that he offered politicians a chance to make a fortune in a promising speculation. The first petition, in June 1769, asked for a grant of 2,500,000 acres of the land ceded at Fort Stanwix. Hillsborough, who was president of the Board of Trade as well as secretary of state for America, referred the petitioners to the treasury, to find out if the Crown had a right to sell land to private persons. But he advised them not to be so modest. Ask for 20,000,000 acres. In December the company was reorganized at a meeting held at the Crown tavern. Besides Franklin and Wharton fourteen men were present. Anthony Todd was there, secretary of the British post office, and John Foxcroft, joint-deputy for North America. More than half the men were English. Thomas Walpole, a London banker and nephew of the great Sir Robert, lent his influential name. (The Grand Ohio Company came to be usually known as the Walpole company or grant.) Thomas Pownall, formerly governor in turn of New Jersey, Massachusetts, and South Carolina, author of the valuable *Administration of the Colonies*, and member of Parliament for Tregoney, gave the group an official cast. The new company was to be divided into seventy-two shares, held not only by the projectors but also by as many officials as could be interested in the enterprise.

These then or later numbered among them Lord Camden, lord chancellor (who as Charles Pratt, attorney-general, had been friendly when Franklin came on his Pennsylvania mission a dozen years before); Lord Hertford (another nephew of Sir Robert Walpole), lord chamberlain, and close to the king; Earl Temple, brother to George Grenville who died in 1770 but had favoured the enterprise; Lord Gower, president of the Privy Council; Lord Rochford, secretary of state for the northern department. Only Camden among the noblemen had any respect or liking for the colonies, and some of them had political as well as financial motives for taking shares. Grey Cooper, a secretary of the treasury, joined them, with Richard Jackson, William Strahan and his son Andrew, and under-secretaries from several government departments. The names of the two Franklins, Sir William Johnson, and Croghan were on the list, and even more American Whartons than English Walpoles. Thomas Bradshaw, a henchman of the Duke of Grafton, furnished expert aid in rounding up desirable shareholders.

The Grand Ohio Company petitioned for a grant of 20,000,000 acres. They offered to pay £10,460 7s. 3d. (the exact amount which the treaty of Fort Stanwix had cost the Crown in presents and expenses) and a quit-rent of two shillings for every hundred acres of cultivable land after twenty years. The proposal came before the treasury on 4 January. The treasury agreed to the sale, provided the company would support the civil establishment of the colony which was to be founded. Hillsborough later said he had advised the company to ask for such an immense tract in the belief that the treasury would either refuse or else demand more money than could be raised. Now the proposal came back to the Board of Trade and the American department, and his unwilling hands were full.

Shelburne, whose ideas owed much to Franklin, had hoped to settle three colonies in the west, with local autonomy, and freedom to develop—exploit—the country. Hillsborough's ideas, so far as they are clear, were more cautious. As an administrator he was afraid of another Indian uprising against new colonies, and as a landlord with large estates in Ireland he was afraid he would lose tenants and labourers to America. Though he seemed at first to encourage Wharton's project, Hillsborough probably felt with most of the members of the Board of Trade that remoter colonies were dangerous to British interests. It had been a settled policy, as he later said, to confine "the western extent of settlement to such a distance from the sea coast as that those settlements should lie within the reach of the trade and commerce of this kingdom, upon which the strength and riches of it depend, and also of the exercise of that authority and jurisdiction which was conceived to be necessary for the preservation of the colonies in a due subordination to, and dependence upon, the mother country." It would be hard to regulate the trade of the western colonies, and hard to govern them. Population might be drawn off from the older colonies, and the value of their land and their production of raw materials diminished. It would be better to leave the country west of the Alleghenies wholly to the Indians and the fur trade, forbidding white emigration there until the eastern colonies were solidly populated. Hillsborough seemed not to understand, as Shelburne understood, that emigration was irresistible and had already more than begun.

For a year or so Hillsborough did not show himself opposed to the Ohio company. In April 1771 Franklin thought the affair was near a conclusion. But Hillsborough delayed and objected. Virginia under its charter claimed the territory in question, and Virginia officers and soldiers were asking for land for their services in the French and Indian war. Washington had titles for 32,373 acres on the Ohio and the Great Kanawha. Wharton got the Virginians to merge their claims with those of the Walpole company. Still Hillsborough delayed. New names for the colony were thought of. At first it was to be called Indiana. Then Pittsylvania, as a compliment to Chatham. Finally Vandalia, because the queen was said to be descended from the royal line of the Vandals. Wharton enlisted Lord Rochford, dissolute and needy, and Lord Gower, head of the Bedford party. The Bedfords wanted to oust Lord North from the ministry and thought it might be done by defeating Hillsborough, who was North's closest ally in the cabinet. Hillsborough still did not act. By roundabout avenues Wharton reached even George III. Strahan, David Hume's publisher, wrote to Hume in Edinburgh. Hume, who had formerly been secretary to Lord Hertford, wrote to the lord chamberlain.[45] Hertford possibly talked to the king. The king asked a friend of Hillsborough when the Ohio petition would be ready for the Privy Council. Hillsborough dared not delay it any longer. On 25 March 1772 the Board of Trade took the petition under consideration, and Hillsborough reported against it to the Council on 29 April.

No nicety of sentiment troubled the members of the Council— Gower and Rochford—who had here to decide whether they approved of selling Crown lands at a negligible price to themselves and their friends, for what might be enormous profits. Gower as president announced that the report was open to evidence against it. On 5 June, at a committee hearing at the Cockpit, Walpole, Franklin, Wharton, William Trent for the Pennsylvania traders, and James Mercer for the Virginia soldiers appeared. Walpole spoke, but the day was Wharton's. He had prepared and had had printed the *Observations on and Answers to the Foregoing Report*[46] long ascribed to Franklin. Wharton brilliantly observed and answered for several hours, and won the committee, who on 1 July advised the Privy Council against accepting Hillsborough's adverse judgment. Hillsborough furiously said that if the grant were made and the Vandalia colony undertaken by the government, he would resign rather than carry it out. This was what Gower wanted, not the expansion of America. Rochford was willing, if he might make a fortune. A majority in the Privy

Council stood with them. It was not the "interest of the Ohio
planters" that undid Hillsborough, Franklin wrote to his son on
17 August, so much as the dislike of his "brother ministers." "Seeing that he made a point of defeating our scheme, they made
another of supporting it, on purpose to mortify him, which they
knew his pride could not bear. . . . The king too was tired of
him and his administration, which had weakened the affection and
respect of the colonies for a royal government; of which (I may say
it to you) I had used proper means from time to time that His
Majesty should have due information and convincing proofs."[47]
Hillsborough resigned on 1 August, and was made an English earl.
North, in spite of the snub to one of his favoured colleagues,
remained in power.

　Chagrined at having lost his place, Hillsborough put too much
blame on Franklin, whom he said he would never forgive for writing the company's answer to his report. When Anthony Todd
assured Hillsborough that Franklin had not written it, Hillsborough was displeased with Todd, and insisted that Franklin was
"one of the most mischievous men in England." Yet the enemies
met amicably enough at Oxford the next year. "Lord H.," Franklin wrote to his son on 14 July 1773, "called upon Lord Le
Despencer, whose chamber and mine were together in Queen's
College. I was in the inner room shifting, and heard his voice but
did not see him, as he went downstairs immediately with Lord
Le D.; who mentioning that I was above, he returned directly and
came to me in the pleasantest manner imaginable. 'Dr. F.,' says he,
'I did not know till this minute that you were here, and I am come
back to make you my bow. I am glad to see you at Oxford, and
that you look so well,' etc. In return for this extravagance I complimented him on his son's performance in the theatre, though
indeed it was but indifferent; so that account was settled. For as
people say, when they are angry: 'If he strikes me, I'll strike him
again'; I sometimes think it may be right to say: 'If he flatters me,
I'll flatter him again.' This is *lex talionis*, returning offences in
kind." Of all the men he had ever met, Franklin thought, Hillsborough was "surely the most unequal in his treatment of people,
the most insincere, and the most wrong-headed. Witness, besides
his various behaviour to me, his duplicity in encouraging us to ask

for more land; 'Ask for enough to make a province' (when we at first asked only for 2,500,000 acres) were his words, pretending to befriend our application, then doing everything to defeat it; and reconciling the first to the last by saying to a friend that he meant to defeat it from the beginning. . . . Thus, by the way, his mortification becomes double. He has served us by the very means he meant to destroy us, and tripped up his own heels into the bargain."[48]

Hillsborough was succeeded as colonial secretary by Lord Dartmouth, looked upon as a friend of the Americans, who had named a college for him in New Hampshire. Dartmouth had been Franklin's first choice for the place, and Franklin was hopeful. He believed that the administration would now be more attentive to American rights, more considerate of American interests. The Vandalia grant might not move as fast as his associates expected. "I do not clearly yet see land," he wrote to Joseph Galloway on 6 April 1773. "I begin to be a little of the sailor's mind, when they were handing a cable out of a store into a ship, and one of 'em said: ' 'Tis a long, heavy cable. I wish we could see the end of it.' 'D——n me,' says another, 'if I believe it has any end; somebody has cut it off.' "[49] But the grant might be carried out, and Franklin's old idea of a barrier colony realized, with an incidental profit to him. He knew that the older colonies had been founded in much the same way. He himself was interested in a plan to colonize twenty-one townships in Nova Scotia, where a group of Pennsylvania speculators had a patent from the king and where Franklin's share was two thousand acres. So far the scheme had been mismanaged by John Hughes. The settlers sent to Nova Scotia in 1766 had not gone prepared for the winter and had barely survived. Their experience had given the colony a bad reputation.[50] Yet the older colonies too had had early reverses. Franklin was willing to be patient. (But the next year, insulted and dismissed by the ministry, he gave up his share in the Ohio company, which he was no longer able to serve; though he still had some hopes for profit in Nova Scotia.[51])

August 1772 was probably as triumphant and serene a month as Franklin ever passed in England. "As to my situation here," he wrote to his son on the 19th, "nothing can be more agreeable, especially as I hope for less embarrassment from the new ministry: a general respect paid me by the learned, a number of friends and acquaintances among them with whom I have a pleasing intercourse; a character of so much weight that it has protected me when some in power would have done me injury, and continued me in an office they would have deprived me of; my company so much desired that I seldom dine at home in winter and could spend the whole summer in the country houses of inviting friends if I chose it. Learned and ingenious foreigners that come to England almost all make a point of visiting me; for my reputation is still higher abroad than here. Several of the foreign ambassadors have assiduously cultivated my acquaintance, treating me as one of their corps; partly I believe from the desire they have, from time to time, of hearing something of American affairs, an object become of importance in foreign courts who begin to hope Britain's alarming power will be diminished by the defection of her colonies; and partly that they may have an opportunity of introducing me to the gentlemen of their country who desire it. The king too has lately been heard to speak of me with great regard."

Sometimes he was seized by a violent homesickness "which I can no otherwise subdue but by promising myself a return next spring or next fall, and so forth. As to returning hither, if I once go back, I have no thoughts of it. I am too far advanced in life to propose three voyages more." If he stayed another winter it was because of the new minister in the colonial department. He added a postscript three days later to say that "last night I received a letter from Paris . . . acquainting me that I am chosen *Associé Étranger* (foreign member) of the Royal Academy there. There are but eight of these *Associés Étrangers* in all Europe, and those of the most distinguished names of science." This was a moving mark of respect from "the first academy in the world."[52]

Philosopher in England

IN THE spring of 1768 James Boswell, whose *Account of Corsica* had just been published, came from Edinburgh to enjoy among great men in the capital the stir caused by his first book. Corsica was the fashion, and Englishmen of various principles were full of sympathy for the brave island fighting for its freedom from the Genoese. Confined by an amorous malady to his lodgings in Half-Moon Street, Boswell was called upon by more great men than ever in any other three weeks of his whole life: Lord Lyttelton and General Oglethorpe, David Hume and Dr. Johnson, Sir John Pringle and Benjamin Franklin, and dozens less important. But Boswell, in no condition to do justice to his journal, made only brief notes of what was said. On 14 May Pringle, Franklin, William Rose, schoolmaster and translator, and James Burgh, schoolmaster and pamphleteer, dined with Boswell. "All was elegant," he wrote in his journal, as if he were talking the scene over with himself. "You maintained that an author should never correct his book. Sir John opposed this. 'But,' said I, 'Lord Kames has made his *Elements of Criticism* so 'tis not the same book.' Sir John: 'Then it's another book'—very well said. Burgh was always saying: 'Ah, that came off so fine and dry!' And Sir John sat with one leg crossed over the other and talked with shrewd gravity and satisfaction. . . . Burgh and Rose drank tea. Franklin asked whether infidels or protestants had done most to pull down popery. We disputed the price of Robertson's book, and the good done by preaching, and agreed that the English tone was superior to the Scotch, possibly because there was more music here, except whistling."

Franklin seems then to have impressed Boswell less than Pringle did. On 15 September 1769 Boswell called on Pringle and found him and Franklin playing chess. "Sir John, though a most worthy man, has a peculiar sour manner. Franklin again is all jollity and pleasantry. I said to myself: Here is a prime contrast: acid and alkali." On the 21st: "I went to a club to which I belong. It meets every other Thursday at St. Paul's coffee house. It consists of clergymen, physicians, and several other professions. There are of it: Dr. Franklin, Rose of Chiswick, Burgh of Newington Green, Mr. Price who writes on morals, Dr. [Joseph] Jeffries, a keen supporter of the bills of rights, and a good many more. We have wine and punch upon the table. Some of us smoke a pipe, conversation goes on pretty formally, sometimes sensibly, and sometimes furiously. At nine there is a sideboard with Welsh rabbits, apple puffs, porter, and beer. Our reckoning is about 18*d*. a head. Much was said this night against Parliament. I said that, as it seemed to be agreed that all members of Parliament become corrupted, it was better to choose men already bad and so save good men. Dr. Franklin informed me that Paoli was actually arrived in London; for he had seen Mr. [Robert] Wood, the under-secretary of state, who had been with him."[1]

Franklin nowhere mentions Boswell, though he learned from the Corsican discussions that every lady in Genoa imagined she was a queen of Corsica, and he more than once applied it to the attitude of the English toward America. His few meetings with Boswell gave that genius among chroniclers little opportunity, if he had had the inclination, to reproduce the look and manner of Franklin, the form and colour of his conversation. All that appears from Boswell's notes is that Franklin was amiable rather than aggressive, spent much time with Pringle, belonged to a club of unofficial men, but was himself close enough to officials to know before Boswell that Boswell's hero the Corsican leader Pasquale Paoli had come to his refuge in England. Nor did any other skilful diarist or letter-writer preserve for later times the visible and audible Franklin who moved with his large renown through London.

Painters did more for him. When Benjamin Wilson, member of the Royal Society and writer on electricity, painted Franklin's portrait in 1759, he saw, or at least set down, a suaver countenance within a smoother wig than had appeared in Franklin's American portraits." London had soon refined the provincial agent. Mason

Chamberlin in 1762 noted further changes. Still elegant in wig and ruffles, with conventionalized hands holding conventional pen and paper, Franklin had become—as Chamberlin saw him— more shrewd in his appearance, but also more benign. Benignity seemed somehow underneath the shrewd surface, ready to come through. In 1767 the Scottish David Martin at last caught sight of the essential American that Franklin had become in his conflict with the England which had at first refined him. Now he was past sixty and easy in the fame which had followed his examination before the House of Commons. Here were the heavy-rimmed glasses which he wore and the moles on his left cheek and lower lip which no earlier painter had put into a portrait of him. One strong, square hand rested a realistic thumb speculatively against his chin. Reading a manuscript held in the other hand, he looked intent, detached, humorous, kind, firm, and wise: no longer a man of the current fashion but a self-made man who with knowledge and experience had passed through changing fashions to the more lasting status of scholar and philosopher.

II

In Craven Street during the years 1764–75 Franklin lived, as before, in serene comfort and affection, less a lodger than the head of a household. Mrs. Stevenson made room for the English Sally Franklin, and later for William's son Temple. The boy was sent to a school in Kensington kept by Strahan's brother-in-law, the eccentric philologist James Elphinston; but spent his vacations with his grandfather. Sally was "nimble-footed and willing to run of errands and wait upon me,"[2] Franklin wrote to his wife on 1 December 1772, and he gave up keeping the man John whom he had brought with him. Mrs. Stevenson's maid Nanny had once lived in Philadelphia. When the rascal she married made away with her money she came back to Craven Street. Polly Stevenson was most of the time with her aunt Mrs. Tickell. Since Mrs. Stevenson did not like to write letters, Franklin wrote Polly the news of the household. He tried to cheer her when she complained of her aunt's bad temper. "Nothing is more apt to sour the temper of aged people," he wrote on 28 October 1768, "than the apprehension that they are neglected; and they are extremely apt to entertain such suspicions. It was therefore that I did propose asking her to be of our late party; but, your mother disliking it, the motion was dropped, as some others have been by my too great easiness, contrary to my judgment. Not but that I was sensible her being with us might have lessened our pleasure, but I hoped it might have prevented you some pain."[3] The Franklins and Stevensons had parties like members of one family, and all of them together might be invited to dinner with the Strahans.

Letters between Franklin and his wife, who he said was his best correspondent, kept the two families of Philadelphia and London in close touch. He still sent her and Sally clothes and trinkets which Mrs. Stevenson and Polly helped him choose, and his wife sent him corn meal, buckwheat flour, apples, cranberries, dried peaches, and nuts. (Early in 1768, when America was angrily protesting against the Townshend acts, Franklin made a smiling present to Lord Bathurst, lord chancellor, and Lady Bathurst of some of the American nuts and apples: "which he prays they will accept as a tribute from that country, small indeed but voluntary."[4]) Messages of affection went back and forth. After Benjamin Franklin Bache, Sally's first child, was born in August 1769, the grandmother's letters were filled with him. Franklin teased her about it, but asked for more of that charming history, and complained if a letter came with no fresh chapters. He reported everything to Mrs. Stevenson, and consulted with Sir John Pringle about the inoculation of the baby. After Polly Stevenson had married and had a child, Franklin replied to his wife's stories about her grandson with his stories about his godson: his teething, his weaning, his beginning to walk and talk. "He was with us a few days last week," Franklin wrote to her on 2 February 1773 when Billy Hewson was not quite two, "grew fond of me, and would not be contented to sit down to breakfast without coming to call 'Pa,' rejoicing when he had got me into my place. When seeing me one day crack one of the Philadelphia biscuits into my tea with the nutcrackers he took another and tried to do the same with the tea-tongs. It makes me long to be at home to play with Ben."[5]

The house in Craven Street was run to suit Franklin's convenience, but he was easy to please. He got up early and took his tonic bath, he told Barbeu Dubourg on 28 July 1768. That is, he sat in his bedroom "without any clothes whatever, half an hour or an hour according to the season, either reading or writing. . . . And if I return to bed afterwards before I dress myself, as sometimes happens, I make a supplement to my night's rest of one or two hours of the most pleasing sleep that can be imagined."[6] He shaved himself every day, breakfasted lightly, and did most of his private work in the forenoon. As always he saved all the letters, notes, invitations, documents he received, and kept copies of those he sent. Now and then his papers and accounts got in disorder. In the winter of 1770–71 two young grandnephews from Boston, Jonathan and Josiah Williams, came to visit Franklin, and Jonathan went over the accounts and made up a complete new set of books. Franklin did not have too many mornings free to work at home, for there were for ever great men to see about America. His coach would come for him and take him on his lobbying, patriotic rounds. Dinner then was usually at three or four, and he dined in his busy seasons more often than not away from home. He might have tea in Craven Street and play cards there in the evening, or he might go to taverns or to the houses of his friends. He seems to have seen little of the theatre. After convivial evenings he frequently went late to bed.

He had spells of gout and recurrent colds. It was hard to find time for the exercise he knew he needed. Thinking about it, he concluded that the amount of exercise was to be measured "not by time or by distance but by the degree of warmth it produces in the body," he wrote to his son on 19 August 1772. "Using round numbers without regard to exactness but merely to mark a great difference . . . there is more exercise in one mile's riding on horseback than in five in a coach; and more in one mile's walking on foot than in five on horseback; to which I may add, that there is more in walking one mile up and down stairs than in five on a level floor. The two latter exercises may be had within doors when the weather discourages going abroad; and the last may be had when one is pinched for time, as containing a great quantity of exercise in a handful of minutes. The dumb-bell is another exercise of the latter compendious kind. By the use of it I have in

forty swings quickened my pulse from sixty to one hundred beats
in a minute, counted by a second watch; and I suppose the warmth
generally increases with quickness of pulse."[7] He insisted always
on ventilation and fresh air, and heretically kept his windows open
at night. "What caution against air, what stopping of crevices, what
wrapping up in warm clothes, what shutting of doors and windows, even in the midst of summer!" he wrote to Thomas Percival
on 25 September 1773. "Many London families go out once a day
to take the air; three or four persons in a coach, one perhaps sick;
these go three or four miles, or as many turns in Hyde Park, with
the glasses both up close, all breathing over and over again the
same air they brought out of town with them in the coach, with
the least change possible, and rendered worse and worse every
minute. And this they call taking the air."[8] The house in Craven
Street might be sometimes crowded but it was always ventilated.

The warm, gay friendship between Franklin and Polly Stevenson never varied, except that he no longer corresponded with her
about natural philosophy. Her friends Dorothea Blount, daughter
of Sir Charles Blount who lived at Bromley, and a Miss Barwell,
who lived in London, were his friends too. When he came back
from his second visit to Paris in the summer of 1769 Polly could
hardly wait to send him her "welcome to England, my dear, my
honoured friend," and to tell him about a young doctor she had
first met the day before at Margate, where she was visiting. She
might marry him, she told Franklin, though the young doctor still
knew nothing of her impulse. "How strangely I let my pen run on
to a philosopher; but that philosopher is my friend, and I may
write what I please to him." Franklin, "just home from a venison
feast where I have drank more than a philosopher ought," wrote
to her the evening he got her letter, 2 September. "Possibly if
the truth were known I have reason to be jealous of this same
insinuating, handsome young physician; but, as it flatters more
my vanity, and therefore gives me more pleasure, to suppose you
were in spirits on account of my safe return, I shall turn a deaf ear
to reason in this case, as I have done with success in twenty others."[9]

When the doctor, William Hewson, proposed the following May,
Polly asked Franklin's advice. When, a few weeks later, she was
married, she wrote to Franklin about her new life and her new

relatives. "I am apt to love everybody that loves you," he wrote her on 24 July, "and therefore I suppose I shall in time love your new mother and new sister and new Dolly. I find I begin to like them already, and if you think proper you may tell them so. But your old Dolly [Dorothea Blount] and I have agreed to love each other better than ever we did, to make up as much as we can our supposed loss."[10] By September the Hewsons had come to live in Craven Street. Mrs. Stevenson with Sally Franklin went to Rochester on the 22nd, leaving Polly in charge. And Franklin, to let them know how they were missed, and to tease Polly, wrote *The Craven Street Gazette*[11] in a daily parody of newspaper gossip about the court. A lazy man who was as busy as Franklin would not have found time to write more than a note. Franklin, whose industry was so great that he thought of himself as lazy, took time to write almost a whole newspaper to entertain the young people of his household.

"This morning Queen Margaret, accompanied by her first maid of honour, Miss Franklin, set out for Rochester. . . . It is whispered that the new family administration, which took place on Her Majesty's departure, promises, like all other new administrations, to govern much better than the old one.

"We hear that a certain Great Person (so called from his enormous size) of a certain family in a certain street is grievously affected at the late changes, and could hardly be comforted this morning, though the new ministry promised him a roasted shoulder of mutton and potatoes for his dinner.

"It is said that the same Great Person intended to pay his respects to another great personage this day, at St. James's, it being coronation day; hoping thereby a little to amuse his grief; but was prevented by an accident, Queen Margaret, or her maid of honour, having carried off the key of the drawers so that the lady of the bedchamber could not come at a laced shirt for His Highness. Great clamours were made on this occasion against Her Majesty.

"Other accounts say that the shirts were afterwards found, though too late, in another place. And some suspect that the wanting a shirt from those drawers was only a ministerial pretence to excuse picking the locks, that the new administration might have everything at command.

"We hear that the lady chamberlain of the household [Polly] went to market this morning by her own self, gave the butcher whatever he asked for the mutton and had no dispute with the potato woman, to their great amazement at the change of times. . . .

"We have good authority to assure our readers that a cabinet council was held this afternoon at tea; the subject of which was a proposal for the reformation of manners and a more strict observation of the Lord's day. The result was a unanimous resolution that no meat should be dressed tomorrow; whereby the cook and the first minister [Polly and her husband] will both be at liberty to go to church, the one having nothing to do and the other no roast to rule. It seems the cold shoulder of mutton and the apple pie were thought sufficient for Sunday's dinner. All pious people applaud this measure, and it is thought the new ministry will soon become popular. . . .

"It is now found by sad experience that good resolutions are easier made than executed. Notwithstanding yesterday's solemn order of council nobody went to church today. It seems the Great Person's broad-built bulk lay so long abed that the breakfast was not over till it was too late to dress. At least this is the excuse. In fine, it seems a vain thing to hope reformation from the example of our great folks. . . .

"Lord and Lady Hewson walked after dinner to Kensington to pay their duty to the Dowager [Hewson's mother]; and Dr. Fatsides made four hundred and sixty-nine turns in his dining room, as the exact distance of a visit to the lovely Lady Barwell, whom he did not find at home; so there was no struggle for and against a kiss, and he sat down to dream in the easy chair that he had it without any trouble. . . .

"We are credibly informed that the Great Person dined this day with the Club at the Cat-and-Bagpipes in the City on cold round of boiled beef. This, it seems, he was under some necessity of doing (though he rather dislikes beef) because truly the ministers were to be all abroad somewhere to dine on hot roast venison. It is thought that if the Queen had been at home he would not have been so slighted. And though he shows outwardly no marks of dissatisfaction it is suspected that he begins to wish for Her Majesty's return. . . .

"This evening there was high play at Craven Street House. The Great Person lost money. It is supposed the ministers, as is usually supposed of all ministers, shared the emoluments among them. . . .

"This morning my good Lord Hutton [James Hutton the bookseller] called at Craven Street House and inquired very respectfully and affectionately concerning the welfare of the Queen. He then imparted to the Big Man a piece of intelligence important to them both and but just communicated by Lady Hawkesworth [wife of John Hawkesworth], viz., that the amiable and delectable companion Miss D[orothea] B[lount] had made a vow to marry absolutely him of the two whose wife should first depart this life. It is impossible to express the various agitations of mind appearing in both their faces on this occasion. Vanity at the preference given them over the rest of mankind; affection to their present wives, fear of losing them, hope, if they must lose them, to obtain the proposed comfort; jealousy of each other in case both wives should die together, etc., etc., etc.: all working at the same time jumbled their features into inexplicable confusion. They parted at length with professions and outward appearances indeed of ever-during friendship, but it was shrewdly suspected that each of them sincerely wished health and long life to the other's wife; and that, however long either of these friends might like to live himself, the other would be very well pleased to survive him. . . .

"A terrible accident had like to have happened this afternoon at tea. The boiler was set too near the end of the little square table. The first Ministress was sitting at one end of the table to administer the tea; the Great Person was about to sit down at the other end where the boiler stood. By a sudden motion the lady gave the table a tilt. Had it gone over, the G. P. must have been scalded, perhaps to death. Various are the surmises and observations on this occasion. The godly say it would have been a just judgment on him for preventing, by his laziness, the family's going to church last Sunday. The opposition do not stick to insinuate that there was a design to scald him, prevented only by his quick catching the table. The friends of the ministry give it out that he carelessly jogged the table himself and would have inevitably been scalded had not the Ministress saved him. It is hard for the public to come at the truth in these cases. . . .

"We hear that from the time of Her Majesty's leaving Craven Street House to this day, no care is taken to file the newspapers; but they lie about in every room in every window and on every chair, just where the Great Person lays them when he reads them. It is impossible government can long go on in such hands."

To vary the bulletins, Franklin wrote a letter to himself, as from a reader who called himself "Indignation": "I make no doubt of the truth of what the papers tell us, that a certain Great Person is half starved on a blade-bone of a sheep (I cannot call it of mutton, there being none on it) by a set of the most careless, worthless, thoughtless, inconsiderate, corrupt, ignorant, blundering, foolish, crafty, and knavish ministers that ever got into a house and pretended to govern a family and provide a dinner. Alas for the poor old England of Craven Street! If they continue in power another week the nation will be ruined. Undone, totally undone, if I and my friends are not appointed to succeed them." Then Franklin answered himself as from "A Hater of Scandal": "The wickedness of writers in this age is truly amazing. I believe that if even the angel Gabriel would condescend to be our minister and provide our dinners he could scarcely escape newspaper defamation from a gang of hungry, ever-restless, discontented, and malicious scribblers. It is, sir, a piece of justice you owe our righteous administration to undeceive the public on this occasion by assuring them of the fact; which is that there was provided, and actually smoking on the table under his royal nose at the same instant, as fine a piece of ribs of beef roasted as ever knife was put into, with potatoes, horse-radish, pickled walnuts, etc., which His Highness might have eaten if he had so pleased to do; and which he forbore to do merely from a whimsical opinion (with respect be it spoken) that beef doth not with him perspire well but makes his back itch, now that he has lost the little Chinese ivory hand at the end of a stick, commonly called a scratchback, presented to him by Her Majesty."

Then random notices, and a final compliment to Polly's housekeeping: "*Marriages.* None since our last, but Puss begins to go a-courting. *Deaths.* In the back closet and elsewhere, many poor mice. *Stocks.* Biscuit—very low. Buckwheat and Indian meal—both sour. Tea—lowering daily, in the canister. Wine—shut. *Wednesday, September 26th. Postscript.* Those in the secret of affairs do not scruple to assert roundly that our first Ministress is very notable, having this day been at market, bought mutton chops and apples four a penny, made an excellent apple pie with her own hands, and mended two pair of breeches."

The next May or June Polly had her first child, and the philosopher was godfather. On the way home from Scotland late in the year Franklin found at the Baches' house in Lancashire a joint letter from Polly and Dorothea Blount, part of it about his godson. "His being like me in so many particulars," Franklin wrote to Polly on 25 November, "pleases me prodigiously; and I am persuaded there is another which you have omitted, though it must have occurred to you while you were putting them down. Pray let him have everything he likes; I think it of great consequence while the features of the countenance are forming; it gives them a pleasant air, and, that being once become natural and fixed by habit, the face is ever after the handsomer for it; and on that much of a person's good fortune and success in life may depend. Had I been crossed as much in my infant likings and inclinations as you know I have been of late years, I should have been—I was going to say—not near so handsome; but as the vanity of that expression would offend other folk's vanity, I change it, out of regard for them, and say a good deal more homely." As to Polly's telling that her mother had a new gallant, Franklin said he was not surprised; "for I have been used to rivals, and scarce ever had a friend or a mistress in my whole life that other people did not like as well as myself." Before he could write the second half of his letter to Dorothea Blount he was called to dinner, and could add only: "Dear Dolly, I love you more than you can imagine."[12]

With Polly and the other young women who adored him in London Franklin was at once philosopher, father, philanderer, and friend, in a mixture of his own. About one of them, Judith Osgood, there has been some mystery. She lived in King Street, and was married in August 1770 to Franklin's colleague John Foxcroft, who had come to England on the affairs of the Ohio grant. The minister of the ceremony was Thomas Coombe of Philadelphia, who had been for a time another lodger in the Craven Street house, and was chaplain to Lord Rockingham.[13] It is natural that Franklin should have met her, and not unnatural that in letters to Foxcroft he should have referred to her as "my daughter." This has caused the suspicion that she was another illegitimate child of his. But as she seems to have been English and young in 1770, she can hardly have been the actual daughter of a man who was in America from 1726 to 1757. She was simply another of the young women whom Franklin called daughter and who liked being called that. During 1765 he frequently saw Elizabeth Graeme from Philadelphia, whom his son had jilted. "Miss Betsy Graeme lodges not far from me," he told his wife on 14 February, "and is pretty well."

In October 1772, when Polly had had one child and was expecting a second, Mrs. Stevenson gave her house up to the Hewsons and moved, with Franklin, to another house in the same street. "I am almost settled in my new apartment," Franklin wrote to his son on 3 November; "but removing and sorting my papers and placing my books and things has been a troublesome job. I am amazed to see how books have grown upon me since my return to England. I brought none with me, and now have a roomful; many collected in Germany, Holland, and France; and consisting chiefly of such as contain knowledge that may hereafter be useful to America." In the spring of 1774, a dark time for Franklin, the two little Hewson boys had smallpox, and their father, who had infected himself during an operation, died, leaving Polly to bear a posthumous daughter. By the death of her aunt that summer she came into a reasonable fortune. The Revolution soon sent Franklin to America and then to France, but Polly and he managed to get letters to each other. She called her children his grandchildren, and talked of marrying her daughter to Benny Bache. After the peace she visited Franklin at Passy with her young family. Later she followed him to Philadelphia to settle in the country which was hers because it was his. Neither time nor war could estrange them.

"You cannot conceive how shamefully the mode here is a single life," Franklin had written to his wife during his earlier stay in

England. "One can scarce be in the company of a dozen men of circumstance and fortune but what it is odds you find on inquiry eleven of them are single. The great complaint is the excessive expensiveness of English wives."[14] A friend to marriage and a lover of children, Franklin knew only a few households besides his own in which he could enjoy the swarming familiar life which he liked. He took a special pleasure in his visits to Twyford, the home of Jonathan Shipley, bishop of St. Asaph. How the two became acquainted is not certain. But the bishop's brother William Shipley, originator and registrar of the Society of Arts, had invited Franklin to become a member while he was still in Philadelphia, and in London presumably introduced him to the bishop, perhaps while he was dean of Winchester. In April 1768 Franklin went to Winchester on an errand which he does not explain.[15] The next year Jonathan Shipley was consecrated bishop of Llandaff and the same year translated to St. Asaph in Wales, where he had one of the smallest cathedrals in Britain and a dilapidated palace in which he spent no more than one month out of twelve, preferring London or his country house at Twyford near Winchester. When he was given a bishopric he must have had the favour of the king and of the Duke of Grafton. But Shipley, who is known to history best as the friend of Franklin, soon shifted to the opposition. Almost alone among the bishops he upheld the rights of the American colonists and of the British dissenters.

In June 1771 Franklin went for a week to Twyford, and left with the promise to return shortly. Business kept him away longer than he had expected. "I now breathe with reluctance the smoke of London, when I think of the sweet air of Twyford," he wrote to the bishop on the 24th. "I have taken the liberty of sending . . . one of my books for Miss Georgiana, which I hope she will be good enough to accept as a small mark of my regard for her philosophic genius; and a specimen of the American dried apples for Mrs. Shipley, that she may judge whether it will be worth while to try the practice."[16] Toward the end of July he went again, this time for nearly three weeks. It was a happy and memorable visit. The bishop had a son who was already in orders and five daughters ranging from twenty-three to eleven: Anna Maria, Amelia, Elizabeth, Georgiana, Catherine. Franklin captivated old and young so that they became his friends for life. Perhaps he told them stories of his own boyhood in remote Boston and Philadelphia and was told that such stories ought to be saved for the world. At least he began at Twyford, "expecting the enjoyment of a week's uninterrupted leisure," to write his *Autobiography* in the form of a letter to his son.

"I have ever had pleasure in obtaining any little anecdotes of my ancestors." Perhaps his son might like to read about "the circumstances of my life, many of which you are yet unacquainted with." William, thanks to his father, had had very different fortunes and at little more than thirty had become governor of a province. Their later posterity might find in the story of Franklin's rise in the world some hints for their own conduct. "Were it offered to my choice, I should have no objection to a repetition of the same life from its beginning, only asking the advantages authors have in a second edition to correct some faults of the first. . . . But though this were denied, I should still accept the offer." Since he could have no such chance, the next best thing was remembering and recording. Perhaps, Franklin admitted, he was simply indulging "the inclination so natural in old men, to be talking of themselves and their own past actions; and I shall indulge it without being tiresome to others who, through respect to age, might conceive themselves obliged to give me a hearing; since this may be read or not as any one pleases. And lastly (I may as well confess it, since my denial of it will be believed by nobody), perhaps I shall a good deal gratify my own vanity. . . . Most people dislike vanity in others, whatever share they have of it themselves; but I give it fair quarter wherever I meet with it, being persuaded that it is often productive of good to the possessor and to others that are within his sphere of action; and therefore, in many cases, it would not be altogether absurd if a man were to thank God for his vanity among the other comforts of life."[17]

There had been almost no famous autobiographies before Franklin, and he had no models for his kind. St. Augustine had written of his conversion, Cellini of his adventures as artist and scapegrace. Rousseau in his still unpublished *Confessions* had poured out the tumults of his heart, and Casanova was soon to begin the chronicle of his loves. Franklin's conversions, adventures, tumults, loves were of a sort new to literature. He had been bred a tradesman in an age of reason, and he wrote for a middle class which had had few historians. His book was the first master-piece of autobiography by a self-made man: made, that is, neither in war nor in art but in peaceful business. What he told his son was the "little anecdotes" of a tradesman's household in Boston; of the apprentice aiming higher than his craft; of the journeyman on his inconspicuous, ambitious travels; of the master setting up his own shop, gathering private friends about him for the public benefit, and himself making his way through trade to prosperity and wis-dom. Here were the homeliest memoirs that had ever been written, in the plainest language. With his swift, powerful ease, Franklin in his week or so wrote nearly a half of the *Autobiography*, on the whole the best part. It is said he read the book to the Shipley family as he wrote it. The room in which he worked came to be known as Franklin's room.

Something of the pleasant life there appears in a letter to his wife on 14 August. "The bishop's lady knows what children and grandchildren I have, their ages, etc. So when I was to come away on Monday the 12th in the morning, she insisted on my stay-ing that one day longer, that we might keep my grandson's birth-day. At dinner, among other nice things, we had a floating island, which they always particularly have on the birthdays of any of their own six children; who were all but one at table, where there was also a clergyman's widow now above a hundred years old. The chief toast of the day was Master Benjamin Bache, which the venerable old lady began in a bumper of mountain [a variety of Malaga wine]. The bishop's lady politely added: 'And that he may be as good a man as his grandfather.' I said I hoped he would be much better. The bishop, still more complaisant than his lady, said: 'We will compound the matter and be contented if he should not prove quite so good.' This chitchat is to yourself only, in return for some of yours about your grandson, and must only be read to Sally, and not spoken of to anybody else; for you know how people add and alter silly stories that they hear, and make them appear ten times more silly."[18]

Kitty, the youngest daughter, was going back to school in Lon-don, and accompanied Franklin in the post chaise. Not all philosophers would have been at ease with a schoolgirl of eleven, or been able to keep her from feeling shy. Franklin seems to have had no difficulty. She was soon talking freely, he reported to her mother, about what men she thought the sisters ought to marry. Georgiana should have a country gentleman, Betty a rich city merchant. Emily (Amelia), who was Kitty's favourite, deserved an earl. Anna Maria should have a very rich man with many possessions, because she liked managing. Franklin suggested a duke. No, come to think about it, let Emily have a duke, and Anna Maria the earl. Then perhaps Kitty herself might choose a soldier, Franklin said, perhaps a general. Not unless he were very old, Kitty insisted. " 'I like an old man, indeed I do, and somehow or other all the old men take to me; all that come to our house like me better than my other sisters. I go to 'em and ask 'em how they do, and they like it mightily; and the maids take notice of it, and say, when they see an old man come: "There's a friend of yours, Miss Kitty." ' 'But then [from Franklin], as you like an old general, hadn't you better take him while he's a young officer, and let him grow old upon your hands, because then you'll like him better and better every year as he grows older and older?' 'No, that won't do. He must be an old man of seventy or eighty, and take me when I am about thirty. And then, you know, I may be a rich young widow.' "[19] Kitty did not marry her old general, but she never forgot this journey with Franklin, who fifteen years later, when he was president of Pennsylvania, found time to write for her his bagatelle on *The Art of Procuring Pleasant Dreams*.

As a present for the Shipley girls Franklin got through his wife a grey squirrel from Philadelphia. It became a favourite in the Twyford family and was called Mungo or Skugg—Skugg was as common a name for pet squirrels in England as Puss for cats. But Mungo got out of his cage, wandered away, and was killed by a dog. The girls buried him in the garden, and Georgiana asked Franklin to write an epitaph for the monument. The philosopher gravely complied, in a letter of 26 September 1772. "I lament with you most sincerely the unfortunate end of poor Mungo. Few squirrels were better accomplished; for he had had a good education, travelled far, and seen much of the world. As he had the honour of being, for his virtues, your favourite, he should not go, like common skuggs, without an elegy or an epitaph. Let us give him one in the monumental style and measure, which, being neither prose nor verse, is perhaps the properest for grief; since to use common language would look as if we were not affected, and to make rhymes would seem trifling in sorrow." He wrote her an epitaph which happily parodied the pompous style of many epitaphs in the grand style of contemporary graveyards. Then he reduced even that to a simile which has become proverbial. "You see, my dear Miss, how much more decent and proper this broken style is than if we were to say, by way of epitaph:

> Here Skugg
> Lies snug
> As a bug
> In a rug.

And yet there are people in the world of so little feeling as to think that this would be a good enough epitaph for poor Mungo."[20]

III

Franklin left London on his travels chiefly for his health, but there was a kind of system in his curiosity, and he managed to see a good deal of the world which was then most important to London and to him. After his journeys to Hanover in 1766 and to Paris in 1767 he was kept close to London for two years, though during that time he frequently went out of town to the houses of his friends. In July and August 1769 he visited Paris again, again with Pringle, whose French was better than Franklin's. Having been elected president of the American Philosophical Society in January, Franklin was now a more or less official representative of American learning, which through him began to be regarded in Europe. D'Alibard and his wife were as obliging as before. The Academy of Sciences welcomed him, and the congenial physiocrats. There was talk of the comet of that year and of the transit of Venus in June, which had been accurately observed in Philadelphia. "Would to God," Franklin wrote to du Pont de Nemours on 2 October 1770, "I could take with me [to America] Messrs.

du Pont, Dubourg, and some other French friends, with their good ladies. I might then, by mixing them with my friends in Philadelphia, form a little happy society that would prevent my ever wishing again to visit Europe."[21] It pleased Franklin to find that France was interested in the colonies. "All Europe (except Britain) appears to be on our side the question," he wrote to Samuel Cooper on 30 September 1769. "But Europe has its reasons," he went on to explain. "It fancies itself in some danger from the growth of British power, and would be glad to see it divided against itself. Our prudence will, I hope, long postpone the satisfaction our enemies expect from our dissensions."[22] In Paris Franklin carefully studied the way the French built their houses to avoid the danger of fires.[23]

During 1770 he was too busy to leave London, but in 1771 he travelled more than in any other of his English years. In May he went with friends to see the manufacturing towns in the north, and called on Priestley and John Smeaton (builder of the Eddystone lighthouse) at Leeds and Thomas Percival, physician, at Manchester. On this journey Franklin and his friends may have seen Erasmus Darwin at Lichfield. After Franklin's two visits to the Shipleys in June and July he set out in August for the long journey to Ireland and Scotland which kept him away from London till the end of November. In June 1772 he travelled north again for a month. "I spent some days at Preston," he wrote to his wife on 14 July, "visited several friends in Cumberland, Westmoreland, Yorkshire, and Staffordshire. Rachel Wilson sent her love to you and our children, as did our remaining relations at Birmingham, where I likewise stayed several days. In Cumberland I ascended a very high mountain where I had a prospect of a most beautiful country, of hills, fields, lakes, villas, etc., and at Whitehaven went down the coal mines till they told me I was eighty fathoms under the surface of the sea which rolled over our heads; so that I have been nearer both the upper and lower regions than ever in my life before."[24] In October he made what seems to have been his first visit to Lord Le Despencer at West Wycombe in Buckinghamshire, where he went again in the summers of 1773 and 1774. In July 1773 he accompanied Le Despencer to Oxford, where Lord North was being installed as chancellor. In October

Franklin journeyed to Portsmouth with several friends to study the effect of pouring oil on the rough water off Spithead.

Only now and then do the records show how he looked and talked. In April 1772 the Abbé Morellet came to England on Lord Shelburne's invitation and spent five or six days at Shelburne's house at Wycombe, along with Colonel Barré, John Hawkesworth, David Garrick, and Franklin. Morellet had little English, but the others all knew enough French to understand his clear enunciation and strong voice, on which Garrick complimented him. The abbé discoursed with Franklin about the freedom of commerce, population, and the American colonies; about music, which Franklin loved, and physics and ethics. Franklin spoke briefly and slowly (*en peu de mots et à des intervalles assez longs*). Morellet thought no man was ever more economical of time and words. But the sage was not too grave to play a joke on his friends. One day when they were walking in the park at Wycombe he said that he could quiet the waves on a small stream which was being whipped by the wind. He went two hundred paces above where the others stood, made some magic passes over the water, and waved his bamboo cane three times in the air. The waves gradually sank and the stream became as smooth as a mirror. After they had marvelled Franklin explained. He carried oil in the hollow joint of his cane, and a few drops of it spreading on the water had caused the miracle.[25]

When the dissolute, half-mad young Christian VII of Denmark, first cousin to George III and married to his sister, was in England between August and October 1768, "he sent me," Franklin wrote, "a card expressing in strong terms his esteem for me and inviting me to dinner with him at St. James's." The dinner was on 1 October, and besides Franklin the only philosophers were Lord Morton of the Royal Society and Matthew Maty of the Honest Whigs.[26] In the midst of flamboyant excesses the visiting king still wanted to meet the philosophers of England, of whom Franklin was the one best known to him, as later he met the philosophers of France. The virtuous George III cared nothing for the philosopher and disliked the colonial patriot. And so generally with the lords who ruled the nation. They were as indifferent to science as they were remote from trade, and Franklin was a scientist who had been a tradesman. He received in England few of the splendid and delicate attentions which delighted him across the Channel. Lady Bathurst might graciously accept his present of American apples. Lady North, seeing that North avoided speaking to Franklin at a country house, might come and sit on the sofa beside him, "as if to make amends."[27] But the ladies of England followed their lords in thinking of him as without rank or wealth and so outside the oligarchy, annoying it with his demands in behalf of his everlasting Americans.

Though Franklin had friends as eminent as Shelburne, as exemplary as the bishop of St. Asaph, and as notorious as Le Despencer, he belonged most to London and to plainer men of learning. The Royal Society, which then had a house in Crane Court, was almost a club for him. Pringle became president in November 1772, and Franklin was for the fourth time chosen a member of the council (as in 1760, 1765, 1766). Many of the scientific papers sent from America, and some from England, were transmitted through him. He concerned himself with the election of his American and French friends to the Royal Society, and with the election of his French and English friends to the American Philosophical Society. As with his young tradesmen and his early scientific correspondents in the colonies, he wanted now to bring the scholars of all Europe and all America together in common pursuits. Nor did his scientific friends confine themselves to science. John Fothergill wrote a pamphlet advocating the repeal of the Stamp Act, and Richard Price attacked the American policies of the ministry. Priestley supported first the American Revolution and then the French, and in the end emigrated to Pennsylvania. He probably owed in part to Franklin, as well as to Price, his appointment to be Shelburne's librarian and companion at Bowood, near Calne in Wiltshire, where Priestley lived for eight years and where he discovered oxygen in 1774. In England as in America Franklin never spared himself when there was a chance to be useful to any of his friends. He recommended Americans for honorary degrees at Edinburgh till he was embarrassed. He procured books for the Library Company of Philadelphia and scientific instruments for Harvard.

Franklin seems somewhat irregularly to have met with a group of friends at the Dog tavern,[28] and more regularly at the George and Vulture,[29] but his favourite club was the Honest Whigs,[30] of which Boswell attended a meeting in September 1769. At that time it met every other Thursday evening at a coffee house in St. Paul's Churchyard, but by March 1772 the manager had left St. Paul's to set up the London coffee house on Ludgate Hill, and the club had followed. Boswell on the evening of the 26th was bored at the theatre and after three acts went to the London, where Franklin had promised to meet him. "When I got thither," Boswell noted in his journal, "neither he nor any one else whom I knew was there. One of the men here came out, but could recollect nothing of me. This was very awkward."[31] Another member recognized him. Boswell was admitted and found Priestley there.

The club was Whig in politics, philosophical rather than literary in its interests. The membership seems to have been elastic, and the lists recorded are inexact and discrepant. Bishop Shipley is said to have belonged, but the other clergymen were nonconformists: Priestley, Richard Price, and Andrew Kippis, who later edited the second edition of the *Biographia Britannica*. John Canton, the electrician, had been a schoolmaster, as were James Burgh and William Rose. John Hawkesworth was a dramatist, essayist, and editor. John Stanley was a composer and organist. Peter Collinson was a merchant and naturalist. The profession most represented was medicine. There were William Watson, Franklin's old rival in electricity, now physician to the Foundling Hospital; Matthew Maty, principal secretary of the Royal Society and principal librarian of the British Museum; Peter Templeman, keeper of the reading room at the British Museum; James Parsons, doctor and philologian. And there were Franklin's close friends Fothergill and Pringle.

When the club was first formed is not known, or how long it lasted, or whether all these men were actually members or came often to the meetings. Perhaps, like other clubs, the Honest Whigs had a few who regularly met and a scattering of others who came when they pleased. Franklin, Price, and Canton appear to have been the earliest and, with Priestley when he was in London, the most faithful of the members. The club was a group of Franklin's friends, held together by shared opinions and tastes, and the varieties of knowledge in which he was at home. They met on their Thursday evenings, drank, smoked (Franklin did not use tobacco), talked "pretty formally, sometimes sensibly, and sometimes furiously," and had supper at nine. Except for one brief evening they had no Boswell to take even the briefest notes of what was said. But it may be guessed that most of their topics are to be found here or there in the writings of Franklin.

IV

Franklin's scientific interests in England were, as they had been in America, the somewhat casual results of his almost universal curiosity. "Everything of difficult discussion," he wrote to Alexander Colden on 2 June 1773, "and that requires close attention of mind and an application of long continuance, grows rather irksome to me; and where there is not some absolute necessity for it, as in the settlement of accounts or the like, I am apt to indulge the indolence usually attending age, in postponing such business from time to time, though continually resolving to do it."[32] If Franklin lacked the patience to carry out long scientific tasks, his observations were still endless, free, and bold, and often original and fundamental as well as inventive. To go with him month by month as inquiries rose to his mind is to range through the world of contemporary science.

Some time during 1767 Filippo Mazzei consulted Franklin about the stove which he had invented but which the English makers changed from the original design. Franklin helped him look for a true model and had two made for him to send to the Grand Duke Leopold.[33] On 5 August of that year Franklin was writing to George Croghan about the mastodon tusks and teeth which Croghan had sent to London. Nothing of the sort, Franklin said, had been found in any other part of America except Peru. He noticed that the teeth had "knobs, like the grinders of a carnivorous animal; when those of the elephant, which eats only vegetables, are almost smooth. But then we know of no other animal, with tusks like an elephant, to whom such grinders might belong." It was remarkable, he reflected, that though elephants were now unknown outside of hot countries they seemed once to have lived in Siberia as well as on the Ohio; "which looks as if the earth had anciently been in another position, and the climates differently placed from what they are at present."[34] In November he was asked by the council of the Royal Society to give his opinion, "as the best judge present," of the electrical experiments for which it was proposed that Priestley be given the Copley medal.[35] To Cadwallader Evans on 20 February 1768 Franklin wrote that he had long believed lead poisoning to be due "to a metallic cause only; observing that it affects, among tradesmen, those that use lead, however different their trades: as glaziers, letter-founders, plumbers, potters, white-lead makers, and painters."[36] He was a pioneer in the diagnosis of this disease. On 28 February 1768 Franklin wrote to Lord Kames at some length about the chimneys in the new house Kames had bought. "I . . . think happiness consists more in small conveniences or pleasures that occur every day than in great pieces of good fortune that happen but seldom to a man in the course of his life. Thus I reckon it among my felicities that I can set my own razor and shave myself perfectly well; in which I have a daily pleasure, and avoid the uneasiness one is sometimes obliged to suffer from the dirty fingers or bad breath of a slovenly barber."[37]

On 10 May, writing to Pringle, Franklin reported an experiment he had made. In Holland, Pringle would remember, they had been told that canal boats went more slowly when the water was low in the canal than when it was high. "After our return to England, as often as I happened to be on the Thames, I inquired of our waterman whether they were sensible of any difference in rowing over shallow or deep water. I found them all agreeing in the fact that there was a very great difference, but they differed widely in expressing the quantity of the difference." Franklin reasoned that the boat in the canal "must in every boat's length of her course move out of her way a body of water equal in bulk to the room her bottom took up in the water; that the water so moved must pass on each side of her and under her bottom to get behind her; that if the passage under her bottom was straitened by the shallows more of the water must pass by her sides, and with a swifter motion, which would retard her, as moving the contrary way: or that, the water becoming lower behind the boat than before, she was pressed back by the weight of its difference in height, and her motion retarded by having that weight constantly to overcome."

But Franklin had not merely reasoned the matter out. He had put it to experiment. "I provided a trough of planed boards fourteen feet long, six inches wide, and six inches deep, in the clear, filled with water within half an inch of the edge, to represent a canal. I had a loose board of nearly the same length and breadth that, being put into the water, might be sunk to any depth and fixed by little wedges where I would choose to have it stay, in order to make different depths of water, leaving the surface at the same height with regard to the sides of the trough. I had a little boat in form of a lighter or boat of burden, six inches long, two inches and a quarter wide, and one inch and a quarter deep. When swimming, it drew one inch water. To give motion to the boat I fixed one end of a long silk thread to its bow, just even with the water's edge, the other end passed over a well-made brass pulley, of about an inch diameter, turning freely on a small axis; and a shilling was the weight. Then placing the boat at one end of the trough, the weight would draw it through the water to the other." Not having a watch with a second hand, Franklin had to count while his boat was drawn along his canal, and he supposed there might be some "little inequalities in my counting." But he repeated his experiment several times, and found that the mean number of counts was 101 when the water was 1½ inches deep, 89 when it was two, and 79 when it was 4½. "They serve sufficiently to show that the difference is considerable. Between the deepest and shallowest it appears to be somewhat more than one-fifth. . . . Whether this difference is of consequence enough to justify a greater expense in deepening canals is a matter of calculation which our ingenious engineers in that way will readily determine."[38]

On 2 July Franklin wrote on several topics to John Winthrop of Harvard: the astronomical instruments that Winthrop had ordered from London; the plans being made to observe, from many parts of the earth, the transit of Venus the next year; the objections to lightning rods on churches; and the behaviour of the pulse-glass which Franklin had brought from Hanover. Later that summer, too busy for his annual journey, Franklin turned sharply but easily from physical science to phonetics and spelling reform.

There was then no science of phonetics for him to know. He was a printer and writer who had observed the disorderly confusion of English spelling. But instead of proposing surface changes he went straight to the first principles of the matter. The letters used in English did not match the sounds. Six of the letters, he thought, were unnecessary: *c, j, q, w, x, y.* In their places six others were needed: for the sounds of *a* as in *ball* or *o* as in *folly,* of *th* as in *think,* of *th* as in *thy,* of *sh* as in *ship,* of *ng* as in *repeating,* of *u* as in *unto.* The new letter for *sh* in combination with other letters could stand for *(d)j* or *(d)g* as in *James* or *gentle,* for *(t)ch* as in *cherry,* or for *(z)j* as in *jamais.* Each letter would always represent the same sound. There would be no superfluous letters used. Franklin, having designed the new letters he proposed, reformed his alphabet in a phonetic order which he had worked out himself, obviously, by noting the part played by throat, breath, tongue, teeth, and lips in the pronunciation of various sounds. He did not distinguish all the sounds in English or provide for them, and he left *A Scheme for a New Alphabet and Reformed Mode of Spelling*[39] unfinished. But his analysis was as fundamental, if not as detailed, as any that has been made since.

His alphabet was not published till 1779, in his *Political, Miscellaneous, and Philosophical Pieces.* He seems to have taken no interest in it after September 1768, when he showed or sent it to Polly Stevenson, received a letter in which she used it, and on the 28th answered her objections, writing with some slips in the new mode (here transcribed to the old for want of the new letters which he had designed). "The objection you make to rectifying our alphabet, 'that it will be attended with inconveniences and difficulties,' is a natural one; for it always occurs when any reformation is proposed, whether in religion, government, laws, and even down as low as roads and wheel carriages. The true question then is not whether there will be no difficulties or inconveniences but whether the conveniences will not, on the whole, be greater than the inconveniences. In this case, the difficulties are only in the beginning of the practice; when they are once overcome the advantages are lasting.

To either you or me, who spell well in the present mode, I imagine the difficulty of changing that mode for the new is not so great but that we might perfectly get over it in a week's writing. As to those who do not spell well, if the two difficulties are compared, viz., that of teaching them true spelling in the present mode and that of teaching them the new alphabet and the new spelling according to it, I am confident that the latter would be by far the least. They naturally fall into the new method already, as much as the imperfection of their alphabet will admit of; their present bad spelling is only bad because contrary to the present bad rules; under the new rules it would be good. The difficulty of learning to spell well in the old way is so great that few attain it, thousands and thousands writing on to old age without ever being able to acquire it. 'Tis, besides, a difficulty continually increasing, as the sound gradually varies more and more from the spelling; and to foreigners it makes the learning to pronounce our language, as written in our books, almost impossible."

Franklin could not agree with Polly that the new spelling by obscuring the etymologies of words would obscure their meaning. "Etymologies are at present very uncertain; but such as they are, the old books would still preserve them and etymologists would there find them. Words in the course of time change their meanings as well as their spelling and pronunciation; and we do not look to etymology for their present meanings. If I should call a man a knave and a villain he would hardly be satisfied with my telling him that one of the words originally signified only a lad or servant, and the other an under-ploughman or the inhabitant of a village. It is from present usage only the meaning of words is to be determined."

Nor did Franklin concede to Polly that the new alphabet would destroy "the distinction between words of different meaning and similar sound." "That distinction is already destroyed in pronouncing them; and we rely on the sense alone of the sentence to ascertain which of the several words similar in sound we intend. If this is sufficient in the rapidity of discourse it will be much more so in written sentences, which may be read leisurely and attended to more particularly in case of difficulty than we can attend to a past sentence while a speaker is hurrying us along with new ones.

"Your third objection is that 'all the books already written would be useless.' This inconvenience would only come on gradually, in a course of ages. You and I, and other now living readers, would hardly forget the use of them. People would long learn to read the old writing though they practised the new. And the inconvenience is not greater than what has actually happened in a similar case, in Italy. Formerly its inhabitants all spoke and wrote Latin; as the language changed the spelling followed it. It is true that at present a mere unlearned Italian cannot read the Latin books, though they are still read and understood by many. But if the spelling had never been changed he would now have found it much more difficult to read and write his own language; for written words would have had no relation to sounds, they would only have stood for things; so that if he would express in writing the idea he has when he sounds the word *vescovo* he must use the letters *episcopus*. In short, whatever the difficulties and inconveniences now are, they will be more easily surmounted now than hereafter; and some time or other it must be done, or our writing will become the same with the Chinese as to the difficulty of learning and using it. And it would already have been such if we had continued the Saxon spelling and writing used by our forefathers."

The bookish arguments of people who like to see traditional spelling because they have always seen it, Franklin did not bother to discuss. He philosophically viewed the language as a whole. Language was first speech, then writing. He knew enough about etymology and the history of language—perhaps from talks with James Parsons of the Honest Whigs—to understand that speech had moved faster than writing, and that in 1768 writing had become a drag on language, stiffening it to the printed usage of dictionaries. Children who knew their English by ear had to master by eye what was almost an ancient dialect so far as its spelling showed. Here, Franklin thought, were a great waste and a great unreason. Let speech prevail, since it was the true source and guide of language, and let writing adapt itself to speech. The conservative objections to the new alphabet were less weighty than the advantages of the new one. Sooner or later spelling would have to be simplified. It might as well be undertaken now. In matters of reason Franklin was likely to be a thoroughgoing revolutionary, and he was never more so than in his scheme for the reform of spelling, which concerned everybody.

When in January 1769 he was elected president of the American Philosophical Society he was publishing in England a "revised, methodized, and improved" fourth edition of his *Experiments and Observations on Electricity*, to which he added *Letters on Philosophical Subjects*. Here were his plain, penetrating notes, chiefly in letters to friends in America, England, and France, not only on electricity but also on population, smallpox, whirlwinds and waterspouts, geology, evaporation, salt mines, Scottish tunes and modern music, the origin of north-east storms in America, sound, tides in rivers, insects, the absorption of heat by different colours, the effect of oil on water, the pulse-glass. Some of the pieces had been written many years before, and some as recently as the letter of July 1768 from Winthrop, whose permission Franklin had not had time to ask. If he ranged widely in his subjects, he ranged no less widely in his friends: the physician to the queen, the governor of New York, an astronomer at Harvard, Franklin's brother Peter, and his young friend Polly Stevenson. The world was his field of knowledge and its inhabitants were his friends.

John Bartram had been appointed American botanist to the king, and Franklin sent him seeds that might grow in America. On 9 July 1769 he urged Bartram to digest and publish the observations he had made in his travels. "It is true, many people are fond of accounts of old buildings and monuments; but there is a number who would be much better pleased with such accounts as you could afford them. And, for one, I confess that if I could find in any Italian travels a receipt for making Parmesan cheese it would give me more satisfaction than a transcript of any inscription from any old stone whatever."[40] On 7 September Franklin wrote to Cadwallader Evans that he had sent him a treatise on the management of silkworms. "There is no doubt with me but that it might succeed in our country. It is the happiest of all inventions for clothing. Wool uses a good deal of land to produce it, which, if employed in raising corn, would afford much more subsistence for man than the mutton amounts to. Flax and hemp require good land, impoverish it, and at the same time permit it to produce no food at all. But mulberry trees may be planted in hedgerows on walks or avenues, or for shade near a house, where nothing else is wanted to grow. The food for the worms which produce the silk is in the air, and the ground under the trees may still produce grass or some other vegetable good for man or beast. Then the wear of silken garments continues so much longer, from the strength of the materials, as to give it greatly the preference. Hence it is that the most populous of countries, China, clothes its inhabitants with silk while it feeds them plentifully, and has besides a vast quantity both raw and manufactured to spare for exportation."[41] Anything might happen in America, and Americans go in silk for their common garments. Franklin hereafter followed the experiments at silk-growing in Pennsylvania with steady attention.

On 29 October he wrote to Anthony Todd of the British post office about the Gulf Stream, which Franklin seems to have studied before any other scientist. This first information he had received from his kinsman Timothy Folger of Nantucket, who told Franklin what the Nantucketer had learned about the current from hunting whales along the edge of it. Captain Folger had marked "the dimensions, course, and swiftness of the stream" on a chart which, with other written directions, Franklin sent to Todd to be used by the masters of the mail packets in shortening their voyages from England to America.[42] On 11 January 1770 he sent John Bartram "some of the true rhubarb seed."[43] The garden rhubarb known as pie-plant was common in America, but not the Chinese rhubarb used in medicine which Franklin was the first to introduce. He sent over what is believed to be the first kohlrabi (cabbage turnip) and Scotch cabbage seed to be grown west of the Atlantic.[44]

For the two years 1770–72 politics and economics almost wholly absorbed him, though he wrote letters on astronomy, the use of copper for roofs, the protection of houses from fire, silk culture in Pennsylvania, and spectacles for different eyesights. On 13 January 1772 he told Ezra Stiles, not yet president of Yale, of a new work published in Paris on Zoroaster. "I have cast my eyes over the religious part," said the critical philosopher; "it seems to contain a nice morality, mixed with abundance of prayers, ceremonies, and observances. . . . There is no doubt of its being a genuine translation of the books at present deemed sacred as the writings of Zoroaster by his followers; but perhaps some of them are of later date though ascribed to him; for to me there seems too great a quantity and variety of ceremonies and prayers to be directed at once by one man. In the Romish church they have increased gradually in a course of ages to their present bulk. Those who added new ones from time to time found it necessary to give them authority by pretences of their antiquity. The books of Moses, indeed, if all written by him, which some doubt, are an exception to this observation."[45]

That year the Board of Ordnance asked Franklin how the powder magazines at Purfleet might be protected from lightning. He visited them on 28 May and recommended lightning rods,[46] which by his advice had been erected on St. Paul's three years before.[47] The matter was taken to the Royal Society, which appointed a committee to investigate. Franklin, who was on the committee (with Henry Cavendish, William Watson, John Robertson, and Benjamin Wilson), drew up the report on 21 August and wrote a long paper in explanation.[48] Wilson, the electrician who had painted Franklin's portrait, dissented from the committee majority. They proposed pointed rods, which he thought would "solicit" the lightning and draw it into the magazines. Blunt rods would be better. Pointed rods were used, but Wilson published adverse, angry pamphlets. Franklin refused to answer them. The controversy had an incredible consequence. After the Revolution had begun the powder magazines were struck by lightning, though not damaged. George III at once sided with Wilson and ordered blunt conductors for the magazines and for his own palace, as if to spite the rebel Franklin. Because Pringle would not sustain the king in this prejudice he was forced to resign as president of the Royal Society and dismissed from his post as royal physician.

On 19 September Franklin wrote to Priestley, who could not quite make up his mind whether to become Shelburne's librarian. Such cases of indecision, Franklin said, "are difficult chiefly because while we have them under consideration all the reasons pro and con are not present to the mind at the same time; but sometimes one set present themselves and at other times another, the first being out of sight. . . . To get over this, my way is to divide half a sheet of paper by a line into two columns; writing over the one 'Pro' and over the other 'Con.' Then during three or four days' consideration I put down under the different heads short hints of the different motives that at different times occur to me for and against the measure. When I have thus got them all together in one view I endeavour to estimate their respective weights; and where I find two, one on each side, that seem equal I strike them both out. If I find a reason pro equal to some two reasons con, I strike out the three. If I judge some two reasons con equal to some three reasons pro I strike out the five; and thus proceeding I find at length where the balance lies . . . and come to a determination accordingly. And, though the weight of reasons cannot be taken with the precision of algebraic quantities, yet when each is thus considered separately and comparatively and the whole lies before me, I think I can judge better and am less liable to make a rash step; and in fact I have found great advantage from this kind of equation in what may be called moral or prudential algebra."[49]

By December Franklin was in active correspondence with Barbeu Dubourg, who had undertaken to translate the collected *Observations and Experiments* into French and who wanted new material for his edition. The book aimed to give the body of Franklin's philosophy, with letters to him as well as from him on the matters he discussed. Colonial politics, left out of the English collection, appeared in the letters of 1754 to Governor Shirley. *The Way to Wealth* was translated as *Le moyen de s'enrichir*, and Poor Richard became *le pauvre Henri* (to avoid the pun in *pauvre* and *richard*). Franklin's two remarkable letters on swimming[50] here reached the public first in French, and are known in English only as translated, along with his account of flies apparently drowned in wine but revived by the sun. "I wish it were possible, from this instance, to invent a method of embalming drowned persons in such a manner that they may be recalled to life at any period, however distant; for, having a very ardent desire to see and observe the state of America a hundred years hence, I should prefer to any ordinary death the being immersed in a cask of Madeira wine, with a few friends, till that time, to be then recalled to life by the solar warmth of my dear country."[51] In July 1773 Dubourg's two volumes— *Œuvres de M. Franklin*—were nearly printed, and on 1 September Franklin wrote about them to his wife. "To the French edition they have prefixed a print of me which, though a copy of that by

Chamberlain, has got so French a countenance that you would take me for one of that lively nation. I think you do not mind such things or I would send you one."[52]

Six years earlier Franklin had called the French, in a letter to his son, "that intriguing nation." With the two handsome French quartos of the summer of 1773 the philosopher took a great step towards being the legendary figure he was to become in France. Philadelphia, Dubourg explained in his preface, had been founded in the midst of the savages of America. But its founder was wiser than Lycurgus, and Philadelphia in less than a century had gone so far in the exercise of the purest virtues and the practice of the most useful arts that it would be hard to find in the ancient world anything comparable to these beginnings in the new. In all this Franklin had taken a great part: scientist, statesman, and sage. A hero who seemed to come from Plutarch had sprung up among the peaceful Quakers in America and now brought something of the heroic age to intricate, troubled Europe. And he came looking, to judge by his picture, like a Frenchman.

During that same year in England Franklin wrote to correspondents about seeds for Bartram, seeds sent from America to England, sun spots, magnetism, a new method of making carriage wheels, the consumption of smoke in stoves, toads living in stone (about which Franklin wondered), the electrocution of animals to be eaten, the making of better glass for use in electrical experiments, Cadwallader Colden's *Inquiry into the Principles of Vital Motion*, the proof that the electric ray (the torpedo) was actually electric, heating a church in Boston, the increasing use of lightning rods in England, France, and Tuscany, the census in China, his own proposal more than twenty years before for printing from copperplates on earthen-ware, the purifying of air by vegetation, the vegetable origin of coal.

Franklin's chief studies for the year were of the common cold and of the effect of oil on rough water. In June he made notes[53] for what would have been a long essay on colds, but had no time to write it out; "and my opinions on that head are so singular here," he told Dubourg on the 29th, "that I am almost afraid to hazard them abroad."[54] Though he could never, of course, have heard of germs, and though he used some expressions which have become obsolete, he guessed in his unsanitary century almost as much about colds as anybody now knows. "I hope," he wrote to Benjamin Rush on 14 July, "that after having discovered the benefit of fresh and cool air applied to the sick, people will begin to suspect that possibly it may do no harm to the well. . . . I have long been satisfied from observation that besides the general colds now termed influenzas (which may possibly spread by contagion as well as by a particular quality of the air) people often catch cold from one another when shut up together in close rooms, coaches, etc., and when sitting near and conversing so as to breathe in each other's transpiration; the disorder being in a certain state. I think, too, that it is the frowzy, corrupt air from animal substances and the perspired matter from our bodies which, being long confined in beds not lately used and clothes not lately worn and books long shut up in close rooms, obtains that kind of putridity which occasions the colds observed upon sleeping in, wearing, and turning over such bedclothes or books; and not their coldness or dampness. From these causes, but more from full living with too little exercise, proceed in my opinion most of the disorders which for about one hundred and fifty years past the English have called colds. . . . Travelling in our severe winters, I have suffered cold sometimes to an extremity only short of freezing, but this did not make me catch cold. And, for moisture, I have been in the river every evening two or three hours for a fortnight together, when one would suppose I might imbibe enough of it to take cold if humidity could give it; but no such effect ever followed."[55] The way to avoid colds was to eat and drink temperately, take enough exercise, and breathe as much fresh air as possible.

As to oil on water he wrote to William Brownrigg on 7 November: "I had, when a youth, read and smiled at Pliny's account of a practice among the seamen of his time, to still the waves in a storm by pouring oil in the sea. . . . I think . . . that it has been of late too much the mode to slight the learning of the ancients. The learned, too, are apt to slight too much the knowledge of the vulgar." Franklin had always taken knowledge where he found it. At sea in 1757, bound for London, he noticed that two of the ships left wakes which were smoother than the others. The captain supposed the cooks had emptied greasy water through the scuppers.

Franklin did not quite believe the explanation, but he remembered Pliny. Again at sea in 1762, on his way to America, he noticed the quietness of the oil on the agitated water in a hanging lamp he had devised.[56] A fellow-passenger told him that the Bermudians put oil on water to smooth it "when they would strike fish, which they could not see if the surface of the water was ruffled by the wind." Franklin heard of other uses, by fishermen and divers, of oil to make water smooth. "All these informations I at times revolved in my mind, and wondered to find no mention of them in our books of experimental philosophy.

"At length, being at Clapham, where there is on the common a large pond which I observed one day to be very rough with the wind, I fetched out a cruet of oil and dropped a little of it on the water. I saw it spread itself with surprising swiftness upon the surface; but the effect of smoothing the waves was not produced; for I had applied it first on the leeward side of the pond where the waves were largest, and the wind drove my oil back upon the shore. I then went to the windward side where they began to form; and there the oil, though not more than a teaspoonful, produced an instant calm over a space several yards square, which spread amazingly and extended itself gradually till it reached the lee side, making all that quarter of the pond, perhaps half an acre, as smooth as a looking-glass. After this I contrived to take with me, whenever I went into the country, a little oil in the upper hollow joint of my bamboo cane, with which I might repeat the experiment as opportunity should offer, and I found it constantly to succeed"— as at Shelburne's house.

How so little oil could spread so far over the water Franklin could not understand, and he could only conjecture that the water grew quiet because the wind could not catch it, with its smooth film of oil, and stir it into waves. "Therefore we might suppress the waves in any required place, if we could come at the windward place where they take their rise. This in the ocean can seldom if ever be done. . . . But discoursing lately [August 1773[57]] on this subject with his Excellency Count Bentinck of Holland, his son the Honourable Captain Bentinck, and the learned Professor Allemand (to all whom I showed the experiment of smoothing in a windy day the large piece of water at the head of the Green Park), a letter was mentioned which had been received by the count from Batavia, relative to the saving of a Dutch ship in a storm by pouring oil into the sea." Franklin had been reading the narrative— edited by his friend John Hawkesworth—of James Cook's recent voyage around the world, "particularly where accounts are given of pleasant and fertile islands which they much desired to land upon, when sickness made it more necessary, but could not effect a landing through a violent surf breaking on the shore." Might they not, Franklin suggested to Captain Bentinck, have poured oil into the sea and lessened the surf? Bentinck, then stationed at Portsmouth, offered to furnish men and boats for the experiment if Franklin would come and direct it.

About the middle of October Franklin went to Portsmouth. With him were three members of the Royal Society. Joseph Banks and Daniel Charles Solander had both sailed with Captain Cook on the *Endeavour*. Charles Blagden was a medical officer in the army. It is noteworthy that of these three, and Bentinck, the eldest was thirty years younger than Franklin, that ageless man with his ageless energy. "A day of wind happening, which made a lee-shore between Haslar hospital and the point near Jillkecker, we went from the *Centaur* with a longboat and barge towards that shore. Our disposition was this: the longboat was anchored about a quarter of a mile from the shore; part of the company were landed behind the point (a place more sheltered from the sea), who came round and placed themselves opposite to the longboat, where they might observe the surf and note if any change occurred in it upon using the oil. Another party, in the barge, plied to windward of the longboat, as far from her as she was from the shore, making trips of about half a mile each, pouring oil continually out of a large stone bottle, through a hole in the cork somewhat bigger than a goose-quill. The experiment had not, in the main point, the success we wished, for no material difference was observed in the height or force of the surf upon the shore; but those who were in the longboat [Franklin apparently among them] could observe a tract of smoothed water the whole of the distance in which the barge poured the oil, and gradually spreading in breadth towards the longboat. I call it smoothed; not that it was laid level but because, though the swell continued, its surface was not roughened by . . . wrinkles or smaller waves . . . and none or very few whitecaps (or waves whose tops turn over in foam) appeared in that whole space, though to windward and leeward of it there were plenty; and a wherry that came round the point under sail, in her way to Portsmouth, seemed to turn into that tract of choice and use it from end to end as a piece of turnpike road."

Franklin tried to explain their failure, for the benefit of future experimenters. "Waves once raised, whether by the wind or any other power, have the same mechanical operation by which they continue to rise and fall, as a pendulum will continue to swing a long time after the force ceases to act by which the motion was first produced; that motion will, however, cease in time; but time is necessary. Therefore, though oil spread on an agitated sea may weaken the push of the wind on those waves whose surfaces are covered with it, and so by receiving less fresh impulse they may gradually subside; yet a considerable time, or a distance through which they will take time to move, may be necessary to make the effect sensible on any shore in a diminution of the surf; for we know that, when wind ceases suddenly, the waves it has raised do not as suddenly subside but settle gradually and are not quite down till after the wind has ceased. So, though we should by oiling them take off the effect of wind on waves already raised, it is not to be expected that those waves should be instantly levelled. The motion they receive will for some time continue; and, if the shore is not far distant, they arrive there so soon that their effect upon it will not be visibly diminished. Possibly, therefore, if we had begun our operations at a greater distance the effect might have been more sensible. And perhaps we did not pour oil in sufficient quantity."[58]

Franklin's letter to Brownrigg was read before the Royal Society on 2 June 1774 and published in their *Transactions*. It reappeared in the *Journal des Sçavans* in Paris in November, and from that was translated into Dutch. In Manchester and Birmingham and Leyden the experiment was successful on small bodies of water. No one had Franklin's knack at the large experiments which could stir a general curiosity. He had found out how to tame the lightning. He might find out how to still the waves.

Scapegoat

THE serene elation in which Franklin wrote to his son in August 1772 could not last long. With his triumph over Hillsborough he had brought upon himself a ministerial animosity which, already stronger than he realized, was soon to be angry and open. Hillsborough had been North's friend, and North might partly blame on Franklin the loss of an ally in the cabinet. By the following July they were on the coolest terms when they met at Le Despencer's house. "Displeased with something [North] said relating to America," Franklin wrote to his son on the 14th, "I have never been at his levees, since the first. Perhaps he has taken that amiss. . . . He seemed studiously to avoid speaking to me. I ought to be ashamed to say that on such occasions I feel myself to be as proud as anybody. . . . We dined, supped, and breakfasted together without exchanging three sentences."[1]

But during the latter part of 1772 Franklin was still serene in his varied friendships, which ranged from the children of Bishop Shipley to one of the most notorious men in England: Lord Le Despencer, better known as Sir Francis Dashwood. Though the affairs of the post office had brought them together—Le Despencer had been postmaster-general since 1766—they do not appear to have been close friends before October 1772, when the philosopher spent sixteen days at the rake's house at Wycombe in Buckinghamshire. "I am in this house," Franklin told his son concerning a later visit, "as much at my ease as if it was my own; and the gardens are a paradise. But a pleasanter thing is the kind countenance, the facetious and very intelligent conversation of mine host, who, having been for many years engaged in public affairs, seen all parts of Europe, and kept the best company in the world, is himself the best existing."[2] That best company had included not only Thomas

Gray and Horace Walpole and Lady Mary Wortley Montagu and
the household of Frederick Prince of Wales, but also the scandalous and blasphemous Knights of St. Francis of Wycombe, the
so-called monks of Medmenham abbey, whom Dashwood had
gathered around him about 1745, which had been Franklin's
bawdy year in Philadelphia. Dashwood, immensely rich, had restored an old Cistercian abbey for meetings where he, Bute,
Sandwich, Charles Churchill, Paul Whitehead, and—for a time—
John Wilkes, with others, had devoted themselves, gossip more or
less credibly said, to nameless orgies and obscene parodies of religious rites. In 1762, fifty-four years old, Dashwood had entered
Parliament and been made chancellor of the exchequer through
the influence of Bute—who that year got William Franklin made
governor of New Jersey. The next year Dashwood had succeeded
to his father's title of Le Despencer. As premier baron of England,
he had settled down to respectability, and now made friends with
a philosopher.

Franklin enjoyed the seasoned old sinner, who enjoyed Franklin,
and they spent parts of three summers together at Wycombe. Le
Despencer, once a blasphemer, had recently undertaken a deistic
revision of the Prayer Book. Occupied with the Liturgy, he asked
Franklin to help him "by taking the rest of the book, viz., the
Catechism and the reading and singing Psalms. These," Franklin
later remembered, "I abridged by retaining of the Catechism only
the two questions: 'What is your duty to God?' 'What is your duty
to your neighbour?' with answers. The Psalms were contracted by
leaving out the repetitions (of which I found more than I could
have imagined), and the imprecations, which appeared not to suit
well the Christian doctrine of forgiveness of injuries and doing
good to enemies. The book was printed for Wilkie, in St. Paul's
Churchyard, but never much noticed. Some were given away, very
few sold, and I suppose the bulk became waste paper."[3] Published
as *Abridgment of the Book of Common Prayer* (1773), it had a
preface by Franklin, who economically suggested that shorter services would save the time of both congregations and ministers.

The single recorded episode of Franklin at Wycombe shows his
reputation as an American and a wit. His sly *Edict by the King of
Prussia* appeared in a newspaper in September 1773. Franklin "was

down at Lord Le Despencer's when the post brought that day's papers. Mr. Whitehead was there too (Paul Whitehead, the author of *Manners*), who runs early through all the papers and tells the company what he finds remarkable. He had them in another room, and we were chatting in the breakfast parlour, when he came running in to us, out of breath, with the paper in his hand. 'Here,' says he, 'here's news for ye. Here's the king of Prussia claiming a right to this kingdom.' All stared, and I as much as anybody; and he went on to read it. When he had read two or three paragraphs a gentleman present said: 'Damn his impudence, I dare say we shall hear by next post that he is upon his march with one hundred thousand men to back this.' Whitehead, who is very shrewd, soon after began to smoke [see through] it, and, looking in my face, said: 'I'll be hanged if this is not some of your American jokes upon us.' The reading went on and ended with abundance of laughing, and a general verdict that it was a fair hit; and the piece was cut out of the paper and preserved in my lord's collection."[4]

It was possibly at Le Despencer's that Franklin played what may have been another American joke on the company. John Adams, who had the story from Franklin himself, told it long afterwards, giving the date only as "before his return to America in 1775" and the place "I believe at Lord Spencer's."[5] The conversation, whenever and wherever it was, turned to Æsop, La Fontaine, and Gay. One of the men present said he thought that all the imaginable beast fables had been written. Franklin said the subject was inexhaustible. Challenged to furnish a new fable, he promptly wrote out one about the eagle and the cat, which has till lately been known only in Adams's version. If, as is likely, this happened at Le Despencer's, not Spencer's, and during Franklin's final years in England, it was a hoax when Franklin pretended to improvise his fable. For he had already written it and two others and published them anonymously in the *Public Advertiser* for 2 January 1770, where they have remained unknown to his editors.

The fable had originally been curter than Adams remembered it. "An eagle, king of birds, sailing on his wings aloft over a farmer's yard, saw a cat there basking in the sun, mistook it for a rabbit, stooped, seized it, and carried it up into the air, intending to prey on it. The cat, turning, set her claws into the eagle's breast;

who, finding his mistake, opened his talons and would have let her drop; but Puss, unwilling to fall so far, held faster; and the eagle, to get rid of this inconvenience, found it necessary to set her down where he took her up." With this fable had been another somewhat similar, of the mastiff and the growing lion whelp, and a third about the cows and the farmer. "A herd of cows had long afforded plenty of milk, butter, and cheese to an avaricious farmer, who grudged them the grass they subsisted on, and at length mowed it to take money of the hay, leaving them to shift as they could, and yet still expected to milk them as before; but the cows, offended with his unreasonableness, resolved for the future to suckle one another."[6] All three of these fables, as the company at Spencer's or Le Despencer's saw in the one they heard, were pointed warnings to England not to make mistakes about America.

II

The feelings of the ministry towards Franklin were both irritation and boredom. It was irritation enough to have to hear now and then from the remote Americans, steadily and ingeniously resisting every effort to bring them profitably into the Empire and tax them, and invariably raising the cry of tyranny and slavery. The ministers did not think of themselves as tyrants nor did they design to make slaves of the Americans. They simply wanted the Americans to help support the Empire. When the Americans still objected to the methods of raising the money the ministers still saw in this no more than an objection to paying anything at all. What were those provincial legislatures that the Americans should set such store by them? What were the rights of man they could never stop clamouring about? The ministers did not understand either the political sentiments of the Americans or their political language, only their boycotts and their mobs. These were rebellion against Parliament, which the ministers were sure ought to be paramount throughout the Empire no less than in the realm. Mildness could go only so far. Sooner or later, if the Americans persisted, they would have to be compelled. How difficult it would be to compel them, so far away and so numerous, the ministers seem not to have reckoned. But they could think of force more easily than of reasons for reducing the conflict to its first principles and then ending it by the concession of local self-government. After all, such a thing had never been granted to any colony in history, and the king and his ministers were not the men to invent it out of prophetic wisdom.

Irritating as it was for unphilosophical British politicians to listen to distant Americans who, it must have seemed, could find philosophical excuses even for riots, it was still more irritating to have an American philosopher almost at court, almost an ambassador. There might be temporary quiet overseas, but there was never any relief from Franklin. Touch American interests at any point, and he was instantly aware and active. Close to the opposition, he was close also to manufacturers, merchants, and tradesmen, to men of learning, and through his writings to the public. His long stay in England had not changed him except to make him even more firmly an American. Realistic in his arguments, he was not afraid of large principles, without which he believed there could be no political realism. By his own prestige he gave prestige to America, which had to be answered because he had to be. In a sense, his arguments were too good. That is, conservative and stubborn officials resented having to feel that, though their actions gave them the last word, his arguments had been better than their answers. Instinctively they held him to be somehow responsible for all America, and instinctively focused on him their animosities. The resignation of Hillsborough had been forced by his own colleagues in the Privy Council, but some of the ministers suspected Franklin's crafty hand. This was a disturbing power for an American to have. Irritated and bored by Franklin and his Americans, the ministers wished they could get rid of him, and by 1772 had instinctively begun to wait for a chance to do it.

Franklin was not long in giving them an excuse. He had hoped, when Dartmouth succeeded Hillsborough in August 1772, that the new minister for America would deal more wisely with the colonies. Dartmouth was in the country till the end of October, when he returned to London "and had his first levee on Wednesday, at which I attended," Franklin wrote to his son on 3 November. "He received me very politely in his room, only Secretary Pownall present, expressing some regret that he happened to be from home when I was near him in the country, where he had hoped for the pleasure of seeing me, etc. I said I was happy to see his lordship in his present situation, in which for the good of both countries I hoped he would long continue; and I begged leave to recommend my son to his protection, 'who,' says I, 'is one of your governors in America.' The secretary [Pownall] then put in: 'And a very good governor he is.' 'Yes,' says my lord, 'he has been a good governor, and has kept his province in good order during times of difficulty.' I then said that I came at present only to pay my respects, and should wait on his lordship another day on business; to which he said he should always be ready to hear me and glad to see me. I shall attend his levee again today, on some New England affairs, and hope we may now go on more smoothly; but time will show."[7]

What time showed was that Dartmouth, however friendly, was willing or able to go no great distance to meet the Americans. Franklin brought up his New England business, which was another petition to the king from the Massachusetts Assembly. They knew it was an innovation and thought it a grievance that their new governor, Thomas Hutchinson, received his salary from the Crown, not the Assembly, and so was free to disregard their wishes. "A few days after my leaving your petition with Lord Dartmouth," the agent reported to Thomas Cushing on 2 December, "his lordship sent for me to discourse upon it. After a long audience he was pleased to say that, notwithstanding all I had said or that could be said in support of the petition, he was sure that presenting it at this time could not possibly produce any good." The king and Parliament would be offended and would reprimand the Assembly. "Minds had been heated and irritated on both sides the water, but he hoped those heats were now cooling, and he was averse to the addition of fresh fuel." He would present the petition if Franklin as agent insisted, but he wished the Assembly might reconsider it.

"I answered that the great majority with which the petition and the resolves on which it was founded were carried through the House made it scarce expectable that their order would be countermanded; that the slighting, evading, or refusing to receive petitions from the colonies, on some late occasions by the Parliament, had occasioned a total loss of the respect for and confidence in that body formerly subsisting so strongly in America, and brought on a questioning of their authority; that his lordship might observe petitions came no more from thence to Parliament but to the king only; that the king appeared now to be the only connexion between the two countries; and that, as a continued union was essentially necessary to the well-being of the whole Empire, I should be sorry to see that link weakened, as the other had been; that I thought it a dangerous thing for any government to refuse receiving petitions and thereby prevent the subjects from giving vent to their griefs."[8]

Dartmouth said that he asked for delay only out of "pure good will to the province." Franklin, reflecting that the petition had been drawn while Hillsborough was minister, concluded that it might be better not to embarrass Dartmouth so early in his administration. For the Assembly to reconsider would do no harm, and in the meantime both sides might become more reasonable. Then, in the same letter to Cushing, Franklin made the move which his enemies in England were waiting for. Here began the famous affair of the Hutchinson letters.

"On this occasion I think fit to acquaint you," he went on, "that there has lately fallen into my hands part of a correspondence that I have reason to believe laid the foundation of most if not all our present grievances. I am not at liberty to tell through what channel I received it; and I have engaged that it shall not be printed, nor copies taken of the whole or any part of it; but I am allowed to let it be seen by some men of worth in the province, for their satisfaction only. In confidence of your preserving inviolably my engagement, I send you enclosed the original letters, to obviate every pretence of unfairness in copying, interpolation, or omission. The hands of the gentlemen will be well known. Possibly they may not like such an exposal of their conduct, however tenderly and privately it may be managed. But if they are good men, or pretend to be such, and agree that all good men wish a good understanding and harmony to subsist between the colonies and their mother country, they ought the less to regret that, at the small expense of their reputation for sincerity and public spirit among their compatriots, so desirable an event may in some degree be forwarded. For my own part, I cannot but acknowledge that my resentment against this country for its arbitrary measures in governing us, conducted by the late minister, has, since my conviction by these papers that those measures were projected, advised, and called for by men of character among ourselves, and whose advice must therefore be attended with all the weight that was proper to mislead and which could therefore scarce fail of misleading; my own resentment, I say, has by this means been exceedingly abated. I think they must have the same effect with you; but I am not, as I have said, at liberty to make the letters public. I can only allow them to be seen by yourself, by the other gentlemen of the Committee of Correspondence, by Messrs. Bowdoin and [James] Pitts of the Council, and Drs. [Charles] Chauncy, Cooper, and Winthrop, with a few other such gentlemen as you may think fit to show them to. After being some months in your possession you are requested to return them to me."⁹

Franklin was not one of those little conspirators for whom secrecy is a delectable science. He kept nothing secret about the transaction except the name of the man who had got hold of the letters, and consequently the means that had been used. These were the other man's secrets. As much as Franklin was free to tell he told frankly. In conversation, he later said, with "a gentleman of character and distinction," he had been assured that the sending of troops to Boston and "all the other grievances we complained of, took their rise not from government here but were projected, proposed to administration, solicited, and obtained by some of the most respectable among the Americans themselves, as necessary for the welfare of that country. As I could not readily assent to the probability of this, he undertook to convince me and, he hoped, through me (as their agent here) my countrymen. Accordingly he called on me some days after and produced to me these very letters."¹⁰ Franklin found that six of them were from Thomas Hutchinson, written in 1768–69 before he became governor, and four from Andrew Oliver, written in 1767–69 before he became lieutenant-governor. Hutchinson had at that time been chief justice and lieutenant-governor, and Oliver secretary of the province: certainly "some of the most respectable among the Americans."

The letters said little that both men were not known to believe. They were Boston officials who, while natives of Massachusetts, disliked and distrusted the popular party. Their houses had been wrecked or destroyed by senseless mobs during the Stamp Act agitation. It was not to be wondered at that Hutchinson thought, as he said in one of his letters, "there must be an abridgment of what are called English liberties"; or that Oliver suggested the officers of the Crown should be made "in some measure independent" of the Assembly; or that the two agreed on the need of a firm hand—even of armed forces—to keep the colony in order. But these letters made it clear, as Samuel Adams had suspected of Hutchinson, that influential Americans had been, directly or indirectly, in secret correspondence with British ministers. To Franklin, shocked by the discovery, this seemed a kind of treason to New England and a betrayal of the best interests of the whole Empire.

There is no reason to doubt that Franklin thought the letters might lessen Boston's resentment against the mother country as they had lessened his. They had been put into his hands to convince him that the ministry had been misguided rather than oppressive. Let Boston know the truth, and the embittered town, laying the blame where it belonged, might be patient again in the hope of a better understanding with London. Nor was Franklin alone in thinking this. Besides the man who brought him the letters there were two others in England who knew about them, and aimed at reconciliation with America. The English were of two parties in the controversy, as the Americans were. If there were Americans, like Hutchinson and Oliver, who urged a stricter British rule over the colonies, there were Englishmen who favoured an increase of colonial self-government. So long as the conflict could be made to seem a difference of opinions, on both sides of the Atlantic, there was the prospect that reason might keep the peace.

Franklin accepted the stipulation that the letters were on no account to be published in Boston, for fear they might, if generally read, "occasion some riot of mischievous consequence. I had no other scruple in sending them, for as they had been handed about here to prejudice that people, why not to them for their advantage? . . . To whom they were directed here I could only conjecture; for I was not informed, and there was no address upon them when I received them."[11] But he must have supposed, as he later knew, that they had been written to Thomas Whately, who had held office under both Grenville and North and who had died the past June. Franklin explicitly says that the letters were not among the papers which fell to Whately's executor,[12] and that they had been "shown about here to several persons"[13] before they were brought to Craven Street. Whately had been out of office, with Grenville, when the letters were written, but he was a member of Parliament and intimate with Grenville and the opposition. The letters, Franklin considered, though called private by the writers of them, "were not of the nature of private letters between friends. They were written by public officers to persons in public stations, on public affairs, and intended to procure public measures; they were therefore handed to other public persons who might be influenced by them to produce those measures."[14] "Mr. Grenville, who was the centre to which flowed all the correspondence inimical to America, to whomsoever directed, had these letters put into his hands, lent them to another, and, dying before they were returned, gave an opportunity for their falling into ours."[15] "Had not a person died in whose hands they were, probably we should not soon have seen them."[16] The course of the letters seems clear. Written to Whately in 1767–69, they had reached Grenville in time for him to lend them before his death in 1770. They had not been returned to Whately, who died two years later. Still a third man had had them when he also died. And there is no telling how many public men had read them. They might be secret, but they were hardly private.

Franklin knew, too, that his own correspondence with his son and with the Massachusetts Assembly had been intercepted and read. Within six months after he heard he had been appointed agent he wrote to Thomas Cushing, on 10 June 1771: "The letters I have received from my friends in Boston have lately come to hand badly sealed, with no distinct impression, appearing as if they had been opened, and in a very bungling way closed again." He thought it might have been done by a prying person in the coffee house to which they were addressed, but he suggested that letters from Boston might be sent "under cover to some merchant of character who would forward them to me more safely."[17] On the day Franklin sent the Hutchinson-Oliver letters to Cushing, he wrote to his son that he suspected their letters were being opened not by the post office but by somebody close to Hillsborough. "When a packet arrives [from America], a special messenger goes directly from the office with the public letters before the sorting is finished. Mine has been sometimes sent by the same messenger, who called on me in his way to Lord H.'s, sometimes in his return." Possibly the messenger had been obliging to William Knox, now under-secretary of state for America, who had opposed the repeal of the Stamp Act and been dismissed as agent for Georgia in favour of Franklin. Since Hillsborough's resignation Franklin thought the correspondence had not been tampered with. The post office had no right to open letters without an order from a secretary of state, and that order was not likely to have been given. "It is seldom used but in times of war, rebellion, or on some great public occasion."[18] This was not, Franklin assumed, anything of the kind.

III

The letters went off on their long voyage, and Franklin for months knew nothing of the enormous trouble they were to cause. He still put his faith in peaceful, legal resistance on the part of America. "Our great security lies, I think," he wrote to Cushing on 5 January 1773, "in our growing strength both in numbers and wealth; that creates an increasing ability of assisting this nation in its wars, which will make us more respectable, our friendship more valued and enmity feared; thence it will soon be thought proper to treat us not with justice only but with kindness, and thence we may expect in a few years a total change of measures with regard to us; unless, by a neglect of military discipline, we should lose all martial spirit, and our western people become as tame as those in the eastern [Asiatic] dominions of Britain, when we may expect the same oppressions; for there is much truth in the Italian saying: 'Make yourselves sheep, and the wolves will eat you.' In confidence of this coming change in our favour, I think our prudence is meanwhile to be quiet, only holding up our rights and claims on all occasions in resolutions, memorials, and remonstrances; but bearing patiently the little present notice that is taken of them. They will all have their weight in time, and that time is at no great distance."[19] And again on 9 March: "In the meantime I must hope that great care will be taken to keep our people quiet; since nothing is more wished for by our enemies than that by insurrections we should give a good pretence for increasing the military among us and putting us under more severe restraints."[20]

From the ministry Franklin expected little. "We govern from hand to mouth," he wrote to his son on 6 April. "There seems to be no wise regular plan."[21] Almost any ministry but North's, with the king behind them, might have seen that if the Americans kept on resisting the tax on tea there must be something wrong with the tax in principle. As it was, the ministers and their master saw only that smuggling had not been stopped and that tea was being shipped to America by French, Dutch, and Danish merchants. The East India Company had so much unsold tea in its London warehouses that its credit suffered and the price of its stock had fallen by January 1773 from 280 to 160. The ministry made a bargain with the Company whereby it was to have a monopoly of the colonial tea business. By a new act passed in April no duties were to be charged in England, and the tea could be sold in America at a lower price than ever. But it was still to bear the tax to which the Americans objected. The ministry was determined, Franklin wrote to Cushing on 4 June, "to keep up the exercise of the right. They have no idea that any people can act from any other principle than that of interest; and they believe that threepence in a pound of tea, of which one does not perhaps drink ten in a year, is sufficient to overcome all the patriotism of an American."[22]

Franklin on 5 May had a conversation with Dartmouth. Though the Hutchinson letters had reached Boston, the news of their reception had not yet come to England, and Dartmouth was troubled with nothing worse than the debates between the governor and the Assembly over the rights of the colonists. The Assembly had strongly declared its legislative independence of Parliament, and Hutchinson had reported the declaration in his dispatches. Dartmouth was embarrassed. He wanted to keep matters quiet. If he laid the dispatches before Parliament, Parliament might take some angry step that would make matters worse. If he delayed, the administration might later be charged with neglect.

" 'What can now be done?' " Dartmouth asked Franklin. " 'It is impossible that Parliament can suffer such a declaration . . . to pass unnoticed.' 'In my opinion,' says I, 'it would be better and more prudent to take no notice of it. It is words only. Acts of Parliament are still submitted to there. No force is used to obstruct their execution. And while that is the case, Parliament would do well to turn a deaf ear and seem not to know that such declarations had ever been made. Violent measures against the province will not change the opinion of the people. Force could do no good.' 'I do not know,' says he, 'that force would be thought of; but perhaps an act may pass to lay them under some inconveniences till they rescind that declaration.' " Franklin thought such an act unwise. " 'It is likely that it will only put them as heretofore upon inventing some method of injuring this country till the act is repealed; and so we shall go on injuring and provoking each other instead of cultivating that good will and harmony so necessary to the general welfare.' "

Dartmouth was " 'sensible our divisions must weaken the whole; for we are yet one Empire,' says he, 'whatever may be the sentiments of the Massachusetts Assembly.' " But he thought he could not avoid bringing the dispatches before Parliament. " 'What,' his lordship was pleased to say, 'if you were in my place, would or could you do?' . . . I said his lordship could best judge what in his situation was fittest for him to do; I could only give my poor opinion, with regard to Parliament, that, supposing the dispatches laid before them, they would act most prudently in ordering them to lie on the table, and take no farther notice of them. For were I as much an Englishman as I am an American, and ever so desirous of establishing the authority of Parliament, I protest to your lordship I cannot conceive of a single step the Parliament can take to increase it that will not tend to diminish it; and after abundance of mischief they must finally lose it. The loss in itself perhaps would not be of much consequence, because it is an authority they can never well exercise for want of due information and knowledge, and therefore it is not worth hazarding the mischief to preserve it.' "[23]

These were the words of a peacemaker not conspirator. But the Hutchinson letters were already in Boston. Seen at first by a few, they came to be talked about by so many that Samuel Adams in June read them to the Assembly, in secret session. In spite of Franklin's stipulation the letters had been copied, and with slippery reasons were printed. The Assembly petitioned the king to remove Hutchinson and Oliver from office.

Only three persons in London and three in Boston seem to have known that Franklin had sent the letters. When he heard that they had been made public he did not complain to Cushing. Cushing wanted it kept a secret that they had been sent to him. Franklin wrote him on 25 July: "I did not accompany them with any request of myself being concealed; for, believing what I did to be in the way of my duty as agent, though I had no doubt of its giving offence not only to the parties exposed but to administration here, I was regardless of the consequences. However, since the letters themselves are now copied and printed, contrary to the promise I made, I am glad my name has not been heard on the occasion; and, as I do not see it could be of any use to the public, I wish it may continue unknown, though I hardly expect it. As to yours, you may rely on my never mentioning it, except that I may be obliged to show your letter in my own vindication to the person only who might otherwise think he had reason to blame me for breach of engagement." He thought it impossible that the Crown would leave Hutchinson and Oliver in their posts: "it can never be for its interest to employ servants who are under such universal odium." On the same day Franklin wrote to John Winthrop against violence. "I trust the general prudence of our countrymen will see that by our growing strength we advance fast to a situation in which our claims must be allowed; that by a premature struggle we may be crippled and kept down another age; that as between friends every affront is not worth a duel, between nations every injury not worth a war, so between the governed and the governing every mistake in government, every encroachment on rights, is not worth a rebellion."[24]

Hutchinson in Boston believed that Franklin was "the great director" of the Massachusetts radicals. But Franklin's letters to America in that critical July were so moderate and pacific that the radicals themselves suspected him of being "too much of an Englishman." He insisted that the ministry did not represent the

British people. "The friends of liberty here," he wrote to Cushing on the 7th, "wish we may long preserve it on our side the water, that they may find it there if adverse events should destroy it here. They are therefore anxious and afraid lest we should hazard it by premature attempts in its favour. . . . With regard to the sentiments of people in general here, concerning America, I must say that we have among them many friends and well-wishers. The dissenters are all for us, and many of the merchants and manufacturers. There seems to be, even among the country gentlemen, a general sense of our growing importance, a disapprobation of the harsh measures with which we have been treated, and a wish that some means may be found of perfect reconciliation. A few members of Parliament in both houses, and perhaps some in high office, have in a degree the same idea; but none of these seem willing as yet to be active in our favour, lest adversaries should take advantage and charge it upon them as betraying the interests of this nation." There was no chance of any sudden change in the feelings or the policy of Britain. The colonists must still bear "a little with the infirmities of her government, as we would with those of an aged parent."[25]

But in that same month Franklin for the first time, in a letter to his son on the 14th, showed that he had come to look behind the ministry for an explanation of its American policies. "Between you and I, the late measures have been, I suspect, very much the king's own, and he has in some cases a great share of what his friends call firmness. Yet, by some painstaking and proper management, the wrong impressions he has received may be removed, which is perhaps the only chance America has for obtaining soon the redress she aims at."[26] These mild words, which said as much as it was safe to say in a letter which might be read by some officer of the Crown, meant more than appeared in them. For Franklin, who had long contended that the colonies were bound to the Empire only through the king, was now admitting that the king himself was a partisan, not a dispassionate ruler over all his people. And on 24 August Franklin wrote to Cushing that "some great persons about the court"[27] did not think the Hutchinson letters gave any ground for removing the governor. The governor had done nothing that the king and his ministers did not approve.

In September, when most of the royal ministers were still out of town, Franklin wrote for the *Public Advertiser* the two most stinging satires of all his years in England. *Rules by Which a Great Empire May Be Reduced to a Small One*[28] carried on Franklin's feud with Hillsborough, to whom it was fictitiously said to have been presented when he took office, for the use of all ministers. "You are to consider," Franklin said with a belittling homeliness in his first rule, "that a great empire, like a great cake, is most easily diminished at the edges." Begin with the remotest provinces, and then get rid of nearer ones. Be sure, of course, to see that the provinces are never incorporated with the mother country: "like a wise gingerbread baker, who, to facilitate a division, cuts his dough half through in those places where, when baked, he would have it broken to pieces."

Rule by rule, Franklin went through the steps the ministry had taken, he insinuated, in American affairs to estrange America. Forget that the colonies were founded at their own expense. Resent it that they have become important to the Empire and expect some consideration from the imperial government. "Suppose them always inclined to revolt, and treat them accordingly. . . . By this means, like the husband who uses his wife ill from suspicion, you may in time convert your suspicions into realities." Choose inferior, rapacious, and pettifogging men for governors and judges in the provinces. Support them against all complaints from the governed. Reward them for having governed badly, when at last they have to resign or be recalled. When you want money from the colonies, "despise . . . their voluntary grants, and resolve to harass them with novel taxes." If they petition for redress, scorn their petitions. "Nothing can have a better effect in producing the alienation proposed; for though many can forgive injuries, none ever forgave contempt." Disregard the wealth which the mother country draws from the colonies, and not only tax them but publicly declare "that your power of taxing them has no limits; so that when you take from them without their consent one shilling in the pound you have a clear right to the other nineteen." Deprive them of their constitutional liberties, such as the right of habeas corpus or trial by jury or freedom from seizure of property without warrant. Send "indiscreet, ill-bred, and insolent" officials to collect the unpopular revenues. Use the revenues to pay salaries or pensions "to every governor who has distinguished himself by his enmity to the people and by calumniating them to their sovereign." If the provincial parliaments claim any rights, dissolve them or adjourn their meetings to some inconvenient place.

"XV. Convert the brave, honest officers of your navy into pimping tide-waiters and colony officers of the customs. Let those who in time of war fought gallantly in defence of their countrymen, in peace be taught to prey upon it. Let them learn to be corrupted by great and real smugglers; but (to show their diligence) scour with armed boats every bay, harbour, river, creek, cove, or nook throughout the coast of your colonies; stop and detain every coaster, every wood-boat, every fisherman; tumble their cargoes and even their ballast inside out and upside down; and, if a penn'orth of pins is found unentered, let the whole be seized and confiscated. Thus shall the trade of your colonists suffer more from their friends in time of peace than it did from their enemies in war. Then let these boats' crews land upon every farm in their way, rob the orchards, steal the pigs and the poultry, and insult the inhabitants. If the injured and exasperated farmers, unable to procure other justice, should attack the aggressors, drub them, and burn their boats, you are to call this high treason and rebellion, order fleets and armies into their country, and threaten to carry all the offenders three thousand miles to be hanged, drawn, and quartered. Oh, this will work admirably!"

Never believe that the discontents of the colonies are general or in any way justified. Listen to all the governors say, to nothing you hear from the friends of the people. Think nothing of it if rival nations rejoice "at the prospect of your disunion with your provinces." You are aiming at that yourself. Do not hesitate, if any colony has built a fortress for defence from foreign enemies [such as Castle William at Boston] to "turn it into a citadel to awe the inhabitants and curb their commerce." "Send armies into their country under pretence of protecting the inhabitants; but, instead of garrisoning the forts on their frontiers with those troops to prevent incursions, demolish those forts and order the troops into the heart of the country, that the savages may be encouraged to attack the frontiers, and that the troops may be protected by the inhabitants."

"XX. Lastly, invest the general of your army in the provinces with great and unconstitutional powers, and free him from the control of even your own civil governors. Let him have troops enow under his command, with all the fortresses in his possession; and who knows but (like some provincial generals in the Roman empire, and encouraged by the universal discontent you have produced) he may take it into his head to set up for himself? If he should, and you have carefully practised these few excellent rules of mine, take my word for it, all the provinces will immediately join him; and you will that day (if you have not done it sooner) get rid of the trouble of governing them and all the plagues attending their commerce and connexion from henceforth and for ever. Q. E. D."

Here was the boldest tone Franklin had ever taken in public, and all the bolder because his hard arguments were edged with insulting irony. He talked back to the ministers, from whom he had borne too much. Hillsborough had shown contempt for him; "and none ever forgave contempt." Franklin, for all his imperturbability, was proud. In the draft scheme of his *Autobiography* he made only one note on "My character: Costs me nothing to be civil to inferiors; a good deal to be submissive to superiors."[29] Now from the ministers he turned his satire still higher, and wrote *An Edict by the King of Prussia* [Frederick the Great],[30] a parody of the English king's claim to arbitrary rule over America.

The edict, circumstantial hoax, proclaimed that Britain had been settled by colonists from Germany, had never been emancipated, and had hitherto yielded little revenue to "our august house." "And whereas we ourself have in the last war fought for and defended the said colonies against the power of France, and thereby enabled them to make conquests from the said power in America, for which we have not yet received adequate compensation; And whereas it is just and expedient that a revenue should be raised from the said colonies in Britain, towards our indemnification; and that those who are descendants of our ancient subjects, and thence still owe us obedience, should contribute to the replenishing of our royal coffers as they must have done had their ancestors remained in the territories now to us appertaining: We do hereby ordain and command"—that duties be laid on all goods exported from Britain or imported into it, and that all ships to and from Britain "touch at our port of Koningsberg, there to be unladen, searched, and charged with the said duties."

No iron might be manufactured in Britain, and no hats, though the raw materials might be sent to Prussia, there manufactured, and returned; "the people thus favoured to pay all costs and charges of manufacturing, interest, commission to our merchants, insurance, and freight going and returning." "We do not, however, think fit to extend this indulgence to the article of wool; but, meaning to encourage not only the manufacturing of woollen cloth but also the raising of wool in our ancient dominions, and to prevent both as much as may be in our said island, we do hereby absolutely forbid the transportation of wool from thence, even to the mother country, Prussia"; and no wool raised in any British county, or goods made of wool, might be carried by any means from one county to another. "Nevertheless, our loving subjects there are hereby permitted (if they think proper) to use all their wool as manure for the improvement of their lands."

"And lastly, being willing farther to favour our said colonies in Britain, we do hereby also ordain and command that all the thieves, highway and street robbers, housebreakers, forgers, murderers, s–d——tes, and villains of every denomination, who have forfeited their lives to the law in Prussia but whom we in our great clemency do not think fit here to hang, shall be emptied out of our gaols into the said island of Great Britain, for the better peopling of that country." (Here Franklin returned to the subject of his earliest satire against England: his proposal in 1751 to exchange American rattle-snakes for British convicts.) The king of Prussia was sure that his English colonists would not object to these "just and reasonable" regulations. They were copied from their own statutes—he cited them—"and from other equitable laws made by their parliaments; or from instructions given by their princes; or from resolutions of both Houses, entered into for the good government of their own colonies in Ireland and America."

"Such papers," Franklin wrote to his son on 3 November, "may seem to have a tendency to increase our divisions; but I intend a contrary effect, and hope that by comprising in a little room and setting in a strong light the grievances of the colonies, more attention will be paid to them by our administration; and that, when their unreasonableness is generally seen, some of them will be removed, to the restoration of harmony between us."[31] Franklin himself preferred the *Rules* to the *Edict*, but at first the *Edict* was more popular. "My clerk went the next morning to the printer's and wherever they were sold. They were all gone but two. . . . I have heard [it] spoken of in the highest terms, as the keenest and severest piece that has appeared here for a long time. Lord Mansfield, I hear, said of it that it was very able and very artful indeed; and would do mischief by giving here a bad impression of the measures of government; and in the colonies, by encouraging them in their contumacy."[32] Like the retired rakes at Le Despencer's house, many people were at first taken in, and then, when they saw through the American joke, laughed at it. The *Rules* kept on being read. It was copied in other papers, including Strahan's *Chronicle* and the *Gentleman's Magazine*, and "reprinted some weeks after" in the *Advertiser*, "the printer giving for reason that he did it in compliance with the earnest request of many private persons and some respectable societies."[33] Franklin felt justified in his bold language, and wrote to Cushing on 1 November that "the general sense of the nation is for us; a conviction prevailing that we have been ill used and that a breach with us would be ruinous to this country."[34]

IV

Franklin's efforts to make men reasonable by satirizing them had no more effect than his attempt, that October, to quiet the troubled water off Spithead by pouring oil on it. The ministry were once more irritated by seeing the Americans put patriotically in the best light and the British government satirically in the worst. In July Franklin had thought he would return to America in September. In October he decided to stay in England that winter, to watch events. November was almost quiet, with Parliament adjourned to January, and Dartmouth and other ministers staying late in the country. Then in December things happened, simultaneously in Boston and London, which turned out to mean the end of peace between the two countries and of Franklin's work in England.

If Parliament was short-sighted in giving to the East India Company a monopoly of the colonial tea trade, it was blind in allowing the Company to be its own exporter in England and its own importer in America. The merchants, British and American, who had been used to handling tea between the countries, were excluded from a business which had been large in spite of the partial boycott. The American merchants, conservative towards talk about English liberties and natural rights, were sensitive enough to a blow at their own interests, and they joined the political radicals in opposition to the monopoly. Although the Company's tea, when it came, was rejected at every American port, it was most dramatically rejected in Boston. There, where Hutchinson was at the height of his unpopularity because of his letters to England, the tea was to be distributed, for the Company, by two of his sons and a nephew. Here seemed to be new evidence that Hutchinson was the head of a little family oligarchy, looking out for itself at the expense of the public. (Oliver was Hutchinson's brother-in-law, and Hutchinson's daughter was married to another Oliver.) The patriots, the merchants, and the mob demanded that the tea agents resign their offices and return the tea, which reached Boston early in December. The agents took refuge in Castle William, protected by cannon. The people would not allow the three tea ships to land their cargo. The governor would not sign a permit for the ships to leave, and he set two war vessels to keep them from escaping. Noisy meetings were held, led chiefly by Samuel Adams, the most fervent of the patriots. After the largest gathering, on 16 December, had learned that the governor would not yield, something like two thousand men, from Boston and neighbouring towns, resorted to direct action. They stood by at the wharf and approvingly watched a smaller group of them, disguised as Indians, throw the tea into the harbour.

Franklin, when he heard of the Boston Tea Party, thought it "an act of violent injustice"[35] for which Boston should make voluntary and speedy reparation. The news came at a time when the worst of his troubles in England was just ready to break over him.

During the early days of December the affair of the Hutchinson letters produced a London scandal. William Whately, brother and executor of the Whately to whom they had been written, had been accused by gossip, as early as September, of having allowed the letters to become public. Whately, a banker, denied that he was at fault. He remembered that in October 1772, shortly before the letters were sent to America, John Temple, an officer in the customs, known to Franklin since they crossed the Atlantic together in 1757, had asked to see letters which he himself had written from America to Thomas Whately, and with the executor's permission had taken some of them away with him. Temple replied that the offending letters had not been among those he looked over, and that he had taken none but his own and his brother's. Whately and Temple carried their argument to the newspapers.[36] Temple challenged Whately, and they fought a bungling duel in Hyde Park on 11 December, with pistols and swords. Whately was wounded. Both remained angrily dissatisfied.

In this controversy the name of Franklin was not mentioned. He himself said nothing at first, because he had promised Cushing he would not tell that the letters had been sent to him, and could not reveal his own secret without at the same time revealing Cushing's. "I suffered that altercation to go on without interfering, supposing it would end, as other newspaper debates usually do, when the parties and the public should be tired of them." Franklin was out of town when the duel took place and did not know about it till later. "Imagining all now over between them, I still kept silence till I heard that the duel was understood to be unfinished, as having been interrupted by persons accidentally near, and that it would probably be repeated as soon as Mr. Whately, who was mending daily, had recovered his strength. I then thought it high time to interpose. And as the quarrel was for the public opinion, I took what I thought was the shortest way to settle that opinion." On Christmas Day he issued a statement in the *Public Advertiser* saying that both men were "totally ignorant and innocent" of the whole transaction. "I alone am the person who obtained and transmitted to Boston the letters in question. Mr. W. could not communicate them, because they were never in his possession; and, for the same reason, they could not be taken from him by Mr. T."[37]

On 5 January Franklin wrote to his son that he had admitted sending the letters, in which "our friend Temple . . . had no concern. . . . This has drawn some censure upon myself, but as I grow old I grow less concerned about censure when I am satisfied I act rightly; and I have the pleasure of having exculpated a friend who lay undeservedly under an imputation much to his dishonour."[38] That same day Franklin wrote also to Cushing, saying that he had acted to "rescue Mr. Temple's character from an undeserved and groundless imputation. . . . I did this with the more pleasure, as I believe him a sincere friend of our country. I am told by some that it was imprudent in me to avow the obtaining and sending those letters, for that administration will resent it. I have not much apprehension of this, but if it happens I must take the consequences."[39]

Franklin, who took the consequences because he took the responsibility, never divulged the secret history of the episode, which has always been a mystery. Nor is the mystery made much less by Temple's later assertions. Temple, born in America, married to a daughter of James Bowdoin, had as commissioner of customs in Boston sided with the popular party against Governor Bernard, and had been dismissed. Going to England for redress, he had won the favour of his kinsman Earl Temple and of Earl Temple's younger brother George Grenville, and had been made surveyor-general of the customs in England. When he was accused by Whately and the newspapers of having had something to do with the Hutchinson letters, he insistently denied it, and Franklin supported him. But Temple was dismissed from his post by Lord North, who declined to give any reason. Suspected and watched by the government, Temple stayed on in England till 1778, when he was at last able to return with his family to Boston. There he told the men who had received and handled the letters that he had been Franklin's confidant and was surprised to find that Franklin had said nothing to them about it. In Holland in 1781 Temple told John Adams.[40] On 26 July Temple wrote from Holland to Franklin, at Passy, insisting on his share of credit for the affair.

"You know we were dismissed from our several employments under the Crown of England at one and the same time and for one and the same cause." If the promise of secrecy had not been violated in Boston, Temple pointed out, he would not have lost a post worth £1000 a year. He had told the Bostonians that: "I had been privy to the whole transaction; that it was through my means that you were able to obtain them; that they were obtained in an honourable way; but, to save an innocent person whose bread depended on the ministry and who would have been suspected, the most positive injunction from you, at my request, accompanied those letters." As he had suffered from the breaking of the pledge, he hoped Franklin would furnish him a testimonial to take to America.

Franklin received this letter, and kept it among his papers, but there exists no answer from him. Temple was back in Boston the following October, still asking to be compensated for his loss. On 1 September 1782 he wrote to the president of the Senate and the speaker of the House, in Massachusetts, rehearsing his good deeds and his misfortunes, and saying: "Dr. Franklin acquainted me with every step he took in that memorable transaction. He showed me every line he wrote and every line written to him upon the occasion; and commented upon the contents of one of the letters written to him palliating the violation of his injunction, with more asperity than I ever before knew him to discover." (Samuel Cooper mentioned Temple's claim to Franklin, who received the letter.[41]) Massachusetts did not compensate Temple, and after the peace he got a different reward from the British government, which made him consul-general at New York. With his salary, his wife's share of the Bowdoin fortune, and the baronetcy which he inherited in 1792, he seems to have been content.[42]

It is hard to believe that Temple, if he had not done what he said he had, would have dared so openly to claim it while Franklin was still alive and could so easily contradict him. But it is also hard to understand why Franklin never bothered—so far as is known—to say a word about Temple's claim. The simplest explanation probably is that Temple did have a hand in obtaining the letters, and was at least one of the three men who knew they were being sent to Boston; but that, having tried to avoid his share of the blame, he later found it difficult to get his share of the credit. He could not win by betting both ways. When in 1778 he was ready to claim credit, in the hope that he might profit by it, he was known by the Americans to be an office-seeker and suspected of being a British secret agent. (As he was—with the promise of a baronetcy and a pension if he could help bring about a peace with the Americans on terms which he, privately devoted to their cause, thought favourable to them.[43]) By the time Franklin came back from France to America, and might have testified, Temple was a British official who could not want it known that he had ever had anything to do with the affair. Franklin kept the mysterious secret.

Whatever the facts were in January 1774, and whatever wary agreements were made among the four men in London who knew the truth, Franklin took the whole responsibility, and the ministry turned on him their full anger. The attack was sudden. On the 5th Franklin had "not much apprehension." On the afternoon of the 8th, which was Saturday, he was notified that the Lords Committee of His Majesty's Privy Council for Plantation Affairs would hear the petition of the Massachusetts Assembly for the removal of Hutchinson and Oliver on the following Tuesday. The petition had been delivered to Dartmouth in August, and the king by 3 December had asked that it be laid before the Privy Council. Franklin sent first for Arthur Lee, who was associated with him as agent for the Assembly. Lee was at Bath. Then Franklin called on William Bollan, an English solicitor who was agent for the Massachusetts Council. Bollan advised against employing legal aid in support of the petition. "He had sometimes done it in colony cases, and found lawyers of little service. Those who are eminent, and hope to rise in their profession, are unwilling to offend the court; and its disposition on this occasion was well known. But he would move to be heard in behalf of the Council of the province, and thence take occasion to support the petition itself."[44] Late in the afternoon of Monday the 10th Franklin received notice that Israel Mauduit, agent for the governor and the lieutenant-governor, had asked and been given leave to be heard by counsel. This short notice, Franklin thought, was meant to put him at a disadvantage.

The next day, at the Cockpit where the hearing was held, more lords than usual were present, and Alexander Wedderburn, the solicitor-general, appeared for Hutchinson and Oliver.

After the petition had been read, Franklin was asked what he had to offer in support of it. He said that Bollan would speak. The Committee refused to hear Bollan because he represented the Massachusetts Council, not the Assembly from which the petition had come. The ministry's business was with Franklin. Franklin said he would lay before them the resolutions of the Assembly and a copy of the letters on which the resolutions were founded. The resolutions were read. But when the letters were taken up, Wedderburn intervened.

"*Mr. Wedderburn*. The address [petition] mentions 'certain papers.' I would wish to be informed what are those papers.

"*Dr. Franklin*. They are the letters of Mr. Hutchinson and Mr. Oliver.

"*Court*. Have you brought them?

"*Dr. Franklin*. No; but here are attested copies.

"*Court*. Do you not mean to found a charge upon them? If you do, you must produce the letters.

"*Dr. Franklin*. These copies are attested by several gentlemen at Boston, and a notary public.

"*Mr. Wedderburn*. My lords, we shall not take advantage of any imperfection in the proof. We admit that the letters are Mr. Hutchinson's and Mr. Oliver's handwriting; reserving to ourselves the right of inquiring how they were obtained.

"*Dr. Franklin*. I did not expect that counsel would have been employed on this occasion.

"*Court*. Had you not notice sent you of Mr. Mauduit's having petitioned to be heard by counsel on behalf of the governor and lieutenant-governor?

"*Dr. Franklin*. I did receive such notice; but I thought that this had been a matter of politics and not of law, and I have not brought any counsel.

"*Court*. Where a charge is brought, the parties have a right to be heard by counsel or not, as they choose.

"*Mr. Mauduit*. My lords, I am not a native of that country, as these gentlemen are. I know well Dr. Franklin's abilities, and wish to put the defence of my friends more upon a parity with the attack. He will not therefore wonder that I choose to appear before your lordships with the assistance of counsel. . . .

"*Court.* Dr. Franklin may have the assistance of counsel, or go on without it, as he shall choose.

"*Dr. Franklin.* I desire to have counsel.

"*Court.* What time shall you want?

"*Dr. Franklin.* Three weeks."[45]

This is the record of the first hearing as published by Mauduit for the ministry. Franklin's account, written to Cushing on 15 February, adds a few details. When Wedderburn reserved the right to inquire how the letters were obtained, " 'Certainly,' replied Lord Chief Justice De Grey, somewhat austerely, 'and to whom they were directed; for the perfect understanding of the passages may depend on that and other such circumstances. We can receive no charge against a man founded on letters directed to nobody, and perhaps received by nobody. The laws of this country have no such practice.' Lord President [Gower], near whom I stood as I was putting up my papers, asked me if I intended to answer such questions. In that, I said, I shall take counsel."[46] The day appointed for the hearing was 29 January.

"A report now prevailed through the town that I had been grossly abused by the solicitor-general at the Council board. But this was premature. He had only intended it and mentioned that intention. I heard, too, from all quarters, that the ministry and the courtiers were highly enraged against me for transmitting those letters. I was called an incendiary, and the papers were filled with invectives against me. Hints were given me that there was some thoughts of apprehending me, seizing my papers, and sending me to Newgate. I was well informed that a resolution was taken to deprive me of my place; it was only thought best to defer it till after the hearing; I suppose because I was there to be so blackened that nobody should think it injustice. Many knew, too, how the petition was to be treated; and I was told, even before its first hearing, that it was to be rejected with some epithets, the Assembly to be censured, and some honour done the governors. How this could be known one cannot say. It might be only conjecture."[47]

Bollan changed his mind and urged Franklin to employ counsel.

He retained John Dunning, formerly solicitor-general, and John Lee, afterwards to be. Dunning assured Franklin that he "was not and could not be obliged" to answer questions as to how he had obtained the letters, "being under a promise." But both Dunning and Lee thought nothing was to be gained by arguing that passages in the letters supported the charges made in the Assembly's resolutions and petition. "The counsel observed we wanted evidence to prove those passages false; the counsel on the other side would say they were true representations of the state of the country; and, as to the political reflections of the writers and their sentiments of government, their aims to extend and enforce the power of Parliament and diminish the privileges of their countrymen, though these might appear in the letters and need no other proof, yet they would never be considered here as offences, but as virtues and merits." It would be more advisable to state as facts that the people of Massachusetts were discontented and the governors odious: "facts of which the petition was itself full proof, because otherwise it could not have existed; and then show that it must in such a situation be necessary for His Majesty's service, as well as the peace of the province, to remove them."[48]

No preparations could be made against Wedderburn's expected attack on Franklin, since he admitted having obtained the letters and refused to tell how. He would have to endure whatever Wedderburn might say. That the solicitor-general had been chosen to defend the governors was evidence of what the ministers wanted done. He was the government's master of abuse. He had left the Scottish bar at twenty-four because the judges of the Court of Session asked him to apologize to the president, seventy-two, whom he had insulted in open court. In his Edinburgh days he had been intimate with men of letters and had defended Hume against church censure. In England Wedderburn had taken pains to cure himself of his native accent, made friends with Bute, and within four years become a Tory member of Parliament. Eight years more, and he had deserted his party to join in the popular defence of John Wilkes. Promptly given a Whig borough by Lord Clive, Wedderburn had opposed the North ministry with such virulence that in two years he had to be bought off. North had made him solicitor-general. There was no change in the ministerial policy, but Wedderburn, once in office, supported it with a canny zeal that made him duly baron, lord chancellor, and earl. It does not appear that he had had any dealings with Franklin before 1774, except possibly in the matter of the Ohio company. The company was still pressing the royal lawyers for a favourable opinion, and Wedderburn was strongly against the grant. Franklin told Shelburne that Wedderburn felt a "personal animosity." Wedderburn said he felt only a deep attachment to the memory of Thomas Whately.[49] Personal motives need not be particularly suspected. Wedderburn would do what he had talents for. The ministry saw they had the most dangerous American bull tied to the stake, and they called on the most ferocious British dog.

Naturally the petition was to be rejected. The king and the majority of his ministers—Lord North less than the others— thought the government had been too mild too long. Crediting the reports of their own governor rather than those of a colony agent, they believed that the unrest in Massachusetts was traceable to a few wrangling agitators and a lawless mob. Men of substance did not hold those opinions or tolerate those actions, which were mere democracy and a menace to civil order. The accused governors must be sustained, with further force if necessary. It was not they who had disturbed the harmony between the two countries, but the rhetorical legislators. Look at the furor raised by the Hutchinson-Oliver correspondence. The passages which had given offence in Boston seemed to the ministers in London to be soundly reasoned. There could be no yielding to such wrong-headed petitioners. The ministers were angry as well as stubborn. The ringleader of the tumults was close at hand. Franklin had got hold of the letters and sent them across the Atlantic. Here at last was a chance to punish him for his persistence and excellence in the long, irritating dispute. Here was a chance to get rid of him, and perhaps of the trouble with America. The best charge to bring was that he had made a public use of private letters. No minister thought such an act seriously objectionable when he did it himself. All the ministers did it or knew it was done by the government. Franklin's letters had been opened and read. Dartmouth had received some of them, obtained in Boston and sent to London. But Franklin had been found out, through his own acknowledgment, and the ministers need wait no longer. They could make a resounding moral issue of the episode and at the same time accuse him of any other crimes that Wedderburn could think of.

Busy with plans for the 29th, Franklin was surprised by a sub-pœna ordering him to appear at once in a suit in chancery brought against him by William Whately as administrator of his brother's estate. The bill alleged that Franklin, having obtained letters which belonged to the estate, had, "carrying on the trade of a printer," through "his agents or confederates printed and published the same letters in America and disposed of great numbers" and now "threatened to print the same in England"; that Whately had asked Franklin to return the letters, stop printing and publishing them, and account to the administrator for the profits already made; and that Franklin had refused. All these allegations were entirely false except that Franklin had obtained the letters. In chancery practice the plaintiff was not put upon oath, but the defendant must swear to the truth of his answer. Whately, praying the lord chancellor to require Franklin to tell how he came by the letters as well as what number he had sold, seemed to be trying to get at the secret. Franklin was mystified. Though he had barely known Whately, he had helped him establish his title to some land—worth £5000—which his grandfather had long ago bought in Pennsylvania without leaving a clear record of it; and Franklin had put himself in jeopardy to prevent Whately's second duel with Temple. There appeared to be no good reason why Whately, however perturbed he might be over the use of the letters to his brother, should bring a suit based upon lies.

Strahan, calling one day in Craven Street, furnished what might be an explanation. He was on his way home from the treasury, where he had been given "what he styled a pretty thing" to take to a friend of his. "It was an order for £150 payable to Dr. Johnson, said to be one-half of his yearly pension, and drawn by the secretary of the treasury on this same Mr. Whately."[50] Franklin, having discovered that Whately was a banker to the government for the pension money, made a guess—which was no more than a guess— that Whately had brought his suit as a roundabout service to the ministers. The great men in office, it appeared to Franklin, were so angry that they were capable of this nagging stratagem.

The many lords who had gone to the Cockpit on the 11th to hear Wedderburn abuse Franklin might some of them have been cooler by the 29th, if a day or so before the second hearing the news had not come to London that Boston had destroyed the tea.

V

Edmund Burke, who was agent for New York and friend to other colonies, came early to the anteroom of the Privy Council chamber with Priestley, whom he had met in the street. The anteroom was already filled, but the orator, holding the preacher by the arm, made his imperious way to the inner door, and they were the first to enter when it was opened to the public. The Committee was seated at a long table, with Gower as president at the head. There were no chairs for the spectators. Burke took his place behind the first chair next the president's, Priestley behind the chair next to that. North himself, who arrived late, stood behind the chair opposite Priestley. The parties to the hearing and the rest of the spectators packed the chamber. "All the courtiers were invited, as to an entertainment, and there never was such an appearance of privy councillors on any occasion, not less than thirty-five [actually thirty-six], besides an immense crowd of other auditors."[51] Lord Camden, who knew what was planned, refused to come.

Of the privy councillors, the archbishop of Canterbury and the bishop of London were there, and the Duke of Queensberry. The eight earls present included Dartmouth, who for a year and a half had had Franklin on his hands; Hillsborough, who thought he had lost his place in the cabinet on account of Franklin; Rochford, who, hoping to make a fortune in Franklin's Ohio company, had joined with Gower in forcing Hillsborough's resignation; and Sandwich, Franklin's superior and enemy in the post office. Among the nine other peers at the table, only Le Despencer was clearly a friend to Franklin. General Conway and Thomas Townshend were in the opposition to North, but most of the remaining councillors were the king's friends. Charles Jenkinson was the leader of their party, and Sir Jeffery Amherst was a soldier of the king.

Wedderburn and Mauduit appeared for the Massachusetts governors, Bollan for the Council, and Franklin for the Assembly through Dunning and John Lee. Arthur Lee of Virginia, already chosen to succeed Franklin in the Massachusetts agency, had come; Ralph Izard of South Carolina, who had carried Temple's challenge to Whately; and Edward Bancroft of Massachusetts, not yet the double-dealer of the Revolution. Franklin stood at the left of the fireplace which was at one end of the room, facing the lords at the table. Somewhere among the spectators were Lord Shelburne and the young Jeremy Bentham, who both admired the American philosopher.

"The hearing began," Franklin wrote, "by reading my letter to Lord Dartmouth enclosing the petition, then the petition itself, the resolves, and lastly the letters, the solicitor-general making no objections nor asking any of the questions he had talked of at the preceding board. Our counsel then opened the matter, upon their general plan, and acquitted themselves very handsomely; only Mr. Dunning, having a disorder on his lungs that weakened his voice exceedingly, was not so perfectly heard as one could have wished."[52] This was not, Dunning explained, a suit at law, and not an impeachment. There was no evidence to offer except the resolutions and the petition of the Assembly, which were proof of the discontents in the province. The Assembly appealed to the king's wisdom and goodness, and asked, as a favour, that the governors be removed, to quiet the present unrest and restore the ancient peace and unity.

Wedderburn, standing between the chairs of two of the privy councillors at the right of the president, so close to the table that he could pound on it, defended the governors by attacking first the Assembly and then Franklin. The question, he said, which had brought so many lords and so large an audience to the hearing was "of no less magnitude than whether the Crown shall ever have it in its power to employ a faithful and steady servant in the administration of a colony." The history of Hutchinson's and Oliver's past ten years in colonial affairs, which Wedderburn related, showed no misconduct. The Assembly merely "disliked" the men. It was the misconduct of the Assembly which had brought the armed forces from England, not the appeal of the governors.

Wedderburn rightly pointed out that the decision to send troops had been made in London before the appeal came. The letters, he wrongly declared, had caused the first and only objection ever made to the Crown's servants. "They owe therefore all the ill will which has been raised against them, and the loss of that confidence which the Assembly themselves acknowledge they had heretofore enjoyed, to Dr. Franklin's good offices in sending back these letters to Boston. Dr. Franklin therefore stands in the light of the first mover and prime conductor of the whole contrivance against His Majesty's two governors; and, having by the help of his own special confidants and party leaders first made the Assembly his agents in carrying on his own secret designs, he now appears before your lordships to give the finishing stroke to the work of his own hands."

How Franklin had obtained the letters was still a mystery. Wedderburn said that he had lived for years in the strictest intimacy with Thomas Whately, who was always very careful with his papers. "These letters I believe were in his custody at the time of his death. And I as firmly believe that without fraud they could not have been got out of the custody of the person whose hands they fell into."[53] (So Wedderburn was quoted by Mauduit, who published a ministerial version of the speech. But as Franklin's friends remembered it, the solicitor-general had said: "Nothing then will acquit Dr. Franklin of the charge of obtaining them by fraudulent or corrupt means, for the most malignant of purposes; unless he stole them from the person who stole them. This argument is irrefragable." And then or later Wedderburn was remembered to have said: "I hope, my lords, you will mark and brand this man, for the honour of this country, of Europe, and of mankind. . . . He has forfeited all the respect of societies and of men. Into what companies will he hereafter go with an unembarrassed face or the honest intrepidity of virtue? Men will watch him with a jealous eye; they will hide their papers from him and lock up their escritoires. He will henceforth esteem it a libel to be called a man of letters: *homo trium literarum*"[54]—that is, *fur*, or thief, as in an epithet from Plautus.[55])

"Wherein had my late worthy friend or his family offended Dr. Franklin, that he should first do so great an injury to the memory of the dead brother by secreting and sending away his letters, and then, conscious of what he had done, should keep himself concealed till he had nearly, very nearly occasioned the murder of the other?" Wedderburn read the letter in which Franklin, on Christmas Day, had taken full responsibility upon himself to clear William Whately and Temple: "a letter," Wedderburn said, "which it is impossible to read without horror; expressive of the coolest and most deliberate malevolence." Wedderburn cited a villain in Edward Young's tragedy *Revenge* who had boasted:

> I forged the letters; I disposed the picture;
> I hated, I despised, and I destroy.

"My lords, what poetic fiction only had penned for the heart of a cruel African, Dr. Franklin has realized and transcribed from his own."[56] (Again according to Mauduit. Franklin's friends remembered: "Here is a man who, with the utmost insensibility of remorse, stands up and avows himself the author of all. . . . I ask, my lords, whether the revengeful temper attributed, by poetic fiction only, to the bloody African is not surpassed by the coolness and apathy of the wily American?"[57])

Nothing could be more sacred, Wedderburn went on, than "the private letters of friendship." He picked out the three or four sentences in the Hutchinson-Oliver letters that had any personal bearing, and grieved over the crime of making them public. "Other receivers of goods dishonourably come by may plead as a pretence for keeping them that they don't know who are the proprietors. In this case, there was not the common excuse of ignorance. The Doctor knew whose they were, and yet did not restore them to the right owner. This property is as sacred and as precious to gentlemen of integrity as their family plate or jewels are. . . . Can then a man in a public station have no private friends and write no private letters? Will Dr. Franklin avow the principle that he has a right to make all private letters of your lordships his own and apply them to such uses as will best answer the purposes of party malevolence?"

Franklin's own letters to Boston were of course not private. Wedderburn apparently knew about some of them, through the watchful care of the government. Franklin had, in fact, when he sent over the governors' letters, named five men besides Cushing to whom they might be shown. They had been sent, Wedderburn told the lords, to a junto of six persons: "If the Doctor choose it, I will name the six." But the solicitor-general said that Franklin's accompanying letter was anonymous, which it was not, and did not say that Franklin had given Cushing leave to increase the number of readers if he saw fit. The guilt must be centred in Franklin. The "innocent, well-meaning farmers which comprise the bulk of the Assembly" had been duped by "the arts of these leaders" who were Franklin's tools. Franklin was not so much "an agent for the Assembly's purposes" as "a first mover and prime conductor of it for his own . . . the actor and secret spring . . . the inventor and first planner of the whole contrivance." Wedderburn had begun to repeat his epithets.

"With a whole province set in flame . . . with all this weight of suspicion and with all this train of mischiefs before his eyes, Dr. Franklin's apathy sets him quite at ease, and he would have us think that he has done nothing more than what any other colony agent would have done." Wedderburn knew several colony agents and he had gone to them with a moral question. "My lords, they received the proposal with horror. One of them said it was profaning the word duty to apply it to such a purpose; another, that if he had been their agent he would sooner have cut off his right hand than have done such a thing."

Franklin was so far from being an honourable colony agent that he had perhaps forgotten he was an agent at all. "My lords, Dr. Franklin's mind may have been so possessed with the idea of a Great American Republic that he may easily slide into the language of the minister of a foreign independent state." A foreign ambassador might "bribe a villain to steal or betray any state papers; he is under the command of another state and is not amenable to the laws of the country where he resides; and the secure exemption from punishment may induce a laxer morality. But Dr. Franklin, whatever he may teach the people at Boston, while he is here, at least, is a subject; and if a subject injure a subject he is answerable to the law." The court of chancery before which Franklin had been summoned in Whately's suit would "not much attend to his new self-created importance."

"My lords, the rank in which Dr. Franklin appears is not even that of a province agent; he moves in a very inferior orbit." He was agent only for the Assembly. Thundering and thumping the table, Wedderburn half undid his accusation that the Assembly were the tools and dupes of Franklin. "The party by whom the Assembly is now directed did not want a man who should think himself bound in duty to consult for the peace and harmony of the whole government; they had their own private, separate views, and they wanted an agent of their own, who should be a willing instrument and instructor in accomplishing their own separate purpose." Franklin, who was the instrument of the Assembly who were his instruments, was ambitious. For his own purposes he had made it his duty "to furnish materials for dissensions; to set at variance the different branches of the legislature; and to irritate and incense the minds of the king's subjects against the king's governor." He and "his constituents" had been able to bring about the removal of one governor (Bernard) and now aimed at the removal of another. "They wish to erect themselves into a tyranny greater than the Roman." The motive behind all this was Franklin's design to become governor himself. "Nothing surely but a too eager attention to an ambition of this sort could have betrayed a wise man into such conduct as we have now seen. . . . I hope that Mr. Hutchinson will not meet with the less countenance from your lordships from his rival's being his accuser. Nor will your lordships, I trust, advise the having Mr. Hutchinson displaced in order to make room for Dr. Franklin as a successor."

As to the petition asking for the removal of the governors because their letters had upset the province, it was unfounded and absurd. "Was it," Wedderburn inquired with a deft confusion of the order of events, "to confute or prevent the pernicious effect of the letters that the good men of Boston have lately held their meetings, appointed their committees, and with their usual moderation destroyed the cargo of three British ships? If an English consul in any part of France or Spain, or rather Algiers or Tripoli (for European powers respect the law of nations), had not called this an outrage on his country he would have deserved punishment. But if a governor at Boston should presume to whisper to a friend that he thinks it somewhat more than a moderate exertion of

English liberty to destroy the ships of England, to attack her officers, to plunder their goods, to pull down their houses, or even to burn the king's ships of war, he ought to be removed; because such a conduct in him 'has a natural and efficacious tendency to interrupt the harmony between Great Britain and the colony' [inexactly quoted from the petition] which these good subjects are striving by such means to establish."

The governors against whom the petition had been brought were merciful. "They are convinced that the people, though misled, are innocent." The conduct of their leaders might "provoke a just indignation," but the governors would be the first to urge that these men might be excused and not punished. The governors "love the soil, the constitution, the people of New England; they look with reverence to this country and with affection to that. For the sake of the people they wish some faults corrected, anarchy abolished, and government re-established. But these salutary ends they wish to promote by the gentlest means and the abridging of no liberties which a people can possibly use to its own advantage. A restraint from self-destruction is the only restraint they desire to be imposed upon New England." On this benevolent note Wedderburn ended.

For nearly an hour Franklin, who had just passed his sixty-eighth birthday, stood, in his old-fashioned full-bottomed wig and his suit of figured Manchester velvet, without the slightest change of expression in this wind of abuse, under all the curious, exulting eyes of that hostile room. Not all those who heard were hostile. Burke thought Wedderburn's attack "beyond all bounds and measure."[58] Shelburne called it in a letter to Chatham, "as is agreed on all hands . . . scurrilous invective."[59] Bentham was stunned.[60] Priestley was so outraged that when, afterwards in the anteroom, Wedderburn came forward to speak to him, he turned away and hurried out of the place.[61] Ralph Izard knew that if he had been so insulted he would have struck back, whatever the consequences. Bollan wrote that Wedderburn's reproaches seemed to him "incompatible with the principles of law, truth, justice, propriety, and humanity."[62] North was grave and quiet throughout the tirade, and so, it must be supposed, were Le Despencer, Conway, and Townshend. But, as Franklin told Cushing, "not one of their lordships checked and recalled the orator to the business before them, but on the contrary, a very few excepted, they seemed to enjoy highly the entertainment, and frequently broke out in loud applauses."[63] Resentments had been long accumulating in the members of the Privy Council. They honestly believed that Massachusetts had no sensible grievances, and that all the trouble had been caused by a few mischief-makers. Now, they were ready and pleased to be told, the plotters had been brought to light, and with them the "prime conductor"—a clever hit at the electrician who had meddled with politics, which were for lords and gentlemen. The old philosopher had been caught at his tricks. He was fair game, and it was good sport to stand by while the lively Wedderburn barked and bit at him.

For Franklin there was only one course if he was to get any victory out of the occasion. He would not be allowed to interrupt, and he could not afford to risk replying to a speaker more dexterous and unscrupulous than he. To keep silent before that hostile audience would be to seem, temporarily, to admit his guilt. But to hold out without word or sign through all the bawling lawyer could say would make Franklin seem, in the long run, to have been the strong man of the two. Silence like that would be taken for both contempt for Wedderburn, which it was, and magnanimity, which it was no less. If Franklin, exposed to this lightning of abuse, had made the most far-sighted calculations, he could not have chosen a shrewder behaviour. He did not have to choose. In emergencies men behave, not according to what they later reflect would have been wise, but according to their characters at the time. Franklin already had the instinct to be patient under stress, the habit of magnanimity, and the schooled knowledge of the world which made him realize that the longer Wedderburn went on the sooner his words would come to be held against him, as so much injustice and inhumanity. Yet it was the heaviest strain on Franklin to stay perfectly quiet. Anger, which he had once called "that momentary madness," runs almost irresistibly along the nerves of the wisest man at sufficient provocation. Again and again it must have flared up in Franklin, close to the surface, raging for relief.

He knew he had no right to complain if he were accused of

getting the letters dishonourably. He had laid himself open to that by keeping the method secret. But the charge that he was a thief in general, and had vengefully conspired against the Whately brothers, was unsupported by anything in the record. If he had done William Whately a civil wrong, the Privy Council was not the place to try him. The matter was already before the court of chancery, where Wedderburn had had most of his practice. That the charges against Franklin in relation to Massachusetts were insolently distorted, Wedderburn knew or had a chance to know. The ministry had read enough of Franklin's letters to Boston to be aware that he had always urged temperate measures and insisted on the complete unwisdom of any violence whatever. And of course it was rancorous nonsense to say that Franklin had set himself up for an ambassador from the Great American Republic or that he had schemed to be governor of Massachusetts. Worst of all, Wedderburn in what was to be his defence of the governors had shown what was the Privy Council's scorn for the petition, which was after all the true concern of this hearing, and a thing at least as close to Franklin as his own reputation before that body.

"It may be supposed," he wrote to Cushing on 15 February, "that I am very angry on this occasion. . . . But indeed what I feel on my own account is half lost in what I feel for the public. When I see that all petitions and complaints of grievances are so odious to government that even the mere pipe which conveys them becomes obnoxious, I am at a loss to know how peace and union are to be maintained or restored between the different parts of the Empire. Grievances cannot be redressed unless they are known; and they cannot be known but through complaints and petitions. If these are deemed affronts, and the messengers punished as offenders, who will henceforth send petitions? And who will deliver them? It has been thought a dangerous thing in any state to stop up the vent of griefs. Wise governments have therefore generally received petitions with some indulgence, even when but slightly founded. Those who think themselves injured by their rulers are sometimes by a mild and prudent answer convinced of their error. But where complaining is a crime, hope becomes despair."[64]

With anger for himself, despair for America, Franklin heard

Wedderburn to the end, with a shrewdness which was wisdom, a wisdom which was drama. Wedderburn said he was ready to examine Franklin. Through Dunning as counsel he declined to be examined. The Committee—whether before or after the spectators left the room is not clear—voted at once to report to the Privy Council that the petition "is founded upon resolutions formed upon false and erroneous allegations; and that the same is groundless, vexatious, and scandalous; and calculated only for the seditious purposes of keeping up a spirit of clamour and discontent in the said province." Wedderburn had a triumphant reception in the anteroom. Franklin went quietly home alone. This was late Saturday afternoon. The day following, he says, he received a letter telling him he had been dismissed from his office as Deputy Postmaster-General. The records of the post office show that on Monday the 31st he was ordered to make up his accounts, and his successor was appointed. There had been no delay because the authorities had been ready in advance of the hearing. Franklin had no regrets. At breakfast on Sunday he told Priestley that he considered this one of the best actions of his life and would do it again in the same circumstances.

On 7 February the Privy Council approved of their Committee's report, which meant that the king rejected the petition. Mauduit for the ministry published the letters from the governors, with an account of the proceedings of the government, and Wedderburn's speech so far as it touched upon the letters. "This part of his speech," Franklin wrote to Cushing on the 15th, "was thought so good that they have since printed it, in order to defame me everywhere, and particularly to destroy my reputation on your side of the water; but the grosser parts of the abuse are omitted, appearing, I suppose, in their own eyes too foul to be seen on paper, so that the speech, compared to what it was, is now perfectly decent."[65] Only a few of the worse things Wedderburn actually said were ever printed, and that by Benjamin Vaughan five years later, "as well as they could be collected."[66]

"My friends advise me to write an answer," Franklin wrote to Cushing in the same letter, "which I purpose immediately." Though his *Tract Relative to the Affair of Hutchinson's Letters*[67] was soon written, it was not published then, nor till after his death.

He had, he said, often been censured for the part he took in public affairs. "Such censures I have generally passed over in silence; conceiving, when they were just, that I ought rather to amend than defend; and when they were undeserved, that a little time would justify me. Splashes of dirt thrown upon my character I suffered while fresh to remain. I did not choose to spread by endeavouring to remove them, but relied on the vulgar adage that they would all rub off when they were dry." Circumstances had delayed his vindication, he explained on 18 March to his Dutch friend Jan Ingenhousz, who had written from Vienna to tell Franklin of his distress over the news. The chancery suit was still pending, as it was to be as long as he remained in England. And he had other reasons for not keeping an older controversy alive in the midst of new ones. His letter to Ingenhousz was serene. "Be assured, my good friend, that I have done nothing unjustifiable, nothing but what is consistent with the man of honour and with my duty to my king and country; and this will soon be apparent to the public as it is now to all here who know me. I do not find that I have lost a single friend on the occasion. All have visited me repeatedly with affectionate assurances of their unaltered respect and affection, and many of distinction with whom I had before but slight acquaintance. You know that in England there is every day, in almost every paper, some abuse of public persons of all parties; the king himself does not always escape; and the populace, who are used to it, love to have a good character cut up now and then for their entertainment. On this occasion it suited the ministry to have me abused, as it often suits the purpose of their opposers to abuse them. And having myself been long engaged in public business, this treatment is not new to me. I am almost as much used to it as they are themselves, and perhaps can bear it better. I have indeed lost a little place that was in their power, but I can do very well without it."[68]

Franklin could expect that this letter, sent to a foreign country, might be opened and read, and he may have written it as much for some inquiring secretary as for Ingenhousz. But it does not appear that the attack by Wedderburn brought about the dramatic change in Franklin's sentiments that some of his biographers have insisted on. Franklin had only lost another degree of hope in the wisdom of the North ministry. He had too rich and mobile a mind to settle easily into a narrow, obsessive resentment. On 17 February, he told Richard Bache, he was "fixed to return homewards in or about May next."[69] But in another month he decided to stay longer, and he spent more than a year in further mediation. The one evidence that he kept a grudge may be looked upon, no less plausibly, as another of his American jokes. When, four years later, he was to sign the treaties of commerce and alliance with France, he got out his suit of figured Manchester velvet, which had been laid aside for many months, and wore it at the ceremony. The news of this went straight to England, presumably by way of the double-dealing Bancroft, and was held to mean that Franklin was still angry.[70] There was as much humour in it as hatred.

End of an Imperialist

FRANKLIN'S life went on much as before, except that he had no dealings with the ministry. On 12 February, two weeks after the scene at the Cockpit, he was at David Hartley's house in Putney, with the bishop of Carlisle, Priestley, Price, "and lords and others," to see Hartley's experiment for making houses fireproof.[1] That same day Franklin began a correspondence with the dean of Gloucester, who wrongly accused him of having sought to become one of the stamp officers for America under the act he had later worked to have repealed. "I persuade myself," Franklin said in his third letter, "that by this time you begin to suspect you may have been misled by your informers. I do not ask who they are, because I do not wish to have particular motives for disliking people who in general may deserve my respect."[2] In March he wrote to Beccaria about a new electrical discovery, and to the Marquis de Condorcet in answer to various questions about Pennsylvania. The free Negroes there, he said, were generally "improvident and poor. I think they are not deficient in natural understanding, but they have not the advantage of education. They make good musicians."[3] He had lately taken a growing interest in plans to abolish slavery or at least to improve the condition of slaves.[4] On 10 April he wrote to Priestley about marsh gas. Franklin had heard of its being set on fire in New Jersey in 1764 but never in England, though he had tried the experiment twice and had got only a fever for his pains. On 17 April he and Le Despencer went to hear Priestley's friend, Theophilus Lindsey, preach in his new Unitarian chapel in Essex Street, Strand. Priestley was there, and Le Despencer made a handsome contribution.[5] Polly Hewson's children were recovering, one of them from smallpox and the other from inocu-

lation, in their house near by in Craven Street. Polly's husband
died on 1 May, to the grief of both households.

Writing to his son on 2 February about the loss of the postmastership, Franklin assumed that the governor had now no official
prospects, and wished he were settled on his farm. "You will hear
from others the treatment I have received. I leave you to your own
reflections and determinations upon it."[6] And again on the 18th:
"Some tell me that it is determined to displace you likewise, but I
do not know it as certain. . . . Perhaps they may expect that your
resentment of their treatment of me may induce you to resign and
save them the shame of depriving you when they ought to promote. But this I would not advise you to do. Let them take your
place if they want it, though in truth I think it is scarce worth
your keeping, since it has not afforded you sufficient to prevent
your running every year behindhand with me. But one may make
something of an injury, nothing of a resignation."[7] William Franklin did not resign, nor did he share his father's political sentiments.
"You," Franklin wrote to him on 7 September, "who are a thorough courtier, see everything with government eyes."[8] The older
of the two was the rebel, and their close relationship was soon
to end.

With difficulties enough for anybody, Franklin had one near at
hand which he did not know about. Arthur Lee, from Virginia,
Eton, and Edinburgh, had turned from medicine to law and been
admitted to the English bar, and had taken to writing on public
affairs, both British and American, in a language congenial to
Samuel Adams. Chosen in 1770 as associate and future successor to
Franklin in the Massachusetts agency, Lee could not help being
eager to come into the influential position and the substantial
salary. Though he admired Franklin, he was exasperated by
Franklin's staying on year after year, and he became acutely suspicious. In letters to Boston Lee had more than hinted that Franklin was under the influence of the ministers—of Hillsborough
even—and was cautious on account of his Crown office and his
hopes of a better one. The Massachusetts radicals, who thought
Franklin's methods and language too moderate, were inclined to
agree with Lee. Franklin was half suspected by some of the very
men who Wedderburn said had looked to him to lead them into

sedition. Wedderburn's attack on Franklin cleared his name generally in America, where he was again a hero, as after his examination in 1766 before the House of Commons. Though he at once wrote that he could be of no further use to the province, he still kept an eye on the Assembly's affairs in London, "as a private man,"[9] while Lee left for France and Italy in April to be gone for perhaps a year.

There was much for Franklin to do in London and to report to Boston. Since all his letters were now apparently being read, even those from his innocent and devoted sister Jane, he could not speak out to his correspondents, and his course during this last year in England is not always easy to follow. Yet it was one of his busiest years. He published little himself. His *Parable against Persecution*, which had been printed in Strahan's *London Chronicle* ten years before, was included by Lord Kames in a book of his own in 1774, not only for itself but perhaps also to give Kames a chance to say, in the face of adverse opinion, that Franklin was "a man who makes a great figure in the learned world, and who would make still a greater figure for benevolence and candour were virtue as much regarded in this declining age as knowledge." The *Poor Richard* preface for 1758, which had appeared in the *Chronicle* that year, was issued separately in London in 1774 as *The Way to Wealth*. Franklin's *Causes of the American Discontents*, now six years old, was reprinted in two parts in the *Chronicle* for 30 August and 1 September, this time not expurgated as before and probably from the original text. Rivington in New York, issuing it in December as a pamphlet by "F. B." and changing the *Discontents* of the title to *Distractions*, said in his advertisement in his *Gazetteer* for the 29th: "From which initial letters the reader may possibly choose to impute this excellent piece to Sir Francis Bernard; those who think the reverse may give the palm to the celebrated Dr. Benjamin Franklin."

Franklin this year furnished the materials for Arthur Lee's *True State*, which presented the cause of Massachusetts somewhat as Richard Jackson's *Historical Survey* had sixteen years before presented that of Pennsylvania. At the request of Franklin and Fothergill, Priestley wrote his *Address to Protestant Dissenters*, on liberty in England and America. Bishop Shipley in his *Speech*

Intended to Have Been Spoken gave to the public what he might have said to the House of Lords when they were altering the charter of Massachusetts. "With regard to the people of Boston," he said, "I am free to own that I neither approve of their riots nor their punishment"; he considered their "violences as the natural effects of such measures as ours on the minds of freemen." This was the "greatest national concern that ever came under your deliberation. . . . My lords, I look upon North America as the only great nursery of freedom now left upon the face of the earth." There were readers who thought that Franklin had written the bishop's speech, though he had not. In America, Thomas Jefferson wrote his *Summary View of the Rights of British North America*, printed in Williamsburg and reprinted in London that same year. There was no more reason, Jefferson said, why Britain should rule the English colonists in America than why Saxony should claim that right over the Saxon peoples in Britain. Franklin's *Edict by the King of Prussia* had thrown out as satire a point which Jefferson now powerfully argued. On 30 September Franklin wrote to his son-in-law a letter of introduction for "Mr. Thomas Paine . . . very well recommended to me as an ingenious, worthy young man. . . . I request you to give him your best advice and countenance, as he is quite a stranger there."[10]

The destruction of the tea at Boston was a lawless affront to the British government which the king and the ministry could not ignore. "I suppose," Franklin wrote to Cushing on 22 March, "we never had since we were a people so few friends in Britain. . . . I cannot but hope that the affair of the tea will have been considered in the Assembly before this time, and satisfaction proposed if not made; for such a step will remove much of the prejudice now entertained against us, and put us again on a fair footing in contending for our old privileges as occasion may require."[11] The Americans living in London disapproved of Boston's misbehaviour and sent a remonstrance against it, drawn up by Arthur Lee, to Parliament. Parliament supported North almost without opposition in the bills which were quickly voted. Burke might ridicule the idea of punishing Boston to preserve British dignity; the bishop of St. Asaph insist that Boston had done only what any freemen would do under like grievances; General Burgoyne favour persuasion rather than the sword; and Colonel Barré warn that this was the first vengeful step and therefore very dangerous. But even Barré, who was Shelburne's spokesman in the Commons, voted for the bill to close the port of Boston from 1 June till the tea, valued at £15,000, should have been paid for. Another act changed the constitution of Massachusetts, to decrease the power of the legislature, increase that of the governor. And it was further provided that officers who might be brought to trial for enforcing the law should not be tried in Boston, but sent to some other colony or to Great Britain.

"Divine Providence," Franklin had said in January, "first infatuates the power it designs to ruin."[12] There was, of course, infatuation on both sides. Angry nations, like angry men, accuse each other of having first offended, and excuse themselves by claiming that they have acted merely in rightful self-defence. Anger has no accurate, just chronology. But the rulers of a great empire should be wiser than angry men. The king and North were not, though North was wiser than the king. They listened to Hutchinson instead of Franklin. Refusing to see that the principle of taxation was important no matter how small the amount of the tax might be, and believing that only a noisy minority in Massachusetts were discontented, they struck hard to put an end at once to what they thought was mere disorder. Franklin could have told them that they struck too hard.

The bill to close the port to the commerce of a whole province was bad enough. But, as Franklin wrote to Cushing at the first news about the tea, "though the mischief was the act of persons unknown, yet as probably they cannot be found or brought to answer for it, there seems to be some reasonable claim on the society at large in which it happened."[13] Plenty of men in Boston thought the tea ought to be paid for. They became less reasonable when the port was closed almost without warning, and General Gage, who had been commander-in-chief of the British army in America, was made governor of Massachusetts, with so many soldiers in the town that there was one of them to every five inhabitants. Throughout the conflict of the past ten years the provincial legislature had stood on what it thought its rights under the provincial constitution. Now Parliament remodelled that constitution as it pleased. This seemed to Massachusetts as arbitrary as if the stronger of two parties to a contract should revise the terms of the contract by force.

The port of Boston was left open to coastwise ships bringing food and fuel to its people, with permits from the customs officers at Salem. But if there was to be no general commerce there would be no money to pay for supplies. Even before the act went into operation Massachusetts called on the other colonies for aid. The response was prompt and generous. South Carolina sent cargoes of rice, Virginia money and nine thousand barrels of flour, Connecticut flocks of sheep, one of them driven by Israel Putnam. Rhode Island undertook a new meeting house, in Providence, to give work to unemployed Boston carpenters. For the first time in their history the scattered colonies were united in a common sentiment. Many things had happened in the twenty years since they had snubbed Franklin's Plan of Union as adopted and proposed by the Albany Congress. Sympathetic towards Boston, the colonies were apprehensive for themselves, in view of what now appeared to be the drastic temper of Parliament. An act that same year made it unlawful to export from England any tools for American use in the manufacture of cotton, linen, wool, and silk. The Quebec Act, wisely guaranteeing to the Canadians the free exercise of French judicial procedure and the Catholic religion, extended the boundaries of Quebec south to the Ohio, west to the Mississippi. In New England and elsewhere in America many intolerant Protestants bitterly objected to the toleration of Catholics, even in the old province of Quebec. And other Americans saw in the extension of Quebec a move to shut the English colonies out of territory claimed by some of them, and to set up behind them a barrier of alien laws and religion supported by the British government.

The common feeling among the colonies led to a common action. There was already a loose intercolonial organization in the committees of correspondence. Virginia in March 1773 had urged all the colonies to set up such committees to keep each other—and the legislatures—informed as to the state of public opinion in the interests of unity. Franklin had been one of the earliest to expect that something more than correspondence might come of the scheme. "I am glad," he wrote in a private letter to Cushing on 7 July, "to see the resolves of the Virginia House of Burgesses.

There are brave spirits among that people. I hope their proposal will be readily complied with by all the colonies. It is natural to suppose, as you do, that if the oppressions continue, a congress may grow out of that correspondence. Nothing would more alarm our ministers; but if the colonies agree to hold a congress, I do not see how it can be prevented."[14] That same day, writing officially to Cushing, he was more specific: "Perhaps it would be best and fairest for the colonies, in a general congress now in peace to be assembled, or by means of the correspondence lately proposed, after a full and solemn assertion and declaration of their rights, to engage firmly with each other that they will never grant aids to the Crown in any general war till those rights are recognized by the king and both Houses of Parliament; communicating at the same time to the Crown this their resolution."[15]

This was in July 1773. In May 1774 Virginia invited all the colonies to meet at a congress, which was held at Philadelphia in September with delegates from every colony except Georgia. Most of the delegates were members of the committees of correspondence. Franklin again put off his return to America. "I have been advised by our friends," he wrote to Cushing on 3 September, "to stay till the result of your congress should arrive. The coolness, temper, and firmness of the American proceedings; the unanimity of all the colonies, in the same sentiments of their rights and of the injustice offered to Boston; and the patience with which those injuries are at present borne, without the least appearance of submission, have a good deal surprised and disappointed our enemies; and the tone of public conversation, which has been violently against us, begins evidently to turn. . . . All who know well the state of things here agree that if the non-consumption agreement should become general and be firmly adhered to, this ministry must be ruined, and our friends succeed them, from whom we may hope a great constitutional charter to be confirmed by king, Lords, and Commons, whereby our liberties shall be recognized and established as the only sure foundation of that union so necessary for our common welfare."[16]

The union which Franklin thought necessary was still that of the whole British Empire which he had so long and so ardently desired. Its worst enemies, he believed, were the North ministry, who he kept on thinking could not stand much longer. "I have seen no minister since January, nor had the least communication with them," he wrote to his sister Jane on the 26th.[17] But the next day he wrote to Cushing that the friends of America "have frequent communications, for the purpose of dropping their private misunderstandings and uniting in the public cause, which at present needs all their joint assistance, since a breach with America, hazarded by the late harsh measures, may be ruinous to the general welfare of the British Empire. In forwarding this good work among them, as far as my little endeavours may amount to, I have been for some time industriously engaged. I see some letters in your newspapers, said to be written from hence, which represent Lord Chatham as having deserted your cause. I can of my own certain knowledge assure you of the contrary."[18] All that was needed, Franklin thought on 6 October, was for the Continental Congress to agree on a boycott of British manufactures and for the people to observe it. As this "would in a peaceable and justifiable way do everything for us that we can wish, I am grieved to hear of mobs and violence and the pulling down of houses, which our friends cannot justify and which give great advantage against us to our enemies. . . . I am in perpetual anxiety lest the mad measure of mixing soldiers among a people whose minds are in such a state of irritation, may be attended with some sudden mischief; for an accidental quarrel, a personal insult, an imprudent order, an insolent execution of even a prudent one, or twenty other things may produce a tumult, unforeseen and therefore impossible to be prevented, in which such a carnage may ensue as to make a breach that can never afterwards be healed."[19]

Not, Franklin wrote again to Cushing three days later, that much could be hoped for from Parliament at the best. "If the temper of the Court continues there will doubtless be a majority in the new Parliament for its measures, whatever they are; for as most of the members are bribing or purchasing to get in, there is little doubt of selling their votes to the minister for the time being, to reimburse themselves. Luxury introduces necessity even among those that make the most splendid figures here; this brings most of the Commons as well as Lords to market; and if America would save for three or four years the money she spends in fashions and fineries and fopperies of this country she might buy the whole Parliament, minister and all."[20]

II

Parliament was dominated by a man who never once doubted that his aims were virtuous. After fourteen years on the throne George III was still unalterably bent on being a patriot king, ruling his people, still for their own good, above the interference of faction. He believed in his right to rule, and he felt a deep, stubborn sense of responsibility. Single-minded himself, he did not in the least understand the opposition in England and America in the name of liberty. He saw it as a form of disorder, if not disobedience. Bewildered by statesmen like Chatham, Shelburne, and Burke, the king could not have dealt with them even if he had been willing to. He looked for politicians who would be less philosophical and more pliable. Many members of Parliament were already corrupt, and a good many of them agreed with the king in his kingly principles. He was too certain of his good ends to question his bad means. The patriot king must have friends who could be relied on always to support his policy, though they might have to be bribed, as Franklin said, "to vote according to their consciences."[21] A seat in Parliament was a place of profit, with contracts to be let and minor offices given to grateful beneficiaries. Candidates could afford to pay high prices to the electors or to the lords who had boroughs in their pockets. A member who had got a seat through the bounty or the influence of the king was expected to be friendly to him. By the time the trouble with Boston reached its crisis the king could regularly count on a majority in Parliament, and North, by no means willingly, would manipulate it.

Franklin had lost faith in the king and the ministry, but he believed that the landowners and the king's friends might not hold out against the commercial interests of the realm if the Americans should refuse to trade with Britain. The Massachusetts acts might be repealed as the Stamp Act had been. The danger was that violence would lead to larger violence, and all interest and reason be overwhelmed. Generally speaking, the mother country wanted to exploit the colonies and the colonies did not want to be exploited. But in both America and England there were sensible men who saw the advantages of a common trading system and wished only to correct the inequalities that had grown up. Generally speaking, the Crown and the Parliament wanted to extend their authority over the colonies, and the colonies wanted to maintain, if not augment, their rights to make and administer their domestic laws. But in both England and America there were enlightened men who, valuing, admiring, and loving the idea of the Empire, were convinced that wisdom might work out a scheme of government which would bind the whole together in a common satisfaction. Wisdom is long, violence is short. Franklin knew that he was working against time, and he waited for the news from America in a restless uncertainty.

Chatham too was aware of the crisis. After three years of sickness and virtual retirement, he now emerged to add his great strength to the opposition. George III had in July talked with Hutchinson, just from Boston, and had understood the governor to say that the Port Bill was effective and the Bostonians dispirited. Chatham in August consulted Franklin.

Since January Franklin had left the ministry alone. "I made no justification of myself from the charges brought against me; I made no return of the injury by abusing my adversaries; but held a cool, sullen silence, reserving myself to some future opportunity." He spent August in the country, part of the time with Le Despencer. Towards the end of the month, returning from Brighthelmstone (Brighton), Franklin stopped to visit his friend John Sargent in Kent. Sargent told him that Lord Stanhope, who lived in the neighbourhood, expected them to call. (Sargent, member of Parliament for Seaford, was one of Franklin's partners in the Ohio company. Franklin had in 1773 recommended Stanhope and his son to membership in the American Philosophical Society.) "We accordingly waited on Lord Stanhope that evening, who told me Lord Chatham desired to see me; and that Mr. Sargent's house, where I was to lodge, being in the way, he would call for me there the next morning and carry me to Hayes [Chatham's house]. This was done accordingly. That truly great man received me with abundance of civility, inquired particularly into the situation of affairs in America, spoke feelingly of the severity of the late laws against the Massachusetts, gave me some account of his speech in opposing them, and expressed great regard and esteem for the people of that country, who he hoped would continue firm and united in defending by all peaceable and legal means their constitutional rights. I assured him that I made no doubt they would do so; which he said he was pleased to hear from me, as he was sensible I must be well acquainted with them.

"I then took occasion to remark to him that in former cases great empires had crumbled first at their extremities" because they were too remote to be understood by the central government and had been left in the hands of bad governors. "But that this Empire had happily found and long been in the practice of a method whereby every province was well governed, being trusted in a great measure with the government of itself; and that hence had arisen such satisfaction in the subjects, and such encouragement to new settlements, that had it not been for the late wrong politics (which would have Parliament to be omnipotent though it ought not to be so unless it could at the same time be omniscient), we might have gone on extending our western empire, adding province to province, as far as the South Sea. That I lamented the ruin which seemed impending over so fine a plan, so well adapted to make all the subjects of the greatest empire happy; and I hoped that, if his lordship with the other great and wise men of this nation would unite and exert themselves, it might yet be rescued out of the mangling hands of the present set of blundering ministers, and that the union and harmony between Britain and her colonies, so necessary to the welfare of both, might be restored.

"He replied with great politeness that my idea of extending our Empire in that manner was a sound one, worthy of a great, benevolent, and comprehensive mind. He wished with me for a good understanding among the different parts of the opposition here, as a means of restoring the ancient harmony of the two countries which he most earnestly desired." But Chatham thought a coalition against the ministry was hardly to be expected. The friends of America, trying to win others to her cause, found many Englishmen doubtful about further concessions. They believed that "America aimed at setting up for itself as an independent state; or at least to get rid of the Navigation Acts. I assured him that, having more than once travelled almost from one end of the continent to the other and kept a great variety of company, eating, drinking, and conversing with them freely, I never had heard in any conversation, from any person drunk or sober, the least expression of a wish for a separation or hint that such a thing would be advantageous to America." The "main material part" of the Navigation Acts, Franklin said, was "as acceptable to us as it could be to Britain." Americans were not opposed to regulations of their general commerce by Parliament, "providing such regulations were *bona fide* for the benefit of the whole Empire, not for the small advantage of one part to the great injury of another." Chatham thought that some of the restraining acts might be amended.

"In fine, he expressed much satisfaction in my having called upon him, and particularly in the assurances I had given him that America did not aim at independence; adding that he should be glad to see me again as often as might be. I said I should not fail to avail myself of the permission he was pleased to give me of waiting upon his lordship occasionally, being very sensible of the honour and of the great advantage and improvement I should reap from his instructive conversation: which indeed was not a mere compliment."[22]

Franklin in September could tell Cushing that Chatham was still a friend to America, but there was little America's friends could just then do in England. The ministry, disturbed by the news that other colonies had taken the side of Massachusetts, and alarmed by the prospect of a continental boycott of English manufactures, suddenly dissolved the old Parliament and ordered the election of a new one in as short a time as the law permitted. Haste seemed necessary. To delay was to give the possible boycott a chance to be felt in the trading and manufacturing towns, which might then vote against the ministry in the election. At first Franklin was hopeful. By the middle of October he had concluded that the new Parliament would again take its orders from the Court. "My situation here," he wrote to Galloway on the 12th, "is

thought by many to be a little hazardous; for that if by some accident the troops and people of New England should come to blows
I should probably be taken up; the ministerial people affecting
everywhere to represent me as the cause of all the misunderstanding; and I have been frequently cautioned to secure my papers,
and by some advised to withdraw. But I venture to stay, in compliance with the wish of others." He might be of some use when
the American Congress had been heard from. "I confide in my
innocence, that the worst which can happen to me will be an
imprisonment on suspicion, though that is a thing I should much
desire to avoid, as it may be expensive and vexatious as well as
dangerous to my health."[23] He moved guardedly the next three or
four months, and seems to have risked few letters.

It must have been at about this time—though the precise date is
not certain—that he had a cartoon drawn, engraved on copper,
and struck off on cards on the back of which he wrote occasional
notes to his friends, and on half-sheets of paper with an explanation and a moral. "Great Britain," he said of the mutilated figure
in the drawing, "is supposed to have been placed upon the globe;
but the colonies (that is, her limbs) being severed from her, she is
seen lifting her eyes and mangled stumps to heaven; her shield,
which she is unable to wield, lies useless by her side; her lance has
pierced New England; the laurel branch has fallen from the hand
of Pennsylvania; the English oak [under which Britannia sits] has
lost its head, and stands a bare trunk with a few withered branches;
briers and thorns are on the ground beneath it; the British ships
[in the background] have brooms at their topmast heads, denoting
their being on sale; and Britannia herself is seen sliding off the
world (no longer able to hold its balance), her fragments overspread with the label: *Date obolum Belisario*." The moral was
clear. "History affords us many instances of the ruin of states by
the prosecution of measures ill suited to the temper and genius of
their people. The ordaining of laws in favour of one part of a
nation, to the prejudice and oppression of another, is certainly the
most erroneous and mistaken policy. An equal dispensation of
protection, rights, privileges, and advantages is what every part is
entitled to and ought to enjoy; it being a matter of no moment to

the state whether a subject grows rich and flourishing on the Thames or the Ohio, in Edinburgh or Dublin. These measures never fail to create great and violent jealousies and animosities between the people favoured and the people oppressed; whence a total separation of affections, interests, political obligations, and all manner of connexions necessarily ensue, by which the whole state is weakened and perhaps ruined for ever."[24]

Between the dissolution of the last Parliament and the first session of the next on 29 November Franklin wrote an *Intended Speech*[25] for the king to deliver at the opening. Shipley's *Speech Intended to Have Been Spoken* to the House of Lords had been sold by thousands and, Franklin thought on 6 October, had "had an extraordinary effect in changing the sentiments of multitudes with regard to America."[26] Now he would say for the king what the king would say if he had sense enough. The speech as Franklin wrote it was too blunt to be printed, and Franklin can hardly have meant it to be. Perhaps he only showed it to his friends. The manuscript was left in England with David Hartley, who returned it after the Revolution had justified much of the prophecy which Franklin had put so ironically into the king's mouth.

The king told his lords and gentlemen that none of the measures of the former Parliament had had the "salutary effects" upon America which the ministry had promised him. "I therefore sent that Parliament a-packing rather abruptly, and have called you in their place to pick a little advice out of your wise heads upon some matters of the greatest weight and importance relating to a sort of crusade that I have upon my hands. I must needs tell you that the business, if you choose to undertake it for me, will be a seven or ten years' job at least." The ministry wanted him to coax the new Parliament into believing that the affair would soon be over, because the Americans were "no better than a wretched pack of cowardly runaways, and that five hundred men with whips would make them all dance to the tune of *Yankee Doodle*." The king would tell them no such thing. "If you undertake this job it will cost you at the least farthing a good round sum of forty or fifty millions; forty or fifty thousands of your constituents will get knocked on the head; and then you are to consider what the rest of you will be gainers by the bargain even if you succeed. The trade of a ruined and desolated country is always inconsiderable, its revenues trifling; the expense of subjecting and retaining it in subjection certain and inevitable. On the other side, should you prove unsuccessful, should that connexion which we wish most ardently to maintain be dissolved, should my ministers exhaust your treasures and waste the blood of your countrymen in vain, will they not deliver you weak and defenceless to your natural enemies?" The king could never forget that Rockingham had advised him not to tax America: "that it was ten to one against our making any hand of it at all, that they were not worth shearing, and at best that we should raise a cursed outcry and get but little wool."

"And now, my lords and gentlemen: I have stated the whole matter fairly and squarely before you. It is your own business, and if you are not content as you are, look to the rest for yourselves. But if I were to give you a word of advice it should be to remind you of the Italian epitaph upon a poor fool that killed himself with quacking: *Stava bene, por star meglio, sto qui.* That is to say: I was well, I would be better, I took physic and died."

On 17 November Josiah Quincy arrived from Boston and had tea with Franklin the same day. This was the son of that other Josiah Quincy who in 1755 had come to Philadelphia and with Franklin's help had persuaded the Assembly to vote money for the use of Massachusetts in the expedition against Crown Point. The younger Quincy, intensely American, brought with him a suspicion that Franklin was lukewarm, as Arthur Lee had told the Bostonians. The suspicion hardly outlasted the two hours of that first call, and in a week Quincy wrote his wife that Franklin was "explicit and bold," and that "his hopes are as sanguine as my own of the triumph of liberty in America." Jonathan Williams was then living in Craven Street, and he told Quincy that Franklin was glad he had come. He dined with Franklin and Edward Bancroft the next day, and heard that Hutchinson had assured the ministry the colonies would not unite and would soon submit. Various great men—North, Pownall, Dartmouth, Shelburne— whom Quincy soon talked with told him the same thing. North said the authority of Parliament must be upheld in America. Shelburne said that if the Americans persisted they would get all they asked. The ministry could not carry on a civil war against them. Within two weeks Quincy was so close to Franklin that Hillsborough in the House of Lords bracketed them as men walking the streets of London who ought to be in Newgate or Tyburn: "though not by name, yet so that everybody knew whom he meant."[27]

Quincy dined often alone with Franklin or with Franklin and his friends. On the afternoon of 24 November Franklin and Price introduced Quincy to a meeting of the Royal Society. That evening they took him to the London coffee house, where he met the Honest Whigs. Franklin admitted that he had written the *Rules by Which a Great Empire May Be Reduced to a Small One* and *An Edict by the King of Prussia*. Early in December he invited Quincy to go with him to spend Christmas at Bishop Shipley's house. Neither of them went, and for a time they were separated, Quincy leaving for Bath and Shelburne's house at Calne, and Franklin staying in London in intricate negotiations about which Quincy knew nothing. On 17 January Quincy "dined with Mrs. Stevenson, with a number of ladies and gentlemen, in celebration of Dr. Franklin's birthday, who made one of the festive company, although he this day enters the seventieth year of his age."[28] Two evenings later Franklin, Quincy, Priestley, Price, and many others were again at the London coffee house. Franklin the next day was Chatham's guest at the House of Lords, and Quincy took the notes of the speeches which Franklin thought were "by much the best account of that day's debate."[29] On the 25th they dined, along with Priestley, Price, Dunning, John Lee, and others, at Shelburne's. But Quincy was now a sick man. ("His zeal for the public," Franklin wrote to James Bowdoin on 25 February, "like that of David for God's house, will I fear eat him up."[30]) Fothergill, Franklin's physician and friend, took charge of Quincy, refusing any fee, and sent him off for a month to Islington, where all his busy friends found time to visit him. His journal and letters furnish almost the only details of Franklin's life during these weeks. The rest are in the secret history, *An Account of the Negotiations in London for Effecting a Reconciliation between Great Britain and the American Colonies*,[31] which Franklin wrote on his voyage home.

III

About the beginning of November, he wrote, "being at the Royal Society, Mr. Raper, one of our members, told me there was a certain lady who had a desire of playing with me at chess, fancying she could beat me, and had requested him to bring me to her; it was, he said, a lady with whose acquaintance he was sure I should be pleased, a sister of Lord Howe's, and he hoped I would not refuse the challenge. I said I had been long out of practice, but would wait upon the lady when he and she should think fit. He told me where her house was, and would have me call soon and without farther introduction, which I undertook to do; but, thinking it a little awkward, I postponed it; and on the 30th, meeting him again at the feast of the Society election, being the day after the Parliament met, he put me in mind of my promise, and that I had not kept it, and would have me name a day when he said he would call for me and conduct me. I named the Friday following [2 December]. He called accordingly. I went with him, played a few games with the lady, whom I found of very sensible conversation and pleasing behaviour, which induced me to agree most readily to an appointment for another meeting a few days after; though I had not the least apprehension that any political business could have any connexion with this new acquaintance."[32]

There was politics behind the chess, reaching at least to the secretary of state for America. Dartmouth's physician was Franklin's friend Fothergill. Whether Dartmouth or Fothergill suggested it, Fothergill had been authorized—or permitted—to consult with Franklin about some plan of reconciliation between the government and the colonies. Fothergill was to undertake this in company with David Barclay, a rich Quaker banker, brewer, and merchant in the American trade. Barclay too had a friend in a ministerial post, Lord Hyde, formerly in the diplomatic service and the post office, and now chancellor of the duchy of Lancaster. The actual first suggestion may have come from Hyde to Barclay, and Barclay, as he later told Franklin, may have taken it to Fothergill. The beginnings are still somewhat mysterious because they were mysterious then. There was no reason why Dartmouth, if he wanted Franklin's help, should not have gone straight to Franklin. That would have been too direct for ministers. Both Dartmouth and Hyde had been present in the Cockpit, and might expect that Franklin would be resentful. Great lords could not chance a rebuff. They preferred to work indirectly through Fothergill and Barclay, who as Quakers could hold no public office and so were outside of politics, and who while Englishmen (or at least Scots) were friends of America and of Franklin. The chess was an incident. It would give the brother of Miss Howe (called Mrs. Howe according to the usage of that century) a chance to talk with Franklin. The Howes knew America. Their eldest brother had been killed by the French on Lake George, and Massachusetts had erected a memorial to him in Westminster Abbey. A third brother, General Sir William Howe, had fought at Louisbourg and Quebec. The present Lord Howe, rear-admiral and member of Parliament, desired to make friends with Franklin and through him with his countrymen.

Franklin, whom the ministry had abused and done its best to disgrace, was now turned to as never before in England. Ministers, members of the opposition, merchants, men of learning, and even a lady of fashion believed that he better than anybody else might find a way out of the angry difficulties which baffled them. But the ministers moved by stealth.

On the Thursday before the first chess match Barclay called on Franklin to talk about a petition to Parliament from the merchants trading to America. Barclay spoke of the dangerous situation of affairs, and "the great merit that person would have who could contrive some means of preventing so terrible a calamity and bring about a reconciliation. He was then pleased to add that he was persuaded, from my knowledge of both countries, my character and influence in one of them, and my abilities in business, no man had it so much in his power as myself. I naturally answered that I should certainly be very happy if I could in any degree be instrumental in so good a work, but that I saw no prospect of it." The Americans were, Franklin was sure, "willing and ready to agree upon any equitable terms," but not the ministry. So far as he could judge, "they rather wished to provoke the North American people into an open rebellion which might justify a military execution and thereby gratify a grounded malice which I conceived to exist here against the Whigs and dissenters of that country." Barclay thought Franklin too hard on the ministers. Some of them, Barclay was sure, "would be very glad to get out of the embarrassment on any terms, only saving the honour and dignity of government." He wished Franklin would give the proposal further thought and talk with him again. Franklin said he would do it, but believed any efforts of the kind useless.[33]

Barclay did not let the matter rest. Two days later he wrote that on his way home he had run into Fothergill, who invited both of them to his house at five o'clock the next day. "The time thus appointed," Franklin wrote in his history, "was the evening of the day on which I was to have my second chess party with the agreeable Mrs. Howe, whom I met accordingly. After playing as long as we liked we fell into a little chat, partly on a mathematical problem and partly about the new Parliament then just met; when she said: 'And what is to be done with this dispute between Great Britain and the colonies? I hope we are not to have a civil war.' 'They should kiss and be friends,' says I, 'what can they do better? Quarrelling can be of service to neither, but is ruin to both.' 'I have often said,' says she, 'that I wished government would employ you to settle the dispute for 'em; I am sure nobody could do it so well. Don't you think that the thing is practicable?' 'Undoubtedly, Madam, if the parties are disposed to reconciliation; for the two countries have really no clashing interests to differ about. It is rather a matter of punctilio, which two or three reasonable people might settle in half an hour. I thank you for the good opinion you are pleased to express of me; but the ministers will never think of employing me in that good work; they choose rather to abuse me.' 'Aye,' says she, 'they have behaved shamefully to you. And indeed some of them are now ashamed of it themselves.' I looked upon this as mere accidental conversation, thought no more of it, and went in the evening to the appointed meeting at Dr. Fothergill's, where I found Mr. Barclay with him."[34]

Fothergill hoped that Franklin would have already drawn up a preliminary plan of conciliation. Franklin still thought there was no use in making any such attempt. "He said I might be mistaken;

that whatever was the violence of some, he had reason, good reason, to believe others were differently disposed; and that if I would draw a plan which we three upon considering should judge reasonable, it might be made use of and answer some good purpose; since he believed either himself or D. Barclay could get it communicated to some of the most moderate among the ministers, who would consider it with attention; and what appeared reasonable to us, two of us being Englishmen, might appear so to them." Franklin suggested they should wait till there was word from the Continental Congress. Both Fothergill and Barclay urged all possible speed. There was no telling what message might come from the Congress, or when, or what might happen in the meantime. Franklin consented to draw up a plan and meet them at the same place on Tuesday.[35]

On that Tuesday, Quincy reported to his wife, one of the ministerial members, in a coffee house adjoining the House of Commons, offered to bet seventy-five guineas to twenty-five that by this time General Gage had reduced Boston to ashes. If there was danger of violence in America, so was there in Parliament. Franklin brought to Fothergill's house no mollifying scheme of compromise. It was too late, he thought, to smooth the quarrel over. There must be fundamental action if there was to be a durable union. He did not content himself with general terms, which he knew might mean different things to different persons. Instead he took up seventeen specific points, which he had written out as *Hints for Conversation*, and which he read to his friends, telling them his reasons for each point as he went along.[36]

His first point was that the tea which had been destroyed must be paid for. On this, he says, "I observed that when the injury was done Britain had a right to reparation, and would certainly have had it on demand, as was the case when injury was done by mobs in the time of the Stamp Act; or she might have a right to return an equal injury if she chose rather to do that; but she could not have a right both to reparation and to return an equal injury; much less had she a right to return the injury ten- or twentyfold, as she had done by blocking up the port of Boston. All which extra injury ought in my judgment to be repaired by Britain. That therefore if paying for the tea was agreed to by me, as an article fit to be proposed, it was merely from a desire of peace, and in compliance with their opinion expressed at our first meeting: that this was a *sine qua non*, that the dignity of Britain required it, and that if this was agreed to everything else would be easy." Barclay and Fothergill, who knew that the ministry had made the destroyed tea an essential issue, must have been struck by Franklin's counterclaim against the government. They said his reasoning was just, but thought the tea would have to be paid for unconditionally.

Franklin went on with his remaining points, on most of which the others agreed with him. The act laying a duty on tea was to be repealed. He further insisted that the money which had been collected under the act should be repaid to the several provinces, though Barclay and Fothergill were sure this would not be done and advised against asking it. The Navigation Acts were to be re-enacted in the colonial legislatures, the duties arising from them paid into the colonial treasuries for public use, and the customs officers appointed by the governors in America, not sent from England. America was to maintain its own military establishment in time of peace, with no requisition from Britain. This "was at first objected to, on the principle that all under the care of government should pay towards the support of it." Franklin pointed out that "new countries had many public expenses which old ones were free from, the works being done to their hands by their ancestors: such as making roads and bridges, erecting churches, courthouses, forts, quays, and other public buildings, founding schools and places of education, hospitals and almshouses, etc." Since Britain was to have a monopoly of American commerce, America would pay indirectly, in higher prices for goods bought, as much as her share in the imperial peace establishment amounted to. In time of war the colonies might be expected, on requisition from the king with consent of Parliament, to contribute to the government annually at least a fourth and possibly a half as much as the sum of their last provincial peace tax. Fothergill had suggested at the first meeting that the government would not be satisfied with the promise of voluntary grants from the colonies, and might justly ask that the amounts be fixed on some stipulated basis. Franklin had his own reason for agreeing: "that the view of the proportion to be given in time of war might make us the more frugal in time of peace."

Castle William in Boston harbour was to be restored to Massachusetts and no fortress built in any province except with the consent of its legislature. "The gentlemen had not much to say against this article, but thought it would hardly be admitted." The acts changing the constitution of Massachusetts and the Quebec Act were to be repealed. Here it was pointed out that the ministry would think the older colonies had no right to meddle with the affairs of Canada. Franklin, who cannot have wanted to deprive the French Canadians of their own religion and law, spoke chiefly of the enlargement of Quebec to the south and west: "an arbitrary government on the back of our settlements might be dangerous to us all; and . . . loving liberty ourselves, we wished it to be extended among mankind." He was on stronger ground when he said that the Americans could not have their laws and charters altered by Parliament at will. "This was a situation we could not be in, and must risk life and everything rather than submit to it." Provincial judges and governors were to be paid by order of the assemblies. Parliament was to disown its threat to try Americans for treason under a statute of Henry VIII. The American admiralty courts were to have the same power as in England. And, finally, Parliament was to disclaim all powers of internal legislation in the colonies—which Barclay and Fothergill thought "could hardly be obtained but might be tried."

On certain of Franklin's points they firmly disagreed. Not that they themselves necessarily thought him wrong, but "they wished, they said, to have this paper or plan that they might show, as containing the sentiments of considerate, impartial persons, and such as they might as Englishmen support." For instance, his point that no troops were "to enter and quarter in any colony but with the consent of the legislature." The king, "who is to defend all parts of his dominions, should of course have a right to place his troops where they might best answer that purpose. I supported the article upon principles equally important, in my opinion, to Britain as to the colonies; for that if the king could bring into one part of his dominions troops raised in any other part of them, without the consent of the legislature of the part to which they were brought, he might bring armies raised in America into England without consent of Parliament, which probably would not like it, as a few years since they had not liked the introduction of the Hessians and Hanoverians." If there were any real emergency in America, the legislatures would consent to the troops. Franklin, instead of being ready to drop the article, thought he ought to add another requiring that the troops now in America be withdrawn. No just treaty could be made if one party to it was acting under compulsion from the other.

Barclay and Fothergill could not agree to the demand that all the acts restraining manufactures in the colonies be repealed. That would alarm the English. But the acts might be reconsidered. Franklin accepted the change. He struck out entirely his proposal that if Britain would give up its monopoly of American commerce, then America would contribute to the British government as much in time of peace as in time of war. "The monopoly of the American commerce," his colleagues said, "could never be given up, and the proposing it would only give offence."

There was little evidence in all this that Franklin felt a personal resentment or that he was diplomatically jockeying for a favourable position. His terms were his convictions, most of them held for years. As to the Boston emergency, Massachusetts by paying for the destroyed tea would make the first confession of wrongdoing. The British government could then with good grace repeal the duty on tea, as impracticable. The colonies would concede to the British the right to a monopoly of their commerce, and pledge themselves to help the mother country in a foreign war. The government could then afford not to levy peace taxes. The experience of the past ten years had made it plain that Parliamentary legislation for the colonies disturbed them, and consequently both countries. Parliament would serve the common welfare by leaving American legislation to Americans. This would put an end, Franklin held, to the disorder which the British troops had been sent to quiet. The troops might safely be withdrawn, with assurances that no more of them would be quartered in America except against a foreign enemy. Franklin here turned the argument squarely on the British. How would they like to see American troops in England? He spoke not as a colonial but as an equal in the Empire.

When his points had been discussed, the plan behind the meeting showed itself. Fothergill said he would like to communicate the proposed terms to Dartmouth, and Barclay asked if he might take them up with Hyde. "I had drawn the paper at their request, and it was now theirs to do with it what they pleased." Franklin said he had no objection to being named to the ministers so far as he was concerned, but he thought they were prejudiced against him and would be against any scheme of his. The three decided that he was not to be mentioned. "I kept this whole proceeding a dead secret." On the 8th he sent Barclay a fair copy of the paper. On the 11th Barclay wrote a guarded note saying that he had been with "a person" (presumably Hyde) and had walked with him "to another noble person's house" (presumably Dartmouth's or North's— Franklin did not know which). Hyde—if it was Hyde—had told Barclay "that he could say that he saw some light."[37] On the 13th Hyde wrote to Barclay that the *Hints* seemed to him "rather high." He supposed that Fothergill had "certainly imparted them to the proper officer" (presumably Dartmouth).[38]

But on the 18th the petition from the Continental Congress arrived in London, sent, in care of Franklin, to him and all the colonial agents, who were asked to present it to the king. For a time Franklin was too busy over the petition to do anything else. Only the agents for Massachusetts were willing to act without instructions from their colonies. Franklin, Bollan, and Lee—who had returned from the Continent—waited on Dartmouth, through whom as secretary of state for America the petition would officially be presented. Dartmouth told them it was decent and proper, and gave them a hope that it might bring about a change of measures. The king had received it graciously, and would lay it before Parliament as soon as they met. As it was now near the Christmas holidays the three conspirators for peace let their plan rest, and Barclay and Franklin put off till later their other plan for a protest from the British merchants against a policy that had brought on a new American boycott. Although the proceedings of Congress were published in the London newspapers, the petition was held back till it could reach Parliament in form. Rumours got around that Franklin, acting for Congress, had settled the dispute with North, and stocks rose. Thereafter he was inconveniently thought to have more diplomatic authority than he had.

(In the midst of these troubles Deborah Franklin was dead in Philadelphia, without Franklin's presence or even knowledge. She had told her son that if her husband did not come back that winter she would never see him again, for she was sure she would not live through it. She had a stroke on 14 December, felt better on the 18th, died without a sound on the 19th, and was buried on the 22nd—the day Franklin in London dined with Barclay and heard that Hyde thought the *Hints* "too hard." Richard Bache sent his clerk express to Amboy, and William Franklin, in wind and snow, was able to get to Philadelphia only half an hour before her body left the house for the churchyard. He and Richard Bache were chief mourners. Hugh Roberts, the governor wrote, and several other friends of Franklin were "carriers," and "a very respectable number of the inhabitants" were at the funeral.[39] "It seems but t'other day," Franklin had written to her two years before, "since you and I were ranked among the boys and girls, so swiftly does time fly. We have, however, great reason to be thankful that so much of our lives has passed so happily."[40])

Franklin called again on Miss Howe on Christmas Day. "She told me, as soon as I came in, that her brother, Lord Howe, wished to be acquainted with me; that he was a very good man, and she was sure we should like each other. I said I had always heard a good character of Lord Howe and should be proud of the honour of being known to him. 'He is but just by,' says she; 'will you give me leave to send for him?' 'By all means, Madam, if you think proper.' She rang for a servant, wrote a note, and Lord H. came in a few minutes."

Howe too was alarmed over America, and was sure nobody understood the situation better than Franklin. He knew Franklin had been badly treated by the ministry, but hoped he would not let that weigh too much with him. If Franklin hesitated about having any communication with the ministers, Howe would be willing to act as go-between, in perfect secrecy. Miss Howe here offered to leave the room, but Franklin said he had no secrets in the matter which he could not trust to her. "As to what his lord-ship mentioned of the injuries done me, those done my country were so much greater that I did not think the other, at this time, worth mentioning . . . besides, it was a fixed rule with me not to mix my private affairs with those of the public . . . I could join with my personal enemy in serving the public, or, when it was for its interest, with the public in serving that enemy." Howe then asked Franklin to draw up a set of terms on which the countries might be reconciled. Franklin at first declined, and said the peti-tion from Congress covered all the ground. He read a part of the petition, which he seems to have had with him, and thought they were affected by it. But Howe still wanted to see Franklin's terms, in case those of Congress should not be accepted. Franklin agreed to draw up another paper.[41]

The next day he went to Hayes to show Chatham the petition, as well as the proceedings which had been sent ahead as soon as they arrived from Philadelphia. "He received me with an affec-tionate kind of respect that from so great a man was extremely engaging; but the opinion he expressed of the Congress was still more so. They had acted, he said, with so much temper, modera-tion, and wisdom that he thought it the most honourable assembly of statesmen since those of the ancient Greeks and Romans, in the most virtuous times." Chatham did not agree with Congress on one point, but "the rest he admired and honoured." If his health permitted he might speak on America in the House of Lords after the holidays, and he "should wish to have previously my senti-ments." Franklin pointed out the hazard of keeping the troops in Boston, in a time of such unrest. (The hazard was greater than Franklin knew. General Gage, who had said that with four regi-ments he could put down all the disorder, was now urging the ministry to hire 20,000 Hessians and Hanoverians to make a com-plete conquest of New England.) Chatham, listening to Franklin, "seemed to think these sentiments had something in them that was reasonable." After a night at Sargent's house, Franklin spent an-other night with Lord Camden at Chislehurst. Camden, who had called the Stamp Act unconstitutional, had been lord chancellor under Chatham, and was now powerful in the opposition, heartily approved the actions of Congress.[42]

On Wednesday Franklin again met Howe at his sister's house. "I apologized for my not being ready with the paper I had promised, by my having been kept longer than I intended in the country. . . . His lordship told me he could now assure me of a certainty that there was a sincere disposition in Lord North and Lord Dartmouth to accommodate the differences with America." He asked what Franklin would think of a scheme to send some person or persons to America to try to bring about an understanding. "I said that a person of rank and dignity, who had a character of candour, integrity, and wisdom, might possibly, if employed in that service, be of some use. . . . Mrs. Howe said: 'I wish, brother, you were to be sent thither on such a service; I should like that much better than General Howe's going to command the army there.'" The ministry had already thought of replacing Gage with the younger Howe. "'I think, Madam,' says I, 'they ought to provide for General Howe some more honourable employment.' Lord Howe here took out of his pocket a paper and, offering it to me, said smiling: 'If it is not an unfair question, may I ask whether you know anything of this paper?'" It was a copy, in Barclay's handwriting, of Franklin's *Hints*. Franklin, seeing that Barclay had not kept the secret, acknowledged it. Howe "said he was rather sorry to find that the sentiments expressed in it were mine, as it gave him less hopes of promoting, by my assistance, the wished-for reconciliation, since he had reason to think there was no likelihood of the admission of those propositions." He hoped Franklin would reconsider the subject and form some more acceptable plan. "He expatiated on the infinite service it would be to the nation, and the great merit in being instrumental in so good a work; that he should not think of influencing me by any selfish motive, but certainly I might with reason expect any reward in the power of government to bestow.

"This to me was what the French call 'spitting in the soup.'" Franklin was too shrewd not to see a ministerial bait in the suggestion. He had asked too much. If he were willing to ask less he might do the ministry a favour and be entitled to a reward. "However, I promised to draw some sketch of a plan, at his request, though I much doubted, I said, whether it would be thought preferable to that he had in his hand. But he was willing to hope that it would; and, as he considered my situation, that I had friends here and constituents in America to keep well with; that I might possibly propose something improper to be seen in my handwriting; therefore it would be best to send it to Mrs. Howe, who would copy it, send the copy to him to be communicated to the ministry, and return me the original." That is, if Franklin were to accept the bribe, there would be no incriminating document to prove it. "This I agreed to, though I did not apprehend the inconvenience he mentioned. In general I liked his manner, and found myself disposed to place great confidence in him on occasion; but in this particular the secrecy he proposed seemed not of much importance."[43]

In a day or two Franklin sent Miss Howe, for her brother, another paper[44] in which he left out nothing he had asked before. "It is supposed to be the wish on both sides," he began, "not merely to put a stop to the mischief at present threatening the general welfare, but to cement a cordial union and remove not only every real grievance but every cause of jealousy and suspicion." The Continental Congress had explicitly named the American grievances and promised that if they were removed the future conduct of the Americans would show them worthy of the regard in which "in their happier days" they had been held by the government. Britain had only to repeal the laws that had caused the trouble, and withdraw the ships and troops from Boston. Let the government give authority to the Congress by appointing "a person of weight and dignity of character" to preside over it in behalf of the Crown. Then Congress could be asked for such pledges as were required, including payment to the East India Company for its tea.

On 2 January Howe, who had received the paper, wrote to his sister that the terms made him afraid he would have more difficulty with the ministers than he had expected. About a week later Miss Howe asked Franklin to call on her, and showed him another letter from her brother. "He desired to know from their friend, meaning me, through her means, whether . . . if that friend should engage for their payment of the tea as a preliminary," Congress would approve; and whether Franklin was still of the same mind as to the aids that America would be willing to give in case of a foreign war. Franklin at once wrote an answer which Miss Howe copied and sent to her brother that same evening. He still thought, Franklin said, about aids as he had thought before; he believed it was evident from his revised terms. As to payment for the tea, the Americans looked upon the tax as an injury to them before the tea was destroyed, and the closing of the port a greater injury since. They would probably not be willing to make the first move in reparation.

Howe, and no doubt the ministers, had discovered that the prospect of a bribe had not made Franklin pliable. On 19 January "Lord Howe returned to town, when we had another meeting at which he lamented that my propositions were not such as probably could be accepted." He thought, with the ministers, that Franklin "had powers or instructions from the Congress to make concessions on occasion that would be more satisfactory. I disclaimed the having any of any kind but what related to the presenting of their petition." The ministry, who had made the mistake of thinking Franklin less honest than he was, now made the mistake of thinking him more crafty. But he finally said "that if what I proposed would not do I should be glad to hear what would do; I wished to see some propositions from the ministers themselves. His lordship was not, he said, as yet fully acquainted with their sentiments, but should learn more in a few days. It was, however, some weeks before I heard anything further from him."[45]

The negotiations through Barclay and Fothergill with Hyde went on no better than those with Howe. During Howe's absence in the country Barclay had been so busy with the merchants' petition that he had not seen Hyde, and Fothergill was slow in bringing an answer from Dartmouth. At length Fothergill called on Franklin and told him that Dartmouth thought some of the *Hints* "reasonable," some "inadmissible or impracticable." Another patient of Fothergill's, Sir Fletcher Norton, the Speaker of the House of Commons, had been let into the secret. Though he was anxious for a reconciliation, he "had said it would be very humiliating to Britain to be obliged to submit to such terms. But the Doctor told him she had been unjust and ought to bear the consequences and alter her conduct; that the pill might be bitter, but it would be salutary, and must be swallowed. . . . Sooner or later these or similar measures must be followed or the Empire would be divided and ruined."[46]

The 19th was the day on which Parliament met after the holiday recess. Lord North laid before them letters from the colonial governors which put it beyond doubt that the whole of America was resolute and that Massachusetts, though the chief victim, was not ahead of some of the other colonies in what the king, in his opening speech, had called criminal resistance and disobedience. Parliament was overwhelmed. The opposition had no programme to match the king's. The grave and temperate petition of the Congress "came down," Franklin wrote to Charles Thomson on 5 February, "among a great heap of letters and intelligence from governors and officers in America, newspapers, pamphlets, handbills, etc., from that country, the last in the list, and was laid upon the table before them, undistinguished by any particular recommendation of it to the notice of either House."[47] The mind of America had gone into the petition. The mind of England could not be brought to listen. But British anger instinctively responded to American anger.

The only men in England who had something like Franklin's public wisdom—Chatham, Camden, Shelburne, Burke, and now the young Charles James Fox—were of course with Franklin. On the first day of the session he "received a card from Lord Stanhope acquainting me that Lord Chatham, having a motion to make on the morrow in the House of Lords, concerning America, greatly desired that I might be in the House, into which Lord S. would endeavour to procure me admittance. At this time it was a rule of the House that no peer could introduce more than one friend. The next morning his lordship let me know by another card that if I attended at two o'clock in the lobby Lord Chatham would be there about that time and would himself introduce me. I attended, and met him there accordingly. On my mentioning to him what Lord Stanhope had written to me he said: 'Certainly; and I shall do it with the more pleasure as I am sure your being present at this day's debate will be of more service to America than mine'; and so, taking me by the arm, was leading me along the passage to the door that enters near the throne, when one of the doorkeepers followed and acquainted him that, by the order, none were to be carried in at that door but the eldest sons or brothers of peers; on which he limped back with me to the door near the bar, where were standing a number of gentlemen waiting for the peers who were to introduce them and some peers waiting for friends they expected to introduce; among whom he delivered me to the door-keepers, saying aloud: 'This is Dr. Franklin, whom I would have admitted to the House'; when they readily opened the door for me accordingly."[48]

The manuscript from which Chatham read his motion that day he presented the next day to Franklin. In a sense it was Franklin's motion, for it proposed that the king be asked to withdraw the troops from Boston. With the highest praise for the actions of the Congress, Chatham justified American resistance to oppressive laws. The Americans were doing what the English must not forget how to do: defending English liberty. "Lord Camden, another wonderfully good speaker and clear, cool reasoner, joined him in the same argument, as did several other lords who spoke excellently well; but all availed no more than the whistling of the winds."[49] Sixteen Scottish peers and twenty-four bishops voted against the motion, in a majority of sixty-eight to eighteen.

"As in the course of the debate some lords in the administration had observed that it was common and easy to censure their measures, but those who did so proposed nothing better, Lord Chatham mentioned that he should not be one of those idle censurers; that he had thought long and closely upon the subject and purposed soon to lay before their lordships the result of his meditation, in a plan for healing our differences and restoring peace to the Empire. . . . I much desired to know what his plan was, and intended waiting on him to see if he would communicate it to me; but he went the next morning to Hayes, and I was so much taken up with daily business and company that I could not easily get out to him. A few days after, however, Lord Mahon called on me and told me Lord Chatham was very desirous of seeing me; when I promised to be with him the Friday following, several engagements preventing my going sooner.

"On Friday the 27th, I took a post chaise about nine o'clock and got to Hayes about eleven; but, my attention being engaged in reading a new pamphlet, the postboy drove me a mile or two beyond the gate. His lordship, being out on an airing in his chariot, had met me before I reached Hayes, unobserved by me, turned, and followed me, and, not finding me there, concluded as he had seen me reading that I had passed by mistake, and sent a servant after me. He expressed great pleasure at my coming and acquainted me in a long conversation with the outlines of his plan, parts of which he read to me." Chatham had shown it only to Camden and now Franklin. Nobody else was to see it before it was presented to the House of Lords. "He requested me to make no mention of it; otherwise parts might be misunderstood and blown upon beforehand, and others perhaps adopted and produced by ministers as their own. I promised the closest secrecy, and kept my word, not even mentioning to anyone that I had seen him. I dined with him, the family only present, and returned to town in the evening."[50]

It did not promise too well for the success of Chatham's plan that he had so few confidants. Even the greatest of the Whigs needed other Whigs with him. The opposition was scattered enough as it was. The followers of Rockingham, now out of office for nine years, still clung to the principle of the Declaratory Act which had made it possible for them to repeal the Stamp Act. They knew that Chatham disagreed with them. They had not supported him when he moved to withdraw the troops, and they watched him with a jealous fear that he might succeed in opposition where they had failed.

"On the Sunday following, being the 29th, his lordship came to town and called upon me in Craven Street. He brought with him his plan transcribed in the form of an act of Parliament, which he put into my hands, requesting me to consider it carefully and communicate such remarks upon it as should occur to me. His reason for desiring to give me that trouble was, as he was pleased to say, that he knew no man so thoroughly acquainted with the subject or so capable of giving advice upon it; that he thought the errors of ministers in American affairs had been often owing to their not obtaining the best information; that therefore, though he had considered the business thoroughly in all its parts, he was not so confident of his own judgment but that he came to set it right by mine, as men set their watches by a regulator." Chatham, after talking with Franklin, decided that the plan should be offered to the

Lords as soon as possible, and set the date for the next Wednesday. "He wished to see me upon the preceding Tuesday, when he would again call upon me unless I could conveniently come to Hayes. I chose the latter, in respect to his lordship, and because there was less likelihood of interruption. . . . He stayed with me near two hours, his equipage waiting at the door; and, being there while people were coming from church, it was much taken notice of and talked of, as at that time was every little circumstance that men thought could possibly any way affect American affairs. Such a visit from so great a man, on so important a business, flattered not a little my vanity; and the honour of it gave me the more pleasure as it happened on the very day twelvemonth that the ministry had taken so much pains to disgrace me before the Privy Council."[51]

Chatham, whose wide vision saw the Americans as compatriots of the British, still held, his plan showed, that Parliament had a right to bind the colonies in the interest of the Empire, and the Crown the right to send troops without consent of the provincial assemblies. But he held also that only Americans could tax Americans and that their charters were inviolable. He proposed that the Continental Congress be made official and permanent; that it be asked to make a free grant for imperial purposes; and that Parliament suspend for the present the acts of which the colonists complained. Franklin, reading and considering the transcript Chatham had left with him, wrote out notes for the comments he had been invited to bring to Hayes on Tuesday. But on that day, "though I stayed near four hours, his lordship, in the manner, I think, of all eloquent persons, was so full and diffuse in supporting every particular I questioned that there was not time to go through half my memorandums. He is not easily interrupted; and I had such pleasure in hearing him that I found little inclination to interrupt him. Therefore, considering that neither of us had much expectation that the plan would be adopted entirely as it stood . . . that, to have it received at all here, it must seem to comply a little with some of the prevailing prejudices of the legislature [Parliament]; that, if it was not so perfect as might be wished, it would at least serve as a basis for treaty, and in the meantime prevent mischiefs; and that, as his lordship had determined to offer it the next day, there was not time to make changes and another fair copy: I therefore ceased my querying." Franklin, he later told his son, had had no hand in writing the original plan and had been responsible for only the single word "constitutions" added after "charters."

"On Wednesday Lord Stanhope, at Lord Chatham's request, called upon me and carried me down to the House of Lords, which was soon very full. Lord Chatham, in a most excellent speech, introduced, explained, and supported his plan. When he sat down, Lord Dartmouth rose and very properly said it contained matter of such weight and magnitude as to require much consideration, and he therefore hoped the noble earl did not expect their lordships to decide upon it by immediate vote but would be willing it should lie upon the table for consideration. Lord Chatham answered readily that he expected nothing more." Franklin, hearing what Dartmouth said, believed he had been affected by the negotiations through Barclay and Fothergill. "But Lord Sandwich"— who hated both Franklin and America—"rose and in a petulant, vehement speech opposed its being received at all, and gave his opinion that it ought to be immediately rejected with the contempt it deserved. That he could never believe it to be the production of any British peer. That it appeared to him rather the work of some American; and, turning his face towards me, who was leaning on the bar, said he fancied he had in his eye the person who drew it up, one of the bitterest and most mischievous enemies this country had ever known. This drew the eyes of many lords upon me; but, as I had no inducement to take it to myself, I kept my countenance as immovable as if my features had been made of wood. . . .

"Lord Chatham, in his reply to Lord Sandwich, took notice of his illiberal insinuation that the plan was not the person's who proposed it; declared that it was entirely his own. . . . That it had been heretofore reckoned his vice not to be apt to take advice; but he made no scruple to declare that if he were the first minister of this country and had the care of settling this momentous business, he should not be ashamed of publicly calling to his assistance a person so perfectly acquainted with the whole of American affairs as the gentleman alluded to and so injuriously reflected on: one, he was pleased to say, whom all Europe held in high estimation for his knowledge and wisdom and ranked with our Boyles and Newtons; who was an honour not to the English nation only but to human nature. I found it harder to stand this extravagant compliment than the preceding equally extravagant abuse; but kept as well as I could an unconcerned countenance, as not conceiving it to relate to me."[52]

Camden and Shelburne, the Dukes of Richmond and Manchester, and several other lords spoke in favour of considering Chatham's plan, but the ministers, and Hillsborough, agreed with Sandwich who as first lord of the admiralty had built up a powerful system of patronage and bribery. Dartmouth did not dare hold out against his colleagues. He quickly changed his mind, said he was now ashamed of his earlier stand, and was ready to reject the plan at once. "Lord Chatham's bill," Franklin wrote to Charles Thomson four days later, "though on so important a subject, and offered by so great a character, and supported by such able and learned speakers . . . was treated with as much contempt as they could have shown to a ballad offered by a drunken porter."[53] To Franklin, the wisest man there though unheeded or despised, these lords who claimed "sovereignty over three millions of virtuous, sensible people in America . . . appeared to have scarce discretion enough to govern a herd of swine. Hereditary legislators! thought I. There would be more propriety, because less hazard of mischief, in having (as in some university of Germany) hereditary professors of mathematics. But this was a hasty reflection; for the elected House of Commons is no better, nor ever will be while the electors receive money for their votes and pay money wherewith ministers may bribe their representatives when chosen."[54]

Franklin's great patience was nearly at an end. The next day North proceeded to measures for suppressing the "rebellion." Six thousand men were to be sent to join the armed forces already in the colonies. In answer to the non-importation and non-exportation agreements recommended by the Congress, Parliament voted that New England was to be restrained from all trade with Great Britain, Ireland, and the West Indies, and excluded from the Newfoundland fisheries. But there was opposition in and out of Parliament, and the coercive measures, North announced, would cease as soon as the colonies should submit. Franklin on 4 February thought it still worth while to confer again with Barclay and Fothergill, who assured him that the administration—which

must mean Dartmouth and North—was not completely hostile.
While Fothergill talked about the horrors of war, Barclay hinted
at the reward which a successful peacemaker might expect. Franklin
was disgusted at the hint, but he went with them again over his
seventeen points and heard the observations which he was told the
ministers had made. Three of the points were rejected outright,
four accepted, the others modified in varying degrees. "We had not
at this time a great deal of conversation upon these points; for I
shortened it by observing that while the Parliament claimed and
exercised a power of altering our constitutions at pleasure there
could be no agreement; for we were rendered unsafe in every
privilege we had a right to, and were secure in nothing. And it
being hinted how necessary an agreement was for America, since
it was so easy for Britain to burn all our seaport towns, I grew
warm; said that the chief part of my little property consisted of
houses in those towns; that they might make bonfires of them
whenever they pleased; that the fear of losing them would never
alter my resolution to resist to the last that claim of Parliament;
and that it behoved this country to take care what mischief it
did us, for that sooner or later it would certainly be obliged to
make good all damages with interest. The Doctor smiled, as I
thought, with some approbation of my discourse, passionate as it
was, and said he would certainly repeat it tomorrow to Lord
Dartmouth."[55]

On Thursday the 16th the three met again. Barclay, who had
talked with Hyde, brought with him a draft of a revised plan
which he thought a basis for compromise between Franklin and
the ministers. More than anything else the ministry desired some
act of confession and submission from Massachusetts. They, or
Barclay, proposed that the agent or agents of the colony, "in a
petition to the king, should engage that the tea destroyed shall be
paid for"; and when payment had been made the port should
again be opened. Franklin said he was willing to make the engagement himself, but that he thought there was no time to wait for
Massachusetts to approve; "that if such an engagement were entered into, all the Massachusetts acts should be immediately
repealed."

Fothergill the same day (apparently not on the 6th as has been thought[56]) wrote to Dartmouth that the negotiations had failed. There had been, he wrote, "no opposition or refractory disposition in Dr. Franklin." He would have no objection to meeting the ministers and discussing "the whole affair with the utmost candour and privacy"; to petitioning the king for the restoration of peace; to offering "on the part of Boston to pay the East India Company for the tea, though at the risk of his own private fortune." But he would do these things only if the Massachusetts acts were repealed. There was, Fothergill assumed, no hope that the other ministers would accept these terms, though Dartmouth might. Franklin, Fothergill was convinced, would not yield further.

"Weighing now the present dangerous situation of affairs in America, and the daily hazard of widening the breach there irreparably," Franklin on Friday drafted a petition to the king and a memorial and a letter to Dartmouth, and met Barclay and Fothergill. His language to them was much crisper than that he had used in his formal papers. "If we mean a hearty reconciliation," he said, "we must deal candidly, and use no tricks." The Massachusetts Assembly could not meet under the new constitution without acknowledging the right of Parliament to alter their old one. To propose that they meet was to say: " 'Try on your fetters first, and then, if you don't like 'em, petition and we will consider.' " Barclay and Fothergill advised him against sending his petition and memorial, but they undertook, with however little confidence, to report his sentiments to their superiors.

Barclay on Thursday evening must have told Hyde that Franklin had undertaken to pay for the tea, and Hyde must have told Howe, who wanted to go to America as commissioner for settling its grievances. Howe through his sister made an appointment to see Franklin at her house at eleven o'clock on Saturday. Cheerfully and wordily Howe again said how much he valued Franklin and hoped to be able to take him to America "as a friend, an assistant, or secretary." Franklin replied that he did not know what proposals were to be made to the Americans. "If they were reasonable ones in themselves, possibly I might be able to make them appear such to my countrymen; but if they were otherwise I doubted whether that could be done by any man, and certainly I should not undertake it." These were more outspoken words than a viscount was used, in England, to hearing from a philosopher. Howe quickly went on to say that he would insist on Franklin's being well rewarded, both now and for the future. As proof in advance of the ministry's good will, Franklin might have the arrears of his salary as agent for Massachusetts, which the ministry had held up. That is, what was already Franklin's would be an earnest of benefits to come. (The sum of arrears and charges was £1851 when Franklin finally received it from the Assembly in October, when he had gone to Cambridge to see Washington take command of the Continental army.[57]) Mean and insulting as Howe's offer was, Franklin merely said that he must not accept any "previous favour from ministers; my accepting them would destroy the very influence you propose to make use of; they would be considered as so many bribes to betray the interest of my country. Only let me see the propositions; and if I approve of them, I shall not hesitate a moment, but will hold myself ready to accompany your lordship at an hour's warning." Howe asked if Franklin would talk to Hyde. Franklin answered that he would. Howe said he would speak to Hyde and send word when Franklin might see him. But when, on Monday, Howe had spoken to Hyde, he wrote to Franklin that the minor minister thought nothing could come of a meeting. Barclay, it appears, had again been with Hyde and had told him that Franklin would pay for the tea only if all the Massachusetts acts were repealed at once.[58]

That Monday in Parliament North made a conciliatory motion. If any colony should see fit to contribute voluntarily to imperial defence and also support its colonial officers, it might be excused from the payment of any taxes or duties except those for the regulation of commerce. Though the motion was carried, it aroused general confusion and dissatisfaction. Anger on both sides had spoiled their taste for any but thoroughgoing measures. Franklin on the 25th wrote to James Bowdoin saying that if the Americans would continue firm and united in their boycott the ministry could not possibly last another year. But there must be no surrender. "The eyes of all Christendom are now upon us, and our honour as a people is become a matter of the utmost consequence to be taken care of. If we tamely give up our rights in this contest, a century to come will not restore us in the opinion of the world; we shall be stamped with the character of bastards, poltroons, and fools, and be despised and trampled upon, not by this haughty, insolent nation only, but by all mankind. Present inconveniences, therefore, are to be borne with fortitude, and better times expected."[59]

The same day he wrote to Galloway, who had drawn up a plan of union which the Continental Congress had rejected. Galloway's plan provided for an imperial legislature and a written constitution. Franklin had shown it to Chatham and Camden, but he put no trust in it. England and America were too far apart. "When I consider the extreme corruption prevalent among all orders of men in this old rotten state, and the glorious public virtue so predominant in our rising country, I cannot but apprehend more mischief than benefit from a closer union. I fear they may drag us after them in all the plundering wars which their desperate circumstances, injustice, and rapacity may prompt them to undertake; and their wide-wasting prodigality and profusion is a gulf that will swallow up every aid we may distress ourselves to afford them. Here numberless and needless places, enormous salaries, pensions, perquisites, bribes, groundless quarrels, foolish expeditions, false accounts or no accounts, contracts and jobs devour all revenue and produce continual necessity in the midst of natural plenty. I apprehend, therefore, that to unite us intimately will only be to corrupt and poison us also. . . . However, I would try anything, and bear anything that can be borne with safety to our just liberties, rather than engage in a war with such near relations, unless compelled to it by dire necessity in our own defence."[60] A little more, and Franklin, in disgust and desperation, would be ready for independence.

On the 28th he met Howe again. Franklin had just heard of his wife's death and said he must go by the first ship to Philadelphia, unless Howe still needed him on his mission. Howe urged him to call on Hyde. Franklin knew that Hyde was an early riser, and was at his house at eight the next morning. Hyde was full of Tory platitudes about America. "I answered all, but with little effect; for, though his lordship seemed civilly to hear what I said, I had reason to believe he attended very little to the purport of it, his mind being employed the while in thinking on what he himself purposed to say next." Franklin had got beyond the bland idiom of diplomacy. North's latest proposal, he said, "was similar to no mode of obtaining aids that ever existed, except that of a highwayman who presents his pistol and hat at a coach window, demanding no specific sum, but if you will give all your money or what he is pleased to think sufficient, he will civilly omit putting his own hands into your pockets; if not, there is his pistol." Even if North's scheme were adopted, it would still apply only to taxes. And taxes were now less important to America than the inviolability of their charters and laws.

Hyde could not give up his belief that Franklin was bargaining. With authority to come to an agreement, he was being "extremely reserved" for the sake of his constituents. "But my expectations might deceive me; and he did think I might be assured I should never obtain better terms than what were now offered by Lord North." Hyde said all over again that Franklin had been badly treated—and that if he would only "bring about a reconciliation on terms suitable to the dignity of government" he might be "honoured and rewarded, perhaps, beyond my expectations." Franklin, bored as well as disgusted, "replied that I thought I had given a convincing proof of my sincere desire of promoting peace when, on being informed that all wanted for the honour of government was to obtain payment for the tea, I offered, without any instruction to warrant my so doing or assurance that I should be reimbursed or my conduct approved, to engage for that payment, if the Massachusetts acts were to be repealed: an engagement in which I must have risked my whole fortune, which I thought few besides myself would have done. That . . . I was not the reserved man imagined, having really no secret instructions to act upon. That I was certainly willing to do everything that could reasonably be expected of me. But if any supposed I could prevail upon my countrymen to take black for white, and wrong for right, it was not knowing either them or me; they were not capable of being so imposed on, nor was I capable of attempting it."[61]

Except for one polite and futile meeting with Howe a week

later this ended the negotiation with the ministers. "And I heard no more of that with Messrs. Fothergill and Barclay. I could only gather from some hints in their conversation that neither of them were well pleased with the conduct of the ministers respecting these transactions. And a few days before I left London I met them by desire at the Doctor's house, when they desired me to assure their friends from them that it was now their fixed opinion that nothing could secure the privileges of America but firm, sober adherence to the terms of the Association made at the Congress, and that the salvation of English liberty depended now on the perseverance and virtue of America."[62]

In his last week in England Franklin, disappointed, disgusted, bored too long, flew into an unreasonable rage. Members of both Houses of Parliament had in the course of debate contemptuously accused the Americans of every dishonesty and cowardice. Even Franklin's old friend Strahan, now printer to the king and member for Malmesbury, believed the story that a Scottish sergeant had disarmed forty American soldiers and brought them into Boston.[63] "General Clarke," Franklin afterwards remembered, "had the folly to say in my hearing at Sir John Pringle's that with a thousand British grenadiers he would undertake to go from one end of America to the other, and geld all the males, partly by force and partly by a little coaxing."[64] Franklin drew up an insolent memorial to Dartmouth, protesting against the blockade of Boston and the exclusion of Massachusetts from the fisheries, and demanding satisfaction. "But consulting my friend Mr. [Thomas] Walpole upon it, who is a member of the House of Commons, he looked at it and me several times alternately, as if he apprehended me a little out of my senses. As I was in the hurry of packing up, I requested him to take the trouble of showing it to his neighbour, Lord Camden, and ask his advice upon it." Walpole was troubled. He wrote Franklin a note telling him it would be dangerous to present any such memorial, called on him when he was out, and followed him to the House of Lords to caution him. Since he had no instructions for his demand, it would seem a national affront. "I had no desire to make matters worse, and, being grown cooler, took the advice so kindly given."[65]

IV

To the very last Franklin hoped against hope that the friends of America and of the Empire might yet gather enough strength to overthrow the North ministry. In a letter to Charles Thomson as late as 13 March he said that even the ministers were not "cordially united" and that they were supported "chiefly by accounts from America that all was fluctuating there. . . . Our only safety is in the firmest union and keeping strict faith with each other."[66] On the 3rd Franklin had had a solemn conference with Josiah Quincy, who, dying of tuberculosis, was to sail the next day for Boston. Quincy had not wanted to go, and Fothergill had advised against it. But various Americans in London urged the need of a messenger who could carry information and counsel which it was not safe to write. Quincy, dining with Franklin, talked for three hours with him alone. If Franklin, as is probable, told him of the secret negotiations, Quincy did not mention it in the sparse notes he took.[67] "Dissuades from France or Spain," he wrote. "Intimate with both the Spanish and French ambassadors, the latter a shrewd great man." Quincy might tell his friends in Boston that some of the Americans in London had already thought of looking for help to France or Spain, but that Franklin was not yet of their opinion, or believed the time had not yet come. "By no means take any step of great consequence, unless on a sudden emergency, without advice of the Continental Congress. Explicitly, and in so many words, said that only New England [that is, New England alone] could hold out for ages against this country, and if they were firm and united, in seven years would conquer. Said he had the best intelligence that the manufacturers were bitterly feeling and loudly complaining of the loss of the American trade. Let your adherence be to the non-importation and non-exportation agreement a year from next September, or to the next session of Parliament, and the day is won."

What else Quincy had to say he never told, for he died on the voyage. Franklin, who outlived so many young disciples, went on with his work in London. "My time was . . . much taken up, by friends calling continually to inquire for news from America; members of both Houses of Parliament to inform me what passed in the Houses, and discourse with me on the debates and on motions made or to be made; merchants of London and of the manufacturing and port towns, on their petitions; the Quakers upon theirs, etc., etc."[68] He planned to sail on 21 March, but was not sure he could in so short a time wind up more than ten years in England. The chancery suit was still over his head, and was soon, after many delays, at last to be argued. Whately, afraid Franklin would sail and so be outside the jurisdiction of the court, consulted Wedderburn. Wedderburn, who might have been glad to strike again at Franklin, consulted Edward Thurlow, the attorney-general. Thurlow, no friend of America or Franklin, thought it unwise to hold him. The ministry would be blamed for persecution.[69]

Nothing else interfered, and Franklin made his farewells, which he did not know were his last as a subject of the Empire. He thought he might come back in the fall, though he finally turned the agency for Massachusetts over to Arthur Lee.[70] On the 19th Franklin spent several hours with Burke, who made his great and unavailing speech on conciliation three days later. Burke moved, almost as Franklin might have done, that Parliament repeal its objectionable acts and leave American taxation to Americans. His last day in London Franklin spent alone with Priestley, from morning till night. Strangers, Priestley wrote, often thought Franklin cold and reserved. But that day he was deeply stirred by the prospect of civil war, which he thought he had done all he could to prevent. He was reading newspapers from America, telling Priestley what to extract from them for the English papers. Now and then the philosopher could not read for the tears that filled his eyes and ran down his cheeks. If there should be a war, he was sure America would win, but it would take ten years, and he would never live to see the end.[71] In the evening he received a letter from Fothergill, who asked Franklin to get their friends together in Philadelphia and tell them how the peaceful negotiations had failed. Tell them, as to the British government, that " 'whatever specious pretences are offered, they are all hollow; and that to get a larger field on which to fatten a herd of worthless parasites is all that is regarded.' The Doctor, in the course of his daily visits among the great in the practice of his profession, had full opportunity of being acquainted with their sentiments, the conversation everywhere at this time turning upon the subject of America."[72]

Posting to Portsmouth from which he was to sail on the Pennsylvania packet, Franklin had his grandson Temple with him, who was at last to be acknowledged by his father. They made a pleasant voyage of six weeks, "the weather constantly so moderate that a London wherry might have accompanied us all the way."[73] On the very first day out Franklin began to write for his son the secret history of his recent dealings with the ministry. The details were fresh in his mind, he had brought the documents with him, and he told the story with grave power and homely ease. In the second half of the voyage he began to take the daily temperature of the air and water, studying the Gulf Stream.

Six years before he had learned from his Nantucket cousin that if the American captains of merchant ships made faster time from London to Rhode Island than the English captains of the mail packets from Falmouth to New York, it was because the American captains understood the Gulf Stream and crossed it directly instead of running against it for days. Franklin had had a chart made, with the help of his cousin, and had furnished it to the packet captains, "who slighted it." Now for the week of 26 April–2 May he lowered his thermometer into the ocean from two to four times a day, from as early as seven in the morning to as late as eleven at night, while the ship kept along the eastern edge of the stream and then cut across it into colder water. He had seen a whale on the 26th, before they entered, but saw none in the stream itself. He noticed that the water of the stream had its own colour and more gulf weed than the surrounding water, and "that it does not sparkle in the night." It might be studied and understood like a river. "A vessel from Europe to North America may shorten her passage by avoiding to stem the stream, in which the thermometer will be very useful; and a vessel from America to Europe may do the same by the same means of keeping in it. It may have often happened accidentally that voyages have been shortened by these circumstances. It is well to have command of them."[74]

Franklin wrote to Priestley on 16 May that he had made "a valuable philosophical discovery which I shall communicate to you when I get a little time."[75] It was not till ten years later, on his last voyage home to America, that he found or took time to write out his conclusions. For when he arrived at Philadelphia on 5 May he heard of the bloody outbreaks at Lexington and Concord while he was on the Atlantic. The next morning he was chosen by the Assembly to be one of its deputies to the Second Continental Congress, which was to meet in Philadelphia in four days.

Paris

Postmaster-General

MEN of seventy seldom make revolutions. Franklin, the oldest man in the Continental Congress, was nearly a generation older than half the members. At a time when most Americans of his years held back in opposition, uncertainty, or dread, he brought to the insurgents the prestige of the first American name: first in science, letters, and international reputation. Congress, sending him as commissioner to Canada, called him in the formal commission: "Benjamin Franklin, LL.D., member of the Royal Academy of Sciences at Paris, F.R.S., etc., etc." In Europe, where he was better known than any of his compatriots, he was thought of as the leader of the colonies. Many Englishmen melodramatically believed, whether in sympathy or anger, that he had hurried to America after the insult at the Privy Council to organize a rebellion for revenge. But in America, presuming upon neither his name nor his grievances, Franklin absorbed himself in the general cause. Though his year and a half in Congress was perhaps the busiest period of his life, he kept and left only the scantiest personal records.

As Galloway later remembered it, Franklin on his return did not at once show his hand and for five or six weeks stayed at home when not away on public business.[1] He tried to persuade his son to give up his post as governor, and Galloway to sit in the Continental Congress to which he had been nominated by the Pennsylvania Assembly. The governor had long been Franklin's confidant, Galloway his lieutenant in the conflict with the proprietors; but now both the younger men were more conservative than he. Finally, when the three had met one evening and talked and drunk till late, Franklin announced that he was for independence. His son and Galloway, Franklin must have thought, would be almost two sons to him in the dangerous undertaking. It was bound to mean much to the Americans if a royal governor should join them in their resistance to the British ministry, and a colonial statesman of Galloway's standing and ability. Franklin's arguments and his example could not persuade them. William Franklin remained faithful to his office, and after a term in prison was president of the Associated Loyalists in New York. Galloway, after three complicated years in Pennsylvania, became the exiled spokesman of the American loyalists in London. Franklin seems to have formed no intimate new friendships in Philadelphia, even with the congenial delegates from Massachusetts and Virginia.

He is hardly ever mentioned in the diaries and letters which speak of dinners and excursions for the members of Congress. This was no longer London, not yet Paris. He lived quietly in the house in Market Street, ten years old but new to him, with his devoted daughter Sarah and her husband Richard Bache, and the grandchildren Franklin had never seen before, though his wife had written him so much about their little histories. Temple had gone to his father at Perth Amboy. Franklin on 13 June wrote affectionately to him, telling him that a long letter had come from their landlady in London with all the news. The little Bache boys, Benjamin and William, were playing soldier. "Will has got a little gun, marches with it, and whistles at the same time by way of fife."[2]

Philadelphia was full of voluntary soldiers. The Associators, heirs of the association which Franklin had organized against the French almost thirty years before, drilled, marched, enlisted recruits, and paid harsh attention to men who were loyal to the government they had lived under all their lives. The news from Lexington called for armed resistance to the ministerial forces that threatened—the phrase invariably ran—"the liberties of America." Four days before Franklin's arrival the Associators gathered in all the wards of the city to form defensive companies. On 9 May the South Carolina delegates to Congress landed from the Charleston packet. The same day delegates from North Carolina, Virginia, Maryland, and Delaware rode in from the south, met six miles out by five hundred mounted officers and gentlemen, two miles out by riflemen and infantry, and conducted with playing bands and ringing bells through the town, with fifteen thousand persons watching the slow, solemn march. The next day there were military ceremonies for the delegates from Massachusetts, Connecticut, and New York.

Congress assembled on the 10th in the Pennsylvania State House, to elect Peyton Randolph of Virginia as president and Charles Thomson of Pennsylvania as secretary. (The delegates from New Jersey had come quietly, and those from Rhode Island and Georgia were late.) On the second day the session heard the letter sent in February, from Franklin, Bollan, and Arthur Lee in London, which reported the neglect by king and Parliament of the petition from the First Continental Congress. But most of the session was taken up with depositions about the affair at Lexington. On the fourth day, Saturday, the whole Congress dined together at the City Tavern, where they drank the health of Edmund Burke, along with others, for his far-sighted speech on conciliation. Franklin, writing to Burke on Monday, spoke of the first hostilities: "You will see by the papers that General Gage called his Assembly together to propose Lord North's pacific plan; but before they could meet, drew the sword and began the war. His troops made a most vigorous retreat—twenty miles in three hours—scarce to be paralleled in history; the feeble Americans, who pelted them all the way, could scarce keep up with them."[3] And the next day Franklin wrote further about Gage to Priestley: "All America is exasperated by his conduct, and more firmly united than ever. The breach between the two countries is grown wider, and in danger of becoming irreparable."[4]

One of the firmest and boldest of the delegates, Franklin was one of the most silent. "I served," Jefferson said long afterwards, "with General Washington in the legislature of Virginia before the Revolution, and during it with Dr. Franklin in Congress. I never heard either of them speak ten minutes at a time, nor to any but the main point which was to decide the question. They laid their shoulders to the great points, knowing that the little ones would follow of themselves."[5] Washington left for Cambridge in June to take command of the Continental army, and Jefferson, a third silent man, came to Congress. In temper he was closer to Franklin than any other delegate, though so much younger, and there were now two philosophers among the politicians. John Adams, habitually an orator, wondered that Franklin, "from day to day sitting in silence, a great part of the time fast asleep in his chair,"[6] was appointed to all the most important committees, Adams to few of them. It may have been good fortune, Adams thought, for Franklin, Washington, and Jefferson that they had no love of debate.

Certainly Franklin had none. He adjusted himself to the tone of Congress and was patient during its deliberations. In his own mind he had gone through these issues before, some of them long before, and had to watch younger men learn what he already knew. When Congress voted in July to send one more humble petition to the king, Franklin, who knew the king and his ministry better than any other American, believed it useless, as it turned out to be. Dartmouth did not present it when it reached London. A royal proclamation on 23 August had declared the Americans to be rebels and warned all persons not to give them aid and comfort. Franklin, while the petition was being drawn, wrote to John Sargent in Kent: "It now requires great wisdom on your side the water to prevent a total separation; I hope it will be found among you. We shall give you one opportunity more of recovering our affections and retaining the connexion; and that I fear will be the last."[7] He was willing to take a chance on any hope of reconciliation as long as there was the least possibility of it. He did what he could to preserve wisdom and good humour in Congress while the debates went on. But his own taste and gift ran to action. The colonies must arm themselves, if only to gain a strength which would force the ministry to deal peaceably with them. If that could not be done, then there was even better reason for being armed. England was the most powerful nation in the world, with a disciplined army to send against the straggling colonial militia, with an incomparable navy to blockade or burn the undefended seaports which were the chief American towns.

An omniscient historian, if there were one, might point out what particular steps in the conflict from 1760 to 1776 decisively led to war and independence rather than to peace and the imperial unity which Franklin had desired. To anything less than omniscience almost all the steps seem unavoidable incidents in a historical process. The transplanted English had been made new men by a new land: that is, Americans. As they lost the sense of feudal subordination to the old aristocracy they increasingly resented their commercial subordination under the mercantile system. The British government, first by taxation, tried to keep them subordinate. They replied to taxation, in the form of import duties, by partly ceasing to import British goods. With taxation and non-importation went agitation and anger in both America and Britain. Franklin had early come to fear that growing anger. Angry nations do not know what their reasons are, much less state them clearly. Besides the international antagonism there was internal strife. In England a reactionary king and ministry were opposed by liberal and imaginative Englishmen who demanded for themselves in the realm something like the same extension of liberty as the Americans were demanding. The restive Americans, encouraged by British Whigs, saw themselves as defending ancient English rights. But there were other Americans who sympathized with the king and his ministers, and believed that the American patriots were a democratic—proletarian—threat to an established civil order. The ministry were the more ready to use force because they thought they would be supported by the American Tories, and the American patriots the more ready to resist because they thought they would be supported by the British Whigs. During 1775 both sides were armed or arming, both determined, and both certain they must not yield.

Franklin, who had steadily counselled non-importation as the best answer to taxation, had no less steadily urged a firm resistance to force. Now there seemed no resort but to armed measures. At his age he might with credit have retired from public life, as his son urged him to do. Instead he gave himself with ageless energy to defensive schemes, looking forward also to possible aggression. He had so long faced the prospect of an open breach that it did not horrify him as it did many conservatives in Congress. Of all Americans he had had the largest vision of the Empire that might be shaped by political wisdom, and perhaps the strongest affection for the idea. But he had always known that it could not be brought about by the subordination of the colonies. To keep a part of the Empire weak was not the way to make the whole of it strong. That was to deny potential life, for the benefit of short-sighted privilege. If the ministry's plan for the Empire was to compel the Americans to be less than they had the power to become, then they would be better off outside it, whatever they might lose by separation. Franklin might leave his mind open for some unforeseen accident of fortune, but his heart had let his old vision go.

II

His history from May 1775 to October 1776 is a synopsis and calendar of activities which touch almost every phase of the Revolution except actual fighting. Appointed by Congress as chairman of a committee (29 May) to establish a postal system, he brought in their report on 25 July and the next day was elected Postmaster-General, at a salary of a thousand dollars a year, which he gave for the relief of wounded soldiers. Since his dismissal from the royal post office it had become unpopular in America, and a rival system had been set up by William Goddard, now of Baltimore, whose father had been postmaster at New London under Franklin and who himself had learned the printing trade under Franklin's partner in New York. Congress took over Goddard's "constitutional post" and Franklin reorganized it with the help of Richard Bache as controller. With Philadelphia as the central office, the line ran from Falmouth (Portland) to Savannah. By December of that year the royal post office had been discontinued.[8] The present American post office descends in an unbroken line from the system Franklin planned for the Continental Congress. When the first postage stamps came into use in 1847 the two denominations issued bore one of them the face of Washington (ten cents), the other that of Franklin (five cents).

He had more than postal matters on his hands. During June he was assigned to committees to report the petition to the king, to promote the manufacture of saltpetre for gunpowder in the colonies, to draw up the declaration by Washington on taking command, to arrange for the printing of paper money. Franklin avoided drafting state papers and left it to more oratorical men, whom Congress preferred. But as a scientist he was active on the saltpetre committee, and he was a master at printing money. He made sketches for the new currency.[9] Having observed in some of his studies that the veins of leaves are never alike, he suggested the leaf designs used on Continental bills, a different leaf for each denomination, to make counterfeiting difficult. Richard Bache was one of three men chosen to supervise the printing.

Franklin had more than Congressional matters on his hands. On 30 June, when the Pennsylvania Assembly adjourned to September, it appointed a Committee (or Council) of Safety to defend the province during the recess. John Dickinson was named first, and was presumably to be chairman, but when the Committee met on 3 July Franklin was elected president. "My time," he wrote to Priestley on the 7th, "was never more fully employed. In the morning at six I am at the Committee of Safety . . . which . . . holds till near nine, when I am at the Congress, and that sits till after four in the afternoon. Both those bodies proceed with the greatest unanimity, and their meetings are well attended." No need to tell even Priestley, at that British distance, about the furious arguments which were still going on in Congress about the petition to the king. "It will scarce be credited in Britain that men can be as diligent with us from zeal for the public good as with you for thousands per annum. Such is the difference between uncorrupted new states and corrupted old ones."[10]

The minutes of the Committee of Safety,[11] little noted by Franklin's biographers, show him busy day by day at such devices as an unready populace must make shift with against trained soldiers and ships of war. At the second meeting (4 July) he was instructed by the Committee to furnish a model of a pike for infantrymen. The Americans might be brilliant marksmen but, as had lately appeared at Bunker Hill, they could not yet match the British with the bayonet. Men who had no muskets or ammunition—and America was short of both—might stand up against a bayonet charge if they were armed with pikes. Charles Lee, once colonel in the British army but now an American major-general, believed so, and Franklin agreed with him. He brought in his model the next day. The Committee ordered one made, and afterwards a hundred for their armed boats on the Delaware. (As late as February Franklin, writing to Lee, still wished pikes might be introduced into the army, and even bows and arrows. He gave arguments in favour of them and quoted Polydore Virgil, in

Latin.[12] He had in mind, of course, the want of powder and lead, and the defects of the common musket of the time.)

The Committee, having decided they could not lay an obstructing boom across the river, on 15 June ordered "machines for the interruption of navigation" which were in effect gigantic *chevaux de frise*, of logs and iron, planted in the channel to keep British war vessels from coming up within range of the town. These may or may not have been devised by Franklin, but they were one of his special projects.[13] An effort was made to keep their whereabouts secret except from the ten pilots who were selected to guide peaceful vessels through the difficult passage. Along with these the Committee were building armed boats fifty feet long, called row-galleys or gondolas, which were driven by twelve oarsmen on a side. With a crew of thirty to fifty each, and a brass gun, they were little movable forts. A more substantial fort was built below the town, at Gloucester. A watchman was stationed near Cape Henlopen to send word of the approach of armed vessels. The lighthouse-keeper would signal as soon as one was sighted. By the end of September the Committee had provided seventeen *chevaux de frise* and thirteen armed boats (among them the *Experiment* and the *Congress*, the *Burke* and the *Camden*, the *Washington* and the *Franklin*).

Busy as Franklin was with the Committee, he was as busy with Congress, which did not adjourn till 1 August. On 12 July he was appointed to the committee to devise ways and means to protect the trade of the colonies: which meant, partly, to arrange for importing munitions of war while maintaining the non-importation agreements against Great Britain. The next day he became one of three commissioners (with Patrick Henry and James Wilson) to have charge of the Indians of the middle department, living west of Pennsylvania and Virginia. On 21 July Congress resolved itself into a committee of the whole to "take into consideration the state of America," and Franklin read the *Articles of Confederation and Perpetual Union*[14] which he had drawn up for "The United Colonies of North America." This was his Albany Plan of Union, revised to fit the changed conditions. If approved by the assemblies and ratified in the ensuing Congress, "the union thereby established is to continue firm till the terms of reconciliation proposed in the petition of the last Congress to the king are agreed to; till the acts since made, restraining the American commerce and fisheries, are repealed; till reparation is made for the injury done to Boston by shutting up its port, for the burning of Charlestown, and for the expense of this unjust war; and till all the British troops are withdrawn from America. On the arrival of these events"—which Franklin must have felt certain would be never—"the colonies return to their former connexion and friendship with Britain; but on failure thereof, this confederation is to be perpetual." Congress as a whole was not ready for any such scheme, though Jefferson and some others were,[15] and Franklin did not press it. The next day he was appointed chairman of a committee (with Jefferson, John Adams, and Richard Henry Lee) to consider North's February motion for conciliation. They reported against the motion on the 31st, and Congress voted to reject it. Franklin, now Postmaster-General, was the same day appointed to a committee which during the recess was to make inquiries about lead and lead ore throughout the colonies, and the cheapest and easiest way of making salt.

The Committee of Safety took no recess. On all but two week days of August, till the 26th, Franklin was present, working still at the home-made defences of the province, carrying on the organization of the militia, selecting officers for the armed boats, obtaining medicines for the troops, sending powder from the Philadelphia magazine to the Committee of Safety in New York, requisitioning some of the lead captured by Ethan Allen and Benedict Arnold at Ticonderoga. In the last days of August Franklin went to Perth Amboy for a brief visit to his son. They could agree only to continue each in his own course.

Back in Philadelphia Franklin was again absorbed in the Committee of Safety and after 13 September in Congress. The day Congress met he was given permission to land his books, papers, and furniture from the ship in which they had come from England, as not excluded by the boycott. On the 18th he was appointed to the secret committee for the importation of gunpowder, and on the 22nd to the committee on American trade. On the 27th at the meeting of the American Philosophical Society, of which he had been president for almost seven years, he for the first time took the chair. On the 29th he signed, and probably wrote, a memorial from the Committee of Safety to the Assembly, proposing that persons who had conscientious scruples against war—Quakers and Moravians—be excused from military service but required to pay a fixed sum towards the cost of defence. The same day the Committee made a summary report of its summer's activities. The next day Congress chose Franklin (with Thomas Lynch of South Carolina and Benjamin Harrison of Virginia) to go to Cambridge to confer with Washington and the New England authorities on the support of the army. On 3 October, the day before he left, he wrote cheerfully to Priestley: "Britain, at the expense of three millions, has killed one hundred and fifty Yankees this campaign, which is twenty thousand pounds a head. . . . During the same time sixty thousand children have been born in America."[16]

Two weeks later the Congressional committee and their three servants were in Washington's camp. Gage had been replaced by Sir William Howe, but the British forces were still shut up in Boston under the deadly fire, if they showed themselves, of the militia and of backwoods riflemen from Pennsylvania, Maryland, and Virginia. The New England companies which Congress had adopted as the Continental army were made up of volunteers who would soon be free to go home, as many of them meant to do, and Washington asked that a new army be formed, of twenty thousand men enlisted for at least a year, with better discipline and more abundant supplies. The Council sat for four days, planning the reorganization of the army, revising the articles of war, making rules for the exchange of prisoners and for the disposal of prizes taken at sea by the armed schooners (one of them named the *Franklin*) which, the beginnings of the American navy, harassed the British supply ships. At the end of the conference Washington still had hopes and promises rather than an army, but New England had some reason to believe that the other colonies would continue their support, and Congress had shown itself willing to assume, so far as it could, a general responsibility.

Franklin had brought with him a hundred pounds raised by friends in England for the benefit of Americans who had been wounded at Lexington and Concord, or for the widows and orphans of men killed that day. He paid the money over to the

Massachusetts Assembly, and collected from them the sum due him
for his services as agent in London. One day at dinner he met
Abigail Adams, who sent a letter by him to John Adams in Philadelphia. Franklin's character, she said, "from my infancy I had
been taught to venerate. I found him social but not talkative, and
when he spoke something useful dropped from his tongue. He was
grave, yet pleasant and affable. You know I make some pretensions
to physiognomy, and I thought I could read in his countenance
the virtues of his heart; among which patriotism shone in its full
lustre, and with that is blended every virtue of a Christian: for a
true patriot must be a religious man."[17] Nathanael Greene, at the
head of the Rhode Island regiments, met the committee from
Congress on the evening of its arrival. "I had the honour," he wrote
the next day, "to be introduced to that very great man, Dr. Franklin, whom I viewed with silent admiration the whole evening.
Attention watched his lips, and conviction closed his periods."[18]

The studious young general must often have heard of Franklin,
for Greene was from Warwick in his native colony, a kinsman of
Catherine Ray Greene, and had been married the year before to
her niece and namesake Catherine Littlefield. General Greene also
might have sent a letter by Franklin, who on his way home stopped
in Rhode Island. He had learned in May, from John Adams, that
his sister Jane had left Boston for Warwick. Guessing that she
must be with the Greenes, Franklin had at once written to her
there, and his answer had been a joint letter from Jane and her
hostess: "your affectionate friend as long as life." Now, in his
pleasant stay with his favourite sister and his dear friend, he went
with Catherine to visit her uncle at Pastuxet, where Judge Philip
Greene told his daughter Betty, Catherine's cousin, that Franklin
was the most famous man in the world. But Betty, according to a
family tradition, was shocked by the philosopher's bold speech and
did not like him.[19] Franklin took Catherine's son Ray, now ten,
with him to enter school in Philadelphia.

Just before Franklin set out for Cambridge he had been elected
a member of the Pennsylvania Assembly, which was in session
when he got back by 15 November. In his absence he had again
been appointed to the Committee of Safety and to the delegation
to Congress. The Assembly sat for only ten days after his return,

and he was often absent from the meetings of the Committee. In Congress he was at once appointed (16 November) to arrange for two swift packets for the mails; the next day to another on vessels and cargoes of the enemy taken by the colonies; on the 23rd to yet another on what to do with persons who refused to accept the Continental currency. Then on the 29th he was assigned to what was to be the most important of all his committees, with Harrison, Thomas Johnson of Maryland, Dickinson, and John Jay of New York. The five had "the sole purpose of corresponding with our friends in Great Britain, Ireland, and other parts of the world."[20] It was a secret committee, the first on foreign affairs, and the origin of the American Department of State.

For more than a year various Americans had talked of appeals to European states which might be glad to help the colonies as a means of reducing the disproportionate strength of England. "We have not yet," Franklin wrote to Priestley on 7 July, "applied to any foreign power for assistance, nor offered our commerce for their friendship. Perhaps we never may; yet it is natural to think of it, if we are pressed."[21] By the end of November Congress had thought of it as justified. Their petition had been disregarded, and Americans proclaimed rebels. The British had burned Charlestown in June and Falmouth in October. News had come that troops from Brunswick and Hesse were to be hired to put the rebellion down. That Englishmen had been lukewarm and slow in enlisting for the American service might be a sign that England was divided, as many Americans believed. But that foreign mercenaries had been called in was proof of the purposes of the king and the ministry. Congress too would look abroad for aid.

The diplomatic committee did not have to look far. France had been watching Congress, and within a few days a secret agent, Achard de Bonvouloir, arrived in Philadelphia. He made himself known to Franklin through a French bookseller in the town, and through Franklin to other members of the committee. They met at night, each of them coming conspiratorially alone.[22] Though Bonvouloir had only verbal instructions, he was from the French foreign minister, Vergennes, authorized to convey the cautious wish that the colonies might become independent—and give their trade to France. During December, six months before the formal

Declaration, the committee in three meetings convinced Bonvouloir that Congress had made up its mind for independence: so
he reported to Vergennes on the 28th.[23] The situation of Congress
was a vicious circle. Its strongest weapon against England, the non-
importation and non-exportation agreements, was wholly defensive. America could not make war without importing manufactures, particularly arms and ammunition, nor without the money
derived from trade. To open her ports to other countries besides
England was in effect to declare independence. On that, Congress
had reason to suppose, public opinion was much divided. But trade
was all Congress had to offer France in return for assistance, and
France, risking a war with England, could not afford to help the
colonies if there was a chance they might make up their quarrel
with the mother country. That is, the colonies could not declare
independence without being sure of assistance from France, and
could not be sure of assistance from France till they had declared
independence.

These matters were by no means clear in Philadelphia in December 1775, when the Committee of Secret Correspondence still
knew nothing of Vergennes's actual plans and could not even be
sure that Bonvouloir had the authority he claimed. The first moves
of the committee were discreet and tentative. Jointly on 12 December they wrote to Arthur Lee in London, instructing him to find
out how foreign powers were disposed to America, and sending
him two hundred pounds for expenses. But most of the early
diplomatic correspondence fell upon Franklin alone, and was with
friends in Europe to whom he already had some occasion to write.

Ever since his return in May he had now and then written
letters to England. There was the famous letter to his old friend
Strahan on 5 July. Strahan, in spite of his devotion to Franklin,
had seen the Americans as rebels and had voted with the ministry.
"Mr. Strahan," Franklin began, not "Dear Sir" or "Dear Friend"
or "Dear Straney," as was customary with him: "You are a member
of Parliament, and one of that majority which has doomed my
country to destruction. You have begun to burn our towns and
murder our people. Look upon your hands! They are stained with
the blood of your relations. You and I were long friends. You are
now my enemy, and I am   Yours, B. Franklin."[24] This letter was

never sent, and Franklin in two days wrote a friendly letter to which he had a friendly answer. But letter-writing with him was a form of art. Some time during that long day at the Committee of Safety or in Congress, or earlier or later, the thought of Lexington and Bunker Hill came to him, and of his friend who had voted for the measures which had led to the battles; and the thought became a letter as in another man it might have become a lyric. One plain sentence of statement, another of hard accusation. Then the third and fourth suddenly throbbed with strong feeling and a bitter image. But the moment of lyric anger passed, and Franklin tempered his sixth and last sentence with his deft conclusion.

With graceful skill Franklin wrote to Don Gabriel of Bourbon on 12 December. The prince had sent Franklin, through the Spanish ambassador in London, a fine edition of Sallust. Franklin, thanking him, delicately invited his attention to the American colonies, neighbours to Spanish Florida. "I wish I could send from hence any American literary production worthy of your perusal; but as yet the Muses have scarcely visited these remote regions. Perhaps, however, the late proceedings of our American Congress, just published, may be a subject of some curiosity at your court. I therefore take the liberty of sending your highness a copy, with some other papers which contain accounts of the successes wherewith Providence has lately favoured us. Therein your wise politicians may contemplate the first efforts of a rising state which seems likely soon to act a part of some importance on the stage of human affairs, and furnish materials for a future Sallust. I am very old and scarcely hope to see the event of this great contest; but looking forward I think I see a powerful dominion growing up here, whose interest it will be to form a close and firm alliance with Spain (their territories bordering), and who, being united, will be able not only to preserve their own people in peace but to repel the force of all the other powers in Europe."[25]

Franklin wrote to his friend Charles William Frederick Dumas, who had sent him some books from Holland, and a little later to Barbeu Dubourg, translator and editor of Franklin's works in French. Both of them, Franklin hoped, would report as much as they could about the possibility of a foreign alliance, would suggest to persons in authority the value of American trade, and recommend military engineers, whom the Americans much needed. All this, of course, had to be managed with the greatest secrecy, because of British cruisers lying in wait for treasonable communications. The letters to Don Gabriel, Lee, and Dumas went by Thomas Story, a special messenger who was to visit London, the Hague, and Paris, and bring answers back. The letter to Dubourg went by a private commercial agent, Penet, who had come to Philadelphia and was returning to France with contracts from Congress for munitions, to be paid for by American exports. Dubourg and Dumas, as Franklin had expected, at once gave themselves up to the cause of America, and Dumas became Congress's official observer in Holland. But it was months after December 1775 before they could be heard from. Congress hesitated for a time, and then on 3 March voted to send Silas Deane, recently delegate from Connecticut, to represent Congress in France, or wherever he might find friends, assistance, or a willingness to trade with the United Colonies. Deane carried instructions written by Franklin— a masterpiece of diplomatic counsel[26]—and letters to all Franklin's friends in Paris. Outwardly a merchant buying goods for trade with the Indians, Deane was to proceed through Dubourg to the foreign minister, to assure him that the colonies showed every sign of being ready to declare independence soon, and not to stay too long at the first visit if Vergennes seemed reserved.

Occupied with Congress and new committees, his eyes so tired that he could hardly write at night, Franklin during the winter months had little to do with the Committee of Safety or the Assembly, and on 27 February resigned from both. "It would be a happiness to me," he said, "if I could serve the public duly in all these stations; but, aged as I am, I feel myself unequal to so much business and on that account think it my duty to decline a part of it."[27] The day before he had moved that Congress open American ports to foreign trade. The motion had been voted down by a majority not yet ready for it. But he had on the 15th been assigned by Congress to the laborious and hopeless task of going to Canada to win the French Canadians to the side of the English colonies. With Franklin on the commission were three men from

Maryland: Samuel Chase (a Protestant), Charles Carroll of Carrollton, a rich and influential Catholic layman, and John Carroll, a Jesuit priest.

The affair of Canada had been a bungling fiasco. So long as the British held Quebec, with its fortress on the St. Lawrence, there was always danger that they might proceed up the river and by way of Lake Champlain, Lake George, and the Hudson reach New York. Washington had sent two hasty armies against Canada. General Richard Montgomery, formerly a British captain, had taken Montreal in November, and in December had joined Colonel Benedict Arnold before Quebec, to which Arnold's army had come by a classic march through the Maine woods. Their assault on the city had been a failure, and Montgomery had been killed and Arnold wounded. Though what was left of Arnold's forces kept the British in Quebec, the Americans were not equipped for a Canadian winter. Sick, cold, hungry, without credit, and undisciplined, they were lawless and violent towards the French Canadians, who learned to detest and fear them. The army undid whatever Congress had been able to do, which was little enough.

In the protests against the Quebec Act of 1774 the colonists had abused the Catholic church with a bigotry which the French Catholics could not forget when Congress urged them in 1775 to join the Revolution and make it continental. The French were better satisfied under British rule than they had been under the French bureaucracy. Most of them were peasants, indifferent one way or the other, but their leaders did not sympathize with the Americans or trust their promises. On 14 February Franklin's committee on foreign affairs reported—the report is in his handwriting—that the Canadian noblesse and clergy had turned the people against the American colonies and that agents should be sent to explain the situation. Only Franklin and Chase were members of Congress. Charles Carroll as a third commissioner, and John Carroll as an associate, were asked to go along because they were Catholics and had been educated in France. Franklin was seventy. Only one of the others was barely over forty.

(On 20 March Franklin was chairman of a meeting, at the Indian Queen tavern, of the Ohio company.[28] Though he no longer held a share he was proxy for his son, with whom he seems to have been in some kind of financial if not political communication. The speculators, seeing there was little further chance of a grant from the Crown, were scheming to obtain the land in some other way. Franklin believed, as he had shown by his Articles of Confederation, that Congress should take charge of boundary disputes between the old colonies "and the planting of new colonies, when proper.")

In the last week of March the commissioners for Canada set out on their mission. The British had evacuated Boston, and Washington was moving his headquarters to New York. It was not, John Carroll saw, the "gay, polite place it used to be esteemed," for the people were expecting a bombardment, and those who could had gone or were going elsewhere. Franklin called on a friend, Mrs. Barrow. "Mr. Barrow had been from her two or three months to keep Gov[ernor] Tryon and other Tories company on board the *Asia*, one of the king's ships which lay in the harbour; and in all that time [that] naughty man had not ventured once on shore to see her. Our troops were then pouring into the town, and she was packing up to leave it, fearing, as she had a large house, they would incommode her by quartering officers in it. As she appeared in great perplexity, scarce knowing where to go, I persuaded her to stay; and I went to the general officers then commanding there and recommended her to their protection; which they promised."[29]

After two days in New York the commission took a sloop for Albany, at five in the afternoon of 2 April. They sailed thirteen miles before they anchored. In the night they heard cannonading and saw fire on what they thought was Bedloe's Island. "Dr. Franklin went upon deck, and saw waving flashes of light appearing suddenly and disappearing, which he conjectured to be the fire of musketry, although he could not hear the report."[30] The next day, passing St. Anthony's Nose, they met a squall which split their mainsail. All that day and the next they waited for the wind to quiet, while the crew repaired the damage. At five on the 5th they anchored off West Point, and Chase and Charles Carroll rowed ashore to inspect Constitution Fort, which looked so weak that the commissioners sent an express to Congress urging that the fort be put in better state. On the 6th they saw two frigates on the stocks at Poughkeepsie, being built for the United Colonies. Sailing all that night they made ninety-six miles by morning and arrived early at Albany. General Philip Schuyler, commander of the Continental forces in New York, met them and took them to his house about a mile from town, where they dined. "He behaved with great civility, lives in a pretty style; has two daughters (Betsy and Peggy), lively, agreeable, black-eyed girls." After two days in Albany, where they noted that Dutch was still chiefly spoken but that English was gaining ground, they went on the 9th in a wagon, with the whole Schuyler family, to the Schuyler seat at Saratoga. What with bad roads and two ferry crossings they were till sunset in travelling thirty-two miles.

At Saratoga, under six inches of April snow, they spent a week, pleased "with the ease and affability with which we were treated, and the lively behaviour of the young ladies." (Betsy married Alexander Hamilton four years later.) Franklin, who left it to the two Carrolls to keep a record of the journey, felt overtaxed. "I am here on my way to Canada," he wrote to Josiah Quincy on the 15th, "detained by the present state of the lakes, in which the unthawed ice obstructs navigation. I begin to apprehend that I have undertaken a fatigue that at my time of life may prove too much for me; so I sit down to write to a few friends by way of farewell. . . . I thought, when I sat down, to have written by this opportunity to Dr. Cooper, Mr. Bowdoin, and Dr. Winthrop, but I am interrupted."[31] He wrote with his habitual strong serenity, and went with the others the next day, deeper into the American wilderness than he had ever been before. They rowed laboriously up the Hudson, seven miles in four hours, and spent the night at a frontier inn at Fort Edward. On the way to Fort George on the 17th they were halted by a message from Schuyler telling them the lake was not yet open and asking them to spend another night at Wing's tavern half-way between the two forts. Schuyler had left Saratoga ahead of them and was already with his command at Fort George, although ill. A letter,[32] hitherto unpublished, which Franklin wrote in reply shows that he had come on horseback from Saratoga, that the commissioners had been accompanied by a sergeant sent by Mrs. Schuyler, and that Chase had not stayed with the others at the tavern but had gone on to Fort George, with the sergeant and on Franklin's mount.

At Mr. Wyng's, April 17. 76

Dear Sir

We are all concern'd to hear of your Indisposition, and join in requesting you earnestly to take care of your self. We purpose staying here as you advise in your kind Note of this Morning. We left all well at your House. The Sergeant has a Letter that I brought for you. Mrs Schuyler requests that you would send him back as soon as may be. I return inclos'd the Papers you favour'd us with. Our respects to Mr Chase: I desire him to send back my Mare by the Sergeant. Our best Wishes attend you. I am,

Dear Sir

[signature cut off]

We have sent forward Mr Chase's Bed & Portmanteau Trunk, on a Supposition that he intends not to return hither.

Gen. Schuyler

Leaving Wing's tavern the next day at noon, the party joined Schuyler, and with him embarked on Lake George in clumsy open flatboats that had to fight their way through the ice. From time to time they landed on the rough shore to build fires, warm themselves, and drink tea. At night some of them slept in the woods, the others (including Franklin) under awnings on the boats, in beds which they had had the forethought to bring with them. On the 20th they met the post coming from Montreal. "Dr. Franklin found in the Canada mail, which he opened, a letter for General Schuyler."[33] After a tedious portage the commissioners embarked on Lake Champlain on the 25th. Daily they set out at four or five in the morning, landed when they were hungry or cold, fell in with the current, and came to St. John's on the afternoon of the 27th. In calèches ordered from Montreal they drove, over bad roads, to the St. Lawrence, again took to water, and at Montreal on the 29th were met by Arnold, now a general, with a salute from the cannon of the citadel to the "Committee of the Honourable Continental Congress . . . with the celebrated Dr. Franklin at their head."[34] At Arnold's headquarters they passed the evening in the company of friendly ladies and gentlemen, with "decent mirth" and the singing of the ladies, which was pleasant after the wilderness. Late that night, very tired, they were taken to their lodgings in the handsome house of Thomas Walker, an ardent friend of the United Colonies who had already suffered for his zeal. The next day they were given a ceremonial dinner.

Franklin must have seen from the first conference with Arnold and his officers on the 30th that the mission could not succeed. The French Catholics of the province were incurably hostile. There were not more than four hundred English Protestants, at least half of whom were loyalists, and the others unable to make any stand against the royal government. The American invaders had no money and less credit. Franklin advanced them £353 of his own, in gold.[35] When word reached Montreal of the arrival on 6 May of British reinforcements by sea at Quebec, he could have no doubt, knowing the condition of the American army, that it would be driven out of Canada—as it was in June. He was suffering from boils and a swelling of his legs he thought was dropsy. He might as well go back at once to Philadelphia where he could be of some use. On 11 May he suddenly decided to leave, and John Carroll followed him to St. John's the day after. Charles Carroll and Chase waited to retire with the garrison. "It was with the greatest difficulty," Franklin wrote to Schuyler from St. John's on the 12th, "I got a conveyance here." The Canadians were afraid to let it be known that they had carriages, apparently for fear the Americans would requisition them. Unless provisions were sent, Franklin said, "the army must starve, plunder, or surrender."[36] He had to wait at St. John's for two days before he and John Carroll could begin their journey to Albany.

Since Montreal was now nearly as unsafe a place for American sympathizers as Boston for loyalists, the Montreal hostess of the commissioners left with Franklin. Walker overtook them at Saratoga, "where," as Franklin dryly recounted, "they both took such liberties, in taunting at our conduct in Canada, that it came almost to a quarrel. We continued our care of her, however, and landed her safe in Albany with her three wagon-loads of baggage, brought hither without putting her to any expense, and parted civilly though coldly. I think they both have an excellent talent at making themselves enemies, and I believe, live where they will, they will never be long without them."[37] From Albany they went by land as arranged by General Schuyler, to whom Franklin wrote from New York on the 27th. "We arrived here safe yesterday evening, in your post chaise driven by Lewis. I was unwilling to give so much trouble, and would have borrowed your sulky and driven myself; but good Mrs. Schuyler insisted on a full compliance with your pleasure, as signified in your letter, and I was obliged to submit; which I was afterwards very glad of, part of the road being very stony and much gullied, where I should probably have overset and broken my own bones, all the skill and dexterity of Lewis being no more than sufficient. Through the influence of your kind recommendation to the inn-keepers on the road we found a great readiness to supply us with a change of horses. Accept our thankful acknowledgments; they are all we can at present make."[38]

Franklin was worn out by the journey. "I find I grow daily more feeble," he wrote from New York to the other commissioners the same day; "and I think I could hardly have got along so far but for Mr. Carroll's friendly assistance and tender care of me." (Eight years later the Papal Nuncio in Paris told Franklin that on his recommendation John Carroll would probably be made a bishop; and he became the first archbishop in America.[39]) "Some symptoms of the gout now appear, which makes me think my indisposition has been a smothered fit of that disorder, which my constitution wanted strength to form completely."[40] Yet Franklin had not forgotten Mrs. Barrow, whom he found "still in quiet possession of her house. I inquired how our people had behaved to her. She spoke in high terms of the respectful attention they had paid her and the quiet and security they had procured her. I said I was glad of it; and that, if they had used her ill, I would have turned Tory. Then says she, with that pleasing gaiety so natural to her: 'I wish they had.' For . . . she is a Toryess. . . . I drank tea with her." Later Franklin heard that the street she lived in had been "chiefly burnt down," but "had no opportunity of knowing whether she suffered any loss in the conflagration. I hope she did not, as, if she did, I should wish I had not persuaded her to stay there."[41]

Once more in Philadelphia, Franklin recovered slowly. His gout, he wrote to Washington on 21 June, "has kept me from Congress and company ever since you left us, so that I know little of what has passed except that a declaration of independence is preparing."[42]

III

The public feeling in favour of independence had grown rapidly since December when the Committee of Secret Correspondence told Bonvouloir that Congress had made up its mind. On New Year's Day Norfolk, Virginia, was burned by the British. On 10 January Thomas Paine, now a journalist in Philadelphia, published his *Common Sense*, which rose above the confusion like a trumpet, giving every reason for independence its most infectious statement. Franklin in October had proposed to Paine that he write "a history of the present transactions" to appear the following spring. Paine, who had already written a part of his Tyrtæan argument, "without informing him of what I was doing, got it ready for the press as fast as I conveniently could, and sent him the first pamphlet that was printed off."[43] While *Common Sense* ran through the continent news came that Parliament had prohibited trade and intercourse with the colonies, whether from Great Britain or any other country, and declared an absolute blockade. Congress declared its ports open to the commerce of all countries except Great Britain. One by one the colonies, beginning with North Carolina on 12 April, instructed their delegates to Congress to vote for independence.

Pennsylvania lagged. Though Franklin had been, with the Adamses and Jefferson, earliest and firmest for separation, the Pennsylvania members of Congress were divided, and bound by a conservative Assembly which met in another room in the State House. The Quakers were averse to any war. The proprietary party as a whole was loyal to the Crown, or at least unwilling to break yet from its allegiance. Since Philadelphia, as the meeting-place of the Continental Congress, was in a sense the capital of the nation, Congress took a hand in the provincial turmoil. In May it passed a resolution urging colonies which had no adequate governments to form them. A mass-meeting in the State House yard condemned the Assembly, declared that the old charter from the king was antiquated, and demanded a new constitution and a new legislature. The Assembly made concessions and on 14 June just before adjournment gave the delegates carte blanche in any Congressional vote on independence. It was too late to save the Assembly, which four days after it adjourned was virtually superseded by a meeting of county committees which called for a constitutional convention to meet in July.

Franklin had been on his expedition to Canada during much of this struggle, and too ill, as he told Washington, for "Congress or company" for some weeks after his return. But as the most eminent and influential man among the Pennsylvania patriots he was particularly blamed by the Philadelphia conservatives, who long held his stand against him and hated him for having ruined the Assembly and thrown away the venerable and admirable charter on which the government of Pennsylvania had been founded. For Franklin June must have been a disturbing month. Hardly had Richard Henry Lee on the 7th introduced his resolution declaring that "these United Colonies are, and of right ought to be, free and independent states" when word came to Congress that the New Jersey Assembly had ordered the arrest of Governor Franklin and put him under guard at his farm near Burlington. Congress on the 24th, when Franklin may have been present, resolved that the governor should be sent from New Jersey to Connecticut. "He is son to Dr. Benjamin Franklin," a contemporary newspaper said, "the genius of the day and the great patron of American liberty."[44] But though William Franklin might have some consideration shown him on account of his father, he was still a loyalist at a time of bitter feeling against all loyalists, and in Connecticut, whether on parole or in actual confinement in the Litchfield jail, he was a prisoner for more than two years.

On 10 June Congress appointed a committee to prepare a declaration which might be published, with all possible eloquence and effect, to the world: Jefferson, John Adams, Franklin, Roger Sherman of Connecticut, and Robert R. Livingston of New York. Sherman and Livingston seem to have had little to do with the document. The five men met and chose Jefferson to write a first draft. He submitted it to Franklin and Adams, perhaps more than once to each of them. Franklin, when he wrote to Washington on the 21st, may have seen it. On the 28th the committee reported it to Congress. On 1 July the Lee resolution came up for debate.

Three of the five Pennsylvania members were still opposed, with Franklin and John Morton in the minority. On the 2nd, by whatever pressure, Dickinson and Robert Morris were induced not to take their seats, and James Wilson joined Franklin and Morton. The resolution was voted. On the 4th the committee's version of the declaration, as revised by Congress, was agreed to. On the 8th it was read at noon to a crowd of Philadelphians gathered before the State House. On the 10th it was published in the *Pennsylvania Journal*. The engrossed copy of what has ever since been called the Declaration of Independence was not signed by the members till 2 August, and then not by all those who had voted for the resolution, some of whom signed it later. Others signed who had not voted for it at all.

Franklin, like Adams, made only a few verbal changes in the ringing text of the Declaration, which remains essentially Jefferson's. Where Jefferson had said: "We hold these truths to be sacred and undeniable," Franklin—for the correction seems to be in his handwriting—changed "sacred and undeniable" to the cooler and sharper "self-evident." Where Jefferson had said: "reduce them to arbitrary power," Franklin made it read "reduce them under absolute despotism." Jefferson said the king had made American judges dependent on his will "for the tenure of their offices, and amount of their salaries." Franklin made it more precise by changing the last four words to "the amount and payment of their salaries." To Jefferson's charge that the king had given his assent to acts "for taking away our charters, and altering fundamentally the forms of our governments" Franklin added a third clause, inserted between the other two: "abolishing our most valuable laws"—in recollection of the many acts passed by the Pennsylvania Assembly and invalidated by Parliament. The petitions of America, Jefferson said, had been "answered by repeated injury." Franklin strengthened if not exaggerated it to "answered only by repeated injury." Jefferson's accusation that foreign mercenaries were being sent to "deluge us in blood" was modified by Franklin to the less rhetorical "destroy us."[45] (Congress dropped the whole accusation as brought against the British people.)

Characteristically, Franklin's most memorable contribution to the Declaration, besides the support he gave to it early and late, is the one humorous story and the one witty remark associated with the grave, momentous episode. While Congress was at work on the committee's draft, Jefferson afterwards remembered, "I was sitting by Dr. Franklin, who perceived that I was not insensible to these mutilations. 'I have made it a rule,' said he, 'whenever in my power, to avoid becoming the draftsman of papers to be reviewed by a public body. I took my lesson from an incident which I will relate to you. When I was a journeyman printer one of my companions, an apprentice hatter, having served out his time was about to open shop for himself. His first concern was to have a handsome signboard with a proper inscription. He composed it in these words: "John Thompson, hatter, makes and sells hats for ready money," with a figure of a hat subjoined. But he thought he would submit it to his friends for their amendments. The first he showed it to thought the word "hatter" tautologous, because followed by the words "makes hats" which show he was a hatter. It was struck out. The next observed that the word "makes" might as well be omitted, because the customers would not care who made the hats. If good and to their mind, they would buy, by whomever made. He struck it out. A third said he thought the words "for ready money" were useless, as it was not the custom of the place to sell on credit. Everyone who purchased expected to pay. They were parted with, and the inscription now stood: "John Thompson sells hats." "Sells hats?" says his next friend. "Why, nobody will expect you to give them away. What then is the use of that word?" It was stricken out; and "hats" followed it, the rather as there was one painted on the board. So his inscription was reduced ultimately to "John Thompson" with the figure of a hat subjoined.' "[46]

When Congress came to sign the Declaration, John Hancock, as president writing his name first, is said to have said: "We must be unanimous; there must be no pulling different ways; we must all hang together." "Yes," Franklin is said to have said, "we must indeed all hang together, or most assuredly we shall all hang separately." Though it would have been like him to make a pun at that dramatic moment and this is such a pun as he might have made, there seems to be no contemporary record to show that he did. His early biographers do not tell the story, not even the anecdotal Parson Weems (1815, 1821) or Peter Parley (1832) or John Sanderson and his colleagues anywhere in their nine volumes of *Biography of the Signers to the Declaration of Independence* (1820–27). Jared Sparks in his edition of Franklin's works (1840) admitted the story to the canon "as also another anecdote related of Franklin."[47] Thus a traditional anecdote, real or invented, found its way into history, and has since then lived on in legend with authority from Sparks.

IV

Though the Declaration had closed one difficult chapter of the Revolution it opened a more difficult one. Governor Carleton of Canada, with Burgoyne second in command, was moving by way of the St. Lawrence towards New York, with reinforcements from England and the first German mercenaries from Brunswick and Waldeck. The American forces had been routed, and the British advance from St. John's was delayed only by Benedict Arnold and his remnant of an army, building a rough flotilla on Lake Champlain. An expedition sent first from Boston to North Carolina under Clinton, with another from Ireland under Cornwallis, had combined in an attack on Charleston late in June. Driven off by the fire of Fort Moultrie, their fleet might any day be expected at some other port. (They arrived at New York early in August.) General Howe, who had withdrawn from Boston to Halifax in March, on the day before the Declaration landed his Boston army, reinforced, on Staten Island. Within a week after the Declaration Admiral Lord Howe, with a fleet and transports, joined his brother. Besides British troops and sailors they had nine thousand Hessians. All together they outnumbered Washington's army on Manhattan by perhaps two to one, and were immeasurably superior in training and equipment. The British military plan was by the co-operation of Carleton from Canada and General Howe from New York to cut New England off from the other colonies and so mortally divide the rebellion. As a more pacific venture the two Howes had been named as special commissioners to offer full pardon to all rebels, with the secret exception of John Adams. It was soon believed in America, however, that Samuel Adams, Richard Henry Lee, and Franklin also were excepted.[48]

Franklin, like other members of Congress, must have felt that there was everything to be done, all at once, and much of it impossible. The demands on him tested even his versatility. On the day of the Declaration he was appointed with John Adams and Jefferson to devise a seal for the United States. This committee did not report till 20 August, when it recommended an elaborate device of which nothing was kept by Congress but the motto *E Pluribus Unum* and the Eye of Providence. Which of these was suggested by which members of the committee does not appear. But on the reverse of the seal, as recommended by them, was the device proposed by Franklin: "Pharaoh sitting in an open chariot, a crown on his head and a sword in his hand, passing through the divided waters of the Red Sea in pursuit of the Israelites. Rays from a pillar of fire in the cloud, expressive of the Divine presence and command, beaming on Moses, who stands on the shore and, extending his hand over the sea, causes it to overflow Pharaoh. Motto: 'Rebellion to tyrants is obedience to God.' "[49]

On 18 July Franklin and John Adams reported for a committee—Dickinson, Franklin, Adams, Harrison, Robert Morris—which had been appointed on 12 June, during Franklin's illness, to draw up treaties of alliance to be proposed to foreign powers. Dissatisfied with the first report, Congress added Richard Henry Lee and James Wilson to the committee. A modified report, with a set of articles for treaties of commerce and amity, was adopted on 17 September, with instructions to the proposed commissioners on the 24th and on 16 October. These documents made up the Plan of 1776 on which the later treaties with France, and other countries, were based. Franklin wrote out a private *Sketch of Propositions for a Peace* with England, which the committee did not make use of. Commissioners carrying such a proposal, he thought, might get some protection from it if they were taken at sea. France might be more ready for an alliance if she had reason to think that America considered making peace with England. And England might be divided if the opposition could show that peace with America was possible. "As the having such propositions to make," Franklin wrote, "or any powers to treat of peace, will furnish a pretence for B. F.'s going to England, where he has many friends and acquaintances, particularly among the best writers and ablest speakers in both Houses of Parliament; he thinks that he shall be able when there, if the terms are not accepted, to work up such a division of sentiments in the nation as greatly to weaken its exertions against the United States and lessen its credit in foreign countries."[50]

What most immediately claimed Franklin's attention after 4 July was the politics of Pennsylvania. On the 8th Philadelphia elected its delegates to the constitutional convention, with Franklin at the head of the list. On the 15th the convention met, with Franklin as president, and on the 20th he was chosen by the largest number of votes to be one of its delegates to Congress. His time and strength taken up by Congress, he seems to have been chiefly an absentee adviser to the convention, though he presided during some of the debates and spoke at least once, late in the session.[51] But the constitution as adopted in September embodied two of his favourite provisions. One was for a plural executive council, not a governor, and the other for a legislature of a single chamber. A bicameral parliament reminded Franklin, he then said and later wrote, of "the famous political fable of the snake with two heads and one body. . . . She was going to a brook to drink, and in her way was to pass through a hedge, a twig of which opposed her direct course. One head chose to go on the right side of the twig, the other on the left, so that time was spent in the contest; and before the decision was completed the poor snake died with thirst."[52]

On the day Franklin took his seat as delegate from Pennsylvania Congress resolved that he might answer the letter which had reached him from Lord Howe. Since the British government did not yet recognize the existence of the American Congress, the royal commissioners could not address it as an official body, and Howe's offer of pardon, made to private subjects, had been officially disregarded. But Howe, remembering his conversations with Franklin in London, sent him an amicable, complimentary letter as soon as the flagship reached Sandy Hook. Franklin's answer, dated 30 July, began with a Congressional grimness.

"Directing pardons to be offered to the colonies," he said, "who are the very parties injured, expresses indeed that opinion of our ignorance, baseness, and insensibility which your uninformed and proud nation has long been pleased to entertain of us; but it can have no other effect than that of increasing our resentments. It is impossible we should think of submission to a government that has with the most wanton barbarity and cruelty burnt our defence-less towns in the midst of winter, excited the savages to massacre our peaceful farmers and our slaves to murder their masters, and is even now bringing foreign mercenaries to deluge our settle-ments with blood." Franklin himself had modified the violent expression "deluge us in blood" in Jefferson's draft of the Declara-tion. Here he was writing for Congress almost as much as for Howe. He went on with an observation upon injury and forgiveness which sounds more like the moral philosopher he was. "These atrocious injuries have extinguished every remaining spark of affection for that parent country we once held so dear; but, were it possible for us to forget and forgive them, it is not possible for you (I mean the British people) to forgive the people you have so heavily injured."

As to the peace which Howe said the king was desirous of pro-moting: "If by peace is here meant a peace to be entered into between Britain and America, as distinct states now at war, and His Majesty has given your lordship powers to treat with us of such a peace, I may venture to say, though without authority, that I think a treaty for that purpose not yet quite impracticable, before we enter into foreign alliances. But I am persuaded you have no such powers. Your nation" might, by suitable reparations, "recover a great share of our regard and the greatest part of our growing commerce, with all the advantage of that additional strength to be derived from a friendship with us; but I know too well her abound-ing pride and deficient wisdom to believe she will ever take such salutary measures. Her fondness for conquest as a warlike nation, her lust of dominion as an ambitious one, and her wish for a gainful monopoly as a commercial one (none of them legitimate causes of war) will all join to hide from her eyes every view of her true interests and continually goad her on in those ruinous distant expeditions, so destructive both of lives and treasure, that must prove as pernicious to her in the end as the Crusades formerly were to most of the nations in Europe.

"I have not the vanity, my lord, to think of intimidating by thus predicting the effects of this war; for I know it will in England have the fate of all my former predictions, not to be believed till the event shall verify it.

"Long did I endeavour," Franklin went on, now fully in his own person, "with unfeigned and unwearied zeal to preserve from breaking that fine and noble china vase the British Empire; for I knew that, once being broken, the separate parts could not retain even their shares of the strength and value that existed in the whole, and that a perfect reunion of those parts could scarce ever be hoped for. Your lordship may possibly remember the tears of joy that wet my cheek when, at your good sister's in London, you once gave me expectations that a reconciliation might soon take place. I had the misfortune to find those expectations disappointed, and to be treated as the cause of the mischief I was labouring to prevent. My consolation under that groundless and malevolent treatment was that I retained the friendship of many wise and good men in that country, and among the rest some share in the regard of Lord Howe."

Franklin, saying he would always feel esteem and even affection for Howe, said he was sorry to see his friend engaged in a war which was largely aimed, according to Howe's own words, at keeping American trade in British hands. "To me it seems that neither the obtaining or retaining of any trade, how valuable soever, is an object for which men may justly spill each other's blood; that the true and sure means of extending and securing commerce is the goodness and cheapness of commodities; and that the profit of no trade can ever be equal to the expense of compelling it, and of holding it, by fleets and armies. I consider this war against us, therefore, as both unjust and unwise; and I am persuaded that cool, dispassionate posterity will condemn to infamy those who have advised it; and that even success will not save from some degree of dishonour those who voluntarily engaged to conduct it. I know your great motive in coming hither was the hope of being instrumental in a reconciliation; and I believe, when you find that to be impossible on any terms given you to propose, you will relinquish so odious a command, and return to a more honourable private station."[53]

Franklin's letter, which Howe said was very warmly expressed but which he must have known had Congress back of it, temporarily blocked Howe's scheme for peace. Congress was busy with the actual war. At the end of July Franklin took a more outspoken stand in debate, apparently, than ever before, on the plan for a new confederation. Most of all he insisted that the states must be represented in proportion to the number of their people and the amount of their contributions. In a permanent legislature it could not be fair for each state, no matter how small, to have the same vote as the largest. "Let the smaller colonies," he said on the 31st, "give equal money and men, and then have an equal vote. But if they have an equal vote without bearing equal burdens, a confederation upon such iniquitous principles will never last long." Pennsylvania with his advice was forming a democratic constitution, and for a time he wished that the Pennsylvania convention might publicly dissent from the Congressional plan for equal votes, which would give the smaller states an undemocratic advantage. Lynch of South Carolina, one of the average states, said that slaves should not be counted as population when taxes were assessed, since slaves were property and no more to be taxed than sheep. Franklin on the 30th pointedly observed: "Slaves rather weaken than strengthen the state, and therefore there is some difference between them and sheep: sheep will never make any insurrections."

On 1 August Franklin moved that the votes in Congress be in proportion to population. "I hear," he said, supporting his motion, "many ingenious arguments to persuade us that unequal representation"—that is, equal votes—"is a very good thing. If we had been born and bred under an unequal representation"—like the English with their pocket boroughs—"we might bear it; but to set out with an unequal representation is unreasonable. It is said that the great colonies will swallow up the less. Scotland said the same thing at the Union."[54] So Adams here quotes the gist of Franklin's speech. Jefferson adds the turn Franklin gave to his argument. "At the time of the union of England and Scotland the Duke of

Argyle was most violently opposed to that measure, and among other things predicted that, as the whale had swallowed Jonah, so Scotland would be swallowed by England. However, when Lord Bute came into the government, he soon brought into its administration so many of his countrymen that it was found, in event, that Jonah had swallowed the whale."[55] Congress, Jefferson said, laughed itself into good humour.

While debate brought Congress no nearer to confederation the war went badly for the Americans. Washington, beaten on Long Island on 27 August, had the luck to get his army back to Manhattan, but could not hope to hold it long. The Howes, instead of attacking, made another conciliatory move. Lord Howe paroled General John Sullivan, who had been captured by the British, and sent him to Philadelphia with the request that Congress appoint some of its members to confer privately with Howe about a possible settlement before any decisive blow had been struck on either side and while neither could feel compelled to treat. Congress drew a distinction. Being the representatives of the free and independent United States of America, they could not send any of their members as private citizens to confer with him, but they would send a committee to find out what authority he had to deal with persons authorized by Congress, and to hear whatever proposals he might see fit to make. Franklin, John Adams (not aware that the Privy Council had excluded him from pardon), and Edward Rutledge of South Carolina were chosen on 6 September to go on the questioning errand.

Franklin wrote to Howe that the committee would come to meet him on the 11th either at the governor's house at Perth Amboy (so lately Governor Franklin's) or at the Billopp house on Staten Island opposite Perth Amboy. Howe chose the Staten Island place of meeting, and promised, weather permitting, to send a boat to ferry them over under a flag of truce. On the way from Philadelphia the committee, Adams on horseback and the other two in "chairs" (probably chaises), found the roads thronged with soldiers marching to join Washington, and the inn at New Brunswick so crowded that Franklin and Adams had to share a bed in a room hardly larger than the bed itself, with one small window. "The window was open," Adams remembered, "and I, who was an invalid and afraid of the air of the night, shut it close. 'Oh!' says Franklin, 'don't shut the window; we shall be suffocated.' I answered I was afraid of the evening air. Dr. Franklin replied: 'The air within the chamber will soon be, and indeed is now, worse than that without doors. Come, open the window and come to bed, and I will convince you. I believe you are not acquainted with my theory of colds.'" Adams had so much curiosity about the theory, which he thought a paradox, that he opened the window and risked the cold. But he fell asleep while Franklin was still explaining it, and noticed that the last words he heard were spoken very sleepily.[56]

Howe's barge met the committee, with an officer who had been sent as hostage, subject to their orders, to guarantee their safe return. They thought it would be childish to depend on such a pledge and took the officer back with them. Howe was at the shore when they arrived at Staten Island, with a double line of Hessians drawn up from the beach to the house. Pleased to see that his hostage had not been held, Howe cordially greeted Franklin, who introduced his companions. "A general and immaterial conversation from the beach to the house," the minutes noted. "The Hessian guard saluted as they passed." Inside the house, which had been occupied by soldiers and was neglected and dirty, one of the rooms had been hung with moss and branches till it was, Adams thought, "not only wholesome but romantically elegant." There they dined on cold ham, tongue, mutton, bread, and good claret, with Howe's secretary Henry Strachey and the Hessian colonel. The colonel withdrew before they began their conference. Strachey kept brief minutes[57] of a meeting which, with dinner, lasted for three hours.

Howe did most of the talking. He had long believed, he said, that the differences between the two countries might be accommodated to the satisfaction of both of them. He was known to be a well-wisher to America, particularly to Massachusetts for the honours paid to his eldest brother.

(Here, as Adams later remembered though the minutes do not show it, Howe said he felt for America as for a brother and should lament, as for the loss of a brother, if America should fall. Franklin with a smile and an air of simplicity said: "My lord, we will use our utmost endeavours to save your lordship that mortification."

Howe, stung, retorted with a hint at some foreign alliance: "I suppose you will endeavour to give us employment in Europe."[58] Nobody said anything, and Howe went on.)

He was sorry he had not arrived till after the Declaration of Independence. Of course he had no powers to treat with the colonies as independent states, and never expected to have. Nor could he acknowledge Congress, since the king did not. The committee must be considered "merely as gentlemen of great ability and influence . . . now met to converse together and to try if any outline could be drawn to put a stop to the calamities of war." Howe hoped they would bear in mind the delicacy of his situation, and in no way imply that he had met them as delegates from Congress. He had perhaps gone too far as it was.

Franklin, according to a note in the margin of the minutes, reassured him: "You may depend upon our taking care of that, my lord."

The idea of a Congress, Howe continued, "might easily be thrown out of the question at present; for that, if matters could be so settled that the king's government should be re-established, the Congress would of course cease to exist; and that if they meant such accommodation, they must see how unnecessary and useless it was to stand upon that form which they knew they were to give up upon the restoration of legal government.

"Dr. Franklin said that his lordship might consider the gentlemen present in any view he thought proper; that they were also at liberty to consider themselves in their real character; that there was no necessity on this occasion to distinguish between the Congress and individuals; and that the conversation might be held as amongst friends." To this Adams and Rutledge agreed in very few words.

Howe, having dismissed Congress from the argument, explained that the king's "most earnest desire was to make his American subjects happy, to cause a reform in whatever affected the freedom of their legislation, and to concur with his Parliament in the redress of any real grievances"; that the committee "knew we expected aid from America; that the dispute seemed to be only concerning the mode of obtaining it.

"Dr. Franklin here said: '*That* we never refused, upon requisition.'"

Money, Howe declared, was the smallest consideration. America could "produce more solid advantages to Great Britain" in "her commerce, her strength, her men."

"Here Dr. Franklin said with rather a sneering laugh: 'Aye, my lord, we have a pretty considerable manufactory of men'—alluding as it should seem to their numerous army." (So the secretary guessed. But Howe, or somebody who knew Franklin better, wrote in pencil in the margin: "No; to their increasing population.")

"Lord Howe continued. 'It is desirable to put a stop to these ruinous extremities, as well for the sake of our country as yours. When an American falls England feels it. Is there no way of treading back this step of independency and opening the door to a full discussion?' Lord Howe concluded with saying that, having thus opened to them the general purport of the commission and the king's disposition to a permanent peace, he must stop to hear what they choose to observe.

"Dr. Franklin said he supposed his lordship had seen the resolution of the Congress which had sent them hither; that the resolution contained the whole of their commission; that if this conversation was productive of no immediate good effect it might be of service at a future time; that America had considered the Prohibitory Act as the answer to her petition to the king; [that] forces had been sent out and towns destroyed; that they could not expect happiness now under the domination of Great Britain; that all former attachment was obliterated; that America could not return again to the domination of Great Britain and therefore imagined that Great Britain meant to rest it upon force. 'The other gentlemen will deliver their sentiments.'"

Adams said he did not care what he was considered on this occasion, so it was not as a British subject. Congress had declared for independence at the instruction of all the colonies, and had no power to treat with Howe except as a Congress. "He mentioned warmly his own determination not to depart from the idea of independency." Rutledge spoke, seemingly, at greater length. Great Britain, he suggested, might profit more from an alliance with the independent states than from her former relationship. South Carolina had accepted its new government and would not become a colony again even if Congress desired it.

Howe could only repeat that he had no authority whatever, "nor did he expect he ever should have, to treat with the colonies as states independent of the Crown of Great Britain; and that he was sorry the gentlemen had had the trouble of coming so far to so little purpose; that if the colonies would not give up the system of independency, it was impossible for him to enter into any negotiation.

"Dr. Franklin observed that it would take as much time for them to refer to, and get an answer from, their constituents as it would the commissioners to get fresh instructions from home, which he supposed might be done in about three months. Lord Howe replied that it was in vain to think of his receiving instructions to treat upon that ground.

"After a little pause Dr. Franklin suddenly said: 'Well, my lord, as America is to expect nothing but upon unconditional submission ——'

"Lord Howe interrupted the doctor at the word 'submission'; said that Great Britain did not require unconditional submission; that he thought what he had already said to them proved the contrary; and desired the gentlemen would not go away with such an idea."

Franklin went on: " '—and your lordship has no proposition to make us, give me leave to ask whether, if we should make propositions to Great Britain (not that I know or am authorized to say we shall) you would receive and transmit them?' "

Howe thought he could not well avoid receiving any papers that might be put into his hands, but he was doubtful about the propriety of transmitting them; still, he could not say that he would decline it. On this note of muddled uncertainty the conference ended.

The committee reported to Congress that Howe appeared to have no authority except to grant pardons if America would submit; and there was no certainty that, if America submitted, her grievances would be redressed. The commissioners for peace, with no power to recognize the independence which Congress would not give up, had nothing to do but resume hostilities.

With fleet and army the two Howes moved promptly against Washington on Manhattan and drove him northward first to Harlem Heights and then to White Plains. During the evacuation New York caught fire and a third of the town was burned. The loyalists blamed the patriots. Nathan Hale, taken within the British lines on an errand for Washington, was hanged on 22 September as a spy. Congress, with every reason for anxiety, looked again to France. A long letter to Franklin arrived from Dubourg, full of zeal for the American cause and assurances that the French ministry favoured it. In the Congressional debates Franklin gave it as his opinion "that a virgin state should preserve the virgin character, and not go about suitoring for alliances, but wait with decent dignity for the applications of others. I was over-ruled; perhaps for the best."[59] On 26 September Congress in what was to be strict secrecy chose commissioners to represent it at the court of France: Franklin, Jefferson, and Silas Deane already in Paris.

In the midst of these events Franklin had a happy visit from his sister Jane and William and Catherine Greene, who were in Philadelphia the week the committee of Congress returned from their meeting with Lord Howe. Though Catherine had been devoted to Franklin for more than twenty years he had spent most of them in Europe and she had seen him only three times, for only a few days at a time. Now she found him so busy that even the day she left, the 16th, he had to be away at Congress. She seems not to have regretted this. "Parting from those we love is sorrow," she wrote him after the nine days' journey home. She hoped he might soon visit them. "We feasted upon you a great deal since you left your house, for all there is but such a morsel of you left."[60] Jane Mecom remained in Philadelphia with her brother. Franklin on the 28th wrote a letter, heretofore unpublished, to Temple at Perth Amboy. "I hope you will return hither immediately, and that your mother [stepmother] will make no objection to it, something offering here that will be much to your advantage if you are not out of the way."[61] He could not risk mentioning the French mission, which was being kept as secret as possible. But he wanted his grandson with him, not with Temple's loyalist father or within reach of his influence.

On 1 October Franklin, preparing for his voyage, conferred with Robert Morris, the only other member of the Committee of Secret Correspondence who was in town. Thomas Story, sent on his stealthy mission ten months before, had returned with semi-official news. France was not yet ready to form an alliance, which would mean war with England, but would soon ship £200,000 worth of arms and ammunition to some port in the West Indies where Congress might claim them. Franklin and Morris decided that, for the sake of France, they would keep the news from Congress, which was too large for secrecy. There were already rumours in Philadelphia that ambassadors had been appointed. Morris was on other committees which could arrange to bring the supplies to the continent, and Franklin would manage the affair in Europe.[62]

Before he sailed Franklin turned the post office over to Richard Bache as deputy, and "all the money he could raise, between three and four thousand pounds," into a loan to Congress, "which, demonstrating his confidence, encouraged others to lend their money in support of the cause."[63] With Galloway, now retired to the country, Franklin left a trunk "containing all my correspondence, when in England, for near twenty years. . . . As he was a friend of my son's, to whom in my will I had left all my books and papers, I made him one of my executors, and put the trunk of papers into his hands, imagining them safer in his house (which was out of the way of any probable march of the enemies' troops) than in my own."[64] The trunk contained the only manuscript of the *Autobiography*.

At the last moment Congress, having learned that Jefferson on account of his wife's health could not go, chose Arthur Lee, then in London, to be the third commissioner. On 26 October Franklin quietly left Philadelphia and the next day embarked on the armed sloop *Reprisal*, which carried a cargo of indigo to pay the expenses of the mission. Exhausted by long hours and lack of exercise during his time in Congress, troubled with boils which had kept breaking out on him ever since his trip to Canada, he lived on his passage "chiefly on salt beef, the fowls being too hard for my teeth."[65] Though the *Reprisal*, commanded by Lambert Wickes, was making a perilous American venture into European waters, Franklin had brought two grandsons with him: Temple, now near seventeen, and Benjamin Franklin Bache, seven. The indomitable old man, who was almost certain to be hanged for high treason if the *Reprisal* should be captured, noted the temperature of air and water every day, again studying the Gulf Stream. About four weeks from Cape Henlopen, within two days of France, Captain Wickes took two British prizes and brought them into Quiberon bay off the coast of Brittany. He had intended to sail up the Loire to Nantes, but the wind was difficult and Franklin was impatient. After three or four days of waiting on board he landed at Auray on 3 December, to finish his journey to Nantes by land.

"The carriage was a miserable one," Franklin wrote in his journal, "with tired horses, the evening [of the 5th] dark, scarce a traveller but ourselves on the road; and, to make it more comfortable, the driver stopped near a wood we were to pass through, to tell us that a gang of eighteen robbers infested that wood who but two weeks ago had murdered some travellers on that very spot." The next day: "On the road yesterday we met six or seven country women in company, on horseback and astride; they were all of fair white and red complexions but one among them was the fairest woman I ever beheld."[66] Arriving at Nantes on the 7th, Franklin, who at Auray had been so weak from the voyage that he could hardly stand, was at once given a grand dinner by the friends of America. He took refuge at the country house of a partner of Penet, the commercial agent who was busy with shipments from Nantes to the revolutionists. But crowds of visitors that afternoon and evening, and throughout Franklin's stay, came to offer him their greetings and homage, and he was the hero of the ball given in his honour. His arrival was the first news of his appointment as emissary, about which he kept quiet. The news ran ahead of him to Paris, where every morning it was said that he had come there and every evening that he had not. Accompanied by Penet he reached Versailles the 20th, and Deane drove out to meet him. The next day Franklin was in Paris, the famous philosopher who had come as a patriot to France in the name of that liberty which was just then the darling theme of French philosophy and French society.

Commissioner

AT ONCE Franklin was cast for the heroic role in an international melodrama. Ever since 1763 the French ministry had been bent on revenge for the hard terms they had had to accept at the treaty of Paris. Choiseul, foreign minister of Louis XV, had watched the Stamp Act controversy and been disappointed at the peaceful settlement. The courtesies shown Franklin on his visit to Paris in 1767 were ministerial as well as friendly. Three months after the episode in the Cockpit of January 1774, Louis XVI (not yet twenty) came to the throne, and his foreign minister, Vergennes, saw another opportunity for France in the new controversy between England and the colonies. Perfectly willing to help them with a primary aim at hurting England, Vergennes was cautious. If this quarrel also were settled peacefully, England would be free to turn on any country which had interfered. Chatham even might come back to power and resume the war which had been ended against his judgment. While Franklin was vainly negotiating in the winter of 1774–75 Vergennes was hearing from London that some of the Americans there were ready to appeal to France for help. And during the summer of 1775, while Congress in Philadelphia still hoped that a final breach might be avoided, one of Vergennes's secret agents in London made up his mind that the collapse of British imperial unity was near and that France should strike while England's hands were full of her domestic difficulties. The secret agent was the adventurer, courtier, and dramatist Caron de Beaumarchais.

In September 1775 Beaumarchais returned to Paris with melodramatic reports of the situation in England. He had talked, he said, with an inhabitant of Philadelphia who, just arrived from America, had conferred with the British ministers and terrified them. The Americans, who were fighting as the Corsicans had fought the Genoese, were invincible. Even if they lost the seaboard towns, which they had not yet done, they could take refuge for ever in the back country. In London the strife between Whigs and Tories was so violent that seven or eight members of the opposition would probably go to the Tower. At the first misfortune of the royal army in America the king might lose his crown and his ministers their heads. France and Spain must be ready to profit by whatever bad luck England might have.

Vergennes that same month sent the enigmatic Bonvouloir to Philadelphia, to encourage Congress, and soon began with Beaumarchais to make specific plans for aiding the colonies. For want of documents it is impossible to say which of the two proposed their scheme, but it was theatrical with intrigue. Using many of Beaumarchais's arguments, Vergennes undertook to persuade the king and his council that it would be wise to send the Americans secret military supplies under the pretence of lawful commerce. Beaumarchais would set up a bogus commercial house to carry out the transactions, for which France and Spain were to furnish the initial capital. Turgot, the great controller-general of finance, objected on the prophetic ground that the American colonies of all the European powers were sure to become independent in time; and that England, instead of losing her strength with her colonies, would be better off when trading with them as independent states than now while exercising her colonial monopoly. France, Turgot thought, could not afford a needless war, in view of her own financial circumstances. The king and his council listened to Vergennes, with Beaumarchais behind him. By March, when Silas Deane left America to ask for help from France, France had already agreed with Spain to furnish Beaumarchais one million livres (francs) each. By the time Deane arrived in Paris in July Beaumarchais had already received the French million and was ready to establish the fictitious Roderigue Hortalez and Company, trading to America.

But Beaumarchais in London had talked with Arthur Lee, representing the American Committee of Secret Correspondence, who either did not understand Beaumarchais or was misled by his excitement. Lee sent word to the Committee that France and

Spain were making a gift of the money, which he believed was
£200,000. When Deane arrived, authorized to pay in promised
goods for the arms and ammunition shipped to America, Beaumarchais made a contract with him on that basis. Here was something that would complicate the plot as soon as the suspicious Lee
should find out that Beaumarchais—and Lee suspected Deane as
well—was asking payment for what had been furnished him for
nothing. Certainly the French government did not expect to be
repaid, and almost as certainly Beaumarchais meant to pocket
whatever he could make. Deane probably entered into the agreement in good faith, though he seems also to have done private
trading in goods and stocks.[1]

Roderigue Hortalez set about the clandestine shipment of munitions, most of them from French arsenals, to Haiti and Martinique,
where American agents received and reshipped them. Vergennes,
who denied the right of the British to hinder this trade, had already
defended the right of American ships to enter French ports along
with ships of any other flag. French naval squadrons were stationed
off the Channel ports and sent to the French West Indies to deter
the British from molesting commerce to or from them. As early
as May 1776 France had in effect recognized the Americans as
belligerents. But France put off declaring war on England. In
August Vergennes, who had heard of the evacuation of Boston and
the Declaration of Independence, was willing to begin hostilities,
and Spain by October was ready to join France, in the hope of
conquering Portugal and Minorca and of making terms with the
American colonies which would enable Spain to hold her own
colonies in America. The news of the defeat of Washington on
Long Island and the loss of New York to the British temporarily
checked Vergennes's programme. He did not mean to pick the
losing side.

Affairs were in this posture when Franklin reached Paris and
two days later informed Vergennes that the three commissioners—
Lee had come from London—were "fully empowered by the Congress of the United States of America to propose and negotiate a
treaty of commerce between France and the United States. The
just and generous treatment their trading ships have received by a
free admission into the ports of this kingdom, with other considera-

tions of respect, has induced the Congress to make this offer first to France."² On the 28th the envoys saw Vergennes, who complimented Franklin on his fame and knowledge and recognized his wit, but was averse to breaking with England so long as the prospects of America were uncertain. (Spies reported the meeting to London, and another on 9 January.) Franklin did not need to be told that the Americans, though favoured in France, would have to wait till the government could see a clear advantage to itself in helping them.

The melodrama in which Franklin found himself was intricate. The British ambassador Stormont watched every move the French made and protested every favour shown to America. Vergennes, friendly in private, in public made large gestures to quiet England: such as forbidding ships to sail for America with military stores, though allowing them to escape. Beaumarchais was spectacularly busy with Deane, to whom Franklin left the execution of their contract. Lee was angry and bitter. Superseded by Deane, he was eclipsed by Franklin. Edward Bancroft, confidant of Deane and later of the whole commission, from December 1776 was in the pay of the British government, smuggling American secrets off to London. Though Franklin trusted Bancroft, he knew that Paris was full of secret agents. He was careful but imperturbable. To Juliana Ritchie, who warned him three weeks after his arrival that he was surrounded by spies, he wrote on 19 January that he had no doubt he was. "As it is impossible to discover in every case the falsity of pretended friends who would know our affairs; and more so to prevent being watched by spies when interested people may think proper to place them for that purpose; I have long observed one rule which prevents any inconvenience from such practices. It is simply this: to be concerned in no affairs that I should blush to have made public, and to do nothing but what spies may see, and welcome. . . . If I was sure, therefore, that my *valet de place* was a spy, as probably he is, I think I should not discharge him for that, if in other respects I liked him."³

These were the words of a sage whose cunning was wisdom. It was no hardship for Franklin to assume the role he found waiting for him, because it was his nature to be thoughtful, witty, benevolent, cheerful, and homely. He was not a Quaker, as the French thought, but he was willing to let them think it. Paris admired the sect for its gentle, resolute merits and spoke of William Penn as a Lycurgus. Franklin, by no means a philosopher of the backwoods, for thirty years had lived among scholars and scientists, merchants and politicians, clergymen and men of fashion. His manners were as urbane and expert as his prose. But the French were looking for a hero who should combine the reason and wit of Voltaire with the primitive virtues celebrated by Rousseau, and they were sure they had found their hero in Franklin. He denied them nothing they expected. He had landed in Brittany wearing the fur cap that had kept his head warm on the November voyage. When the French delightedly took the cap for some kind of badge of transatlantic philosophy, he went on wearing it, even in Paris, for a time and for particular occasions. Having too much curiosity and too little vanity to go without the spectacles he needed, he unfashionably wore them too. If they amused Paris, they amused him. "Figure me in your mind," he wrote to a friend on 8 February, "as jolly as formerly, and as strong and hearty, only a few years older; very plainly dressed, wearing my thin grey straight hair that peeps out under my only coiffure, a fine fur cap, which comes down to my forehead almost to my spectacles. Think how this must appear among the powdered heads of Paris."[4] The French police, describing him for their records, noted not only his spectacles, fur cap, brown coat, and the stick he carried instead of a sword, but also his "very white" linen.[5]

No one could have foreseen the outburst of enthusiasm which made Franklin overnight the most famous man in the world of French opinion. The British ambassador insisted that France ought not to receive the emissary of the rebels, since England was a friendly power. Vergennes on 10 December, while Franklin was still at Nantes, ordered the police not to allow Frenchmen in cafés to say that they were going with the approval of France to join the American army.[6] In the cafés Franklin became a chief topic. Here was something Utopian yet flesh-and-blood. Here was a sage who seemed to come from the exalted past yet to belong to the shining future. The state of nature Rousseau talked about had been perhaps an abstraction. There was nothing abstract about Franklin, who was leading—the French thought—the rebellion of a natural state against the corruptions of an old order. Since he was rarely seen in public, likenesses of him were so quickly and widely called for that before the middle of January it was the fashion for everybody to have an engraving of him over the mantelpiece. The fashion did not pass. Two years later he told his daughter that his portrait had appeared in many medallions of different sizes: "some to be set in the lids of snuffboxes and some so small as to be worn in rings; and the numbers sold are incredible. These, with the pictures, busts, and prints (of which copies upon copies are spread everywhere), have made your father's face as well known as that of the moon, so that he durst not do anything that would oblige him to run away, as his phiz would discover him wherever he should venture to show it."[7] Aware as Franklin was of his popularity, he was not self-conscious. He enjoyed his honours and serenely lived up to them.

If he profited by the enthusiasm of France for the cause of the Americans, so did America profit by France's passion for Franklin. Merely by being himself to the utmost he dignified and glorified his country. Vergennes could not have found a more useful colleague in his plan to make war on England. While the minister pulled dynastic and diplomatic strings the philosopher won public sentiment. The king was only slowly persuaded to help a rebellion against another king, and there were plenty of noblemen who hesitated with him. Other financiers besides Turgot held that the French budget could not stand a war. The merchants and traders who were prospering in peace did not want to see it disturbed. But there was a part of the public, sentimental and ardent, which believed that the cause of America was the cause of humanity and that France by taking sides would directly serve it. It was this public which adored Franklin, and which was rapidly enlarged by his influence. Vergennes guessed that he could make the best use of Franklin by leaving him to his own devices. Franklin had the tact to fall in masterfully with Vergennes's programme. He demanded nothing that the minister could not yet give, asked for no compromising pledges, and after two conspicuous months in Paris withdrew to Passy, then a suburban village, where he set up his reticent little court.

But in the few crowded weeks in Paris, at the Hôtel d'Hambourg in the Rue de l'Université, Franklin had firmly established his mission as well as his character in France. While the commissioners had no outright promises from France, they received, a few days after the meeting with Vergennes, a secret subsidy of two million livres with no fixed terms regarding payment. They sent Captain Wickes out with the *Reprisal*, and in a month he had brought in five British prizes which were sold, in spite of Stormont's very proper protests, at Lorient. Franklin renewed his acquaintance with the physiocrats and other scholars, and was present on 15 January at the meeting of the Academy of Sciences. He was taken, wearing his fur cap, to the salon of the famous, old, blind, witty Madame du Deffand, who wrote to Horace Walpole whom she loved that she was not for the insurgents.[8] (She was more Tory than Walpole, who wrote to another correspondent on the following 11 December: "Were I Franklin, I would order the [British] cabinet council to come to me at Paris with ropes about their necks, and then kick them back to St. James's.") On 26 January Franklin dined with the young Duc de La Rochefoucauld d'Enville,[9] who began promptly to translate the constitutions of the thirteen American states. On account of Lafayette, nineteen and eager to win renown and avenge his father's death by fighting against England, Franklin met the Noailles family, one of whose daughters was Lafayette's wife. The Prince de Broglie, whose connexions were as powerful as those of La Rochefoucauld and Noailles, offered himself to America as a sympathetic dictator of the nation, perhaps another William of Orange. The Duc de Choiseul hoped through Franklin to be restored to royal favour. By such great persons as hardly noticed Franklin in England, he was now sought and treasured in France. He bore himself always as the wise and simple philosopher they desired him to be. Even his bad French, which gradually became more fluent but was always inaccurate, charmed them. It pleased them that, though they all knew he had come on a burdensome mission, he seemed to have time for light-hearted society.

England knew that Franklin was in France as soon as Paris did. His enemies in London gave out that he had ignominiously run away from the hopeless rebellion he had started. But Rockingham, first minister when the Stamp Act was repealed and now a leader of the opposition in the House of Lords, saw Franklin's coming in a different light. "The horrid scene at a Privy Council," Rockingham wrote, "is in my memory, though perhaps not in his. It may not excite his conduct. It certainly deters him not. He boldly ventures to cross the Atlantic in an American little frigate, and risks the dangers of being taken and being once more brought before an implacable tribunal. The sight of Banquo's ghost could not more offend the eyes of Macbeth than the knowledge of this old man being at Versailles should affect the minds of those who were principals in that horrid scene. Depend upon it, he will plead forcibly." The British ministers, Rockingham supposed, would minimize the danger of Franklin's appeal to France, but "inwardly they will tremble at it."[10] Charles James Fox, in Paris when Franklin arrived, approved his saying, as to Howe, that England's war on America would be as costly and useless as the Crusades. George III through his excellent secret service kept close watch on "that insidious man"[11] from Philadelphia.

Franklin renewed his correspondence with a few friends in England, and sent them optimistic news. To Polly Hewson during his driven January he wrote twice, telling her about his grandchildren, asking affectionately about her children and her mother, and—as on his holiday visit ten years before—remarking on the current fashions. "Temple observes them more than I do. He took notice that at the ball at Nantes there were no heads [headdresses] less than five, and a few were seven, lengths of the face above the top of the forehead. . . . Yesterday we dined at the Duke de Rochefoucault's, where there were three duchesses and a countess, and no head higher than a face and a half. So, it seems, the farther from court the more extravagant the mode."[12]

In spite of the British secret service letters reached Franklin from England. Not all were political. One of them, addressed to "Monsieur Francis" in care of a friend in Passy, was from Georgiana Shipley, now eighteen or so, daughter of the bishop of St. Asaph. "You are the first man," she said, "who ever received a private letter from me." Her father had thought it imprudent for any of them to risk a letter, in view of the war, but she was "not of an age to be so very prudent," and she was afraid if she did not write Franklin might misunderstand her silence. "I could not support the idea of your believing that I love and esteem you less than I did some few years ago." The other members of her family felt as she did; "nor can any time or event in the least change their sentiments." They were all in good health, and one of the sisters was married. Had Franklin read Adam Smith's *Wealth of Nations*, which she had begun? She thought it the only recent book worth mention except the first volume of Gibbon's history. She had been reading everything she could about Socrates, "for I fancy I can discover in each trait of that admirable man's character a strong resemblance between him and my much-loved friend." She wished Franklin were in England to answer the questions she would like to ask him about electrical matters. "I find a strong inclination to envy your grandson the having it in his power to show you any kindness and attention."[13]

Besides letters to his friends Franklin wrote for the press and public. If he did not edit or help edit the periodical *Affaires de l'Angleterre et de l'Amérique*, which ran to eighty-two numbers (*cahiers*) during his first four years in France,[14] he was at least its most eminent contributor. It reprinted his *Examination* before the House of Commons, his *Edict* of the King of Prussia, his *Rules* for reducing a great empire. It printed his correspondence with Lord Howe and with Strahan, and brief new pieces aiming to win general European sympathy for the American rebels. His *Comparison of Great Britain and the United States in Regard to the Basis of Credit in the Two Countries*, put into various languages throughout Europe for the sake of the loan Congress was trying to get, argued that: "from the general industry, frugality, ability, prudence, and virtue of America, she is a much safer debtor than Britain; to say nothing of the satisfaction generous minds must have in reflecting that by loans to America they are opposing tyranny and aiding the cause of liberty, which is the cause of all mankind."[15]

The Sale of the Hessians, published originally and only in French,[16] is thought to be the satire which Franklin sent to John Winthrop on 1 May. "The conduct of those princes of Germany," he wrote, "who have sold the blood of their people, has subjected them to the contempt and odium of Europe. The Prince of Anspach, whose recruits mutinied and refused to march, was obliged to disarm and fetter them, and drive them to the seaside by the help of his guards; himself attending in person. In his return he was publicly hooted by mobs through every town he passed in Holland, with all sorts of reproachful epithets. The king of Prussia's humour of obliging those princes to pay him the same toll per head for men they drive through his dominions as used to be paid him for their cattle, because they were sold as such, is generally spoken of as containing a just reproof of those tyrants."[17] While *The Sale of the Hessians* is not certainly known to be by Franklin, it can hardly have been by anybody else. In style and temper it is another Franklin hoax, and vitriol in print. Ostensibly a letter from the Count de Schaumbergh, safe in Rome, to Baron Hohendorf, commanding the Hessians in America, and dated 18 February, it must have been written later, when Franklin had had time to hear—not until March—of the capture of the Hessians at Trenton the day after Christmas.

Count de Schaumbergh was delighted by the news that 1605 of his Hessians had been killed. The report of the British ministry had made the number only 1455. He had no doubt that Hohendorf would correct Lord North's error, which if allowed to stand would cheat the count out of money he was entitled to for his dead subjects. He hoped the baron had not taken too much trouble to keep wounded men alive. "I am sure they would rather die than live in a condition no longer fit for my service. . . . I am about to send you some new recruits. Don't economize them. Remember glory before all things. Glory is true wealth. There is nothing degrades the soldier like the love of money. He must care only for honour and reputation, but this reputation must be acquired in the midst of dangers. A battle gained without costing the conqueror any blood is an inglorious success, while the conquered cover themselves with glory by perishing with their arms in their hands. Do you remember that of the three hundred Lacedæmonians who defended the defile of Thermopylæ, not one returned? How happy should I be could I say the same of my brave Hessians!"[18] There was an actual Count Schaumburg who, as agent for George III, tried in 1777 to buy soldiers from the young Duke of Saxe-Weimar, patron of Herder, Goethe, and Schiller. Franklin satirically gave the name of the British agent to the Hessian prince.[19]

II

By the first of March Franklin had established his household in Passy, "a neat village on a high ground, half a mile from Paris, with a large garden to walk in."[20] Benjamin Bache was at a boarding school in the village and spent his Sundays with his grandfather. Temple acted as Franklin's secretary. Franklin's grandnephew Jonathan Williams had come from London, and was now at Passy, now at Nantes overseeing the shipments to America. Living in a kind of patriarchal nepotism, Franklin had Deane often with him in the same house, but not Arthur Lee. The commission's quarters in Passy were in the grounds of the great Hôtel Valentinois, occupied by the owner, Donatien Le Ray de Chaumont, an ardent partisan of the United States—and also a large contractor furnishing goods to the insurgents—who refused for the present to accept any rent. Though Franklin kept a carriage and a pair of horses he stayed much at home during the middle months of 1777, and was said to go to Paris chiefly for the meetings of the Academy of Sciences, though he went more than the public realized. Once that year or early the next, according to Silas Deane: "a celebrated cause being to be heard before the Parliament of Paris, and the house and streets leading to it crowded with people, on the appearance of Dr. Franklin way was made for him in the most respectful manner, and he passed through the crowd to the seat reserved for him, amid the acclamations of the people. An honour seldom paid to the first princes of the blood. When he attended the opera and plays similar honours were paid him."[21] His retirement to Passy made the public more curious about him than ever.

While the commissioners waited to see how Vergennes would decide on their proposal in March for a triple alliance of the United States, France, and Spain against England, and while Vergennes waited for a decision from Spain, there was much to do at Passy. At least three cruisers were fitted out in French ports and sent against British shipping in the Channel, with such success that insurance rates rose sharply in London. Franklin tried in

April to arrange with Stormont for the exchange of prisoners. The letter was returned, seemingly unopened though Stormont had read it, with the unsigned note: "The king's ambassador receives no letters from rebels but when they come to implore His Majesty's mercy." To this Franklin replied with humorous hectoring, to the amusement of Paris. When Stormont gave out news that the Americans had lost four thousand men in a battle and their general had been killed, Franklin said that truth was one thing and Stormont another (*la vérité et le stormont sont deux*). Chaumont told one of Vergennes's agents, who reported it to Vergennes on 11 August.[22] Perhaps Franklin varied his expression. At any rate, Parisian slang made to stormont (*stormonter*) a synonym for to lie (*mentir*).

But Stormont, though the French laughed at him, still had his spies, still knew what Franklin was doing, still was able to notify his chief at home that Franklin was probably carrying on a correspondence with Shelburne, Camden, Thomas Walpole, Samuel Wharton, Thomas Wharton, and John Williams, under the names Jones, Jackson, Johnson, Watson, and Nicholson.[23] And Stormont did have news which was unfavourable to America: about Washington's evacuation of New York, his ragged campaigns in New Jersey, Howe's advance on Philadelphia (where Franklin's *chevaux de frise* helped to delay the passage of the British boats up the Delaware), and the march of Burgoyne's army south from Canada with his German mercenaries and Indian allies. Until there should be better news the commissioners could hope for nothing more than surreptitious help from France. The summer and fall at Passy were full of tense anxiety.

(To this summer belongs the famous story of the meeting of Franklin and Gibbon at an inn which Horace Walpole spoke of in a letter of 25 April 1781. Franklin, according to the story, arrived at the inn, learned that Gibbon was there, and sent to ask for the pleasure of his company. Gibbon answered with a note saying that, much as he admired Franklin as a man and a philosopher, he could not in loyalty to his king have any conversation with a rebel. The rebel, with his flair for the last word, wrote that he still had the greatest respect for the historian. When Gibbon came to write of the decline and fall of the British Empire, Franklin would be happy to furnish him with the ample materials in his possession.

Gibbon was in Paris that year, and between 12 May and 16 June dined once somewhere with Franklin "by accident."[24] There is no other record of their meeting. The story was told because it was in character, and it may have been invented for the same reason.)

At Passy Franklin, with his fame and his cause, was overwhelmed by correspondents and visitors. Everybody who thought he had anything to say about America wrote it to Franklin. There were endless applications from merchants who had goods to sell and traders who hoped to make a profit out of dealing with America. The heaviest demands came from French—and other European—officers who wanted to be recommended to the American army. These, Franklin wrote, "are my perpetual torment. People will believe, notwithstanding my continually repeated declarations to the contrary, that I am sent hither to engage officers. In truth, I never had any such orders. . . . Not a day passes in which I have not a number of soliciting visits, besides letters. . . . You can have no conception how I am harassed. All my friends are sought out and teased to tease me. Great officers of all ranks, in all departments; ladies, great and small, besides professed solicitors, worry me from morning to night. The noise of every coach now that enters my court terrifies me. I am afraid to accept an invitation to dine abroad, being almost sure of meeting with some officer or some officer's friend who, as soon as I am put in good humour with a glass of champagne, begins his attack upon me. Luckily I do not often in my sleep dream myself in these vexatious situations, or I should be afraid of what are now my only hours of comfort."[25]

Franklin could make exceptions. Though he did not meet Lafayette before his departure for America, Franklin in August wrote to Washington, asking a favour. The friends of "that amiable young nobleman" had sent him money and would send more; "but on reflection, knowing the extreme generosity of his disposition, and fearing that some of his necessitous and artful countrymen may impose on his goodness, they wish to put his money into the hands of some discreet friend [Washington himself], who may supply him from time to time, and, by that means knowing his expenses, may take occasion to advise him, if necessary, with a friendly affection and secure him from too much imposition."[26] Lafayette was virtually adopted by Washington. The other most valuable officer who crossed the Atlantic that year was also recommended by Franklin, and with some craft. This was—to give him the name he used in America—Frederick William Augustus von Steuben.

Steuben had served on the Prussian general staff, as an aide to Frederick the Great, and so had as good military training as was then possible. But in the summer of 1777 he was a needy captain in Baden looking for employment. There he met an English friend of Franklin who sent Baron von Steuben to Paris with a letter of introduction. Already known to the French minister of war, Saint-Germain, who had a high opinion of the Prussian army, Steuben was earnestly recommended to Franklin, who saw him at Passy. After some hesitation Franklin—with Deane—decided to send the baron to America. But they raised his rank in their letters, to make Congress more willing to accept another foreigner. "The gentleman who will have the honour of waiting on you with this letter," Franklin wrote to Washington on 4 September, "is the Baron de Steuben, lately a lieutenant-general in the king of Prussia's service, whom he attended in all his campaigns, being his aide-de-camp, quartermaster-general, etc."[27] Coming as a Prussian general, Steuben impressed Congress and was assigned to Washington at Valley Forge. Literally within a few weeks he had made the army over, and thereafter it matched the British in discipline. But without the calculated, imaginary promotion in Paris Steuben might never have gone or been so promptly accepted and given his chance to drill the militiamen into soldiers.[28]

Much as Franklin came to dread or resent the pressure on him for recommendations to America, he was a humorist in the model letter he drew up on 2 April for routine use. "The bearer of this, who is going to America, presses me to give him a letter of recommendation, though I know nothing of him, not even his name. This may seem extraordinary, but I assure you it is not uncommon here. Sometimes, indeed, one unknown person brings another, equally unknown, to recommend him; and sometimes they recommend one another. As to this gentleman, I must refer you to himself for his character and merits, with which he is certainly better acquainted than I can possibly be. I recommend him, however, to those civilities which every stranger of whom one knows no harm has a right to; and I request you will do him all the good offices, and show him all the favour, that on further acquaintance you shall find him to deserve."[29] It is not known how often Franklin used his model letter, or to what effect. He may have drawn it up chiefly for his own amusement.

Though Franklin might be imperturbable about spies, the British secret service had put a fantastic net around him. The service was organized in London by William Eden (later Lord Auckland), an ambitious under-secretary of state. Eden's chief of spies for the Paris business was Paul Wentworth, probably born in America, who had been colonial agent for New Hampshire and had remained loyal to the Crown. Wentworth, with a salary and an expense account, and promises of a baronetcy, a seat in Parliament, a sinecure, superintended the work of the other agents, and himself made frequent rapid trips between London and Paris. It was he who persuaded Edward Bancroft to become a spy.

Deane had brought to Paris a letter from Franklin to Bancroft, formerly Franklin's friend in London and a member of the Royal Society. Bancroft joined Deane in the summer of 1776, with a salary which was paid him throughout the Revolution. Wentworth offered him a larger salary. Bancroft took money from both of them, and gave most of his confidence to Wentworth. On the list of spies Bancroft was called Edward Edwards. Hired as a secret agent in December, he was present with the American commissioners, as their secretary, at their meeting with Vergennes on 9 January, and duly reported it. Then he settled down to his career of double-dealing. He lived in Franklin's household for the first year, and then or later was never suspected by Franklin. Bancroft furnished Wentworth regular bulletins on the negotiations with France and Spain, the means of obtaining credit, the correspondence with Congress. He furnished Stormont the names of ships and masters employed by the commissioners, details of their sailings, and news of privateers and prizes. Writing his reports in invisible ink, on the white spaces of letters otherwise "on gallantry," Bancroft deposited them in a sealed bottle in a hole in a tree on the south terrace of the Tuileries, where they were picked up at half-past nine every Tuesday evening by a messenger who left in another bottle any communications to Bancroft from Stormont, through whom while he remained in Paris the Bancroft-

Wentworth correspondence was transmitted. Arthur Lee, who suspected everybody but his own secretary, who was a spy, suspected Bancroft. To quiet doubts about him Bancroft made occasional trips to London to get unimportant secret information for Franklin, and was once arrested there on trumped-up charges.

Thanks to Bancroft, Stormont could make accurate protests to Vergennes against French violations of neutrality, and British cruisers could know where to watch for shipments and mail to America. Wentworth put another spy, less brilliant than Bancroft, on a different task in France. This was Joseph Hynson, a nautical man from Maryland, who was a stepbrother of Wickes of the *Reprisal.* Hynson came complicatedly into the plot. Deane had as voluntary secretary William Carmichael, also of Maryland, a young man of fortune who had been enjoying himself in London when the Revolution broke out. Carrying letters from Arthur Lee, Carmichael started for America but stopped in Paris and met Deane. The secretary was set to find ship captains who might become privateers, and found Hynson. Together they arranged that a cutter should be obtained in Dover, cleared ostensibly for an innocent voyage, and at some port of France fitted out as an armed packet to carry dispatches to Congress. At this point, as if on the most melodramatic stage, appeared John Vardill, a loyalist clergyman who was a British spy in London because he hoped to become an American professor of divinity in New York. Hynson, in London in February 1777, boasted to a girl that he was close to Franklin. Vardill heard about it and made offers to Hynson if he would betray the Americans. Hynson pretended, to the girl, to reject the offers, but actually accepted them. The admiralty, being in the secret, allowed the cutter to sail. While it—or some other vessel— was being made ready Hynson was in Paris with the commissioners and able to give information to Stormont's secretary.

Hynson's great task, proposed by Vardill and approved by North, was to steal the American dispatches. After long delays the packet was ready, but Franklin and Deane, though they did not yet suspect Hynson, decided to give the command on the first voyage to John Folger—from Nantucket and Franklin's distant cousin. The dispatch pouch was forwarded to Folger in care of Hynson, now at Havre. Hynson substituted blank paper for the dispatches and turned the pouch over to Folger. The originals went in Hynson's hands straight to Wentworth and, arranged and digested, to the king in October. The king and the ministry, at about the time of Burgoyne's surrender, had authoritative records of all the commissioners had been doing for months.[30]

A special duty of Vardill was to look out for any agents that Franklin might send to London. Assistant minister of Trinity church in New York, Vardill (only twenty-two) had come to London in 1774 to obtain a charter which would make King's College (Columbia) a university. For an appointment as regius professor of theology when the rebellion should have been put down, and a salary in the meantime, he became a spy. When the Abbé Raynal arrived in London with letters from Franklin, Vardill managed to get at them. He spied on Jonathan Loring Austin when he brought Franklin's messages to Shelburne. Jacobus Van Zandt came to London, and Vardill engaged him, a young New Yorker of good connexions, to go to spy on the commissioners in Paris. Calling himself George Lupton, he hung about Deane's circle at the Hôtel d'Hambourg, sneaking out bits of information such as the names used on letters from London addressed to the commissioners. Once he was assigned to carry instructions to Nantes, and noted the ships and shipments then in port. Arthur Lee's secretary was named Thornton. Because Lee was not always in the confidence of Franklin and Deane, Thornton could not learn much. He represented himself as an American spying on the British, and brought false military information which Lee forwarded to Congress. The list of spies might be made longer if they were worth it, and the story of their schemes.[31]

While the British spies watched the commissioners, the spies of Vergennes and Beaumarchais hunted for suspicious Englishmen in France, and the French police kept an eye on everybody. Franklin steadily refused to pay too much attention to the tangled net. His trust in Bancroft, through whom the admiralty learned about sailings, cost America a good many shipments and dispatches. But they could not all—or perhaps most—of them have escaped the alert British cruisers, even if these had been unwarned. The papers Hynson stole merely confirmed what Bancroft had been reporting to Wentworth. On the whole Franklin profited more by the British spies than he lost. His policy of unexpected candour confused them. When finally he met Wentworth, the chief spy, Franklin outdid him in cunning and turned his zeal to use in hastening the alliance with France which Wentworth had come to prevent.

Wentworth was less trouble to Franklin than Arthur Lee, who bred trouble if he did not find it. The commissioners were officially of equal rank, but Franklin's renown and popularity made him overwhelmingly first among them. Deane felt it honour enough to be known as Franklin's friend and countryman. Lee, though he still could not help admiring Franklin, as in London, was miserable in that great shadow. His missions to Spain, Vienna, and Berlin during the first half of 1777 were unsuccessful, and in Berlin he had his papers filched by the active British minister Hugh Elliott. Back in Paris in July, Lee was at once dissatisfied with the supplies being furnished to America. He objected, in particular, to the blue and buff of the Continental uniforms, and insisted that scarlet was the only colour fit to fight in. He wrangled over buttons and lapels till the French contractors refused to have any dealings with him. Learning that bills were being rendered to Congress, and remembering what Beaumarchais had said about free gifts before Deane came over, Lee was convinced that Beaumarchais and Deane were both stealing public funds. Because Franklin seemed to side with Deane, or at least left the matter of the contracts in his hands, Lee by 12 September 1778 had decided that Franklin himself was "concerned in the plunder, and that in time we shall collect the proofs."[32] Lee suspected that Franklin's nephew Jonathan Williams, overseeing the shipments from Nantes, was another dishonest beneficiary; and he complained of Franklin's having his grandson for his secretary.

Letters to Richard Henry Lee (Arthur Lee's brother) and Samuel Adams carried suspicions to Congress. From Congress, not quite intending it, support for Arthur Lee came to Paris. In May 1777 he had been commissioned to Spain and two new commissioners appointed: William Lee (a third brother) to Berlin and Vienna and Ralph Izard to Tuscany—both of them already in France. Since none of these courts would recognize the independence of the United States, the three Americans stayed in or near Paris, disturbing the embassy. William Lee and Izard took Arthur Lee's view of Deane, but it was Arthur Lee's letters to America which had most to do with causing Congress in December to order Deane home to report on "the state of affairs in Europe." What Lee had wanted in October, when he wrote his letters, was to see Deane shipped off to Holland and Franklin to Vienna, so that he himself could take full charge in Paris, "the great wheel that moves them all."[33]

If Deane had been a peculator, and Franklin indifferent if not worse, then Lee would have been in fact the unhappy and mistreated victim he always thought he was. There was no doubt in his own mind that he, the most virtuous of the commissioners, had caught the others at mischief. But he was doubly in the minority, because Franklin was a majority in himself. Though Lee might, it proved, get Deane recalled, he could not budge the sage, serene, humorous philosopher who was master no less in strategy than in wisdom. Lee was shrill with suspicion and fury. As long as he was in France he never ceased his backbiting and talebearing. And through the anxious months of 1777, when the commissioners were waiting for news of Howe and Burgoyne, Lee perpetually dissented. As he was, he thought, the only honest man of the three, so was he the only thorough patriot, unshakably for independence. The others might be willing to compromise. British spies in Paris thought the same thing, and so reported to London. When Wentworth came to France in December he would not talk with Lee, believing the commissioners were of two minds and Franklin and Deane more likely than Lee to listen to British reason.

III

In July Vergennes told the king that secret assistance was no longer enough to keep up the war in America and that France must either withdraw altogether or else do more—that is, declare war on England. What was needed was an offensive and defensive alliance with the United States and Spain, each of them agreeing not to make peace without the consent of the others. The king was willing only if Spain would join them. But Spain held back, having made a truce with Portugal and being still opposed to independence for any American colonies. The news from America did not encourage France to go on alone. Burgoyne easily took Ticonderoga in July. Howe, though dilatory, promised to capture Philadelphia. If Philadelphia as well as New York were to be in the hands of the British, and New England isolated by Burgoyne, the rebellion must fail, Vergennes assumed. He continued his waiting for some hopeful occasion to strike.

To the French Franklin still showed the calm, smiling face which reassured and charmed them. Even when bad news came and Gérard (or someone) said: "Well, Doctor, Howe has taken Philadelphia," Franklin replied: "I beg your pardon, Sir, Philadelphia has taken Howe."[34] Pleased with Franklin's spirit in public, Paris thought his wit better than it was. Privately he knew that American affairs were in the worst way. Letters from Congress said they did not see how they could continue without alliances and loans. Few letters arrived. British men-of-war had almost cut off the service of communications, and a squadron outside the mouth of the Loire effectually shut up American vessels in the port of Nantes: privateers eager to invade the Channel, cargo ships with munitions for the United States. While the British army threatened to divide New England from the other colonies, the British navy threatened to divide Washington, heading the Revolution at home, from Franklin, heading it abroad. Both of them suffered from lack of supplies and money. Both of them had to endure quarrels and cabals among their associates. Both of them had fallen back on the last deep resources of their minds and wills.

Late in September the commissioners presented a memorial to Vergennes, pressing him to recognize the independence of their country and to grant a loan—they mentioned fourteen million livres—which would bring real relief. Through the sly Bancroft and the protesting Stormont the ministers heard about the memorial before it reached them. Vergennes, in a temporizing answer, told the envoys they did their work unguardedly. It must not leak out. They argued among themselves over the ministerial reproof. Lee thought they laid their affairs "open to all the world"; Deane that the accusation was untrue; Franklin that Vergennes had only found a pretext for refusing help.[35] The month went on with no decisive answer.

On 25 October Lee had a long talk with Franklin at Passy and that day wrote out at unusual length in his journal what Franklin had said about the American beginnings of the Revolution which Lee, in England, had not seen. "He seemed to agree with me in thinking that France and Spain mistook their interest and opportunity in not making an alliance with us now, when they might make better terms than they could expect hereafter. That it was well for us they left us to work out our own salvation; which the efforts we had hitherto made, and the resources we had opened, gave us the fairest reason to hope we should be able to do.

"He told me the manner in which the whole of this business had been conducted was such a miracle in human affairs that, if he had not been in the midst of it and seen all the movements, he could not have comprehended how it was effected. To comprehend it we must view a whole people for some months without any laws or government at all. In this state their civil governments were to be formed, an army and navy were to be provided for those who had neither a ship of war, a company of soldiers, nor magazines, arms, artillery, or ammunition. Alliances were to be formed, for they had none. All this was to be done, not at leisure nor in a time of tranquillity and communication with other nations, but in the face of a most formidable invasion, by the most powerful nation, fully provided with armies, fleets, and all the instruments of destruction, powerfully allied and aided, the commerce with other nations in a great measure stopped up. . . .

"Nor was this all; they had internal opposition to encounter which alone would seem sufficient to have frustrated all their efforts. The Scotch, who in many places were numerous, were secret or open foes as opportunity offered. The Quakers, a powerful body in Pennsylvania, gave every opposition their art, abilities, and influence could suggest. To these were added all those whom contrariety of opinion, Tory principles, personal animosities, fear of so dreadful and dubious an undertaking, joined with the artful promises and threats of the enemy, rendered open or concealed opposers, or timid neutrals, or lukewarm friends to the proposed revolution." But Franklin was convinced that the Revolution was supported by a genuine majority. "Consequently the feebleness, irresolution, and inaction which generally, nay, almost invariably attends and frustrates hasty popular proceedings, did not influence this. . . . Those who acted in council bestowed their whole thoughts upon the public; those who took to the field did with what weapons, ammunition, and accommodations they could procure. . . . Dr. Franklin assured me that upon an average he gave twelve hours in the twenty-four to public business." Multitudes of men, "not of inferior abilities," had worked as hard.

"The consequence was that in a few months the governments were established; codes of law were formed which, for wisdom and justice, are the admiration of all the wise and thinking men in Europe. Ships of war were built, a multitude of cruisers were fitted out, which have done more injury to the British commerce than it ever suffered before. Armies of offence and defence were formed, and kept the field through all the rigours of winter in the most rigorous climate. Repeated losses, inevitable in a defensive war, as it soon became, served only to renew exertions that quickly repaired them. The enemy was everywhere resisted, repulsed, or besieged. On the ocean, in the Channel, in their very ports, their ships were taken and their commerce obstructed. The greatest revolution the world ever saw is likely to be effected in a few years; and the power that has for centuries made all Europe tremble, assisted by twenty thousand German mercenaries and favoured by the universal concurrence of Europe to prohibit the sale of warlike stores, the sale of prizes, or the admission of the armed vessels of America, will be effectually humbled by those whom she insulted and injured, because she conceived they had neither spirit nor power to resist or revenge it."[36]

The voice of Franklin sounds through the words of Arthur Lee. In the light of all that is now known about those first years, Franklin's version of the Revolutionary beginnings seems at many points romantic. But versions like his were a part of the Revolution itself. Here was the grand style by which the humorous philosopher lived, in the midst of his realistic cares and plans. That grand style in the Revolutionary leaders was a force which the cynical British ministry could not learn to take into account.

In November news came by way of England that Philadelphia had fallen to Howe. Franklin, all of whose property was in the town, with his daughter and her younger children so far as he knew, was the firmest of the commissioners when they met on the 27th to make up their next dispatches to Congress. "He was clearly of opinion," according to Arthur Lee's journal, "that we could maintain the contest, and successfully too, without any European assistance; he was satisfied, as he had said formerly, that the less commerce or dependence we had upon Europe the better, for that we should do better without any connexion with it." Nor would he consent to warn the French ministry that without a French alliance the envoys must make terms with England: "the effect of such a declaration upon them was uncertain; it might be taken as a menace, it might make them abandon us in despair or in anger."[37] Better wait till the news was better, and they could make better terms. Just before noon on 4 December Jonathan Loring Austin arrived from Boston with the news that Burgoyne's entire army had surrendered at Saratoga.

Beaumarchais, who was there or came soon after Austin, rushed off to Paris, presumably to speculate on the report, and drove so recklessly that his carriage was overturned and his arm injured. Bancroft left for London, certainly in part to look after his own speculations. (He had already written a London friend that Burgoyne was in danger and that stocks were likely to fall.) The envoys at once drew up a dispatch for Vergennes. Lee wrote to the Spanish ambassador. Two days later Conrad-Alexandre Gérard of the foreign office called at Passy, bringing Vergennes's congratulations and inviting the Americans to renew their proposal for an alliance. Franklin drafted the proposal on the 7th, and on the 8th Temple delivered it. Sir George Grand, dining with Franklin that day, told him that a note just come from Vergennes referred to the envoys as "our friends," not "your friends" as formerly. On the 12th the envoys went by stealth—for fear of possible spies—to a place some distance from Versailles and sent word to Gérard. A coach called for them and took them to a house half a mile out of town, where Gérard and Vergennes were waiting. Nothing could be done of course, Vergennes said, without Spain, but he complimented and encouraged them. His courier could travel to and from Madrid in three weeks. In only five days Gérard came to Passy to say that the king's council had decided upon the alliance, though they would, as a mark of respect to Spain, not technically conclude it till the courier returned. Vergennes's haste was due largely to the presence in Paris of Paul Wentworth, chief of the British spies.

Wentworth now distrusted Bancroft because Bancroft had withheld from him the private information about the danger Burgoyne was in. A speculator in stocks himself, Wentworth resented being left out of what might be a lucrative secret. At least Bancroft had meant to leave him out, even though Wentworth had got hold of the message to Bancroft's partner. George III, who hated speculation, disliked both Bancroft and Wentworth for their financial activities. And he disliked them, too, for the information they had furnished about the prospect of a French alliance, which he obstinately refused to believe in. But after the news of Saratoga the king could no longer oppose North's plans for a prompt though belated move toward conciliation. Wentworth was sent to Paris, without authority to offer terms but with instructions to learn how Franklin and Deane stood, and to watch developments. Arthur Lee's spy-secretary had reported Lee to be so set on absolute independence that there could be no point in dealing with him. Wentworth left London on 6 December, and was in Paris by the time the American commissioners had their clandestine meeting with Vergennes.

Within a few days Wentworth had had two conferences with Deane. The spy said the British ministry had been forced into the war with America against their will, and now wanted to undo that mistake. They were ready to return to the imperial status before 1763 and repeal the obnoxious acts passed since then. Wentworth suggested a general armistice by land and sea, the British troops to be withdrawn everywhere except from the New York islands. Long Island might remain temporarily British as a kind of barrier fortress, and the smaller islands neutralized. This was to last while a commission went from England to readjust American affairs on the "grand basis of the Navigation Acts." The British would still have their colonial monopoly over the Americans, who would still be colonists. Deane said that America must be independent. Wentworth promised that any Americans who helped to bring about an understanding might expect everything from the Crown in the way of reward: titles of honour, wealth, high administrative posts.

Franklin, who knew that Deane was seeing Wentworth, refused himself to see him. Nobody knew better than Franklin how much the best policy honesty was. He turned over to Vergennes a letter to Bancroft from an unidentified correspondent in London asking whether the Americans would accept something "a little short of independence." This was on the 17th, the very day Gérard came to Passy to say that the French had decided, but must formally wait for Spain. The presence of British emissaries in Paris gave rise to the rumour that, if France did not recognize American independence, the Americans might be reunited with England and join in the conquest of the French and Spanish islands in the West Indies. Vergennes, without crediting it, used the rumour to influence the king. A reunion between Great Britain and the colonies, Vergennes knew, would put a French war on England out of the question. And Vergennes could not be sure—any more than Franklin was—what Wentworth's errand amounted to. Had he been sent to coax the envoys out of a French alliance, or only to cause the French to distrust them? Might he not—even—have been craftily brought over by Franklin for the purpose of troubling and hurrying up the French? Was he, as Wentworth pretended, merely an agreeable cosmopolitan speculator, or was he a British spy? Vergennes's own spies watched Wentworth so closely that he burned his papers, and his friends avoided him. He was worried over being thought a spy. Stormont, to give Wentworth a character, presented him to Louis XVI. Vergennes, to have a closer look at him, asked him to dinner.

Franklin waited. So long as Bancroft was in London it was hard for Wentworth to find out much about the commissioners. After Bancroft's return Wentworth learned that letters had come to Franklin from the British opposition. On 25 December Wentworth wrote to Eden that it would be wise to promise the envoys anything, no matter whether the promises were to be kept or not. The alliance must be prevented. In spite of Wentworth's efforts, made through Bancroft, Franklin still refused an interview. By the 31st Vergennes had his answer from Spain, which was against signing the treaty. France must act alone. Franklin gave Vergennes a few days more, and then consented to talk with Wentworth on 6 January, stipulating that Wentworth must not say a word about personal rewards to the commissioners. The master spy came to Passy.

"I called on Franklin yesterday," Wentworth reported to Eden (using numbers for names: 72 for Franklin), "and found him very busy with his nephew [grandson], who was directed to leave the room, and we remained together two hours. . . . Franklin received me very kindly. I introduced the conversation by some compliments, to which he is very open. . . . I concluded with wishing to be honoured with his opinion of the temper of the Congress, the terms and the means he would suggest to induce reconciliation. Hinted that his opinion, in my opinion, would be that of the Congress." Wentworth reminded Franklin that he had formerly favoured an imperial union rather than American independence. "He said that any of the different opinions he had given would have done at the time they were given, because they were, as they necessarily must be, formed from the circumstances of the epocha; that Mr. Barclay and Dr. Fothergill had one set in writing which only subjected him to abuse. Another set was obtained by Lord Hyde and Lord Howe, and again by Lord Howe in America." As to the present, propositions in writing were impossible, and Franklin had learned to be cautious about verbal ones, which were "liable to be not sufficiently or over-explained." After recalling many details of the Barclay-Fothergill negotiations, Franklin, according to Wentworth, "worked himself up into passion and resentment. I told him . . . that his resentments should be lost in the cause of his country; that this was too great to mix private quarrels with. . . . He replied that his warmth did not proceed from a feeling of personal injuries, but that, they going all along with the barbarities inflicted on his country, the remembrance of these roused in an old man, constitutionally phlegmatic, the resentments of high-mettled youth; and it should serve to convince me of the resentments of those on the spot, seeing the regular system of devastation and cruelty which every general had pursued. Here he lost breath in relating the burning of towns, the neglect or ill-treatment of prisoners." They spoke of Major Thornton, Lee's secretary, who had gone to London with a letter to North about American prisoners held by the British.

How large, Wentworth went on, Franklin's satisfaction must be "if he could turn the torrent of vigour and resolution of an opulent and courageous people into affection, union, and prosperity. Britain and America could be the greatest empire on earth. He answered he believed he might do a great deal, but that the spirit of America was so high nothing but independence would be at all listened to." Other nations were willing to make "candid and fair" terms with the United States. "Nay, the savages of America would soon be more so than the savages of G[reat] Britain. Here he apostrophized again, and talked of Englishmen to be barbarous!" Wentworth tried to moderate him by changing the subject, and read—on a pledge of secrecy—a letter from Eden, who was not named. Franklin thought it a sensible letter, as far as it went. "He said he was glad to find honour and zeal so near the throne." A row of dashes in the letter probably hinted to Eden of things which Franklin said about George III but which Wentworth did not care to write. By this time Wentworth had given up reporting Franklin's talk so fully as at first. "I never knew him so eccentric"—that is, so out of centre with royal and ministerial opinion. "Nobody says less, generally, and keeps a point more closely in view, but he was diffuse and unmethodical today." Wentworth offered to try to get safe conduct for Franklin to go to London. Franklin said he might deal with a commission properly authorized. As it was, he had no powers himself and could merely hold polite conversation. Any discussions between representatives of England and America would have to be "on the broad bottom of reciprocal advantages." Before anything had been settled Deane came in, and he and Franklin dined with Wentworth and Bancroft, the two spies. "The conversation at dinner was offering bets that 7 [America] would be 107 [independent]; that Vandalia was to be the paradise on earth"; and that Chaumont with his whole family would emigrate.[38]

Wentworth, who noted and reported a letter lying on Franklin's table and all the bits of news he picked up at dinner, seems not to have perceived that Franklin was playing with him, talking against time at canny length. The spy returned to London with no real answer, and perhaps without the uncomfortable knowledge that Franklin had seen him for the effect the meeting would have on Vergennes. The next day after the interview, when Wentworth thought it not worth while to call again as he had intended, the king's council voted in favour of a treaty and an alliance.

On the 8th Gérard came to Deane's lodgings in Paris to meet the commissioners. Having put three questions, he withdrew for an hour so they might discuss them. "Dr. Franklin began to write," Lee's journal says, "and the other two to talk."[39] Franklin wrote out two questions with their answers. The commissioners had not yet agreed on the second, when Gérard returned. Gérard thought the first question and answer sufficient for the time being. "*Question.* What is necessary to be done to give such satisfaction to the American commissioners as to engage them not to listen to any proposition from England for a new connexion with that country? *Answer.* The commissioners have long since proposed a treaty of amity and commerce which is not yet concluded. The immediate conclusion of that treaty will remove the uncertainty they are under with regard to it, and give them such a reliance on the friendship of France as to reject firmly all propositions made to them of peace from England which have not for their basis the entire freedom and independence of America, both in matters of government and commerce."[40] The king, Gérard now said he was at liberty to tell them, had given his word that the treaty would be concluded. After a year's delay, Gérard did not say, the French desired the alliance as much as the Americans did, and were offering it, asking only the pledge that America would not make peace with England. Franklin had won a diplomatic campaign equal in results to Saratoga.

IV

It was nearly a month before the treaties were signed. The French still hoped that Spain might come into the alliance, and Franklin, Arthur Lee heard from Temple, worked slowly because he dined out every day. In substance the treaty of amity and commerce followed the Plan of 1776. France was to help the United States achieve its independence. The United States was to make common cause with France if war should break out between France and Great Britain. Neither should conclude either truce or peace with England without the consent of the other, and they mutually agreed not to lay down their arms till American independence should have been assured by treaty. In the matter of commerce, France and the United States were to be most-favoured nations to each other, with certain stipulations, and their ports freely open to trade in general. But there were many detailed clauses in the treaty, and the American envoys were far from harmonious. Not till 5 February was the document at last engrossed on parchment and ready to be signed that evening. Gérard, the French plenipotentiary, had a cold. The signing was put off to the evening of Friday the 6th, at the office of the ministry for foreign affairs in the Hôtel de Lautrec in Paris. Franklin, who had got out an old blue coat for the 5th, wore it again the next day, as both Deane and Bancroft noticed. Deane asked him why. "To give it a little revenge," he said. "I wore this coat on the day Wedderburn abused me at Whitehall."[41] At the final ceremony Gérard signed first, then Franklin, and the two stood talking before the fireplace while Deane and Lee added their names, with some argument over whether Lee should or should not sign twice, since he was commissioner to both France and Spain. The treaty was put in charge of Franklin.[42]

Bancroft later claimed—not very credibly—that he was able to get a copy of it to England in forty-two hours. On the 17th Fox in the House of Commons asked North if such a treaty had been made. On the 23rd Gibbon, then a member, remarked that the two greatest nations in Europe were "fairly running a race for the favour of America."

There was an almost literal race across the Atlantic. Eden, whose secret service had kept Congress in ignorance of affairs in France, had drawn up the bills of conciliation which North introduced in Parliament on 17 February. Three years to a day after Franklin had engaged to pay for the tea if the worst American grievances should be redressed, the ministry offered substantially what he had asked. Commissioners were to be sent to treat with Congress, with full powers to negotiate a peace, proclaim a truce, grant general pardons, suspend the objectionable acts passed since 1763, and assure the colonies home rule within the Empire. Without waiting for the conciliatory bills to become laws the ministry sent copies of them over, with the announcement that commissioners would follow. The French dispatched the treaties. The British outran the French, and the bills (enacted 9 March) reached Congress first. For a time there were more than a few members of Congress who thought it might be wise to deal with the British commissioners. But the treaties arrived on 2 May and were ratified two days afterwards. In the meantime the French ambassador to England had informed the government (13 March) of the new alliance. The two ambassadors were recalled. England and France were at war, though for some months without hostilities. The English commissioners, it turned out, had no success whatever in the colonies. A French fleet commanded by the Comte d'Estaing appeared at the mouth of the Delaware on 8 July, bringing Gérard, an accredited minister to the recognized United States.

On 20 March Louis XVI avowed the treaty by receiving the commissioners. When they arrived by coach and went first to the apartments of Vergennes, the crowd gathered about Versailles thought Franklin had dressed like a Quaker. Without wig or sword, in brown (*mordoré*) velvet, white hose, his hair hanging loose, his spectacles on his nose, and a white hat under his arm, as Mme. du Deffand reported,[43] he was as much the most conspicuous among the envoys as he was the most eminent. Still in his dramatic role, he came to court like the rustic philosopher France admired. The other envoys wore court dress as prescribed by the chamberlain. With William Lee and Ralph Izard, and several other American friends, the commissioners were taken by Vergennes to the king. The courtiers in the corridors and the antechamber, many brilliant shows as they had seen, thought they had never seen anything so striking as this republican simplicity in such a place. (Franklin had known what they would think.)

Louis XVI was uncermonious in his dressing room, but the Duc de Croÿ, who was present, noticed that the king spoke with unusual care and grace. "Firmly assure Congress," he said, "of my friendship. I hope that this will be for the good of the two nations." He praised the conduct of Franklin and his compatriots in France. "Mr. Franklin very nobly thanked him in the name of America, saying: 'Your Majesty may count on the gratitude of Congress and its faithful observance of the pledges it now takes.'"[44]

When the party crossed the courtyard to be presented to other members of the cabinet, the crowd forgot the etiquette of the palace and loudly cheered the insurgents. The five envoys at a dinner given them by Vergennes in his apartments met a great company of the French nobility, and later made a call on the royal family. The queen desired Franklin to stand beside her, and talked to him whenever she was not too much occupied by the royal gambling, which appeared to be for high stakes.

Just before the king received the Americans someone connected with the British ministry seems to have made a final and authoritative offer to Franklin, to detach him from France and win his approval of the Parliamentary scheme for conciliation. A "negotiator" came to Paris with the terms, which were to be kept secret if not accepted. The terms are still a mystery, though Franklin gave a copy to Deane, who was hastily leaving on 31 March for Toulon, where he was to sail with the French fleet in company with the new minister Gérard. On 1 April, in a farewell note to Gérard, Franklin may have been referring to this offer. "Mr. Deane . . . will show you the propositions. They would probably have been accepted if they had been made two years ago. I have answered that they have come too late; and that every kind of acknowledgment of the government of Great Britain, how small soever, is now become impracticable."[45] But on the 7th Franklin wrote to Deane: "The negotiator is gone back, apparently much chagrined at his little success. I have promised him faithfully that since his propositions could not be accepted they should be buried in oblivion. I therefore earnestly desire that you would put that paper immediately in the fire on receipt of this, without taking or suffering to be taken any copy of it, or communicating its contents."[46] Possibly there were two sets of "propositions," and Franklin in his letter to Gérard may have referred to one less secret[47] than the one Deane had and destroyed. The ministry had clearly offered so much that they did not dare to have their failure known. Whatever their terms were, they did not include independence.

Other Englishmen came to Paris on pacific errands. James Hutton the Moravian—"my good lord Hutton" of the *Craven Street Gazette*—hoped the dreadful war might not be prolonged. David Hartley and William Pulteney, both members of Parliament, believed that with Franklin's help peace might be made and the Empire saved. Franklin would not yield an inch in his stand on independence or his conviction that nothing could be done with the North ministry. Yet as late as 26 February he wrote to Hartley: "I am of opinion that if wise and honest men, such as Sir George Savile, the bishop of St. Asaph, and yourself, were to come over here immediately with powers to treat, you might not only obtain peace with America but prevent a war with France."[48] Franklin sent Austin, who had brought the Saratoga news, to London during February and March to confer with Shelburne and other members of the opposition and convince them of the uselessness of keeping up the war. They were powerless against the stubborn king and his majority. Moreover, those who were best disposed to the Americans, like Chatham and Shelburne, also had the strongest attachment to the Empire as a whole, and looked upon American independence as tragic and fatal. "When that happens," Shelburne said in Parliament on 5 March, "England's sun is set." And of course the war with France called forth a loyalty to Britain that the opposition did not feel for the British ministry.

When Deane, who had managed most of the accounts of the embassy, returned to America, Franklin was left to carry on its affairs with Bancroft, who was a spy, Temple, who was a boy, and the Lees and Izard, who were angrily disaffected. The departure of Deane with Gérard brought on fresh trouble with Arthur Lee. He had not been consulted as to the choice of Gérard as minister to America. He had wanted to send a special ship with the news that the envoys had been publicly received by the king, and Franklin and Deane had united against him in thinking this expensive and unnecessary when the signed treaties were already on their way. Deane had taken possession of all the vouchers, and the public accounts had not been settled. Lee resented being left out. "Had you studied to deceive the most distrusted and dangerous enemy of the public," he wrote to Franklin on 2 April, "you could not have done it more effectually. I trust, Sir, that you will think with me that I have a right to know your reasons for treating me thus. If you have anything to accuse me of, avow it, and I will answer you. If you have not, why do you act so inconsistently with your duty to the public and injuriously to me? . . . Is this the example you in your superior wisdom think proper to set, of order, decorum, confidence, and justice?"[49]

Franklin answered the next day in as impatient a letter as he ever wrote. "It is true I have omitted answering some of your letters. I do not like to answer angry letters. I am old, cannot have long to live, have much to do and no time for altercation. If I have often received and borne your magisterial snubbings and rebukes without reply, ascribe it to the right causes: my concern for the honour and success of our mission which would be hurt by our quarrelling, my love of peace, my respect for your good qualities, and my pity of your sick mind, which is for ever tormenting itself with its jealousies, suspicions, and fancies that others mean you ill, wrong you, or fail in respect for you. If you do not cure yourself of this temper it will end in insanity, of which it is a symptomatic forerunner, as I have seen in several instances. God preserve you from so terrible an evil; and for His sake pray suffer me to live in quiet."[50] But probably Franklin, having relieved himself in this letter, did not send it, for on the 4th he answered in different terms in a longer letter which more patiently took up Lee's clamours point by point. He might, he said, not send either yesterday's letter or today's. "I believe I shall not unless exceedingly pressed by you, for of all things I hate altercation."[51]

Though Lee's own disposition had put him on bad terms with his colleagues and the French with whom they had to deal, he still knew he was excluded from some of the commission's affairs and still had no doubt that there was trickery somewhere. He was sure that Deane had pocketed a fortune out of the public funds in a conspiracy with Beaumarchais. Deane's later poverty ought now to be disproof of this. But Lee, who could see that Beaumarchais and Deane were asking payment from Congress for supplies which Lee had understood were to be gifts from France and Spain, had not been shown all the accounts. Franklin, declining to busy himself with the contracts made before he came to Paris, said on 17 May he wished "that if practicable he might be excused from any concern in matters of commerce, which he so little understands."[52] In this Lee could still see nothing less than collusion. After all, money was being made out of the American contracts. Beaumarchais, though complaining that he had not been paid for the eight shiploads he had sent to Congress, lived in splendour. Chaumont, Franklin's landlord at Passy, was not only a contractor for supplies but also a buyer and seller of American prizes taken at sea. Jonathan Williams, Franklin's grandnephew at Nantes, did business for Chaumont. Franklin's friends of the Vandalia company, Thomas Walpole and Samuel Wharton, still in London, speculated in stocks no less than Bancroft and Wentworth. Lord North declared, according to a letter from Benjamin Vaughan written in April 1779, that Franklin was the only man in Paris who during the Revolution did not stain his hands with stock jobbery.[53] But Lee suspected Franklin as well as almost everybody else. Lee's own honesty supported his bad temper, and there was a kind of mad punctilio behind his wrangling, in which he had William Lee and Izard as allies. "I bear all his rebukes with patience for the good of the service," Franklin wrote to Deane on 7 April; "but it goes a little hard with me."[54]

The arrival the next day of John Adams in place of Deane took some of the burden off Franklin. Adams occupied a part of Franklin's house, and his son John Quincy, then ten, went to Benjamin Bache's school in Passy. Franklin greeted the new commissioner with an invitation from Turgot to dine with him. That evening the two Americans had cheese and beer together. Franklin at once and Arthur Lee a little later told Adams of the bad blood in the embassy. He seems to have tried to avoid being a partisan of either side, and to devote himself to straightening out the confused accounts and disorderly methods of official business into which the envoys had fallen. They lived extravagantly for republicans, he thought. Deane besides his apartments in Franklin's house had had another house in Paris. With Lee's, this made three houses which Congress was maintaining for one legation. Their quarters at the Hôtel Valentinois ought to be enough for all of them. Thinking it improper to accept this as a gift from Chaumont, Adams offered to pay him rent. Chaumont insisted that, so long as the future of America was uncertain, it was enough of a reward to him that his house had been immortalized by Dr. Franklin and his associates. Whatever profit Chaumont might be making out of American contracts, there can be no doubt as to his affection for Franklin.

"Franklin's reputation," Adams began to discover, "was more

universal than that of Leibnitz or Newton, Frederick or Voltaire; and his character more beloved and esteemed than any or all of them. . . . His name was familiar to government and people, to kings, courtiers, nobility, clergy, and philosophers, as well as plebeians, to such a degree that there was scarcely a peasant or a citizen, a *valet de chambre*, coachman or footman, a lady's chambermaid or a scullion in a kitchen who was not familiar with it and who did not consider him a friend to human kind. . . . When they spoke of him they seemed to think he was to restore the golden age. . . . His plans and his example were to abolish monarchy, aristocracy, and hierarchy throughout the world."[55]

Yet it is plain that Adams never liked Franklin. He thought the philosopher too bland and benevolent, too ready to flatter and be flattered, taken up with too many friends, too much amused by too many frivolous pleasures. "He loves his ease, hates to offend, and seldom gives any opinion till obliged to do it. . . . Although he has as determined a soul as any man, yet it is his constant policy never to say yes or no decidedly but when he cannot avoid it."[56] Adams seemed to think that Franklin's reserve gave him an almost unfair advantage over the public which adored the sage. "His rigorous taciturnity was very favourable to this singular felicity. He conversed only with individuals, and freely only with confidential friends. In company he was totally silent."[57] Adams preferred the more outspoken manners he had learned in Boston and brought to Paris. But here as in Congress the honours went most of them to Frankln. For even a great man, like Adams, living day by day with a very great one, it is hard to see that there is much difference between them or why that difference should seem to others so immense.

Adams soon saw that affairs in Paris would be better off in the hands of a single commissioner than loosely divided among three of them, who were bound to disagree. His letters home advised the change, though he did not, like Arthur Lee, suggest himself as the man for the single post, nor quarrel with Franklin. Without too many altercations Franklin got through his remaining months as joint commissioner. When Adams agreed with the Lees that Jonathan Williams—who had been a clerk in Adams's law office in Boston—should be dismissed from his agency at Nantes, Franklin did not argue. After the Lees had accused Williams of embezzling funds, and a committee of merchants had investigated and exonerated him, the next year, Franklin did not appoint his nephew again to the public service. Williams took to private business ventures, married a daughter of one of Franklin's friends, returned to America with Franklin, attracted the attention of Jefferson, and finally became the first superintendent of West Point.

Both Deane and Franklin supposed that Deane's recall to America was due to Arthur Lee, but they could only guess what had been charged. In Philadelphia Deane found himself blamed for recommending too many European soldiers to the American army, and accused of trying with Beaumarchais to defraud Congress. In the state of American finances Congress was perfectly unwilling to pay for supplies that had been given to them, if the money was to go no further than to dishonest agents. Deane, summoned on short notice, had not been able to collect the papers which, if they existed, might have supported his claim. He had spent his own money, expecting to be reimbursed at the final settlement. Congress refused to pay the bills without better proof of indebtedness than Deane had brought, and there was a long, dreary contention which Deane recklessly took to the newspapers in December. After a fruitless year and a half in America he returned to Paris to have his accounts audited. A year more, with the auditing still delayed, and Deane had grown so bitter against Congress that he wrote letters which, intercepted and published in New York in 1782, were taken to prove that he was a traitor as well as a cheat. "I had an exceeding good opinion of him when he acted with me," Franklin wrote after he had read these letters, "and I believe he was then sincere and hearty in our cause."[58] Beyond this Franklin seems never to have made up his mind, or to have committed himself, on Deane's guilt or innocence. Having nothing left but his claim, which Congress no longer even considered, Deane lived the rest of his life in distress, with hardly any friend but the spy Bancroft. Not till 1842 did Congress finally pay the claim—or about half of it—to his heirs.

Throughout 1778, as ever since the first letter of the commissioners to Stormont, Franklin worked for the exchange of prisoners. The British government, since it did not recognize the independence of the United States, naturally did not consider captured Americans prisoners of war, but kept them in prison in Plymouth or Portsmouth, on charges of high treason. The American ships which brought British prisoners into French ports had either, before the treaty, to hold them on shipboard or let them go. After the treaty had made French prisons available Franklin no less earnestly and persistently kept up his efforts on humane grounds. During the year's delay before the exchanges began in March 1779, he sent money for the relief of the American prisoners to David Hartley, who got further subscriptions from generous Englishmen. When Hartley came to Paris to talk about peace he talked also about the prisoners. The other commissioners, who thought he was probably a spy, suspected that his humane concern might be ministerial policy. Franklin, as he had written to Ralph Izard, made it a rule "always to suppose one's friends may be right till one finds them wrong, rather than to suppose them wrong till one finds them right."[59] He took it for granted that Hartley's interest in the prisoners was genuine—as it was—and frankly told Vergennes of Hartley's offer of peace terms.

Vergennes, who had the greatest confidence in Franklin, dealt always with him alone if he could. This was true also of the other ministers. In June Franklin alone of the American commissioners knew of the plans which the ministry of marine was making for John Paul Jones. Jones had come from America in the *Ranger* to Brest, and in April and May had raided the English and Scottish coasts in retaliation for the burning of American towns, captured a British naval sloop, and taken seven prizes. Sartine, the French minister of marine, decided to put Jones in charge of the frigate *Indien* which had been built for the Americans in Holland but transferred to the French navy. Franklin wrote him of it on 10 June. "It is now settled (observe that this is to be a secret between us, I being expressly enjoined not to communicate it to any other person, not even to the other gentlemen) that you are to have the frigate from Holland, which actually belongs to government and will be furnished with as many good French seamen as you shall require. But you are to act under Congress's commission."[60] These plans did not work out. There were difficulties in placing an American commander over French officers, and France needed all the ships she could muster against England. Jones was kept idle till February 1779, when he was given the old, decrepit French *Duras*, forty guns. He renamed it *Bonhomme Richard* in honour of Poor Richard.

In June 1778 came the mysterious, melodramatic episode of Charles de Weissenstein. Some unknown person threw "into one of our grates"—presumably grated doorways—at Passy a long communication written in English, ostensibly at Brussels, and dated 16 June. It was marked "secret and confidential." On the cover it requested Franklin, to whom it was addressed, to read it in private and show it to no one till he had considered it thoroughly. The pseudonymous Weissenstein enclosed with his letter detailed projects for conciliation and for the future government of America.[61] He was an Englishman, he said, who thought the ministry had been often mistaken in their dealings with the colonies. But he was sure that independence was impossible and that America would be betrayed by France. Why should the leaders of America not take their cause up with their king himself? In this Weissenstein could be useful. Let Franklin come to Notre Dame between twelve and one on either 6 July (Monday) or the following Thursday. There, inside the iron gates at the side of the choir or in the right-hand aisle, as he entered, he would see a man sketching or taking notes, with a rose in his hat or button-hole. Franklin's answer was to be left where the messenger could pick it up. The messenger knew nothing about the business, and believed this was some affair of gallantry.

In the project for "allaying the present ferments in North America" Weissenstein proposed benefits to come for Americans who might contribute to a reconciliation. "As the conspicuous public part which some American gentlemen have taken may expose them to the personal enmity of some of the chief persons in Great Britain, and as it is unreasonable that their services to their country should deprive them of those advantages which their talents would otherwise have gained them, the following persons shall have American offices or pensions for life at their option, according to the sums opposite their respective names: Messieurs Adams, Hancock, Washington, Franklin, etc., etc., etc." The sums were not specified, as if left to those who might accept them. They should be the first American peers, if any should be created, and Washington immediately be made a lieutenant-general.

Franklin was convinced, from various expressions in the letter, that it came directly from George III, and on 1 July he wrote an answer which was meant not only to defend the course of America but also to ridicule and insult the king, who Franklin supposed would read it. As to independence: "We have never asked it of you; we only tell you that you can have no treaty with us but as an independent state; and you may please yourselves and your children with the rattle of your right to govern us. . . . Your Parliament never had a right to govern us, and your king has forfeited it by his bloody tyranny." As to the terms of peace which the commissioners had been invited to propose: "You would have me give them to, or drop them for, a stranger whom I may find next Monday in the church of Notre Dame, to be known by a rose in his hat. You yourself, Sir, are quite unknown to me; you have not trusted me with your true name. . . . I may be indiscreet enough in many things; but certainly, if I were disposed to make propositions (which I cannot do, having none committed to me to make), I should never think of delivering them to the Lord knows who, to be carried the Lord knows where, to serve no one knows what purposes." As to the bribes hinted at: "This proposition of delivering ourselves, bound and gagged, ready for hanging, without even a right to complain and without a friend afterwards among all mankind, you would have us embrace upon the faith of an act of Parliament. Great God! An act of your Parliament! This demonstrates that you do not yet know us and that you fancy we do not know you. But it is not merely this flimsy faith that we are to act upon; you offer us hope, the hope of places, pensions, and peerages. . . . This offer to corrupt us, Sir, is with me your credential, and convinces me that you are not a private volunteer in your application. It bears the stamp of British court character. It is even the signature of your king."[62] Franklin rejected what he thought the royal offers, with indignation but with an obvious pleasure in his opportunity.

The letter was not sent. It and Weissenstein's were submitted to Vergennes, who had the police keep the appointment at Notre Dame. "A gentleman appeared and, finding nobody, wandered about the church, gazing at the statues and pictures and other curiosities of that magnificent cathedral, never losing sight, however, of the spot appointed, and often returning to it, looking earnestly about, at times, as if he expected somebody. . . . He remained two hours in the church and then went out, was followed through every street and all his motions watched to the hotel where he lodged." He was a "Colonel Fitz-something, an Irish name that I have forgotten," Adams later remembered.[63] Nothing further came of the episode and letter and answer remained in the French archives. Nor is there any evidence that this was a communication from George III. Some busybody may have added another mystery to the general melodrama.

Still a further mystery belongs to 1778. A British privateer captured a Dutch smuggler on its way to Ireland, carrying printed copies of *An Address to the Good People of Ireland, on behalf of America*, signed with Franklin's name and dated at Versailles 4 October. They were turned over to the commander of the *Portland* and sent to the Admiralty, where they remained harmless among the files. Nothing more is known about the *Address*, which shows few marks of Franklin's hand. But it was printed in Dublin, in the *Hibernian Journal* for 4 November, and may have affected some Irish readers, restless under English rule.

On the Fourth of July Franklin and Adams celebrated the Declaration at Passy with a dinner to their compatriots and their French friends in the neighbourhood, about fifty of them all together. Franklin would not invite Izard, but he made no objection to Adams's doing it. Izard thought there should have been some of the gentlemen of France, not mere philosophers and republicans. But the day was pleasant, without animosities, with many flowers on the table and a "handsome posy" for each guest, the American flag and the Cap of Liberty displayed, and merry toasts after dinner.

In French opinion the most dramatic episode of the year was probably the meeting of Franklin and Voltaire, who came back to Paris in February to spend the last four months of his life there after an absence of twenty-eight years. They met more than once. The envoys went at once to call on Voltaire. He insisted on showing that he could speak the language of Franklin, and solemnly blessed Temple.[64] "When I gave the benediction to the grandson of the illustrious and wise Franklin, the man of all America most to be respected," Voltaire wrote on 21 February, "I pronounced only the words: God and Liberty. All who were present shed tears of tenderness." At the initiation of Voltaire into the Masonic lodge of the Nine Sisters (Neuf Sœurs) on 9 April he entered on the arm of Franklin. Their most conspicuous meeting was at the Academy of Sciences on 29 April. John Adams dryly recorded it in his diary. "Voltaire and Franklin were both present, and there presently arose a general cry that M. Voltaire and M. Franklin should be introduced to each other. This was done, and they bowed and spoke to each other. This was no satisfaction; there must be something more. Neither of our philosophers seemed to divine what was wished or expected; they however took each other by the hand. But this was not enough. The clamour continued until the explanation came out: *Il faut s'embrasser à la française.* The two aged actors upon this great theatre of philosophy and frivolity then embraced each other by hugging one another in their arms and kissing each other's cheeks, and then the tumult subsided. And the cry immediately spread throughout the kingdom, and I suppose all over Europe: *Qu'il est charmant de voir embrasser Solon et Sophocle.*"[65] Solon and Sophocles should embrace, but it must be in the manner of the French.

In this year of renown 1778 Houdon executed his marble bust of Franklin, and Turgot devised for him the most famous of modern Latin epigrams: *Eripuit cælo fulmen sceptrumque tyrannis* (He snatched the lightning from the sky and the sceptre from tyrants). There had been versions of almost the same thought and image before Turgot, and his own may have been: *Eripuit cælo fulmen mox sceptra tyrannis* (meaning that as Franklin had wrested the lightning from heaven he would soon wrest the sceptre from George III).[66] But the common version became almost universal, even with people who knew few Latin words besides these. Franklin three years later protested against being given more credit by the epigram than he deserved: "It ascribes too much to me, especially in what relates to the tyrant; the Revolution having been the work of many able and brave men, wherein it is sufficient honour for me if I am allowed a small share."[67]

Minister Plenipotentiary

A FTER Arthur Lee had hinted to Congress that he might well
be given charge of the Paris mission, and Adams had plainly
said that one man could do the work better than three, Franklin
on 22 July, in a letter to James Lovell of the Committee for Foreign Affairs, said the easy last word which was the best. "Speaking
of commissioners in the plural puts me in mind of inquiring if it
can be the intention of Congress to keep three commissioners at
this court. We have indeed four with the gentleman intended for
Tuscany [Izard], who continues here and is very angry that he was
not consulted in making the treaty, which he could have mended
in several particulars; and perhaps he is angry with some reason, if
the instructions to him do, as he says they do, require us to consult
him. We shall soon have the fifth; for the envoy to Vienna [William
Lee], not being received there, is I hear returning hither. The
necessary expense of maintaining us all is, I assure you, enormously
great. I wish that the utility may equal it. . . . Whatever advantage there might be in the joint counsels of three for framing and
adjusting the articles of the treaty, there can be none in managing
the common business of a resident here. On the contrary, all the
advantages in negotiation that result from secrecy of sentiment and
uniformity in expressing it, and in common business from dispatch, are lost. In a court, too, where every word is watched and
weighed, if a number of commissioners do not every one hold the
same language in giving their opinion on any public transaction,
this lessens their weight. . . . And where every one must be consulted on every particular . . . and one of them is offended if the
smallest thing is done without his consent," there was certain to be
dissension and delay. The delay might be less if the three could
live in one house. But Franklin thought it almost impossible to

"find three people whose tempers are so good, and who like so well one another's company and manner of living and conversing," as to live in harmony. "And in consideration of the whole, I wish Congress would separate us."[1]

The three commissioners seemed to agree that one was enough. Gérard, the French minister in Philadelphia, took pains to let Congress understand that Franklin would be more acceptable to France than Lee.[2] On 14 September Congress revoked the joint commission and elected Franklin sole plenipotentiary. The only state which voted against him was Pennsylvania, and its opposition was due not only to his conservative enemies but also to others who disliked his having Temple—son of a notorious loyalist—for secretary. "Methinks," Franklin wrote to Richard Bache when he heard of this, "it is rather some merit that I have rescued a valuable young man from the danger of being a Tory and fixed him in honest republican Whig principles. . . . It is enough that I have lost my son; would they add my grandson?" He knew that the objection had been raised by the Lees and Izard along with their other complaints to Congress. "Those gentlemen have plenty of ill will to me, though I have never done to either of them the smallest injury or given the least just cause of offence. But my too great reputation, and the general good will this people have for me, and the respect they show me, and even the compliments they make me, all grieve those unhappy gentlemen; unhappy indeed in their tempers and in the dark uncomfortable passions of jealousy, anger, suspicion, envy, and malice. It is enough for good minds to be affected at other people's misfortunes; but they, that are vexed at everybody's good luck, can never be happy. I take no other revenge of such enemies than to let them remain in the miserable situation in which their malignant natures have placed them."[3]

Lafayette was sent on a leave of absence to Paris with Franklin's commission and Congressional instructions. Delivering the documents in February 1779, the young man who had sought renown and revenge but who in Washington's company had grown ardent for the American cause, became the devoted friend of Franklin. Adams, having honestly recommended himself out of office, generously approved the action of Congress. Arthur Lee raged and sulked. When Franklin wrote on the 18th to ask him for the public papers in his files, Lee answered that he had no papers belonging to the minister plenipotentiary. All he had were the property of the joint commission. He would keep them as proofs of his own rectitude, and would furnish Franklin copies. Franklin mildly told him that copies would be satisfactory. "I assure you I had not the least intention of depriving you of anything you might think necessary for your vindication."[4] If he himself had any papers which Lee might think he needed, Franklin would be glad to give him the originals and keep only copies for the embassy.

Though there were further difficulties with Lee, and with William Lee and Izard, they were all recalled by Congress during the year. "No soul regrets their departure," Franklin wrote on 7 April 1780, after they had left Paris. "They separately came to take leave of me, very respectfully offering their services to carry any dispatches, etc. We parted civilly, for I have never acquainted them that I know of their writing against me to Congress. But I did not give them the trouble of my dispatches."[5] About Arthur Lee, Franklin wrote to Joseph Reed in Philadelphia: "I caution you to beware of him; for in sowing suspicions and jealousies, in creating misunderstandings and quarrels, in malice, subtilty, and indefatigable industry, he has I think no equal."[6]

Suffering from gout, Franklin could not at once appear in form as minister, but on Tuesday 23 March 1779 "I thought myself able to go through the ceremony and accordingly went to court, had my audience with the king in the new character, presented my letter of credence, and was received very graciously. After which I went the rounds with the other foreign ministers, in visiting all the royal family. The fatigue, however, was a little too much for my feet and disabled me for near another week."[7] Franklin, who always bore pain like a stoic, humorous animal, thought less of his gout than of his happiness in being settled among the French. "I find them here a most amiable people to live with," he wrote to his Boston friend Josiah Quincy on 22 April. "The Spaniards are by common opinion supposed to be cruel, the English proud, the Scotch insolent, the Dutch avaricious, etc., but I think the French have no national vice ascribed to them. They have some frivolities, but they are harmless. . . . They are only the effects of the tyranny of custom. In short, there is nothing wanting in the character of a Frenchman that belongs to that of an agreeable and worthy man. There are only some trifles surplus, or which might be spared."[8]

What pleased the French in Franklin, whom they persisted in thinking a rustic philosopher, was of course his civilized taste, which drew him to them at a time when many Americans were still suspicious of their ancient foes as Catholic, despotic, and immoral. But Franklin had, beyond and above his civilized taste, the natural grace which came from his quick imagination and wide humanity. Not many old philosophers, gouty and overworked, would have exchanged such farewells with a boy of eleven as Franklin did with John Quincy Adams, waiting at Brest for the ship which would take him and his father to America. This boy addressed this philosopher not as "Honoured Sir," which would have been customary, but as "Dear Friend," sent him letters to be distributed among other correspondents in Passy, told him about the French fleet, and broke off one letter "—but as the boat is just now a-going I cannot write any more, and so conclude myself your affectionate friend, John Q. Adams." Franklin, writing to "Dear Master Johnny," on 22 April, said he had seen to it that the boy's letters were carefully delivered, but had not yet received answers to send him. "Benjamin [Bache], whom you so kindly remember, would have been glad to hear of your welfare, but he is gone to Geneva. As he is destined to live in a Protestant country, and a republic, I thought it best to finish his education where the proper principles prevail. I heartily wish you a good voyage and happy sight of your mamma, being really your affectionate friend."[9]

The philosopher who knew how to write to a friendly child knew no less well how to write to the stately commander of the armies in America. Lafayette brought from Washington a letter of commendation to Franklin, but was too modest to show it to him for a year. Then Franklin, acknowledging it on 5 March 1780, and remembering what Washington too had had to endure from rivals, paid him the compliment of such high praise as only one great man can pay to another. "Should peace arrive after another campaign or two, and afford us a little leisure, I should be happy to see your Excellency in Europe and to accompany you, if my age and strength would permit, in visiting some of its ancient and most famous kingdoms. You would, at this side of the sea, enjoy the great reputation you have acquired, pure and free from those little shades that the jealousy and envy of a man's countrymen and cotemporaries are ever endeavouring to cast over living merit. Here you would know, and enjoy, what posterity will say of Washington. For a thousand leagues have nearly the same effect with a thousand years. The feeble voice of those grovelling passions cannot extend so far either in time or distance. At present I enjoy that pleasure for you, as I frequently hear the old generals of this martial country (who study the maps of America and mark upon them all your operations) speak with sincere approbation and great applause of your conduct; and join in giving you the character of one of the greatest captains of the age.

"I must soon quit the scene, but you may live to see our country flourish, as it will amazingly and rapidly after the war is over: like a field of young Indian corn, which long fair weather and sunshine had enfeebled and discoloured, and which, in that weak state, by a thunder-gust of violent wind, hail, and rain seemed to be threatened with absolute destruction; yet the storm being past, it recovers fresh verdure, shoots up with double vigour, and delights the eye not of its owner only but of every observing traveller."[10]

II

Though Franklin might feel easier in his official household, now that he was its unquestioned head, he still had the burden of enormous and complex responsibilities. He was involved, perhaps even more than he realized, in a fierce struggle of European powers which were concerned with America chiefly for the sake of their own dynastic ends.[11] France, the most absolute monarchy in Europe, had allied itself with a rebel republic much less out of love for America than out of hatred for England. England had humiliated France in the last war. England had grown intolerably strong. Vergennes, ambitious for France, had set himself to weaken the British Empire by dividing it. He had to coax and push the young king into the alliance and the war. He took advantage of a public sentiment in favour of natural liberty and republican virtue, because it brought influential adherents to his foreign policy.

Having no desire for American territory, Vergennes made no claim on Canada, and opposed American plans to invade and capture it. France was not to appear to be seeking an empire for itself, and so alarming other European nations with the prospect that it in turn might grow intolerable. In the treaty of commerce France did not demand exclusive trading privileges with the United States, but left trade open to European neutrals whom France wanted to propitiate. The British had monopolized the commerce of their colonies. If France asserted a monopoly, the neutrals would have no more concern with America than before, and no special reason to side with France rather than with England.

By the Family Compact of 1761 Louis XVI and his uncle Charles III—that is, France and Spain—were bound to assist each other in war and peace. But in the matter of America Spain moved more slowly than France and had different designs. Having important American colonies herself, as against France's few islands in the West Indies, Spain would do nothing to further the dangerous idea of American independence. Holding Louisiana as a buffer province between the United States and Mexico, and claiming not only the Mississippi river but also protective territory along its east bank, Spain wanted to limit the English colonies. The ends of Spain would be best served if England and America could go on being at strife, though not actually separated, and neither of them a menace to other nations. In Europe Spain desired above all things to recover and control Gibraltar. In spite of the Family Compact Spain during 1778 made diplomatic efforts to persuade England to give up Gibraltar as the price of Spanish neutrality. England refused. In April 1779 Spain and France made a treaty which was kept secret from the Americans. France, committed with America to a war for American independence, now committed herself to Spain for the restoration of Gibraltar, with which America had nothing to do. America, aiming only to become independent of England, was involved, through its open alliance with France and France's secret alliance with Spain, in European affairs almost as remote from America's as any could be. Spain declared war on England in June 1779.

Austria, France's defensive ally, and Prussia, France's recent enemy, were guardedly at war during 1778 over the Bavarian succession. Each of them tried to bring France into their conflict. Vergennes, unwilling to turn aside from his campaign against England, helped arrange a peace between Austria and Prussia on terms which pleased Prussia rather than Austria. The friendship of Frederick the Great meant more to France than the Austrian alliance. Frederick had no sympathy with the American Revolution, and little interest in it, but he was glad to see England and France too busy on the Atlantic to pay much attention to central Europe, and he hated England for deserting him in the negotiations at the close of the Seven Years' War. Frederick's attitude was that of most of the Continental powers: indifference to American aims, disapproval of rebellion against a king, more or less active dislike of England. Though in all Europe there was a good deal of liberal or academic enthusiasm for the American cause, it affected the governments hardly at all. Portugal, traditional ally of Great Britain, was the only country that closed its harbours to American ships engaged in innocent trade. But Denmark, the Netherlands, and Austria forbade their subjects to supply contraband to the rebel colonies; and none of them (nor Sweden, Russia, the German states, the Holy Roman Empire, Tuscany) would recognize an American diplomatic agent.

The Austro-Prussian peace of May 1779, quieting central Europe, allowed Vergennes to go ahead with his policy of organizing the neutrals against England. The British fleet in the Channel and the North Sea stopped Baltic, Scandinavian, and Dutch ships carrying naval supplies—tar, pitch, hemp, cordage, canvas, wrought iron—to France, and protected similar cargoes on their way to England. Both countries had to import materials for shipbuilding. The British superiority at sea by cutting down neutral trade to France put France at a disadvantage in her programme for the increase of her navy. France, upholding the neutral right of free ships free goods, was of course furthering French ends. Vergennes, making war, became the champion of the neutrals.

In the Netherlands, especially, a diplomatic war went on between the French and English ambassadors. The Dutch, the principal bankers of Europe, were thriving on the clandestine trade to America, through their West Indian island of St. Eustatius, and had heavy foreign investments which would suffer if neutral trade

in general were to be restricted. The French support of the neutrals was a service to the Dutch. But the Netherlands had conflict-
ing treaty relations with England. An old maritime treaty provided
that if either party were belligerent and the other neutral, the
belligerent was to permit the neutral the right of free ships free
goods, except for contraband of war (not including ship's timbers
and naval stores). By reason of this treaty the Dutch might insist
on being allowed to trade with France and Spain without interference from England. But there was also an old Anglo-Dutch
treaty of alliance providing that either power must come to the aid
of the other when attacked or threatened. If the Dutch were to
demand their rights under the maritime treaty, the English might
counter with demands for their rights under the treaty of alliance.
In theory each country had one advantage over the other. In fact,
the advantage lay distinctly with England because of her superior
fleet. The Netherlands, demanding neutral rights, could not enforce them. The English, calling upon the Dutch for assistance
against France and Spain, could, if refused, then abrogate the
maritime treaty and deal with Dutch shipping at will.

Franklin's friend Dumas at The Hague kept up his reports to
Franklin and his liberal propaganda in the Netherlands in favour
of America. But he worked under the guidance both of Franklin
and of the French ambassador, through whom Vergennes brought
pressure to bear upon the Dutch. France by a decree of July 1778
guaranteed to neutrals the right of free ships free goods for six
months, but said the right would be withdrawn in six months if
England did not accord similar treatment. This was to encourage
neutral governments, particularly the Netherlands, to insist upon
their rights from England. Though the Dutch did not desire war,
they did desire the profits of neutral trading. During 1779 they
sent armed vessels to convoy their cargo ships to France. Some of
these were taken by the British early in 1780 and confiscated.
Dutch opinion, still divided, swung further toward France. This
was a victory for Vergennes, though Dutch shipping, which the
French were not strong enough to safeguard, was almost ruined
by the British. Help came from Russia, where also there was a
diplomatic war between the English and French ambassadors. In
February Catherine the Great declared that Russia would protect

her shipping against all belligerents, and invited the other neutral nations to join with Russia in the Armed Neutrality. Before the Netherlands could complete the formalities of joining, England declared war. The Dutch as belligerents would be less formidable than as protected neutrals. St. Eustatius was destroyed as a port through which munitions might be shipped to America. But the British gave up interfering in the Baltic trade and observed specific treaties already in force between various neutrals and Great Britain. Nearly all the European maritime states joined the Armed Neutrality, and England was isolated by the diplomacy of Vergennes.

In this large outline of European conflicts the affairs of America were incidental. What Vergennes wanted primarily from the United States was that they should continue their demand for independence, and so continue to draw British efforts away from Europe. With different motives France and America had the same end. But the situation was full of ironies. France in order to strengthen her own monarchy was creating a republic which was to set a new example to the European peoples. America to gain her independence from the European dynastic and commercial system was entangled in a European quarrel. Vergennes, one of the most devoted subjects of the monarchy, was the amicable colleague of Franklin, one of the most democratic citizens of the republic. Each of them helped and used the other. Franklin's prestige as a philosopher was an asset to Vergennes: it kept articulate French opinion alive and favourable to the war for American liberty. Vergennes was for Franklin—and America—the source of ships, soldiers, munitions, and money which it weakened France to give. Perhaps it is the oddest irony of all that the realistic minister seems, in view of the outcome, to have been altruistic, while the genial philosopher obtained for his country the solid and lasting benefits of the alliance.

III

Franklin had for years been of the opinion, as he said to the other commissioners just before the French alliance was made, that

America ought to get along with the least possible dependence upon Europe. Though English corruption and English wars were what he had usually objected to, he knew that these were not special to England. But in France, though he was candidly a republican and made jokes about kings,[12] he was on the best of terms with the royal government. He still worked with the tools he had and dealt with circumstances as they came.

For all his versatility, Franklin was sometimes overwhelmed by the range of demands upon him. Besides his own office he held also in effect that of United States consul-general, director of naval affairs, and judge of admiralty. He saw countless persons who had advice to give America, asked for information, desired favours, or hoped to emigrate. The line of them ran with a deadly monotony of interruption through his whole time in France. He was called upon for help and counsel in matters outside his experience. Representing Congress, he planned with the French ministry of marine in 1779 for a joint attack on the British coast, the sea forces to be in command of John Paul Jones, the land forces led by Lafayette, who had proposed the scheme. "I have not enough of knowledge in such matters to presume upon advising it," Franklin wrote to Lafayette on 22 March, "and I am so troublesome to the ministers on other accounts that I could hardly venture to solicit it if I were ever so confident of its success." Franklin was for the boldest measures. "On the whole it may be encouraging to reflect on the many instances of history which prove that in war attempts thought to be impossible do often, for that very reason, become possible and practicable because nobody expects them and no precautions are taken to guard against them."[13]

When Lafayette's part in the scheme was given up, and Jones set out alone in August with the *Bonhomme Richard* and his makeshift fleet, he carried instructions which Franklin had drawn up on 28 April. Jones was particularly to take care that his men, several of whom had escaped from English prisons, should not retaliate upon any prisoners whom they might take. And "although the English have wantonly burnt many defenceless towns in America, you are not to follow this example, unless where a reasonable ransom is refused; in which case your own generous feelings, as well as this instruction, will induce you to give timely notice of your intention, that sick and ancient persons, women and children, may be first removed."[14] (But after Franklin had heard of the burning of Fairfield in July, by British and Hessian troops, he wrote on 17 October that these new acts "have at length demolished all my moderation; and were such another expedition [as Jones's] to be concerted, I think so much of that [moderate] disposition would not appear in the instructions."[15]) The *Bonhomme Richard's* bloody defeat of the *Serapis* in September was the first major victory of the American navy. Afterwards Franklin had to investigate the charges brought by Jones against Pierre Landais of the *Alliance*, which had fired only a few shots during the battle and damaged the American flagship more than the enemy. Unable to settle the long dispute, Franklin at last referred it to Congress.[16] He had been quick to recognize the merits of Jones and had insisted that he be given an opportunity to use them. Jones, back in Paris, was another American hero, and he and Franklin, never envious, were close friends.

Franklin commissioned the American privateers which used French ports as their base for raids against British ships. When they came back with prizes, he served—in Paris—as judge in the proceedings of condemnation and sale. This he found troublesome and exhausting, in part because he disapproved of the whole system. By June 1780 he was not only in favour of the Armed Neutrality's stand on free ships free goods but wished "they would extend it still further, and ordain that unarmed trading ships, as well as fishermen and farmers, should be respected, as working for the common benefit of mankind, and never be interrupted in their operations, even by national enemies; but let those only fight with one another whose trade it is, and who are armed and paid for that purpose."[17] One of Franklin's earliest official acts as minister plenipotentiary was to write, on 10 March 1779, a "passport" for Captain Cook, whom Franklin had known in London. Cook had actually been killed in the Hawaiian islands a month before, but the news had of course not yet reached Europe and he was expected soon to return from his third voyage. Franklin instructed the commanders of armed ships acting under commissions from Congress, so far as he could reach them, that if Cook's ship should fall into their hands, "you would not consider her an enemy, nor suffer any plunder to be made of the effects contained in her, nor obstruct her immediate return to England by detaining her or sending her into any other part of Europe or to America; but that you would treat the said Captain Cook and his people with all civility and kindness, affording them, as common friends to mankind, all the assistance in your power which they may happen to stand in need of."[18]

If Franklin was nearly an overseas secretary of the navy for America, he was emphatically its secretary of the treasury in Europe. From the beginnings of the Revolution Congress had been always in need of money, to buy munitions from abroad and to pay soldiers at home. It had no federal authority to tax the people of the states, and the states were wary about taxing themselves. Colonial taxes in the years of peace had been low. In every state, so divided on the question of independence that the Revolution was also a kind of civil war, the legislature faced the prospect that adequate taxation might turn popular sentiment against the patriot cause. Congress in 1775 had been able to decide on nothing better than two issues of Continental paper money, to a total amount of £6,000,000. Franklin, then a member, had been opposed. Taxes were sounder. Bills would depreciate. "I took all the pains I could in Congress," he wrote to Samuel Cooper on 22 April 1779, "to prevent the depreciation by proposing, first, that the bills should bear interest; this was rejected. . . . Secondly, after the first emission, I proposed that we should stop, strike no more, but borrow on interest those we had issued. This was not then approved of. . . . When, from the too great quantity, they began to depreciate, we agreed to borrow on interest; and I proposed that, in order to fix the value of the principal, the interest should be promised in hard dollars. This was objected to as impracticable. . . . The Congress did at last come into the proposal of paying the interest in real money. But when the whole mass of the currency was under way in depreciation, the momentum of its descent was too great to be stopped by a power that might at first have been sufficient to prevent the beginning of the motion. The only remedy now seems to be a diminution of the quantity by a vigorous taxation."

But this was the fourth year of the war and Congress had gone on printing money which had gone on depreciating. "The effect of paper currency," Franklin commented, "is not understood on this side the water. And indeed the whole is a mystery even to the politicians: how we have been able to continue a war four years without money, and how we could pay with paper that had no previously fixed fund appropriated specifically to redeem it. This currency, as we manage it, is a wonderful machine. It performs its office when we issue it; it pays and clothes troops and provides victuals and ammunition; and when we are obliged to issue a quantity excessive, it pays itself off by depreciation."[19]

These miracles happened only in America. In Europe actual money was needed. France and Spain in 1776 had advanced Beaumarchais two million livres for America, a virtual subsidy, and France had granted another two million at the beginning of 1777. That year the French Farmers-General had lent Congress one million livres, to be repaid in tobacco. The French government accompanied the alliance early in 1778 with a first loan of three million, in a series which amounted to eighteen million in 1782.[20] All these sums Franklin had to obtain from a ministry burdened with France's own war against England. He was not left to the exercise of his judgment as to when to apply for loans. Congress would authorize him to apply and then, without waiting to hear from him, would draw upon the funds which he had been told to apply for. There might be delays in getting the money transferred from the French treasury to Congress's banker in Paris, but there was no delay in the drafts from Congress. "The drafts of the treasurer of the loans coming very fast upon me," Franklin wrote to the Committee for Foreign Affairs on 26 May 1779, "the anxiety I have suffered and the distress of mind lest I should not be able to pay them has for a long time been very great indeed. To apply again to this court for money for a particular purpose, which they had already over and over again provided for and furnished us, was extremely awkward." The ministry pointed out that France by sending a fleet to America had given expensive aid to the Revolution and ought not to be asked for money too. Spain had granted or lent but small sums, and the loan asked from the Netherlands had made no progress. Franklin lived in dread that drafts would come which could not be met, with the "consequences of ruin to our public credit both in America and Europe."[21]

"The storm of bills which I found coming upon us both," Franklin wrote to John Jay in Spain on 2 October 1780, "has terrified and vexed me to such a degree that I have been deprived of sleep, and so much indisposed by continual anxiety as to be rendered almost incapable of writing."[22] Congress, he thought, should dig more and beg less. "I have long been humiliated," he wrote to John Adams in Holland the same day, "with the idea of our running about from court to court begging for money and friendship, which are the more withheld the more eagerly they are solicited, and would perhaps have been offered if they had not been asked. The supposed necessity is our only excuse. The proverb says: God helps them that help themselves. And the world too in this sense is very godly."[23] France operated upon an annual budget, settled in advance, and the ministers disliked what Frankin called the "afterclap" demands made by Congress. It was deeply embarrassing to him to have to present them, to avoid the worse embarrassment of having no money to meet the drafts upon him. But the drafts never ceased. Agents buying supplies for Congress here or there in Europe would draw on Franklin, each of them insisting that American credit depended on the prompt payment of each draft. Jay had been sent as minister to Spain, where he arrived in January 1780. Congress drew on him against the loan he had gone to arrange, but had found impossible, and those drafts came to Franklin. John Adams went to the Netherlands in July, to negotiate a Dutch loan. Congress drew on Adams, who had yet obtained nothing, and more drafts came to Franklin. All these endless demands, Franklin wrote on 12 February 1782, had made him "quite sick of my Gideonite office: that of drawing water for the whole congregation of Israel."[24] There was no relief, but Franklin by incessant labour met the drafts.

On 6 August 1781 he was in a mood of impatience with Holland, which had once been a rebel province in the hard grip of alien Spain. "Though it was formerly in the same situation with ourselves," he wrote to Dumas, "and was glad of assistance from other nations, it does not seem to feel for us or to have the least inclination to help us; it appears to want magnanimity. Some writer, I forget who, says that Holland is no longer a nation, but a great shop; and I begin to think it has no other principles or sentiments but those of a shopkeeper."[25] Four days later he apologized: "I apprehend I may have expressed myself perhaps a little too hardly of your country. . . . I was a little out of humour when I wrote."[26] He stood firm against the demands of the Spanish government, which was not willing to make an alliance unless the United States would yield to it the control of the Mississippi. "The very proposition," Franklin wrote to Jay on 2 October 1780, "can only give disgust at present. Poor as we are, yet, as I know we shall be rich, I would rather agree with them to buy at a great price the whole of their right on the Mississippi than sell a drop of its waters. A neighbour might as well ask me to sell my street door."[27]

For France, the one real source of help, Franklin had unvarying respect and affection. His temper no less than his judgment kept him amiable and made him successful with the French ministers. John Adams, recalled to America in 1779, had hardly reached there when he was sent back to Europe to begin negotiations for peace. Vergennes, through Gérard in Philadelphia, had urged Congress to send a peace mission and had specifically commended Adams. But Adams in Paris, where he arrived the following February, found that his errand was not to be publicly recognized, and was officially a secret even from Franklin. Not that Franklin was blind or deaf. He wrote to David Hartley on the 2nd of that month that if Congress had "entrusted to others rather than to me the negotiations for peace, when such shall be on foot, as has been reported, it is perhaps because they may have heard of a very singular opinion of mine, that there hardly ever existed such a thing as a bad peace or a good war; and that I might therefore easily be induced to make improper concessions."[28] He left Adams strictly alone in his dealings with Vergennes, who was soon so offended by Adams's manner that the dealings came to an end. Adams blamed Franklin, and grew more convinced than ever that France had selfish aims and would prolong the war to gain them without consideration for America. Franklin, Adams was sure, was subservient to France.

After Adams had gone to Holland Franklin on 9 August explained the situation—and defended his own methods—in a letter to Samuel Huntington, president of Congress. "Mr. Adams has given offence to the court here by some sentiments and expressions contained in several of his letters written to the Count de Vergennes. . . . Mr. Adams did not show me his letters before he sent them. . . . It is true that Mr. Adams's proper business is elsewhere [with England]; but, the time not being come for that business, and having nothing else here wherewith to employ himself, he seems to have endeavoured to supply what he may suppose my negotiations defective in. He thinks, as he tells me himself, that America has been too free in expressions of gratitude to France; for that she is more obliged to us than we to her; and that we should show spirit in our applications. I apprehend that he mistakes his ground, and that this court is to be treated with decency and delicacy." Louis XVI, Franklin believed, took a pleasure in reflecting that he was benevolently aiding an oppressed people. "I think it right to increase this pleasure by our thankful acknowledgments, and that such an expression of gratitude is not only our duty but our interest. . . . Mr. Adams, on the other hand, who at the same time means our welfare and interest as much as I or any man can do, seems to think a little apparent stoutness and greater air of independence and boldness in our demands will procure us more ample assistance. . . .

"M. Vergennes, who appears much offended, told me yesterday that he would enter into no further discussions with Mr. Adams, nor answer any more of his letters. He is gone to Holland to try, as he told me, whether something might not be done to render us less dependent on France. He says the ideas of this court and those of the people in America are so totally different that it is impossible for any minister to please both. He ought to know America better than I do, having been there lately, and he may choose to do what he thinks will best please the people of America. But . . . I cannot but imagine that he mistakes the sentiment of a few for a general opinion. It is my intention, while I stay here, to procure what advantages I can for our country, by endeavouring to please this court; and I wish I could prevent anything being said by our countrymen here that may have a contrary effect."[29] It was hard for the downright John Adams to realize that pleasanter manners than his were more effective with France. Franklin knew well enough that France had her own interests and would look out for them. But so long as those interests were on the whole the same as America's, Franklin could see no reason why the allies should not conduct their diplomatic affairs with cosmopolitan good breeding.

IV

The war went badly for the Americans in 1780. The combined French and American forces in the south failed to win Savannah from the British, and a British expedition took Charleston. Cornwallis, marching inland, routed Gates at Camden. In the north, Benedict Arnold's treason came near to giving the British, who still held New York, control of the Hudson. In December, now that England was at war with Holland, St. Eustatius was captured and the chief West Indian source of American supplies cut off. At the beginning of the new year there was a money crisis. Congress had in March 1780 been forced to a qualified repudiation of its paper currency, and had called in the old bills at a ratio of forty dollars to one dollar of a sounder new issue. Many holders of the old bills were ruined. There was no money for army expenses, and angry, hungry soldiers mutinied. Washington wrote to Franklin that America must have either peace or money from France.[30] Rochambeau, commanding the French army which had spent the winter in Rhode Island, reported to Paris that conditions were desperate. The early successes of 1781 were the result of desperate efforts. Nathanael Greene, Franklin's young admirer, brilliantly changed the course of the war in the Carolinas. Lafayette, with New England and later Pennsylvania troops, harassed Cornwallis, moving northwards into Virginia. Then in May Rochambeau in Newport learned that another French fleet under the Comte de Grasse had been sent to America by way of the West Indies, and that the king had granted the Americans a fresh subsidy of six million livres for the prosecution of the war.

Though Congress had sent John Laurens, with Thomas Paine[31] and other advisers, as a special commissioner for the emergency loan, the six million had been promised before Laurens arrived in March. On the 12th Franklin wrote to Huntington. He had, he said, drawn a memorial presenting the requests from America as soon as they reached him in February. "The ministry being extremely occupied with other weighty affairs, and I obtaining for some time only general answers . . . I wrote again and pressed strongly for a decision on the subject; that I might be able to write explicitly by this opportunity what aids the Congress were, or were not, to expect; the regulation of their operations for the campaign depending on the information I should be enabled to give. Upon this I received a note appointing Saturday last for a meeting with the minister, which I attended punctually. He assured me of the king's good will to the United States; remarking, however, that being on the spot I must be sensible of the great expense France was actually engaged in, and the difficulty of providing it." The loan of twenty-five millions asked was very large, and the depreciation of American currency had hurt the credit of the United States in Europe. Nor could the king "favour a loan for us in his dominions, because it would interfere with, and be a prejudice to, those he was under the necessity of obtaining himself to support the war; but that, to give the states a signal proof of his friendship, His Majesty had resolved to grant them the sum of six millions, not as a loan but as a free gift." The money was to be drawn upon by Washington for the supply of the American army. "I . . . remarked that it was not the usage with us for the general to draw, and proposed that it might be our treasurer who should draw the bills. . . . But I was told that it was His Majesty's order. And I afterwards understood . . . that . . . it was thought best to put it into the general's hands, that it might not get into those of the different boards or committees who might think themselves under a necessity of diverting it to other purposes. There was no room to dispute on this point, every donor having the right of qualifying his gifts with such terms as he thinks proper."[32]

In the same letter Franklin went on with a personal matter which was probably politic. He knew that the Lees and Izard were talking against him in America. Adams had been chosen by Congress to negotiate peace. John Laurens was coming as special commissioner. Franklin for once thought it better to resign than run the risk of being dismissed. "I have passed my seventy-fifth year, and I find that the long and severe fit of the gout which I had the last winter has shaken me exceedingly, and I am yet far from having recovered the bodily strength I before enjoyed. I do not know that my mental faculties are impaired; perhaps I shall be the last to discover that; but I am sensible of great diminution in my activity, a quality I think particularly necessary in your minister for this court. I am afraid, therefore, that your affairs may some time or other suffer by my deficiency. I find also that the business is too heavy for me and too confining. . . . I have been engaged in public affairs, and enjoyed public confidence, in some shape or other during the long term of fifty years, and honour sufficient to satisfy any reasonable ambition; and I have no other left but that of repose, which I hope the Congress will grant me by sending some person to supply my place." He had no doubt of the success of America, nor any grievance. "As I cannot at present undergo the fatigues of a sea voyage (the last having been almost too much for me), and would not again expose myself to the hazard of capture and imprisonment in this time of war, I purpose to remain here at least till the peace; perhaps maybe for the remainder of my life; and if any knowledge or experience I may have acquired here may be thought of use to my successor, I shall freely communicate it and assist him with any influence I may be supposed to have or counsel that may be desired of me."[33] He asked only that Congress might "be pleased to take under their protection my grandson, William Temple Franklin." Temple had served in Paris an apprenticeship to a diplomatic career, and though he was still too young for a responsible post, Franklin hoped that Congress could see fit to employ him as secretary to the minister at some European court.

Franklin had meant, he said, if his resignation were accepted to go with his grandson for a tour in Italy and Germany, and then "spend the evening of life more agreeably in philosophic leisure."[34] But Congress promptly refused. Franklin seems to have been more gratified than disappointed. "I must . . . buckle again to business," he wrote to William Carmichael on 24 August, "and thank God that my health and spirits are of late improved. I fancy it may have been a double mortification to those enemies you have mentioned to me, that I should ask as a favour what they hoped to vex me by taking from me, and that I should nevertheless be continued. . . . I call this continuance an honour, and I really esteem it to be a greater than my first appointment, when I consider that all the interest of my enemies, united with my own request, were not sufficient to prevent it."[35]

Franklin thought that Laurens "brusqued the ministers too much, and I found after he was gone that he had thereby given more offence than I could have imagined."[36] But Laurens was a soldier, who knew at first hand the wants of the armies in America, and his mission was able to obtain not only the six million livres already promised but also ten million more, if this could be borrowed in Holland on French security. The Dutch loan was not completed till November. In the meantime there was controversy over the six millions Franklin had obtained. Laurens in June set out for America with 2,500,000 in cash, having sent 1,500,000 to Holland to be shipped from there, and having left orders in France for military stores to the amount of 2,200,000, to be paid for by Franklin. It had been assumed that the Dutch loan would supply him. When he found that it was delayed, he stopped the shipment of the money from Holland. William Jackson, in charge of the shipment, was furious. Franklin was steadfast. It was, he believed, more important to hold the money in reserve to meet bills already outstanding than to send it to America, however much it might be needed, and so ruin American credit in Europe, from which future money must come. "I cannot suffer the credit of our country to be destroyed," he wrote to Jackson on 5 July, "if by detaining this money it may be saved. . . . I applaud the zeal you have both [Jackson and Laurens] shown in the affair; but I see that nobody cares how much I am distressed, provided they can carry their own points. I must therefore take what care I can of mine, theirs and mine being equally intended for the service of the public."[37] Jackson later apologized, saying Franklin had been right at every point.

In August Franklin learned that his resignation as minister to France had been refused; in September that he, Adams, and Jay had been chosen as commissioners to negotiate a peace with Great Britain. "I have never known a peace made," he wrote to Adams, "even the most advantageous, that was not censured as inadequate, and the makers condemned as injudicious or corrupt. 'Blessed are the peacemakers' is, I suppose, to be understood in the other world; for in this they are frequently cursed. Being as yet rather too much attached to this world, I had therefore no ambition to be concerned in fabricating this peace. . . . I esteem it, however, as an honour."[38]

To another correspondent, who told Franklin he was now the keystone of the American arch, Franklin wrote that the metaphor was "very pretty. . . . But I suppose you have heard our story of the harrow. If not, here it is. A farmer in our country sent two of his servants to borrow one of a neighbour, ordering them to bring it between them on their shoulders. When they came to look at it, one of them, who had much wit and cunning, said: 'What could our master mean by sending only two men to bring this harrow? No two men upon earth are strong enough to carry it.' 'Poh!' said the other, who was very vain of his strength, 'what do you talk of two men? One man may carry it. Help it upon my shoulders and see.' As he proceeded with it, the wag kept exclaiming: 'Zounds, how strong you are! I could not have thought it. Why, you are a Samson. There is not such another man in America. What amazing strength God has given you! But you will kill yourself. Pray put it down and rest a little, or let me bear a part of the weight.' 'No, no,' said he, being more encouraged by the compliments than oppressed by the burden; 'you shall see I can carry it quite home.' And so he did. In this particular I am afraid my part of the imitation will fall short of the original."[39]

In October Franklin exchanged friendly letters with Edmund Burke regarding the exchange of Burgoyne, now in England but still on parole. "If I were not fully persuaded of your liberal and manly way of thinking," Burke wrote, "I should not presume, in the hostile situation in which I stand, to make an application to you. But in this piece of experimental philosophy I run no risk of offending you. I apply, not to the ambassador of America, but to Dr. Franklin the philosopher; my friend; and the lover of his species." And Franklin replied on the 15th: "Since the foolish part of mankind will make wars from time to time with each other, not having sense enough otherwise to settle their differences, it certainly becomes the wiser part, who cannot prevent those wars, to alleviate as much as possible the calamities attending them." Burke read Franklin's letter to the House of Commons, infuriating the ministry. In November came the news of Cornwallis's surrender, the month before, at Yorktown. At eleven on the night of the 19th Vergennes wrote Franklin a note informing him; and Franklin sent copies, made on the copying press he had invented, to certain of his friends at dawn.[40]

"It is a rare circumstance," Franklin wrote to Adams on the 26th, "and scarce to be met with in history, that in one war two armies should be taken prisoners completely, not a man in either escaping." The capture of Cornwallis, four years after Burgoyne, seemed to Franklin, at that distance, to have a kind of classical simplicity and irony. "It is another singular circumstance that an expedition [that against Cornwallis] so complex, formed of armies of different nations, and of land and sea forces, should with such perfect concord be assembled from different places by land and water, form their junction punctually without the least retard by cross accidents of wind or weather or interruption from the enemy; and that the army which was their object should in the meantime have had the goodness to quit a situation from whence it might have escaped, and place itself in another from whence an escape was impossible."[41] Franklin later had a medal struck, by Dupré at the Mint,[42] commemorating Saratoga and Yorktown, with an infant Hercules strangling two serpents in his cradle, while France (in the figure of Minerva) contended with the British lion.

But Franklin declined to be too hopeful. He had not the slightest faith that Tory England could ever learn everything from any experience: "at least," as he had written to Lafayette, "while the present ministry continues; or rather, while the present madman has the choice of ministers."[43] "Depend upon it, the king hates us cordially, and will be content with nothing short of our extirpation."[44] Hardly had the news of Yorktown reached England when Franklin began to hear from English friends, sounding him out as to possible terms of peace. He would have nothing to do with anyone not authorized to treat. To David Hartley, who throughout the war kept desiring peace and writing about it to Franklin, he said firmly on 15 January that America would not even consider Hartley's suggestion for a truce between England and the United States while England settled her European quarrel with France. "The Congress will never instruct their commissioners to obtain a peace on such ignominious terms; and though there can be but few things in which I should venture to disobey their orders, yet, if it were possible for them to give me such an order as this, I should certainly refuse to act, I should instantly renounce their commission and banish myself for ever from so infamous a country."[45]

As closely as he could in Paris Franklin followed the course of British opinion and Parliamentary action: the king's obstinate speech implying that the war must go on, the remonstrances from London and other cities, the enormous budget asked of an empty treasury, the swift increase in the strength of the opposition, the brilliant attacks on the ministry by Fox, William Pitt the younger (Chatham had died in 1778), and Richard Brinsley Sheridan, the general disgust with the incompetent if not corrupt ministers who were the best the king had been willing to use, or able to find, to direct his army and navy. On 22 February General Conway, who had moved the repeal of the Stamp Act and had refused to serve against the colonists, moved an address to the king praying that the war might no longer be pursued for the impracticable purpose of reducing the inhabitants of that country to obedience by force. The motion was lost by a single vote which Franklin saw as North's own. When it was carried six days later Burke at once wrote the news to Franklin: "I congratulate you, as a friend of America; I trust, as not the enemy of England; I am sure, as the friend of mankind."

"The ministry," Franklin wrote on 4 March, ". . . declare that the war in America is for the future to be only defensive. I hope we shall be too prudent to have the least dependence on this declaration."[46] The next day Conway moved, and carried, a resolution to the effect that all who advised or attempted a further prosecution of offensive war on the continent of America should be considered enemies to the king and the country. On the 7th, after the king had been privately informed by North that he could no longer remain in office, Franklin was still cautious. "We must not . . . be lulled by these appearances. That nation is changeable. And though somewhat humbled at present, a little success may make them as insolent as ever. I remember that, when I was a boxing boy, it was allowed, even after an adversary said he had enough, to give him a rising blow. Let ours be a douser."[47]

○○○

Sage in France

IN THE portrait of Franklin which the younger Cochin painted
in 1777 the philosopher looked, or was made to look, like a sly
French peasant with a fur cap and spectacles, sharp eyes, and
amused but determined mouth. The next year Duplessis painted
for Chaumont a more venerable likeness. In this Franklin's thin-
ning hair was brushed back from his high, wide forehead and fell
straight to the fur collar of his coat. His eyes were full and bright,
not brooding, his mouth bland. Strong lines across his forehead,
between his eyebrows, beside his nose, marked his face with old
age, but an old age robust and ruddy. "I do not find that I grow
any older," he wrote at seventy-four to Thomas Bond in Philadelphia. "Being arrived at seventy, and considering that by travelling
further in the same road I should probably be led to the grave, I
stopped short, turned about, and walked back again; which having
done these four years, you may now call me sixty-six. Advise those
old friends of ours to follow my example; keep up your spirits, and
that will keep up your bodies; you will no more stoop under the
weight of age than if you had swallowed a handspike."[1] The French,
who commonly thought Franklin older than he was, admired and
praised his ageless spirit, but they found it charming in him to be
patriarchal, and the portraits made of him in France were all
meant to show him old as well as wise.

"I have at the request of friends," Franklin wrote to one of them
in 1780, "sat so much and so often to painters and statuaries that I
am perfectly sick of it. I know of nothing so tedious as sitting
hours in one fixed posture. I would nevertheless do it once more
to oblige you if it was necessary; but there are already so many
good likenesses of the face that if the best of them is copied it will
probably be better than a new one; and the body is only that of

a lusty man which need not be drawn from the life; any artist can add such a body to the face."[2] Franklin was, he told a French friend the same year, neither rich nor vain enough (*ni assez riche ni assez vain*[3]) to pay eight or ten louis (about thirty to forty dollars) for portraits to give away. If he gave the time his friends would have to pay the painter. Duplessis painted at least a dozen portraits, some of them possibly without sittings. Greuze and J.-F. de l'Hospital painted Franklin in 1777–79. Houdon and Jean-Jacques Caffieri modelled busts, in marble, bronze, and plaster. There were other paintings and busts, miniatures, medallions, statuettes, drawings, and prints, endlessly reproduced, first on snuff-boxes and rings and in time on watches, clocks, vases, dishes, hand-kerchiefs, and pocket-knives. Probably no man before Franklin had ever had his likeness so widely current in so many forms.[4] It was such a fad that Louis XVI, bored with the Comtesse Diane de Polignac's ardours over her American hero, is said to have presented her at New Year's with a *vase de nuit* of Sèvres porcelain elegantly if surprisingly adorned with Franklin's picture and his Latin epigram.[5]

Franklin might speak of turning back his age at seventy, but during his first years in France he noted changes in his powerful constitution, and on 4 October 1778 began a clinical commentary on his health. While still in England he had been "sometimes vexed with an itching on the back which I observed particularly after eating freely of beef. And sometimes after long confinement at writing with little exercise I have felt sudden pungent pains in the flesh of different parts of the body which I was told were scorbutic. A journey used to free me of them." The most persistent symptom was a "scab or scurf" on his head. Pringle had "advised my abstaining from salted meats and cheese, which advice I did not much follow, often forgetting it." The voyages to and from America, with dry, salt food on shipboard, and the exhausting, confining work for Congress had not only weakened Franklin when he arrived in France but had brought on new scorbutic symp-toms, "the scurf extending all the small of my back, on my sides, my legs, and my arms, besides what continued under my hair. . . . I found that bathing stopped the progress of the disorder. I there-fore took the hot bath twice a week, two hours at a time till this last summer." He tried to remember not to eat beef, salt meat, and cheese, though he was fond of all of them, and to drink less wine than he would have liked.[6] But he was no ascetic. In October– November 1780 he had a bad spell of the gout that lasted for six weeks. With a humour which the pain could not touch he wrote his *Dialogue between Franklin and the Gout*,[7] in which the personified malady told him he deserved all his discomfort.

"Let us examine your course of life," the Gout said. "When the mornings are long and you have plenty of time to go out for a walk, what do you do? Instead of getting up an appetite for breakfast by salutary exercise you amuse yourself with books, pamphlets, and newspapers most of which are not worth the trouble. Yet you eat an abundant breakfast, not less than four cups of tea with cream, and one or two slices of buttered toast covered with strips of smoked beef. . . . Immediately afterwards you sit down to write at your desk or talk with people who come to you on business. This lasts till an hour after noon, without any kind of bodily exercise. . . . But what do you do after dinner? Instead of walking in the beautiful gardens of the friends with whom you have dined, like a man of sense, you settle down at the chess-board and there you stay for two or three hours. . . . Wrapped in the speculations of this wretched game, you destroy your constitution. . . . Do not flatter yourself that when you ride for half an hour in your carriage you are taking exercise. Providence has not given carriages to everybody, but it has given everybody a pair of legs. . . . Remember how often you have promised yourself to walk tomorrow morning in the Bois de Boulogne, in the garden at La Muette or in your own, and then have not kept your word; alleging sometimes that it was too cold, at other times too warm, too windy, too damp, or too something else; when in truth it was too much nothing which hindered you but too much laziness. . . . You know M. B[rillon]'s gardens and how good they are for walking; you know the fine flight of a hundred and fifty steps which lead from the terrace down to the lawn. You have been in the habit of visiting this amiable family twice a week in the afternoon. A maxim you yourself invented says that a man may have as much exercise in going a mile up and down stairs as in walking ten on level ground. What an opportunity for you to take exercise in both

these ways! . . . What have you done? You have sat on the terrace, praised the fine view, and looked at the beauties of the
gardens below; but you have never stirred a step to descend and
walk about in them. On the contrary, you call for tea and the
chess-board. . . . And then, instead of walking home, which
would stir you up a little, you take your carriage. . . .

"*Franklin*. What would you have me do with my carriage?

"*Gout*. Burn it if you like . . . or, if that proposal does not suit
you, I have another. Observe the poor peasants who till the soil in
the vineyards and fields about the villages of Passy, Auteuil, Chaillot, etc. Every day you may find among these good creatures four
or five old women and old men, bent and perhaps crippled by the
weight of years and by labour too hard and unrelieved, who after
a long, fatiguing day have to walk a mile or two to their cottages.
Order your coachman to pick them up and take them home. That
will be a good deed, and good for your soul! And if at the same
time, after your visit to the B[rillon]s, you return on foot, that will
be good for your body.

"*Franklin*. Ah! how tiresome you are . . . Oh! oh! for heaven's
sake leave me! and I promise faithfully that from now on I shall
play no more chess but shall take daily exercise and live temperately.

"*Gout*. I know you too well. You promise beautifully; but, after
a few months of good health, you will go back to your old habits;
your fine promises will be forgotten like the forms of last year's
clouds." (But on 20 November 1782 Franklin told John Adams:
"I walk a league every day in my chamber. I walk quickly and
for an hour, so that I go a league. I make a point of religion of it."[8])

Humorous about the gout, Franklin was cheerful about the
bladder stone which suddenly disabled him in the last week of
August 1782, in the midst of the peace negotiations, and never left
him during the rest of his life. Within a year it was so painful he
could not bear the jolting of his carriage over the pavement. He
gave up going regularly on Tuesdays to court, and sent his grandson in his place. In view of the few years he had to live at best,
Franklin would not risk an operation and took no drugs. "You
may judge that my disease is not very grievous," he wrote to John
Jay on 6 January 1784, "since I am more afraid of the medicines

than of the malady."⁹ It always gave him "more or less uneasiness," he wrote to Jan Ingenhousz on 29 April, "unless when I am laid in bed; and when I would write it interrupts my train of thinking so that I lay down my pen and seek some light amusement."¹⁰ On 23 May he remembered the old song he had sung so often in Philadelphia, wishing he might govern his passions and not suffer from gout or stone. "But what signifies our wishing? Things happen, after all, as they will happen. I . . . now find at fourscore that the three contraries have befallen me, being subject to the gout and the stone and not yet being master of all my passions. Like the proud girl in my country who wished and resolved not to marry a parson nor a Presbyterian nor an Irishman, and at length found herself married to an Irish Presbyterian parson."¹¹

Franklin's real malady was old age. But he might have put off the ill effects of his daily indolence if he had been able to make such annual journeys as he had made in England. Travel always roused and cured him. His multifarious duties gave him no opportunity for it in France. From the time he arrived in Paris till he left it, eight and a half years after, to return to America, he never went beyond the city or its suburbs. Minister plenipotentiary, he was bound as closely to his office as he had ever been to his shop when he was a tradesman in Philadelphia. At any time something might come up which called for his decision. If he dined out every day he came home every night to sleep and wake the next morning to his perpetual responsibilities.

His house in Passy, in what is now the Rue Raynouard, has been replaced by the chapel of the Friars of the Christian Doctrine. In his day the street was a paved road along the crest of a hill which sloped to the Seine, which he could see from his terrace. Passy was less a village than a group of villas, with four royal châteaux, in a region of forests and vineyards. There were a parish church, a few shops and houses, and the huts of the labourers on the estates. The grounds of the Hôtel Valentinois were laid out in formal gardens, with grass plots around an octagonal piece of water, and alleys of clipped lindens. Franklin's house, on which he installed a lightning rod, has been described as a pavilion in the grounds, a dependency of the Hôtel Valentinois, a wing of the building. The Duc de Croÿ, who called on Franklin in March 1779, spoke of him

as then lodged with three servants in a small house at the rear,
approached by a little-used road from Chaillot. (Elkanah Watson,
calling on Franklin in September, noted that "at the hour of
dinner he conducted me across a spacious garden of several acres,
to the princely residence of M. Le Ray de Chaumont.") In February 1783 the duc said he found Franklin in the main house,
with a fine prospect from his windows.[12] It seems clear that he
lived first in one house and then in another. John Adams in 1778,
a year before the duc's first call, thought the embassy was extravagantly housed in the Petit Hôtel, with superfluous servants. But
Franklin, in 1782, apparently moved to the Hôtel itself. It was
built in two wings which were really separate, parallel houses
joined by a colonnade and an archway between them over the
entrance, to a common courtyard, from the Rue Raynouard (then
the Rue Passy). Benjamin Franklin Bache made a drawing[13] of the
Hôtel which, like another contemporary drawing,[14] shows the two
wings apparently the same size. Franklin's was to the left of persons
entering the courtyard. It was large enough for his household and
his guests, the printing press he set up, the experiments he had
time to make, and (at least from January 1783) nine servants.

Certain neglected papers and accounts of the Passy household
make it appear that Franklin and his grandson at first had their
dinners at Chaumont's table or from Chaumont's kitchen, paying
six livres apiece for each meal for themselves or for any guests they
might bring. If they chose, they might dine separately at the same
price. When Franklin gave a large dinner in his own apartments it
would be furnished by Chaumont, and Franklin would pay the
entire costs, providing his own wine in addition.[15] The weekly
charges for the Franklin meals began 9 March 1777 and ran to
August,[16] which may have been the end of this joint arrangement
with Chaumont. For the last quarter of 1782 and thereafter Franklin paid rent at an annual rate of 6000 livres.[17] From January 1783
he had a maître d'hôtel, Jacques Finck, who was always saying he
was an honest man, though Franklin suspected—and afterwards
found out—that the man was "mistaken."[18] Finck undertook to
pay all expenses for food (not drink) for a household of five members and nine servants out of an allowance to him of 1300 francs a
month.[19] Breakfast, at eight on week days and at nine or ten on

Sundays, was bread and butter, honey, and coffee or chocolate, or fair equivalents such as Franklin's tea. For dinner there was a joint of beef or veal or mutton, followed by fowl or game, with two sweets, two vegetables, pastry, hors d'œuvres, butter, pickles, radishes, two fruits in winter, four in summer, two compotes, cheese, biscuits, bonbons, and ices twice a week in summer and once in winter. The cellar was as generous as the table. In February 1779 Franklin had 1040 bottles of wine: more red and white Bordeaux, less Burgundy, a little champagne, a great deal of sparkling white wine, a good deal of vin rouge ordinaire (probably for the servants), and 48 bottles of rum. In September 1782 his stock was 1203 bottles. The hire of his carriage and horses, and the wages and clothes of his coachman, cost 5018 livres a year. Franklin's annual salary from Congress was 11,428 livres, with "reasonable expenses." Arthur Lee found out that in fifteen months Franklin drew $12,214 from the bank for his private account. He must have spent that much or more on an average every year in France.[20] Some of his compatriots thought him lavish, and he himself said in June 1782 that frugality was "a virtue I never could acquire in myself."[21] But, economical for his country, he lived more plainly than any other ambassador in Paris.

His sober unembroidered brown coat, with a fur collar in cold weather, became almost his uniform. He carried his crab-tree stick wherever he went, and always wore glasses. By August 1784 he could not, without them, "distinguish a letter even of large print."[22] Before that year he had used "two pair of spectacles which I shifted occasionally, as in travelling I sometimes read and often wanted to regard the prospects. Finding this change troublesome and not always sufficiently ready, I had the glasses cut and half of each kind associated in the same circle." That is, he invented bifocals. "This I find more particularly convenient since my being in France, the glasses that serve me best at table to see what I eat not being the best to see the faces of those on the other side of the table who speak to me; and when one's ears are not well accustomed to the sounds of a language, a sight of the movements in the features of him that speaks helps to explain; so that I understand French better by the help of my spectacles."[23]

Franklin's permanent household was himself, Temple Franklin, and a French clerk. Benjamin Bache until he was sent to Geneva lived at his school in Passy, with John Quincy Adams for a year or so and other American boys from time to time. They had dinner on Sunday with Franklin, who unlike many ageing men was not bored or irritated by children. When John Jay and his family were living in Franklin's house, Maria Jay, a year and a half old, formed a "singular attachment" to the philosopher which he said he could never forget.[24] In the summer of 1784 Franklin, urging Polly Hewson to come from London with her children to visit him, told her he had a pool for them to swim in, "besides the river in view. I like your monthly account of them, and in return send you my daughter's account of my grandchildren at Philadelphia."[25] Polly came with the children and a maid for the whole winter, and when she left about the first of May Franklin wrote in reply to her letter from Dover: "You talk of obligations to me, when in fact I am the person obliged. I passed a long winter in a manner that made it appear the shortest of any I ever passed. . . . My love to William and Thomas and Eliza, and tell them I miss their cheerful prattle. Temple being sick, and Benjamin at Paris, I have found it very *triste* breakfasting alone, and sitting alone, and without any tea in the evening."[26] The children of all his friends in Passy were his friends too. Unknown French schoolboys wrote him letters.

Passy was as much his home as Craven Street had been, and more than Philadelphia had been for years. During the British occupation of Philadelphia in 1777–78 the Baches lived in the country and Captain John André was quartered in Franklin's house. When Howe withdrew his army and the Baches returned, they found that the British had carried off musical instruments, Temple's schoolbooks, and some of the electrical apparatus. Captain André, later a major and a tragic spy, took the Benjamin Wilson portrait of Franklin as a souvenir of the arch-rebel. (The portrait got to England, where it remained till 1906, when Earl Grey restored it to America and a permanent place in the White House.) The war made the mails so uncertain that Franklin once had no letter from his daughter for eighteen months. But, though he might scold her for extravagance, he kept up an affectionate correspondence with her, and longed to see the four younger children born to her in his absence.

II

Franklin's closest friends in France were for the most part his nearest neighbours. He was on good terms with the parish priest and the village tradesmen. He and the Chaumont family, in the Hôtel Valentinois, saw each other almost daily. Franklin teasingly called the daughter Sophie his wife, which delighted her. Passy was then famous for its mineral springs, down the slope near the river. Louis Le Veillard, who managed the drinking, bottling, and bathing at the Eaux and became in 1789 the first mayor of the town, lived there, like Franklin, all the year round, and he and his wife and daughter were Franklin's friends for life. Across the street from Franklin was the Château de Passy, which belonged to the Comte de Boulainvilliers. His daughter was another of Franklin's favourites. When she became engaged to the Comte de Clermont-Tonnerre, all Passy said that Franklin's lightning rod (*paraton-nerre*) had not been able to protect her. William Alexander, a Scot whom Franklin had known in Edinburgh and London, now lived with his family at Saint-Germain. His daughter Marianne was married in 1779 to Franklin's grandnephew Jonathan Williams.

Franklin, John Adams disapprovingly said, "at the age of seventy-odd had neither lost his love of beauty nor his taste for it."[27] But there is no support for the tradition which insists that the philosopher was a lively lecher in France. "You mention the kindness of the French ladies to me," he wrote to his Boston stepniece Elizabeth Partridge on 11 October 1779. "I must explain that matter. This is the civilest nation upon earth. Your first acquaintances endeavour to find out what you like, and they tell others. If 'tis understood that you like mutton, dine where you will you find mutton. Somebody, it seems, gave it out that I loved ladies; and then everybody presented me their ladies (or the ladies presented themselves) to be embraced; that is, have their necks kissed. For as to the kissing of lips or cheeks it is not the mode here; the first is reckoned rude, and the other may rub off the paint. The French ladies have, however, a thousand other ways of rendering themselves agreeable; by their various attentions and civilities and their sensible conversation."[28]

Some of the attentions paid him were in the elaborate, Arcadian mode of the old regime which was so near its downfall. Madame Campan, companion of Marie Antoinette, later remembered a ceremonial occasion—of no given time or place—when the most beautiful of three hundred women placed a crown of laurel on Franklin's white head and kissed both his cheeks.[29] In April 1781 he was the hero of a *fête champêtre* arranged by the Comtesse d'Houdetot (the Sophie of Rousseau's *Confessions*) at her house at Sannois, ten miles from Passy. She and her party came on foot half a mile to meet his carriage, and she welcomed him with verses she had composed herself. Liberty, the verses sighed, was far off, but here was a mortal who had made happy citizens. Hosts and guests (the gouty philosopher too?) walked to the château and dinner. At each glass of wine there was another stanza to be sung or spoken. There would be altars in America for Benjamin, the chorus said; let Sannois drink to his renown. He freed men by enlightening them, said a stanza, and virtue took its very countenance from him. William Tell was brave, but savage; our dear Benjamin, shaping the destiny of America, could laugh at this civilized table. Long live Philadelphia, sang the comtesse; its independence so tempted her that she would like to live there, though it had no balls or comedies.

After dinner Franklin was led by the whole family into the gardens where, under a rural arbour, he planted with his own hands a Virginia locust treet. More verses, to be engraved on a marble pillar beside it, near another for Voltaire. Sacred tree, durable monument of a sage's visit to these grounds, receive now homage and incense, and hereafter live as long as his name, his laws, and his works. The tree would never be struck by lightning, for the sage had mastered that, while destroying still worse evils. At farewell, when Franklin was in his carriage, the comtesse read her final verses to the legislator of one world, the benefactor of two, discharging as well as she could the debt that all the ages would continue to owe him. Three years later she solicitously planned a second visit to Sannois, in June, by boat and the easiest stages on land. He was now too feeble to make the journey. Six years later she wrote to him, in Philadelphia, saying it was sweet to think of him under that venerated tree, where she paid her sort of devotions and he was one of her saints.[30]

Silent, smiling, Franklin went through these literary rites, too much pleased by the affectionate honours shown him to laugh at the artificial forms they took. But his close friendships with women were easier and more humorous. There was Madame Brillon, wife of a treasury official who was much older than she and less imaginative. She seems to have been in her thirties when she met Franklin soon after he arrived in Paris. From the first she loved the philosopher. He told her how the savages in America sometimes adopted their prisoners, in the place of kinsmen who had died. She adopted Franklin to succeed her father whom she had loved and still missed.[31] "Oh, my Papa," she wrote in November 1778, "I beg for your friendship, your healthy philosophy; my heart listens and submits to you. . . . Never call me anything but 'my daughter.' Yesterday you called me 'Madame,' and my heart shrank." She confided to him, as she might have to her father, her difficulties with her husband, her jealousy of her daughters' governess, the ingratitude she had to bear. Franklin sent her, in his own French, the fatherly advice she asked for. Bad as ingratitude was, she must not try to pay it back. "If they have done you injuries, reflect that although they may formerly have been your equals they have by those means put themselves beneath you. If you avenge yourself and punish them in kind, you restore them to the state of equality which they have lost. But if you pardon them without any punishment, you will fix them in the low state to which they have fallen and from which they can never rise without true repentance and full reparation."[32] Poor Richard had said almost the same thing in his almanac for 1749.

Still, Franklin and Madame Brillon were not father and daughter, and there was the spice of gallantry in their friendship. "People have the audacity," she wrote him, "to criticize my pleasant habit of sitting on your knee, and yours of always asking me for what I always refuse." She decided to be more discreet in the future, but at least once, while in her covered bath, she began a game of chess with him, and they were so absorbed that he found it was eleven when he got home that evening.[33] Twice a week during the summer (usually Wednesday and Saturday) he came with Temple to her house after dinner, to idle on the terrace in the sun, with chess and tea, or to listen indoors to her and her daughters at their music. After Saratoga Madame Brillon composed for Franklin a *March of the Insurgents*.[34] Sometimes he played on the harmonica. These concerts he called his opera, for he rarely went to the opera in Paris. The family gatherings were discreet enough. But during the winter when she was in Paris, and between their regular days of the week in summer, letters went back and forth between them in which he often urged his claim to be more than father, and she as often rejected it—without ever choosing to end the piquant debate.

"How am I going to spend the Wednesdays and Saturdays?" she asked after she had left Passy in November 1779. Perhaps another life might be better than this, with its enforced separations. "In paradise we shall be reunited, never to leave each other again. We shall there live on roast apples only; the music will be made up of Scotch airs; all parties will be given over to chess . . . everyone will speak the same language; the English will be neither unjust nor wicked there; the women will not be coquettes, the men will be neither jealous nor too gallant. . . . We shall never suffer from gout there nor from our nerves. . . . Ambition, envy, pretensions, jealousy, prejudices, all these will vanish at the sound of the trumpet. . . . Every day we shall love one another in order that we may love one another still more the day after; in a word, we shall be completely happy. In the meantime, let us get all the good we can out of this poor world of ours."

Franklin in reply said he had been thinking about how the two of them would manage their affairs in paradise. In the course of nature he would die forty years before her and have to wait that long till she came. He could not without scruple think of asking her to desert her husband, who was good and generous and loved them as they did him. "However, the idea of an eternity in which I shall be favoured with no more than permission to kiss your hands, or sometimes your cheeks, and to pass two or three hours in your sweet society on Wednesdays and Saturdays, is frightful." But he would leave it for her to decide in paradise. "If you reject me, perhaps I shall address myself to Madame d'Hardancourt [her mother], and she may be willing to live with me; then I shall pass my hours at home agreeably with her. . . . In forty years I shall have time to practise on the armonica, and perhaps I shall play well enough to be worthy to accompany you on your pianoforte. From time to time we shall have little concerts." All their friends from Passy would be the audience. Her daughters and certain young angels would sing. "And we shall pity those who are not dead."[35]

Madame Brillon relented—for the future. "I give you my word of honour that I will become your wife in paradise, on condition, however, that you do not make too many conquests among the heavenly maidens while you are waiting for me. I want a faithful husband when I take one for eternity." She would tell her mother of his "good intentions" towards her, but it might cause jealousy between the two women, devoted as they were to one another. He must not apologize for his French. If it was not very pure, it was at least very clear.[36] As she said in another letter, it was "always very good French to say: *Je vous aime.*" Leave grammar to the academicians. She corrected the errors in his paradisal plans and he kept the manuscript.[37] The matter of genders, he said, had bothered him for sixty years, and at seventy-eight he still found the French feminines a plague. This made him more content to go to paradise, where such distinctions, he had heard, would be abolished. When she accused him of inconstancy he insisted it was as plain as Euclid that whoever was constant to several persons was more constant than he who was constant to only one.

Consider his plight. "When I was a young man and enjoyed more favours from the sex than at present, I never had the gout. If the ladies of Passy had more of that Christian charity which I have so often recommended to you, in vain, I would not have the gout now."[38] He returned more than once to this idea of Christian charity, and she more than once called him a sophist. She said there were many pains in life which must be borne with patience. He agreed with her. "But it seems to me that there are also many pleasures. That is why I love to live. We must not blame Providence inconsiderately. Reflect how many of our duties it has ordained to be naturally pleasures; and that it has had the goodness, besides, to give the name of sin to several of them so that we might enjoy them the more."[39] She undertook to serve as his confessor. "I lay fast hold on your promise," he wrote, "to absolve me of all sins, past, present, and future, on the easy and pleasing condition of loving God, America, and my guide above all things. I am in rapture when I think of being absolved of the future. . . . And now I am consulting you upon a case of conscience, I will mention the opinion of a certain father of the Church which I find myself willing to adopt, though I am not sure it is orthodox. It is this: that the most effectual way to get rid of a certain temptation is, as often as it returns, to comply with and satisfy it. Pray instruct me how far I may venture to practise upon this principle?"[40]

"If I had wings I should have flown to you," he wrote, "and I think I should sometimes scratch at the window of your bed-chamber. It is very mischievous of nature to deny us the advantages that she has wasted so profusely on all the little good-for-nothing birds and flies."[41] Another time he turned (in his own English) to mythology for his image. "My poor little boy [Amor], whom you ought methinks to have cherished, instead of being fat and jolly like those in your elegant drawings is meagre and almost starved to death for want of the substantial nourishment which you, his mother, inhumanly deny him, and yet would now clip his little wings to prevent his seeking it elsewhere."[42] And a third time Franklin spoke of wings, this time Scriptural. Madame Brillon in October 1781 was in Marseilles on her way to Nice for the winter, and found a letter waiting for her. "It gave me much pleasure," she wrote. "I found in it evidences of your friendship and a touch of that gaiety and gallantry which makes all women love you, because you love all women. Your proposition to carry me on your wings, if you were the angel Gabriel, made me laugh; but I would not accept it, though I am no longer very young nor a virgin. That angel was a sly fellow, and your nature united to his would become too dangerous. I would be afraid of miracles' happening; and miracles between women and angels might not always bring a redeemer."[43]

The game of love and kisses ran through their correspondence, but their friendship included more than gallantry. In April 1781 Franklin formally proposed his grandson—whom the Brillons called Franklinet—as husband of their eldest daughter. The philosopher, believing he might not outlive the war and would have to remain in France, hoped to make his friends his family there. Temple might be given some diplomatic post in Europe, and would not have to take his wife away to America. As to the difference in religion, Franklin thought that unimportant. "In each religion there are essential things, and others which are only forms and fashions; as a loaf of sugar may perhaps be wrapped in brown or white or blue paper, and tied with a string of flax or wool, red or yellow; but the sugar is always the essential thing."[44] Madame Brillon, for herself and her husband, affectionately declined the offer. Temple, they were sure, belonged to America, and they required a husband for their daughter who could assume, as Temple was too young to do, the responsibilities which Brillon wished to give up to a successor in his post. But the Brillons, though not Franklin's children, would always be his friends and care for him as if he were their father. When their daughter was married to another man Franklin was happy, and delighted at the birth of her first child in November 1784. He had known Madame Brillon's mother and grandmother; and now she was a grandmother herself: five generations of women he admired and loved. Remain in France fifteen or sixteen years more, Madame Brillon urged him, and he might see a sixth with his patriarchal eyes.[45]

If Franklin was disappointed, he had had no worse luck in trying to make a match for Temple than he had had in London, planning a marriage between Temple's father and Polly Stevenson. That earlier episode was doubly repeated. Temple in 1785 became the father of a short-lived son by Blanchette Caillot, the wife of a neighbour in Passy. The Franklin line of illegitimacy was international: Franklin's son born in Philadelphia, William's born in London, Temple's born in Passy.

If the gallantry between Madame Brillon and Franklin went along with domestic sentiments, so did it with literature and politics. To commemorate a day which they and their friends had spent at the Moulin Joli, the home of Claude-Henri Watelet on an island in the Seine, Franklin in 1778 wrote for her *The Ephemera*, the first of his bagatelles.[46] As a further comment on her description of paradise and her conclusion that men should make the best of this world while it lasted, he wrote for her his story of *The Whistle* on 16 November 1779.[47] Foolish men, he said, were always putting false values on things; court favour, popularity, wealth, pleasure, outward appearances. He himself, he hinted, might ruin himself if something which she knew he very much desired were for sale—as it was not. Madame Brillon was perfectly devoted to the cause of America. When in Nice she heard of the surrender of Cornwallis she pouted to Franklin, in a letter, because he had not taken the trouble to be the first to send her the news. On Christmas Day he replied that it was too soon to be too triumphant. "In bad fortune I hope for good, and in good I fear bad. So I play at this game [war] with almost the same calm spirit as you have seen me play at chess."[48] In March she sent him, drawn up with all the legal forms of a court action, a complaint that he had not written to her often enough. In July, absorbed in the peace negotiations and harassed by the gout, he wrote out for her the articles which he proposed for a treaty of peace between them. "I fancy we shall neither of us get anything by this war, and therefore, as feeling myself the weakest, I will do what indeed ought always to be done by the wisest: be first in making the propositions for peace."[49] The merry war was not given up, but their affection and their letters continued to the end of his life, whether he was in Passy or in remote Philadelphia, after her husband died and her fortune was reduced and the French Revolution overturned her captivating world.

And there was Madame Helvétius, widow of the rich farmer-general who had been a philosopher and had given brilliant Tuesday dinners for philosophers. Since his death in 1771 his widow had lived with her two daughters at Auteuil, the village next to Passy. On the edge of the Bois de Boulogne, in a little park planted with hortensias and rhododendrons and swarming with cats, dogs (Temple Franklin brought a bulldog from England), chickens, pigeons, canaries, and wild birds from the Bois, Madame Helvétius kept up her spirited salon. When Voltaire came to call she met him at the gate, like a king. After Turgot had brought Franklin for his first visit she regretted that she had not shown him the same honour. He may have come, as he went to Madame du Deffand's, to win an influential woman to the side of America. But he and Madame Helvétius became instantly and permanently friends. She had been so beautiful that Fontenelle, who lived to be a hundred, was said to have paid her one of the most famous compliments of the age: "Ah, Madame, if I were only eighty again!" And at sixty she was still so pleasing that Franklin paid her, it is said, another which became as famous. There are different versions of the story, told of different women and different situations.[50] The classic account is that Madame Helvétius accused Franklin of having put off a visit she expected. "Madame, I am waiting till the nights are longer."

Abigail Adams, arriving from Boston by way of congenial London in August 1784 and asked to dinner at Franklin's house with Madame Helvétius, thought her untidy, noisy, and brazen. She called Dr. Franklin merely Franklin, kissed his cheeks and forehead when she greeted him, and sat beside him at dinner sometimes holding his hand and sometimes carelessly throwing her arm around his neck (her other arm now and then on the back of John Adams's chair). "I should have been greatly astonished at this conduct if the good Doctor had not told me that in this lady I should see a genuine Frenchwoman, wholly free from affectation or stiffness of behaviour, and one of the best women in the world. For this I must take the Doctor's word; but I should have set her down for a very bad one."[51] Taught from her childhood to venerate the great Franklin, the Puritan lady was shocked to find that Madame Helvétius was bold with him and that he liked it.

Franklin could hardly have made clear to his American admirer why he enjoyed his French friend. But he explained it to Madame Helvétius. "I see that statesmen, philosophers, historians, poets, and men of learning of all sorts are drawn around you, and seem as willing to attach themselves to you as straws about a fine piece of amber. . . . I would not attempt to explain it by the story of the ancient who, being asked why philosophers sought the acquaintance of kings and kings not that of philosophers, replied that philosophers knew what they wanted, which was not always the case with kings. Yet thus far the comparison may go: that we find in your sweet society that charming benevolence, that amiable attention to oblige, that disposition to please and be pleased, which we do not always find in the society of one another. It springs from you; it has its influence on us all; and in your company we are not only pleased with you but better pleased with one another and with ourselves."[52]

Yet the casual records which are all that survive of the friendship of Franklin and Madame Helvétius seldom even mention the other great men who visited her. This was the friendship of country neighbours, narrowed largely to the members of the two households. Franklin gave Madame Helvétius the name she had in their circle: Notre Dame d'Auteuil. He named her daughters the Étoiles, from the story of the mother who told her children that old moons were cut up to make new stars. The witty Abbé Morellet, who had met Franklin in England, lived near Madame Helvétius if not in her house. The book-loving Abbé de La Roche was comfortably domesticated with her, and the young Pierre-Jean-Georges Cabanis, later eminent as a physiologist. All of them might come to dinner with Franklin regularly once a week, and he, with Temple, dined another day each week at Auteuil. They went back and forth to breakfast together.

"Behold your friend at Auteuil," the Gout said reprovingly to Franklin in the dialogue between them. "When she honours you with a visit she comes on foot. . . . But you go to Auteuil in your carriage, though it is no further from Passy to Auteuil than from Auteuil to Passy." Once, as it appears from a little-known letter (in primer French) to Madame La Freté, Franklin took his Gout's advice. "I decided to go on foot; my shoes were a little too tight; I got there almost crippled. Entering the courtyard, I was somewhat surprised to find it so empty of carriages, and to see that we [he and Temple] were the first arrivals. We went up the stairs. Not a sound. We went into the breakfast room. Nobody but the Abbé [de La Roche] and M. C[abanis]." Franklin had made a mistake and was not expected that day, and Madame Helvétius was dressing to go to Paris. When she had left, another breakfast was served. "We began to eat. The butter was soon gone. The abbé asked if we wanted more. Yes, of course. He rang, but nobody came. We went on talking, and he forgot the butter. I scraped the plate; then he snatched it up and ran into the kitchen to look for more. After a while he came back, saying sadly that there was no more in the house. To amuse me, the abbé suggested a walk; my feet forbade that. So we left the table and went up to his room, to finish our feast among his books."[53]

In conversation, according to Morellet, Franklin was invariably good-natured, simple, gentle, with a serenity that passed often into gaiety. He rarely spoke at length, and then for the most part in the form of little stories which he told to make his points. Once, speaking of the Scotch songs which he loved, he recalled a night he had spent in a frontiersman's house beyond the Alleghenies. (Or so Morellet supposed, though Franklin had never actually crossed the mountains.) There he had heard a young girl sing *Such merry as we have been* (Morellet's version) so touchingly that he could hear it still after thirty years.[54] More and more of his stories, as he grew old and older in Europe, dealt with America, the country of his youth. Morellet remembered several of them and, when the news of Franklin's death first reached him, sent them to the *Gazette Nationale* of 15 July 1790, where they have lain hitherto unnoted.[55]

For savages, Franklin said, even an extraordinary fact was only a fact, and they never traced facts back to causes. An Indian in Philadelphia came to see him make the experiment of lighting brandy with an electric spark. "These white men are clever rascals," the Indian said, without the least surprise or any reflection on what he had seen. When Franklin was a printer in Philadelphia he knew another printer who worked only half of each week. He had an uncle in London, he explained, who meant to work hard for twenty years and then live like a gentleman. That, the nephew thought, was to become a gentleman by wholesale. He himself preferred the retail way, for he would rather have half a week now than a whole week twenty years from now. After the Declaration of Independence, when the states were forming their new constitutions, the Pennsylvania convention debated for two or three months and got nowhere. Meanwhile, life went on with no disorder. Franklin said one day to the delegates: "Gentlemen, you see that in the anarchy in which we live society manages much as before. Take care, if our disputes last too long, that the people do not come to think that they can very easily do without us." As an apologue on the correction of faults Franklin told his friends, in his slow French, the story of the man and the speckled axe which

he wrote out in his happier English for the new section of the
Autobiography begun in 1784.[56] And he told a Parisian anecdote
at his own expense. At a public gathering, where there were many
speeches, Franklin, not always understanding them, watched
Madame Boufflers and applauded when she did. Afterwards his
grandson told him that he had been applauding praises of himself,
and more loudly than anybody.

Cabanis in his recollections of Franklin said that he never
seemed hurried, kept open house, and was always ready for an
hour with any friend. He explained that he and his small staff, only
his grandson and a clerk, could do more than the large French
governmental offices where needless assistants made needless work
for each other and got in one another's way. He continued in
France to sleep with his windows open and often sat naked in his
room, both in the morning and at night. When he talked it was
without gestures or movements of his head or body. Once, speaking of good conduct, in "his French to which even his incorrectness
almost always gave an added force or grace," he said: "If the rascals
knew the advantages of virtue they would become honest men out
of rascality." He said that in dealing with politicians he took pains
to speak the exact truth. "That is my only cunning; and the politicians are so corrupt that I always fool them by this means."[57]

Conversation, moral tales, chess, Scotch songs, and the harmonica
did not take up all the time which Franklin, in the midst of his
official duties, found to give to Madame Helvétius. He made their
circle into a kind of little academy of arts and letters. Morellet
wrote drinking songs, some of them in praise of Franklin. In
return Franklin wrote his "Christian, moral, and philosophical
reflections" on wine in the undated bagatelle *À Monsieur l'Abbé
Morellet*,[58] with drawings to illustrate the argument that the
human elbow was providentially devised to make drinking natural
and easy. "Let us then, glass in hand, adore this benevolent wisdom. Let us adore and drink." To the Abbé de La Roche, who had
lent Franklin a copy of Helvétius's poems, Franklin sent a song
which he himself had written forty years ago on happiness, which
was one of Helvétius's subjects. "I have often noted, in reading
the works of M. Helvétius, that, though we were born and brought
up in two countries so remote from each other, we have often hit

upon the same thoughts; and it is a reflection very flattering to me that we have loved the same studies and, so far as we have known them, the same friends, and the same woman."[59]

Franklin's devotion to Madame Helvétius was frank and open, and he wrote about it to Cabanis in the full assurance that she would be shown the letters. "As he has already given her many of his days," he wrote on 19 September 1779, in the third person and in French, "although he has so few of them left to give, it seems ungrateful in her that she has never given him a single one of her nights."[60] And again to Cabanis: "M. Franklin being up, bathed, shaved, combed, beautified as best he could, all dressed, and on the point of going out, with his head full of the four Helvétius ladies and the sweet kisses he intends to steal from them, is much mortified to find the possibility of this happiness put off to next Sunday. He will be as patient as he can, hoping to see one of these ladies at M. de Chaumont's on Wednesday. He will be there early, to see her enter with that grace and that dignity which have charmed him for seven weeks at the same place. He even plans to capture her and keep her with him for life. The three others left at Auteuil ought to be enough for the canaries and the abbés."[61]

Just when Franklin proposed marriage to Madame Helvétius and how seriously he meant it are neither of them certain. A letter to La Roche on 7 December 1778 refers to an "exercise" which Franklin was sending for the abbé to correct, "en forme de billet à Notre Dame d'Auteuil."[62] This has been commonly thought to be *À Madame Helvétius*,[63] the most graceful and felicitous of all his bagatelles. But the bagatelle itself speaks of Franklin as having been married long enough to bring the date to January 1780. In any case, he seems to have proposed, and she to have said that she had resolved to be faithful to the memory of her husband. (She had said the same thing to Turgot, her oldest friend, who had proposed to her after Helvétius died.) Franklin, according to his humorous account (here newly translated), went home mortified and dreamed that night that he was in the Elysian Fields, where he met Helvétius.

"He received me with much courtesy, having known me by reputation, he said, for some time. He asked me many things about the war and about the present state of religion, liberty, and government in France. 'You ask nothing then,' I said to him, 'about your dear friend Madame Helvétius; and yet she still loves you to excess; I was with her less than an hour ago.' 'Ah!' he said, 'you remind me of my former happiness. But we must forget if we are to be happy here. For several years at first I thought of nothing but her. At last I am consoled. I have taken another wife; the most like her I could find. She is not, it is true, altogether so beautiful, but she has as much good sense and plenty of wit, and she loves me infinitely. She studies continually to please me, and she has just now gone out to search for the best nectar and ambrosia to regale me with this evening. Stay with me and you will see her.' 'I perceive,' I said, 'that your former friend is more faithful than you; she has had several good offers and has refused them all. I confess to you that I have loved her, to madness; but she was cruel to me and absolutely rejected me for love of you.' 'I pity you,' he said, 'in your misfortune; for she is indeed a good and beautiful woman, and very amiable.'" Here Helvétius, Franklin said, advised him to make use of the abbés in his courtship. Morellet might argue in favour of her suitor, La Roche against him; both would be of service. Then "the new Madame Helvétius came in with the nectar; immediately I recognized her as Madame Franklin, my former friend. I claimed her again, but she said coldly: 'I was a good wife to you for forty-nine years and four months, almost half a century. Be content with that. I have formed a new connexion here which will last for eternity.'

"Indignant at this refusal from my Eurydice, I at once resolved to quit those ungrateful shades, return to this good world, and see again the sun and you. Here I am. Let us avenge ourselves."

Madame Helvétius, partly on the advice of Turgot, persisted in her resolution. Franklin had never been a tragic lover and was not one now. Whatever frustration or mortification he may have felt, he kept the affair on the most engaging level and teased her with a devotion at which he smiled himself. As he printed for her, and for their friends, his Elysian conference with Helvétius, so he printed *Les Mouches à Madame He——s,*[64] his little-known petition from the flies in his house. They would have been happy with him, they told her, but for the spiders which he tolerated. She had ordered them and their webs swept out, and now the flies desired only one thing more to make them happy: to see her and Franklin joined in one household. His proposal and her refusal had no effect on their friendship. During his last four years in France he seems to have spent more time with her than with Madame Brillon, but the two women were not jealous of each other. (Madame Brillon wrote to him one Saturday morning that she could not see him at tea that afternoon and he might give the day to her amiable rival.[65] Madame Helvétius pretended to be jealous of Madame de Forbach, Dowager Duchess of Deux-Ponts, who gave Franklin his crab-tree cane.[66]) On his trying journey to the ship which was to take him home Franklin wrote twice to Madame Helvétius. "It seems to me that things are badly arranged in this world, when I see that two beings so made to be happy together are obliged to separate."[67] "Often in my dreams," he wrote to her from Philadelphia three years later, "I have breakfast with you, I sit beside you on one of your hundred sofas, I walk with you in your beautiful garden."[68] She wrote him scrawling, misspelled letters, sent news through her abbés, inquired about his grandsons, shopped for his daughter in Paris, and added presents to what she had bought. She had always loved him and always would. Though they would never see each other again in this world, perhaps in the next "we shall meet again, with all those who have loved us, I a husband and you a wife—but I believe you have been a rogue and will find more than one."[69]

If in France there were new women whom Franklin loved and who loved him, he lost none of his old friends. In spite of the British he kept up an intermittent correspondence with Catherine Greene, whose husband was now governor of Rhode Island and who delighted the French officers who met her and told her about Franklin. Letters still found their way back and forth between him and Polly Hewson and Georgiana Shipley in England. The long life of all his affectionate friendships helps to define them. Without the brevity of ordinary lust, or the perseverance of obsession, they had a general warmth which, while no doubt sexual in origin, made them strong, tender, imaginative, and humorous beyond the reach of mere desire, with its hard, impersonal appetite. Always a person himself, Franklin treated every woman as if she were a person too, and made her feel more truly one than ever. Because he loved, valued, and studied women, they were no mystery to him, and he had no instinctive fear of them. Statesman and scientist, profoundly masculine, he took women into account as well as any other force of nature.

Even in his political or moral writings, the sexes might furnish him with images or examples. "What would you think of a proposition if I should make it," he wrote to David Hartley on 16 October 1783, "of a family compact between England, France, and America? America would be as happy as the Sabine girls, if she could be the means of uniting in perpetual peace her father and her husband."[70] And to Priestley on 7 June 1782: "Men I find to be a sort of beings very badly constructed, as they are generally more easily provoked than reconciled, more disposed to do mischief to each other than to make reparation, much more easily deceived than undeceived, and having more pride and even pleasure in killing than in begetting one another; for without a blush they assemble in great armies at noonday to destroy, and when they have killed as many as they can, they exaggerate the number to augment the fancied glory; but they creep into corners, or cover themselves with the darkness of night, when they mean to beget, as being ashamed of a virtuous action. A virtuous one it would be, and a vicious one the killing of them, if the species were really worth producing or preserving; but of this I begin to doubt."[71]

III

The cards which Franklin's callers left at Passy, and which with his passion for records he preserved, show how generally the noblesse and learning of the old regime paid their friendly respects to the philosopher. The ministers to France from courts which had not recognized the United States did not call on him, nor he on them. As late as May 1782, he noted with amusement, the Comte du Nord, son of Catherine the Great, and later Paul I, came to Paris and ordered cards sent to all the ambassadors. One arrived for Franklin, bearing the name of the comte and of Prince Bariatinski, ambassador from Russia. As was customary, Franklin stopped at the door of the Russian embassy and had his name written in the visitors' book. The next day a servant came to Passy "in great affliction, saying he was like to be ruined by his mistake in bringing the card here. . . . In the afternoon came my friend, M. Le Roy, who is also a friend of the prince's, telling me how much he, the prince, was concerned at the accident, that both himself and the comte had great personal regard for me and my character, but that, our independence not yet being acknowledged by the court of Russia, it was impossible for him to permit himself to make me a visit as minister." Franklin sensibly thought no harm had been done, since none had been intended. "I thought the remedy was easy; he [Bariatinski] had only to erase my name out of his book of visits received, and I would burn their card."[72] But privately Franklin was friends with the foreign ministers whom he met at Versailles each Tuesday, and exchanged counsel with them.

Franklin would not have been Franklin without a club, and his club in France was the Masonic lodge of the Nine Sisters, which admitted him to membership during 1777. On 28 November 1778 he took part in their fantastic ceremonial in honour of Voltaire, who had died in May. Voltaire's niece was present, and the Marquise de Villette at whose house he had died. There were music and addresses, in the darkened hall, and then a sudden light which revealed an immense picture—by Gauget—of the apotheosis of Voltaire, emerging from his tomb to be presented by Truth and Beneficence to Corneille, Racine, and Molière. Minerva in the picture was seen driving Envy away, and Fame publishing Voltaire's renown. Lalande the astronomer, Greuze the court painter, and Madame de Villette solemnly put crowns upon the head of La Dixmerie the chief eulogist, Gauget, and Franklin; and they in turn laid their crowns at the foot of Voltaire's picture. At the dinner which followed, for two hundred guests, the first toast included the United States and their great emissary.[73] Franklin found, sitting between him and a poet, a representative of the chamber of commerce of Languedoc, sent to ask him about the products of the United States.[74] The next year Franklin was chosen Grand Master (*Vénérable*) of the lodge. While his health allowed it he presided at their meetings. On 6 March 1783 a celebration was held at the new Masonic hall in Paris, and the bust of

Franklin was garlanded with myrtle and laurel to the sound of music. In 1786, after he had returned to Philadelphia, the Nine Sisters announced a prize of six hundred francs for the best eulogy of him.[75]

Freemasonry in America had been social and local, with little influence in politics. In France it was freethinking and opposed to absolutism. The Nine Sisters lodge greeted Franklin as a brother of their order who had carried out its reforming aims in his own country. He joined them not only because he was a Mason but also because they were men who could be of benefit to his diplomatic mission. The Nine Sisters was another Junto, and he worked through it as he had worked through his Leather Apron club when he was young, poor, and unknown. The Masons of the most eminent lodge in France became his informal colleagues in the service of the new republic. It is as easy to exaggerate as it is impossible to trace the specific help they gave him. They were simply a valuable group of his close friends in a whole nation which was friendly. He seems to have had little to say about the French affairs in which they were interested, since he was an accredited minister to their king and had to be discreet. But it was one of them, La Rochefoucauld d'Enville, who on Franklin's suggestion translated the American state constitutions. By order of Congress Franklin in 1783 gave two copies to every ambassador in Paris and dispersed copies throughout Europe.[76]

Among the Masons of the Nine Sisters the American constitutions were looked upon as a grammar of liberty. This was a lodge of constitutionalists, hoping that France might put constitutional limits to its monarchy. Moderate men, several of them were guillotined during the Terror: Bailly the astronomer; Brissot de Warville, who had been to America and who urged that France adopt a constitution like America's; Danton; Camille Desmoulins, who believed that America had revived the pure democracy of Greece; Le Veillard, Franklin's neighbour in Passy. Condorcet died in prison, possibly poisoned, and La Rochefoucauld d'Enville was assassinated. Among those who escaped death were Bonneville, translator of Thomas Paine, who had come to France with letters from Franklin; Hilliard Auberteuil, who had written a history of the American Revolution and was a friend of Jefferson as well as

Franklin; and the Abbé Sieyès.[77] In the unsuspecting years before violence began they talked of constitutions with the sage who, it seemed to them, had made a revolution with benevolent wisdom.

Nor did Franklin, apparently, in the least perceive that France was on the way to a more fundamental revolution than America's. Confined to Paris and its neighbourhood, moving in circles of wealth and privilege, he was little aware of the misery and desperation of the French people. He must have known that the system of farming out the taxes was corrupt and wasteful, but he obtained money for America from the farmers-general, and Madame Helvétius was the widow of one of them. Though Franklin's economic ideas became increasingly radical in France, he seems to have believed with his constitutional friends that a constitution was all France needed. He knew of Robespierre only as a young lawyer of Arras who in October 1783 sent to Passy a printed copy of the plea he had made in court against an ordinance prohibiting the use of lightning rods in Saint-Omer.[78] He knew of Marat only as an obscure student of the nature of fire, who in 1779 appealed to Franklin for help in bringing the new ideas before the Academy of Sciences: help which Franklin gave.[79]

From his arrival in France till after the peace had been negotiated Franklin had almost no leisure for learning. "I should rejoice much," he told Priestley on 7 June 1782, when at last there seemed some prospect of it, "if I could once more recover the leisure to search with you into the works of nature; I mean the inanimate not the animate or moral part of them: the more I discovered of the former the more I admired them; the more I know of the latter the more I am disgusted with them." The day before he wrote Franklin had watched Lavoisier, at the Academy of Sciences, perform an experiment with oxygen, which Priestley had been first to identify.[80] During these years when Franklin was too busy for the studies he liked best he kept his ranging scientific curiosity alive. He visited Lavoisier in his laboratory,[81] he went to the meetings of the Academy of Sciences and of the Royal Society of Medicine, to which he was elected in 1777. His old friend Le Roy was in charge of the king's laboratory at La Muette, a royal château in Passy. Franklin was often there, and at Le Roy's house. He called Madame Le Roy a pocket-wife (*femme de poche*). After his return to Philadelphia he exchanged affectionate letters with both of them, though the two had separated.[82]

In a letter to Ingenhousz on 26 April 1777 Franklin commented on the apparent differences between the Leyden jar and Volta's new electrophorus. In August he wrote again at considerable length on the effects of lightning which had struck a steeple in Cremona. But he asked Ingenhousz not to publish the notes, "as it perhaps may occasion disputes and I have no time to attend to them."[83] In October, for the same reason, he declined to take up the controversy over pointed and blunt conductors in England, where George III had decided against Franklin. By December 1778 he had written his paper on the *Aurora Borealis* which seems to have been read at a meeting of the Academy of Sciences after Easter of the following year and was published in both French and English.[84] "The rapid progress true science now makes," he wrote to Priestley on 8 February 1780, "occasions my regretting sometimes that I was born so soon. It is impossible to imagine the height to which may be carried, in a thousand years, the power of man over matter. . . . O that moral science were in as fair a way of improvement, that men would cease to be wolves to one another, and that human beings would at length learn what they now improperly call humanity."[85] During his attack of gout in 1780 Franklin wrote on 13 November to Edward Nairne, a former friend in London, about hygrometers with observations on the humidity of the air in London, Philadelphia, and Passy. Possibly in this same painful leisure he set down for Ingenhousz, who had visited Passy that summer, answers to various questions on electricity.[86] On 1 May 1781 he replied to Turgot's questions about a new kind of smoke-consuming stove which Franklin had invented in London but had not yet had time to describe for the public.

In a letter to Court de Gebelin on 7 May Franklin touched on American linguistics: "As the Indians had no letters they had no orthography. The Delaware language being differently spelt from the Virginian may not always arise from a difference in the languages; for strangers who learn the language of an Indian nation, finding no orthography, are at liberty in writing the language to use such compositions of letters as they think will best produce the sounds of the words. I have observed that our Europeans of different nations who learn the same Indian language form each his own orthography according to the usual sounds given to the letters in his own language. Thus the same words of the Mohawk language written by an English, a French, and a German interpreter often differ very much in the spelling; and, without knowing the usual powers of the letters in the language of the interpreter, one cannot come at the pronunciation of the Indian words." Court de Gebelin thought some of the Indian words looked Phœnician. "If any Phœnicians arrived in America," Franklin commented, "I should rather think it was not by the accident of a storm but in the course of their long and adventurous voyages; and that they coasted from Denmark and Norway over to Greenland, and down southward by Newfoundland, Nova Scotia, etc., to New England; as the Danes themselves certainly did some ages before Columbus."[87]

On 20 July he sent Félix Vicq d'Azyr, physician to Marie Antoinette and secretary of the Royal Society of Medicine, some notes (read or heard) on the length of time infection might remain in dead bodies, pointing out that the data still had to be confirmed by exacter observation. To Francis Hopkinson in Philadelphia Franklin remarked on 13 September: "You have a new crop of prose writers. I see in your papers many of their fictitious names, but nobody tells me the real. You will oblige me by a little of your literary history."[88] On 2 October he began a long letter to Ingenhousz, in answer to several letters he had received, but was so much interrupted that he could not finish it till the following June. But on 6 April, being with Chaumont at his quarry in Passy, Franklin questioned the workmen about some living toads they claimed to have found shut up in solid stone. He supposed, if the workmen were correct in what they thought they had found, that the toads may have needed no food because they had not perspired and so had lost none of their substance.[89] Having been sent William Cowper's *Poems* from England, Franklin on 8 May wrote that, though "the relish for reading of poetry had long left me," he had been pleased with the book and had read the whole of it, some of it more than once.[90]

Absorbed by the peace negotiations, Franklin neglected all his sciences through the summer of 1782. But on 22 September, in constant pain with the stone, he was speculating on the structure of the earth, in a letter to the Abbé Soulavie. From what he had noticed of the geology of England, with coal mines under the sea at Whitehaven and oyster shells in the Derbyshire mountains, Franklin was sure there had been great changes in the surface of the island. "Such changes in the superficial parts of the globe seemed to me unlikely to happen if the earth were solid to the centre. I therefore imagined that the internal parts might be a fluid more dense, and of a greater specific gravity, than any of the solids we are acquainted with; which therefore might swim in or upon that fluid. Thus the surface of the globe would be a shell, capable of being broken and disordered by the violent movements of the fluid on which it rested. . . . You see," Franklin ended after some random guesses at geological history, "I have given a loose to imagination; but I approve much more your method of philosophizing, which proceeds upon actual observations, makes a collection of facts, and concludes no farther than those facts will warrant."[91]

That these were Franklin's true scientific principles had no effect on the general legend which made him out a mysterious wizard, taming lightning, stilling waves. Horace Walpole on 27 February 1778 contemptuously declared that even the British ministry shared the superstition. "The natural philosophers in power believe that Dr. Franklin has invented a machine of the size of a toothpick case and materials that would reduce St. Paul's to a handful of ashes." But Franklin's solid reputation as scientist and philosopher grew at a more natural rate. His *Political, Miscellaneous, and Philosophical Pieces* was published in London in 1779, by Benjamin Vaughan, who called Franklin on the title-page "Minister Plenipotentiary at the Court of Paris for the United States of America"—though the British government recognized the existence of no such independent nation. "The times appear not ripe enough," Vaughan said in his preface, "for the editor to give expression to the affection, gratitude, and veneration he bears to a writer he has so intimately studied. Nor is it wanting to the author; as history lies in wait for him, and the judgment of mankind balances already in his favour." In 1780 the materials of Dubourg's French edition (1773) and of Vaughan's were translated into German as Franklin's collected works (*Sämmtliche*

Werke) in three volumes at Dresden. There were Italian translations published at Padua as *Opere filosofiche* in 1782 and *Opere politiche* in 1783. Already a member of learned societies in Philadelphia, London, Edinburgh, Göttingen, Rotterdam, and Paris, Franklin was made a fellow of the American Academy of Arts and Letters at Boston in 1781; a foreign member of the Academy of Science, Letters, and Arts of Padua in 1782, and of that of Turin in 1783; and honorary fellow of the Royal Society of Edinburgh in 1783. Along with these graver events and honours went continual new editions of *The Way to Wealth*, called *La Science du Bonhomme Richard* in France after 1777, in Paris (five issues within a year), London, Dublin, Paisley, Canterbury, Edinburgh.

With his genius for combining and alternating work and play, Franklin set up a private press at Passy, apparently in 1777. His first intention may have been only to print the official forms and documents needed by the mission. The earliest dated piece of printing is an invitation to dinner for 5 July 1779 (in celebration of the Fourth, which had fallen that year on Sunday). Franklin's old trade was in his blood, and his press came to occupy a good deal of his time at Passy. He cast type in his own foundry, where during 1779–80 he employed, besides the foreman Hemery, two or three other men and a girl.[92] It is possible that he composed and printed off some of the bagatelles with his own skilful hands. The exact dates of printing are unknown, the number of copies, and the pleasant uses he put them to. Yet from a few facts and reasonable guesses something of their obscure history may still be traced.

On the day he spent with his friends at the Moulin Joli in the summer of 1778 he noticed many dead and living ephemeras on the island, and the company spoke of the brevity of their insect lives. Franklin remembered that years before (4 December 1735) he had published in the *Pennsylvania Gazette* an essay on *Human Vanity* by some writer, unknown to him, who had imagined an insect philosopher declaiming on the flight of time. As a souvenir of the day for Madame Brillon (*belle et brillante*) Franklin turned his hand to the same theme in French in *The Ephemera*, probably on 20 September. It was too charming to be kept a secret. "A friend of this lady," Franklin wrote on 17 June 1780 to William Carmichael in Madrid, "having obtained a copy of it under a promise not to give another, did not observe. that promise; so that many have been taken, and it is become as public as such a thing may well be that is not printed."[93] Even in Madrid Carmichael had heard of it. As Franklin then furnished him a manuscript copy, the printing must have come later.

Having written a bagatelle for Madame Brillon, Franklin had to do as much for Madame Helvétius and on 7 December he gave her, through the Abbé de La Roche, as is supposed, the story of his interview with Helvétius in Elysium. According to Morellet, this came to Auteuil one morning after an evening which Madame Helvétius and Franklin had spent together with much gay nonsense.[94] No manuscript of it is known to exist, nor any English version known to be Franklin's. But he printed *À Madame Helvétius* twice, the second time with some corrections, and continued his printed courtship in his petition of the flies which wished she would come and live in his house. His account of the breakfast he missed, printed as *M. F. à Madame La Fr—té*, was as much for Madame Helvétius as for the lady to whom it was addressed.

To be fair to his two favourites he returned to Madame Brillon with *The Whistle*, dated 16 November 1779, written in English, written also in French and carefully corrected, printed in English and French versions. It had been suggested by their reflections on paradise and on getting the most out of mortal life. But this was more than a paragraph in a letter. It was a distinct small work of art and called for type. The next October, shut up at home with the gout, Franklin wrote the dialogue (in French) between him and the disease, with agreeable compliments to both Madame Brillon and Madame Helvétius. Madame Brillon wrote for him, or had perhaps already written, a rhymed fable *Le Sage et la Goutte* in which she laid his malady not only to his indolence and greediness but also to his amorous disposition. In the letter in which he insisted that the ladies of Passy could probably cure him with Christian charity if they would, he apologized to her for printing her fable against, it proved, her wishes. He had only hoped that if he gave her the handsome edition of it which it deserved she might let him keep the manuscript. "I have been at fault, I confess, but as you have had the goodness to forgive it I shall not repeat it till some other occasion."[95] During this same illness he wrote in

English *The Handsome and Deformed Leg*.[96] It must have soon been printed (in French as *La belle et la mauvaise jambe*), for by the following May Georgiana Shipley had received it and the dialogue with the Gout.

Not all of Franklin's bagatelles were gallantries for the ladies of his circle. So fond of chess that he once at Passy played from six in the evening till sunrise, he wrote his *Morals of Chess*[97] "with a view to correct (among a few young friends) some little improprieties in the practice of it." Dubourg had seen the manuscript by 28 June 1779. If Franklin printed it at Passy, no copy is known. Published, apparently for the first time, in the *Columbian Magazine* for December 1786, the *Morals* has since then appeared in many languages, a minor classic of the game. For friends whose taste ran to the broadest humour Franklin wrote his *Letter to the Academy at Brussels*, which in 1782 he asked William Carmichael not to print and of which he sent a manuscript copy to Richard Price on 16 September 1783. But the *Essay on Perfumes*, as it is sometimes called, was eventually printed in English at Passy, with the French *Conte* of Montrésor who, like countless heroes of countless stories since, went to heaven (or dreamed it) and talked with St. Peter at the gate. At Passy Franklin printed his *Parable against Persecution* in French. And there he may have printed, though no copies are known, his modernized version of *The Lord's Prayer* and his delightful parodies, *The Levee* and *Proposed New Version of the Bible*.[98] Franklin, making the Lord and Satan talk like a modern king and one of his ministers, ironically ridiculed the king and the minister by setting them in contrast with a god and a devil.

Out of respect for the memory of an old friend, now dead, Franklin printed Dubourg's *Petit Code de la raison humaine*, apparently in 1782. He printed something which Polly Hewson had translated (possibly from Dubourg) but which seems to have been wholly lost.[99] In 1779 Pierre-André Gargaz, near the end of twenty years as a galley-slave, wrote to Franklin sending him a project for universal and perpetual peace. After his release in 1781 Gargaz walked all the way from Provence to Paris to consult the great men there about his scheme. Rustic and shabby, he could get no access to men in office, and came to Passy. Franklin read his manuscript and thought it should be printed. Gargaz had no money. Franklin printed the project as *Conciliateur de toutes les nations de l'Europe* in 1782 and gave Gargaz as many copies as he wanted to take away.[100] That same year, during the negotiations for peace, Franklin produced the first of three Passy titles which belong to his later history: *Supplement to the Boston Independent Chronicle, Information to Those Who Would Remove to America*, and *Remarks concerning the Savages of North America*.

The Passy imprints, as Franklin wrote and issued them in French and English, were hardly known until the twentieth century, and still wait for the edition they deserve. The issues of no other private press are more desired by collectors or would bring higher prices if they could be found. Most of the surviving copies are unique. But these "little scribblings" even in the casual translations from the French in which some of them have usually been read, are not mere rarities for bibliographers. They are the happy records of a wise and witty man in the midst of overwhelming work. The resolute *Ça ira* which Franklin said again and again during the American Revolution and which is said to have given the French Revolution its first song,[101] was no more characteristic of the philosopher than his *Vive la bagatelle*.

Peacemaker

VERGENNES, impresario of the general war, was in a
difficult position between his two allies. Spain in violation of
her secret treaty with France during 1780 carried on discussions
with England for a separate peace, secretly until the presence of
the British agents in Madrid compelled Floridablanca, the Spanish
minister, to admit it to Vergennes. The recovery of Gibraltar was
still the chief European aim of Spain, still of no interest to
America. Holding West Florida and Louisiana and claiming territory east of the Mississippi, Spain was sharply at odds with the
United States over the boundaries which Congress had come to
demand: the Mississippi on the west and the line of 31° north
latitude on the south. The United States insisted upon independence, while Spain, fearing aggression in America from an independent power, preferred some kind of long unsettled truce between Great Britain and her colonies. Vergennes had chosen to
appear fairly neutral in these controversies, satisfying neither Spain
nor America. But through the French minister at Philadelphia
Vergennes had during 1779 done what he could to persuade Congress to consider the boundaries Spain proposed and to put the
American peace commission under French control. Congress for
its commissioner had selected John Adams, thought less susceptible
than Franklin to French influence, and had instructed him in no
case to yield on the point of either independence or boundaries.

When Vergennes in June 1780 learned of the Spanish negotiations with England, which came to nothing, he was alarmed. That
year the British fleet under Rodney won a victory over the Spanish
and temporarily relieved the garrison at Gibraltar, enduring a
stubborn siege, and the British armies in America were ominously
successful. At a time when it was by no means certain that America

could maintain the struggle, Adams in Paris was demanding not only American independence, to which France was pledged, but also boundaries which the Franco-American treaty of alliance had not set forth. Moreover, Adams wanted to notify the British government at once of his peace powers, and even to go to London on the chance that the ministry might consider stopping the war. In this Vergennes saw separate negotiations as inconvenient to him as those between Spain and England. His objections to Adams's manner were no stronger than his disapproval of Adams's plans. Adams, leaving for Holland where he found that the Dutch too were under French influence, formed once for all his passionate conviction that France for the sake of her own interests was ready to neglect those of America. And there can be no doubt that Vergennes, in view of the military losses and dangerous costs of the war, was already thinking of what terms might be made, if necessary, to save France from the possible consequences of a British triumph.

In February 1781 he wrote out a confidential statement of his policy.[1] France would agree to a truce between Great Britain and the colonies, with each combatant in possession of the territory it then held. That is, the British would continue to hold New York and Long Island, much of Georgia and the Carolinas, and fortified posts in Maine, on Lake Champlain, and throughout the Great Lakes country. Since France could not propose any such arrangement and uphold its treaty obligations to the United States, Vergennes left the proposal to be made by some neutral mediator. Russia and Austria jointly offered themselves in mediation. Vergennes in March wrote to the French minister in Philadelphia, through him suggesting that Congress make its peace terms moderate and instruct Adams to let Vergennes take charge of the whole negotiation—as he would in fact do if there should be an emergency with no time to hear from Congress. Russia and Austria, in May inviting the belligerents to meet with the mediators at Vienna, did not invite the United States. France as ally would represent America. Great Britain was to make its own peace with the colonies, subject to confirmation by the other powers. Vergennes called Adams, now American minister to Holland though not yet recognized there, to Paris in July. Adams, who saw that the scheme was essentially for European ends, refused to have anything to do with it unless he were admitted to the Vienna congress as a member, which would mean that the other members recognized the independence of the United States. Great Britain rejected the mediation as a foreign interference in its domestic concerns. George III here did a valuable service to America, for the next instructions from Congress, inspired by Vergennes, would have hampered Adams, and the powers at Vienna might have done what they liked with America's demands, even for independence.

It does not appear that Franklin, busy with obtaining money and supplies for the year's campaign and leaving the peace negotiations to Adams, was at all disturbed by Adams's outraged belief that Vergennes would not be faithful to the letter of the Franco-American alliance if it were to France's obvious disadvantage. Franklin said he had perfect confidence in "the sincerity of this upright and able minister, who never promised me anything which he did not punctually perform";[2] and he was pleased with the new Congressional instructions. With the instructions came word that Franklin, John Jay, Henry Laurens of South Carolina, and Jefferson had been appointed to serve on the peace commission with Adams. Adams had to return to his post in Holland. Jay was minister to Spain, unrecognized but in Madrid. Laurens, who had been captured at sea in 1780 on his way to Holland, was a prisoner in the Tower of London. Jefferson did not go to France for three years. After the surrender of Cornwallis and the fall of the North ministry the preliminary peace discussions with England were for three months in the hands of Franklin alone.

"Great affairs," he said in his *Journal of the Negotiations for Peace with Great Britain*[3] begun on 9 May 1782, "sometimes take their rise from small circumstances. My good friend and neighbour, Madame Brillon, being at Nice all last winter for her health, with her very amiable family, wrote me that she had met with some English gentry there whose acquaintance proved agreeable; among them she named Lord Cholmondeley, who she said had promised to call in his return to England and drink tea with us at Passy. He left Nice sooner than she supposed, and came to Paris long before her." Cholmondeley called on 22 March. "He told me that he knew Lord Shelburne had a great regard for me, that he was sure his lordship would be pleased to hear from me, and that if I would write a line he should have a pleasure in carrying it." Franklin, who did not yet know of North's resignation two days before, wrote to Shelburne congratulating him on the new temper in England and the prospect of peace. He told Shelburne that the gooseberry bushes he had sent Madame Helvétius had arrived in five days, in excellent order.

"Soon after this we heard from England that a total change had taken place in the ministry and that Lord Shelburne had come in as secretary of state. But I thought no more of my letter till an old friend and near neighbour of mine many years in London [Caleb Whitefoord] appeared in Passy and introduced a Mr. Oswald, who, he said, had a great desire to see me; and Mr. Oswald, after some little conversation, gave me . . . letters from Lord Shelburne and Mr. Laurens." Shelburne explained that Richard Oswald was "a pacifical man and conversant in these negotiations. . . . This has made me prefer him to any of our speculative friends or to any person of higher rank. He is fully apprised of my mind. . . . I have few or no secrets." Laurens wrote that Franklin was believed in England to be a very cunning man. "I have remarked to Mr. Oswald: 'Dr. Franklin knows very well how to manage a cunning man; but when the Doctor converses or treats with a man of candour there is no man more candid than himself.' "[4]

Franklin could only guess at the confusion in London. The king, almost ready to abdicate rather than yield to rebels, would not offer the government to Fox or any member of the opposition who had favoured independence, and offered it to Shelburne, who still hoped the colonies might be somehow joined in a federal union with Great Britain, though with separate sovereign parliaments. Shelburne had no party strong enough to warrant his accepting the responsibility. Rockingham, under whom the Stamp Act had been repealed, became titular first minister, but the king insisted on dealing with Rockingham through Shelburne. Shelburne was secretary of state for colonial affairs, Fox for foreign affairs. This meant that the treaty with the unrecognized United States would come under Shelburne's department, that with France, Spain, and Holland under Fox's. The two secretaries became jealous and bitter rivals. But it was Shelburne who took up the negotiations with Franklin as soon as Franklin's friendly note reached him.

Oswald was chosen as negotiator because he had lived in America and had relatives and property there, was an old retired merchant (army supplies and slaves) turned philosophical, would be willing to carry out Shelburne's instructions without question, and might prove congenial to Franklin. The Rockingham ministry was anxious about Franklin's wizard cunning and expected to have to make up to him for the injuries and insults he had suffered from the North ministry in 1774–75. Franklin had applied through Burke for the exchange of Henry Laurens for Burgoyne, and Laurens had been released on heavy bail, furnished in part by Oswald. Now Oswald and Laurens crossed the Channel together to Ostend, Laurens to confer with Adams at Haarlem, Oswald with Franklin at Passy.

At the first meeting on 15 April Franklin was able to find out from Oswald only that the new ministry sincerely wished for peace and thought France and America had gained their object, American independence. If that was agreed to, there was no other point in dispute. But if France "should insist upon terms too humiliating to England, they could still continue the war, having yet great strength and many resources left." Franklin did not need to be told that this was a hint to America to be satisfied with independence and not to endanger or postpone it by supporting the special demands of France. He said that America and France would act only in concert and that he could do nothing of importance without his fellow-commissioners. Two days later he took Oswald to call on Vergennes. The minister explained that France was under engagements to her allies and could treat for nothing less than a general peace. Oswald, an informal negotiator without plenipotentiary powers, wished he might take specific demands to Shelburne. Vergennes suggested that England, having no allies to consult, was in a position to know at once what it wanted and might more naturally state its demands first.

Oswald, who was a trader too, could see that this suggestion had been made in the hope the British government would commit itself. On the way back from Versailles he undertook a little trading of his own. If France demanded too much, England would again be unanimous for the war and would continue it. "He said there was no want of money in the nation; that the chief difficulty lay in finding out new taxes to raise it." England could stop payment of interest on the public funds and apply that money to the support of the war. Franklin, at least as good a trader as either Vergennes or Oswald, "made no reply to this; for I did not desire to discourage their stopping payment, which I considered as cutting the throat of their public credit and a means of adding fresh exasperation against them with the neighbouring nations. Such menaces were besides an encouragement with me, remembering the adage that they who threaten are afraid."

Oswald set out the next day for London to report to Shelburne, with a letter from Franklin in which he said that he was fully empowered, with the other American commissioners, to treat for a general peace and that he hoped Oswald might bring similar powers back to Paris. Franklin showed Oswald the letter to Shelburne, to be sure it was not in conflict with any of Oswald's impressions. "On his saying that he was obliged to me for the good opinion I had expressed of him to Lord Shelburne in my letter, and assuring me that he had entertained the same of me, I observed that I perceived Lord S. placed great confidence in him; and as we had happily the same in each other we might possibly by a free communication of sentiments, and a previous settling of our own minds on some of the important points, be the means of great good by impressing our sentiments on the minds of those with whom they might have influence and where their being received might be of importance." Oswald, who had fallen under Franklin's spell, was pleased at being made a confidant.

Franklin was not talking at random, but had a specific point in view. Oswald in an earlier conversation had said he thought it had been politic of France to cede Canada to England at the peace of 1763, because "it had weakened the ties between England and her colonies"—in the controversy over the Quebec Act. Now Franklin, desiring to sound out the British ministry on the subject of Canada and Nova Scotia, discreetly made the bold proposal that they be ceded by England to the United States. He began by talking of the reparations England owed for having been the aggressor in the war and for having used Indians in "scalping and burning parties." The use of Indian auxiliaries on the unprotected frontier had been strongly opposed, Franklin knew, by the liberal men who had at last come into office. Perhaps they might feel with him that reparation was due. Nothing, he told Oswald, would do more to bring about a reconcilement than some voluntary offer of England to make amends. "I then touched upon the affair of Canada. . . . I spoke of the occasions of future quarrel that might be produced by her [England's] continuing to hold it; hinting at the same time . . . that such a situation, to us so dangerous, would necessarily oblige us to cultivate and strengthen our union with France."

While Franklin spoke he now and then looked at a paper he had brought with him, being no man to improvise on a complex topic. Oswald asked to see the paper. "After some little delay I allowed him to read it." What Oswald read was substantially what he had heard. "He then told me that nothing in his judgment could be clearer, more satisfactory and convincing, than the reasonings in that paper; that he would do his utmost to impress Lord Shelburne with them; that as his memory might not do them justice, and it would be impossible for him to express them so well or state them so clearly as I had written them, he begged I would let him take the paper with him, assuring me he would return it safely into my hands. I at length complied with this request also. We parted exceeding good friends."[5] (No doubt Franklin remembered his land in Nova Scotia, which would be more surely his if Nova Scotia became a part of the United States. It is impossible to tell how much this minor economic motive affected him.)

The memorandum had suggested that if Canada were given up, enough of its vacant land might be sold "to pay for the houses burnt by the British troops and their Indians; and also to indemnify the royalists for the confiscation of their estates." But after Oswald's departure Franklin was dissatisfied with himself for "hinting a reparation to the Tories" and "a little ashamed of my weakness in permitting the paper to go out of my hands." Since this hint was on its way to Shelburne and Franklin could not recall it, he quickly acted to offset his error—if it should prove to be that— by carrying America's grievance to the public. Oswald left on the 18th. On the 22nd Franklin sent to Adams a copy of the Passy *Supplement to the Boston Independent Chronicle*.[6] It was as skilful a hoax as Franklin ever put his hand to, and was deliberate propaganda. To any casual eye it would seem to be an actual supplement to the actual *Independent Chronicle* of Boston, even to mentioning the editor's name, which was Willis; being called No. 705, the number of a real issue for March which might just have reached Europe; and containing circumstantial advertisements. ("Strayed or stolen from the subscriber, living at Salem, a bay horse, about seven years old, a stocky well set horse, marked I. C. on his off thigh, trots all. Whoever shall take up said horse and return him to the owner, shall be handsomely rewarded. Henry White.")[7]

The feature of the *Supplement*, printed in Franklin's first issue on only one side of a broadsheet, was part of a letter from Captain Gerrish of the New England militia, who had, he said, intercepted eight large packages of American scalps sent by the Seneca Indians as a present to the governor of Canada. There were 43 scalps of Congress soldiers, 98 of farmers killed in their houses, 97 of farmers killed in their fields, 102 of farmers killed in different places and in different ways: "Most of the farmers appear by the hair to have been young or middle-aged men; there being but 67 very grey heads among them; which makes the service more essential." There were 88 scalps of women (their hair long and braided in the Indian fashion to show they were mothers), 193 of boys, 211 of girls "big and little," and 122 of mixed varieties, among them 29 of infants labelled to show that "they were ripped out of their mothers' bellies." With the scalps was a formal speech by a Seneca chief, taken down in writing by a British trader. "We wish you," the chief said to the governor, "to send these scalps over the water to the great king, that he may regard them and be refreshed; and that he may see our faithfulness in destroying his enemies and be convinced that his presents have not been made to ungrateful people." A news item said that the scalps had been brought to Boston. "Thousands of people are flocking to see them this morning, and all mouths are full of execrations. . . . It is . . . proposed to make them up in decent little packets, seal, and direct them: one to the king, containing a sample of every sort for his museum; one to the queen, with some of women and little children; the rest to be distributed among both Houses of Parliament, a double quantity to the bishops."

Franklin admitted to Adams that the form of his accusation might be untrustworthy (as it was), not the substance; "for I believe the number of people actually scalped in this murdering war by the Indians to exceed what is mentioned in invoice." He knew that the British and the loyalists had used savage allies who had done savage deeds on the frontier. His hoax was gruesome propaganda, to turn public opinion against the late British ministry and to make it more difficult for the present one to deny American claims. Copies of the *Supplement* were sent to Dumas in Holland, to be broadcast from that centre of European news. By 1 October Horace Walpole had read the hoax in an English newspaper and was sure it was too good not to be by Franklin. The first issue at Passy, probably not circulated, was followed by a second printed on both sides of the paper and containing a long letter as from John Paul Jones to Sir Joseph Yorke, British ambassador to the Netherlands, abusing George III with all Franklin's polemic energy.

II

Before Oswald's return Franklin had time to write to Adams and Laurens in Holland about the conference with Oswald, and to hear from Adams that he and Laurens agreed upon the importance of Canada and Nova Scotia to the United States. But Franklin, who kept Vergennes scrupulously informed about the other details of the negotiations, did not tell him about the mention of Canada to Oswald, much less about the memorandum which Oswald had carried to Shelburne. Vergennes would certainly not have approved of demands made separately and privately by the United States in advance of the general negotiations. Franklin, keeping the matter of Canada from Vergennes, had made a first move to disassociate the interests of America from those of Europe. What was above all to be desired between England and America, he thought, was a durable peace. The cession of Canada might bring that by removing the most likely causes of resentment in the present and of conflict in the future. "The settlers on the frontiers of the American provinces are generally the most disorderly of the people," he said in his memorandum—foreseeing the main causes of the second war with England if not the later peaceful management of the Canadian boundary line.

Oswald returned on 4 May with a letter from Shelburne which said little except that England desired peace, that Laurens had been given his full liberty, and that Fox was sending over another agent to treat with Vergennes for peace with France. The British ministry, Oswald assured Franklin, trusted him to be honest and open and were sure he still had some of his "ancient affection and regard for Old England." They trusted him with nothing else but the chance which Oswald gave him to look at an extract from the minutes of a cabinet council, agreeing to treat for a general peace at Paris and to allow the independence of America, provided "England be put into the same situation that she was left in by the peace of 1763." Shelburne had actually told Oswald that there could be no reparations to America and that the loyalists must be compensated. Independence was to be granted only on various conditions to be met by the Americans, and only if the United States were independent also of France.[8] Oswald seems to have been uncommunicative on these points, merely suggesting that Franklin's Canada scheme be put off till "towards the end of the treaty." The second agent, Oswald said, was Thomas Grenville, who would arrive in a few days. Vergennes, to whom Franklin again took Oswald, was able to get nothing more out of him. They waited for Grenville, who on the 8th brought Franklin a highly complimentary letter from Fox. That Grenville was the son of George Grenville would not, Fox was confident, be held against the young man by the magnanimous philosopher. On inquiry Franklin found that Grenville had come first to him and expected through him to meet Vergennes. Franklin arranged a meeting for the next day.

All that Grenville had to say, it turned out, was that if England gave America her independence France would be expected to return the British islands she had taken during the war, receiving back the French islands she had lost. "The minister seemed to smile at the proposed exchange and remarked that the offer of giving independence to America amounted to little. 'America,' says he, 'does not ask it of you. There is Mr. Franklin. He will answer you as to that point.' 'To be sure,' I said, 'we do not consider ourselves as under any necessity of bargaining for a thing that is our own.' " Grenville thought that France, having obtained her original object in American independence, should be content with that. Vergennes reminded him that in the last war England's original object had been some uninhabited tracts on the Ohio and on the frontiers of Nova Scotia, but that she had in the end taken Canada, Florida, Grenada and other West India islands, and the greatest part of the northern fisheries, besides her conquests in Africa and the East Indies. Grenville said the war had been provoked by France, encouraging the Americans to revolt. Vergennes warmly insisted that independence had been declared long before France had given the least encouragement. " 'There sits,' says he, 'Mr. Franklin, who knows the fact and can contradict me if I do not speak the truth.' " Franklin, well as he must have remembered the secret emissary who came to Philadelphia six months before the Declaration with a hint from Vergennes that the colonies must first declare their independence if France was to help them, did not contradict the minister. Vergennes said he would notify Spain and Holland and wait for their answers. He asked Grenville to come to see him again on the 10th. Franklin was not present at this second meeting.[9]

On Saturday 11 May Franklin had Oswald and Grenville to breakfast in Passy to meet Lafayette. "The gentlemen . . . had a good deal of conversation at and after breakfast, stayed till after one o'clock, and parted much pleased with each other." But the English agents were still extremely cautious in what they said to Franklin about the peace. In three days Oswald, without giving Franklin any reason, was off for London again. Grenville, calling at Passy, returned to his argument that if France should insist on more for itself than the concession of independence to America, then America would not be bound to support her. It seemed to Grenville, as he reported to Fox, that Franklin did not care who held Gibraltar and that he thought a treaty between England and the United States, friends before the Revolution, would not be the same thing as a treaty between such habitual enemies as England and France. But Franklin, though earnestly and unaffectedly desirous of peace, was still in favour of strict adherence to the treaties America had made with her allies.[10] He looked upon the British order for the general and absolute release of American prisoners (the news reached Franklin on 13 May) as a happy step toward reconciliation.

From these mixed manœuvres of the British government Franklin could and did guess the main outlines of the policy which both Shelburne and Fox were following. The ministry had no doubt that the four enemy allies would be harder to deal with together than separately. Although even Shelburne could now have small hope of reconciliation with the revolted provinces, he could see that he might offer independence to the Americans in such a way as to make them feel that their great aim had been achieved and their treaty with France fulfilled. Nor did the ministry limit itself to the American commissioners in Europe. Even before Oswald came to Paris plans were made to inform Congress and the American people, through Sir Guy Carleton who had been sent to prepare for the withdrawal of the British forces, that the British government had begun negotiations for peace in France and was ready to acknowledge independence at the outset. Congress refused to have any dealings with Carleton and left everything to its commissioners.

Adams, deeply involved in raising a loan in Holland, could not then come to Paris, as Franklin urged him to do on 22 April. To Jay in Spain Franklin wrote on the same day "to press his coming hither; and, being a little out of humour with that court, I said: 'They have taken four years to consider whether they should treat with us. Give them forty and let us mind our own business.' And I sent the letter under cover to a person at Madrid who I hoped would open and read it."[11] Though Jay left Madrid as soon as he could, he did not reach Paris till 23 June. Laurens on the plea of ill-health put off taking part. Franklin went capably on with the negotiations. On 26 May Grenville called to report that a courier had brought him "full powers in form to treat for a peace with France and her allies. . . . He lent me a London gazette, containing Admiral Rodney's full account of his victory over M. de Grasse [12 April], and the accounts of other successes in the East Indies;

assuring me, however, that these events made not the least change in the sincere desires of his court to treat for peace."

But the victory had put England in a stronger position. Vergennes found that the powers received by Grenville from London applied only to France and did not mention her allies. Franklin conferred with Vergennes. " 'They want,' said he, 'to treat with us for you. But this king [of France] will not agree to. He thinks it not consistent with the dignity of your state. You will treat for yourselves; and every one of the powers at war with England will make its own treaty. All that is necessary to be observed for our common security is that the treaties go on hand in hand and are signed all on the same day.' "[12] By this arrangement Vergennes deftly gave the English what they had asked for, without in fact conceding anything. Whatever separate treaties might be in progress, he would remain the impresario of the peace.

("Prince Bariatinski, the Russian ambassador," Franklin here entered in his *Journal*, "was particularly civil to me this day at Court. . . . The Comte du Nord came to M. Vergennes while we were drinking coffee after dinner. He appears lively and active, with a sensible, spirited countenance. There was an opera at night for his entertainment. The house, being richly finished with abundance of carving and gilding, well illuminated with wax tapers, and the company all superbly dressed, many of the men in cloth of tissue and the ladies sparkling with diamonds, formed altogether the most splendid spectacle my eyes ever beheld.")

Grenville on 1 June, when Franklin talked with him, could explain his insufficient powers from London only as some mistake which he said he had more reason to complain of than Vergennes. "That to convince me of the sincerity of his court respecting us," Grenville palavered, "he would acquaint me with one of his instructions, though perhaps the doing it now was premature and therefore a little inconsistent with the character of a politician, but he had that confidence in me that he should not hesitate to inform me (though he wished that at present it should go no further): he was instructed to acknowledge the independence of America previous to the commencement of the treaty." Then Grenville proceeded to praises of Franklin which must have sounded oddly like those he had heard from Howe and Hyde in London seven years before: "the firm and general belief in England that no man was so capable as myself of proposing the proper means of bringing about such a reconciliation; adding that if the old ministers had formerly been too little attentive to my counsels the present were differently disposed, and he hoped that in treating with them I would totally forget their predecessors."[13]

Franklin was not cajoled by these flatteries or affected by Grenville's arguments in favour of a separate peace. Nothing could be done till England had empowered her agents to go beyond discursive preliminaries to authentic treaty-making. It was likely, Franklin wrote to Adams the next day, that George III was reluctant to mention the United States as one of France's allies, since this would "itself be a kind of acknowledgment of our independence." The day after that Oswald came, with more flatteries. "He . . . repeatedly mentioned the great esteem the ministers had for me; that they, with all the considerate people of England, looked to and depended on me for the means of extricating the nation from its present desperate situation; that perhaps no single man had ever in his hands an opportunity of doing so much good as I had at this present; with much more to that purpose. . . . Mr. Oswald said he had told them [the ministers] . . . that nothing was to be expected of me but consistence, nothing unsuitable to my character or inconsistent with my duty to my country. I did not ask him the particular occasion of his saying this, but thought it looked a little as if something inconsistent with my duty had been talked of or proposed."

Oswald this time brought and gave to Franklin a memorandum from Shelburne with specific points in it. Countering the demands for reparation to Americans whose houses had been burned by the British, Shelburne said that one of the first points to be considered must be compensation to the loyalists. Franklin repeated what he had said before to Oswald: that the property of the loyalists had been confiscated by the various states and that Congress could give its commissioners no power to treat concerning them. "That if there were justice in compensating them, it must be due from England rather than America; but in my opinion England was not under any very great obligations to them, since it was by their misrepresentations and bad counsels she had been drawn into this miserable war. And that if an account was brought against us for their losses we should more than balance it by an account of the ravages they had committed all along the coasts of America." Shelburne said further in his memorandum that he left it to Franklin and Oswald to settle between them who should serve on the British commission for the peace. This Oswald in turn left to Franklin, who had no objection to Grenville but preferred Oswald. "He seems to have nothing at heart but the good of mankind and putting a stop to mischief; the other, a young statesman, may be supposed to have naturally a little ambition of recommending himself as an able negotiator." So Franklin commented later in his *Journal*. At the conference he said that he would write to Shelburne, recommending that Oswald be given a special commission to treat with America, but would wait till they heard from London about the commission's powers to treat.[14]

On 15 June Grenville came to Passy and said he had received a new document giving him power to treat with France or "with any other prince or state whom it might concern." Franklin pointed out that the British had "always hitherto affected to consider us only as rebellious subjects," and that the terms "any other prince or state" need not include "a people whom they did not allow to be a state." Grenville was certain that his powers were now sufficient. Moreover, he was authorized to offer what he had prematurely mentioned to Franklin on the 1st: the independence of America without any condition. This declared, England would then separately propose a return to the status of 1763 as between her and France. "He would have entered into conversation on the subject of reconciliation," Franklin noted in the *Journal*, "but I chose still to waive it till I should find the negotiation more certainly commenced." There had been too much loose talk already. He showed Grenville a London newspaper which misrepresented their first conversation. Grenville "seemed to treat the newspaper lightly, as of no consequence." But the philosopher observed "that before he had finished the reading of the article he turned to the beginning of the paper to see the date; which made me suspect that he doubted whether it might not have taken its rise from some of his letters."[15]

The negotiations could not legally begin till Parliament had passed an act enabling the king to treat with the lost colonies. Waiting for this, Franklin now and then had inconclusive discussions with Oswald and Grenville, who seemed to be rival agents as Shelburne and Fox were rival ministers. Grenville was already empowered to treat with France and her allies. Nobody had the power to treat specially with America. If Franklin must take care what he said, he must also take care whom he said it to. To his relief Jay arrived on the 23rd, left his family in apartments in Paris engaged for them by Temple Franklin, and went that afternoon to Passy. For several days he was continually with Franklin, learning the state of the negotiations, calling with him on Vergennes and on the Spanish ambassador. But then Jay caught the influenza which was epidemic in Paris and through July could have little hand in the complicated business. On 1 July Rockingham died. Shelburne succeeded him, Fox resigned, and Grenville was replaced at Paris by Alleyne Fitzherbert. There were now better prospects for a uniform policy towards the peace. But Franklin on the 1st suddenly gave up his *Journal*, and his ample and graphic record ended with these preliminary skirmishes.

III

Talking informally with Oswald on the 9th, Franklin produced a memorandum of what he thought the essential points of peace. Four of them he called necessary: (1) Full and complete independence and the withdrawal from the United States of all the British forces; (2) A settlement of the boundaries between the independent states and the loyal colonies; (3) The confinement of the boundaries of Canada to at least what they had been before the Quebec Act of 1774 extended them below the Great Lakes to the Ohio; (4) Freedom for Americans to fish on the Newfoundland banks, for fish as well as whale. Four more points he called advisable, and were what Franklin, as a friend to England, did advise: (1) Reparation to Americans for damage done them by the British burning of their towns; (2) Some sort of acknowledgment by Parliament of its error "in distressing those countries so much" in the conduct of the war ("A few words of that kind, the Doctor said, would do more good than people would imagine"); (3) Each country to give the same privileges to the ships and trading of the other as to its own; (4) The cession of the whole of Canada.

Since Franklin would not allow Oswald to take or copy this memorandum its terms can be known only from the words in which Oswald transmitted them to Shelburne.[16] But the terms were Franklin's in substance, and they outlined all the basic provisions of the final treaty except the one with regard to drying fish on shore. Franklin in his three months without Jay or Adams had established a tolerably cordial if cautious understanding with Shelburne, and had been allowed to choose the easy and amiable Oswald to go back and forth between them. He had maintained friendly relations with Vergennes, from whom he might soon have to ask, as minister to France, for another loan to Congress. And yet at the same time he had gone decidedly further in separate negotiations with England than would have suited Vergennes if he had known about Franklin's terms through Oswald to Shelburne. If Vergennes had secrets from Franklin, as he had, Franklin had secrets from Vergennes.

The coming of Jay brought a new tone, if not altogether a new element, into the negotiations. During his two years in Spain he had made no headway in his proposal for an alliance and a loan. He had learned that Spain was chilly towards the idea of American independence and was opposed to the American demand for the Mississippi as a western boundary. It seemed to Jay, who did not know how many difficulties France was having on her own account with Spain, that France had done nothing to win Spanish sympathy for America. In Paris it seemed clearer and clearer to him that France and Spain were united in their own interests and that the American commissioners must defend America against European plots. Early in August, when he had recovered from his illness, word came from Shelburne to Franklin that England was now ready to make an unequivocal acknowledgment of American independence. Shelburne hoped that Franklin's four advisable points might be dropped and the four necessary ones be the basis of discussion for a treaty to be carried out as soon as possible. But when Oswald on the 7th called on Jay, whom he now met for the first time, he found that Jay was not satisfied with Oswald's new commission to treat with commissioners named by "the said colonies or plantations." Those former colonies, Jay insisted, had become the United States of America. They had declared themselves independent and must be so considered by the British government before a treaty could begin. If the American commissioners were to treat with Oswald, commissioned as he was, they would be accepting a colonial status and bargaining for independence. This would mean that they might have to yield on other points in order to buy something they already owned. Adams from Holland agreed with Jay by letter.

Franklin had all along been firm against admitting that independence was subject to treaty, but he was not a lawyer and not much disposed to argue over formal expressions. On 19 August, when he and Jay called on Vergennes, Jay still objected to the terms "colonies or plantations." Vergennes thought they did not signify. The king of France was willing to treat with the king of England, who traditionally called himself king of France. The general treaty would be the cause of which independence was the effect. The American commissioners could not reasonably expect the effect before the cause. If they exchanged powers with Oswald, and Oswald's government accepted their powers, which were explicitly from the United States, that would be a tacit British admission of American independence. Vergennes asked Franklin what he thought. "The Doctor said he believed the commission would do." After the conference Jay was sure that Vergennes did not want independence acknowledged so long as the United States might be of use to France in supporting her claims and those of Spain. "The Doctor imputed this conduct to the moderation of the minister, and to his desire of removing every obstacle to speedy negotiations for peace. He observed that this Court had hitherto treated us very fairly and that suspicions to their disadvantage should not be unduly entertained. He also mentioned our instructions as further reasons for our acquiescence in the advice and opinion of the minister."[17] Jay began to feel sure that the commissioners must, in the interests of America, follow their own judgment rather than their instructions.[18]

Jay, vehement for the independent rights of America, ironically seemed to Oswald more attached to the French alliance than Franklin, who urged the need of acting in concert with Vergennes. Oswald had understood from their earlier conversations that Franklin, once assured of independence, would think America under little further obligation to France. But Jay, demanding independence in advance of the treaty, talked of how much America owed to France, even to Spain and Holland. He meant it as a threat of what America might help its allies to win if independence were not granted outright. Oswald took it to mean that America, certain of independence whatever England did, would try to force on England a peace satisfactory to all the allies. In particular Oswald was struck by both Jay's and Franklin's talk about a lasting peace. Could it be, Oswald asked himself, that the Americans had in mind to guarantee a future peace in Europe by promising to side with the allies against England in any later trespass? Troubled, he went to call on Franklin at Passy on the morning of Sunday 11 August.

Franklin seemed as friendly and good-natured as ever. Oswald, afraid of what he might hear, asked how the peace could be made lasting. "The Doctor replied that the method was very plain and easy: which was to settle the terms in the first projection on an equal, just, and reasonable footing." He was reminded of a story from Roman history, "in the early time of the republic; when, being at war with the state of Tarentum, and the Tarentines having the worst of it, they sent to the Senate to ask for peace. The ambassador being called in, the Senate told him they agreed to give them peace, and then asked how long he thought it would last; to which he answered: 'That would be according to their conditions; if they were reasonable, the peace would be lasting; if not, it would be short.' "[19] Oswald was much relieved to find that Franklin so philosophically agreed with him as to what would make a peace endure. On the 15th Oswald showed part of his instructions to Jay. Convinced by this that England was ready to acknowledge American independence in the first article of the treaty, Jay accepted Oswald's assurance that he would recommend to England the form of recognition which the Americans desired.

Oswald reported to Shelburne. The British cabinet on 29 August agreed in principle to an absolute and irrecoverable acknowledgment of independence in advance of the treaty, if this could not be avoided, and if the Americans would consent to treat on the basis of Franklin's four necessary points. But Oswald was instructed not to let Franklin and Jay know of this without a further effort to persuade them to accept independence as an article of the treaty itself. Franklin was incapacitated by the stone before Oswald's courier reached Paris, and through September and October the burden of the treaty fell chiefly on Jay, who was too much troubled over Spain and France to press as hard on England as he might have done to the advantage of America. Neither Jay nor Franklin ever knew that the British cabinet had resolved to meet their full demands.

At the conference with Vergennes on 10 August Jay had discovered that, while Vergennes himself was reserved on the matter of the western boundary of the United States, his secretary Gérard de Rayneval thought the Americans went too far in demanding the Mississippi. This was what Jay had heard constantly in Madrid, and what he was now hearing from the Spanish ambassador in Paris, Aranda, with whom Jay was still vainly trying to arrange a Spanish-American alliance. Jay had little further doubt that France was in league with Spain. Franklin did not agree as to France, but on the 12th he wrote to Robert R. Livingston, secretary of the American department of foreign affairs, that Spain had manifested its "design to coop us up within the Allegheny mountains. . . . I hope Congress will insist on the Mississippi as a boundary and the free navigation of the river." Jay was ready to disregard the Congressional instructions. Franklin hoped for new ones. Yet the two men were equally positive that any narrower western limit was not even to be thought of.

The true difference between them and Vergennes lay in their irreconcilable conceptions of the American Revolution. For Franklin and Jay this had been in large part a crusade for liberty and the sacred rights of man. For Vergennes it had been a phase of a dynastic conflict. They insisted that the new republic categorically must have its independence recognized at once, and must extend from the Atlantic to the Mississippi. Vergennes saw nothing more imperative in these demands than in Spain's for Gibraltar and for protective territory in the American west. He had engineered the alliance of France and America against England in the belief that France would profit if England lost her colonies. The war had cost France more than he had expected in the form of aids to the United States, and the French treasury was close to exhaustion. Vergennes now needed the support of America, if France were to get any profit out of the war. The Americans, he felt sure, would lose interest in France's other aims as soon as independence had been recognized. To put off recognition for a while he advised Franklin and Jay to let independence wait upon the treaty. He did not want them to insist on Canada and the fishing rights, which France had never undertaken to obtain or guarantee. If England should yield she would then be less willing to meet whatever France, America's ally, might demand in other quarters. The Americans thought their territorial claims important. So did the French think their claim to have their port of Dunkirk fully restored to them after seventy years during which the English had not allowed it to be fortified.

And there was Gibraltar. Spain, little help as she had given France in the war, still demanded that France help her regain the fortress, according to the treaty between them. Vergennes could not know whether this was possible or how long it might take, but it furnished him another reason for postponing American independence and looking for continued American support. He allowed Rayneval to propose a scheme of compromise on the western boundary which alienated Jay and disquieted Franklin. This compromise would be a benefit to Spain in her treaty with England. If Spain held western territory she might recognize the part north of the Ohio as British, and possibly make better terms with regard to Gibraltar.

In his involved negotiations Vergennes presumably thought of himself as taking care of the interests of France first—as his duty required—but also of being careful to pay so much attention to the interests of his allies as would preserve the general alliance. He could no more satisfy them all than a governor can satisfy all the antagonistic parties in a state. Jay saw Vergennes's apparent partiality for France and Spain as a kind of treason to America. When he found out on 9 September that Rayneval, after an early morning conference with Vergennes and Aranda, had mysteriously left Versailles for London, Jay was certain that the French and

Spanish ministers had sent an agent to interfere in American affairs. Rayneval had gone primarily to discuss the French and
Spanish treaties with England, but he did hint to Shelburne that
France did not support the whole of the American demands and
that the American commissioners need not be told of what the
French, Spanish, and English were doing.[20] On the 10th Jay was
shown a copy of a dispatch, intercepted by the British, to Vergennes from Barbé-Marbois of the French legation in Philadelphia. That enterprising young diplomat reported that Americans
were not fully agreed on the fishing rights and suggested a means
by which the United States might be excluded from them. Though
the letter was to Vergennes, not from him, Jay took it to be a fresh
indication that French policy was hostile to America.

Franklin thought that the letter (which was genuine) might be
only a British forgery, and that Rayneval may have gone to England, in good faith, only in the interests of France and the general
peace.[21] Jay decided that he must act at once, even without Franklin and in violation of his instructions, to save America from
dangerous conspirators. On the 10th he notified Oswald that the
Americans to avoid delay would accept independence as an article
of the treaty, provided Oswald's commission empowered him,
under the great seal, to treat with the commissioners of "the
United States of America" in so many words. Franklin knew of
this. He did not know that on the 11th Jay sent Benjamin
Vaughan, Franklin's friend and editor who was then in Paris as a
secret agent of Shelburne, back to Shelburne to insist on the new
commission for Oswald and to offset any damage Rayneval might
have done. Vaughan was to tell Shelburne that prompt action on
the part of the British government would cut the cord which tied
America to France. The American commissioners had still to fulfil
their treaty obligations, but were determined not to let the French
alone say what those obligations were. The British government,
which had from the first been trying to detach America from
France, waited no longer. On the 19th the cabinet resolved to
make out the new commission, which reached Oswald in Paris on
the 27th.

Desirous as Shelburne was of a separate peace with America,
and so of an advantage in the treaty with France, he knew that his

expedient was perilous. Haste might be as bad as delay. To deal quickly with the Americans meant to accept more or less their own terms. This would be humiliating and was bound to cause much public resentment in England. Shelburne was unpopular, his hold on the government insecure. But it might be worth while to run risks in the hope of settling with France while Gibraltar was still in British hands. Though it had held out for three years, the combined French and Spanish forces were making enormous efforts to capture it. If it should be taken, then England by delay would have lost more, when it came to treating with France, than she could have lost by haste when treating with America. Shelburne, deciding to go secretly ahead with the American commissioners, thought he had put the greatest confidence in them that had ever been put in men. Let this plan fall through, and England would be distressingly involved in new difficulties with France and the Shelburne ministry ruined.

Franklin was ill, but the British and American commissioners formally exchanged their powers, and Jay on 5 October gave Oswald the first draft of the terms the Americans proposed. They were the same as Franklin's four necessary points of 9 July, with a further stipulation that both England and America should have freedom of navigation and commerce on the Mississippi and elsewhere throughout their dominions on the terms of nationals. Though Franklin agreed to this fifth point, it originated with Jay, bent on keeping Spain out of the territory east of the Mississippi. If America gave England full rights to trade on that river and into the interior of the continent by way of the St. Lawrence and the Great Lakes, England would probably make no claim either to hold the country north of the Ohio for herself or to deal for it with Spain, as Spain hoped with the approval of Vergennes. Jay even suggested to Oswald that England at the final peace should obtain West Florida, with its ports of entry to the interior. Franklin's advisable plan for Canada was dropped. The fishing rights granted the Americans were to include the right to dry fish on the shore in Newfoundland. Specific boundary lines were proposed.

This trial version of the treaty, not shown to Vergennes, reached London on the 11th, after the news that the great September attack on Gibraltar had failed. The ministry felt less need of hurry than before. On the 17th the cabinet recorded its objections to Jay's draft. Oswald, some of the ministers thought, seemed to be acting on the side of the Americans. Henry Strachey, who had been secretary to Lord Howe at the time of his meeting with Franklin and Adams on Staten Island, was now an under-secretary of state in the colonial office. Shelburne sent Strachey to Paris to stiffen Oswald. The loyalists must be compensated, or at least a strong fight made in their behalf. The debts due British merchants from America must be honestly paid in honest money. The right of Americans to dry their fish on the Newfoundland shore would lead to trouble with British fishermen; better limit American fishermen to deep water. Shelburne urged that the boundary line between Canada and the United States be made more favourable to England. When Strachey arrived in Paris on the 28th he found that John Adams had arrived from Holland two days before.

Adams, having been appointed first to the peace commission, was officially its head, but he could not know all that had happened and he came full of suspicion. On his second day in Paris he called on Jay but did not find him at home. Another friend, Matthew Ridley, told Adams some of the news. Franklin had given up his large Sunday dinners at Passy, but his health had lately improved and he was now able to sit at table. He had been, Ridley said, much less firm than Jay in dealing with Oswald, much more bound by the instructions from Congress. Adams confided to his diary that he saw he would have "a delicate, a nice, a critical part" to act between "two as subtle spirits as any in the world." Jay was probably honest, Adams thought, but "Franklin's cunning will be to divide us; to this end he will provoke, he will insinuate, he will intrigue, he will manœuvre." The next morning Adams spent three hours with Jay and found that they were of one mind as to what to do and how to do it. Jay had a chance to tell Adams that Rayneval, dining four days before with Franklin and Jay at Passy, had said he thought the Americans asked too much as to boundaries and fishing rights.[22] On both these points Franklin was as firm as Jay, or Adams. Jay, who admired and respected Franklin in spite of their differences of opinion, noted in his diary only that Adams "spoke freely what he thought" of their colleague. Adams had worked up such an aversion to Franklin that he could hardly bear to call on him. But on the 29th, after a meeting in Paris with Jay, Oswald, and Strachey, Adams went to Passy. There, some time during the evening, he told Franklin "without reserve" his opinion of the policy of France, praised the "principles, wisdom, and firmness" which Jay had shown, and announced that he would support Jay to the utmost of his power. "The Doctor heard me patiently, but said nothing." At the conference of all three commissioners the next morning with Oswald and Strachey, Franklin turned to Adams and Jay and said: "I am of your opinion, and will go on with these gentlemen in the business without consulting this court."[23]

IV

For a week the negotiators met at eleven every day and dined four times together to continue their work into the evening. The British commission had Caleb Whitefoord for a secretary. (He had lived next door to Franklin in Craven Street and had been his friend for more than twenty years.) Temple Franklin was secretary to the American commission. (He had been appointed by Franklin and Jay before Adams reached Paris. Adams thought this an affront to him, and was sure that Franklin was scheming to get his grandson made minister to France while he himself went as minister to England—where Adams wanted to go.) The discussions were intricate and detailed. Strachey thought the Americans great quibblers. But they stood solidly together, and the agreed articles which were drawn up on 5 November, to be sent to London, were close to the original American demands. Independence was to be unconditionally acknowledged. The boundaries were to be the Mississippi on the west, the Atlantic and the St. Croix on the east. On the north the Americans asked as alternatives either the present Canadian line by river and lake from the St. Lawrence to Lake of the Woods or the line of 45° due west from the Connecticut to the Mississippi. On the south the line was to run along latitude 31° eastward from the Mississippi to the Chattahoochee and then by the northern boundary of Florida to the Atlantic.(They used the great map published in 1755 by John Mitchell, one of Franklin's

earliest scientific correspondents.) In a secret article it was provided that if England held West Florida at the final peace its
boundary should be the latitude of the mouth of the Yazoo, about
32° 28'. Navigation on the Mississippi was to be free from its source
to its mouth.

There was no conflict over independence, and not too much
over boundaries. The points particularly disputed were debts, fisheries, and loyalists. Franklin and Jay had earlier taken the dubious
stand that the private debts owed to British merchants at the outbreak of the war had been counterbalanced by the confiscations of
American property by the British forces. Adams bluntly said he
had no idea of cheating anybody. American debts incurred before
1775 were validated, and nothing then said about money owed to
American creditors. In the debates over fishing rights Adams took
the lead. But it seems to have been Franklin who proposed that
Americans be allowed to fish as before, not only on the Newfoundland banks but also in the Gulf of St. Lawrence; and that, though
not allowed to dry their fish on the shore in Newfoundland, they
might dry them on the uninhabited coasts of Nova Scotia. "Are
you afraid there is not fish enough," he asked, "or that we should
catch too many; at the same time that you know that we shall bring
the greatest part of the money we get for that fish to Great Britain
to pay for your manufactures?"[24] Loyalists were to be allowed six
months in which to remove their property from America and the
states might extend just and reasonable clemency.

About the loyalists Franklin was, for a moralist, strangely implacable. This was a main point with the British. London was
full of refugees (including Franklin's former friend Galloway) who
for their loyalty to the Crown had been ruthlessly driven from
America as traitors, their estates confiscated. They had the sympathy of king and Parliament and never ceased their demand on
Shelburne that the treaty right their wrongs. He had good reason
to expect that his ministry could not last unless the loyalists were
compensated. Refusing to cede Canada, as Franklin had suggested,
Shelburne told Strachey that Maine and West Florida, if retained
by the British, might somehow produce the necessary compensation. In any case, Strachey was ordered to see that the loyalists had
an article in the treaty, if only to prove that the British govern-

ment had made an effort for them. The American commissioners refused to look upon the loyalists as loyal victims of successful rebels. The Revolution had been, from the first, a deadly civil war in America between loyalists and patriots. Though the patriots had won it, they had no inclination to show more mercy than they believed they would have been shown if they had lost. In the last years of the war, the commissioners held, the loyalists had been responsible for many British raids on the coast and had themselves committed unforgivable outrages on the frontier. Jay, who condemned the confiscation act proposed by his own brother in New York as thoroughly unjust, and Adams thought the loyalists deserved nothing from America, yet they would possibly have come to some agreement on the point rather than break off the treaty. Franklin could not be moved. His own son, president of the Associated Loyalists, had the past summer left America charged by both Congress and a British court-martial with responsibility for the hanging of a New Jersey militia officer under the lawless authority of the association.[25] It is not known how far Franklin was aware of these facts or whether they consciously affected him. But the civil war in America had been a civil war in his own heart and loins and had gone too deep for him to make peace with his closest enemies.

Strachey took the proposed articles to London, and for three weeks the American and British commissioners saw little of each other. Franklin, as minister to France, now had the unpleasant task of asking for another loan. He had put it off as long as he could. On 25 June he had written Livingston that France had promised six million livres for the year, but "that it was all the king could spare us, that we must not expect more. . . . Under this declaration, with what face could I ask for another six millions?" as Congress insisted. "It would be saying: 'You are not to be believed, you can spare more; you are able to lend me twice the sum if you were but willing.' "[26] Urgent letters came from Congress, and Franklin on 8 November sent Vergennes Congress's resolves and letters. Franklin added only that the slow progress of the Anglo-American treaty made him fear another campaign could hardly be avoided: "our enemies being well informed of our present distresses for want of money and conceiving great hopes that we shall nowhere find a supply."[27] If the war was to be continued to the satisfaction of both America and France, it was to the interest of both France and America, Franklin hinted, to share the costs.

The American and English peace commissions met again on the morning of 25 November, after Strachey's return. Oswald had been instructed to take counsel with Strachey and with Fitz-herbert, in charge of the negotiations between England and France. During five days of minute discussion the articles of the 5th were agreed on with few changes. There was particular strife over the loyalists. Shelburne had already decided that it would be better to give them up than to delay the conclusion of the treaty beyond the opening of Parliament on 5 December. But since he knew that Parliament would angrily blame him for neglect of them, Oswald and his associates were to make every effort in a final stand for compensation. At the close of the first conference in Paris Jay asked Strachey if his demand was an ultimatum from the ministry. Strachey had reluctantly to say no. The next morning at breakfast Adams and Jay agreed with Franklin not to consent. He read them a letter he had written to Oswald.[28] On Oswald's suggestion it was finally provided that Congress should "earnestly recommend" to the several states the restitution of confiscated estates which had belonged to British subjects. The American commissioners made it plain that Congress had no authority to enforce its recommenda-tion. The British commissioners knew what they were accepting. It would not compensate the loyalists, but it was a promise on paper which might save the ministers' honour and places.

On the 29th the British were willing to sign but not quite willing to admit it. Fitzherbert said they could not go beyond their instructions on the disputed last points in the fisheries debate. Unlike the Americans, men of weight and authority in their coun-try, he and Strachey and Oswald were little more than obedient pens in the hands of the ministers who had instructed them. Adams said there was time to ask further advice from London. In that case, Franklin interposed, he had another article to suggest for the treaty. He took a paper out of his pocket and read it. Since Con-gress was to recommend compensation to the loyalists, George III, according to Franklin's article,[29] would recommend to his Parlia-ment that it compensate Americans for all the goods seized in

Boston by Gage and carried away from Philadelphia by Howe; for the tobacco, rice, indigo, and slaves taken by Arnold, Cornwallis, and others in Virginia, the Carolinas, and Georgia; for the American ships and cargoes captured by the British navy before the declaration of war; and for the towns, villages, and farms burned and destroyed by the British troops or their adherents during the war. He mentioned his own library in Philadelphia. Adams and Jay added details. Laurens, who had arrived in time for this last day of the negotiations, spoke of plunder in the Carolinas. The British commissioners, who had thought that the danger of delay might make the Americans yield on their last points, now saw a difficult earlier issue raised again. They went into another room, agreed that it would be better for them to yield than to give the Americans a chance to think of still other demands, and came back to say that Oswald would accept the American terms.

They met the next morning (Saturday) at Oswald's lodgings and signed the provisional treaty, which was not to become final "until terms of a peace shall be agreed upon between Great Britain and France." After that they all went out to Passy to dine with Franklin.[30] This time he did not bring out the old blue coat in which he had been abused by Wedderburn, but came to the ceremony in black because the French court was then in mourning for some German prince.[31]

V

In signing the treaty without consultation with Vergennes the Americans had deliberately violated their instructions from Congress. Jay and Adams, only guessing how far those instructions were Vergennes's own, believed that to follow them would be to betray true interests of America which Congress did not know were threatened by the designs of France and Spain. Franklin looked upon the instructions less as an evidence of French craft than, simply, as a method of bringing about a unified conduct of affairs. But the distance was too great and the time too short to explain the need of new instructions and get them from Congress. The commissioners, he later wrote, had to do "what appeared to all of us best at the time." Congress by choosing five men, four of whom were in Paris, had seemed to show "some dependence on our joint judgment, since one alone could have made a treaty by direction of the French ministry as well as twenty."[32] He may have thought, more than the others did, that there was a chance Congress might not confirm the treaty. But both Jay and Adams testified that Franklin worked in perfect harmony with them during the negotiations.[33] He had himself first drawn the plan on which the treaty was constructed, and he was on no point of American interest less firm than any of his colleagues.

Left to himself he would probably have kept up the most courteous relations with Vergennes. They understood each other. Neither of them would have expected the other to accept less for his country than he could contrive to get. Each would have his strategic secrets. When Vergennes—or Rayneval for him—at various times suggested that the Americans should compromise as to boundaries, agree to limitations in the fishing rights, and compensate the loyalists, Franklin thought it natural enough. Vergennes was "afraid that we, relying too much on the ability of France to continue the war in our favour and supply us constantly with money, might insist on more advantages than the English would be willing to grant, and thereby lose the opportunity of making peace, so necessary to all our friends."[34] But it was also natural, Franklin thought, for him to aim at every possible advantage for America and to work for it in the ways most likely to succeed. If Jay had not objected to the language of Oswald's commission the terms of peace might conceivably have been agreed upon in August or September. If Franklin and Jay had submitted them to Vergennes he could not have disapproved of them without plainly putting the special interests of France ahead of America's, and so probably losing an ally at once. Jay did object, and the terms were not then agreed on. Adams arrived. "He means well for his country," Franklin later observed, "is always an honest man, often a wise one, but sometimes, and in some things, absolutely out of his senses."[35] Franklin was in a minority, not as to the interests of America but as to the deference to be shown to France in the negotiations. Being only one man in three he fell in with the suspicious policy of the others.

But the burden of reporting to Vergennes fell entirely upon Franklin. On the evening of the 29th he wrote a note telling the minister that the preliminary articles had been settled. The next day he sent a copy of the treaty with the information that it had been signed that morning. It was perhaps on Tuesday of the following week, Franklin's usual day at Versailles, that he called on Vergennes, who amicably said that the haste in signing "had not been particularly civil to the king." Franklin excused himself and his colleagues as best he could.[36] Vergennes said they had managed well for their country and by securing their independence had overcome a difficult obstacle to the general peace.[37] He gave no sign of feeling that France had been cheated by her American ally. The agreement just signed would technically not be valid till peace had been made between England and France. Technically the only fault of the Americans was incivility. Though he meant to hold Franklin responsible for that, he did not blame him for anything worse. Vergennes had tried to drive the allies abreast to the treaty. He had known that the Americans, thanks in part to their distance from Europe, had an advantage. The matter of their independence was more simple than the adjustment of European claims. He would have been willing to hold America back for the possible benefit of France and Spain, and he had not hesitated to make secret efforts to do it. Since the United States had won their independence he could hardly count on further support from them in claims which were wholly European. What had happened was an incident of statecraft. If he had been in Franklin's place he would have done the same thing. The Anglo-American agreement might even be a help to him. France had been uncomfortably involved with Spain, relentlessly demanding Gibraltar. Now there was little hope that Gibraltar could be won and Spain could not persist much longer in her demand, which was holding up the Anglo-French agreement.

There remained the delicate question of the French loan. Franklin on 5 December, after he had talked with Vergennes, wrote to Livingston that the sum had not been fixed. He reminded Congress "that there are bounds to everything and that the faculties of this nation are limited like those of all other nations. Some of you seem to have established as maxims the suppositions that

France has money enough for all her occasions and all ours besides; and that if she does not supply us it is owing to her want of will or to my negligence."[38] (As he commented two weeks later, he thought "our people certainly ought to do more for themselves. It is absurd, the pretending to be lovers of liberty while they grudge paying for the defence of it."[39]) But on the 15th Franklin wrote to Vergennes saying that an American ship, with a British passport, was ready to sail for America with dispatches to Congress. "I hoped I might have been able to send part of the aids we have asked, by this safe vessel. I beg that Your Excellency would at least inform me what expectations I may give in my letters. I fear the Congress will be reduced to despair when they find that nothing is yet obtained."[40] Vergennes, master of the muffled language of diplomacy, knew that Franklin was not only pressing him for money but also telling him that without it Congress would probably do nothing more for France, if any unforeseen new need should arise.

This gave Vergennes the chance he had been waiting for. He was surprised, he answered the same day, to learn that Franklin and his colleagues, after disregarding their instructions from Congress, were now "about to hold out a certain hope of peace to America without even informing yourself on the state of the negotiation on our part. You are wise and discreet, Sir; you perfectly understand what is due propriety; you have all your life performed your duties. I pray you to consider how you propose to fulfil those which are due to the king. I am not desirous of enlarging these reflections; I commit them to your own integrity. When you shall be pleased to relieve my uncertainty I will entreat the king to enable me to answer your demands."[41] Vergennes's words were essentially a gesture. Though he intended to grant the loan which, bad as the French finances were, he thought he could not afford to withhold so long as there was any chance of further hostilities, he must write some disapproval of America's conduct into the record of the whole transaction. He put it, in that immensely punctilious age, in the form of a courteous reproach to Franklin for his discourtesy.

Franklin on the 17th replied in one of the most famous of all diplomatic letters, after he had shown it to the other commissioners and they had approved it.[42] He had thought, he said, of the

American ship with its British passport as partly a convenience to Vergennes. If the American dispatches did not go promptly Congress might be left to hear of the agreement from the English first, which would surely be improper. As to the agreement itself, he again reminded Vergennes that it was only a provisional one, dependent on the French treaty of peace. As to the hurried closing of these preliminary articles, Vergennes's "observation" was "apparently just: that in not consulting you before they were signed we have been guilty of neglecting a point of *bienséance* [propriety]. But, as all this was not from want of respect for the king, whom we all love and honour, we hope it will be excused; and that the great work which has hitherto been so happily conducted, is so nearly brought to perfection, and is so glorious to his reign, will not be ruined by a single indiscretion of ours. And certainly the whole edifice sinks to the ground immediately if you refuse on that account to give us any further assistance." Franklin went on to say how much he and his countrymen loved and respected the king. Then with a flash of genius, as if the idea had suddenly been brought to his mind, Franklin wrote a sentence which he underlined. "*The English, I just now learn, flatter themselves they have already divided us.*" Of course they did, and of course they had. But "I hope," Franklin added with the brilliant assumption that France and America were still faithfully united against England, "this little misunderstanding will therefore be kept a secret and that they [the English] will find themselves totally mistaken."[43] (Through Edward Bancroft, still a spy, a copy of Franklin's letter reached Fitzherbert, who, as well as Shelburne, had been in touch with Bancroft during the negotiations.[44])

Two great diplomatic duellists had formally crossed swords, and the philosopher had exquisitely disarmed the minister. The next week Franklin wrote to Robert Morris that the "little misunderstanding" had been "got over" in three days. The first 600,000 of the 6,000,000 would be sent at once and the remainder paid quarterly during 1783. But there was still a chance that Parliament might not ratify the preliminary articles. "A little more success in the West Indies this winter may totally turn the heads of that giddy nation."[45]

The preliminary articles were so unpopular in England that

Shelburne was forced to resign in February 1783 and to give place to the singular coalition of Fox and North. Before that (on 20 January) the Anglo-French and the Anglo-Spanish preliminaries were signed in Vergennes's office in Versailles. Vergennes took care that Franklin and Adams should be present while the diplomats rearranged territories and privileges in America, Europe, Africa, and Asia. At the same time a general armistice was signed between England and each of the three allies. (The settlement with Holland came later.) The Parliamentary turmoil in England postponed the final treaty. Oswald, Shelburne's agent, was recalled, and David Hartley, Franklin's old friend, came to Paris in April. Hartley hoped to bring about some kind of close alliance between England and the United States, providing for mutual defence and reciprocal freedom of trade. Franklin strongly believed "that a state which leaves all her ports open to all the world upon equal terms will by that means have foreign commodities cheaper, sell its own productions dearer, and be on the whole the most prosperous."[46] He especially urged that the final treaty contain an article against privateering in the case of future wars.[47] Adams and Jay had other proposals in the discussions with Hartley. No agreement was reached, and the Americans soon doubted that Hartley's scheme would ever be ratified by the British government.

The preliminary articles (without the secret one dealing with Florida, which England had ceded to Spain) were signed as final at Hartley's lodgings in the Hôtel de York in Paris on 3 September. The treaty between England and France was signed at Versailles the same day. Vergennes, still scrupulous, held up the ceremony till word came that the Americans had signed their treaty. "We are now friends with England and with all mankind," Franklin wrote to Josiah Quincy on the 11th. "May we never see another war! For in my opinion there never was a good war or a bad peace."[48]

It was nearly thirty years since Franklin, talking with Governor Shirley in Boston, had clearly put forth his plans for a wise imperial union of Britain and America. That had been his chief aim, and the aim of the wisest Englishmen, till 1775. Then he had given up his long and patient faith that British wisdom might be able to prevail over a reactionary king and his bought Parliament.

Better for America to lose the benefits of the Empire, Franklin decided, than to be at the mercy of quarrelling English politicians. Once he had set his mind on American independence he seems never to have been haunted by his old imperial vision. He would have preferred to keep America independent of the rest of Europe as well as of England. But for the sake of the Revolution he went to France for European aid in getting free of Europe. Here was the paradox of the American situation. It does not appear that Franklin was ever troubled by the paradox. He took French help as he found it, and was no less grateful to France because he knew that France had her own ends to gain in her war with England. The good done to America was the same, no matter what European motives France may have had. But when it came to making terms of peace Franklin's instinct was towards the completest independence of America from all Europe. A cosmopolitan who had most of his dearest friends in England and France and was himself more renowned and honoured in Europe than in America, he moved boldly to separate the new republic from the parent continent. Let commerce and knowledge bind the continents naturally together. Let there be as few as possible of those artificial bonds which make unnatural wars.

∞∞∞

The Older the Bolder

ON 27 August, exactly a week before the final treaty with
England was signed, Franklin saw Paris's first balloon ascension at the Champ-de-Mars. The brothers Montgolfier had sent up
the first balloon (linen) in history at Annonay near Lyons in June,
inflating it with heated air from burning straw. The capital must
not lag behind the provinces. Now for four days a new balloon
(varnished silk) had been filling up with hydrogen gas made by
pouring oil of vitriol on iron filings, under the direction of the
physicist Jacques-Alexandre-César Charles. There had been daily
bulletins and such public excitement that fifty thousand people,
Franklin estimated, gathered to see the ascent at five o'clock on a
signal given by the firing of cannon. The balloon, wet a little by
the rain "so that it shone and made an agreeable appearance," rose
rapidly "till it entered the clouds, when it seemed to me scarce
bigger than an orange and soon after became invisible." The dripping spectators argued about the utility of the experiment. Franklin, reporting to Sir Joseph Banks of the Royal Society in London,
thought it might "pave the way to some discoveries in natural
philosophy of which at present we have no conception."[1] On the
occasion itself he made an epigram which ran through Paris and
was hurried off by Baron Grimm to his royal correspondents in
Germany, Poland, and Russia.[2] What good, some sceptic asked,
could a balloon be? What good, Franklin replied, was a new-born
baby? (*Eh, à quoi bon l'enfant qui vient de naître?*) The image
rose naturally to his mind, for there was a baby in his own house
at Passy, Ann Jay then two weeks old.

Joseph Montgolfier came from Annonay to Paris for an experiment on 19 September at Versailles. His balloon, with rococo
ornaments painted in oil over its whole outer surface, carried up a

sheep, a cock, and a duck and brought them safely down in the presence of the king and his court. There were at once two factions among the enthusiasts, some siding with Montgolfier and his heated air, some with Charles and his hydrogen gas. Franklin was not a partisan. His malady had kept him from going to Versailles, but he witnessed the first ascent of human passengers in a free balloon at the Château de La Muette in Passy on 20 November. The scientist Pilâtre de Rozier and the Marquis d'Arlandes were lifted about five hundred feet, burning straw as they went in a grate hung underneath the balloon, and were driven across the Seine to land without mishap in Paris. The marquis called on Franklin that evening and brought Montgolfier. "I am sorry," Franklin wrote to Banks the next day, "this experiment is so totally neglected in England, where mechanic genius is so strong. . . . Your philosophy seems to be too bashful. In this country we are not so much afraid of being laughed at. If we do a foolish thing we are the first to laugh at it ourselves."[3] What if aeronautics was at present only an amusement? So had been the first experiments in magnetism and electricity. On 1 December Franklin was present when Charles and one of the brothers Robert, who had constructed another hydrogen balloon, rose two thousand feet from the Tuileries.

"Being a little indisposed, and the air cool and the ground damp, I declined going into the garden of the Tuileries where the balloon was placed, not knowing how long I might be obliged to wait there before it was ready to depart; and chose to stay in my carriage near the statue of Louis XV, from whence I could well see it rise and have an extensive view of the region of air through which, as the wind sat, it was likely to pass. The morning was foggy, but about one o'clock the air became tolerably clear, to the great satisfaction of the spectators, who were infinite; notice having been given of the intended experiment several days before in the papers, so that all Paris was out, either about the Tuileries, on the quays and bridges, in the fields, the streets, at the windows, or on the tops of houses, besides the inhabitants of all the towns and villages of the environs. Never before was a philosophical experiment so magnificently attended. . . . Between one and two o'clock all eyes were gratified with seeing it rise majestically from

among the trees and ascend gradually above the buildings, a most
beautiful spectacle. When it was about two hundred feet high the
brave adventurers held out and waved a little white pennant, on
both sides their car, to salute the spectators, who returned loud
claps of applause. The wind was very little, so that the object,
though moving to the northward, continued long in view. . . . I
had a pocket-glass with which I followed it till I lost sight first of
the men, then of the car, and when I last saw the balloon it
appeared no bigger than a walnut. I write this at seven in the
evening," he told Banks. The next day Franklin added a thankful
postscript saying that the adventurers had before sunset managed
a perfect descent at L'Isle-Adam nearly seven leagues from Paris.[4]

On 6 December, the day Franklin excused himself from going
any more to Versailles, he wondered whether the balloon might
not become a common carriage and relieve him from the jolting
of pavements. Hardly in his time, he supposed. In other ways the
discovery might "possibly give a new turn to human affairs. Convincing sovereigns of the folly of wars may perhaps be one effect
of it; since it will be impracticable for the most potent of them to
guard his dominions. Five thousand balloons, capable of raising
two men each, could not cost more than five ships of the line; and
where is the prince who can afford so to cover his country with
troops for its defence as that ten thousand men descending from
the clouds might not in many places do an infinite deal of mischief
before a force could be brought together to repel them?"[5] Franklin
eagerly kept track of later experiments. He must have been pleased
when the American Philosophical Society soon repeated the experiments of Montgolfier. He was certainly pleased when John
Jeffries, an American though a loyalist who had been surgeon-
major in the British army, made with Jean-Pierre Blanchard the
first flight across the Channel. Jeffries, a busy hero at Versailles
and in Paris, dined several times with Franklin. On the 22nd John
Paul Jones was another guest. He and Jeffries, late enemies,
praised each other's courage. Franklin, implacable towards loyalists, was gentle and courteous.[6] Jeffries brought him a letter from
England, "the first through the air."[7]

The portrait made by Duplessis in pastel the year of the final
peace, and given to Le Veillard, showed Franklin in the happiest

mood he ever felt even in France. There was more light in the soft blue coat than in the familiar sober brown; there was serenity in his eyes. He looked, if not precisely younger than in the portraits made before in France, yet somehow fresher. Though he had had many triumphs in the sixty years since he ran away from Boston to seek his fortune, this latest one was the greatest of them all. But there was more than ordinary triumph in his face. He looked not as if he had gained a point but as if he had found that he and the world were ultimately at peace. He had loved it and he was sure that it loved him as much as a philosopher could reasonably ask.

Franklin at last had some leisure. As soon as the preliminary peace articles were signed he had written to Congress that he wished "for the little time I have left to be my own master."[8] Though his release was put off for more than two years, the burden of his office was much lighter than it had been. Thomas Barclay had come from America to take over Franklin's consular duties. France, suspending payment on some of her own bills, made a final loan to America of six million livres which Franklin negotiated in February 1783, and then would make no more. John Adams had the work of finding money in Holland. There was no war to keep Franklin in anxiety, no admiralty court to distract and confine him. It was pleasant to have the Swedish ambassador say that his king not only desired to be the first in Europe to enter into a treaty of amity and commerce with the independent United States but also particularly desired to deal with Franklin, for whom the king had so much esteem; and pleasant to conclude the treaty in March.[9] It seemed only natural for Anthony Todd, still secretary of the British post office, to apply to Franklin in June for advice on the restoration of postal service between England and America, and for Franklin in the fall to draw up—in French— the *Plan d'arrangement* which the French and British followed in their system of mail packets to and from America.[10] His daily strain had been eased. But he was still officially minister to France, still unofficially ambassador to Europe, and he set himself in his new leisure to answer at large some of the accumulated countless questions he had been asked, year after year, about his country. They occupied him during part of the coldest winter anybody in France could remember, with heavy snow on the ground from Christmas through February. (In May he wrote a paper of *Meteorological Imaginations and Conjectures* on the cold, tentatively ascribing it to the long summer fogs of 1783 which so chilled the ground that the early snows in December did not melt as usual.[11])

Just when he wrote *Information to Those Who Would Remove to America* is not certain, but by 9 March he had printed it in French and in English at Passy.[12] Since he spoke of the war as ended and the armies as disbanded, he cannot have written it before the latter part of 1783. Some time between those dates he used his leisure to write out fully for all Europe a general statement which he could send to inquiring individuals. Too many of the wrong people, he thought, wanted to emigrate to America for the wrong reasons. They believed that the Americans were rich but ignorant; ready to welcome scholars and artists from Europe; waiting for European persons of family to come and fill offices which were above the capacity of natives; willing to reward immigrants with free gifts of transportation, land, slaves, tools, and livestock. "These are all wild imaginations. . . . The truth is, that though there are in that country few people so miserable as the poor of Europe, there are also very few that in Europe would be called rich." Patrons of the arts were so rare that American artists had uniformly had to leave their own country for Europe to find employment and rewards. While Americans valued learning, they had scholars of their own, trained in their own nine colleges. There were not many civil offices, and "no superfluous ones, as in Europe." Office-seekers and soldiers would be wise not to look for careers in America. "Much less is it advisable for a person to go thither who has no other quality to recommend him but his birth. . . . It is a commodity that cannot be carried to a worse market than that of America." The government encouraged any foreigner only by admitting him to equality with natives and to citizenship in one or two years. "If he does not bring a fortune with him he must work and be industrious to live. . . . In short, America is the land of labour, and by no means what the English call Lubberland and the French Pays de Cocagne."

The chief resource of America was cheap land, made so by "the vast forests still void of inhabitants and not likely to be occupied in an age to come." Not till "the lands are all taken up and cultivated, and the excess of people who cannot get land" thrown out of employment, Franklin prophesied, would there be any great poverty in America. For the present, labour was still well paid. Skilled artisans could make a good living and provide for children and old age. Farm labourers could save their wages and become farmers. Men with small capital could lay it out in land and be sure of a rise in price. Meanwhile they could work with their hands and not incur disgrace, as in Europe, but instead win the respect of their neighbours. There was little vice in America because there was little idleness. As he summed it up more pungently in an undated letter to an unidentified correspondent: "Our country offers to strangers nothing but a good climate, fertile soil, wholesome air, free governments, wise laws, liberty, a good people to live among, and a hearty welcome. Those Europeans who have these or greater advantages at home would do well to stay where they are."[13]

He had been asked often about the Red Indians. Now, apparently, he wrote his *Remarks concerning the Savages of North America*[14] which La Rochefoucauld—friendly translator of the American constitutions—had translated into French by 7 January.[15] "Savages we call them," Franklin began with dramatic abruptness, "because their manners differ from ours, which we think the perfection of civility; they think the same of theirs. . . . The Indian men, when young, are hunters and warriors; when old, counsellors; for all their government is by counsel of the sages; there is no force, there are no prisons, no officers to compel obedience or inflict punishment. Hence they generally study oratory, the best speaker having the most influence. The Indian women till the ground, dress the food, nurse and bring up the children, and preserve and hand down to posterity the memory of public transactions. These employments of men and women are accounted natural and honourable. Having few artificial wants, they have abundance of leisure for improvement by conversation. Our laborious manner of life, compared with theirs, they esteem slavish and base; and the learning on which we value ourselves they regard as frivolous and useless."

Franklin told of something which had happened at Lancaster in Pennsylvania at a treaty between the Six Nations and Virginia in 1744. The Virginia commissioners offered to take six Indian boys and educate them at the college in Williamsburg. The Indians, after politely waiting till the next day, declined the offer. Their young men who had gone to college in the northern provinces had come back "bad runners, ignorant of every means of living in the woods, unable to bear either cold or hunger, knew neither how to build a cabin, take a deer, or kill an enemy, spoke our languages imperfectly, were therefore neither fit for warriors, hunters, nor counsellors; they were totally good for nothing." But the Indians would take a dozen Virginia boys and educate them properly in the forest. Most of the *Remarks* were such stories as Franklin had come to be famous for telling to his friends in Paris: stories to prove that "if we could examine the manners of different nations with impartiality we should find no people so rude as to be without any rules of politeness, nor any so polite as not to have some remains of rudeness." At the end of his greatest diplomatic triumph he remembered the Indians to whom he had gone on his first mission, at Carlisle, almost exactly thirty years before. Though the Six Nations had sided with the British during the Revolution Franklin did not hold it against them as against the white loyalists.

His *Remarks* and his *Information* were at once published in London as *Two Tracts* and went that year through three English editions and another in Dublin. There were two Italian translations of them in 1785 at Padua and Cremona. The *Information* appeared in French at Paris in 1784 and in German at Hamburg in 1786. What he had to say about the savages was of interest to readers of a philosophic turn of mind. But his information for emigrants was taken for his advice and interested far more readers. He seemed to stand, a strange angel with a strange sword, at the gate of a new paradise, warning away persons not desired or desirable there. America, he told them, was not for men looking for civil privilege or military adventure. It was a land where all men must work, though where all men who worked might prosper. Most of his friends in Europe—statesmen, soldiers, philosophers, scientists, artists, gentlemen and ladies—would hardly do for

America. The new world, cutting itself off from the old, had left behind rank and privilege, luxury and vice, elegance and some of the graces. His information came from his reasoned opinion, and it boldly undertook to distinguish America from Europe. Franklin was no Rousseau, romantically celebrating a primitive society. These were plain arguments for plain men, appealing to common instincts and pointing an American way to common forms of happiness.

On 26 January of that cold winter he wrote his daughter a long letter which turned his advice upon America.[16] She had sent him newspapers full of the Society of the Cincinnati which had been organized among the former officers of the American army, with Washington as its head. Membership was to be hereditary in the line of eldest sons, like titles of nobility. Franklin thought such titles foolish and ridiculed them. "Honour worthily obtained (as for example that of our officers) is in its nature a personal thing and incommunicable to any but those who had some share in obtaining it. Thus among the Chinese, the most ancient and from long experience the wisest of nations, honour does not descend but ascends." When a Chinese won it the credit went to his parents. "This ascending honour is therefore useful to the state, as it encourages parents to give their children a good and virtuous education. But the descending honour, to posterity who could have no share in obtaining it, is not only groundless and absurd but often hurtful to that posterity, since it is apt to make them proud, disdaining to be employed in useful arts and thence falling into poverty and all the meannesses, servility, and wretchedness attending it; which is the present case with much of what is called the noblesse in Europe."

That descending honours were groundless and absurd Franklin demonstrated by simple mathematics. "A man's son, for instance, is but half of his family, the other half belonging to the family of his wife. His son, too, marrying into another family, his share in the grandson is but a fourth." And so on till "in nine generations, which would not require more than three hundred years (no very great antiquity for a family), our present Chevalier of the Order of Cincinnatus's share in the then existing knight will be but a 512th part." Or look backward from the point of view of that young knight of the ninth generation. He would owe his honour to the 512 persons (existing in 1784) from whom he had descended, and also to the intervening ones through whom the honour had reached him: 1022 in all. So many men and women to make one knight, and each successive knight with a smaller and smaller share of true honour. "I hope, therefore, that the order will drop this part of their project and content themselves . . . with a life enjoyment of their little badge and ribband, and let the distinction die with those who have merited it."

Franklin had been friends with the holders of many hereditary titles in Europe, but now at seventy-eight he thought no more of them in principle than he had when he was seventeen and a young radical in Boston; or when at forty-five in Philadelphia he had figured in *Poor Richard* for 1751 that any contemporary nobleman who traced his line to the Norman conquest would be actually descended from 1,048,576 persons who had been living then. "Carry the reckoning three hundred years farther and the number amounts to above 500,000,000, which are more than exist at any one time upon earth—and shows the impossibility of preserving blood free from such mixtures, and that the pretension of such purity of blood in ancient families is a mere joke."

Incidentally, Franklin said he wished the bald eagle had not been chosen as an emblem of America. "He is a bird of bad moral character; he does not get his living honestly; you may have seen him perched on some dead tree near the river, where, too lazy to fish for himself, he watches the labour of the fishing-hawk; and, when that diligent bird has at length taken a fish and is bearing it to his nest for the support of his mate and young ones, the bald eagle pursues him and takes it from him. With all this injustice he is never in good case; but, like those among men who live by sharping and robbing, he is generally poor and often very lousy. Besides, he is a rank coward; the little kingbird, not bigger than a sparrow, attacks him boldly and drives him out of the district. . . . The turkey is in comparison a much more respectable bird, and withal a true original native of America. . . . He is (though a little vain and silly, it is true, but not the worse emblem for that) a bird of courage, and would not hesitate to attack a grenadier of the British Guards who should presume to invade his farmyard with a red coat on."

The philosopher drew his letter out to an essay, probably intending to print it. This seems to have been the time—from December to May—when his press at Passy was most active, with the printer Maurice Meyer employed for the whole five months.[17] Benjamin Franklin Bache, now fourteen, had come back from Geneva the past July, and Franklin had decided to make a printer of him. "I had thoughts of bringing him up under his cousin [Temple] and fitting him for public business, thinking he might be of service hereafter to his country; but, being now convinced that service is no inheritance, as the proverb says, I have determined to give him a trade, that he may have something to depend on and not be obliged to ask favours or offices of anybody."[18] Franklin's requests to Congress to appoint Temple to some diplomatic office had been silently neglected. Seeing his other grandson at work at his new trade, Franklin felt like a printer again, a master with his press in his house. The *Information* and the *Remarks* were the longest of the Passy imprints, both printed in both French and English. Franklin sent them to Madame Brillon in April, along with other pieces which he did not name, and thought she now had all his bagatelles.[19] The letter on the Cincinnati seemed at first to belong among them.

But he changed his mind about it when the Abbé Morellet, who had translated the letter, advised against letting it be known, even in the Passy circle. On 16 March Franklin wrote that it would probably never appear till after his death, if then.[20] For he agreed with Morellet that it might offend in France, as well as in America. A minister to France was under the strictest obligation not to put on record his contempt for a French institution; and hereditary nobility was part of the very structure of the old regime. The French censors would certainly not allow Franklin's letter to be published. As certainly he ought not to print it. But the ideas in it were still important to him, and he turned them over, by coincidence not with prevision, to the younger Mirabeau, brilliant, intractable son of Franklin's old friend the physiocratic marquis. The American opposition to a new aristocracy led through Franklin to the most eminent orator of the French Revolution which destroyed the old one.

Having received from Philadelphia the *Considerations upon the Order of the Cincinnati* written by Ædanus Burke of South Carolina, Franklin suggested that Mirabeau translate it. On 13 July Franklin's journal noted: "MM. Mirabeau and Chamfort came and read their translation of (American) Mr. Burke's pamphlet against the Cincinnati, which they have much enlarged, intending it as a covered satire against noblesse in general. . . . They say General Washington missed a *beau moment* when he accepted to be of that society (which some affect to call an order). The same of the Marquis de Lafayette."[21] Franklin did more than listen. He must have given Mirabeau a copy of the letter to Sarah Bache. For when Mirabeau's *Considérations sur l'ordre de Cincinnatus* (the first of his writings to which Mirabeau signed his name) appeared in London in or soon after September, it had footnotes on ascending honour among the Chinese and on the mathematics of descending honour which seem more like translations from Franklin's text than mere reports of his conversation.[22] Mirabeau had gone to London in August, where Shelburne was his friend. But it was a letter from Franklin to Benjamin Vaughan on 8 September which helped Mirabeau find a publisher for his dangerous book—and the publisher was John Johnson who had printed Franklin's collected *Pieces* for Vaughan during the war. The next year Mirabeau's work was translated into English by Samuel Romilly, who had in the meantime visited Franklin at Passy, and published in London; and in 1786 the translation appeared in Philadelphia, to which Franklin had by then returned. Though he had not printed his bagatelle for Passy, he had seen his ideas presented to the three chief cities of his world.

If Franklin did not print his letter on the Cincinnati, neither did he print *An Economical Project*[23] which he wrote apparently on 24 March, to inform Paris, with a humour hardly so easy and fresh as usual, that the sun gives light as soon as it rises and that if people would only get up early they might save many candles. He had perhaps lost some of his interest in the press which had amused him during the cold spell. But he had not lost interest in his speculations, which continued clear and bold throughout his remaining months in Paris. On 17 July in a letter to a friend he ridiculed and condemned the "murderous practice of duelling."[24] The next day he advised two young Americans, Mason Locke Weems and Edward Gant, not to be troubled if the archbishop of Canterbury would not permit them to be ordained in the Church of England without their taking the oath of allegiance to the king. The American clergy, like the early Scottish priests, might ordain themselves. "If the British Isles were sunk in the sea (and the surface of this globe has suffered greater changes) you would probably take some such method as this; and if they persist in denying you ordination, 'tis the same thing. An hundred years hence, when people are more enlightened, it will be wondered at that men in America, qualified by their learning and piety to pray for and instruct their neighbours, should not be permitted to do it till they had made a voyage of six thousand miles out and home, to ask leave of a cross old gentleman at Canterbury."[25]

In particular Franklin speculated on the welfare of common men in Europe and America. Luxury, which the moralists of the age thought an evil, was then often defended as a means of giving employment to the poor. Franklin could not altogether accept that defence. "I have not, indeed," he wrote to Benjamin Vaughan on 26 July, "thought of a remedy for luxury. I am not sure that in a great state it is capable of remedy. Nor that the evil is in itself always so great as it is represented. . . . Is not the hope of one day being able to purchase and enjoy luxuries a great spur to labour and industry?" He remembered how, long ago, his wife had once made a present of "a new-fashioned cap" to a country girl at Cape May. All the girls in Cape May resolved to have caps like it, and to earn money to buy them took to knitting worsted mittens for sale in Philadelphia. "I was more reconciled to this little piece of luxury, since not only the girls were made happier by having fine caps, but the Philadelphians by the supply of warm mittens." No doubt now and then "a shilling spent idly by a fool may be picked up by a wiser person who knows better what to do with it." But on the whole, Franklin thought, want and misery were caused by the employment of too many men in making things that had no good use. Because they produced nothing, other men had to make up for them by working more or eating less.[26]

On 14 March 1785 Franklin, in another letter to Vaughan, blamed the cruel penal laws of the time on unjust wealth. "Superfluous property is the creature of society. Simple and mild laws were sufficient to guard the property that was merely necessary. The savage's bow, his hatchet, and his coat of skins were sufficiently secured, without law, by the fear of personal resentment and retaliation. When, by virtue of the first laws, part of the society accumulated wealth and grew powerful, they enacted others more severe, and would protect their property at the expense of humanity. . . . I see in the last newspaper from London that a woman is capitally convicted for privately stealing out of a shop some gauze, value fourteen shillings and threepence. . . . Is not all punishment inflicted beyond the merit of the offence so much punishment of innocence? . . . If I am not myself so barbarous, so bloody-minded and revengeful, as to kill a fellow-creature for stealing from me 14/3, how can I approve of a law that does it?"[27] The next year Franklin's letter was published by Samuel Romilly in his *Observations*, the first book in his long career as a reformer of the English criminal law.

Franklin went on to speak of war as theft and murder. "Justice is as strictly due between neighbour nations as between neighbour citizens. A highwayman is as much a robber when he plunders in a gang as when single; and a nation that makes an unjust war is only a great gang."[28] He accused England particularly of making unjust wars and of privateering, which was theft. But he believed privateering bad wherever practised, and he had already drawn up the article against it and the molestation of non-combatants which was incorporated in the first American treaty of amity and commerce between the United States and Prussia. Franklin's last year in France was given up to the making of such treaties more than to anything else. Jefferson arrived in August to assist Franklin and Adams, who now came from The Hague, to negotiate with European and north African powers. The three met at Franklin's house on the 30th, then daily for some time, and frequently till 9 July when they signed the treaty with Prussia three days before Franklin left for America. He had a hand in all their joint reports to Congress,[29] and he wrote the first draft of the proposed treaty with the piratical Barbary States.[30]

II

When Jefferson reached Paris he found "more respect and veneration attached to the character of Dr. Franklin in France than to that of any other person, foreign or native."[31] Franklin had just come before the public in the last conspicuous episode of his French career. It had to do with Mesmer and mesmerism.

Friedrich Anton Mesmer had been in Paris for six years, trying to win scientific approval of theories already rejected in Vienna and Berlin. Though he had won the favour of the queen and had a fashionable following, he had been steadily opposed by physicians and scientists, who thought him a greedy, unscrupulous charlatan. Denied a licence to practise medicine in France, he had a licensed doctor, Charles Deslon, as disciple and partner and eventually as rival. Mesmer seems to have been honest in his belief that he had made a discovery in the art of healing, as he had. But this pioneer in psychotherapy also believed that his cures were brought about by the action of a universal fluid diffused throughout nature, upholding and governing the stars, and flowing—to put it simply—from healer to patient as animal magnetism. With some skill in curing by suggestion, on the verge of the discovery of hypnotism, Mesmer was occult in his doctrines and flamboyant in his methods. He gave group treatments which were like séances, with hocus-pocus and hysteria. Early in 1784, with the war ended and balloons no longer so exciting as at first, Mesmer became a tremendous fad. Among his ardent followers were Lafayette and many nobles of the highest rank and influence. To assist Mesmer in carrying out his grandiose designs, establishing a hospital, and even setting up a new academy for his new science, a joint stock company was organized and raised 340,000 livres. The matter had become so serious that the king on 12 March appointed a commission to investigate animal magnetism as practised by the licensed Deslon. The first four commissioners were doctors chosen from the Faculty of Paris, one of them Joseph-Ignace Guillotin whose name survives in the guillotine. These four asked that members of the Academy of Sciences be joined with them in the investigation. Five were selected: Franklin, his friends Le Roy, Bailly, and Lavoisier, and the mathematician De Bory.

Franklin on 19 March was sceptical about animal magnetism, but willing to think that the "delusion may, however, in some cases be of use while it lasts. There are in every great rich city a number of persons who are never in health because they are fond of medicines and always taking them, whereby they derange the natural functions and hurt their constitutions. If these people can be persuaded to forbear their drugs in expectation of being cured by only the physician's finger or an iron rod pointing at them, they may possibly find good effects though they mistake the cause."[32] He was too ill to go to Paris and left it to the other commissioners to attend Deslon's clinic and study his modes of healing.

They found that Deslon grouped his patients around a wooden tub (*baquet*) in the centre of a large, handsome, dimly lighted room with a pianoforte in the corner to accompany and stimulate the cures. Through holes in the lid of the tub long iron rods, jointed, reached to the patients and could be applied to whatever parts of their bodies needed treatment. Then the whole group was linked together with cords and each member of it held his neighbour's thumb between his own thumb and first finger. To the sound of music, perhaps of voices singing, the healer walked about and among his patients, now pointing a short iron rod at them, now touching them with his hands on the parts affected or particularly on the lower abdomen. The tub, Deslon explained, was the condenser and conductor of the animal magnetism which streamed through the group. Nature was one, and there was only one disease and one remedy. Animal magnetism, the universal fluid, was the universal means by which all men could be cured of their ills. The treatments went on for hours in a growing tension, with nervous coughing, hiccups, outcries, tears, immoderate laughter, often convulsions which were looked upon as salutary. More women than men got into convulsive states, the investigators noted. They could find no electricity in the tub and were unable to perceive animal magnetism with any of their senses.

Since their presence, they thought, was disturbing to the patients, they decided to go no more to these public clinics, but to make their tests elsewhere. Several of them were carried out at Franklin's house in Passy, in late April and early May,[33] on 19 June and perhaps other days. First they chose for experiment seven persons of a lower class. The asthmatic widow Saint-Amand; the woman Anseaune who had a swelling on her thigh; Claude Renard, six years old, scrofulous and tubercular; Geneviève Leroux, nine, afflicted with something like St. Vitus's dance: all these felt nothing in the stream of Deslon's animal magnetism. François Grenet, who had a tumour in his blind right eye, had a little pain in his left eyeball when Deslon moved his finger back and forth close in front of it. The woman Charpentier, who two years before had been thrown down by a cow and been infirm ever since, suffered when Deslon pressed his hand on her ruptured abdomen. Joseph Ennuyé's sensations were less acute but perceptible. Four out of the seven had not been affected at all.

Then for another test the examiners selected four persons of a higher social class. Madame de Bory and M. Romagni had no sensations. M. Moret,[34] with a tumour on his knee, thought it grew warmer when Deslon's hand came near it. Madame de V——, who had some nervous disorder, almost fell asleep under the treatment—that is, presumably, she was almost hypnotized. At the end of an hour and nineteen minutes she was agitated and in some discomfort. Franklin, his grandsons, his secretary, and an American officer felt nothing. Certain patients whom Deslon had brought with him were more responsive, but when blindfolded they several times thought they were being magnetized when they were not, and when they were being did not perceive it. In the most dramatic of the experiments Deslon magnetized an apricot tree in Franklin's garden so that, he maintained, it would affect anybody who touched it. Deslon when he had done this was required to stand some distance away to prevent any signalling to his subject, a boy twelve years old. The boy was led out of the house, with a bandage over his eyes, and to four unmagnetized trees one after another. At the first tree the boy perspired and coughed. At the second he felt a pain and stupor in his head. At the third he complained of an increasing headache and said he was getting closer to the magnetic tree, though he was further from it than ever. At the fourth tree he fainted. They carried him to a grass plot where Deslon revived him.[35]

Franklin, as the oldest and most eminent of the investigators, signed his name first to the *Rapport* which was made to the king on 11 August and to the briefer *Exposé* which Bailly read to the Academy of Sciences on 4 September. It is not known whether Franklin had a hand, or how much he had, in the writing of these papers.[36] But he agreed with the others in a unanimous opinion that no such thing as Mesmer's animal magnetism had been shown to exist. If there was no universal fluid there could have been no cures by it. The commission had found none that seemed convincing. All the observed effects, they thought, of the public séances were due to familiar causes. The patients were excited by the contact (*attouchement*) of the healers' hands. Expecting to feel powerful sensations, they imagined themselves into them. In the contagion of the group its members involuntarily imitated one another. Since the patients as well as the healers believed that there had to be convulsive states (*crises*) before there could be cures, a séance was commonly drawn out till the whole group was hysterical. The commissioners condemned public treatments as useless and likely to be hurtful. A secret report, not printed at the time, spoke of a special danger from private treatments.[37] Susceptible women, many of them merely idle and curious, were treated at great length by the intimate pressure of the hands of healers who were always men. The magnetic excitement was in such cases partly erotic and no less objectionable when not recognized as such by the women.

Puységur, a disciple of Mesmer, that same summer made valuable discoveries in hypnotism, regarded as a form of magnetic sleep, and used by him if not to much therapeutic purpose at least without the uproar of Mesmer and Deslon. But all of them came under the same condemnation, and hypnotism went undeveloped for half a century. The mesmerists had been so much involved in alchemistic doctrines, extravagant claims, and mountebank ceremonies that the steps they had taken toward mental healing by suggestion were overlooked. The royal commission overlooked them. Its report was taken for the complete exposure of an absolute delusion, what Jefferson called a "compound of fraud and folly." Mesmerism ceased to be a fashion. Mesmer left Paris. Animal magnetism sank again to its earlier level among popular superstitions. Franklin, more widely known than any of his colleagues, was supposed throughout Europe and America to have been their chief in this deathblow to quacks.

Varied international honours came to him during 1784–85 in his election to membership in the Royal Academy of History at Madrid, in academies of sciences and arts at Orléans and Lyons, in the Literary and Philosophical Society of Manchester. From the Papal Nuncio in July 1784 Franklin heard that the Pope, because of what Franklin had said of John Carroll of the Canada expedition of 1776, had named Carroll the Superior of the Catholic clergy in America.[38] The British admiralty through Lord Howe sent Franklin a copy of Captain Cook's *Voyage to the Pacific Ocean* and the Royal Society of London one of the medals which had been struck to commemorate the navigator. George III, though "with a little difficulty," approved the admiralty's friendly gesture to the rebel Franklin who had ordered American cruisers not to interfere with Cook on his return from the South Seas. "The reward," Franklin wrote to Howe on 18 August, "vastly exceeds the small merit of the action, which was no more than a duty to mankind. I am very sensible of His Majesty's goodness in permitting this favour to me, and I desire that my thankful acknowledgments may be accepted."[39] If Franklin and his former king were able now to be, at whatever distance, polite again, the war was over. The king's ambassador to France, the Duke of Dorset, called regularly at Passy, on business and for pleasure.

Banks, for the Royal Society and himself, was eager to make up to Franklin for any share they may have had in "the illiberal treatment towards you," Banks wrote, "with which I fear this country may too justly be accused."[40] Most of Franklin's older friends in England and Scotland had died: Mrs. Stevenson in Craven Street, Fothergill, Pringle, Hume, Lord Kames, Lord Le Despencer. With Strahan, a correspondent for fifty years and even occasionally during the war, Franklin was once more on good terms. He had never ceased being friends with Bishop Shipley and his family. Most of all Franklin remembered the club of

Honest Whigs. "I often think," he wrote to Price on 16 August, "of the agreeable evenings I used to pass with that excellent collection of good men, the club at the London. . . . Perhaps I may pop in some evening when they least expect me"—although, as he explained, his stone made travelling nearly intolerable. Priestley had at last been elected one of the foreign members of the French Academy of Sciences. "I have mentioned him," Franklin told Price, "upon every vacancy that has happened since my residence here, and the place has never been bestowed more worthily."[41]

On that same day Franklin wrote to William Franklin, who had written first to him. "I . . . am glad to find that you desire to revive that affectionate intercourse that formerly existed between us. It will be very agreeable to me; indeed nothing has ever hurt me so much and affected me with such keen sensations as to find myself deserted in my old age by my only son; and not only deserted, but to find him taking up arms against me in a cause wherein my good fame, fortune, and life were all at stake. You conceived, you say, that your duty to your king and regard for your country required this. I ought not to blame you for differing in sentiment with me in public affairs. We are men, all subject to errors. Our opinions are not in our power; they are formed and governed much by circumstances that are often as inexplicable as they are irresistible. Your situation was such that few would have censured your remaining neuter, though there are natural duties which precede political ones and cannot be extinguished by them. This is a disagreeable subject. I drop it." As to his own future plans, he had intended returning to America that year but had not yet been given leave by Congress. In another year "perhaps I may . . . be too old and feeble to bear the voyage. I am here among a people that love and respect me, a most amiable nation to live with; and perhaps I may conclude to die among them; for my friends in America are dying off one after another, and I have been so long abroad that I should now be almost a stranger in my own country."[42] He sent Temple to London for a visit with his father which lasted about two months. During his grandson's absence the philosopher was lonely, apparently afraid the young man might remain in England, and their friends in Passy were solicitous. "I have three invitations to dine out today," he wrote to

Temple on 8 September, "with Madames Brillon, Helvétius, and M. de Chaumont. But it is so excessively hot that I shall stay at home."[43] It was on one of these lonely days that Madame Helvétius dined with Franklin and shocked Abigail Adams.

Franklin now seldom left Passy, but the world came to call on him on all sorts of errands. In particular he was visited by young Englishmen who saw in him the philosopher-hero of the Revolution: William Pitt and William Wilberforce,[44] Samuel Romilly and his friend John Baynes who wrote out all he could remember of what the sage had said about Parliamentary reform, universal suffrage, the resignation of Washington from the American army, the inequality of corruption among men, Quakers, salaries for public officers, imprisonment for debt, the prevention of wars by an international congress, standing armies, luxury, primogeniture, the accumulation of landed estates.[45] Franklin talked with everyone, often with officious busybodies. "It is amazing," he observed in his *Journal* on 18 July, "the number of legislators that kindly bring me new plans for governing the United States."[46] He seems never to have felt the dark need to be alone, and his curiosity was endless. The last thing he wrote in Europe, besides letters, was the engaging *Observations on Mayz, or Indian Corn*[47] which he sent to the chemist Cadet de Vaux on 28 April 1785 and which told all that was then known about the use of corn as food for men or animals: green corn roasted, boiled, or dried, lye hominy, corn meal coarse or fine, hasty pudding, hoecake, corn bread, pop corn, corn syrup, corn liquor, corn fodder.

"You know everything makes me recollect some story," he said in a letter to his daughter. Besides his little moral tales there were his pleasant reminiscences. Talking with John Jay in the summer which the Jays spent at Passy, Franklin told how he had come to be made printer for New Jersey. He had once been at Burlington when the New Jersey Assembly was having some dispute with the governor. No one of the members felt able to write the reply which they thought the governor's message called for. Franklin wrote it for them, and for that and later help was given their public printing. He told Jay stories, of Robert Hunter Morris and of the Pennsylvania Quakers in wartime, which later appeared in his *Autobiography*.[48] That unfinished project was brought back to Franklin's mind by a letter from Abel James in Philadelphia, who had read the manuscript of the first part which Franklin had left with Galloway. Perhaps it had been lost and found again; more likely it had been preserved by Galloway's wife, who had lately died.[49] James, one of her executors, urged Franklin to continue his story. Benjamin Vaughan, then in Paris, was no less urgent. Franklin, who had no copy of his work, could not remember exactly where he had broken off. But some time during 1784 he took up the narrative close to the point where he had stopped thirteen years before. In a short section he told of the founding of the Philadelphia library and his own heroic, mathematical experiments in perfection. Then he broke off again.

John Jay went for his first visit to England in October 1783, leaving his wife and children at Franklin's house and, after they moved to Chaillot early in November, more or less in Franklin's care. On the 6th Mrs. Jay wrote her husband that their slave girl Abigail had become jealous of their French nurse and run away to hide with their English washerwoman. Franklin had the police look for her. Found, she refused to come back. The philosopher suggested they give her fifteen or twenty days to think it over. On 7 December Mrs. Jay wrote again that Abby had changed her mind and wanted to be with them again.[50] Franklin and Temple were the first who came to tea at Chaillot. Once at Passy during November, Franklin teased Mrs. Jay. He showed her and the company two pieces of magnetized steel, one to represent her and one her husband. When they were close, in Chaillot Franklin said, her piece drew Jay's to her. But when Jay's was put at a distance and nearer a third piece, representing an English lady, the English lady had the stronger attraction.[51] Mrs. Jay delighted in Franklin's humorous teasing, which pleased Jay because it showed the Doctor was in high spirits. After Jay's return in January the two families kept up the friendliest relations, though Jay was sometimes troubled a little by Franklin's freethinking. But the Jays returned to America in the spring, and the Adamses, who lived at Auteuil the following winter, were less congenial.

Between Franklin and Jefferson there was perfect harmony. They had been philosophers together in Congress. Franklin introduced his friend to philosophers in France and to the circle of the

Comtesse d'Houdetot. Jefferson had then or later no doubt that Franklin was the greatest American, and felt no envy of him. He thought Franklin had the confidence of the French ministers to such a degree "that it may truly be said that they were more under his influence than he under theirs." It was, Jefferson afterwards said, a school of humility to succeed Franklin as minister to France. No one could replace him, Jefferson always insisted. He was only Franklin's successor. There are few records of their friendship. Seeing each other, they had no reason to write letters, and Jefferson after Franklin's death wrote out only a few of his remarks and his stories. Two of them concerned the Abbé Raynal. Franklin, he told Jefferson, "had a party to dine with him one day at Passy, of whom one half were Americans, the other half French, and among the last was the Abbé. During the dinner he got on his favourite theory of the degeneracy of animals, and even in man, in America, and urged it with his usual eloquence. The Doctor at length, noticing the accidental stature and position of his guests at table, 'Come,' says he, 'M. l'Abbé, let us try this question by the fact before us. We are here one half Americans and one half French, and it happens that the Americans have placed themselves on one side of the table and our French friends on the other. Let both parties rise and we will see on which side nature has degenerated.'" The Americans were tall and large and the French remarkably diminutive, most of all Raynal.

On another day Silas Deane, in the presence of Franklin, told Raynal that the speech of Polly Baker which the Abbé had put into his *Histoire des Deux Indes* could not be true, since there was no such law against bastardy in Massachusetts as the story assumed. Raynal protested that he had documentary authority, though he could not at the moment remember what it was. "Dr. Franklin, who had been for some time shaking with unrestrained laughter at the Abbé's confidence in his authority for that tale, said: 'I will tell you, Abbé, the origin of that story. When I was a printer and editor of a newspaper, we were sometimes slack of news, and, to amuse our customers, I used to fill up our vacant columns with anecdotes and fables and fancies of my own; and this of Polly Baker is a story of my making, on one of these occasions.' The Abbé, without the least disconcert, exclaimed with a laugh: 'Oh, very well, Doctor, I had rather relate your stories than other men's truths.' "[52]

With Polly Hewson and her children in his house during his last French winter Franklin was happy, though still disappointed that Congress, for all his efforts, showed no sign of doing anything for Temple. Perhaps Franklin blamed himself for having trained his grandson only for a public office. Without that, and without special talent or ambition as the most partial grandfather could see, Temple seemed content to be a man of pleasure in Paris or willing to seek his fortune with his father in London. A trade would probably have been better for him. Benjamin Bache, learning a trade, should have the best teaching. In October Franklin installed a master founder at his press in Passy to show the boy how to cast type. In April François Didot, the best printer in France, was persuaded to take Benjamin as apprentice. He ate his meals at Didot's, lodged at Le Roy's in Paris, and came to Passy for weekends. But this arrangement did not last long. On 2 May Franklin received from Congress the long-delayed permission to come home. Ten weeks later he set out from Passy on his boldest journey. He was not sure he could bear the motion of a ship. But his desire for America was so strong that he was willing to travel to Havre to find out. If he could not, then he would have to be put ashore and die in Europe.

III

His last return could hardly have been less like his first, that lusty voyage of an obscure journeyman in the summer of 1726. Now he came back the most famous private citizen in the world. He had the king's miniature set with 408 diamonds, given by the king's government to the departing ambassador. (But the gifts of kings are seldom quite free gifts. Franklin, as was expected of him, gave the official in charge of the present a gold snuffbox worth a tenth as much as the miniature, and fifty louis d'or to his assistant.[53]) With Vergennes Franklin exchanged courtly, complimentary farewells. The minister of marine wrote, too late, that

Franklin might have made the voyage in a royal frigate put at his service in his honour. He was furnished a royal litter from Passy to Havre, and his goods which went by barge down the Seine filled 128 boxes. The litter was ready at his house at four o'clock on the morning of 12 July, but he still had so many accounts to settle that it was late in the afternoon, after dinner with the Chaumonts, before Franklin was helped into his stately conveyance in the courtyard, "in the midst," according to Benjamin Bache, "of a very great concourse of the people of Passy; a mournful silence reigned around him, and was only interrupted by a few sobs."[54]

"When he left Passy," Jefferson said, "it seemed as if the village had lost its patriarch."[55] The Chaumonts, the Brillons, and Madame Helvétius each begged him to spend the rest of his life with them. Infirm and almost eighty, tormented by the stone at any rough motion, how could he risk bad weather on the Atlantic and the conditions, hard at best, of life at sea? Madame Le Veillard accepted his tea table as a sacred relic; Chaumont his table of Mangoni wood which might be ingeniously raised and lowered; the Abbé Morellet his armchair; Cabanis the cane with the hollow joint with which Franklin had played magician. Chaumont and his daughter Sophie accompanied the litter as far as Nanterre; Le Veillard all the way to Havre and then across the Channel to Southampton. Madame Brillon, who could not bear to witness his actual departure, wrote him two days before: "All the days of my life I shall remember that a great man, a sage, wished to be my friend. My prayers will follow him everywhere, my heart will regret him for ever."[56] After her eight years with him she would never have such a friend again. She wept with Madame Helvétius and accused her of letting their great friend go.

He had hardly left when Madame Helvétius wrote a letter to overtake him at Havre. She could not make herself realize that he was no longer at Passy. Yet "I see you in your litter, every step taking you further from us, lost to me and all my friends who love you so much and to whom you leave such long regrets. I am afraid that you are suffering and the journey is tiring you and making your ailment worse. If that is so, come back, dear friend, to us. You will adorn my little retreat. . . . You will increase our happiness and we shall contribute to yours. You cannot doubt this. You could read it in my heart and in the hearts of all my good friends, who are also yours."[57]

Again as fifty-nine years before, though more laconically, Franklin kept a journal.[58] "Having stayed in France about eight years and a half, I took leave of the court and my friends and set out on my return home, July 12th, leaving Passy with my two grandsons at four p.m.; arrived about eight o'clock at St. Germain. . . . We met at St. Germain the Miss Alexanders, with Mrs. Williams our cousin [wife of Jonathan Williams], who had provided a lodging for me at M. Benoît's. I found that the motion of the litter, lent me by the Duke of Coigny, did not much incommode me. It was one of the queen's, carried by two very large mules, the muleteer riding another; M. Le Veillard and my children in a carriage. We drank tea at M. Benoît's and went early to bed." The next morning they said good-bye and went on, Franklin ahead in the litter which swayed easily between the tall Spanish mules "going only foot pace," Le Veillard, the grandsons, and Temple's servant in the two-horse coach behind. That day they made twenty miles, dined at an inn in Meulan, and stopped at Mantes in the evening. "A messenger from the Cardinal de la Rochefoucauld meets us there, with an invitation to us to stop at his house at Gaillon the next day, acquainting us at the same time that he would take no excuse; for, being all-powerful in his archbishopric [Rouen], he would stop us *nolens volens* at his habitation and not permit us to lodge anywhere else. We consented. Lodged at Mantes. Found myself very little fatigued with the day's journey."

They must have started at daylight the day after, for they had breakfast a dozen miles further at Vernon, where the Vicomte de Tilly (father of Madame Le Roy the pocket-wife) and his comtesse called on them. "Arrived at the cardinal's without dining, about six in the afternoon." Their host showed them his château, his picture gallery, his chapel, his magnificent terrace. "We supped early. The entertainment was kind and cheerful. We were allowed to go early to bed, on account of our intention to depart early in the morning. The cardinal pressed us to stay another day with him, offering to amuse us with hunting in his park." They could not waste a day for fear of being late at Havre. "Set out about five in the morning, travelled till ten, then stopped to breakfast and remained in the inn during the heat of the day. . . . We passed a chain of chalk mountains very high, with strata of flints. The quantity that appears to have been washed away on one side of these mountains, leaving precipices of three hundred feet high, gives an idea of extreme antiquity. It seems as if done by the beating of the sea." Chaumont had written to Jean Holker, a merchant who had furnished supplies to the American army during the war, that their friend would come that way. "We got to Rouen about five; were most affectionately received by Mr. and Mrs. Holker. A great company of genteel people at supper, which was our dinner. . . . We lodge all at Mr. Holker's."

Rouen would not let them go. The next morning "a deputation from the Academy of Rouen came with their compliments, which were delivered in form, and a present for me by one of the directors, being a magical square which I think he said expressed my name. I have perused it since but do not comprehend it." There were many guests at dinner, and at six Franklin went in a chair to call on the chief president of the Parlement. "We drank tea there, awkwardly made for want of practice, very little being drunk in France. I went to bed early; but my company supped with a large invited party and were entertained with excellent singing."

On the 17th Holker rode with them for several miles. They dined at Yvetot and got that evening to Bolbec, "being the longest day's journey we have yet made"—perhaps thirty miles. "A linenprinter here offered to remove to America, but I did not encourage him." The next afternoon they reached Havre, where they waited four days for a packet to carry them to England. On the 19th the sculptor Houdon arrived from Paris. He was sailing to America with Franklin, whose bust he had made eight years before, to make a bust of Washington for Virginia. Franklin, writing that day his last letter in France to Madame Helvétius, said he felt stronger than when he left Passy. After continual entertainments in Havre, when they crossed the windy Channel from the morning of the 22nd to the morning of the 24th, Franklin was the only member of the party who was not seasick. They landed at Southampton and all put up at the Star tavern.

Though William Franklin had come from London, there seems to have been no revival of the old affection between father and son. Franklin's journal on four successive days says only: "Met my son, who had arrived from London the evening before. . . . Read over the writings of conveyance, etc., of my son's lands in New Jersey and New York to my grandson. . . . Deeds signed between W. Franklin and W. T. Franklin. . . . Give a power to my son to recover what may be due to me from the British government." (Half of what might be recovered was to be Sarah Bache's.[59]) Franklin was more at ease with his friends. As soon as he landed he sent a note to Bishop Shipley at Winchester, and the bishop with his wife and his daughter Catherine came at once to the Star, where they stayed till Franklin sailed. Catherine was that Kitty who as a child had told Franklin all her plans for the marriage of the Shipley girls.

"*July 25th.*—The bishop and family lodging in the same inn . . . we all breakfast and dine together. I went at noon to bathe in St. Martin's salt-water hot bath and, floating on my back, fell asleep and slept near an hour by my watch without sinking or turning! A thing I never did before and should hardly have thought possible. Water is the easiest bed that can be." Other friends came down from London, bringing Franklin presents. The home secretary sent word that his baggage was not to be opened. Jonathan Williams, whose wife they had left temporarily at Saint-Germain, was in England ready for America again. He had gone bankrupt in France the year before. Benjamin Vaughan arrived. Le Veillard left for France, carrying letters to Franklin's friends. One of them arranged for the payment out of Franklin's account of 48,000 livres to William Franklin for the land conveyed to Temple.[60] Captain Truxtun, later a commodore in the United States navy, on the 27th brought the London packet, 400 tons, into Cowes.

Till the day before the last Franklin hoped, without much confidence, that Polly Hewson and her children might join him in the emigration to Philadelphia which she had almost decided upon. A letter came saying she could not yet decide. "I am sorry," he wrote her, "it did not suit you to go in the ship with me, having engaged places in the cabin that would have accommodated you and yours; not indeed on your account, because I never depended on your going; but I took the whole cabin that I might not be intruded on by any accidental disagreeable company."[61] On the 27th: "We all dine once more with the bishop and family who kindly accept our invitation to go on board with us. We go down in a shallop to the ship. The captain entertains us at supper. The company stay all night." But the next day: "When I waked in the morning found the company gone and the ship under sail."

Stone or no stone, this was probably the most cheerful of all Franklin's eight voyages. He believed that his public life was over and he was finally free for science. On the second day out he began daily records, with Jonathan Williams's help, of the temperature of air and water. On 14 August and 11 September they tried, by letting down a bottle and a keg, to find out the temperature of the water at eighteen or twenty fathoms. As much interested in the Gulf Stream as ever, Franklin took notes on currents and colours and the presence of gulf weed. On the night of 5 September they had the one storm of the voyage, otherwise calm. Franklin wrote more on scientific matters in August than in any other month of his life. His *Maritime Observations*,[62] in form a letter to Julien-David Le Roy, brother of Franklin's electrical friend, took up the rigging of ships; a device to keep hausers from breaking at the sudden swell of a wave; the use of water-tight compartments in a ship to prevent sinking (an early and important contribution); fire, lightning, collision with other ships or icebergs; the construction and operation of Pacific proas, Eskimo kayaks, Indian canoes; paddlewheels to serve as auxiliary to the wind; swimming anchors to retard the motion of vessels during gales in water too deep for anchorage; the Gulf Stream's cause and uses; improved diet for sailors; suggestions for the management of lifeboats and escape from wrecks; advice to passengers as to the stores they should take with them on shipboard. Once Franklin intended to stop, "but the garrulity of an old man has got hold of me, and, as I may never have another occasion of writing on this subject, I think I may as well now, once and for all, empty my nautical budget." He continued in encyclopædic high spirits and ended with a paragraph on the evil uses of navigation in transporting useless luxuries and carrying on the cruel slave trade.

To Ingenhousz in Vienna Franklin on 28 August began a long letter *On the Causes and Cure of Smoky Chimneys*,[63] a fundamental little treatise. He had time at sea to write out a detailed technical *Description of a New Stove for Burning of Pitcoal, and Consuming All Its Smoke*,[64] which he had invented in London in 1771, used three winters there, one in America, and afterwards in Passy. "I have not yet thought of any improvement it may be capable of, though such may occur to others." All these he wrote in his cabin as in a study, too much absorbed to keep up his journal of what happened to him or the forty persons on the ship. More interested in science than in his own life, he did not touch his *Autobiography*, though his friends had urged him to devote the voyage to that. Not till 13 September did he make another journal entry. "The wind springing fair last evening after a calm, we found ourselves this morning, at sun-rising, abreast of the lighthouse and between Capes May and Henlopen. We sail into the bay very pleasantly; water smooth, air cool, day fair and fine. We passed New Castle about sunset and went on near Red Bank before the tide and wind failed; then came to an anchor.

"*Wednesday, September 14th.*—With the flood in the morning came a light breeze which brought us above Gloucester Point, in full view of dear Philadelphia! when we again cast anchor to wait for the health officer, who, having made his visit and finding no sickness, gave us leave to land. My son-in-law came with a boat for us; we landed at Market Street wharf, where we were received by a crowd of people with huzzas, and accompanied with acclamations quite to my door. Found my family well.

"God be praised and thanked for all His mercies!"

The United States

President of Pennsylvania

ANOTHER ship had outsailed the London packet and brought
news of Franklin nine days before him. Philadelphia waited
in hourly excitement. Cannon announced his landing at the
Market Street wharf—where he had as a runaway from Boston
first set foot in the town. Bells rang while he proceeded up the
street four squares to Franklin Court, his daughter, the grandchildren he had only read about, the house the British had occupied and plundered. "The affectionate welcome I met with from
my fellow-citizens," he wrote to Jay in New York a week later,
"was far beyond my expectation."

The welcome was a continuous ceremony for more than that
first week. The public gave him a single night in which to rest,
and then began to call on him. On the next day the Speaker of the
General Assembly, John Bayard, and a member from each county
brought an address of congratulation and felicitation. Franklin
said that he esteemed their "approbation as one of the greatest
honours of my life" and that their kind wishes "for my particular
happiness affect me very sensibly." The day after, John Ewing,
Provost of the University, came with the professors to pay their
special tribute to the scientist and philanthropist who had "first
projected" the Academy, "this favourite child of your youth." "My
best wishes," he said, "will always attend it." On Saturday fifteen
members of the Constitutional Society, led by William Adcock,
came to salute him as the "father of our free and excellent constitution." "In the service you are pleased so kindly to remember,"
he said, "I had great and able assistance from others. My principal
merit, if I may claim any, in public affairs is that of having been
always ready and willing to receive and follow good advice."[1]

Politics had already laid hold on Franklin. The Constitutionalists were the radical majority in the Assembly, increasingly opposed by the more moderate men who desired to amend the state constitution. The Constitutional Society had come to court the greatest Pennsylvanian for their party. The moderates had moved more rapidly. On that same Saturday it was announced that a committee from a "respectable meeting of citizens" at Byrne's tavern had got from Franklin his promise to be the city's candidate, on the Anti-Constitutionalist ticket, for election the next month to the Supreme Executive Council. The Constitutionalists nominated him too, and after them the Mechanical Society: that is, the mechanics of Philadelphia.[2]

Meanwhile the general reception went on. On Monday General James Irvine and the officers of the militia brought their address, and—apparently that day—Plunket Fleeson and the justices of the city and county. On Tuesday morning the *Pennsylvania Packet* outdid itself. Most of history's heroes, "from Macedonia's madman to the Swede," had given themselves to works of destruction; but the celebrated Dr. Franklin's "utmost endeavours have been as invariably turned to promote the prosperity of the human race. . . . The glory of this father of American independence will continue to receive an increase of effulgence. Latest posterity will be wrapt in admiration at the prodigious efforts of native genius which, almost entirely unassisted by the auxiliaries that other famed characters are so much indebted to, shone forth the bright luminary of the western hemisphere." Later in the day, when the Freemasons dedicated a new lodge in Black Horse Alley, they drank a toast first to the king of Prussia, then to George Washington the intended Grand Master of the United States, then to "that dignified philosopher and friend to mankind, Brother Benjamin Franklin,"[3] who seems not to have been present.

The following Monday he met with the members of the Union Fire Company which he had founded nearly fifty years before. Only four of the original members were still alive. Franklin, cheerful among descendants of his old friends, "signed the new articles, and said he would have his bucket, etc., in good order by the next meeting." On Tuesday he took the chair at the American Philosophical Society, meeting at six at the University. Thomas McKean, chief justice of Pennsylvania, read the address of welcome to the philosopher who was "equally distinguished for his philan-thropy, patriotism, and liberal attachment to the rights of human nature." In the "independence which you had so great a share in establishing" the Society hoped it might now go on with enlarging success to its true business. Franklin in his reply was even briefer than usual. They had greatly honoured him by electing him year after year during his absence in Europe. He was grateful, and he gave his warmest wishes for their success in "the promotion of useful knowledge among us, to which I shall be happy if I can in any degree contribute."[4]

Waiting for the election, Franklin wrote a few letters: the first officially to Jay, Congress's secretary for foreign affairs. The next day (20 September) he wrote to Catherine Greene and her hus-band, affectionately telling them of his return and asking about their welfare; and to Washington, introducing Houdon, who at once set out for Mount Vernon. Washington had already heard that Franklin was again in Philadelphia. The two, each without having yet received a letter, sent greetings in the generous lan-guage they always unenviously used with one another. The letter to Jay had gone by Temple Franklin, who his grandfather still hoped might be given some post by Congress, then sitting in New York. Friendly messages came from Jay and his wife, who wished Franklin might be able to bear, as he thought he might, a journey to visit them. Thomas Paine, trying to get from Congress some reward for his services to the country, wrote that he believed he had done nothing to make Franklin regret sending him over from England. "Be assured, my dear friend," Franklin answered on the 27th, "that instead of repenting that I was your introducer into America, I value myself on the share I had in procuring for it the acquisition of so useful and valuable a citizen." As to his situation in Pennsylvania, he had been told he might be able to reconcile the contending parties and "had not sufficient firmness" to refuse to stand for election. "Though I apprehend they expect too much of me, and that without doing the good proposed I shall find myself engaged again in business more troublesome than I have lately quitted."[5]

At the election on 11 October Franklin won his seat in the Council, which he took on the 17th. The Council chose him its president the next day. When the new General Assembly met a week later there was no quorum for two days, but on Saturday the 29th the Assembly proceeded with the Council to the joint election of a president for Pennsylvania. The Council came at eleven to the Assembly chamber in the State House. Franklin was elected, unanimously except for one vote besides his own out of seventy-seven, and Charles Biddle vice-president. The entire body, with all the major and minor officers of the state then in Philadelphia, marched in elaborate order to the courthouse opposite Franklin's first house and shop. There the election of "His Excellency the President and Honourable the Vice-President" was formally proclaimed, "amidst a great concourse of people who expressed their satisfaction by repeated shouts."[6] The procession returned to the State House in the same order. Franklin took the oath of office on Monday.

That day and the next the Council dealt with such routine matters as regularly came before it. George McCrea of Franklin County had been sentenced to pay a fine for selling spirituous liquors without a licence. The Council remitted his fine. It gave an order for the warrant to hang John McDonald on 9 November for the murder of Catherine Kraemer. The records of the conviction and sentence of Robert Elliott for burglary and of Elizabeth Wilson for the killing of her bastard twins were read and postponed for further consideration. John Biddle was appointed measurer of all kinds of corn (grain) and salt imported and brought into the port and city of Philadelphia. The Council decided that John Horn, a minister of the Seventh Day Baptists, was not liable to military duty, and so instructed the lieutenant of militia for his county. Franklin's administration may be said to have begun with his message to the Assembly on 11 November. Along with recommendations as to tax lists and new roads the message proposed that criminals without money be allowed to work out their fines instead of being kept in prison at public charge; and that the test act be amended. "The test laws," he said, "however proper or necessary they may have been at the time or under the circumstances in which they were made, are at present, on various accounts, the cause of much uneasiness in the state. We are, therefore, of the opinion that it is now expedient to revise them."[7]

With this Franklin took his stand against the Constitutionalists who had voted for him in the hope he would support the constitution he had helped make in 1776. On the whole he still favoured its provisions for a single legislative body and a plural executive, with the power in the hands of the people and without any such authoritative governor as he had fought year after year while in the provincial Assembly. The test act, passed after he went to France, could be nothing but repugnant to him. Under it no one could hold office or even vote without taking an oath of allegiance to the constitution. This excluded from a share in the government not only the Quakers and certain German sects who objected to oaths on principle but also many persons who thought the constitution unsatisfactory because of the dominance of the legislature over the executive and judicial branches. At best an emergency act in 1777, when the patriots thought more of keeping affairs in their own hands than of maintaining civil rights, it had since then been used, by the party which had led the war, to shut out the formerly disaffected, indifferent, or pacific elements which now desired a return to a post-war order based on the wishes of all the people.

The move to revise the test act did not originate with Franklin. It had been a chief though unsuccessful aim of his predecessor John Dickinson. But, whether because of a growing general sentiment or because of Franklin's liberal influence, the Assembly turned promptly to revision. On 15 December a bill came before the house and after much debate was carried for a second reading. The Assembly adjourned to the last week of February, then immediately took up the debate again. On 3 March, with the galleries crowded and many people waiting outside the chamber, the bill was carried by a vote of 45 to 23.[8] The changed test act still required voters to swear or affirm that they renounced allegiance to the king of England, were loyal to the commonwealth, and had not since the Declaration of Independence given aid to the British forces; but not that they supported the constitution which was objectionable to so many Pennsylvanians.

The minutes of the Council, which sat every week day, show that during the nearly four months between Franklin's message and the passage of the revising act he was present only about one day in six. His presence in Philadelphia was enough. He was the philosopher-statesman behind the scenes, leaving it to younger men to carry out the business and to Charles Biddle to sign messages and proclamations. Franklin's influence came from his general prestige, his reputation for wisdom, and his known desire for harmony. "We are, I think," he wrote to the bishop of St. Asaph on 24 February, "in the right road of improvement, for we are making experiments. I do not oppose all that seem wrong, for the multitude are more effectually set right by experience than kept from going wrong by reasoning with them. And I think we are daily more and more enlightened."[9] No doubt he could be, when called upon, as shrewd a politician as ever. That was not his present role. Rather, he was a sage who had retired from world affairs to the government of a single province. It must have pleased him when "a numerous company of printers" celebrated his eightieth birthday at the Bunch of Grapes tavern and drank their first toast to the "venerable printer, philosopher, and statesman."[10] But he was distressed when, on 20 February, Benjamin Rush in the annual oration before the American Philosophical Society praised its president, and Pennsylvania's, beyond his endurance. Gently and tactfully Franklin asked Rush, if he should print his oration, to leave out "that most extravagant encomium . . . which hurt me exceedingly in the unexpected hearing and will mortify me beyond conception if it should appear from the press."[11]

The scientific papers Franklin had written on his voyage were read before the Society and printed in the second volume of its *Transactions* (1786). Arranging his books in his library, he wished his arm were longer and by January had invented an instrument for taking books down from high shelves[12]—an instrument which, modified, remains in common use in grocery stores. Then or later he devised a chair which with the seat turned up served as a ladder. He planned an addition to his house and new houses in Market Street, but found building costs high and put off his plans to summer. Temple Franklin had for the present given up hope in Congress and gone to his farm at Rancocas, New Jersey, sixteen miles away. (Word came from Madame Caillot in Passy that their son had died.) It was possibly this year, with a fresh interest in agriculture, that Franklin suggested—as he is said to have done[13]—

writing "This field has been plastered" in large letters traced with gypsum in a field somewhere by the roadside. The grass so fertilized came up a brighter green than the rest and the words could be read by all the passers-by. Washington the next year found that George Logan had done something of the kind at Stenton.[14] Benjamin Franklin Bache was in college. His grandfather made plans to set him up in a printing-house. Franklin was as busy as he had been in Passy. He studiously read even while taking the long hot baths which were his relief from the stone. His tub was copper, shaped like a shoe. "He sits in the heel," Jeremy Belknap gossiped, "and his legs go under the vamp; on the instep he has a place to fix his book; and here he sits and enjoys himself."[15]

His friends in France and England wrote affectionately to him, rather more often than he to them. "The only apology I can make," he told the Abbé Morellet, "and that not a very good one, is that indolence is natural to age and that I am too much engaged in business." But he seldom forgot them long. His first letter telling of his election to office was to Madame Helvétius. Perhaps, he said, writing in French as he rarely did from America, he might be of some further benefit to his people. "Otherwise I shall wish I had accepted your friendly invitation to pass the rest of my days with you."[16] He gave Polly Hewson on 6 May his best account of his way of life in Philadelphia. A letter from her, written in December 1775, had lain all these years unforwarded among Richard Bache's papers. Reading it, with its old gossip of her children and the Craven Street circle, Franklin had come at the end upon her promise to join him in America "as soon as the ministry and Congress agreed to make peace. . . . That peace has been some time made; but alas! the promise is not yet fulfilled. . . .

"The companions of my youth are indeed almost all departed, but I find an agreeable society among their children and grandchildren. I have public business enough to preserve me from ennui, and private amusement besides in conversation, books, my garden, and cribbage. Considering our well-furnished, plentiful market as the best of gardens, I am turning mine, in the midst of which my house stands, into grass plots and gravel walks, with trees and flowering shrubs. Cards we sometimes play here, in long winter evenings; but it is as they play at chess, not for money but for honour or the pleasure of beating one another. This will not be quite a novelty to you, as you may remember we played in that manner during the winter at Passy. I have indeed now and then a little compunction in reflecting that I spend time so idly; but another reflection comes to relieve me, whispering: 'You know that the soul is immortal; why then should you be such a niggard of a little time, when you have a whole eternity before you?' So, being easily convinced and, like other reasonable creatures, satisfied with a small reason when it is in favour of doing what I have a mind to, I shuffle the cards again and begin another game.

"As to public amusements, we have neither plays nor operas, but we had yesterday a kind of oratorio, as you will see by the enclosed paper; and we have assemblies, balls, and concerts, besides little parties at one another's houses in which there is sometimes dancing and frequently good music; so that we jog on in life as pleasantly as you do in England—anywhere but in London, for there you have plays performed by good actors. That, however, is I think the only advantage London has over Philadelphia."[17] Polly Hewson brought her family to Philadelphia later that year. Franklin's account with the bank shows that he let her have $185.30 on 11 January 1787, probably an advance while she was getting settled.[18]

Through the summer of 1786, with the Assembly not in session, Franklin went only four times to the daily meetings of the Council. When Scotosh, son of the half-king of the Wyandots, passed through Philadelphia on his way to New York to visit Congress, he called on 3 July at Franklin's house with an interpreter, strings of white wampum, and a formal message from his people. The late minister to the Court of France received the savage chief with punctilious ceremony, apologizing because the whole Council had not been called together. Though Scotosh had little to say, Franklin followed the Indian code and put off his answer for two days, when he too gave strings of wampum along with his grave reply.[19] On the 21st the American Philosophical Society, at its annual election of new members, included among them William Temple Franklin and a whole list of Franklin's friends in Europe: La Rochefoucauld, Condorcet, Soulavie, Ingenhousz, Charles (the aeronaut); the Passy-Auteuil neighbours Le Roy, Le Veillard,

Cabanis; Franklin's English editor Benjamin Vaughan and his Manchester correspondent Thomas Percival.[20]

During the September session of the Assembly an act was passed to amend the penal code of Pennsylvania, which had hitherto made hanging the punishment for robbery, burglary, rape, arson, sodomy, malicious maiming, manslaughter, and counterfeiting as well as for murder and treason. Under the new act only murder and treason were capital offences, the others punishable by imprisonment at hard labour. Branding with a hot iron, ear-cropping, whipping, and the use of the pillory were abolished. For ten years various Quakers had been working to reform the code, but they were first successful in Franklin's administration.[21] There was more resistance in the Assembly to the Anti-Constitutionalist bill to restore the charter of the Bank of North America, founded in 1782. The charter had been annulled, the day before Franklin arrived in Philadelphia, by a popular majority which held that the state's one bank favoured the moneyed, creditor class at the expense of tradesmen and farmers, Philadelphia to the disadvantage of the inland counties. Franklin believed in banks and in this bank, in which he bought eight shares with an overdraft within three months after his return,[22] and of which his son-in-law Richard Bache was a director. Again, as in the case of the test act, his influence was on the side of the Anti-Constitutionalists, and after a prolonged debate the charter was restored on 17 March 1787.[23] He was re-elected President on 4 November with no vote cast against him but his own.

For almost thirty years, spent in Europe for the public, Franklin had been able to give little time to his private affairs. They had done so well without him that he found his "estate . . . more than tripled in value since the Revolution"[24] by the rise in the price of real property. Almost as soon as he returned he applied to the governor of Georgia for payment of the salary still due Franklin for his services as colonial agent, and obtained a right to take up three thousand acres of Georgia land.[25] "I have a large tract on the Ohio," he wrote to the Abbé Morellet in April 1787. Madame Helvétius might remember "the offer I made her of a thousand acres of woodland out of which she might cut a great garden and have a thousand aviaries if she pleased."[26] He owned a house and lot in Boston and houses and lots in Philadelphia, where he bought others.[27] His chief private concern during his second year at home was building. To get money for it he sold stocks in the French funds.[28] The public market in Market Street was extended that year from Third to Fourth Street in front of his house, which stood so far back, up Franklin Court, that there were houses between him and the street front. Rents rose. "I had begun to build two good houses next the street," he wrote his sister Jane Mecom on 21 September 1786, "instead of three old ones which I pulled down; but, my neighbours disputing my bounds, I have been obliged to postpone till that dispute is settled by law. In the meantime, the workmen and materials being ready, I have ordered an addition to the house I live in, it being too small for our growing family. There are a good many hands employed, and I hope to see it covered in before winter. . . . I hardly know how to justify building a library at an age that will so soon oblige me to quit it; but we are apt to forget that we are grown old, and building is an amusement."[29]

By April 1787 he had nearly completed three houses and was about to begin two more.[30] The two next Market Street, he explained to his sister on 30 May, had an arched passage between them wide enough to admit a carriage to his dwelling. The addition he had built gave him "a large cellar for wood" and on the ground floor a dining room which would seat twenty-four persons. "It has two windows at each end, the north and south, which will make it an airy summer room; and for winter there is a good chimney in the middle, made handsome with marble slabs. Over this room is my library, of the same dimensions, with like windows at each end, and lined with books to the ceiling. Over this are two lodging-rooms; and over all a fine garret. . . . All these rooms are now finished and inhabited, very much to the convenience of the family, who were before too much crowded."[31] When the old lightning rod was taken down the copper point was found to have been melted by a stroke of lightning, rendered harmless by the conductor, while he was in France; "so that at length the invention has been of some use to the inventor."[32] He took special precautions against fire in his new buildings. "None of the wooden work of one room communicates with the wooden work of any other room; and all the floors, and even the steps of the stairs, are plastered close to the boards, besides the plastering on the laths under the joists. There are also trapdoors to go out upon the roofs, that one may go out and wet the shingles in case of a neighbouring fire. But, indeed, I think the staircases should be stone and the floors tiled, as in Paris, and the roofs either tiled or slated."[33]

Franklin on his return hoped he might stand a journey to New York and for two or three years he spoke now and then of going to his native Boston. Temple Franklin at one time expected his grandfather to come by sloop on the Delaware to the farm at Rancocas.[34] But he seems never to have stirred out of Philadelphia. Exercise was painful for him, and riding in a carriage more painful still. He had a sedan chair built and was usually carried in that, though in his first year he sometimes walked the eighth of a mile to the State House. He amused himself with wishing "I had brought with me from France a balloon sufficiently large to raise me from the ground. In my malady it would have been the most easy carriage for me, being led by a string held by a man walking on the ground."[35] A pleasant fiction invented by Crèvecœur[36] after Franklin's death says that the philosopher travelled in 1787 to lay the corner stone of Franklin (now Franklin and Marshall) College; and there have been ingenious arguments explaining why the printed programme and the newspaper report of the dedication ceremonies on 6 June made no mention of him.[37] The facts are that in the state of his health he could not have gone and that he did not go. He was present on the 6th at the meeting of the Executive Council in Philadelphia[38] and had guests at dinner one of whom was Washington.[39] But Franklin contributed £200 to the new college, twice as much as any other of the original subscribers gave. He made a point of keeping none of his annual salary (£1500) for himself.

This year a fort was built at Venango in north-western Pennsylvania and called Fort Franklin. The state already had a Franklin County and Philadelphia a ward named Franklin in December 1785.[40] Massachusetts had given the name to a town in 1778, when a part of Wrentham was set off and incorporated. The town wrote to France asking Franklin to give them a bell. He gave them books instead, "sense being preferable to sound," and asked Richard Price to select "a little parochial library for the use of a society of intelligent, respectable farmers such as our country people generally consist of."[41] The first state set up west of the mountains, what is now Tennessee, called itself Franklin (sometimes Frankland) from 1784 to 1787,[42] and during its contest with North Carolina appealed to Franklin for advice.[43] "Having resided some years past in Europe and being but lately arrived thence," he wrote to William Cocke on 12 August 1786, "I have not had an opportunity of being well informed of the points in dispute between you and the State of North Carolina. I can therefore only say that I think you are perfectly right in resolving to submit them to the decision of Congress and to abide by their determination. . . . It is happy for us all that we have now in our own country such a council to apply to for composing our differences. . . . Let us therefore cherish and respect our own tribunal; for the more generally it is held in high regard, the more able it will be to answer effectually the ends of its institution, the quieting of our contentions, and thereby promoting and securing our common peace and happiness."[44]

II

Franklin, with his immense patience in civil affairs, was less disturbed by the state of the country under the Articles of Confederation than some of the more partisan men who insisted on the need of a stronger central government. Pennsylvania at least seemed to him thoroughly prosperous at the end of 1786. "Our husbandmen," he said in a letter of 24 November, "who are the bulk of the nation, have had plentiful crops, their produce sells at high prices and for ready, hard money. . . . Our working-people are all employed and get high wages, are well fed and well clad. . . . Buildings in Philadelphia increase rapidly, besides small towns rising in every quarter of the country. The laws govern, justice is well administered, and property is as secure as in any country on the globe. Our wilderness lands are daily buying up by new settlers, and our settlements extend rapidly to the westward. European goods were never so cheaply afforded to us as since

Britain has no longer the monopoly of supplying us. In short, all among us may be happy who have happy dispositions; such being necessary to happiness even in paradise."[45] "We discover," he wrote two days later, "some errors in our general and particular constitutions; which it is no wonder they should have, the time in which they were formed being considered. But these we shall mend."[46] He took the populist insurrection known as Shays's rebellion less seriously than Washington did. "The insurgents in the Massachusetts are quelled," he wrote to Jefferson on 19 April, "and I believe a great majority of that people approve the measures of government in reducing them." Franklin thought highly of the delegates to the Constitutional Convention and hoped "good from their meeting. Indeed if it does not do good it must do harm, as it will show that we have not wisdom enough among us to govern ourselves; and will strengthen the opinion of some political writers that popular governments cannot long support themselves."[47]

He was not among the delegates chosen by the Pennsylvania Assembly on 30 December, but was added to them on 28 March. He at first believed that his stone might not permit him to attend, at least with regularity.[48] But during the winter he had taken a new interest in national affairs, particularly after the founding on 9 February of the Society for Political Enquiries which, with him as its president, sought to study political science as the American Philosophical Society studied the natural sciences. "The arduous and complicated science of government" had been too long "left to the care of practical politicians or the speculations of individual theorists."[49] Thomas Paine, one of the members, at the end of March asked Franklin for letters of introduction to his friends in France, where Paine was going with his model for an iron bridge. Franklin, complying, wrote more and longer letters from 15 to 22 April than in any week since his return. "As I live temperately, drink no wine, and use daily the exercise of the dumb-bell," he told Le Veillard, "I flatter myself that the stone is kept from augmenting as much as it might otherwise do and that I may still continue to find it tolerable."[50] He told his French friends all kinds of news, pleased that his two countries were at about the same time to take up the matter of improvements in their government:

France through an assembly of notables, the United States through the Convention to which he was a delegate. Temple, Franklin wrote to Lafayette, "hankers a little after Paris or some other of the polished cities of Europe, thinking the society there preferable to what he meets in the woods of Rancocas; as it certainly is."[51] But Franklin himself seemed content and cheerfully occupied.

The Society for Political Enquiries met at his house on 11 May and Tench Coxe read a paper on the future commercial system of the United States.[52] Washington arrived on the 13th. He "waited on the President, Dr. Franklin, as soon as I got to town," and dined with him the next day.[53] The Convention, set for the 14th, was slow in assembling. All the delegates who had come dined with Franklin on the 16th. They broached a cask of porter which an English friend had sent him. "The company agreed unanimously that it was the best porter they had ever tasted."[54] Once the full Convention had begun its work Franklin was not only present at eleven every day for four months,[55] but often came early enough to the State House to attend also the meetings of the Executive Council of Pennsylvania—more frequently than ever before or after during his term of office. Neither age nor illness had deprived him of his gift for calling at need on his reserves of power.

On Friday 25 May, when at last there was a quorum of states, the Convention was organized. Franklin, the only delegate as eminent as Washington, had been expected to nominate him for president but was kept at home by a heavy rain, and did not take his seat till Monday.[56] (Temple Franklin was nominated by the Pennsylvania delegation for secretary. William Jackson was preferred.) As in the Continental Congress of 1775, Franklin was the oldest man in the Convention. "Dr. Franklin," William Pierce of Georgia wrote later in the session, "is well known to be the greatest philosopher of the present age. . . . But what claim he has to the politician, posterity must determine. It is certain that he does not shine much in public council; he is no speaker, nor does he seem to let politics engage his attention. He is, however, a most extraordinary man, and tells a story in a style more engaging than anything I ever heard. . . . He is eighty-two and possesses an activity of mind equal to a youth of twenty-five years of age."[57]

Franklin's influence in the Convention was, like Washington's, conciliatory, aimed rather at keeping the delegates in agreement than at leading them in a particular direction. His favourite legislative ideas—a single legislature, a plural executive, the non-payment of officers—were none of them adopted. His principal contribution was a compromise. Yet the most single-minded politicians could never long forget that there was a philosopher among them, incomparably able, when he chose, to speak with large wisdom, the pleasantest humour, and a happy grace. When he had more than a few words to say in the midst of debate he wrote out his speech in advance and, because standing was painful, had it read for him. His important speeches have been more accurately preserved than those of any other delegate. (Of course he did not make the speech against the Jews which was impudently forged and maliciously ascribed to him in 1934.[58])

He seems to have spoken first on 31 May in the discussion of the proposed clause which would give the national legislature power to negative state laws contravening the articles of union. Recently concerned in treaty-making, he moved the addition after "the articles of union" of the further words "or any treaties subsisting under the authority of the union." This was agreed to without debate or dissent.[59] On 1 June, when it had been moved that the executive consist of a single person, there was a pause. Franklin "observed that it was a point of great importance and wished that the gentlemen would deliver their sentiments on it before the question was put."[60] The next day he moved that the executive receive no salary. "He said that, being very sensible of the effect of age on his memory, he had been unwilling to trust to that for the observations which seemed to support his motion, and had reduced them to writing, that he might with the permission of the committee [the Convention was then sitting in a committee of the whole] read instead of speaking them. Mr. Wilson made an offer to read the paper, which was accepted." Remembering British politicians, Franklin argued against allowing American posts of honour to be also posts of profit. Alexander Hamilton seconded the motion, merely to bring it before the committee. The motion was postponed and not taken up again. "It was treated with great respect," Madison noted, "but rather for the author of it than from any conviction of its expediency or practicability."[61]

On 4 June Franklin spoke against giving the national executive an absolute veto over the legislature. He cited the abuse of that power by the proprietary governors of Pennsylvania and by the stadtholders in the Netherlands. Absolute executive veto might lead to a monarchy. The Convention was unanimously of Franklin's opinion. The next day, in the debate over the appointment of judges, Franklin humorously intervened. Only two modes of choice had been mentioned, he said: by the legislature and by the executive. Might there not be others? "He then in a brief and entertaining manner related a Scotch mode, in which the nomination proceeded from the lawyers, who always selected the ablest of the profession in order to get rid of him and share his practice among themselves."[62] This was Tuesday. Franklin did not speak again during the rest of the week, which ended on Saturday in an acrimonious clash over the demand of the smaller states to have an equal vote with the larger (Massachusetts, Pennsylvania, and Virginia). On Monday the 11th Franklin brought with him a written counsel of harmony. "It has given me a great pleasure to observe that till this point, the proportion of representation, came before us our debates were carried on with great coolness and temper. If anything of a contrary kind has on this occasion appeared I hope it will not be repeated; for we are sent here to consult not to contend with each other; and declarations of a fixed opinion, and of determined resolution never to change it, neither enlighten nor convince us. Positiveness and warmth on one side naturally beget their like on the other; and tend to create and augment discord and division in a great concern wherein harmony and union are extremely necessary to give weight to our councils and render them effectual in promoting and securing the common good."[63] The matter of representation was only temporarily settled, against the interests of the smaller states, but the debate went on for a time without disruptive anger.

For seventeen days Franklin did not speak except to make two brief remarks on the matter of salaries.[64] In the conflict between the smaller and the larger states neither he nor Washington was partisan, though Luther Martin later accused them both of having stood blandly and approvingly by while the larger states laid plans to enslave the smaller.[65] Franklin had served the whole country for many years, had no sectional prejudices, and did not believe that the individual states would suffer from a government designed for the common welfare of all of them. He might think of the United States as a union of republics, but he felt the country as a nation not as a loose confederation. His desire was to see it as much a unit in fact as it was in his large conception of it. But he soon realized that the jealousy of the states made anything less than some kind of compromise impossible. The smaller states were convinced that unless they had an equal voice with the larger they would be overwhelmed. The combined population of Massachusetts, Pennsylvania, and Virginia (counting three-fifths of its 280,000 Negroes) was estimated at 1,140,000 as against 1,641,000 in the other ten states together.[66] The larger states were convinced that it would be hopelessly unjust for Delaware, for instance, with 37,000 people to have the same representation as Virginia with 420,000. In the first two weeks of the Convention the larger states, with the support of some of the smaller ones, were able to carry votes which would make population determine representation in both houses of the national legislature. Then the smaller states rebelled and insisted on the equal rights they had had under the Articles of Confederation. They had been sent, as had the delegates from the larger states, merely to revise the Articles. And here they were being driven to do away with them completely and set up a new general government which with their local patriotisms they distrusted and feared.

When Franklin spoke again it was, on 28 June, to move that the Convention open its later sessions with prayer. The small progress they had made, he said, was "proof of the imperfection of the human understanding. We indeed seem to feel our own want of political wisdom, since we have been running about in search of it. We have gone back to ancient history for models of government and examined the different forms of those republics which, having been formed with the seeds of their own dissolution, now no longer exist. And we have viewed modern states all round Europe, but find none of their constitutions suitable to our circumstances. . . . How has it happened, Sir [this to Washington as president], that we have not hitherto once thought of humbly applying to the Father of lights to illuminate our understand-ings? . . . I have lived, Sir, a long time, and the longer I live the more convincing proofs I see of this truth: that God governs in the affairs of men. And if a sparrow cannot fall to the ground without His notice, is it probable that an empire can rise without His aid? . . . I . . . believe that without His concurring aid we shall succeed in this political building no better than the builders of Babel. We shall be divided by our little partial local interests; our projects will be confounded; and we ourselves shall become a reproach and byword down to future ages. And, what is worse, mankind may hereafter from this unfortunate instance despair of establishing governments by human wisdom and leave it to chance, war, and conquest."[67]

Though the proposal may have seemed strange from the free-thinking Franklin, it was sincere. He had seen the Revolution triumph against such heavy odds and in spite of so many blunders that he had come first to wonder if Providence had not a directing and favouring hand in it, and then to believe that it had.[68] But there was an immediate reason for his motion. Luther Martin of Maryland had the day before spoken vehemently for three hours against the constitutional plan so far evolved, and he had continued his speech on the 28th. It looked as if the smaller states might force either a return to the former system of representation or else a dissolution of the Convention. Franklin intervened, this time with a grave suggestion which was sure to change the tone of debate. The effect of his motion has been traditionally exaggerated and distorted.[69] While it was received with respect, no action was taken on it. "The Convention," Franklin noted on his manuscript, "except three or four persons, thought prayers unnecessary." But, coming late in the day, the motion cooled the atmosphere and adjournment followed.

Two days later he made a compromise motion which was less important than his general remarks. "The diversity of opinions turns on two points. If a proportional representation takes place, the small states contend that their liberties will be in danger. If an equality of votes is to be put in its place, the large states say their money will be in danger. When a broad table is to be made, and the edges of planks do not fit, the artist takes a little from both and makes a good joint. In like manner here both sides must part with some of their demands, in order that they may join in some accommodating proposition."[70] On 2 July Franklin was elected to the grand committee, one delegate from each state, which was to devise and report a compromise if any could be found. (That day, though he now very seldom dined out, he probably went from the State House to dinner at half-past three with the "gentlemen of the Convention" who lodged at the Indian Queen in Fourth Street.[71]) The next day the grand committee met. Franklin, according to Luther Martin, advocated proportional representation in both houses until it became clear that the delegates from the smaller states would not consent. The delegates from the larger states, according to Elbridge Gerry of Massachusetts, would agree to equal representation in the second branch only if the first controlled the money bills.[72] Finally, on Franklin's motion,[73] the committee arrived at a compromise which was reported to the Convention on the 5th. They recommended: (1) that in the first branch of the national legislature (the House of Representatives) there should be one representative from each state for every 40,000 of its inhabitants; (2) that all bills for raising or appropriating money should originate in the first branch and not be subject to alteration or amendment in the second; (3) that in the second branch (the Senate) the states should have equal votes.

In the debate on the compromise, which lasted to the 11th, Franklin said little. On the 6th, explaining the restriction of money bills to the first branch, "he could not but remark that it was always of importance that the people should know who had disposed of their money and how it had been disposed of. It was a maxim that those who feel can best judge." It was a maxim he himself had made during his examination before the House of Commons. "This end would, he thought, be best attained if money affairs were to be confined to the immediate representatives of the people. This was his inducement to concur in the report."[74] The compromise, as moved by Franklin in committee, was finally adopted in the Convention by a vote of five states (Connecticut, New Jersey, Delaware, Virginia, and North Carolina) to four (Pennsylvania, Maryland, South Carolina, and Georgia), with Massachusetts divided and so not counted. This was Franklin's great victory in the Convention: that he was the author of the compromise which held the delegates together at a time when they were ready to break up without forming any new Federal agreement. The Constitution was not his document. But without the weight of his prestige and the influence of his temper there might have been no document at all.

Manasseh Cutler, visiting Philadelphia from Massachusetts, was taken by Elbridge Gerry to call on Franklin at his house on the afternoon of the 13th. They found him—"a short, fat, trunched old man in a plain Quaker dress, bald pate, and short white locks"—sitting hatless under a mulberry tree in his garden with several men and two or three ladies, one of them his daughter. Franklin, Cutler wrote, "rose from his chair, took me by the hand, expressed his joy at seeing me, and begged me to seat myself close beside him. His voice was low, but his countenance open, frank, and pleasing." He read the letters of introduction Cutler had brought, shook hands with him again, and introduced him to the others. Most of the men were members of the Convention. They sat in conversation till dark, when tea was served under the tree by Sarah Bache. She had three of her children about her. "They seemed to be excessively fond of their grandpapa." Franklin had just been sent a curiosity: a two-headed snake in a phial of spirits. He referred to his fable of such a snake, apparently now a commonplace with him, "and was then going to mention a humorous matter that had that day occurred in the Convention in consequence of his comparing the snake to America; for he seemed to forget that everything in the Convention was to be kept a profound secret. But this secrecy of Convention matters was suggested to him, which stopped him and deprived me of the story he was going to tell." (The records of the Convention for the day do not show what it was he may have said.)

After dark Franklin took the men to his study. "It is a very large chamber and high-studded. The walls are covered with bookshelves filled with books; besides there are four large alcoves, extending two-thirds of the length of the chamber, filled in the same manner." Cutler supposed this was "the largest and by far the best private library in America"—as it was. Franklin showed him other ingenious curiosities: a glass machine for "exhibiting the circulation of the blood in the arteries and veins of the human body"; the rolling press which Franklin had invented for copying letters; "his long, artificial arm and hand for taking down and putting up books on high shelves; and his great armchair, with rockers, and a large fan placed over it, with which he fans himself, keeps off the flies, etc., while he sits reading, with only a small motion of the foot; and many other curiosities and inventions, all his own but of lesser note. Over his mantel he has a prodigious number of medals, busts, and casts in wax or plaster of Paris which are the effigies of the most noted characters in Europe."

Most of all Franklin wanted to show a folio which "contained the whole of Linnæus's *Systema Vegetabilium*" and which was heavy for him to lift; "but . . . he insisted on doing it himself and would permit no person to assist him, merely to show us how much strength he had remaining." Franklin knew that Cutler was a botanist and, talking to his guest, characteristically "lamented that he did not in early life attend to this science. . . . He seemed extremely fond, through the course of the visit, of dwelling on philosophical subjects and particularly that of natural history; while the other gentlemen were swallowed up with politics. This was a favourable circumstance with me; for almost the whole of his conversation was addressed to me, and I was highly delighted with the extensive knowledge he appeared to have of every subject, the brightness of his memory, and clearness and vivacity of all his mental faculties, notwithstanding his age. His manners are perfectly easy, and everything about him seems to diffuse an unrestrained freedom and happiness. He has an incessant vein of humour, accompanied with an uncommon vivacity, which seems as natural and involuntary as his breathing. He urged me to call on him again. . . . We took our leave at ten."[75]

In two months more of the Convention Franklin is known to have uttered only a few sentences. On Sunday 22 July, writing to John Paul Jones, he said he was just recovering from a three days' illness and "so weak as to be scarce able to finish this letter."[76] Yet only two days before he had spoken with his usual point in defence of the clause which would make the national executive impeachable. What, he asked, before the trial of Charles I had been the practice "where the chief magistrate rendered himself obnoxious? Why, recourse was had to assassination, in which he was not only deprived of his life but of the opportunity of vindicating his character. It would be the best way, therefore, to provide in the Constitution for the regular punishment of the executive when his misconduct should deserve it and for his honourable acquittal when he should be unjustly accused."[77] Some of the members of the Convention thought it would be degrading for the executive to be made ineligible for a second term. Franklin on 26 July thought this opinion "contrary to republican principles. In free governments the rulers are the servants and the people their superiors and sovereigns. For the former therefore to return among the latter was not to degrade but to promote them."[78] To the plan to limit the suffrage to freeholders Franklin on 7 August was strongly opposed. "It is of great consequence that we should not depress the virtue and public spirit of our common people. . . . He did not think that the elected had any right in any case to narrow the privileges of the electors."[79]

Foreigners, he held two days later, should not be required to live so long as fourteen years, as had been proposed, in the United States before they could be elected to public office. "The people in Europe are friendly to this country. . . . We found in the course of the Revolution that many strangers served us faithfully—and that many natives took part against their country. When foreigners after looking about for some other country in which they can obtain more happiness give a preference to ours, it is a proof of attachment which ought to excite our confidence and affection."[80] Franklin spoke emphatically on 10 August against a motion to set up a property qualification for officers of the government. "If honesty was often the companion of wealth, and if poverty was exposed to peculiar temptation, it was not less true that the possession of property increased the desire of more property. Some of the greatest rogues he was ever acquainted with were the richest rogues."[81] On 20 August he approved an amendment to the treason clause which would call for two witnesses "to the same overt act" before conviction: "prosecutions for treason were generally virulent, and perjury too easily made use of against innocence."[82] Franklin seconded Mason's motion for the creation of a council of state for the executive: "a council would not only be a check on a bad president but be a relief to a good one."[83] He was appointed to a committee on economy, which never made a report, and made a motion on the government cutting of canals which was lost.

The final day of the Convention, Monday 17 September, when the Constitution had been engrossed over Sunday and was ready for the signing, was dramatically Franklin's and Washington's. First the engrossed document was read by the secretary. Then Franklin rose with a written speech which Wilson read. "I confess that there are several parts of this Constitution which I do not at present approve, but I am not sure I shall never approve them; for, having lived long, I have experienced many instances of being obliged by better information or fuller consideration to change opinions, even on important subjects, which I once thought right but found to be otherwise. It is therefore that the older I grow the more apt I am to doubt my own judgment and to pay attention to the judgment of others. Most men, indeed, as well as most sects in religion think themselves in possession of all truth. . . . But though many private persons think almost as highly of their infallibility as of that of their sect, few express it so naturally as a certain French lady who in a dispute with her sister said: 'I don't know how it happens, sister, but I meet with nobody but myself that's always in the right.' (*Il n'y a que moi qui a toujours raison.*)

"In these sentiments, Sir, I agree to this Constitution with all its faults, if they are such; because I think a general government necessary for us, and there is no form of government but what may be a blessing to the people if well administered; and believe farther that this is likely to be well administered for a course of years and can only end in despotism, as other forms have done before it, when the people shall become so corrupt as to need despotic government, being incapable of any other. I doubt too whether any other convention we can obtain may be able to make a better Constitution. For when you assemble a number of men to have the advantage of their joint wisdom, you inevitably assemble with those men all their prejudices, their passions, their errors of opinion, their local interests, and their selfish views. From such an assembly can a perfect production be expected? It therefore astonishes me, Sir, to find this system approaching so near to perfection as it does. . . . Thus I consent, Sir, to this Constitution because I expect no better, and because I am not sure that it is not the best. The opinions I have had of its errors I sacrifice to the public good. I have never whispered a syllable of them abroad. Within these walls they were born, and here they shall die. . . . On the whole, Sir, I cannot help expressing a wish that every member of the Convention who may still have objections to it would, with me, on this occasion doubt a little of his infallibility, and, to make manifest our unanimity, put his name to this instrument."

Franklin then moved that the Constitution be signed by the delegates as "done in Convention by the unanimous consent of the states present." This ambiguous form had been drawn by Gouverneur Morris of Pennsylvania, who hoped that the dissenting members—Gerry of Massachusetts, Mason and Edmund Randolph of Virginia—might be willing to sign for their states if not for themselves, since a majority in each state's delegation did approve. Morris, according to Madison, had put the proposal into the hands of Franklin "that it might have the better chance of success."[84]

Nathaniel Gorham of Massachusetts proposed a last-minute change, to substitute 30,000 to 40,000 as the unit of population determining the number of Representatives. Washington, putting the question, for the first time in four months ventured to offer his opinion. Many members of the Convention believed there should be more Representatives to secure the rights and interests of the people. He was inclined to believe so himself. "Late as the present moment was for admitting amendments, he thought this of so much consequence that it would give [him] much satisfaction to see it adopted."[85] The change was unanimously agreed to without discussion. The "forty" was erased from the engrossed Constitution, and "thirty" written over it.

Various members spoke, Randolph and Gerry explaining why they could not put their names to the document. But on Franklin's further motion the Convention voted to sign it. Thirty-seven delegates besides Washington signed delegation by delegation, in geographical order from New Hampshire to Georgia. (George Read of Delaware signed for John Dickinson, absent.) "While the last members were signing it," Madison wrote, "Dr. Franklin, looking towards the president's chair at the back of which a rising sun happened to be painted, observed to a few members near him that painters had found it difficult to distinguish in their art a rising from a setting sun. 'I have,' said he, 'often and often in the course of the session, and the vicissitudes of my hopes and fears as to its issue, looked at that behind the president without being able to tell whether it was rising or setting. But now at length I have the happiness to know that it is a rising and not a setting sun.' "[86] The Convention then adjourned to the City tavern to dine together and exchange farewells.

The next morning at eleven the Pennsylvania delegates appeared before the General Assembly, which was then in session, and Franklin addressed the Speaker: "Sir, we have now the honour to present to this house the plan of government for the United States which has been determined upon by the Federal Convention. We sincerely hope and believe that the result of the labours of that honourable body will tend to promote the happiness and prosperity of this commonwealth in particular and of the United States in general." As soon as the Speaker had read the report to the Assembly Franklin presented a letter from the Pennsylvania delegates which recommended that the legislature take prompt steps to vote a tract of land ten miles square to the new Congress in order that the national capital might be within the boundaries of Pennsylvania.[87] After that Franklin had little to do, outwardly, with the Pennsylvania ratification of the Constitution. The Federalists—as the party in favour of ratifying came at once to be called—did not nominate him to the state convention which was to decide the matter. He pleaded his age and infirmity and thought it would be improper for the President to sit in the convention. The Anti-Federalists put his name on their ticket as a ruse to attract votes to other candidates who were opposed to the Constitution. Only 235 votes were cast for him, and those for him as person rather than as candidate.[88] On the night of the election, 6 November, a Federalist mob broke the windows of the house where certain Anti-Federalist assemblymen lodged. Franklin on the 12th issued a proclamation offering a reward of three hundred dollars for the capture and punishment of the rioters.[89] No arrests were made. The state convention met on the 21st, and ratified the Constitution on 12 December. On the 13th the ratification was formally proclaimed at the courthouse, all the officers of the Pennsylvania government marching in due ceremonial procession from the State House and back again.

Franklin's speech of 17 September was looked upon as the literary masterpiece of the Convention, and in spite of the rule of secrecy was soon widely known and printed. Nathaniel Gorham of Massachusetts and Daniel Carroll of Maryland wrote to him asking for copies of it to use in influencing opinion in their states.[90] Franklin freely gave copies to them and others, and no doubt gave consent to the publication of the speech in the *American Museum* for December. As a Boston newspaper complained, the hypothesis that General Washington and Dr. Franklin made" the Constitution, was "too strong an argument in the minds of many to suffer them to examine, like freemen, for themselves."[91] Was Franklin, the wisest American, wise enough to realize that he could now have only a narrowed influence, because he was so old? The other delegates to the Convention had respectfully listened to him, but had rarely followed his advice on specific legislative points. He had nothing but a wise past to affect them with. He had, they knew, no powerful future. His presence among them was a brief triumph over his years. His final speech was a melancholy leave-taking from the life of action in which they, not he, would have to carry out the plans they had made.

III

Franklin was elected President for the third time on 31 October, again unanimously. Throughout that month, as during September, he was often present at the meetings of the Council, as if the energy roused in him by the Convention still persisted. And the Council was occupied with the unrest in the Wyoming district.

The unrest was the climax of a long story. In 1754 a group of speculators from Connecticut had bought land, from the Six Nations, in the Wyoming valley. The territory was claimed by Connecticut on the basis of a royal grant which was older than the overlapping royal grant of the same territory to Pennsylvania. Franklin had at that time drawn up his *Plan for Settling Two*

Western Colonies in North America "to divert the Connecticut emigrants from their design of invading this province and so induce them to go where they would be less injurious and more useful."[92] But they were not diverted and they came into conflict with the Penns and later with various citizens of Pennsylvania who had an interest in the rich valley lands. Connecticut in 1776 set up the county of Westmoreland there, and it elected members to the Connecticut legislature. In 1781 Pennsylvania appealed to Congress to settle the dispute under the Articles of Confederation, and the next year a court of commissioners sitting at Trenton awarded the territory to Pennsylvania. But the Pennsylvania authorities, organizing Wyoming into townships, at first unjustly tried to oust the Connecticut men from the farms they had made out of the wilderness. They resisted during 1783 in a little war in which they were led by the spirited and resolute John Franklin, who looked upon Pennsylvania much as Benjamin Franklin had looked upon England. (The two were not related.) The more just and reasonable Pennsylvanians objected to the action of their legislature (urged on by land-jobbers), and a new law temporarily restored the dispossessed farmers to their homes pending the legal decision of all the rights involved. Here matters might have rested but for the Connecticut speculators of the Susquehannah Company, who in 1785 proceeded to form a militia in Wyoming to defend the settlers in case the law decided against them. Ethan Allen, granted land in the valley, visited it and agreed to fight if Pennsylvania should send an armed force. There was even talk of creating a new state.[93]

Affairs were at this stand when Franklin first became President of Pennsylvania. On 1 January 1786 he wrote to George Clinton, governor of New York, to inform him that "Ethan Allen from Vermont and one Solomon Strong of your state have lately been among the settlers at Wyoming, persuading them to join in erecting a new state to be composed of those settlements, those on the west branch of the Susquehanna, and a part of the state of New York. . . . Chimerical as it appears, and unlikely to succeed, we thought it nevertheless right to acquaint Your Excellency with it, that such inquiries may be made and measures taken as you may judge proper to prevent these restless spirits from exciting disturbances that may divert the people's attention from their industry, and be attended with mischievous consequences."[94]

John Franklin, who did not see the controversy as mere local disorder, on 25 February drew up (with two other settlers) an appeal to the President. On his election, John Franklin said, "every soul here acquainted with Your Excellency's character and capable of sentiment and reflection exulted on the joyous occasion from a conception that something favourable to this settlement might yet be hoped through the instrumentality of such a known friend to the sacred rights of mankind, whose election wrought in our imaginations the affectionate epithet of a political father, who would impartially consider and weigh the opposite claims of his children, dispensing his smiles or his frowns according to their adherence or non-adherence to those pure original laws which can neither be superseded nor abrogated by human tribunals. . . . We know your attention has of late been occupied with greater and more material concerns, which renders it possible, if not probable, that you may not be duly apprised of our many and complicated sufferings."[95] Here was a strange reversal of circumstances. John Franklin was appealing to Benjamin Franklin in the name of the natural rights of man as Benjamin Franklin had appealed to the British king and Parliament.

The Council promptly heard the messenger from Wyoming, who talked also to several members of the Assembly. He "gave so clear and so affecting an account of the situation of your people, their present disposition and former sufferings," the President wrote to John Franklin, "as inclined the government in general to show them every kind of reasonable favour. The Assembly accordingly took the necessary previous steps for a compliance with your request respecting a separate county, which will probably be completed at their next session."[96] The Assembly raised the Wyoming townships to a county, Luzerne, and sent Timothy Pickering as commissioner to organize it and bring about a reconciliation. An act of 1787 gave the lands they claimed to the Connecticut settlers who had been in possession of them at the time of the Trenton decision, and compensated the Pennsylvania claimants with land in another district. But there had been long suspicion and bad blood between the rival parties in Wyoming, and the later comers from Connecticut were not satisfied. John Franklin, leading a final outburst in September, was arrested and brought to Philadelphia, where on 7 October the Council voted that he, "the principal of the banditti lately assembled at Tioga," should be kept in irons for fear of escape, be denied the use of pen, ink, and paper, and permitted to see nobody except with the leave of the Council or a judge of the supreme court.[97]

Benjamin Franklin, sending Colonel Nathan Dennison to Luzerne County on 10 October, gave him instructions to be mild and generous towards the lesser offenders. It appeared that the riots following John Franklin's arrest had been "committed in the heat of passion, occasioned by the supposition that he was carried off illegally"; and that the rioters, now better informed, "were sorry for their conduct in that affair and determined to submit quietly to the operation of the laws, hoping this their offence might be passed over." Dennison was authorized to assure them "that if they hereafter behave orderly, as good citizens of the State of Pennsylvania, no prosecution will be commenced against them." But he was also to assure them that the government, "having already taken every measure for securing to the settlers the future quiet possession of their lands, are now determined to carry into execution the laws of the state, to the full extent of its boundaries, and propose to send immediately into that county a force sufficient to support the public officers in the discharge of their respective functions against all opposers, who if they persist in their evil practices are to expect no further favour."[98] There was little unrest in the remainder of Franklin's administration. John Franklin was later indicted for treason against Pennsylvania, kept in jail over three years, pardoned in 1792, and the same year made high sheriff of Luzerne County.

After October 1787 Franklin went less and less frequently to the meetings of the Council, not once from 3 January to 12 March. He had, he wrote Ingenhousz on 11 February, been "very ill with a severe fit of the stone which followed a fall I had on the stone steps that lead into my garden, whereby I was much bruised and my wrist sprained, so as not to be capable of writing for several weeks." On the Fourth of July, which Philadelphia magnificently celebrated, "his Excellency the President was too much indisposed to attend," the *Gazette* said on the 9th. Perhaps when the procession, three hours long, turned from Fourth Street into Market near Franklin's house, he may have watched it, like many people, from some roof or window; may have been pleased to see all classes and trades in cheerful concord; may have noted, as the committee of arrangements did, that today for the first time in its history Philadelphia saw "the clergy of [almost all the] different Christian denominations, with the rabbi of the Jews, walking arm in arm."

In the last months of Franklin's term the Council met at his house, notably on 16 September 1788 to receive word from Congress that eleven states had ratified the Constitution. Thomas Mifflin was elected to succeed him in October. "Having now finished my term of being President," he wrote to La Rochefoucauld on the 22nd, "and promising myself to engage no more in public business, I hope to enjoy the small remains of life that are allowed me in the repose I have so long wished for." In the first four days of this freedom he wrote a dozen letters to his friends in Europe. "It is true, as you observe," he told Madame Lavoisier, "that I enjoy here everything that a reasonable mind can desire." Yet all these things "do not make me forget Paris and the nine years' happiness I enjoyed there, in the sweet society of a people whose conversation is instructive, whose manners are highly pleasing, and who, above all the nations of the world, have, in the greatest perfection, the art of making themselves beloved by strangers. And now, even in my sleep, I find that the scenes of all my pleasant dreams are laid in that city or in its neighbourhood."[99]

Ending

IN THE summer of 1788 Franklin made his will (signed and witnessed on 17 July) in language which was plainly not only for his executors but also for the public which he knew would be interested.[1] He left his son William the Nova Scotia land, the books and papers in his possession, and the debts which had accumulated during the years when William had lived beyond his governor's salary on money furnished by his father. "The part he acted against me in the late war, which is of public notoriety, will account for my leaving him no more of an estate he endeavoured to deprive me of." Franklin's real estate and household goods in Philadelphia he left to Richard and Sarah Bache. Richard was given "the lands near the Ohio" and forgiven his debt of over two thousand pounds to his father-in-law, who requested that "in consideration thereof he would immediately after my decease manumit and set free his Negro man Bob." The miniature of Louis XVI went to Sarah, with the request "that she would not form any of those diamonds into ornaments either for herself or daughters, and thereby introduce or countenance the expensive, vain, and useless fashion of wearing jewels in this country." Franklin left his sister Jane Mecom his house and lot in Unity Street, Boston, and fifty pounds a year for life. His right to take up land in Georgia he gave to his grandson Temple, with "the bond and judgment I have against him of four thousand pounds sterling." All the types and printing materials in Philadelphia and Franklin's share in the Library Company were to go to Benjamin Franklin Bache. There were small legacies for the surviving descendants of the Boston Franklins, and precise instructions for dividing books, manuscripts, and philosophical and musical instruments among relatives, friends, the Library Company, the American Philosophical Society, and the American Academy of Arts and Sciences in Boston.

Franklin's old uncollected business debts, as "stated in my great folio ledger E," he left to the Pennsylvania Hospital, hoping that his debtors or their descendants, "who now, as I find, make some difficulty of satisfying such antiquated demands as just debts, may, however, be induced to pay or give them as charity to that excellent institution." (But seven years after his death the managers of the hospital found the bequest gave them more trouble than it was worth and returned the ledger to the executors.[2]) To the directors of "the free schools in my native town of Boston" he left a hundred pounds, of which the interest was to be annually "laid out in silver medals and given as honorary rewards." The Franklin medals were awarded first in January 1793 and continuously after that. Always given only to boys, they have since 1867 been given only to boys in the Boston Latin School and other high schools. In 1922 the number of medals was about thirty a year, and the total from 1793 had been about four thousand.[3]

On 23 June 1789 Franklin added the long codicil[4] which has made his will famous. There were a few minor changes and corrections and some further personal bequests. "My fine crab-tree walking-stick, with a gold head curiously wrought in the form of the cap of liberty, I give to my friend, and the friend of mankind, General Washington. If it were a sceptre, he has merited it and would become it." But the feature of the codicil was a scheme of progressive philanthropy meant to run two hundred years. Out of the unused salary Franklin had received as President of Pennsylvania he left a thousand pounds each to Boston and Philadelphia. These sums were to be used for loans to "such young married artificers, under the age of twenty-five years, as have served an apprenticeship in the said town, and faithfully fulfilled the duties required in their indentures, so as to obtain a good moral character from at least two respectable citizens who are willing to become their sureties." Each borrower was to pay five per cent interest and repay a tenth of the principal each year, "which sums of principal and interest, so paid in, shall be again let out to fresh borrowers. . . . It is hoped that no part of the money will at any time be dead, or be diverted to other purposes, but be continually

augmented by the interest. . . . If this plan is executed, and succeeds as projected without interruption for one hundred years, the
sum will then be one hundred and thirty-one thousand pounds."
Of this amount the town of Boston or Philadelphia was to expend
one hundred thousand on public works and to continue the remainder as loans to promising young men for another hundred
years. "At the end of this second term, if no unfortunate accident
has prevented the operation, the sum will be four millions and
sixty-one thousand pounds sterling, of which I leave one million
sixty-one thousand pounds to the disposition of the inhabitants of
the town of Boston [or Philadelphia], and three millions to the
disposition of the government of the state, not presuming to carry
my views further."

Franklin, who owed this expansive scheme to a French correspondent Mathon de la Cour,[5] had had it in mind ever since his
return to Philadelphia. There was in 1789 hardly an American
fortune so large as a million dollars, and Franklin's was perhaps no
more than a fifth of that. But he had always known how to be
patient, and time had served him. He would put money to work,
at benevolent compound interest, for posterity. In a hundred
years, and then in another hundred, his gift would be princely.
Nor would the money lie idle in the meantime. Speculating on
the best use to put it to, Franklin remembered that a loan to him
when he was a married tradesman under twenty-five had set him
on the road to success. Now he might pass the favour on to many
men after him. He could—or did—not foresee the coming changes
in the apprentice system and the rise of an industrialism which
would make young independent tradesmen less and less common,
less and less able to profit by his loans. His calculations as to
the "continually augmenting" fund turned out to have been too
hopeful. But by 1907 the Benjamin Franklin Fund in Philadelphia
amounted to $172,350, of which $133,076.46 was transferred to the
Franklin Institute; and the remainder of the Fund had grown by
1936 to $132,660.24.[6] Boston at the end of the first hundred years
of the Franklin Fund had $391,000. Part of this was withdrawn
for public works, as Franklin had ruled, and with the help of
Andrew Carnegie it built and equipped the Franklin Union, a
technical school for young men already employed and possibly

able to study only in the evening. The part of the Franklin Fund which was reinvested in 1891 had grown in 1935 to $593,000, and at the present rate is expected to be in 1991 about four millions[7] —the most munificent money gift ever made by a philosopher.

Disappointment came to Franklin from Congress. At the settlement of his account in May 1785, Thomas Barclay, serving as Congress's auditor, found that Franklin had 7533 livres and a fraction still due him; "the difference between my statement and his," Franklin told Cyrus Griffin, president of Congress, on 29 November 1788, "being only seven sols which by mistake I had overcharged: about threepence halfpenny sterling. At my request, however, the accounts were left open for the consideration of Congress, and not finally settled, there being some equitable demands, as I thought them, for extra services which he had not conceived himself empowered to allow, and therefore I did not put them in my account. He transmitted the accounts to Congress and had advice of their being received. On my arrival in Philadelphia one of the first things I did was to dispatch my grandson, William T. Franklin, to New York to obtain a final settlement of those accounts; he, having long acted as my secretary and being well acquainted with the transactions, was able to give an explanation of the articles that might seem to require explaining, if any such there were. He returned without effecting the settlement, being told that it could not be made till the arrival of some documents expected from France. . . . It is now more than three years that those accounts have been before that honourable body, and to this day no notice of any such objection has been communicated to me. But reports have for some time past been circulated here, and propagated in the newspapers, that I am greatly indebted to the United States for large sums that had been put into my hands and that I avoid a settlement. This, together with the little time one of my age may expect to live, makes it necessary for me to request earnestly, which I hereby do, that the Congress would be pleased, without further delay, to examine those accounts; and if they find therein any article or articles which they do not understand or approve, that they would cause me to be acquainted with the same, that I may have an opportunity of offering such explanations or reasons in support of them as may be in my power, and then that the accounts might be finally closed."[8]

"I must own, I did hope," Franklin explained on 29 December to his old friend Charles Thomson, still secretary of Congress, "that, as it is customary in Europe to make some liberal provision for ministers when they return home from foreign service during which their absence is necessarily injurious to their private affairs, the Congress would at least have been kind enough to have shown their approbation of my conduct by a grant of some small tract of land in their western country, which might have been of some use and some honour to my posterity." He proudly rehearsed his services.[9] What he most wanted was that Temple be somehow recompensed for his years as unofficial secretary to the legation in Paris. He had given up the study of law for the practice of diplomacy, but Congress had refused him a post. He had returned from Paris to a farm in New Jersey which he liked so little that he spent most of his time in Philadelphia with Franklin. Surely the young man merited a reward.

Congress neither rewarded Temple nor took notice of him. Nor did it even acknowledge Franklin's request for a further settlement of his accounts. Arthur Lee, a member of the treasury board, was not likely to be considerate towards the man he hated; nor was Richard Henry Lee, a member of Congress. John Adams had returned from England, and the Adamses were as good haters as the Lees. The animosity against Franklin in Massachusetts seemed to him "to emanate from the Brantry [Braintree] focus"—that is, from Adams.[10] There had been delegates to the Constitutional Convention from both Massachusetts and Virginia who thought Franklin too fond of France. According to Edmund Randolph the clause which forbade any official of the United States to accept any present or emolument from any foreign king or state was aimed at Franklin on account of the portrait the king of France had given him.[11] And it must have been directly or indirectly through Arthur Lee that Franklin came again to be accused of having withheld money intended for Congress. There was a million livres that neither he nor Ferdinand Grand, banker for America in Paris, could account for.[12] Franklin could only conclude that it had been paid to Beaumarchais before Deane went over. Time was to justify this conclusion,[13] but for the present Franklin was suspected by his enemies, particularly by those who opposed the Constitution in which he had had a hand.

Franklin was grieved but reticent. "This is all to yourself only as a private friend," he told Charles Thomson; "for I have not, nor ever shall, make any public complaint; and even if I could have foreseen such unkind treatment from Congress as their refusing me their thanks, would not in the least have abated my zeal for their cause and ardour in support of it. For I know something of the nature of such changeable assemblies, and how little successors are informed of services that have been rendered to the corps before their admission, or feel themselves obliged for such services; and what effect in obliterating a sense of them, during the absence of the servant in a distant country, the artful and reiterated malevolent insinuations of one or two envious and malicious persons may have on the mind of members, even of the most equitable, candid, and honourable dispositions. Therefore I would pass these reflections into oblivion."[14]

He turned to his *Autobiography*, so long postponed, about which his European friends asked in almost every letter. He explained to Le Veillard that the three scientific articles had been written at sea instead of the promised memoirs because they could be done "out of my own head; the other could not so well be written there for want of the documents that could only be had here."[15] But by 26 November 1786 Franklin had "made some progress in it," he wrote to Edward Bancroft, "and hope to finish it this winter."[16] Apparently he had done no more than go over the manuscript already written. Other matters interfered, and then the Constitutional Convention, and his third term. "I have come to the resolution," he assured Le Veillard on 22 April 1788, "to proceed in that work tomorrow and continue it daily till finished, which, if my health permits, may be in the course of the ensuing summer."[17] Finally he did begin the delayed third part, and noted in the margin: "I am now about to write at home, August 1788."[18] By 22 October he must have written about a fourth more of the whole book, for he that day told La Rochefoucauld: "It is now brought down to my fiftieth year. What is to follow will be of more important transactions." He thought that the earlier years would be "of more general use to young readers; as exemplifying strongly the effects of prudent and imprudent conduct in the commencement of a life of business."[19]

This burden of moralism was heavier on the third part than on the first, written gaily at Twyford, or on the second, written in a philosophic interlude at Passy. Though on the 24th Franklin believed his work should now be done in two months,[20] he was still at his fiftieth year on 9 December.[21] His stone had become worse. "Of late I am so interrupted by extreme pain, which obliges me to have recourse to opium," he wrote to Benjamin Vaughan on the following 3 June, "that between the effects of both I have but little time in which I can write anything." Benjamin Bache was copying what had been written and a copy would go to Vaughan by the next ship.[22] It was not ready till 2 November, when Franklin, no longer "able to bear sitting to write," had begun to dictate to his grandson and wished he had tried the method sooner.[23] Both the copy to Vaughan and another to Le Veillard were sent on the "express condition . . . that you do not suffer any copy to be taken of them, or of any part of them, on any account whatever."[24] Vaughan was to consult with Richard Price, and Le Veillard with La Rochefoucauld. Franklin requested of his French friends that they should read the memoirs carefully, "examine them critically, and send me your friendly, candid opinion of the parts you would advise me to correct or expunge; this in case you should be of opinion that they are generally proper to be published; and if you judge otherwise, that you would send me that opinion as soon as possible, and prevent my taking farther trouble in endeavouring to finish them." And to his English friends: "I shall rely upon your opinions, for I am now grown so old and feeble in mind, as well as body, that I cannot place any confidence in my own judgment."

The two copies went off to England and France to set in train the complex textual history of this simple book: of which three parts appeared first in French, and of which the earliest English editions were retranslations from the French, and of which Temple Franklin published as authorized in 1818 the copy sent to Le Veillard instead of Franklin's original, which was not published entire, as Franklin wrote it, till 1868.[25] At some time after the copies were made, Franklin, in the six painful months left to him, wrote the fragmentary fourth part and then broke off. It seems likely that he himself had made the revisions which in the copy tamed the original. He could no longer trust his taste and could now and then prefer round academic phrases to his own natural sharp, homely ones. He had lived too long, and put off writing too late, to be able to do justice to himself in a book. His greatest years would have to stay unwritten. He might truly have reflected that this was not altogether the loss it seemed. Plenty of other men could find materials for the story of his latest years. Only he had known about his obscure youth, which could never again be obscure.

II

In the year of Franklin's return to Philadelphia Humphry Marshall in his *Arbustrum Americanum* first described the lovely, mysterious flowering tree which John and William Bartram had discovered in Georgia and named *Franklinia alatamaha*.[26] John Fitch, who had tried on 27 September to interest the American Philosophical Society in his model and drawings of a steamboat, turned to Franklin as to a natural patron. Franklin, though polite and friendly, seems not to have seen the importance of the new invention. But his *Maritime Observations*, sent to the Society to be read by Francis Hopkinson on 2 December, included a scheme for propelling boats by machinery. Though it was plainly credited to Daniel Bernoulli, whose device Franklin thought might be improved, and had nothing to do with steam, Fitch when he heard about it was certain Franklin was his rival and wanted to take away his glory. In January Fitch called on Franklin and asked him to subscribe to a company being formed to build the boat Fitch had designed. When Franklin would not Fitch was disappointed, and he was insulted when Franklin, seeing how needy the inventor was, offered him five or six dollars for himself. Fitch had no doubt as to Franklin's selfish aims after Franklin, in May 1788, became a member of the Rumseian Society, organized to carry out the plans of Washington's protégé James Rumsey for using steam in boats, sawmills, grist mills, and pumps. But there is little evidence that Franklin did more than lend his name to the venture, and write some letters to English friends introducing Rumsey to them. On 16 February he told Crevecœur he had been too ill ever to see Fitch's boat, and he foresaw more difficulties than advantages in the invention, though David Rittenhouse did believe in it. Franklin's imagination seems to have been untouched by any prospect of the coming age of steam.[27] He was more interested in the "printing office between my dwelling and the front houses," where Benjamin Bache, now out of college, worked at printing children's books and textbooks under the eye, sometimes too solicitous for the boy's comfort, of his grandfather.[28]

Edward Bancroft in 1787 collected some of Franklin's *Political and Miscellaneous Papers* in London, and Mathew Carey in Philadelphia, who had worked for some months at the Passy press, began to print or reprint a series of Franklin pieces in the *American Museum*. But Franklin did not write much besides his Convention speeches, his *Autobiography*, and his letters, and he published less than he wrote. He withheld *The Retort Courteous*, to the British who said Americans did not pay their debts, for fear he might encourage "any of our people who may be able to pay in the neglect of that duty."[29] *The Art of Procuring Pleasant Dreams*, written probably in the spring of 1786, he sent to Catherine Shipley, a bagatelle for a girl from a busy man.[30] "I am often as agreeably entertained with them as by the scenery of an opera." His *Observations Relative to the Intentions of the Original Founders of the Academy in Philadelphia*, written in June 1789 when the college was being reorganized, did not reach the trustees.[31] So far as writing went, he neglected the natural sciences which he had waited so many years to give his time to. When James Bowdoin was no longer governor of Massachusetts, Franklin, in his own last term in Pennsylvania, wished on 31 May 1788 he might revive their former scientific correspondence. "Our much regretted friend Winthrop once made me the compliment that I was good at starting game for philosophers; let me try if I can start a little for you."[32] But most of Franklin's speculations went on at his house, where the American Philosophical Society and the Society for Political Enquiries held their meetings in his dining room. "My friends indulge me with their frequent visits, which I have now leisure to receive and enjoy."[33]

Benjamin Rush kept a few scrappy notes of things Franklin said to him on his visits during 1786–89. Tobacco was a less common habit than thirty years ago, Franklin thought. Young persons of fashion in Paris no longer used snuff. "He concluded that there was no great advantage in using tobacco in any way, for that he had kept company with persons who used it all his life, and no one had ever advised him to use it. The Doctor, in the eighty-first year of his age, declared he had never snuffed, chewed, or smoked." "Upon another occasion he said that credit produced idleness and vice, and he wished that all debts should like debts of honour or game debts be irrecoverable by law." "He observed that a man lost ten per cent on the value by lending his books; that he once knew a man who never returned a borrowed book, because no one ever returned borrowed books to him." He remarked "that the greatest part of the [foreign] trade of the world was carried on for luxuries most of which were injurious to health or society: such as tea, tobacco, rum, sugar, and Negro slaves." "Quacks were the greatest liars in the world, except their patients." He told of a man who was sentenced to be hanged for peculation in the French army. "Who ever heard," the culprit asked, "of a man being hanged worth two hundred thousand livres?"—and he got off. Pringle once told him, Franklin said, that "ninety-two fevers out of every hundred cured themselves, four were cured by art, and four proved fatal." Greek and Latin Franklin called, in a long disquisition on them, "the quackery of literature."[34] (That same month he called them, in writing, the *"chapeau bras* of modern literature," like the hats which "the politer people in all the courts and capital cities of Europe" felt they must wear, but which, because they could not put them on their heads for fear of disordering their wigs, they carried elegantly and uselessly under their arms.[35])

Franklin, at least as reported by Rush, talked less entertainingly than he wrote. His pen during these years moved with its habitual, varied force and wit and grace through many letters to many correspondents. Here was his true conversation. "I am grown so old as to have buried most of the friends of my youth, and I now often hear persons whom I knew when children, called old Mr. Such-a-one to distinguish them from their sons now men grown and in business; so that, by living twelve years beyond David's period, I seem to have intruded myself into the company of posterity when I ought to have been abed and asleep."[36] If England had gone to any trouble to keep America in a good humour "she might have easily drawn from us much more by our occasional voluntary grants and contributions than ever she could by taxes. Sensible people will give a bucket or two of water to a dry pump, that they may afterwards get from it all they have occasion for."[37] Just after the close of the Constitutional Convention Franklin wrote to a French friend: "If it succeeds, I do not see why you might not in Europe carry the project of good king Henry IV into execution by forming a federal union and one grand republic of all its different states and kingdoms, by means of a like convention."[38] As to Americans: "We are sons of the earth and seas, and like Antæus, if in wrestling with Hercules we now and then receive a fall, the touch of our parents will communicate to us fresh strength and ability to renew the contest. Be quiet and thankful."[39] "During the course of a long life in which I have made observations of public affairs, it has appeared to me that almost every war between the Indians and whites has been occasioned by some injustice of the latter towards the former."[40] "I enjoy the company and conversation of its [Boston's] inhabitants when any of them are so good as to visit me; for, besides their general good sense, which I value, the Boston manner, turn of phrase, and even tone of voice and accent in pronunciation all please and seem to refresh and revive me."[41] "I have sometimes thought that it might be well to establish an office of insurance for farms against the damage that may occur to them from storms, blight, insects, etc. A small sum paid by a number would repair such losses and prevent much poverty and distress."[42] This, written 24 October 1788, seems to have been the earliest suggestion of crop insurance.

"We must not expect that a new government may be formed, as a game of chess may be played by a skilful hand, without a fault. The players of our game are so many, their ideas so different, their prejudices so strong and so various, and their particular interests, independent of the general, seeming so opposite, that not a move can be made that is not contested; the numerous objections confound the understanding; the wisest must agree to some unreasonable things that reasonable ones of more consequence may be obtained; and thus chance has its share in many of the determinations, so that the play is more like *tric-trac* with a box of dice."[43] "I think all the heretics I have known have been virtuous men. They have the virtue of fortitude, or they would not venture to own their heresy; and they cannot afford to be deficient in any of the other virtues, as that would give advantage to their many enemies; and they have not, like orthodox sinners, such a number of friends to excuse or justify them."[44] "If any form of government is capable of making a nation happy, ours I think bids fair now [May 1789] for producing that effect. But, after all, much depends upon the people who are to be governed. We have been guarding against an evil that old states are most liable to, excess of power in the rulers; but our present danger seems to be defect of obedience in the subjects."[45]

In his last summer, so emaciated from the loss of appetite which his opium had caused that, as he said, "little remains of me but a skeleton covered with a skin,"[46] Franklin wrote his sister Jane Mecom one of his most cheerful and charming letters to her. He was pleased to hear that she had not had a misunderstanding with a relative of theirs. "Indeed, if there had been any such, I should have concluded it was your fault; for I think our family were always subject to being a little miffy. By the way, is our relationship in Nantucket quite worn out? I have met with none from thence of late years who were disposed to be acquainted with me, except Captain Timothy Folger. They are wonderfully shy. But I admire their honest plainness of speech. About a year ago I invited two of them to dine with me. Their answer was that they would if they could not do better. I suppose they did better, for I never saw them afterwards, and so had no opportunity of showing my miff, if I had one."[47]

In his last December he told his final story about his earlier years, to explain a letter he had received. It was from "the widow of a Jew who, happening to be one of a number of passengers that were about forty years ago in a stage-boat going to New York, and which by the unskilful management of the boatman overset the canoe from which I was endeavouring to get on board her near Staten Island, has ever since worried me with demands of a gratis for having, as he pretended, been instrumental in saving my life; though that was in no danger, as we were near the shore, and you know what an expert swimmer I am, and he was no more of any service to me in stopping the boat to take me in than every other passenger; to all of whom I gave a liberal entertainment at the tavern when we arrived at New York, to their general satisfaction at the time. But this Hayes never saw me afterwards, at New York or Brunswick or Philadelphia, that he did not dun me for money on pretence of his being poor and having been so happy as to be instrumental in saving my life, which was really in no danger. In this way he got of me sometimes a double johannes, sometimes a Spanish doubloon, and never less; how much in the whole I do not know, having kept no account of it; but it must have been a very considerable sum; and [as] he never incurred any risk nor was at any trouble in my behalf, I have long since thought him well paid for any little expense of humanity he might have felt on the occasion. He seems, however, to have left me to his widow as part of her dowry."[48]

"In this world, nothing can be said to be certain except death and taxes."[49] "The convulsions in France are attended with some disagreeable circumstances; but if by the struggle she obtains and secures for her nation its future liberty, and a good constitution, a few years' enjoyment of those blessings will amply repair all the damages their acquisition may have occasioned. God grant that not only the love of liberty but a thorough knowledge of the rights of man may pervade all the nations of the earth, so that a philosopher may set his foot anywhere on its surface and say: 'This is my country.' "[50]

Franklin died too soon to hear more than the early news from France, and his chief feeling about the French Revolution was anxiety over his friends. But what he heard did not turn him, in the short time he had left, from his long-held belief in the rights of men as against wealth and privilege. In November 1789 he was firmly opposed to the plan to alter the constitution of Pennsylvania so that, as was proposed, the upper house in the legislature should represent the property of the state and the lower house the people, with equal authority between them. "Why should the upper house, chosen by a minority, have equal power with the lower chosen by a majority? Is it supposed that wisdom is the necessary concomitant of riches, and that one man worth a thousand pounds must have as much wisdom as twenty who have only 999? And why is property to be represented at all? . . . The accumulation . . . of property . . . and its security to individuals in every society must be an effect of the protection afforded to it by the joint strength of the society in the execution of its laws. Private property therefore is a creature of society, and is subject to the calls of that society, whenever its necessities shall require it, even to its last farthing; its contributions therefore to the public exigencies are not to be considered as conferring a benefit to the public, entitling the contributors to the distinctions of honour and power, but as the return of an obligation previously received, or the payment of a just debt. . . . The important ends of civil society, and the personal securities of life and liberty, these remain the same in every member of the society; and the poorest continue to have an equal claim to them with the most opulent, whatever difference time, chance, or industry may occasion in their circumstances. On these considerations I am sorry to see . . . a disposition among some of our people to commence an aristocracy by giving the rich a predominancy in government."[51]

The last public matter with which Franklin concerned himself was slavery. In his time he had owned slaves and sold them. But he had also, as far back as 1751, been the first to point out the economic weakness of the institution,[52] and he had from London suggested the establishment of the first school for Negroes in Philadelphia in 1758.[53] The first abolition society, founded by Quakers in 1775 but inactive during the Revolution, had renewed its efforts in 1787 with Franklin as president: The Pennsylvania Society for Promoting the Abolition of Slavery, and the Relief of Free Negroes Unlawfully Held in Bondage. Now on 9 November 1789 it appealed for support and funds in an *Address to the Public* which Franklin signed and may have written.[54] He signed also the memorial which the society presented to the first Congress on 12 February. The memorial was referred after debate to a committee which on 5 March reported that Congress had no authority to interfere in the internal affairs of the states.[55] Franklin on the 23rd, with less than a month still to live, wrote *On the Slave Trade*, a hoax and a parody worthy of his liveliest years.[56]

"Reading last night in your excellent paper," Franklin began, to the editor of the *Federal Gazette*, "the speech of Mr. Jackson [James Jackson of Georgia] in Congress against their meddling with the affair of slavery, or attempting to mend the condition of the slaves, it put me in mind of a similar one made about a hundred years since by Sidi Mehemet Ibrahim, a member of the Divan of Algiers, which may be seen in Martin's account of his consulship, *anno* 1687. It was against granting the petition of the sect called Erika, or Purists, who prayed for the abolition of piracy and slavery, as being unjust. Mr. Jackson does not quote it; perhaps he has not seen it. If, therefore, some of its reasonings are to be found in his eloquent speech, it may only show that men's interests and intellects operate and are operated on with surprising similarity in all countries and climates, when under similar circumstances." Then Franklin went on to parody the American speech in the African speech which he had invented. Jackson's arguments in defence of slavery were matched by Sidi Mehemet Ibrahim's in defence of the right and duty of the Algerines to have Christian slaves, no matter what the canting Erika (Quakers) might say. At a time when the Algerine pirates were detested by all Americans, and their taking of Christian slaves abominated, Franklin compared the American and the Algerine policies and satirically proved that there was nothing to choose between them. "The Divan came to this resolution: 'The doctrine that plundering and enslaving the Christians is unjust, is at best problematical; but that it is the interest of this state to continue the practice, is clear; therefore let the petition be rejected.' And it was rejected accordingly." The dying philosopher feathered his last arrow with a wit still light and swift.

III

There could be no doubt the philosopher was dying. His powerful body, built to last a hundred years, was worn down by pain which was almost unrelieved except when he took opiates. For a year he had been confined largely to his bed or bedroom. His last recorded experiment had been made. "The deafness you complain of," he wrote to Alexander Small on 17 February 1789, "gives me concern, as if great, it must diminish considerably your pleasure in conversation. If moderate, you may remedy it easily and readily by putting your thumb and fingers behind your ear, pressing it outwards, and enlarging it, as it were, with the hollow of your hand. By an exact experiment I found that I could hear the tick of a watch at forty-five feet distance by this means, which was barely audible at twenty feet without it. The experiment was made at midnight when the house was still."[57] But numerous friends came to see him, and he followed the course of the world in the newspapers with his old curiosity. "For my own personal ease," he wrote to Washington on 16 September, "I should have died two years ago; but, though those years have been spent in excruciating pain, I am pleased that I have lived them, since they have brought me to see our present situation"[58]—with the new government at last established and Washington at its head.

Pain seems to have had little effect on Franklin's memory or wit, and none on his cheerfulness. He continued to do some work, with Benjamin Bache as his secretary. He composed the inscription for the corner stone of the Library Company's new building, laid 31 August, leaving out his own name which the committee wrote in. "I have seven promising grandchildren by my daughter," he told Small, "who play with and amuse me, and she is a kind, attentive nurse to me when I am at any time indisposed." The seventh child was another Sarah Bache, then five months old, "a little good-natured girl whom I begin to love as well as the rest."[59] During his last winter his granddaughter Deborah, then nine, came every day after tea to his bedside with her Webster spelling-book, and with unflagging interest he heard her next day's lesson.[60] On 26 December he wrote a long letter to Noah Webster, who had dedicated his *Dissertations on the English Language* to Franklin.[61] One day when Polly Hewson found him in agony, and after it had eased a little undertook to read to him from Johnson's *Lives of the Poets*, he was so much roused by the life of Isaac Watts that he repeated several of the poems from memory.[62] He received a letter from Benjamin West introducing the painter Jonathan Trumbull, whom Franklin already knew. Franklin sent an extract from the letter to the *Pennsylvania Gazette*, where it was printed on 17 February to introduce Trumbull to Philadelphia.

About the first of March Franklin's pain ceased, and he wrote his famous letter to Ezra Stiles, president of Yale. "You desire to know something of my religion. It is the first time I have been questioned upon it. But I cannot take your curiosity amiss, and shall endeavour in a few words to gratify it. Here is my creed. I believe in one God, Creator of the universe. That He governs it by His providence. That He ought to be worshipped. That the most acceptable service we render Him is doing good to His other children. That the soul of man is immortal, and will be treated with justice in another life respecting its conduct in this. These I take to be the fundamental principles of all sound religion, and I regard them as you do in whatever sect I meet with them.

"As to Jesus of Nazareth, my opinion of whom you particularly desire, I think the system of morals and his religion, as he left them to us, the best the world ever saw or is likely to see; but I apprehend it has received various corrupt changes, and I have, with most of the present Dissenters in England, some doubts as to his divinity; though it is a question I do not dogmatize upon, having never studied it, and think it needless to busy myself with it now, when I expect soon an opportunity of knowing the truth with less trouble. I see no harm, however, in its being believed, if that belief has the good consequence, as probably it has, of making his doctrines more respected and better observed; especially as I do not perceive that the Supreme [Being] takes it amiss, by distinguishing the unbelievers in His government of the world with any peculiar marks of His displeasure.

"I shall only add, respecting myself, that, having experienced the goodness of that Being in conducting me prosperously through a long life, I have no doubt of its continuance in the next, without the smallest conceit of meriting it. . . . I confide that you will not expose me to criticism and censure by publishing any part of this communication to you. I have ever let others enjoy their religious sentiments, without reflecting on them for those that appeared to me unsupportable and even absurd. All sects here, and we have a great variety, have experienced my good will in assisting them with subscriptions for building their new places of worship; and, as I never opposed any of their doctrines, I hope to go out of the world in peace with them all."[63] In these tolerant words a great pagan sceptic showed his graceful consideration for the rituals of his time, as Socrates on his deathbed had remembered that he owed a sacrificial cock to Æsculapius.

Jefferson, back from France and on his way from Virginia to New York to take his post as Washington's secretary of state, at Philadelphia early in March "called on the venerable and beloved Franklin. He was then on the bed of sickness from which he never rose. My recent return from a country in which he had left so many friends, and the perilous convulsions to which they had been exposed, revived all his anxieties to know what part they had taken, what had been their course, and what their fate. He went over all in succession, with a rapidity and animation almost too much for his strength. When all his inquiries were satisfied, and a pause took place, I told him I had learned with pleasure that, since his return to America, he had been occupied in preparing for the world the history of his own life. 'I cannot say much of that,' said he; 'but I will give you a sample of what I shall leave'; and he directed his little grandson (William Bache), who was standing by his bedside, to hand him a paper from the table to which he pointed. He did so; and the Doctor, putting it into my hands, desired me to take it and read it at my leisure. It was about a quire of folio paper, written in a large and running hand, very like his own. I looked into it slightly, then shut it, and said I would accept his permission to read it and would carefully return it. He said: 'No, keep it.' Not certain of his meaning, I again looked into it, folded it for my pocket, and said again I would certainly return it. 'No,' said he, 'keep it.' I put it into my pocket and shortly after took leave of him."[64] Jefferson seems to have been the only American, outside of Franklin's family, to whom any part of the manuscript was entrusted. And it was to Jefferson that Franklin, nine days before his death, wrote his last letter, clearly and accurately telling him of the map which the peace commissioners had used in fixing the boundary between Maine and Nova Scotia.[65]

Franklin had already begun to run a temperature and to feel a pain in his chest from an impostume—empyema—in his left lung. (He had many years before had two severe attacks of pleurisy.) The difficulty in his breathing increased till he was almost suffocated, then suddenly left him. He had a day or so of rest. "He rose from his bed," Rush later wrote to Richard Price, "and begged that it be made up for him so that he might die in a decent manner. His daughter told him that she hoped he would recover and live many years longer. He calmly replied: 'I hope not.' Upon being advised to change his position in bed, so that he might breathe easy, he said: 'A dying man can do nothing easy.' "[66] The empyema burst, breathing became almost impossible, and he passed into coma. With his grandsons Temple and Benjamin watching him he died quietly about eleven in the night of 17 April, eighty-four years and three months after he was born.

No other town, burying its great man, ever buried more of itself than Philadelphia with Franklin. He had made and long conducted the *Pennsylvania Gazette* of which No. 3125, black-bordered, announced his death. John Jones, his physician, told the readers of the *Gazette* of Franklin's last illness. Jones was attending physician to the Pennsylvania Hospital, which Franklin had helped to found. The funeral procession assembled on the 21st at the State House, where Franklin had been a familiar figure for more than fifty years, busy and eminent in the affairs of the province, the state, and the nation.[67] First in the cortège from Franklin's house to the graveyard went: All the Clergy of the City, before the Corpse. Franklin, barely a believer, had aided all the churches. The Corpse, carried by Citizens. The Pall, supported by the President of the State, the Chief Justice, the President of the Bank, Samuel Powell, William Bingham, and David Rittenhouse, Esquires. Franklin had been President, and his administration had restored the charter of the bank. William Bingham was vice-president of the Society for Political Enquiries of which Franklin was president. Rittenhouse had served with Franklin on the Committee of Safety during the Revolution. Mourners, consisting of the family of the deceased, with a number of particular friends. The Secretary and Members of the Supreme Executive Council. Franklin had been for three years its president. The Speaker and Members of the General Assembly. This was the single legislature which Franklin had preferred when the state constitution was made. Judges of the Supreme Court, and other Officers of Government. Franklin had been a commissioner of the peace. The Gentlemen of the Bar.

The Mayor and Corporation of the City of Philadelphia. Franklin had been a member of the council and an alderman. The Printers of the City, with their Journeymen and Apprentices. Printing was Franklin's trade. The Philosophical Society. He had founded it, served as its first secretary, and been president for twenty-one years. The College of Physicians. Franklin the past November, as president of the board of trustees of the University, had signed the new *Rules Respecting a Medical Education and a Degree*.[68] The Cincinnati. Franklin, though he had ridiculed its plan to make honour hereditary, had inconsistently accepted an honorary membership.[69] The College of Philadelphia. Franklin had planned and fostered the Academy from which the College had grown. Sundry other Societies—together with a numerous and respectable body of Citizens. It was estimated that twenty thousand people followed or witnessed the funeral: the largest number ever up to that time gathered in Philadelphia. The bells were muffled and tolled. The flags on the ships in the harbour hung at half-mast. When Franklin was lowered into his grave in the Christ Church burying ground, beside his wife, a company of militia artillery fired the funeral guns. Franklin had organized Pennsylvania's first militia, himself a colonel in provincial days.

On 22 April James Madison moved that the House of Representatives, sitting in New York, wear mourning for a month. The motion was unanimously passed without discussion. "The Senate," Jefferson wrote, "refused. I proposed to General Washington that the executive department should wear mourning; he declined it, because he said he would not know where to draw the line if he once began that ceremony. . . . I told him that the world had drawn so broad a line between him and Dr. Franklin, on the one side, and the residue of mankind, on the other, that we might wear mourning for them, and the question still remain new and undecided as to all others. He thought it best, however, to avoid it."[70] In Paris Mirabeau in the Convention on 11 June declared that nations, too long given to take formal note of the death of only those persons in whom courts were interested, should wear mourning, rather, for the benefactors and heroes of humanity. "Would it not become us, gentlemen, to join in this religious act, to bear a part in this homage, rendered, in the face of the world, both to the rights of man and to the philosopher who has most contributed to extend their sway over the whole earth? Antiquity would have raised altars to this mighty genius, who, to the advantage of mankind, compassing in his mind the heavens and the earth, was able to restrain alike thunderbolts and tyrants. Europe, enlightened and free, owes at least a token of remembrance and regret to one of the greatest men who have ever been engaged in the service of philosophy and of liberty. I propose that it be decreed that the National Assembly, during three days, shall wear mourning for Benjamin Franklin." Lafayette and La Rochefoucauld rose to second the motion, which was carried by acclamation.[71]

For the learned in France, Condorcet on 13 November pronounced a eulogy on Franklin before the Academy of Sciences. The Commune of Paris had been prompter, with Claude Fauchet's eulogy at the Rotonde on 21 July,[72] and a celebration throughout the city, in cafés and streets. There were almost as many eulogies as there were orators, almost as many ceremonies as societies, and many charming women wept. While the printers of Paris, gathered at the Couvent des Cordeliers to honour Franklin, listened to an oration by one of them, others set the oration in type as it was delivered, and at the end struck it off and distributed copies as souvenirs.[73] The next 14 March Franklin's friend Vicq d'Azyr spoke yet another eulogy before the Royal Society of Medicine; and on the 1st Franklin's former enemy William Smith, aided in the preparation of his address by Jefferson, Rush, Rittenhouse, and Jonathan Williams, delivered a eulogium in the German Lutheran church in Philadelphia before the American Philosophical Society.[74]

The death of a great man begins another history, of his continuing influence, his changing renown, the legend which takes the place of fact. This is not a biography of the posthumous Franklin. He has here told his story, which ends with his life. Nor should there now be need of a further comment on the record. Let the record stand, and explain itself. It has meant to make clear that

Franklin was not one of those men who owe their greatness merely to the opportunities of their times. In any age, in any place, Franklin would have been great. Mind and will, talent and art, strength and ease, wit and grace met in him as if nature had been lavish and happy when he was shaped. Nothing seems to have been left out except a passionate desire, as in most men of genius, to be all ruler, all soldier, all saint, all poet, all scholar, all some one gift or merit or success. Franklin's powers were from first to last in a flexible equilibrium. Even his genius could not specialize him. He moved through his world in a humorous mastery of it. Kind as he was, there was perhaps a little contempt in his lack of exigency. He could not put so high a value as single-minded men put on the things they give their lives for. Possessions were not worth that much, nor achievements. Comfortable as Franklin's possessions and numerous as his achievements were, they were less than he was. Whoever learns about his deeds remembers longest the man who did them. And sometimes, with his marvellous range, in spite of his personal tang, he seems to have been more than any single man: a harmonious human multitude.

Bibliography

AND

Index

GENERAL BIBLIOGRAPHY

A complete bibliography of Franklin would be almost a bibliography of the eighteenth century. This bibliography, excluding works however valuable which contain nothing about him not given elsewhere, is limited to manuscripts, articles, monographs, and books which furnish, with a maximum of originality and a minimum of repetition, the facts of his life and work.

MANUSCRIPTS AND COLLECTIONS

The principal collection of Franklin manuscripts is in the library of the American Philosophical Society at Philadelphia. Other important Philadelphia collections, of manuscripts and books, are those of the Historical Society of Pennsylvania, the Library of the University of Pennsylvania, Franklin Bache, and A. S. W. Rosenbach (in particular the letters to Jane Mecom and Madame Brillon). The Franklin Papers in the Library of Congress rank next in value to those of the American Philosophical Society. The Mason-Franklin collection, formed by William Smith Mason but now in the Yale University Library, includes, besides books and pamphlets, many manuscripts, notably correspondence with Joseph Galloway and the Shipley family. The William R. Clements Library at the University of Michigan has further Galloway correspondence and other letters to and from Franklin among the Lansdowne (Shelburne) Papers. Franklin's original manuscript of the *Autobiography* is in the Huntington Library at San Marino, California. His letters to Catherine Ray Greene, privately owned, are deposited in the John Carter Brown Library, Providence. In the Morgan Library, New York, are letters to Peter Collinson and the correspondence between William Temple Franklin and Louis Le Veillard. Numerous other Franklin manuscripts and letters exist in widely scattered public and private collections in the United States. In England there are Franklin letters in the British Museum, the Public Record Office, the Royal Society, and King's College, Cambridge; in France, in the Archives du Ministère des Affaires Étrangères, the Bibliothèque du Ministère de la Marine, the Bibliothèque Nationale, and the Archives Nationales, and in various private collections. (Details of the Franklin letters in European public collections may be found in the Stevens *Introduction* and Index cited below.)

COLLECTED WORKS

The first authorized collected edition of Franklin was that published by William Temple Franklin as *Memoirs of the Life and Writings of Benjamin Franklin*, 3 vols. London, 4to, 1818. The editing was inadequate, but the continuation of the memoirs in Vol. I still has value. This was superseded by *The Works of Benjamin Franklin*, edited by Jared Sparks, 10 vols., Boston, 1840. Though there is good reason to find fault with the inaccuracy of Sparks's text, his edition contains useful notes and interesting letters to Franklin. In *The Complete Works of Benjamin Franklin*, edited by John Bigelow, 10 vols., New York, 1887–89, the works were for the first time arranged in chronological order. The best of the collected editions is that of Albert Henry Smyth: *The Writings of Benjamin Franklin*, 10 vols., New York, 1905–07 (with a comprehensive Introduction in Vol. I and a useful Life in Vol. X). A new edition is now needed, at least a supplement to the Smyth. In the Chapter References (below) these four collected editions are referred to as W. T. Franklin; *Works* (Sparks); *Complete Works* (Bigelow); and *Writings* (except for the *Autobiography* in Vol. I, referred to as *Autobiography*).

The passages quoted (with the kind permission of the Macmillan Company) from the Smyth *Writings* in the present biography are modernized as to spelling, capitalization, and punctuation, as are those from other collected, uncollected, and unpublished sources. It has seemed more desirable to present Franklin in his essential clarity than to preserve eighteenth-century fashions of manuscript and type for their own sake. (For sufficient illustration, Franklin's earliest known prose, from the first Dogood paper; his earliest known verse, the *Elegy* (in part); his *Epitaph*; the unpublished letter to General Schuyler; and *The Causes of the Present Distractions* are given as originally written or printed.)

UNCOLLECTED WORKS

Individual letters and minor pieces not in the *Writings* are cited among the Chapter References.

The Causes of the Present Distractions. New York, 1774 (fuller version of *Causes of the American Discontents,* 1768)

A Dissertation on Liberty and Necessity, Pleasure and Pain. Edited by Lawrence C. Wroth. New York, 1930 (facsimile of the first edition)

The Ingenious Dr. Franklin: Selected Scientific Letters. Edited by Nathan G. Goodman. Philadelphia, 1931 (a few pieces hitherto uncollected)

"My Dear Girl." The Correspondence of Benjamin Franklin with Polly Stevenson, Georgiana and Catherine Shipley. Edited by J. M. Stifler. New York, 1927 (contains some of Franklin's letters hitherto unpublished)

Proposals Relating to the Education of Youth in Pensilvania. Edited by William Pepper. Philadelphia, 1931 (facsimile of the first edition, including the notes omitted in *Writings*)

Reflections on Courtship and Marriage: In Two Letters to a Friend. Wherein a Practicable Plan is laid down for Obtaining and Securing Conjugal Fidelity. Philadelphia, 1746

Satires and Bagatelles. Edited by Paul McPharlin. Detroit, 1937 (convenient collection of the lighter pieces, including the surreptitious ones; a good edition of all these still remains to be made)

"The Sayings of Poor Richard." The Prefaces, Proverbs, and Poems of Benjamin Franklin originally printed in Poor Richard's Almanacs for 1733–1758. Collected and edited by Paul Leicester Ford. Brooklyn, 1890

Some Account of the Pennsylvania Hospital; from its first Rise, to the Beginning of the Fifth Month, called May, 1754. Philadelphia, 1754

WORKS RELATING TO FRANKLIN

Adams, John. *Works.* 10 vols. Boston, 1850–56

Becker, Carl. *Benjamin Franklin. Dictionary of American Biography,* VI (1931), 585–98 (best brief account)

Bemis, S. F. *The Diplomacy of the American Revolution.* New York, 1935 (indispensable)

Benjamin Franklin and His Circle. A Catalogue of an Exhibition at the Metropolitan Museum of Art, New York. New York, 1936 (not only portraits but also objects associated with Franklin)

Bigelow, John (editor). *The Life of Benjamin Franklin Written by Himself.* 3 vols. Philadelphia, 1875 (the *Autobiography* with later autobiographical writings arranged as a continuation of it)

Bruce, W. C. *Benjamin Franklin Self-Revealed.* 2 vols. New York, 1917 (a study of Franklin's varied aspects rather than a narrative biography)

Butler, Ruth L. *Doctor Franklin: Postmaster General.* Garden City, 1928

Carey, L. J. *Franklin's Economic Views.* Garden City, 1928

Colonial Records. 16 vols. Harrisburg, 1838–53 (includes: *Minutes of the Provincial Council of Pennsylvania, Minutes of the Council of Safety, Minutes of the Supreme Executive Council*)

Crane, V. W. *Benjamin Franklin: Englishman and American.* Baltimore, 1936 (admirable study of the development of Franklin's mind with regard to public affairs)

De Puy, H. F. *A Bibliography of the English Colonial Treaties with the American Indians including a Synopsis of each Treaty.* New York, 1917 (thirteen of the fifty treaties were printed by Franklin or by Franklin and Hall, 1736–63)

Diller, Theodore. *Franklin's Contributions to Medicine.* Brooklyn, 1912

Doniol, Henri. *Histoire de la participation de la France à l'établissement des États-Unis d'Amérique.* 5 vols. and supplement. Paris, 1886–1900

Duane, William (editor). *Letters to Benjamin Franklin, from his Family and Friends, 1751–1790.* New York, 1859

Eddy, G. S. *The Franklin Library. Proceedings of the American Antiquarian Society,* New Series, XXXIV (1924), 206–26 (best study of Franklin's library, based on a manuscript catalogue the writer has made of books known to have belonged to Franklin)

    Notes and Queries. Colophon, New Series, II, No. 4 (1937), 602–16 (valuable comments on the state of Franklin knowledge and possible directions of research)

    A Ramble through the Mason-Franklin Collection. Yale University Library Gazette, X (1936), 65–90

Eiselen, M. R. *Franklin's Political Theories.* Garden City, 1928

Farrand, Max. *Benjamin Franklin's Memoirs. Huntington Library Bulletin,* No. 10 (1936), 49–78 (discusses the problems of the text and announces a variorum *Autobiography* in preparation)

Faÿ, Bernard. *Franklin, the Apostle of Modern Times.* Boston, 1929 (lively but often inaccurate and given to unsupported conjectures. The third volume of the French edition, Paris, 1929–31, contains a useful *Bibliographie et étude sur les sources historiques relatives à sa vie*)

    The Revolutionary Spirit in France and America. New York, 1927 (notes on Franklin in France)

    The Two Franklins: Fathers of American Democracy. Boston, 1933 (study of Franklin and Benjamin Franklin Bache based on the Franklin Bache collection)

Ford, P. L. *Franklin Bibliography. A List of Books written by, or relating to Benjamin Franklin.* Brooklyn, 1889 (masterly, but needs to be supplemented for materials of later date)

    The Many-Sided Franklin. New York, 1899 (excellent survey of Franklin under the heads of his different activities)

Ford, W. C. *List of the Benjamin Franklin Papers in the Library of Congress.* Washington, 1905

    and others (editors). *Journals of the Continental Congress 1774–1789.* 34 vols. Washington, 1904–37

Goggio, F. *Benjamin Franklin and Italy. Romanic Review,* XIX (1928), 302–08

Gummere, R. M. *Socrates at the Printing Press. Benjamin Franklin and the Classics. Classical Weekly,* XXVI (1932), 57–59

Hale, E. E., and E. E. Hale, Jr. *Franklin in France.* 2 vols. Boston, 1887–88 (fullest account of the French period)

Hays, I. Minis. *Calendar of the Papers of Benjamin Franklin in the Library of the American Philosophical Society.* 5 vols. Philadelphia, 1908 (appendix: *Papers of Benjamin Franklin in the Library of the University of Pennsylvania,* V, 399–510)

    The Chronology of Benjamin Franklin . . . 1706–1790. Philadelphia, 1913

Jefferson, Thomas. *Writings.* 20 vols. Washington, 1905

MacLaurin, Lois M. *Franklin's Vocabulary.* Garden City, 1928

McMaster, J. B. *Benjamin Franklin as a Man of Letters.* Boston, 1887

Minutes of the Provincial Council; Minutes of the Council of Safety; Minutes of the Supreme Executive Council. See *Colonial Records*

Mott, F. L., and C. E. Jorgenson (editors). *Benjamin Franklin: Representative Selections.* New York, 1936 (valuable documented Introduction and Selected Bibliography)

Nolan, J. Bennett. *Benjamin Franklin in Scotland and Ireland 1759 and 1771.* Philadelphia, 1938 (read only after this biography was in page proofs; contains useful supplementary matter for Chapters 12 and 15)

Oswald, J. C. *Benjamin Franklin Printer.* Garden City, 1917

Parton, James. *Life and Times of Benjamin Franklin.* 2 vols. New York, 1864 (superseded at many points by later investigations, but still the best biography of Franklin)

Pennsylvania Archives: Selected and Arranged from Original Documents in the Office of the

Secretary of the Commonwealth. 12 vols. Philadelphia, 1852–56 (has come to be known as *Pennsylvania Archives: First Series*)

Pennsylvania Archives: Fourth Series: Papers of the Governors. 12 vols. Harrisburg, 1900–02

Pennsylvania Archives: Eighth Series: Votes and Proceedings of the House of Representatives of the Province of Pennsylvania. 8 vols. Harrisburg, 1931–35

Pepper, William. *The Medical Side of Benjamin Franklin.* Philadelphia, 1911 (includes most of what Franklin wrote on medical matters)

Peyton, J. L. *Rambling Reminiscences of a Residence Abroad.* Staunton, Va., 1888 (letters to the Shipley family, pages 268, 271–97)

Sachse, J. F. *Benjamin Franklin as a Free Mason.* Philadelphia, 1906

Smythe, J. H., Jr. (editor). *The Amazing Benjamin Franklin.* New York, 1929 (46 contributions, chiefly from officials or experts; most of them are trifling, others furnish material to be found easily nowhere else)

Stevens, B. F. *Facsimiles of Manuscripts in European Archives Relating to America, 1773–1783.* 25 vols. Washington, 1889–98 (indispensable)

   Introduction to the Catalogue Index of Manuscripts in the Archives of England, France, Holland, and Spain Relating to America, 1763 to 1783. London, 1902 (the Index in 180 manuscript vols. is in the Library of Congress)

Victory, Beatrice M. *Benjamin Franklin and Germany. Americana Germanica,* No. 21 (1915)

Weitenkampf, Frank. *Portraits* (of Franklin and his family). *Bulletin of the New York Public Library,* X (1906), 57–83

Wharton, Francis (editor). *Revolutionary Diplomatic Correspondence of the United States.* 6 vols. Washington, 1889

Woody, Thomas. *Educational Views of Benjamin Franklin.* New York, 1931

CHAPTER REFERENCES

References are always to printed sources, when these exist, rather than to manuscripts. Full titles not given under individual chapters will be found in the General Bibliography.

CHAPTER 1

1   *Writings*, III, 453
2   Winsor, II, 270: Winsor, Justin (editor). *Memorial History of Boston*. 4 vols. Boston, 1880–81
3   Hill, I, 331: Hill, H. A. *History of the Old South Church (Third Church)*, Boston, *1669–1884*. 2 vols. Boston, 1890
4   Shurtleff, 617: Shurtleff, N. B. *A Topographical and Historical Description of Boston*. Boston, 1871
5   Shurtleff, 619
6   Sewall, 6 February 1703: Sewall, Samuel. *Diary*. 3 vols. Boston, 1878–82
7   Sewall, 8 September 1708
8   Winsor, II, 271
9   Shurtleff, 618, 630–31
10   Sewall, 29 April 1713
11   Sewall, 23 February 1718
12   Hill, I, 396
13   *Autobiography*, 234–35
14   Kalm, 154: *Peter Kalm's Travels in North America*. 2 vols. New York, 1937
15   *Autobiography*, 235
16   *Writings*, VII, 414–15
17   *Autobiography*, 239–40
18   Cotton Mather, 10 November 1718: Mather, Cotton. *Diary*. 2 vols. Boston, 1921–22
19   *Autobiography*, 240
20   *Autobiography*, 231–32
21   *Autobiography*, 232–33
22   *Writings*, X, 499
23   *Autobiography*, 348
24   *Autobiography*, 233
25   *Autobiography*, 237–38
26   *Autobiography*, 241

See also:

Jordan, J. W. *Franklin as a Genealogist. Pennsylvania Magazine of History and Biography*, XXIII (1899), 1–22 (Franklin's own genealogical chart of his family)

CHAPTER 2

1   *Autobiography*, 238
2   *Autobiography*, 240
3   *Autobiography*, 241–42

4   *Autobiography*, 244
5   *Autobiography*, 242–43
6   W. T. Franklin, I, 447
7   Rush, XXIX, 27: *Excerpts from the Papers of Dr. Benjamin Rush. Pennsylvania Magazine of History and Biography*, XIX (1905), 15–30
8   *Writings*, V, 543, 545
9   *Autobiography*, 246
10   *Courant* No. 3
11   *Courant* No. 1
12   *Courant* No. 5
13   *Courant*, 4 December 1721
14   *Courant* No. 5
15   *Writings*, II, 2–3
16   *Writings*, II, 2–9
17   *Autobiography*, 246
18   *Writings*, II, 11–13
19   *Writings*, II, 21–25
20   *Franklin's Elegy. University of Pennsylvania Library Chronicle*, II (1934), 26–32 (facsimile of the manuscript)
21   *Autobiography*, 248
22   *Courant*, 16 July 1722
23   *Writings*, II, 25–26
24   Facsimile of file in New York Public Library
25   *Writings*, II, 29–31
26   *Writings*, II, 41–43
27   *Writings*, II, 43–45
28   *Autobiography*, 248–49
29   *Autobiography*, 249
30   *Autobiography*, 249–50

See also:

Bleyer, W. G. *Main Currents in the History of American Journalism*. Boston, 1927
Cook, Elizabeth C. *Literary Influences in Colonial Newspapers 1704–1750*. New York, 1912
Ford, W. C. *Franklin's New England Courant. Proceedings of the Massachusetts Historical Society*, LVII (1924), 336–53 (facsimile of the file of the *Courant* in the British Museum; other copies of the facsimile in various American libraries)

CHAPTER 3

1   *Autobiography*, 267
2   *Autobiography*, 250–56

3   *Autobiography*, 256–57
4   *Autobiography*, 258
5   *Autobiography*, 259
6   *Autobiography*, 260–61
7   *Autobiography*, 262
8   *Writings*, IX, 209
9   *Autobiography*, 262
10 *Autobiography*, 263
11 *Autobiography*, 264
12 *Autobiography*, 265
13 *Autobiography*, 269
14 *Autobiography*, 268
15 *Autobiography*, 269
16 *Autobiography*, 270
17 *Autobiography*, 270
18 *Autobiography*, 271–72
19 *Autobiography*, 276
20 *Autobiography*, 276–77
21 *Autobiography*, 279
22 *Autobiography*, 280
23 *The Dunciad*, III, 165–66
24 *Dissertation on Liberty and Necessity,
    Pleasure and Pain*, 16–17, 22, 29
25 *Dissertation*, 10
26 *Autobiography*, 279n.
27 *Writings*, VII, 411–12
28 *Autobiography*, 278
29 *Writings*, II, 52–53
30 *Autobiography*, 281
31 *Autobiography*, 282
32 *Autobiography*, 283
33 *Autobiography*, 283
34 *Autobiography*, 285
35 *Writings*, II, 53–86

CHAPTER 4

1   *Works* (Sparks), I, 104–05n.; Walsh,
    Robert. *Life of Benjamin Franklin.
    Delaplaine's Repository of the Lives
    and Portraits of Distinguished Ameri-
    cans*, Vol. II, Part I (Philadelphia,
    1818), 51–52
2   *Autobiography*, 289
3   In the Historical Society of Pennsyl-
    vania
4   *Autobiography*, 291–92
5   *Autobiography*, 292
6   *Autobiography*, 293–94
7   *Autobiography*, 297–98
8   *Autobiography*, 289–91
9   *Autobiography*, 299–300
10 S. Mather, 56–57: Mather, Samuel.
    *The Life of the Very Reverend and
    Learned Cotton Mather*. Boston, 1729
11 *Writings*, II, 88–90
12 *Autobiography*, 298–99
13 *Works* (Sparks), II, 553–57
14 *Autobiography*, 349–50
15 *Autobiography*, 340
16 *Autobiography*, 341
17 *Writings*, IV, 14
18 *Autobiography*, 342

19 *Autobiography*, 296
20 *Writings*, II, 91–100
21 *Paradise Lost*, V, 153–204
22 *Writings*, II, 157–70
23 *Autobiography*, 326–27
24 *Works* (Sparks), II, 554
25 *Autobiography*, 327–28
26 *Autobiography*, 329
27 *Autobiography*, 329–31
28 *Autobiography*, 333
29 *Autobiography*, 337–38
30 *Autobiography*, 297, 310
31 *Writings*, III, 4
32 *What is Sauce for a Goose is also Sauce
    for a Gander*, 6–7 (anonymous
    pamphlet, Philadelphia, 1764)
33 *Autobiography*, 309–10
34 *Autobiography*, 310–11
35 *Autobiography*, 311
36 *Autobiography*, 300
37 *Autobiography*, 301
38 *Autobiography*, 301
39 *Writings*, II, 106–10
40 *Writings*, II, 110–17
41 *Writings*, II, 126–32
42 *Autobiography*, 308
43 *Writings*, II, 157
44 *Writings*, II, 170–72
45 *Writings*, II, 172–79
46 *Autobiography*, 303
47 *Autobiography*, 304
48 *Autobiography*, 307–08
49 *Writings*, VII, 412
50 *Writings*, II, 133–55
51 *Autobiography*, 306–07
52 *Writings*, II, 182
53 *Writings*, II, 242
54 *Autobiography*, 311–12
55 *Writings*, II, 182–95
56 *Writings*, II, 196
57 *Writings*, II, 200–01
58 *Writings*, II, 213–14
59 *Writings*, II, 300
60 *Writings*, II, 211
61 *Writings*, II, 209
62 *Writings*, II, 218
63 *Writings*, II, 224–25
64 *Autobiography*, 342
65 *Writings*, II, 217–18
66 Smith, W. G. *The Oxford Dictionary
    of English Proverbs*. Oxford, 1935,
    1936
67 *Writings*, II, 218–21
68 Eddy, G. S. *Account Books Kept by
    Benjamin Franklin*. 2 vols. New
    York, 1928–29 (digest of various
    ledgers and journals for 1728–39,
    1730–37, 1739–47)
69 *Writings*, II, 244
70 *Writings*, II, 246–76
71 *Writings*, II, 373
72 *Autobiography*, 348–49
73 *Writings*, X, 166

74 P. L. Ford, *The Many-Sided Franklin*, 209
75 *Writings*, III, 101 (letter wrongly dated November)
76 *Writings*, III, 333–35
77 *Writings*, II, 362
78 Wroth, 186, 216–22, 324: Wroth, L. C. *The Colonial Printer.* New York, 1931; revised ed. Portland, 1938 (here cited)
79 *Writings*, X, 493
80 P. L. Ford, *The Many-Sided Franklin*, 262 (facsimile of epitaph in Franklin's handwriting)

See also:

American Magazine, The. Edited by Lyon H. Richardson. New York, 1937 (facsimile of complete file)
Bleyer, W. G. (References for Chapter 2)
Boyd, Julian P. Note (without title) demolishing the claim and belief that the *Saturday Evening Post* descends from the *Pennsylvania Gazette* and so was founded by Franklin. *Colophon*, New Series, III, No. 2 (1938), 310
Campbell, W. J. *The Collection of Franklin Imprints in the Museum of the Curtis Publishing Company.* Philadelphia, 1918
Cook, Elizabeth C. (References for Chapter 2)
Eames, Wilberforce. *The Antigua Press and Benjamin Mecom. Proceedings of the American Antiquarian Society, New Series*, XXXVIII (1928), 303–48
Eddy, G. S. *A Work Book of the Printing House of Benjamin Franklin and David Hall 1759–1766. Bulletin of the New York Public Library*, XXXIV (1930), 575–89
Ford, P. L. *"The Sayings of Poor Richard."* (General Bibliography)
General Magazine, The. Edited by Lyon H. Richardson. New York, 1938 (facsimile of complete file)
Gray, Austin K. *The First American Library.* Philadelphia, 1936; reissued as: *Benjamin Franklin's Library*, New York, 1937 (on Franklin and early Americana, 24–26)
Hart, C. H. *Who was the Mother of Franklin's Son? Pennsylvania Magazine of History and Biography*, XXXV (1911), 308–14 (argues that Deborah Franklin was the mother)
Hildeburn, C. R. *A Century of Printing: The Issues of the Press in Pennsylvania 1685–1784.* Philadelphia, 1885
Hoch Teutsche und Englische Zeitung, Die. The issue for 25 January 1752 is described by Clarence S. Brigham in the *Proceedings of the Massachusetts Historical Society*, LVI (1923), 301–05
Jorgenson, C. E. *The Sources of Benjamin Franklin's Dialogues between Philocles and Horatio. American Literature*, VI (1934), 337–39 (influence of Shaftesbury)
King, M. R. *One Link in the First Newspaper Chain: The South Carolina Gazette. Journalism Quarterly*, IX (1932), 257–268
Lytle, Charles. *Benjamin Franklin's Change from Radicalism to Conservatism in Religious Thought. Meadville Theological School Quarterly Bulletin*, XXII (1928), 3–20 (exaggerates the change but shows influence of Wollaston)
Mott, Frank Luther. *A History of American Magazines 1741–1850.* New York, 1930
Mustard, W. P. *Poor Richard's Poetry. Nation*, LXXXII (1906), 239, 279
Philadelphische Zeitung. The issues for 6 May and 24 June 1732 are reproduced in facsimile in the *Pennsylvania Magazine of History and Biography*, XXIV (1900), 306–07; XXVI (1902), 91
Poor Richard. The almanacs for 1733, 1749, 1756, 1757, and 1758 are reproduced in facsimile in *Poor Richard's Almanack*, edited by Phillips Russell, Garden City, 1928; that for 1753 in Mott and Jorgenson's *Benjamin Franklin: Representative Selections*
Richardson, Lyon H. *A History of Early American Magazines 1741–1789.* New York, 1931

CHAPTER 5

1 *Writings*, V, 349
2 *Pennsylvania Gazette*, 16–24 November 1738; 21–28 June 1739; 26 July–2 August 1739; 4–11 January 1739
3 Eddy, *Account Books* (1929), 35–41 (References for Chapter 4)
4 *Pennsylvania Gazette*, 15–22 July 1731; 15–22 February 1732; 27 July–3 August 1738; 8–15 June 1738
5 *Pennsylvania Gazette*, 11–18 November 1731; 4–11 May 1732; 16–23 May 1734
6 *Writings*, II, 205–08
7 *Autobiography*, 353–54
8 *Autobiography*, 352–53
9 *Autobiography*, 325–26
10 *Some Observations on the Proceedings against the Rev. Mr. Hemphill; with a Vindication of his Sermons.* Philadel-

phia, 1735; *A Defence of the Rev. Mr. Hemphill's Observations: or, An Answer to the Vindication of the Reverend Commission*. Philadelphia, 1735

11 *Autobiography*, 346–47
12 Sachse, 36–42
13 Sachse, 58–62
14 John Remington
15 *Writings*, X, 162–64
16 *Writings*, II, 214–16
17 *Autobiography*, 354–55
18 *Autobiography*, 358
19 *Autobiography*, 359
20 *Autobiography*, 356
21 *Autobiography*, 355
22 *Autobiography*, 372
23 *Autobiography*, 357
24 *Writings*, II, 228–32
25 *Writings*, II, 276–77
26 *Writings*, II, 289
27 *Works* (Sparks), VI, 74–75
28 *Writings*, II, 288
29 *Writings*, II, 290–93
30 *Writings*, II, 251–52
31 *Writings*, II, 266n.
32 *Writings*, II, 270
33 Watson, I, 408; II, 489: Watson, John F. *Annals of Philadelphia*. Revised ed., 3 vols., Philadelphia, 1884
34 *Writings*, II, 456–59 (wrongly dated 1750?)
35 Hays, *Calendar*, I, 141; Dubourg's edition of Franklin's *Œuvres* (1773) gives the magic square as corrected (II, 274); American Philosophical Society, Franklin Papers, XLIV, 79 (*Calendar*, IV, 387), gives Franklin's rule for making magic squares
36 P. L. Ford, *The Many-Sided Franklin*, 58
37 *Writings*, VII, 434–35
38 M'Vickar, 18–19: M'Vickar, John. *A Domestic Narrative of the Life of Samuel Bard*. New York, 1822
39 *Writings*, IX, 332–33
40 *Port Folio* (Philadelphia), 23 May 1801
41 *Satires and Bagatelles* (1937), 32–34
42 *Writings*, VIII, 369
43 *Writings*, IX, 100
44 *Satires and Bagatelles* (1937), 37–39
45 *Reflections on Courtship and Marriage*, 43
46 *Reflections*, 33, 34
47 *Reflections*, 40–41
48 *Writings*, II, 463–67
49 *Autobiography*, 417
50 *Writings*, II, 302

See also:

Du Ponceau, P. S. *An Historical Account of the Origin and Formation of the Amer-*

ican Philosophical Society. Philadelphia, 1914
Rosengarten, J. G. *The American Philosophical Society*. Philadelphia, 1908

CHAPTER 6

1 *Autobiography*, 417
2 *Writings*, II, 310
3 *Autobiography*, 418
4 *Writings*, II, 302
5 *Writings*, II, 303
6 *Writings*, II, 324–25
7 *Writings*, II, 325
8 *Writings*, II, 362–63
9 *Writings*, II, 402
10 *Writings*, II, 410–11
11 *Writings*, III, 255
12 *Writings*, II, 418
13 *Writings*, II, 420
14 *Writings*, II, 434–38
15 *Writings*, III, 32–34, 35
16 *Autobiography*, 418; *Writings*, III, 7
17 P. L. Ford, *Franklin Bibliography*, 41
18 *Works* (Sparks), V, 288–93
19 Priestley, 171–72: Priestley, Joseph. *History and Present State of Electricity*. London, 1767; 2d ed., 1769 (here cited)
20 *Writings*, III, 99–100
21 *Autobiography*, 420
22 *Writings*, III, 98
23 *Writings*, III, 93–94
24 *Writings*, III, 96
25 *Writings*, III, 149
26 *Writings*, V, 421–22
27 *Writings*, IV, 129
28 Royal Society. *Philosophical Transactions*, XLVII, 567. London, 1753 (account of the electrical kite as written to Collinson 1 October, with the postscript. Collinson in making up Franklin's *Supplemental Experiments and Observations* in 1753 used, not the original letter, but the version in a copy of the *Gazette* which Franklin had sent him. This *Gazette* date has been followed by Franklin's editors, as in *Writings*, III, 99)
29 *Works* (Sparks), V, 375–77
30 *Writings*, III, 124
31 *Writings*, III, 346
32 *Writings*, III, 162
33 *Writings*, III, 258–60
34 *Autobiography*, 419
35 MacLaurin, 55–77; *Oxford English Dictionary*
36 *Writings*, IV, 16–18
37 *Writings*, III, 121
38 *Writings*, II, 312
39 Kalm, I, 160–61 (References for Chapter 1)
40 *Writings*, III, 18

41 *Writings*, II, 383–85
42 *Writings*, III, 61
43 *Writings*, II, 383
44 *Writings*, III, 84–86
45 Keyes, E. L. (editor). *A Letter on Catheters written by Benjamin Franklin*. Fulton, N. Y., 1934 (Franklin's letter of 8 December 1752 to his brother John, reproduced in facsimile with a learned commentary)
46 *Writings*, III, 103
47 *Writings*, III, 187–88
48 *Writings*, III, 273–75
49 *Writings*, II, 429

See also:

Abbe, Cleveland. *Benjamin Franklin as Meteorologist. Proceedings of the American Philosophical Society*, XLV (1906), 117–28
Jernegan, M. W. *Benjamin Franklin's "Electrical Kite" and Lightning Rod. New England Quarterly*, I (1928), 180–96
Potamian, Brother, and J. J. Walsh. *Makers of Electricity*. New York, 1909
Woodward, C. R. *The Development of Agriculture in New Jersey 1640–1880*. New Brunswick, 1927 (for the farms of Franklin and his son)

CHAPTER 7

1 *Autobiography*, 361–62
2 *Writings*, II, 336–53
3 *Works* (Sparks), VII, 23
4 *Autobiography*, 362; *Works* (Sparks), I, 146n. (gives mottoes)
5 *Writings*, II, 356
6 *Autobiography*, 362–63
7 *Pennsylvania Archives: Fourth Series*, II, 30–31
8 *Autobiography*, 374
9 *Autobiography*, 371
10 *Proposals Relating to the Education of Youth in Pensilvania*, 6–9, 10–11, 12, 14–15, 19, 20–21, 25, 26, 27–28, 29
11 *Autobiography*, 371
12 *Autobiography*, 372–73
13 *Writings*, X, 9–10
14 *Writings*, III, 21–29
15 *Autobiography*, 376–77
16 *Autobiography*, 378–79
17 *Writings*, II, 241–42, 278; Winsor, Justin (editor). *Narrative and Critical History of America*, VIII (1889), 33, 68, 81–82
18 *Pennsylvania Archives: Eighth Series*, III, 2373
19 *Autobiography*, 350
20 *Autobiography*, 351
21 *Writings*, II, 279

22 *Writings*, II, 283
23 *Autobiography*, 375
24 *Pennsylvania Archives: Eighth Series*, IV, 3432
25 *Writings*, III, 45–48
26 *Autobiography*, 375
27 *Minutes of the Provincial Council*, V, 666
28 *Minutes of the Provincial Council*, V, 665–86
29 *Writings*, III, 42

See also:

Deutsch, Albert. *The Mentally Ill in America*. Garden City, 1937 (for the founding of the Pennsylvania Hospital)
Franklin, Benjamin. *Some Account of the Pennsylvania Hospital* (General Bibliography)
Montgomery, T. H. *A History of the University of Pennsylvania*. Philadelphia, 1900
Morton, Thomas G. *History of the Pennsylvania Hospital*. Philadelphia, 1897
Philadelphia Contributionship. *Franklin and Fires*. Philadelphia, 1906 (pamphlet issued by the insurance company)
Thorpe, F. N. (editor). *Benjamin Franklin and the University of Pennsylvania*. Washington, 1893

CHAPTER 8

1 *Autobiography*, 364
2 *Writings*, III, 48–50
3 *Pennsylvania Gazette*, 14 January 1752
4 *Writings*, III, 40–42
5 *Writings*, III, 63–73
6 *Writings*, III, 72–73
7 *Pennsylvania Archives: Eighth Series*, V, 3655
8 *Writings*, III, 197–99
9 *Journal of the Congress at Albany. Collections of the Massachusetts Historical Society: Third Series*, V, 41–43
10 *Pennsylvania Archives: Fourth Series*, II, 696–724
11 *Writings*, III, 207–26
12 *Autobiography*, 388–89
13 *Writings*, III, 358–66
14 *Writings*, III, 231–41
15 *Autobiography*, 400–01
16 *Autobiography*, 398
17 *Autobiography*, 399
18 *Writings*, XVII, 262–68
19 Fisher, XVII, 271, 276: Fisher, Daniel. *Diary. Pennsylvania Magazine of History and Biography*, XVII (1893), 263–78
20 *Writings*, III, 265
21 *Writings*, III, 278

See also:

Butler, Ruth L. (General Bibliography)
Kraus, Michael. *Intercolonial Aspects of American Culture on the Eve of the Revolution.* New York, 1928
Mathews, Lois K. *Benjamin Franklin's Plans for a Colonial Union: 1750–1775. American Political Science Review,* VIII (1914), 393–412

CHAPTER 9

1   *Writings,* III, 245–46
2   In the American Philosophical Society
3   *Writings,* III, 282–85
4   *Writings,* III, 285 (letter wrongly given as to John Hancock)
5   *Writings,* III, 288–89
6   *Writings,* III, 344
7   In the American Philosophical Society (dated 13 January 1769 but more likely 1776)
8   *Writings,* X, 4

See also:

Greene, G. S., and Louise B. Clarke. *The Greenes of Rhode Island.* New York, 1903
Lane, W. C. *Harvard College and Franklin. Publications of the Colonial Society of Massachusetts,* X (1906), 229–39
Ray, Catherine (Mrs. William Greene). Unpublished letters to Franklin in the American Philosophical Society. Published letters in Duane and Hale, II, 233–34 (General Bibliography)

CHAPTER 10

1   *Writings,* III, 296–302
2   *Writings,* III, 307–20
3   *Autobiography,* 407–08
4   Nolan, 37: Nolan, J. Bennett. *General Benjamin Franklin.* Philadelphia, 1936 (indispensable account of Franklin as a soldier)
5   *Writings,* III, 321–22
6   *Autobiography,* 412–14
7   *Writings,* III, 323
8   *Minutes of the Provincial Council,* VII, 15–16
9   *Autobiography,* 409–10
10 *Writings,* III, 324
11 *Autobiography,* 411–12
12 *Writings,* III, 327
13 *Autobiography,* 412
14 *Autobiography,* 414
15 *Writings,* III, 348
16 *Writings,* III, 332
17 *Writings,* III, 339
18 *Writings,* III, 348
19 *Autobiography,* 416
20 *Autobiography,* 421–22
21 *Pennsylvania Archives: Fourth Series,* II, 596–97
22 *Minutes of the Provincial Council,* VII, 313–38
23 *Autobiography,* 424

CHAPTER 11

1   *Autobiography,* 425–26
2   *Writings,* III, 396
3   Gratz, XXXIX, 262: Gratz, Simon. *Some Materials for a Biography of Mrs. Elizabeth Ferguson, née Graeme. Pennsylvania Magazine of History and Biography,* XXXIX (1915), 257–321
4   Hart, XXXV, 418: Hart, C. H. *Letters from William Franklin to William Strahan. Pennsylvania Magazine of History and Biography,* XXXV (1911), 415–62
5   *Autobiography,* 430
6   *Writings,* III, 396
7   *Writings,* III, 391
8   *Writings,* III, 382
9   *Writings,* III, 384
10 *Autobiography,* 430
11 *Autobiography,* 431
12 *Autobiography,* 432–33

See also:

Burroughs, Alan (editor). *Harvard Portraits.* Cambridge, 1936 (ascribes the earliest portrait rather to John Greenwood than to Robert Feke)
Foote, H. W. *Robert Feke: Colonial Portrait Painter.* Cambridge, 1930 (ascribes, though tentatively, the Franklin portrait to Feke)
Hart, C. H. *Life Portraits of Great Americans: Benjamin Franklin. McClure's Magazine,* June 1897, 263–72 (reproduces and discusses portrait said to be of Franklin and by Matthew Pratt)

CHAPTER 12

1   *Writings,* X, 198
2   *Works* (Sparks), V, 505–12
3   *Writings,* III, 367
4   *Works* (Sparks), VII, 157–58
5   Mason, XXXIV, 246: Mason, William Smith. *Franklin and Galloway: Some Unpublished Letters. Proceedings of the American Antiquarian Society.* New Series, XXXIV (1924), 227–258
6   *Autobiography,* 435
7   Balch, 110–11: Balch, Thomas. *Let-*

*ters and Papers Relating Chiefly to the
Provincial History of Pennsylvania.*
New York, 1855

8 *Writings,* III, 419–25
9 *Writings,* III, 430–35
10 *Writings,* III, 431
11 *Writings,* V, 394–95
12 *Writings,* III, 426
13 Ferguson, 1–4: Ferguson, James. *Select Mechanical Exercises.* London,
   1773 (contains drawings and description of Franklin's little-known
   clock)
14 *Writings,* III, 435–47
15 *Writings,* III, 446–50
16 *Writings,* III, 451–54
17 *Writings,* III, 457
18 *Writings,* III, 461–67
19 Carlyle, 394–95: Carlyle, Alexander.
   Autobiography. Edinburgh, 1860
20 *Writings,* IX, 21–22n.
21 *Writings,* IV, 3–7
22 *Writings,* VI, 320
23 Mason, XXXIV, 246
24 Quincy, 269–70: Quincy, Josiah.
   *Memoirs of the Life of Josiah Quincy,
   Jun.* Boston, 1825
25 *Writings,* III, 445
26 Eddy, LV, 121: Eddy, G. S. *Account
   Book of Benjamin Franklin kept by
   him during his First Mission as Provincial Agent, 1757–1762. Pennsylvania Magazine of History and Biography,* LV (1931), 97–133
27 *Writings,* IV, 195
28 Mason, XXXIV, 255
29 *Works* (Sparks), III, 529–30
30 Faÿ, *Franklin, the Apostle of Modern
   Times,* 289, 528
31 *Autobiography,* 438
32 *Writings,* IV, 133
33 *Writings,* IV, 32–82
34 *Writings,* IV, 71–72
35 *Writings,* IV, 154
36 *Writings,* IV, 185–86
37 *Writings,* IV, 110–11
38 *Writings,* IV, 121
39 *Writings,* I, 179–81; VI, 254–56
40 *Writings,* IV, 89–95
41 *Writings,* IV, 83–84
42 Low, 199–200: Low, D. M. *Edward
   Gibbon.* New York, 1937
43 *Writings,* IV, 127–29
44 *Writings,* IV, 10–11
45 *Writings,* IV, 20–22
46 *Writings,* IV, 26–31
47 *Writings,* IV, 114–15
48 Pepper, 34–39
49 *Writings,* IV, 163–69
50 *Works* (Sparks), I, 265
51 Sonneck, O. G. *Benjamin Franklin's
   Relations to Music. Music,* XIX
   (1900), 1–14

52 Hays, *Calendar,* IV, 180, 186–87
53 *Writings,* IV, 172
54 *Writings,* IV, 173
55 *Writings,* IV, 176
56 *Writings,* IV, 174
57 *Writings,* IV, 180–81
58 *Writings,* IV, 179

See also:

Livingston, L. S. *Benjamin Franklin's Par-
   able against Persecution with an Account
   of the Early Editions.* Cambridge,
   1916
Macqueen, Edith E. *Benjamin Franklin a
   St. Andrews Doctor of Laws. Scots
   Magazine,* XXI (April 1934), 64–67
Shepherd, W. R. *History of the Proprietary
   Government in Pennsylvania.* New
   York, 1896

CHAPTER 13

1 *Writings,* IV, 194
2 *Writings,* IV, 182
3 *Writings,* IV, 197
4 *Writings,* IV, 207
5 *Writings,* IV, 210
6 *Writings,* IV, 289–314
7 *Writings,* IV, 223
8 *Writings,* IV, 376
9 *Writings,* IV, 223–24
10 Shepherd, 85n. (References for
   Chapter 12)
11 *Writings,* IV, 212–13
12 *Writings,* IV, 243–45
13 *Pennsylvania Archives: Eighth Series,*
   VII, 5590–91, 5595
14 *Writings,* IV, 228
15 *Writings,* IV, 240
16 *Writings,* IV, 314–15
17 *Writings,* IV, 315–38
18 *Writings,* IV, 269–71
19 Reed, I, 37: Reed, W. B. *Life and
   Correspondence of Joseph Reed.* 2 vols.
   Philadelphia, 1847
20 *Writings,* IV, 285
21 *Franklin and Fires,* 15 (References for
   Chapter 7)
22 *Writings,* IV, 288

See also:

*The Scribler, Being a Letter from a Gentle-
   man in Town to his Friend in the
   Country, concerning the present State of
   Affairs.* Philadelphia, 1764 (a defence of Franklin against the
   charges of the proprietary party)

CHAPTER 14

1 *Writings,* IV, 362
2 *Writings,* VI, 200–01
3 *Writings,* IV, 390

4 *Writings*, IV, 367–70
5 M'Vickar, 23 (References for Chapter 5)
6 *Writings*, IV, 373–81
7 *Writings*, IV, 382–83
8 *Writings*, IV, 392
9 *Writings*, IV, 387–88
10 *Writings*, V, 16
11 In the American Philosophical Society, Franklin Papers, L (ii), 51
12 *Writings*, IV, 405
13 *Writings*, IV, 404
14 *Writings*, IV, 408
15 *Writings*, IV, 412–48
16 *Writings*, X, 231
17 *Writings*, X, 232
18 *Writings*, X, 233
19 *Writings*, V, 147
20 *Writings*, IV, 463
21 *Writings*, IV, 449–50
22 *Writings*, IV, 456

See also:

Crane, Verner W. *Benjamin Franklin and the Stamp Act. Transactions of the Colonial Society of Massachusetts,* XXXII (1934), 56–77
Crane, Verner W. *Certain Writings of Benjamin Franklin on the British Empire and the American Colonies. Papers of the Bibliographical Society,* XXVIII (1934), 1–27
Walsh, Robert (References for Chapter 4) (gives Franklin's list of questioners at his examination, 74–77)

CHAPTER 15

1 *Writings*, IV, 459
2 Victory, 53; Hays, *Calendar*, I, 197 (letter from Raspe to Franklin)
3 *Writings*, IV, 465
4 *Writings*, V, 529–30
5 *Writings*, V, 31–32
6 *Writings*, V, 24
7 *Writings*, V, 17–22
8 Crane, XXXII, 58 (References for Chapter 14)
9 *Writings*, IV, 468–71
10 *Writings*, V, 46
11 *Writings*, V, 47
12 *Writings*, V, 48–54
13 *Writings*, V, 95
14 *Writings*, V, 55–60
15 *Writings*, V, 102
16 *Writings*, V, 202
17 *Writings*, V, 68
18 *Writings*, V, 60–65
19 *Writings*, V, 91
20 *Writings*, V, 78–89
21 *Writings*, V, 90
22 *The Causes of the Present Distractions,* 4, 11, 13, 14–16

23 *Writings*, X, 235
24 *Writings*, X, 237
25 *Writings*, X, 237
26 Tucker, XXV, 312n.: Tucker, Josiah. *A Letter from a Merchant in London to his Nephew in North America relative to the Present Posture of Affairs in the Colonies.* London, 1766. Reprinted with Franklin's marginal notes in *Pennsylvania Magazine of History and Biography,* XXV (1901), 307–22, 516–26; XXVI (1902), 81–90, 255–64
27 *Writings*, V, 20–21
28 *Writings*, V, 113–15
29 *Writings*, V, 145–48
30 *Writings*, V, 133
31 *Writings*, V, 296
32 *Writings*, V, 298–304
33 *Writings*, V, 317–19
34 *Writings*, V, 378
35 *Writings*, V, 366
36 *Writings*, V, 366
37 *Writings*, V, 413
38 *Writings*, V, 367–68
39 *Writings*, V, 344
40 *Writings*, V, 379–80
41 *Writings*, V, 376–77
42 *Writings*, V, 362–63
43 Crane, Verner W. *Benjamin Franklin on Slavery and American Liberties. Pennsylvania Magazine of History and Biography,* LXII (1938), 1–11
44 *Writings*, V, 383
45 Hume, I, 452: Hume, David. *Letters.* 2 vols. Oxford, 1932
46 *Writings*, V, 479–527
47 *Writings*, V, 410
48 *Writings*, VI, 98–99
49 *Writings*, VI, 33–34
50 Duane, 36–38; *Writings*, V, 471, 509
51 Abernethey, 111n.: Abernethey, T. P. *Western Lands and the American Revolution.* New York, 1937
52 *Writings*, V, 414–15

See also:

Alvord, Clarence W. *The Mississippi Valley in British Politics.* 2 vols. Cleveland, 1917 (for the Grand Ohio company and the Vandalia colony)
Carey, L. J. (General Bibliography)
Crane, Verner W. (References for Chapter 14)

CHAPTER 16

1 Boswell, VII, 193–94; VIII, 111, 121–22: Boswell, James. *Private Papers.* Edited by Geoffrey Scott and Frederick A. Pottle. 18 vols. New York, 1928–34
2 *Writings*, V, 458

3   Writings, V, 180–81
4   Writings, X, 276
5   Writings, VI, 7–8
6   Writings, V, 153
7   Writings, V, 411–12
8   Writings, VI, 140
9   Writings, V, 225
10 Writings, V, 269–70
11 Writings, V, 272–80
12 Writings, V, 345–47
13 Writings, VI, 102n.
14 Writings, IV, 24
15 Writings, V, 122
16 Writings, V, 329–30
17 Autobiography, 226–27
18 Writings, V, 338–39
19 "My Dear Girl," 216–17
20 Writings, V, 438–39
21 Writings, V, 282
22 Writings, V, 231
23 Writings, V, 266–67
24 Writings, V, 408–09
25 Morellet, I, 197–204: Morellet, Abbé.
    Mémoires inédits. 2 vols. Paris, 1822
26 Writings, VIII, 503; American Philo-
    sophical Society, Franklin Papers,
    XLIX, 78 (seating plan of dinner)
27 Writings, VI, 97
28 Hays, Calendar, I, 118
29 Hays, Calendar, II, 183
30 Writings, VI, 430
31 Boswell, IX, 40
32 Writings, VI, 55
33 Mazzei, I, 305: Mazzei, Filippo.
    Memorie della vita e peregrinazione.
    2 vols. Laguna, 1845
34 Writings, V, 39–40
35 Writings, V, 70
36 Writings, V, 101
37 Writings, V, 107–08
38 Writings, V, 129–32
39 Writings, V, 169–78
40 Writings, V, 221
41 Writings, V, 228
42 Writings, V, 232–33
43 Writings, V, 245
44 Writings, VI, 8
45 Writings, V, 371–72
46 Writings, V, 397–99
47 Weld, II, 94–95: Weld, C. R. *A
    History of the Royal Society.* 2 vols.
    London, 1848
48 Writings, V, 416–30
49 Writings, V, 437–38
50 Writings, V, 542–50
51 Writings, VI, 43–44
52 Writings, VI, 118
53 Writings, VI, 62–72
54 Writings, VI, 61
55 Writings, VI, 100–01
56 Writings, IV, 177–79
57 Hays, Calendar, I, 151
58 Writings, VI, 153–65

See also:

Malone, Kemp. *Benjamin Franklin on Spell-
    ing Reform.* American Speech, I
    (1925), 96–100
Morgan, W. *Memoirs of the Life of the
    Rev. Richard Price.* London, 1815
    (Honest Whigs)
Nichols, John. *Literary Anecdotes of the
    Eighteenth Century.* 9 vols. London,
    1812–15 (Honest Whigs, III, 258)

CHAPTER 17

1   Writings, VI, 96–97
2   Writings, VI, 111
3   Writings, IX, 358
4   Writings, VI, 146
5   John Adams, Works, IX, 268
6   Crane, IX, 503–04: Crane, Verner
    W. *Three Fables by Benjamin Frank-
    lin.* New England Quarterly, IX
    (1936), 499–504
7   Writings, V, 444–45
8   Writings, V, 448–50
9   Writings, VI, 265–67
10 Writings, VI, 262–63
11 Writings, VI, 264
12 Writings, VI, 284
13 Writings, VI, 195
14 Writings, VI, 284
15 Writings, VI, 82
16 Writings, VI, 81
17 Writings, V, 328
18 Writings, V, 461–62
19 Writings, VI, 3–4
20 Writings, VI, 22
21 Writings, VI, 31
22 Writings, VI, 57
23 Writings, VI, 49–50
24 Writings, VI, 273
25 Writings, VI, 78–79
26 Writings, VI, 98
27 Writings, VI, 114
28 Writings, VI, 127–37
29 Autobiography, 225
30 Writings, VI, 118–24
31 Writings, VI, 153
32 Writings, VI, 145
33 Writings, VI, 152–53
34 Writings, VI, 147
35 Writings, VI, 179
36 Almon, III, 242–66: Almon, John.
    *Biographical, Literary, and Political
    Anecdotes.* 3 vols. London, 1797
37 Writings, VI, 283–84
38 Writings, VI, 174
39 Writings, VI, 172–73
40 John Adams, Works, II, 319
41 Hale, II, 221
42 Bowdoin-Temple, IX, 456–63: Bow-
    doin-Temple Letters. *Collections of
    the Massachusetts Historical Society,*

Sixth Series, IX (1897); Seventh Series, VI (1907); Temple's letter to Franklin, 26 July 1781, is in the Library of Congress, Franklin Papers, 846–48

43 Einstein, 88–90: Einstein, Lewis. *Divided Loyalties: Americans in England during the War of Independence.* Boston, 1933 (chapter on John Temple, 72–113)

44 *Writings*, VI, 182–83

45 Mauduit, 77–80: Mauduit, Israel (editor). *The Letters of Governor Hutchinson and Lieut. Governor Oliver . . . and Remarks Thereon . . . Together with the Substance of Mr. Wedderburn's Speech.* London, 1774

46 *Writings*, VI, 185–86

47 *Writings*, VI, 186–87

48 *Writings*, VI, 188

49 Fitzmaurice, II, 298: Fitzmaurice, Lord Edward. *Life of William, Earl of Shelburne.* 3 vols. London, 1875–76

50 *Writings*, VI, 289

51 *Writings*, VI, 188–89

52 *Writings*, VI, 189

53 Mauduit, 90

54 Vaughan, 341: Vaughan, Benjamin (editor). *Political, Miscellaneous, and Philosophical Pieces . . . Written by Benj. Franklin.* London, 1779

55 *Aulularia*, II, iv, 46

56 Mauduit, 91

57 Vaughan, 341

58 Burke, II, 454: Burke, Edmund. *Correspondence.* 4 vols. London, 1844

59 Fitzmaurice, II, 297

60 Bentham, X, 59–60: Bentham, Jeremy. *Works.* 11 vols. London, 1838–43

61 Priestley, XV, 2: *To the Editor of the Monthly Magazine. Monthly Magazine,* XV (February 1803), 1–2

62 Bowdoin-Temple, IX, 338

63 *Writings*, VI, 189

64 *Writings*, VI, 190–91

65 *Writings*, VI, 189–90

66 Vaughan, 341

67 *Writings*, VI, 258–89

68 *Writings*, VI, 219

69 *Writings*, VI, 194

70 Bowdoin-Temple, IX, 416

See also:

Bache, R. M. *The So-Called "Franklin Prayer-Book."* Pennsylvania Magazine of History and Biography, XXI (1897), 225–34

Bancroft, Edward. Account of the Cockpit episode in W. T. Franklin, I, 357–359

Hosmer, James K. *The Life of Thomas Hutchinson.* Boston, 1896 (especially Chapter XII)

Hutchinson, P. O. *Dairy and Letter of . . . Thomas Hutchinson,* 2 vols. Boston, 1883–86 (especially I, 81–93)

Lee, R. H. *Life of Arthur Lee.* 2 vols. New York, 1829 (for the affair of the Hutchinson letters, I, 266–73)

CHAPTER 18

1 Rutt, I, 227: Rutt, J. T. *Life and Correspondence of Joseph Priestley.* 2 vols. London, 1831–32

2 *Writings*, VI, 202

3 *Writings*, VI, 222

4 Pennington, E. L. *The Work of the Bray Associates in Pennsylvania.* Pennsylvania Magazine of History and Biography, LVIII (1934), 1–25

5 Rutt, I, 232

6 *Writings*, VI, 176

7 *Writings*, VI, 197

8 *Writings*, VI, 241

9 *Writings*, VI, 224

10 *Writings*, VI, 248–49

11 *Writings*, VI, 223

12 *Writings*, VI, 173

13 *Writings*, VI, 179

14 *Writings*, VI, 82–83

15 *Writings*, VI, 77

16 *Writings*, VI, 238–39

17 *Writings*, VI, 247

18 *Writings*, VI, 248

19 *Writings*, VI, 249–51

20 *Writings*, VI, 251–52

21 *Writings*, VI, 254

22 *Writings*, VI, 321–24

23 *Writings*, VI, 254

24 *Writings*, VI, 290–91

25 *Writings*, VI, 299–301

26 *Writings*, VI, 250

27 Quincy, 250–58 (References for Chapter 12)

28 Quincy, 317

29 *Writings*, VI, 446

30 *Writings*, VI, 310

31 *Writings*, VI, 318–99

32 *Writings*, VI, 324

33 *Writings*, VI, 325–26

34 *Writings*, VI, 326–27

35 *Writings*, VI, 327–28

36 *Writings*, VI, 328–40

37 *Writings*, VI, 342

38 Fox, 395: Fox, R. H. *Dr. John Fothergill and his Friends.* London, 1919

39 Duane, 57–60

40 *Writings*, VI, 4

41 *Writings*, VI, 345–49

42 *Writings*, VI, 349–52

43 *Writings*, VI, 352–54

44 *Writings*, VI, 354–56

45 *Writings*, VI, 354–59
46 *Writings*, VI, 359–60
47 *Writings*, VI, 304
48 *Writings*, VI, 360–61
49 *Writings*, VI, 362
50 *Writings*, VI, 363
51 *Writings*, VI, 364–65
52 *Writings*, VI, 365–70
53 *Writings*, VI, 306
54 *Writings*, VI, 371
55 *Writings*, VI, 371–74
56 Fox, 332–33
57 Ford, W. C. *Franklin's Accounts against Massachusetts. Proceedings of the Massachusetts Historical Society*, LVI (1923), 94–120
58 *Writings*, VI, 378–86
59 *Writings*, VI, 310
60 *Writings*, VI, 311–12
61 *Writings*, VI, 391–94
62 *Writings*, VI, 395
63 *Writings*, IX, 56
64 *Writings*, IX, 261
65 *Writings*, VI, 396–99
66 *Writings*, VI, 316–17
67 Quincy, 342
68 *Writings*, VI, 395–96
69 Hutchinson, I, 420–21 (References for Chapter 17)
70 *Works* (Sparks), I, 391; VIII, 149n.
71 Rutt, I, 212
72 *Writings*, VI, 399
73 *Writings*, VI, 400
74 *Writings*, IX, 394–98, 405–07
75 *Writings*, VI, 400

CHAPTER 19

1 Hutchinson, II, 237–38 (References for Chapter 17)
2 *Writings*, VI, 406
3 Burke, II, 27 (References for Chapter 17)
4 *Writings*, VI, 400
5 Jefferson, I, 82
6 John Adams, *Correspondence*, IV, 431: *Correspondence between John Adams and Mercy Warren. Collections of the Massachusetts Historical Society*, Fifth Series, IV (1878), 317–511
7 *Writings*, VI, 407
8 Butler, 157–66
9 P. L. Ford, *The Many-Sided Franklin*, 219, 349
10 *Writings*, VI, 409
11 *Minutes of the Council of Safety, Colonial Records*, X, 277–452
12 *Writings*, VI, 438–39
13 *Writings*, IX, 696
14 *Writings*, VI, 420–26
15 Jefferson, XVII, 139
16 *Writings*, VI, 430
17 John Adams, *Familiar Letters*, 122:

Adams, John and Abigail. *Familiar Letters*. Boston, 1876
18 G. W. Greene, I, 116–17: Greene, G. W. *The Life of Nathanael Greene*. 3 vols. New York, 1867–71
19 G. S. Greene, 169–70 (References for Chapter 9)
20 W. C. Ford, *Journals*, III, 392
21 *Writings*, VI, 409
22 Durand, 2–5: Durand, John. *New Materials for the History of the American Revolution*. New York, 1889
23 Doniol, I, 287
24 *Writings*, VI, 407
25 *Writings*, VI, 436–37
26 Burnett, I, 375–77: Burnett, Edmund C. (editor). *Letters of Members of the Continental Congress*. 8 vols. Washington, 1921–36
27 *Pennsylvania Archives: Eighth Series*, VIII, 7410–11
28 Abernethy, 146–47 (References for Chapter 15)
29 *Writings*, VII, 24
30 Charles Carroll, 37: Carroll, Charles. *Journal . . . during his Visit to Canada in 1776*. Baltimore, 1845
31 *Writings*, VI, 445–46
32 In the Schuyler Papers, New York Public Library
33 Charles Carroll, 53
34 John Carroll, V, 1167–68: (Letter from John Carroll, Montreal, 1 May 1776) Force, Peter (editor). *American Archives: Fourth Series*, V (1844)
35 *Writings*, IX, 696
36 *Bulletin of the New York Public Library*, X (1906), 17–18
37 *Writings*, VI, 448
38 *Writings*, VI, 447
39 *Writings*, X, 349
40 *Writings*, VI, 449
41 *Writings*, VII, 24–25
42 *Writings*, VI, 450
43 Conway, I, 67: Conway, M. D. *The Life of Thomas Paine*. 2 vols. New York, 1892
44 Moore, I, 268: Moore, Frank (editor). *Diary of the American Revolution*. 2 vols. New York, 1859–60
45 Becker, 161–69: Becker, Carl. *The Declaration of Independence*. New York, 1922
46 Jefferson, XVIII, 169–70
47 *Works* (Sparks), I, 407
48 Samuel Adams, III, 321: Adams, Samuel. *Writings*. 4 vols. New York, 1904–08
49 W. C. Ford, *Journals*, V, 689–91
50 *Writings*, VI, 454
51 Nevins, 151: Nevins, Allan. *The American States during and after the Revo-*

lution *1775–1789.* New York, 1924 (for Pennsylvania politics 1775–76)

52 *Writings,* X, 57–58
53 *Writings,* VI, 459–62
54 W. C. Ford, *Journals,* V, 554n.; VI, 1079, 1080, 1082
55 Jefferson, XVIII, 167
56 John Adams, *Works,* III, 75–76
57 In the Miscellaneous Papers of Richard Howe, New York Public Library
58 John Adams, *Works,* III, 79
59 *Writings,* VII, 55
60 Duane, 72–73
61 In the American Philosophical Society, Franklin Papers, LXIX, 5
62 Wharton, II, 151–52
63 *Writings,* IX, 696
64 *Writings,* VIII, 304–05
65 Hale, I, 243
66 W. T. Franklin, I, 309

See also:

Graydon, Alexander. *Memoirs of a Life, Chiefly Passed in Pennsylvania, within the last Sixty Years.* Harrisburg, 1811 (brief note on Graydon's meeting with Franklin on his return from Canada, page 126)

Hazelton, J. H. *The Declaration of Independence: Its History.* New York, 1906

Marshall, Christopher. *Extracts from the Diary of Christopher Marshall, kept in Philadelphia and Lancaster, during the American Revolution, 1774–1781.* Edited by William Duane. Philadelphia, 1877

Mathews, Lois K. (References for Chapter 8)

Riddell, W. R. *Benjamin Franklin's Mission to Canada and the Causes of its Failure. Pennsylvania Magazine of History and Biography,* XLVIII (1924), 111–58

CHAPTER 20

1 Abernethy, T. B. *Commercial Activities of Silas Deane in France. American Historical Review,* XXXIX (1934), 477–85
2 *Writings,* VI, 477
3 *Writings,* VII, 11
4 *Writings,* VII, 26
5 Hale, I, 80
6 Stevens, XIV, Nos. 1385, 1389
7 *Writings,* VII, 347
8 Deffand, III, 282–83; Deffand, Marquise du. *Lettres . . . à Horace Walpole (1766–1780).* 3 vols. London, 1912
9 *Writings,* VII, 16

10 Albemarle, II, 302: Albemarle, Earl of. *Memoirs of the Marquis of Rockingham.* 2 vols. London, 1852
11 George III, II, 162: *The Correspondence of George the Third with Lord North from 1768 to 1783.* Edited by W. Bodham Donne. 2 vols. London, 1867
12 *Writings,* VII, 16
13 Hale, I, 91–94
14 Ford, P. L. *Affaires de l'Angleterre et de l'Amérique. Pennsylvania Magazine of History and Biography,* XIII (1889), 222–26
15 *Writings,* VII, 8
16 Lescure, I, 31–33: Lescure, M. de. *Correspondance secrète inédite sur Louis XVI, Marie Antoinette, la cour, et la ville de 1777 à 1792.* 2 vols. Paris, 1866
17 *Writings,* VII, 57–58
18 *Writings,* VII, 28
19 Rosengarten, 26–31: Rosengarten, J. G. *American History in German Archives.* Lancaster, 1904
20 *Writings,* VII, 223
21 Andrews, II, 63: Andrews, Charles M. *A Note on the Franklin-Deane Mission to France. Yale University Library Gazette,* II (1928), 53–68
22 Stevens, XVIII, No. 1648
23 Stevens, XIV, No. 1413
24 Gibbon, I, 313: Gibbon, Edward. *Private Letters 1753–1794.* 2 vols. London, 1896.
25 *Writings,* VII, 81–82
26 *Writings,* VII, 62
27 *Writings,* VII, 63
28 Palmer, 82–99: Palmer, J. M. *General von Steuben.* New Haven, 1937
29 *Writings,* VII, 36
30 Einstein, 51–71 (References for Chapter 17)
31 *Writings,* X, 509–13; Bemis, S. F. *British Secret Service and the French-American Alliance. American Historical Review,* XXIX (1924), 474–95
32 Lee, II, 148 (References for Chapter 17)
33 Lee, II, 113, 115
34 Bentham, X, 527 (References for Chapter 17); Rush, XXIX, 27–28 (References for Chapter 2)
35 Lee, I, 336
36 Lee, I, 343–46
37 Lee, I, 354
38 Stevens, V, No. 489
39 Lee, I, 375
40 Stevens, VIII, No. 774
41 Rush, XXIX, 28
42 Lee, I, 393–94
43 Deffand, III, 423
44 Croÿ, IV, 78: Croÿ, Duc de. *Journal inédit.* 4 vols. Paris, 1906–07

45 *Writings*, VII, 129–29
46 Andrews, II, 66
47 *Writings*, VII, 124–26
48 *Writings*, VII, 109
49 *Writings*, VII, 131
50 *Writings*, VII, 132
51 *Writings*, VII, 136
52 *Writings*, VII, 154
53 Hays, *Calendar*, II, 70
54 Andrews, II, 65
55 John Adams, *Works*, I, 660–63
56 *Warren-Adams Letters*, II, 74: *Warren-Adams Letters. Being Chiefly a Correspondence among John Adams, Samuel Adams, and James Warren.* 2 vols. Boston, 1917–25
57 John Adams, *Works*, I, 661
58 *Writings*, VIII, 393
59 *Writings*, VII, 98
60 *Writings*, VII, 159
61 Stevens, VIII, Nos. 835–37
62 *Writings*, VII, 166–72
63 John Adams, *Works*, III, 179–80
64 Bachaumont, XI, 112–13: Bachaumont, Louis Petit de. *Mémoires secrets.* London, 1784
65 John Adams, *Works*, III, 147; Bachaumont, XI, 210–11
66 Stevenson, 722: Stevenson, B. E. *The Home Book of Quotations.* 3rd edition. New York, 1937
67 *Writings*, VIII, 215

See also:

An Address to the Good People of Ireland, on behalf of America. October 4th, 1778. By Benjamin Franklin. Edited by P. L. Ford. Brooklyn, 1891 (introduction contains almost all that is known about the document)

Bemis, S. F. *The Diplomacy of the American Revolution* (General Bibliography)

Corwin, Edwin S. *French Policy and the American Alliance of 1778.* Princeton, 1916

Deane, Silas. *Papers.* Edited by Charles Isham. 5 vols. New York, 1887–91

Doniol, H. (General Bibliography)

Kite, Elizabeth S. *Beaumarchais and the War of American Independence.* Boston, 1918

Loménie, L. de. *Beaumarchais et son temps.* Paris, 1855. In English, New York, 1856

CHAPTER 21

1 *Writings*, VII, 178–79
2 Loménie, 320 (References for Chapter 20)
3 *Writings*, VII, 344–45
4 *Writings*, VII, 273
5 *Writings*, VIII, 54

6 *Writings*, VIII, 44
7 *Writings*, VII, 278
8 *Writings*, VII, 290–91
9 *Writings*, VII, 288–89
10 *Writings*, VIII, 28–29
11 Bemis, *Diplomacy* (clear outline of the European aims and methods)
12 Jefferson, XVIII, 168; Bentham, X, 527 (References for Chapter 17)
13 *Writings*, VII, 270
14 *Writings*, VII, 299
15 *Writings*, VII, 401
16 Hale, I, 319–41
17 *Writings*, VIII, 80
18 *Writings*, VII, 242–43
19 *Writings*, VII, 293–94
20 Bemis, *Diplomacy*, 93
21 *Writings*, VII, 323–25
22 *Writings*, VIII, 142
23 *Writings*, VIII, 146
24 *Writings*, VIII, 378
25 *Writings*, VIII, 292
26 *Writings*, VIII, 293
27 *Writings*, VIII, 144
28 *Writings*, VIII, 5
29 *Writings*, VIII, 126–28
30 Washington, XX, 142–43: Washington, George. *Writings.* Edited by J. C. Fitzpatrick. Vols. I–XXIII (to 1782). Washington, 1931–37
31 Conway, I, 166–76 (References for Chapter 19)
32 *Writings*, VIII, 217–19
33 *Writings*, VIII, 220–22
34 *Writings*, VIII, 315
35 *Writings*, VIII, 294–95
36 *Writings*, VIII, 295
37 *Writings*, VIII, 275
38 *Writings*, VIII, 316
39 *Works* (Sparks), IX, 72
40 *Writings*, VIII, 319; Watson, 134 (References for Chapter 22)
41 *Writings*, VIII, 333
42 Jusserand, J. J. *Franklin in France.* In: *Essays Offered to Herbert Putnam by his Colleagues and Friends.* Edited by W. W. Bishop and Andrew Keogh. New Haven, 1928 (pages 226–47)
43 *Writings*, VII, 367
44 *Writings*, VIII, 390
45 *Writings*, VIII, 359
46 *Writings*, VIII, 390
47 *Writings*, VIII, 396–97

See also:

Meng, J. J. *The Comte de Vergennes: European Phases of his American Diplomacy (1774–1780).* Washington, 1932

CHAPTER 22

1 *Writings*, VIII, 37
2 *Writings*, VIII, 110

3 *Writings*, VIII, 62–63
4 Oswald, J. C. *Benjamin Franklin in Oil and Bronze*. New York, 1926
5 Campan, I, 233–34: Campan, Madame de. *Mémoires sur la vie privée de Marie-Antoinette*. 3 vols. Paris, 1822
6 Hale, I, 246–30
7 *Writings*, VIII, 154 (not in Franklin's English, as is commonly supposed, but in an anonymous translation first published in Marshall's edition of Franklin's *Complete Works*, 3 vols., London, 1806. The passages quoted in the present biography have been newly translated from Franklin's French)
8 John Adams, *Works*, III, 326
9 *Writings*, IX, 151
10 *Writings*, IX, 308
11 *Writings*, IX, 333
12 Croÿ, IV, 167–69, 271 (References for Chapter 20); also Watson, 87 (below)
13 Faÿ, *The Two Franklins*, 42
14 Grandsaignes, Tabaries de. *Contribution à l'histoire de l'Hôtel Valentinois à Passy. Bulletin No. LXX* (1910) of the Société Historique d'Auteuil et de Passy.
15 University of Pennsylvania, Franklin Papers, IX, 5
16 University of Pennsylvania, Franklin Papers, XII, 2; I, 33–38
17 University of Pennsylvania, Franklin Papers, VIII, 45
18 *Writings*, IX, 470
19 American Philosophical Society, Franklin Papers, LXIII, 2
20 *Writings*, X, 315–17
21 *Writings*, VIII, 459
22 *Writings*, IX, 265
23 *Writings*, IX, 338
24 *Writings*, IX, 325
25 *Writings*, IX, 251
26 *Writings*, IX, 322–23
27 John Adams, *Works*, III, 134
28 *Writings*, VII, 393–94
29 Campan, I, 233
30 *Works* (Sparks), IX, 22–24; Chinard, 5–29: Chinard, G. *Les amitiés américaines de Madame d'Houdetot*. Paris, 1924
31 Ford, W. C. *One of Franklin's Friendships. Harper's Magazine*, CXIII (1906), 626–33
32 *Writings*, X, 411–13
33 *Writings*, X, 431
34 Hays, *Calendar*, I, 314
35 *Writings*, X, 429–30
36 American Philosophical Society, Franklin Papers, XLIII, 64
37 *Writings*, X, 429–30

38 *Writings*, X, 414–15
39 *Writings*, X, 436
40 *Writings*, X, 437–38
41 Rosenbach, A. S. W. *The All-Embracing Doctor Franklin*. Philadelphia, 1932 (page 36)
42 Rosenbach, *Book Hunter's*, 29–30: Rosenbach, A. S. W. *A Book Hunter's Holiday*. Boston, 1936
43 *Writings*, X, 424–25
44 *Writings*, X, 419
45 *Writings*, X, 421–22
46 *Writings*, VII, 206–09
47 *Writings*, VII, 414–16; X, 189–95
48 *Writings*, VIII, 350
49 Rosenbach, *Book Hunter's*, 30
50 *American Museum* (Philadelphia), X (1791), 176
51 Abigail Adams, II, 55–56: *Letters of Mrs. Adams, the Wife of John Adams*. 2 vols., Boston, 1840
52 *Writings*, X, 442
53 Livingston, L. S. *Benjamin Franklin's Letters to Madame Helvétius and Madame La Freté*. Cambridge, 1924
54 Morellet, *Mémoires inédits*, Chapter XV (References for Chapter 16)
55 *Anecdotes sur Francklin. Gazette Nationale, ou Le Moniteur universel*, No. 196, 805–06
56 *Autobiography*, 334
57 Cabanis, V, 230, 248, 269: Cabanis, P. J. G. *Œuvres complètes*. 5 vols. Paris, 1825
58 *Writings*, VII, 436–38; *Works* (Sparks), II, 225–27
59 *Writings*, VII, 434–35; *Works* (Sparks), II, 222
60 *Writings*, VII, 375
61 *Writings*, VII, 376
62 *Writings*, VII, 204
63 *Writings*, VII, 204–06; *Works* (Sparks), II, 204–05
64 Livingston, *Letters to Madame Helvétius*
65 Hays, *Calendar*, I, 557
66 Hays, *Calendar*, II, 187
67 *Writings*, X, 364
68 *Writings*, IX, 678
69 *Writings*, X, 442–44
70 *Writings*, IX, 107
71 *Writings*, VIII, 451–52
72 *Writings*, VIII, 502–03
73 Hale, I, 171–75
74 Hays, *Calendar*, I, 551
75 *Writings*, IX, 558
76 *Writings*, IX, 71, 132
77 Hill, David Jayne. *A Missing Chapter in Franco-American History. American Historical Review*, XXI (1916), 709–19
78 *Writings*, I, 105
79 *Writings*, VII, 286

80 *Writings*, VIII, 431, 435
81 Hays, *Calendar*, I, 254
82 *Writings*, X, 453–56
83 *Writings*, VII, 97
84 *Writings*, VII, 209–15
85 *Writings*, VIII, 10
86 *Writings*, VIII, 189–94
87 *Writings*, VIII, 246–48
88 *Writings*, VIII, 307
89 *Writings*, VIII, 417–18
90 *Writings*, VIII, 448
91 *Writings*, VIII, 598–601
92 American Philosophical Society, Franklin Papers, Cash Book (entries for 16 June 1778–19 October 1780)
93 *Writings*, VIII, 100
94 Morellet, I, 300 (References for Chapter 16)
95 *Writings*, X, 414
96 *Writings*, VIII, 162–64
97 *Writings*, VII, 357–62
98 *Writings*, VII, 427–33
99 *Writings*, VIII, 450–51
100 Eddy, G. S. (editor). *A Project of Universal and Perpetual Peace.* New York, 1922
101 Granier de Cassagnac, B. A. *Histoire des Girondins.* 2 vols. Paris, 1860 (I, 372–73)

See also:

Adams, R. G. (editor). *The Passports Printed by Benjamin Franklin at his Passy Press.* Ann Arbor, 1925
Amiable, L. *Une Loge Maçonnique d'avant 1789.* Paris, 1897 (Neuf Sœurs)
Guillois, Antoine. *Le Salon de Madame Helvétius.* Paris, 1894
Lees, F. *The Parisian Suburb of Passy: Its Architecture in the Days of Franklin.* Architectural Record, XII (1902), 669–83
Livingston, L. S. *Franklin and his Press at Passy.* New York, 1914
Soulavie, J. L. *Mémoires historiques et politiques du règne de Louis XVI.* 6 vols. Paris, 1801 (V, 174–99, what purports to be a faithful dialogue between Soulavie and Franklin on various scientific and political matters, particularly an English plot to foment a revolution among French Protestants)
Turgot, A. R. J. *Œuvres . . . et documents le concernant.* Edited by G. Schelle. 5 vols. Paris, 1913–23 (frequent references to Franklin, particularly V, 192–647)
Watson, Elkanah. *Men and Times of the Revolution; or, Memoirs of Elkanah Watson.* New York, 1856 (Franklin memorabilia, notably 86–88, 92–93, 117–23, 132–34, 157, 181, 286–87)

CHAPTER 23

1 Bemis, *Diplomacy*, 181–82
2 *Writings*, VIII, 302
3 *Writings*, VIII, 459–60
4 *Writings*, VIII, 459–62
5 *Writings*, VIII, 463–73
6 *Writings*, VIII, 437–47
7 Livingston, 58–67 (References for Chapter 22)
8 Hale, II, 51–54
9 *Writings*, VIII, 483–92
10 Hale, II, 55–60
11 *Writings*, VIII, 501
12 *Writings*, VIII, 511–13
13 *Writings*, VIII, 517–18
14 *Writings*, VIII, 523–29
15 *Writings*, VIII, 541–43
16 Hale, II, 68
17 Jay, II, 372–73; Jay, John. *Correspondence and Public Papers.* Edited by H. P. Johnston. 4 vols. New York, 1890–93
18 Monaghan, 194–97: Monaghan, Frank. *John Jay.* New York, 1935
19 Hale, II, 109
20 Bemis, *Diplomacy*, 220–23
21 *Writings*, IX, 60; VIII, 616–17
22 Jay, *Diary*, 13: *The Diary of John Jay during the Peace Negotiations of 1782.* Edited by Frank Monaghan. New Haven, 1934
23 John Adams, *Works*, III, 300, 302, 336
24 Hale, II, 179
25 Mayo, 191, 209: Mayo, Katherine. *General Washington's Dilemma.* New York, 1938
26 *Writings*, VIII, 549
27 *Writings*, VIII, 620
28 *Writings*, VIII, 621–27; John Adams, *Works*, III, 332
29 *Writings*, VIII, 632–33
30 John Adams, *Works*, III, 333–35; Hale, II, 192
31 Whitefoord, 200–01: Whitefoord, Caleb. *Papers.* Oxford, 1898
32 *Writings*, IX, 60
33 John Adams, *Works*, III, 336; Jay. III, 6
34 *Writings*, IX, 61
35 *Writings*, IX, 62
36 Hale, II, 197
37 *Writings*, VIII, 634
38 *Writings*, VIII, 630
39 *Writings*, VIII, 645
40 *Writings*, VIII, 641
41 *Writings*, VIII, 641
42 John Adams, *Works*, III, 349
43 *Writings*, VIII, 642–43
44 Bemis, *Diplomacy*, 24n.

45 *Writings*, VIII, 644–45
46 *Writings*, IX, 63
47 *Writings*, IX, 3–7, 40–41
48 *Writings*, IX, 96

See also:

Bemis, S. F. *The Diplomacy of the American Revolution*. (General Bibliography) (excellent critical essay on the manuscript and printed sources for the peace negotiations, 270–73)

Bemis, S. F. (editor). *The American Secretaries of State and Their Diplomacy.* Vol. I (1927)

Doniol, H. (General Bibliography)

Fitzmaurice, Baron. *Life of William, Earl of Shelburne.* 2d edition. 2 vols. London, 1912

Fox, Charles James. *Memorials and Correspondence.* Edited by Lord John Russell. 4 vols. London, 1853–57

George III. *Correspondence.* Edited by Sir John Fortescue. 6 vols. London, 1927–28

Guttridge, G. H. *David Hartley, M.P., an Advocate of Conciliation, 1774–1783.* Berkeley, 1926

Oswald, Richard. Transcript of "Oswald's Journal; Peace Commission, 1782" among the Franklin Papers in the Library of Congress. Used and cited extensively in Hale, *Franklin in France*, II

Wallace, D. D. *The Life of Henry Laurens.* New York, 1915

Wharton, Francis (General Bibliography)

CHAPTER 24

1   *Writings*, IX, 80
2   Grimm, XIII, 349: Grimm, Baron von (and others). *Correspondance littéraire, philosophique et critique.* 16 vols. Paris, 1877–82
3   *Writings*, IX, 113–17
4   *Writings*, IX, 119–20
5   *Writings*, IX, 155–56
6   Jeffries, John. *Diary.* Edited by B. Joy Jeffries. *Magazine of American History*, XIII (1885), 66–88
7   *Writings*, IX, 480
8   *Writings*, VIII, 636
9   *Writings*, IX, 18
10 Butler, 168–72
11 *Writings*, IX, 215–18
12 *Writings*, VIII, 603–14; IX, 177
13 *Writings*, IX, 150
14 *Writings*, X, 97–105
15 Livingston, 50 (References for Chapter 22)
16 *Writings*, IX, 161–68
17 Livingston, 9 (References for Chapter 22)
18 *Writings*, IX, 279
19 Hays, *Calendar*, III, 541; Livingston, 11
20 Hays, *Calendar*, III, 176, 540; Faÿ, Bernard. *Franklin et Mirabeau collaborateurs. Revue de littérature comparée*, VIII (1928), 5–28
21 *Writings*, X, 354
22 Mirabeau, 72, 74–77: Mirabeau, Comte de. *Considérations sur l'ordre de Cincinnatus.* London, 1784
23 *Writings*, IX, 183–89
24 *Writings*, IX, 237
25 *Writings*, IX, 239–40
26 *Writings*, IX, 243–47
27 *Writings*, IX, 293–95
28 *Writings*, IX, 296
29 *Diplomatic Correspondence*, II, 195–325: *The Diplomatic Correspondence of the United States of America from . . . 10th September, 1783, to March 4, 1789.* 7 vols. Washington, 1833–34
30 Jefferson, V, 27, 42
31 Jefferson, VIII, 129
32 *Writings*, IX, 182–83
33 Hays, *Calendar*, III, 186, 187
34 Hays, *Calendar*, III, 196
35 *Rapport*, 19–37: *Rapport des Commissaires chargés par le Roi, de l'Examen du Magnétisme Animal.* Paris, 1784
36 *Exposé des Expériences qui ont été faites pour l'Examen du Magnétisme Animal.* Paris, 1784; Hays, *Calendar*, III, 207
37 Binet, 18–25: Binet, Alfred, and Charles Féré. *Animal Magnetism.* New York, 1888
38 *Writings*, X, 349
39 *Writings*, IX, 258
40 *Writings*, X, 350
41 *Writings*, IX, 255
42 *Writings*, IX, 252–53
43 *Writings*, IX, 271
44 Wilberforce, 28–29; Wilberforce, R. I. and S. *The Life of William Wilberforce.* Philadelphia, 1839
45 Romilly, I, 69: *Memoirs of Sir Samuel Romilly written by Himself.* 3 vols. London, 1840; Baynes's *Journal* in Franklin, *Complete Works* (Bigelow), VIII, 410–25
46 *Writings*, X, 356
47 *Writings*, V, 553–55; IX, 307; X, xii
48 Jay, *Some Conversations*, 11–15: *Some Conversations of Dr. Franklin and Mr. Jay . . . during 1783–1784.* Edited by Frank Monaghan. New Haven, 1936; *Autobiography*, 389–390, 364–66
49 Farrand, *Benjamin Franklin's Memoirs*, No. 10, 56–58
50 Letters in the Jay Papers, in the Iselin collection

51 Monaghan, *John Jay*, 225 (References for Chapter 23)
52 Jefferson, X, 55; XV, 176; VIII, 131; XVIII, 170–72
53 *Writings*, X, 438
54 Livingston, 127 (References for Chapter 22)
55 Jefferson, VIII, 129
56 American Philosophical Society, Franklin Papers, XLIII, 113
57 American Philosophical Society, Franklin Papers, XLIV, 274a
58 *Writings*, X, 464–71
59 Hays, *Calendar*, III, 351
60 *Writings*, IX, 369
61 *Writings*, IX, 370–71
62 *Writings*, IX, 372–413
63 *Writings*, IX, 414–43
64 *Writings*, IX, 443–62

See also:

Bache, Franklin. *Where is Franklin's First Chart of the Gulf Stream? Proceedings of the American Philosophical Society*, LXXVI (1936), 731–41 (account of Franklin's studies of the Gulf Stream as well as of his charts)

Eddy, G. S. *Correspondence between Dr. Benjamin Franklin and John Walter, regarding the Logographic Process of Printing. Proceedings of the American Antiquarian Society*, New Series, XXXVIII (1928), 349–69 (chiefly 1783–85)

CHAPTER 25

1 *Pennsylvania Gazette*, 21 September 1785
2 *Pennsylvania Packet*, 17 September, 6, 7 October 1785
3 *Pennsylvania Journal*, 24 September 1785
4 *Pennsylvania Gazette*, 5 October 1785
5 *Writings*, IX, 467–68
6 *Pennsylvania Gazette*, 2 November 1785
7 *Minutes of the Supreme Executive Council*, XIV, 576
8 *Pennsylvania Packet*, 6 March 1786
9 *Writings*, IX, 489
10 *Pennsylvania Packet*, 21 January 1786
11 *Writings*, IX, 494
12 *Writings*, IX, 483–85
13 Chaptal, 73: Chaptal, J. A. C. *Chymistry Applied to Agriculture*. Boston, 1836
14 Logan, 44: Logan, Deborah Norris. *Memoirs of Dr. George Logan of Stenton*. Philadelphia, 1899
15 Cutler, II, 234: Cutler, W. P. and Julia P. Cutler. *Life, Journals, and Correspondence of Rev. Manasseh Cutler*. 2 vols. Cincinnati, 1888

16 *Writings*, IX, 471
17 *Writings*, IX, 511–12
18 Bank of North America, Ledger 4
19 *Writings*, IX, 523–25
20 *Pennsylvania Gazette*, 26 July 1786
21 Vaux, 10: Vaux, Roberts. *Notices of the Original, and Successive Efforts, to Improve the Discipline of the Prison at Philadelphia and to Reform the Criminal Code of Pennsylvania*. Philadelphia, 1826
22 Bank of North America, Ledger 3
23 Lewis, 66, 72–75: Lewis, Lawrence. *A History of the Bank of North America*. Philadelphia, 1882
24 *Writings*, IX, 482
25 *Writings*, IX, 474; X, 497
26 *Writings*, IX, 504 (wrongly dated 1786)
27 *Writings*, X, 494–96
28 *Writings*, IX, 536–37
29 *Writings*, IX, 540
30 *Writings*, IX, 576
31 *Writings*, IX, 590
32 *Writings*, IX, 617
33 *Writings*, IX, 613
34 Hays, *Calendar*, IV, 3
35 *Writings*, IX, 572–73
36 Crèvecœur, I, 26–34: Crèvecœur, M. G. J. de. *Voyage dans la haute Pensylvanie et dans l'État de New York*. 3 vols. Paris, 1801
37 Dubbs, 40–58: Dubbs, J. H. *History of Franklin and Marshall College*. Lancaster, 1903.
38 *Minutes of the Supreme Executive Council*, XV, 223
39 Washington, *Diaries*, III, 221: *The Diaries of George Washington 1748–1799*. Edited by J. C. Fitzpatrick. 4 vols. Boston, 1925
40 *Pennsylvania Packet*, 5 December 1785
41 *Writings*, IX, 300
42 Alden, G. H. *The State of Franklin. American Historical Review*, VIII (1903), 271–89
43 *Writings*, X, 483–86
44 *Writings*, IX, 534–35
45 *Writings*, IX, 548
46 *Writings*, IX, 551
47 *Writings*, IX, 574
48 *Writings*, IX, 564
49 *Pennsylvania Packet*, 27 March 1787; printed Rules of the Society in American Philosophical Society
50 *Writings*, IX, 560
51 *Writings*, IX, 571
52 *American Museum*, I (June 1787), 571
53 Washington, *Diaries*, III, 216–17
54 *Writings*, IX, 582
55 *Writings*, IX, 612
56 Farrand, I, 4: Farrand, Max (editor). *The Records of the Federal Convention*

of 1787. Revised edition, 4 vols.
New Haven, 1937

57 Farrand, III, 91

58 The forged speech, called *Franklin's Prophecy,* seems to have appeared first in *Liberation* (Asheville) 3 February 1934; often reprinted. Discussed by Charles A. Beard in *Jewish Frontier* for March 1935, and by Julian P. Boyd in *Pennsylvania Magazine of History and Biography,* LXI (1937), 233–34

59 Farrand, I, 47, 54

60 Farrand, I, 65

61 Farrand, I, 81–85

62 Farrand, I, 120

63 Farrand, I, 197

64 Farrand, I, 216, 427

65 Farrand, III, 152

66 Warren, 287n.: Warren, Charles. *The Making of the Constitution.* Boston, 1928, 1937

67 Farrand, I, 450–52

68 *Writings,* IX, 94

69 Farrand, III, 470–75, 531

70 Farrand, I, 488

71 Farrand, IV, 66

72 Farrand, III, 190, 265

73 Farrand, I, 523

74 Farrand, I, 546

75 Cutler, I, 267–70

76 *Writings,* IX, 605

77 Farrand, II, 65

78 Farrand, II, 120

79 Farrand, II, 204–05

80 Farrand, II, 236–37

81 Farrand, II, 249

82 Farrand, II, 348

83 Farrand, II, 542

84 Farrand, II, 641–43

85 Farrand, II, 644

86 Farrand, II, 648

87 *Pennsylvania Herald,* 20 September 1787

88 McMaster, 13: McMaster, J. B., and F. D. Stone (editors). *Pennsylvania and the Federal Constitution 1787–1788.* Lancaster, 1888

89 *Minutes of the Supreme Executive Council,* XV, 317–19

90 Farrand, IV, 78–80

91 *American Herald,* 14 January 1788

92 *Writings,* III, 265–66

93 Nevins, 583–90 (References for Chapter 19)

94 *Writings,* IX, 477–78

95 *Pennsylvania Archives: First Series,* XII, 296

96 *Writings,* IX, 516

97 *Minutes of the Supreme Executive Council,* XV, 291

98 *Minutes of the Supreme Executive Council,* XV, 293

99 *Writings,* IX, 633, 665, 668

See also:

Boyd, Julian P. (editor). *The Susquehannah Company Papers.* 4 vols. Wilkes-Barre, 1930–33 (does not yet, 1938, bring the account down to the times of Franklin's administration)

Miner, Charles. *History of Wyoming.* Philadelphia, 1845

CHAPTER 26

1   *Writings,* X, 493–501

2   Cobbett, VIII, 188–92: Cobbett, William. *Porcupine's Works.* 12 vols. London, 1801

3   Storer, Malcolm. *The Franklin Boston School Medals. Proceedings of the Massachusetts Historical Society,* LV (1922), 189–98

4   *Writings,* X, 501–10

5   *Writings,* IX, 477

6   Board of Directors of City Trusts of the City of Philadelphia. *Annual Report* for 1907, 1936

7   Franklin Union. *Annual Report of the Director* for 1927, 1935

8   *Writings,* IX, 686–88

9   *Writings,* IX, 691–97

10 *Writings,* IX, 487

11 Farrand, *Records,* III, 327 (References for Chapter 25)

12 *Writings,* IX, 527–28, 553–55

13 Stillé, C. J. *Beaumarchais and the Lost Million. Pennsylvania Magazine of History and Biography,* XI (1887), 1–36

14 *Writings,* IX, 694

15 *Writings,* IX, 560

16 *Writings,* IX, 551

17 *Writings,* IX, 645

18 *Autobiography,* 339

19 *Writings,* IX, 665

20 *Writings,* IX, 673

21 *Writings,* IX, 688

22 *Writings,* X, 32

23 *Writings,* X, 50

24 *Writings,* X, 69

25 Farrand, *Benjamin Franklin's Memoirs*

26 Jenkins, Charles F. *The Historical Background of Franklin's Tree. Pennsylvania Magazine of History and Biography,* LVII (1933), 193–208

27 Westcott, 131–47, 261–62: Westcott, Thompson. *Life of John Fitch, the Inventor of the Steam-Boat.* Philadelphia, 1857; *James Rumsey* in *Dictionary of American Biography;* Mitchell, 271–72: Mitchell, Julia P. *St. Jean de Crèvecœur.* New York, 1916

28 *Writings,* X, 494; Faÿ, *The Two Franklins,* 98–99, 103–06

29 *Writings*, X, 105–16; IX, 560
30 *Writings*, X, 131–37; first printed in
      Columbian Magazine, I (October
      1786), 64–67
31 *Writings*, X, 9–32
32 *Writings*, IX, 652
33 *Writings*, X, 1
34 Rush, XXIX, 131–37 (References
      for Chapter 2)
35 *Writings*, X, 31
36 *Writings*, IX, 588–89
37 *Writings*, IX, 613
38 *Writings*, IX, 619
39 *Writings*, X, 122
40 *Writings*, IX, 625
41 *Writings*, IX, 651
42 *Writings*, IX, 674
43 *Writings*, IX, 659
44 *Writings*, IX, 677
45 *Writings*, X, 7
46 *Writings*, X, 35
47 *Writings*, X, 33
48 *Writings*, X, 74–75
49 *Writings*, X, 69
50 *Writings*, X, 72
51 *Writings*, X, 58–60
52 *Writings*, III, 66–67
53 Pennington, LXIII, 7 (References
      for Chapter 18)
54 *Writings*, X, 66–68
55 *Annals of Congress*, 1 Cong., 2 sess.,
      1197–1205, 1414–15, 1474
56 *Writings*, X, 86–91
57 *Writings*, X, 2
58 *Writings*, X, 41
59 *Writings*, IX, 683
60 Parton, II, 599
61 *Writings*, X, 75–82

62 *Works* (Sparks), I, 532
63 *Writings*, X, 84–85
64 Jefferson, I, 161–62
65 *Writings*, X, 92–93
66 *Works* (Sparks), I, 531
67 *Pennsylvania Gazette*, 21 April 1790
68 *Pennsylvania Gazette*, 13 January 1790
69 *Pennsylvania Gazette*, 21 April 1790
70 Jefferson, X, 421
71 *Gazette Nationale, ou le Moniteur uni-
      versel*, 12 June 1790
72 Condorcet, Marquis de. *Éloge de M.
      Franklin*. Paris, 1791; Fauchet,
      Claude. *Éloge Civique de Benjamin
      Franklin*. Paris, 1790
73 Campan, I, 233n. (References for
      Chapter 22)
74 Vicq d'Azyr, Félix. *Éloge de Franklin*.
      Revue Rétrospective, Second Series,
      (1835), 375–404; Smith, William.
      Eulogium on Benjamin Franklin.
      Philadelphia (printed by Benjamin
      Franklin Bache), 1792

See also:

Carr, Robert. *Personal Recollections of Benjamin Franklin. Historical Magazine*,
   Second Series, IV (1868), 59–60
   (by a former apprentice of Benjamin Franklin Bache)
Gillespie, Mrs. E. D. *A Book of Remembrance*.
   Philadelphia, 1901 (contains notes
   on Franklin's last years by his great-
   granddaughter)
Locke, Mary S. *Anti-Slavery in America . . . (1619–1808). Radcliffe College Monographs* No. II. Boston,
   1901

Notes

The letter to Jared Eliot quoted on pages 177-78 has, since the publication of the original edition of this book, been shown to be not from Franklin but from Charles Read. Franklin had no such farm and made no such experiments as are discussed in that letter.

C. V. D.

The two dialogues between Philocles and Horatio which are quoted and discussed on pages 83-87 have recently been proved not to have been written by Franklin, but taken from the *London Journal*, 1729.
—Publisher's note to the eleventh printing.

Index

FOR THE BEST IN PAPERBACKS, LOOK FOR THE

In every corner of the world, on every subject under the sun, Penguin represents quality and variety—the very best in publishing today.

For complete information about books available from Penguin—including Puffins, Penguin Classics, and Arkana—and how to order them, write to us at the appropriate address below. Please note that for copyright reasons the selection of books varies from country to country.

In the United Kingdom: Please write to *Dept. JC, Penguin Books Ltd, FREEPOST, West Drayton, Middlesex UB7 0BR.*

If you have any difficulty in obtaining a title, please send your order with the correct money, plus ten percent for postage and packaging, to *P.O. Box No. 11, West Drayton, Middlesex UB7 0BR*

In the United States: Please write to *Consumer Sales, Penguin USA, P.O. Box 999, Dept. 17109, Bergenfield, New Jersey 07621-0120.* VISA and MasterCard holders call 1-800-253-6476 to order all Penguin titles

In Canada: Please write to *Penguin Books Canada Ltd, 10 Alcorn Avenue, Suite 300, Toronto, Ontario M4V 3B2*

In Australia: Please write to *Penguin Books Australia Ltd, P.O. Box 257, Ringwood, Victoria 3134*

In New Zealand: Please write to *Penguin Books (NZ) Ltd, Private Bag 102902, North Shore Mail Centre, Auckland 10*

In India: Please write to *Penguin Books India Pvt Ltd, 706 Eros Apartments, 56 Nehru Place, New Delhi 110 019*

In the Netherlands: Please write to *Penguin Books Netherlands bv, Postbus 3507, NL-1001 AH Amsterdam*

In Germany: Please write to *Penguin Books Deutschland GmbH, Metzlerstrasse 26, 60594 Frankfurt am Main*

In Spain: Please write to *Penguin Books S. A., Bravo Murillo 19, 1° B, 28015 Madrid*

In Italy: Please write to *Penguin Italia s.r.l., Via Felice Casati 20, I-20124 Milano*

In France: Please write to *Penguin France S. A., 17 rue Lejeune, F-31000 Toulouse*

In Japan: Please write to *Penguin Books Japan, Ishikiribashi Building, 2–5–4, Suido, Bunkyo-ku, Tokyo 112*

In Greece: Please write to *Penguin Hellas Ltd, Dimocritou 3, GR-106 71 Athens*

In South Africa: Please write to *Longman Penguin Southern Africa (Pty) Ltd, Private Bag X08, Bertsham 2013*